SECOND EDITION

Capital Budgeting

Planning and Control
of Capital Expenditures

John J. Clark
Drexel University

Thomas J. Hindelang
Drexel University

Robert E. Pritchard
Glassboro State College

PRENTICE-HALL, INC., ENGLEWOOD CLIFFS, NEW JERSEY 07632

Library of Congress Cataloging in Publication Data

CLARK, JOHN J.
  Capital budgeting.

  Bibliography: p.
  Includes index.
  1. Capital budget. 2. Cash flow. 3. Capital assets
pricing model. I. Hindelang, Thomas J. II. Pritchard,
Robert E., 1941–   . III. Title.
HG4028.C4C6 1984   658.1′54   83-15998
ISBN   0-13-114348-4

Editorial/production supervision
  and interior design: *Esther S. Koehn*
Cover design: *Wanda Lubelska*
Manufacturing buyer: *Ed O'Dougherty*

Printed in the United States of America

10 9 8 7 6 5 4 3

ISBN 0-13-114348-4

Prentice-Hall International, Inc., *London*
Prentice-Hall of Australia Pty. Limited, *Sydney*
Editora Prentice-Hall do Brasil, Ltda., *Rio de Janeiro*
Prentice-Hall Canada Inc., *Toronto*
Prentice-Hall of India Private Limited, *New Delhi*
Prentice-Hall of Japan, Inc., *Tokyo*
Prentice-Hall of Southeast Asia Pte. Ltd., *Singapore*
Whitehall Books Limited, *Wellington, New Zealand*

For Margaret, Chris, Jody

Contents

PREFACE

In this second edition of *Capital Budgeting*, we seek to implement three objectives: improve the text as a teaching tool; expand certain topics and introduce new materials to keep the subject matter abreast of the times; and correct deficiencies culled from the generally favorable reviews earned by the first edition. It is to be hoped that the product will better serve the needs of those with whom we are primarily concerned: the senior-level undergraduate and graduate students interested in careers in profit and not-for-profit enterprise. They will apply the principles illustrated and, through the interplay of theory and practice, contribute to the advancement of financial management.

To maintain and enhance the strengths of the text for the student use, we pledge to avoid that bane of second (and subsequent) editions; namely, the proliferation of chapter appendixes that undermine the continuity of subject matter. Returning readers will find in *Capital Budgeting, Second Edition*, that new and revised materials are completely integrated with the subject matter under discussion. Moreover, the manuscript has been partitioned into modules. This aspect enables the instructor to pick up the discussion at a level commensurate with the achievements of his or her student group. In this respect, the topics considered assume an acquaintance with finite mathematics and college statistics. Such prerequisites reflect the maturity of computer-assisted decision-making in financial management.

Part I, the first module, introduces the subject and reviews basic tools and concepts relevant to capital budgeting. If the student has had prior exposure to these tools and concepts, the instructor may wish to assign these chapters for the student to read as a refresher and spend only limited classroom time for review. Part II, on the other hand, takes up the details of project evaluation and cost of capital under conditions of unchanging risk. The discussion goes beyond the simple illustration of project-evaluation techniques to explore problems arising in application. All financial models rest upon assumptions and employ either cash flows or book values in their calculations. The majority are static models, making no attempt to trace movements in the variables measured through time. Unless aware of such underlying qualifications, the future practitioner of the art may be entrapped into conclusions that do not square with the reality of a dynamic business environment. Part II constitutes a logical starting point for students with prior course work in financial management.

Part III focuses on computing the incremental cash benefits and expenses traceable to the proposed capital project. More so than in competing texts, emphasis is placed on the role of forecasting in developing the cash flows. Forecasting represents an integral part of capital budgeting. In addition, we treat explicitly the issue of adjusting cash flows for price trends, i.e., long-term upward or downward swings in the general price level. "Inflation" or "deflation," to use the terms loosely, impact cash flows, costs of capital, sustainable growth rates, and so forth. Finally, in putting the cash flows on an after-tax basis, the provisions of the Economic Recovery Tax Act of 1981 and the Tax Equity and Fiscal Responsibility Act of 1982 are employed.

The student is now ready to approach the issue of risk in project evaluation (Part IV). The essence of the discussion lies in the determination of expected return and standard deviation for portfolios of securities and capital projects. An ample number of illustrations and problems depict the use of decision trees in risk analysis, the utilization of probabilities and the calculation of expected NPV or expected IRR, variances, and covariances. The subject matter of Part IV leads ineluctably to a study of the Capital Asset Pricing Model (CAPM). The three chapters of Part V are devoted to the theoretical constructs of CAPM, its application to the capital asset evaluation, and to a critique of CAPM theory. The latter incorporates the contributions of earlier research, as well as the more recent dissents of Roll and others. We attempt in this module to offer a balanced presentation of pros and cons, supported by a bibliography to assist the assignment of research papers.

Part VI turns to mathematical programming for the evaluation of capital projects and the formulation of capital budgets. Linear programming and its variations—integer programming, goal programming, quadratic programming, and dynamic programming—are described with stress on the assumptions of each formulation and the interpretation of outputs. Our objective in this module is to prepare the student for the ever-growing use of such computer-aided models by making him or her capable of stating a capital budgeting problem in terms of an objective function and constraints, interpreting the results of the program, and performing sensitivity analysis on the "optimal" solution.

The last module, Part VII, treats several significant topics in capital budgeting of particular concern in today's economy. These include: leasing, expanded from the first edition to include both lessor and lessee perspectives; capital budgeting in the multinational firm; and business combinations. Each chapter is a self-contained unit and the instructor may use these chapters according to the inclinations of the student body. On the other hand, we deem it appropriate to round out the discussion on a synoptic note. The final chapter looks to strategic planning vis-à-vis capital budgeting, the latter comprising a set of techniques to implement the firm's long-term objectives. This perspective serves to expose areas of possible inconsistency between strategic plans and the naïve application of capital budgeting techniques.

In summary, enumeration of new and expanded materials in the second edition involves the following:

All illustrating problems and student exercises conform to the requirements of the Economic Recovery Tax Act of 1981 and the Tax Equity and Fiscal Responsibility Act of 1982. In addition, a separate chapter is devoted to the new tax law.

Methods are described for adjusting the cash flows for "inflationary" or "deflationary" movements in the general price level.

An expanded treatment of capital asset pricing model is included to incorporate recent dissenting research.

An expanded treatment of leasing includes the issue of lease versus sell, the transferability of tax deductions, and the establishment of a bargaining area between the lessor and lessee.

The nexus between strategic planning and capital budgeting and the issue of sustainable rates of growth at the firm level are discussed.

Collectively, we express our appreciation to reviewers of the first edition who identified areas of possible improvement as well as to our colleagues who devoted time and effort to assessing the present manuscript prior to publication. We are especially indebted to:

Richard H. Bernard
North Carolina State University

Dennis E. Logue
The Amos Tuck School
Dartmouth College

Randolph A. Pohlman
Kansas State University

Arthur C. Gudikunst
Babson University

John F. Muth
Graduate School of Business
Indiana University

George W. Hettenhouse
Graduate School of Business
Indiana University

Francis S. Yeager
University of Houston

Jonathon B. Welch
Northeastern University

In addition, our students at Drexel University provided valuable feedback to the authors on the first edition and the manuscript for the second edition which was extensively class tested at both the graduate and undergraduate levels. To all of our students goes a collective thanks. Several of our graduate students deserve special acknowledgment for their contributions: Daniel W. Davis, Anne G. McGinn, Donald Scholtz, Tom Sheridan, and Pamela S. Wohlschlegel.

Besides the reviewers and our students, we appreciate the contributions of: John D. Benstead, CPA, Tax Partner, Deloitte Haskins and Sells for his review of Chapter 10—Taxation and Depreciation; Oliver H. Winn, Ph.D., Director of the Management Information Systems Center, Glassboro State College for his preparation of the programs for Chapter 9—The Management of Forecasting, Sensitivity Analysis, and Adjustment for Price Trends; Joseph L. Naar of The

Conference Board, Inc., for timely inputs and advice on current business practices; Arthur H. Rosenfeld of Warren, Gorham, and Lamont, Inc., for the use of their comprehensive annuity and discount tables; Dean Paul E. Dascher, College of Business and Administration, Drexel University, for his continuing encouragement and support, and for providing clerical help during the preparation of both editions; and finally David C. Hildebrand, Editor, Economics and Finance, at Prentice-Hall, as well as his staff, provided capable and efficient assistance in producing the final product. Numerous other individuals have helped to improve the quality of the text; to them we offer a collective thank you.

Comments from readers of the second edition are welcomed and encouraged.

John J. Clark
Thomas J. Hindelang
Robert E. Pritchard

1

Introduction to the Management of Capital Assets

Capital budgeting is the decision area in financial management that establishes goals and criteria for investing resources in long-term projects. Capital investment projects commonly include land, buildings, facilities, equipment, vehicles, and the like. The decisions made regarding the acquisition, maintenance, and abandonment of these assets are extremely important to most companies for the following reasons:

1. These assets normally represent relatively large commitments of resources.

2. The funds traditionally remain invested for long periods of time.

3. The need for working capital is generally tied closely to the use of physical assets.

4. The future development of the firm hinges on the selection of capital investment projects, the decision to replace existing capital assets, and the decision to abandon previously accepted undertakings that turn out to be less attractive than originally thought.

Thus, the capital budgeting effort is an integral part of the *strategic management process*. Also, the capital budget constitutes a significant part of a company's business plan.

We refer to capital budgeting in terms of *projects*. Most of these projects have to do with investments in the company's plant and equipment. The expansion and contraction of physical assets is a major application of capital budgeting techniques. But these techniques apply equally well to the valuation of advertising commitments, to the management of the company's financial structure (refunding of a bond issue, for example), to a decision about purchasing or leasing an asset, to the valuation of *other* firms for purposes of combination, and to the management of research and development funds. The methodology of capital budgeting may also be applied to the questions of project termination, divestiture of a segment of the business, and total liquidation of the business.

Capital budgeting offers a method of analysis and decision criteria that can be employed in government, as well as in private enterprise, and in the evaluation of both civilian and governmental projects. In the latter instance, the technique is generally referred to as *cost-effectiveness analysis* or, when placed in a broader context, as *systems analysis*. This has been applied mostly by the Department of Defense, but has since spread to other agencies of the federal government and is now filtering down to the state and local level.

In order for management to establish a procedure for developing a capital budget and for authorizing the acquisition and disposal of assets, it is necessary first to develop a framework that considers the short- and long-term attitudes and needs of such groups as the owners, employees, and customers—that is, to establish a framework for strategic planning. This is the subject of the following section.

THE FRAMEWORK FOR STRATEGIC PLANNING

Strategic planning is necessary because the world is in constant flux—once-reasonable plans frequently turn out to be in error. Thus, management needs a dynamic *planning process* that will flex as conditions change, yet continually meet the needs of the various groups to whom the firm has a responsibility.

The notion of flexibility in planning is not new, but historically the degree of flexibility needed in the short run has been limited more to fine tuning than to major changes. The idea of capital abandonment was linked to managerial "mistakes," and consequently many companies made little effort to follow up on forecasts or to apply strict financial control systems to the acquisition and implementation of projects.

Electric utility companies in particular have felt the brunt of strong criticism from customers and regulatory agencies. Construction cost overruns and—in some instances—excess capacity, combined with increased fuel costs and environmental requirements, have led to steep rate increases. Yet, construction of generating facilities normally takes several years and the plans for construction must be predicated on the best existing forecasts—forecasts based on current economic and demographic trends. Academically, one can easily consider the shutdown of construction if actual demand for electricity does not meet the forecast amount or the purchase of electricity from another company if demand exceeds expectations. But in either case, management will be subject to harsh criticism for poor planning.

Certainly, there are no global remedies to the difficult forecasting problems faced by management. And, many companies do reward executives for *short-term* performance linked to meeting short-term profit objectives. Astute middle managers quickly learn how to maximize short-term profits by cutting back on research, going slow on expensive modernization and retooling, and neglecting maintenance. Once a division is squeezed for all the profit it's worth, the manager normally leaves to take a higher-paying position at another company.

Such scenarios have been played all too frequently. As a result, the top managements of many companies have realized the necessity of structuring management compensation packages to reward employees who think and plan on a long-term basis. Recognizing that long-term commitments of resources can result in lower short-term profits, the banking and financial communities in Japan have entered into long-term growth commitments with Japanese industry —commitments designed to encourage increases in productivity and output and competitiveness in the world markets. This cooperative attitude may well be an indication of changes to come within the American investment community if American industry is to remain competitive.

It is within the context of recognizing the importance of capital budgeting both to the individual firm and to the economy overall that we set forth the following set of assumptions to provide a framework for developing a capital budgeting program.

ASSUMPTIONS BASIC TO THE DEVELOPMENT OF A CAPITAL ACQUISITION PROGRAM

Assumption 1: The primary function of management is to increase the value of the firm as reflected by the price of the common stock. Others would argue that management must satisfy the needs of the many competing interest groups to whom the firm has a responsibility, while maintaining a "satisfactory" level of profits. The problems inherent in both maximizing and "satisficing" are handled through the use of mathematical programming and, specifically, goal programming, the subjects of Chapters 19 through 22.

Assumption 2: Owners have a preference for current, as opposed to future, income. Investors must be compensated for postponing the recovery of their investments and their returns on investment. Since the benefits of capital acquisitions are received over a future period, the *time element* lies at the core of capital budgeting. The firm must time the start of a project to take advantage of short-term business conditions and finance the project to take advantage of trends in the capital markets. In addition, the longevity of capital assets and the large outlays required for their acquisition suggests that the estimates of income and cost associated with the project be *discounted* for the time they are received or paid out. The methodologies of discounting cash flows to their *present values* form the basis upon which projects may be evaluated and ranked. These methodologies are introduced in Chapters 2 and 3 and used throughout the remainder of the text.

Assumption 3: Shareholders are risk-averters. As such, they demand increasingly greater returns as their perceived risk of the firm increases. We examine the problems of capital budgeting under conditions of changing risk in Part IV and deal with utility analysis, which has to do with the relationships between risk and return, in Chapter 12.

Assumption 4: In selecting projects for acquisition or abandonment, it is necessary to evaluate the incremental cash flows attributable directly to the project rather than to historical or sunk costs. The estimation of cash flows is directly related to the process of forecasting, the subject of Chapter 9. Using operating forecasts, relevant tax and depreciation information may be incorporated to produce the cash flows estimates. This process is the subject of Chapters 10 and 11.

Assumption 5: Cash-flow analysis may differ from accounting-income reporting. The analysis for long-term asset management is made on a cash-flow basis, as opposed to the determination of project accounting income. By the end of the project's life, of course, the cash and accounting basis will reconcile, but in any given fiscal period the net return calculated on a cash or accounting basis may diverge quite significantly. A project that appears favorable in the long run may show negative results in the early periods. This can create important political problems for management if it believes that accounting reports influence stock prices and investor decisions. As we shall see, the evidence on this point is not conclusive. In any event, the analyst must bear in mind the effects of the project on each period's accounting results. We deal with the problems of reconciling project cash flows and accounting income in Chapter 21, where goal programming (a multiple criteria model) is examined.

Assumption 6: Since capital acquisition represents long-term commitments, forecasting is essential to the process. Investment decisions are always based upon income information using forecasts of future revenues and costs. We know from experience that such forecasts will always err, and the degree of error may correlate (but not always) with the duration of the project. Short-term forecasts generally display less risk than long-term forecasts. The future dimly seen entails *risk*, and any appraisal of a capital project, therefore, must necessarily comprehend some assessment of the risk accompanying the project.

Assumption 7: The current trend in asset acquisition exhibits management's risk posture. The capital budget concentrates on the benefits and costs of projects and the decisions made determine the composition of the firm's total assets and the business-risk complexion of the enterprise. The capital budget *shapes operating plans for several years in the future* and thus indicates management's risk posture.

Nonetheless, it is not the project that is central to our planning but the firm—its continued existence and development. Hence, although the analysis may yield "reliable" estimates of the project's expected rate of return and risk, the question arises as to what impact these have on the firm's return on assets and risk posture. If the project enhances the rate of return on the firm's assets but makes the operation more risky or increases the possibility of insolvency, do we want the project? The answer may still be affirmative, but the question must be faced, nevertheless. Investors do not simply add new shares to their portfolios without regard to their current holdings; in like manner, financial managers do not (or at least, should not) simply add projects without regard to the firm's overall financial performances. *A high rate of return on a project is not enough to justify its acceptance. The key question is: Does the acceptance of the project increase the market value of the common shares?*

Assumption 8: Every capital project has to be financed and there are no free sources of capital. Most firms strive to maintain a capital structure (a combination of debt capital and equity capital) that will minimize their financing costs. Accordingly, we need to know not only whether the adoption of this or that project increases the market value of the common shares, but also the related question of whether the acceptance of the project increases the debt-carrying capacity of the firm.

In Chapter 8 we provide the methodology for determining the firm's cost of capital and optimal financial structure using "conventional wisdom." The problem of determining the cost of capital is examined again as a part of our study of Capital Asset Pricing in Chapter 17.

Assumption 9: Capital budgeting always involves allocating scarce resources among competing investment opportunities. The constraints are twofold in nature: financial and managerial. The whole capital budgeting process is managerial, and a firm is constrained by the limits of its managerial ability, as well as by its access to the capital needed to carry out a capital budget.

The methods for ranking projects in order of their desirability to the firm are discussed initially in Chapter 4 and further in Parts IV, V, and VI. In addition, the question of leasing as an alternative to purchasing is examined in Chapters 23 and 24. The subject of project financing is discussed in Chapter 27.

Assumption 10: The capital budgeting process is expensive. The applications of capital budgeting techniques are many and varied. In theory, a very large number of problems lend themselves to analysis by the methods described in the following pages. However, analysis absorbs time and money, especially the more sophisticated techniques of ranking and risk management. The cost of these approaches must be justified by the perceived benefits. Theory adapts to circumstances. Conceptually appealing—but costly—techniques of analysis do not merit across-the-board application. Accordingly, in establishing a capital budgeting program within the firm, the first rule involves establishing a cutoff by size of expenditure; that is, projects requiring an investment over a specified amount will be subject to much scrutiny; below this amount, less costly criteria of acceptance will be applied.

There are other important aspects of the capital acquisition process that warrant serious consideration. These come about from the rapidly changing economic conditions, and—in particular—inflation.

CAPITAL BUDGETING IN PERIODS OF INFLATION

The most pervasive economic problem during the past several years has been inflation. The difficulties encountered by management resulting from inflation warrant mention at this time.

First, the measures of inflation, such as the consumer and producer price indices, are misleading and generally do not represent the actual level of inflation experienced by either households or companies. It is therefore necessary for management to compute the inflation rate applicable to its particular company. This is easily accomplished by taking a weighted average of the increases in prices of each input to production. The relative "weighting" is in proportion to the amount of each input used. Projecting an inflation rate may be accomplished using the same methodology, but estimates of cost increases are required for each input.

Second, inflation tends to exaggerate profits and distort many financial ratios and measures of return on investment.

Third, since price changes have differed so greatly among the various inputs to production, the degree of risk associated with a particular project becomes increasingly dependent upon the inputs it will require over its useful life. This necessitates close monitoring of costs and may lead to early capital abandonment. Witness, for example, the large fleets of jet aircraft moored in the desert—abandoned before their time as a result of the quantum leaps in fuel prices that caused the airlines to purchase more efficient airplanes.

Fourth, inflation leads to higher and more volatile interest rates. Irving Fisher was one of the first to argue that the going rate of interest contained a real component, which tended to be constant, plus a premium for inflation, which changed with the inflation rate.[1] Keynesians argue that the real component also changes, but in either event, interest rates are certainly positively correlated to the inflation rates. Volatile interest rates force changes in the timing of capital asset acquisitions; high interest rates force the cost of capital upward and cause postponement or rejection of normally acceptable projects. Further, high interest rates lead to an unexpected anomaly: *the need for accurate long-range planning diminishes in importance in periods of high interest* because the discounted value of funds to be received beyond a 5- or 6-year horizon is generally of negligible importance to the process of project selection.

Fifth, inflation undermines the value of financial statements—and especially of the balance sheet. Historical accounting practices have assumed relative stability of price levels. Ongoing inflation leads to experiments with inflation accounting and the like.

Sixth, inflation encourages mergers, as well as divestiture, of operating divisions. See Chapter 26 for a discussion on mergers and acquisitions.

We discuss the problems of inflation and how to deal with them within the context of capital budgeting in Chapter 9.

The Capital Budgeting Process—A Managerial Overview

As noted earlier, capital budgeting is a managerial process and one that lies at the heart of the company's future. It is ongoing, starting with the determination of owner objectives and, based on those objectives, establishing the basic

---

[1] Irving Fisher, *The Rate of Interest* (New York: Macmillan Publishing Co., Inc., 1907); and *The Theory of Interest* (New York: Macmillan Publishing Co., Inc., 1930).

financial goals of the business. We argue throughout this book that the primary goal of management is to maximize the value of the business, as reflected by the price of the common stock. We are cognizant of other goals, such as maximization of sales, minimization of costs, and maintenance of market share, but we recognize that such goals must be subordinate to maximizing the value of the business.

Nonfinancial goals and environmental, safety, and other regulations must be taken into account. The role of the firm within the community and its relationship to its employees, customers, and the society as a whole must be considered. Such relationships may augur for investments in projects that make little or no contribution to the value of the firm but do reflect the "values" of the owners and management. Further, regulatory agencies force nonproductive capital expenditures that absorb both financial and managerial resources and add to the burden of profitable investments. Priorities for both nondiscretionary and discretionary projects must be established.

Capital budgeting is a part of long-range planning and therefore must be integrated into the firm's business plan. Development of the business plan requires close examination of the company's position within the marketplace in terms of size and penetration of existing and future product lines. This leads to the examination of the physical plant in order to assess the capability of meeting market objectives and securing the necessary inputs to production. The changing marketplace and availability of inputs may suggest vertical or horizontal integration or the divestiture of some existing capability, perhaps as a means of generating funds for more profitable ventures. All of this takes place within a changing economic, political, and tax environment.

The need to collect complete and accurate information throughout the company with respect to needed capital investments requires the development of a capital budgeting manual—a manual that details what information is required, who will supply it, and when it will be supplied. Ground rules must be established for assessing the relative values of competing projects and for deciding which may be delayed or postponed. Typically, most capital expenditures have to do with replacement decisions and thus involve not only operating costs, but such factors as potential obsolescence, in-house fabrication expertise, the cost-effectiveness of rebuilding versus replacement, and leasing versus owning. Of course, these factors relate to new acquisitions as well. As our horizon expands to include industrial engineers, we find that they view production in terms of processes and look at plant and equipment in terms of overall processes rather than as individual entities. Relatively simple questions, such as the replacement of an aging boiler, grow increasingly complex when the boiler is viewed as a part of an aging plant, each component of which will ultimately have to be overhauled or replaced within the planning horizon.

The process of data collection and evaluation immediately suggests that projects fall into various classes with respect to risk. Thus, management must develop rules for classifying projects with respect to their perceived risks in relationship to the firm as a whole. The evaluative and ranking criteria will have to be modified to handle projects that are more or less "risky." In some instances, management will opt to avoid certain projects that have "good numbers" because of preconceived notions or past experiences; the human factors and corporate politics play a large part in the capital acquisition process.

The capital budget must be integrated into the cash budget; expenditures are limited to the availability of funds. In addition, allocation of all available funds to budgeting items would be overly optimistic—historical spending patterns indicate that the unforeseen always happens; contingency planning is a part of capital budgeting.

A budget is simply a plan for spending and does not authorize expenditures. The procedures for expenditure authorization vary from company to company and require the development of a capital budgeting manual. The same procedures for authorizing expenditures must be applied uniformly throughout a company and everyone involved must be aware of them. The Conference Board[2] has researched this aspect of capital budgeting. The results of their study provide valuable insight to the student of financial management.

Once expenditures have been authorized, strict cost controls need to be set into effect. Monitoring costs and establishing crucial "go" and "no-go" decision points are important to limiting cost overruns. PERT/critical-path-monitoring systems are effective tools for controlling larger projects. The lessons learned from close cost control can help improve future estimating procedures, as well as point to problems with projects under completion.

Finally, when acquisition is completed and the project has been implemented, it is time to examine how closely the actual revenues and costs match the estimates. This aspect of capital budgeting has been met with minimal enthusiasm in most companies. Yet, if we are to rely on future estimates, we must know if historical estimates have met the tests of time; if not, we must know the reason for the deviations. For most individuals and companies alike, recognizing and understanding the cause for errors is a most edifying process. But, learning from past successes and mistakes is only one benefit of the monitoring process; the more important benefit has to do with the ongoing evaluative process—should an asset be maintained or liquidated in favor of a potentially more valuable acquisition? Nothing is static. Capital abandonment is a very real part of asset management.

This brief discussion alludes to the numerous facets and intricacies of the capital acquisition process. Our goal is to provide the analytical tools necessary to the process and also some insights into how the process is actually carried out. Initially we will rely upon the analytical methodology of *discounted cash flow*—interest calculations and the reverse function of discounting funds back to their present value. These are the topics of the following two chapters.

QUESTIONS/PROBLEMS

1. What are the basic components of capital budgeting analysis?
2. Explain what is meant by nondiscretionary capital budgeting projects and assess their significance.
3. What is the importance of a business establishing well-defined acceptance criteria for capital investment projects?

[2]Patrick J. Davey, *Capital Investments: Appraisals and Limits*. (New York, The Conference Board, 1974).

4. How can you, as financial manager, explain the possibility of inaccuracies in a forecast cash flow for a given project?

5. The novice to capital budgeting may interpret the term *project* to mean only a new investment in plant and equipment. Evaluate this assumption as it relates to the overall theory of the firm.

6. What are the basic assumptions underlying capital budgeting theory?

7. If a project that enhances the rate of return on a firm's assets is rejected because it increases the possibility of insolvency, other goals of the firm have been brought into the decision process. What are some of the goals of a firm that should be considered in evaluating a capital investment project?

8. Explain the significance of a business plan and indicate how it relates to capital budgeting.

9. Develop an outline for a capital authorization procedure indicating how and at what levels of management authorization decisions may be made.

10. Project: Visit a financial officer involved with capital budgeting in a major company and review the capital budgeting process at that company. If possible, borrow or discuss their capital budgeting manual and the analytical processes which they use to evaluate and monitor expenditures.

INTEREST and ANNUITIES

In Chapter 1 we indicated that central to the process of evaluation of capital investments is the discounting of cash flows to be recovered in the future to their present values. In this chapter dealing with the mathematics of *discounted cash flow*, we detail the computations involving simple and compound interest and the future value of an annuity. Here, we start with a present sum and determine its value in the future. In the following chapter, we reverse the process and ascertain the present value of sums to be received in the future.

SIMPLE AND COMPOUND INTEREST

Simple interest is computed using Equation (1).

$$I = (P)(i)(t) \tag{1}$$

where I = dollar amount of simple interest earned
    P = principal
    i = rate of return (interest rate)
    t = time period for which funds are invested

At the end of the period t, the accumulated fund equals the amount of interest earned (I) plus the original principal (P).

Simple interest is computed on the principal outstanding at the time of the interest calculation. The time of calculation could be the end of a month, quarter, year, and so on. The compound sum after one period is calculated using Equation (2):

$$S = P(1 + i) \tag{2}$$

where S = compound sum.

Funds may be compounded annually or more frequently. The easier case of annual compounding is considered first. If funds are invested with annual compounding, the compound sum after n years is found using Equation (3):

$$S_n = P(1 + i)^n \qquad (3)$$

where S_n = compound sum after n years
n = number of years

□ **EXAMPLE 1**   *Compound Interest*
A depositor puts $3,000 in a bank at 5%, compounded annually, for 3 years. Determine the amount that will have accrued at the end of 3 years.

Solution: Use Equation (3), as follows:

$$S_n = \$3,000(1 + 0.05)^3$$
$$= \$3,000(1.157625)$$
$$= \$3,472.88$$

At the end of 3 years, the depositor will have $3,472.88.   □

The calculations involved in Example 1 are tedious. Use of the first column, "Amount of $1," in Appendix B, "Compound Interest and Annuity Table," greatly simplifies the problem. The factors are referred to as *single payment/compound amount factors.* In Example 1, for instance, reference to the 5% page, 3-year row gives the interest factor 1.157625. This factor is then used rather than raising $(1 + 0.05)$ to the third power.

Frequently, interest is compounded semiannually, quarterly, daily, or continuously. Equation (4) may be used to determine the compound sum in such instances.

$$S_n = P\left(1 + \frac{i}{m}\right)^{mn} \qquad (4)$$

where m = number of times interest is compounded annually
i = the annual interest rate

□ **EXAMPLE 2**   *Compound Interest*
A depositor placed $3,000 in a bank for 5 years, at 6% annual interest, with compounding quarterly. Determine the amount on deposit at the end of the 5-year period.

Solution:

$$S_n = \$3,000\left(1 + \frac{0.06}{4}\right)^{4 \times 5}$$
$$= \$3,000(1.015)^{20}$$
$$= \$3,000(1.347)$$
$$= \$4,041$$

At the end of 5 years the depositor had $4,041.   □

EXPONENTIAL EFFECTS OF COMPOUNDING

Equation (3) is an *exponential function*, which is significant for two reasons. First, the compound sum (S_n) increases at an increasing rate. For example, if $100.00 were invested at 10%, the compound sum would be $110.00, $121.00 and $133.10 after 1, 2, and 3 years, respectively. Second, the compound sum increases at an increasingly faster rate at higher rates of interest. For example, consider the compound sum of $100.00 after 20 years invested at the following rates: 6%, 8%, 10%, and 12%. The compound sums are $320.71, $466.09, $672.75 and $964.63. Notice that the difference between the compound sum at 6% and 8% is $145.38, while the difference between the compound sum at 10% and 12% is $291.88—more than twice the former. The exponential effects of compounding are graphically demonstrated in Figure 2—1.

FIGURE 2–1   Exponential Effects of Compounding

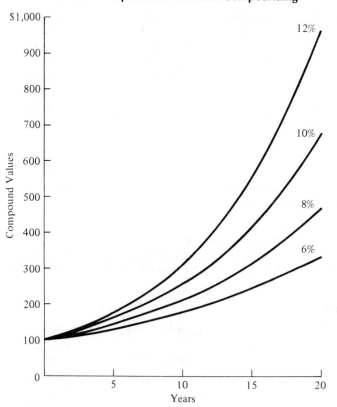

COMPOUND INTEREST AND THE REINVESTMENT RATE

Throughout the sections on compound interest we have implicitly assumed a *constant reinvestment rate*. This means that all interest obtained from an investment is reinvested at the stated rate of return for that investment during the life of the investment. This is a very important assumption, as all interest, annuity, and present-value tables are constructed based on a constant reinvestment rate.

Most investments do *not* have a constant reinvestment rate. An example of one that does is a bank certificate—interest is normally either paid at specified periods *or* may be reinvested at the rate paid on the certificate. In the latter case, the interest is returned to the investor when the certificate matures. An example of an investment that does not have a constant reinvestment rate is a bond. There is a periodic payment of interest (generally semiannually). The reinvestment rate for the interest depends upon the market return available on a security of comparable risk at the time the interest is paid.

CONTINUOUS COMPOUNDING

Some financial institutions utilize continuous compounding. Equation (4) then becomes Equation (5):

$$S_n = P\left[\lim_{m \to \infty} \left(1 + \frac{i}{m}\right)^{mn} \right] \tag{5}$$

Equation (5) can be rearranged as follows:

$$S_n = P\left[\lim_{m \to \infty} \left[\left(1 + \frac{i}{m}\right)^{m/i}\right]^{in} \right]$$

The limit as m approaches infinity of $(1 + i/m)^{m/i}$ is e, the base of the natural or Naperian logarithm system. An irrational number, e has an approximate value of 2.7182.

Equation (5) can be rewritten as Equation (6):

$$S_n = Pe^{in} \tag{6}$$

Values of e^x are contained in Table 2–1.

TABLE 2–1   Values of e^x

x	e^x	x	e^x	x	e^x
0.01	1.0101	0.08	1.0833	0.35	1.4191
0.02	1.0202	0.09	1.0942	0.40	1.4918
0.03	1.0305	0.10	1.1052	0.45	1.5683
0.04	1.0408	0.15	1.1618	0.50	1.6487
0.05	1.0513	0.20	1.2214	0.55	1.7333
0.06	1.0618	0.25	1.2840	0.60	1.8221
0.07	1.0725	0.30	1.3499	0.65	1.9155

□ **EXAMPLE 3**   *Continuous Compounding*

A depositor placed $4,000 in a bank for 5 years, at 5% annual interest, with continuous compounding. How much did the depositor have at the end of the 5 years?

Solution: Using Equation (6) and Table 2–1, we have

$$S_n = \$4,000\, e^{(0.05)5}$$
$$= \$4,000\, e^{0.25}$$
$$= \$4,000(1.2840)$$
$$= \$5,136$$

At the end of 5 years the depositor had $5,136.   □

COMPOUND SUM (FUTURE VALUE) OF AN ANNUITY

Frequently, it is necessary to save a certain sum each year in order to accumulate a required amount within a given time period. In general, savings are made *at the end of the year* and the annuity tables are constructed in that manner.

When a payment is made each year for a period of n years, at interest rate i, the future value is expressed as follows:

$$F = A_1(1 + i)^{n-1} + A_2(1 + i)^{n-2} + \cdots + A_n(1 + i)^0 \qquad (7)$$

where F = future value of the annuity
$A_1, A_2, \ldots, A_n$ = amounts paid into the annuity at the end of the year
i = rate of return
n = number of years

If the payments are equal each period, then Equation (7) may be rewritten as Equation (8):

$$F = A(1 + i)^{n-1} + A(1 + i)^{n-2} + \cdots + A$$
$$= A\left[(1 + i)^{n-1} + (1 + i)^{n-2} + \cdots + (1 + i) + 1\right] \qquad (8)$$

Multiplying both sides of the equation by $(1 + i)$,

$$F(1 + i) = A\left[(1 + i)^n + (1 + i)^{n-1} + (1 + i)^{n-2} + \cdots + (1 + i)\right] \qquad (9)$$

Subtracting Equation (8) from Equation (9),

$$Fi = A\left[(1 + i)^n - 1\right]$$

Dividing by i results in Equation (10),

$$F = A\left[\frac{(1 + i)^n - 1}{i}\right] \qquad (10)$$

Values of $[(1 + i)^n - 1]/i$, commonly referred to as *uniform series / compound amount factors* and symbolized by $S_{\overline{n}|}$, are provided in Appendix B, second column.

□ **EXAMPLE 4**   *Future Value of an Annuity*

An investor plans to put $1,000 per year into an annuity at the *end* of each year for 10 years. If interest is compounded annually at 6%, how much will the investor have at the end of 10 years?

Solution: Use Equation (10) and Appendix B, 6% page, 10-year row:

$$F = \$1,000(13.180795)$$
$$= \$13,180.80$$

At the end of 10 years the investor will have $13,180.80.   □

□ **EXAMPLE 5**   *Future Value of an Annuity*

An investor plans to put $1,000 per year into an annuity at the *start* of each year for 10 years. If interest is compounded annually at 6%, how much will the investor have at the end of 10 years?

Solution: Use Equation (3) to find the value of the initial $1,000 after 10 years. Add this to the future value of an annuity for 10 years (per Example 4), and subtract $1,000. The $1,000 is equivalent to the last payment placed into a year-end annuity, which, of course, is not the case in this example, wherein payments are made at the start of each year. The first payment is denoted by the $1,000 compounded for 10 years.

$$
\begin{aligned}
\$1,000(1.790848) = &\quad \$\ 1,790.85 \\
\$1,000(13.180795) = &\quad 13,180.80 \\
& -\ \underline{1,000.00} \\
\text{Total} \quad &\quad \$13,971.65
\end{aligned}
$$

At the end of 10 years the investor will have $13,971.65. Notice that the accumulated value is $13,971.65 when payments are made at the start of each year, while the value is $13,180.80 with payments made at year's end. The entire $790.85 difference is attributable to the interest earned on the initial $1,000 payment.   □

EXPONENTIAL EFFECTS OF COMPOUNDING ON ANNUITIES

The exponential effects of compounding of annuities are very important, especially in the area of pénsion planning. The rate of return has a very significant effect on the amount accumulated in a fund. The values shown in Table 2–2 represent the accumulations in an annuity based on payments of $2,000 per year at the end of each year.

TABLE 2–2   Annuity Values — $2,000 Year-End Payments

	Accumulation		
Interest Rate	*10 Years*	*20 Years*	*30 Years*
8%	$28,973	$ 91,524	$226,566
10%	31,875	114,550	328,988
12%	35,097	144,105	482,665
14%	38,675	182,050	713,574

SINKING-FUND PAYMENTS

A *sinking fund* is a fund created to provide for payment of a debt or other obligation by setting aside a certain amount at stated intervals, usually at the end of each year. Sinking-fund payments may be determined using *sinking-fund factors*, which are the reciprocals of the uniform series/compound amount factors. Sinking-fund factors are found in Appendix B, third column.

sinking-fund payment = fund obligation $\times$ sinking-fund factor

$$A = F \left[\frac{i}{(1 + i)^n - 1} \right] \tag{11}$$

where the sinking-fund factor is expressed as

$$\frac{1}{S_{\overline{n}|}} = \frac{i}{(1 + i)^n - 1} \tag{12}$$

☐ **EXAMPLE 6** *Sinking Fund*

A corporation needs $15,000,000 in 15 years to pay off a bond issue. The bond indenture requires the establishment of a sinking fund with annual year-end payments. If the corporation can earn 6% annually on its sinking fund, how much must it put into the fund for 15 years to accumulate the full $15,000,000?

Solution: Use Equation (11) and the sinking-fund factor from Appendix B, third column.

sinking-fund payment = $15,000,000 $\times$ 0.04296276

= $644,441.40

The corporation must put $644,441.40 into the fund each year for 15 years to accumulate $15,000,000. ☐

QUESTIONS/PROBLEMS

1. If $1,000 is invested at 6%, 8%, and 10%, determine the compound sum after a period of 20 years and draw graphs for each of the relationships.

2. Mr. Jones wants to know what the compound sum of his $5,000 bank balance will be in 10 years. The interest rate is 5%. He has compound interest tables for 5% and 6%. If he averages the compound interest factors from his tables and uses the average to compute the compound sum, how much error will result?

3. How much must be paid at the end of each year to repay a loan of $10,000 due in 10 years? Assume the funds can be invested at 8% annual interest.

4. An investor placed $1,000 in an 8% investment trust for 20 years, compounded continuously. How much did the investor have at the end of the period?

5. Suppose compounding was semiannually in Problem 4. Calculate the difference between the compound sum and continuous compounding after 20 years?

6. A sinking fund is needed to pay off $10,000,000 in 20 years. If payments are made at the end of each year, determine the amount of each payment for the last 5 years, assuming $250,000 is placed in the fund for the first 15 years and all funds receive 7% interest compounded annually.
7. The state has determined actuarially that it will require $100,000 to fund Ms. Smith's pension. If Ms. Smith has 20 years until retirement, how much must the state place in the retirement system at the end of each year to fund Ms. Smith's retirement, assuming the return is 10% compounded annually?
8. An individual has $2,000 which can be invested in one of two ways. One investment will pay 10% for the next 15 years. As an alternative, the individual can expect to put the investment in an initial 8% savings certificate for 5 years. The expectation is that savings certificate rates will increase 2% every 5 years. Which alternative would you choose? Ignore income taxes.

Present Value, Present Value of Annuities and Perpetuities

Chapter 2 showed how to compute simple and compound interest and the future value of an annuity. In this second chapter on discounted cash flow, we examine the reverse processes of finding the *present value* of an amount to be received in the future, as well as the *present value of an annuity* of future payments (i.e., recovering the initial investment in an asset). We also deal with *perpetuities* (future payments received over an indefinite future) and *capital recovery* in this chapter. The concepts and computations of present value are extremely important to the capital acquisition process, as most projects are expected to yield cash flows over some number of periods in the future.

PRESENT VALUE

When using the discounted-cash-flow procedures for capital investment evaluation, it is necessary to know the present value of a sum to be received at a future time. The present value of a sum to be received in the future may be obtained using Equation (3) of Chapter 2, reproduced here as Equation (1):

$$S_n = P(1 + i)^n \tag{1}$$

Solving Equation (1) for P results in Equation (2), which is the present value (PV) of the sum S_n to be received in n years.

$$PV = \frac{S_n}{(1+i)^n} \quad \text{or} \quad PV = S_n\left(\frac{1}{1+i}\right)^n \quad \text{or} \quad PV = S_n V^n \tag{2}$$

Values for the factor $[1/(1+i)]^n$, symbolized by V^n and called *single payment/present value factors*, are found in Appendix B, fourth column.

In our discussion of compound interest in Chapter 2, we indicate that we are assuming a constant reinvestment rate throughout the life of a given investment and that compound interest, annuity, and present-value tables are developed on this assumption. Thus, we define the present value as an amount that, when compounded at a constant rate over the life of the investment, will equal the future value (compound sum).

□ **EXAMPLE 1**   *Present Value*

A corporation expects to receive $10,000 in 3 years as payment for a note from a customer. The corporation needs cash now and has decided to sell the note to a bank. If the bank discounts the note at 10%, how much will the corporation receive?

Solution: Utilize Equation (2) and Appendix B, fourth column, at 10% as follows:

$$PV = S(\text{present value factor})$$
$$= \$10,000(0.751315)$$
$$= \$7,513.15$$

The corporation will receive $7,513.15 from the bank. Stated another way, the present value of $10,000 to be received in 3 years, discounted at 10%, is $7,513.15.   □

□ **EXAMPLE 2**   *Present Value*

A corporation expects a certain investment to yield cash flows as follows: year 1, $2,000; year 2, $3,000; year 3, $4,000; and year 4, $6,000. If the present value of these cash flows represents the *productive value* of the investment to the corporation, determine the productive value, assuming the company requires a 14% return.

Solution: Use Equation (2) and Appendix B, fourth column, at 14% using the tabular format as follows:

Solution Table for Productive Value at 14%

Time	Cash Flow	Discount Factor	Present Value
Year 1	$2,000	0.877193	$ 1,754
2	3,000	0.769468	2,308
3	4,000	0.674972	2,700
4	6,000	0.592080	3,552
		Productive Value =	$10,314

If the corporation requires a 14% return, the productive value of the asset is $10,314. The productive value will *increase* if the corporation requires a *lower* rate of return and *decrease* if the corporation requires a *higher* rate of return.   □

□ **EXAMPLE 3**   *Present Value*

A corporation has estimated the salvage value of a certain plant to be $1,000,000 in 20 years. Determine the present value of the salvage value at 5-year intervals using 10%, 12%, 14%, and 16% discount rates, and graph the relationships.

Solution: Using Appendix B, the present values are tabulated in Table 3–1.

Figure 3–1 shows that as the rate of return increases, the significance of cash flows to be received many periods in the future becomes increasingly less. Thus, at 16%, the importance of the salvage value to the question of acquiring an asset is much less than if the required return were 10%. Since this is the case, we would want to *allocate more resources* to estimating the salvage value of an asset if the required return were 10% than if it were higher. Also, at higher rates of return, the *relative significance* of an error in estimating the salvage value would be much less important than at lower rates. For example, suppose we made a 20% error in estimating the salvage value to occur at the end of year 20; the actual amount turns out to be $1,200,000, not the estimated $1,000,000. At a 10% discount rate, the error in present value would be $178,397 − $148,664 = $29,733. If,

TABLE 3–1   Present Value of $1,000,000

Present Value (Years to Salvage)

Discount Rate	5	10	15	20
10%	$620,921	$385,543	$239,392	$148,644
12%	567,427	321,973	182,696	103,667
14%	519,369	269,744	140,096	72,762
16%	476,113	226,684	107,927	51,386

FIGURE 3–1   Present Value of $1,000,000

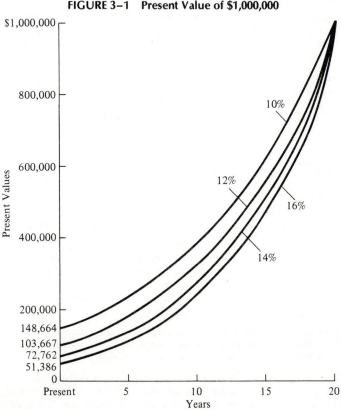

however, the discount rate were 16%, the error in present value would be $61,642 − $51,386 = $10,256. The error in the latter case is about one-third of the error at 10%. Thus, we can conclude that at 16% the error in present value is only about one-third as sensitive to an error in the estimation of the salvage value as at 10%. This is an example of the application of *sensitivity analysis*, an analytical technique that we will be using throughout the remainder of the text.

Table 3–1 and Figure 3–1 also demonstrate the anomaly stated in Chapter 1: The need for long-term accuracy in forecasting decreases as the discount rate employed is increased. □

Present Value of an Annuity

In many capital budgeting problems, funds are expected to be received at the end of each year for a period of years. The present value of a series of payments is the sum of the individual payments to be received each year. The sum is expressed in Equation (3):

$$PV = \frac{S_1}{1+i} + \frac{S_2}{(1+i)^2} + \cdots + \frac{S_n}{(1+i)^n} \tag{3}$$

where PV is the present value of the funds to be received.

If the payments are equal and the discount rate (i) is held constant, Equation (3) can be reduced to Equation (4):

$$PV = \sum_{t=1}^{n} \frac{S}{(1+i)^t} \tag{4}$$

where PV is the present value of a stream of funds to be received in equal amounts at year end, discounted at rate i.

In order to obtain the *uniform series/present worth factors*, symbolized by $A_{\overline{n}|}$ and located in Appendix B, fifth column, start with Equation (10) from Chapter 2.

$$F = A\left[\frac{(1+i)^n - 1}{i}\right] \tag{5}$$

where F = future amount of an annuity
A = equal yearly payment

Recall from Equation (2) that

$$PV = S\left[\frac{1}{(1+i)^n}\right] \tag{6}$$

Since we are concerned with the present value of an annuity, substitute Equation (5) for S in Equation (6):

$$PV = A\left[\frac{(1+i)^n - 1}{i}\right]\left[\frac{1}{(1+i)^n}\right]$$

$$= A\left[\frac{(1+i)^n - 1}{i(1+i)^n}\right] \tag{7}$$

Then,

$$A_{\overline{n}|} = \frac{(1+i)^n - 1}{i(1+i)^n} = \frac{1 - V^n}{i} \tag{8}$$

where $A_{\overline{n}|}$ is the present worth of $1 per period. $A_{\overline{n}|}$ is found in Appendix B, fifth column, commonly referred to as uniform series/present worth factors.

□ **EXAMPLE 4**   *Present Value of an Annuity*

A corporation expects to receive cash inflows of $3,000 each year for 10 years as the result of implementing a new project. Determine the present value of the sum discounted at 8%.

Solution: Utilize Equation (7) and Appendix B, fifth column, 8% for 10 years, as follows:

$$PV = \$3,000(6.710081)$$
$$= \$20,130.24$$

The present value of $3,000 to be received each year for 10 years, discounted at 8%, is $20,130.24.   □

□ **EXAMPLE 5**   *Present Value of an Annuity*

A corporation expects to receive $5,000 per year for 5 years and $8,000 per year for the following 5 years. Determine the present value of these funds at 18%.

Solution: Utilize Equation (8) and Appendix B; write the solution in tabular format, as shown:

Solution Table for Present Value at 18%

Time	Amount	Discount Factor	Present Value
Years 1–5	$5,000	3.127171	$15,636
6–10	8,000	1.366915	10,935
			Present Value = $26,571

The discount factor for years 6–10 may be obtained in two ways. One way is to subtract the annuity factor for years 1–5 from the factor for years 1–10: 4.694086 − 3.127171 = 1.366915. The second requires discounting the discount factor for years 1–5 back 5 years: 3.127171 (0.437109) = 1.366915.   □

PERPETUITIES

A *perpetuity* is an annuity or series of periodic payments that runs indefinitely, differing, therefore, from the annuities previously discussed in terms of duration only. The most common example of a perpetuity is the establishment of an endowment, although bonds lacking any maturity also qualify.

The value of a perpetuity is determined simply by dividing the yearly payment by the rate of return being received on the principal as shown in

Equation (9):

$$PV = \frac{P}{i}$$ (9)

where PV = present value of the perpetuity
P = annual payment
i = rate of return

□ **EXAMPLE 6** *Present Value of Perpetuity*
If a perpetuity yields $1,000 per year, determine the present value based on a 14% required return.

Solution: Use Equation (9) as shown:

$$PV = \frac{\$1,000}{0.14}$$
$$= \$7,143$$

An investor requiring a 14% return would be willing to pay $7,143 for a perpetuity yielding $1,000 per year. From another vantage point, if someone wanted to establish a perpetual endowment of $1,000 per year, $7,143 would be required if the funds could be invested at 14%. □

CAPITAL RECOVERY

In financial problems it is frequently necessary to find the yearly payment needed to repay a debt such as a mortgage. The *capital recovery factor*, which is the reciprocal of the uniform series/present worth factor, may be used for this purpose. These factors are found in Appendix B, sixth column.

$$\text{capital recovery factor} = \frac{1}{A_{\overline{n}|}} = \frac{i(1+i)^n}{(1+i)^n - 1}$$ (10)

$$A = PV\left[\frac{i(1+i)^n}{(1+i)^n - 1}\right] = PV\left[\frac{1}{A_{\overline{n}|}}\right]$$ (11)

□ **EXAMPLE 7** *Capital Recovery*
A borrower needs $20,000. A bank will provide a mortgage at 8% for 25 years with equal annual year-end payments. Determine the amount of the year-end payment.

Solution: Use Equation (11) and Appendix B, sixth column, 8% for 25 years.
$$\text{mortgage payment} = \$20,000(0.09367878)$$
$$= \$1,873.58$$
A borrower would pay $1,873.58 each year for 25 years to repay the $20,000 mortgage. □

QUESTIONS/PROBLEMS

1. A corporation expects an investment to yield cash inflows as follows: year 1, $3,000; year 2, $5000; years 3–9, $4,000; year 10, $6,000. If the present value of these cash flows represents the productive value of the asset, determine the maximum amount the corporation can pay for the asset assuming a required 15% return.

2. A company is considering acquisition of several assets that are expected to last 10 years. When its cost of funds was 8%, management devoted about 20 labor-hours per asset to the estimation of salvage values. Assuming a linear relationship between labor-hours applied to forecasting salvage values and the accuracy of those salvage values, how many labor-hours would you allocate to such activities if the cost of funds increased to 16%?

3. What amount must be deposited today so that $10,000 may be withdrawn at years 12, 13, 14, and 15 if the funds are invested at 8%?

4. A bond pays interest semiannually in the amount of $40.00. If the bond will mature in 10 years paying $1,000 (in principal) at that time, determine the present value of the bond using a 15% discount rate.

5. Mr. Jones wants to purchase a perpetuity that will pay $15,000 per year commencing in 8 years. If perpetuities such as these have 14% yields, determine how much he must pay to purchase the perpetuity now.

6. A bank will provide a $50,000 mortgage at 13% interest for 30 years with equal annual year-end payments. Determine the amount of the year-end payment. Suppose the borrower decides to pay back the remaining loan over a 20-year period after only $2,000 in principal has been repaid. Determine the new year-end payment.

7. An investor bids on a 3-year annuity paying $300 each year at the end of the year. The investor requires a 10% return, but wants an increase in return of 1% per year to compensate for inflation. Determine the amount the investor will pay for the annuity.

8. You have just won the "millionaire" first prize of $50,000 per year for 20 years in the state lottery. You receive your first prize installment immediately and will receive the remaining 19 installments annually. Determine the amount you would accept now in lieu of the $50,000 for 20 years if funds can be invested at 14%. (Ignore tax effects.)

9. You have just won the top prize of $1,000 per week for life in a state lottery. Assuming an investment rate of 13%, how much of the current lottery proceeds must be invested to fund your prize? (Assume a perpetuity.)

10. Ms. Sharpe is 40 years old, anticipates retirement at age 65, and may invest up to $3,500 per year in a Keogh plan. She expects to live to age 80. If she can invest the funds at year's end at an annual rate of 14% and receive a return of 8% after retirement, determine the lump-sum value of her Keogh fund at 65 and the annual pretax payment after retirement.

11. Referring to Problem 10, if Ms. Sharpe wants to receive $100,000 per year, how large an initial payment must she make into a retirement fund in addition to the $3,500 yearly payments?

12. Mr. Jones plans to place $2,500 per year into a retirement fund at the end of each year for 20 years. He has $10,000 in the fund at present. If he obtains a 10% return prior to retirement and 8% return after retirement, determine his pension based on a 20-year payment.

13. Ms. Smith started working for ABC Corporation at age 35. ABC has a defined benefit plan, in which employees receive 2% of their final year's earnings for each year worked. ABC expects salaries to increase an average of 8% a year, and Ms. Smith currently earns $30,000. Most employees retire at age 65. The life expectancies for a person at several ages are given.

Age	Life Expectancy	Years Beyond 65
35	37 years	7 years
50	24	9
60	16	11
65	13	13

Assume ABC will receive an average annual return on its pension fund of 8% and that contributions are made year-end.

(a) Based on Ms. Smith being 35 years old, determine ABC's annual contribution to the pension fund.

(b) When Ms. Smith reaches 50, ABC revises their contribution. Determine the amount needed in the fund when Ms. Smith is 65 based on the assumption that Ms. Smith's salary will continue to increase 8% annually.

(c) If ABC does not change its contribution after Ms. Smith is 50, by how much will the pension fund be overfunded or underfunded?

(d) Determine the revised contribution assuming Ms. Smith's actual salary is then $100,000.

14. ABC Corporation has established a defined benefit pension plan, which provides that at retirement each employee will receive a pension equal to his or her final year's salary multiplied by the number of years employed at the company divided by 60. Thus, if a person were employed for 20 years, the pension would be $20 \div 60$, or one-third, of the last year's salary. The company has been obtaining a 9% return on its pension contributions and it (conservatively) expects the funds to get a 6% return after each employee retires.

Mr. Green, a new employee, is hired. He is age 45 and his life expectancy is 28 years. He is expected to retire at age 65 (giving an expected pension period of 8 years). His current salary is $30,000 per year and it is expected to increase at an average annual rate of 8% per year. Determine the following.

(a) The expected pension at age 65.

(b) The amount needed at age 65 to fund the pension.

(c) The annual contribution to the pension fund.

15. The dividend-valuation model used to determine the cost of common stock equity is

$$K_e = \frac{D_1}{P_0} + g \qquad (12)$$

where K_e = the cost of common stock equity in the present period
D_1 = the dividend in the following period
P_0 = the market price of the common stock in this period
g = the annual expected growth rate of the dividend

Start with Equation (3), assume that S increases at the rate of g each year, and derive Equation (12).

Information for Problems 16–18:

During the life of a firm it is not unusual for the rate of growth of the dividend to change. If the growth rate changes, the value of the firm may be expressed as Equation (13):

$$P_0 = D_0 \sum_{t=1}^{k} \frac{(1+g_1)^t}{(1+r)^t} + D_1 \sum_{t=k+1}^{\infty} \frac{(1+g_2)^{t-k}}{(1+r)^t} \qquad (13)$$

where g_1 = dividend growth rate for periods 1 through k
g_2 = growth rate for periods $k+1$ through infinity
$D_1 = D_0(1+g_1)^k$

For computational purposes, Equation (13) may be rewritten as Equation (14):

$$P_0 = D_0 \sum_{t=1}^{k} \frac{(1+g_1)^t}{(1+r)^t} + D_0 \left(\frac{1+g_1}{1+r}\right)^k \sum_{t=1}^{\infty} \frac{(1+g_2)^t}{(1+r)^t} \qquad (14)$$

In addition to a changing rate of growth for the dividends, the rate of discount may change from period to period. The more general case is described in Equation (15):

$$P_0 = D_0 \sum_{t=1}^{k_1} \frac{(1+g_1)^t}{(1+r_1)^t} + D_1 \sum_{t=1}^{k_2} \frac{(1+g_2)^t}{(1+r_2)^t} + \cdots + D_n \sum_{t=1}^{k_n} \frac{(1+g_n)^t}{(1+r_n)^t} \qquad (15)$$

where n = number of intervals, an interval consists of one or more periods

$g_1, g_2, \ldots, g_n$ = dividend growth rate in intervals $1, 2, \ldots, n$

$r_1, r_2, \ldots, r_n$ = discount rate in intervals $1, 2, \ldots, n$

k_n = number of periods in interval n

D_0 = initial dividend

$D_1, D_2, \ldots, D_n$ = dividend at the beginning of each interval calculated using Equation (16):

$$D_n = D_{n-1} \frac{(1+g_{n-1})^{k_{n-1}}}{(1+r_{n-1})^{k_{n-1}}} \qquad (16)$$

16. A newly formed corporation is offering stock with projected dividends of $2 for the first 3 years and a yearly increase in dividend of 5% per year thereafter. At what current price can the stock be valued, assuming a 10% discount rate and dividend payments at the end of each year?

17. An investor plans to value a stock over a 10-year period. The current dividend is $2. The investor expects dividend growth rates as follows: years 1–3, 8%; years 4–7, 9%; years 8–10, 7%. Determine the dividend valuation for the stock for the 10-year period if the investor's discount rate is 8%.

18. A corporation's dividend is presently $3; it is expected to grow at an annual rate of 5% for 10 years and at an annual rate of 10% thereafter. A shareholder, in valuing the corporation's stock, plans to use an 8% discount rate for the first 5 years and 12% for the next twenty years. Determine the amount at which the shareholder would value the stock.

4

Evaluation of Alternative
Investment Opportunities

Once the firm's management has established its goals and priorities for capital expenditures, it must address the question of evaluating proposed expenditures in some systematic manner. Since in all organizations the amount of funds available for capital expenditures is limited, *management is faced with the dual problem of establishing some basic criteria for the acceptance, rejection, or postponement of proposed investments, and then ranking the projects that meet the criteria for acceptance in order of their value to the firm.* Our studies indicate that at least 35 methods have been devised to guide management in the acceptance or rejection of proposed investments. Some of the methods are general in nature and readily applicable to many firms. Others are designed for particular industries such as utilities. Some are special applications of more general procedures and have been developed to deal, for example, with the question of variability of risk among proposals.

In the course of our study of the methods used to evaluate capital investments, we explore six alternatives: payback, return on investment, equivalent annual charge (also called equivalent annual cash flow), net present value, profitability index, and internal rate of return. The latter four are called *discounted cash-flow procedures* because they consider the time value of money by discounting expected cash flows to their present value. Each method has its own story to tell; consequently, most companies use two or more to provide management with the necessary information to make acquisition and abandonment decisions.

1. *Payback.* This method involves determining the number of years necessary to recover the cost of a project and comparing the recovery period with the *maximum payback period* acceptable to management.

2. *Return on investment.* This name has been given to a variety of methods that divide yearly cash inflows or net income (either before or after taxes) by the project's cost or book value.

3. Equivalent annual charge. This method involves discounting all the expected after-tax cash inflows to present value and then determining their equivalent annual charge over the project's life.

4. Net present value. This method requires discounting all expected after-tax cash flows to present value and taking the difference between the sum of the discounted cash inflows and outflows. This difference is called the *project's net present value.*

5. Profitability index. This method involves dividing the present value of the cash inflows by the present value of the cash outflows. The quotient provides an index for measuring *return per dollar of investment.*

6. Internal rate of return. This method involves determining the discount rate that will exactly equate the present value of the cash inflows with the present value of the cash outflows so that the net present value will be zero. That discount rate is called the project's internal rate of return.

In this chapter we commence with payback and return on investment. The other methods are examined in Chapter 5.

CLASSIFICATION OF PROJECTS

The construction of a capital budget must take note of interrelationships among proposed projects. If the acceptance or rejection of one project does not affect the cash flows of another project, the two are said to be *independent.* On the other hand, dependency effects occur whenever the cash flows of one project influence or are influenced by the cash flows of another. Three situations involving dependency warrant examination:

1. Mutually exclusive projects. If the acceptance of one project precludes the acceptance of another project, the two are mutually exclusive. An airline pondering the future of its fleet may have to choose between the slower 747, which has a larger seating capacity, and the SST, which has a lower passenger capacity but supersonic speed.

2. Complementary projects. If the acceptance of one project enhances the cash flows of another project, the two are complementary. Thus, the cash flows from an automobile service station on a superhighway might be increased by the construction of restaurant facilities.

3. Prerequisite or contingent projects. If the acceptance of one project depends upon the prior acceptance of another project, the acceptance of the former is prerequisite to the acceptance of the latter. The construction of an oil refinery at a given location may depend upon the prior commitment to construct port facilities.

Obviously, dependent projects must be presented together if the manager is to consider the full range of alternatives. In this respect, one of the major problems in capital budgeting lies in the identification of all viable alternatives. *The ranking process is relative and any capital project may appear attractive when compared against a sufficiently poor alternative.*

Some projects are mandatory; they must be accepted if the firm wishes to remain in business. Others are discretionary, acceptable if financially attractive. Utilities, for example, are required by law to make investments needed to provide service on demand, even though more rewarding projects may be available. For the telephone company, switching equipment would fall into the mandatory category, while the installation of new, lower-cost generating equipment would constitute a discretionary investment. On the other hand, *the evaluation of mandatory investments does not exclude the possibility of abandonment, based on a discounted cash-flow analysis. One has the option of going out of business.*

BASIC ASSUMPTIONS

In our initial discussion of capital budgeting, we make several assumptions, which will be relaxed in later chapters. The assumptions are listed below.

1. Projects being evaluated have the same risk posture as the firm overall. We shall assume that the investment decisions made will not alter the firm's existing risk complexion. This does not mean that we are operating in a risk-free atmosphere. *Rather, it means that projects accepted have the same average risk as characterize the firm.*

All firms operate under some degree of business and financial risk. The unique combination of risk elements determines the firm's risk complexion. The risk complexion is integrated by the securities markets and results in the rate at which the market discounts the price of the firm's securities. Types of investments that generally will not affect the risk complexion or market discount rate include replacements for equipment currently in use, where the market and economic structure surrounding the use of the equipment are expected to maintain stable. In Chapters 12 through 15, we examine decision-making techniques that permit us to evaluate the impact of risk on the capital investment decision.

2. Management must set benchmarks for the evaluation of capital expenditures. The benchmark for payback is the maximum number of years required by the firm for the complete recovery of the investment in a project. For rate of return, the benchmark is the minimum rate of return required by management, which may vary appreciably depending on the method used to compute the rate of return. Several methods are in common use, as noted later.

For the discounted cash-flow methods, the criteria for evaluation will initially be assumed to be the firm's marginal cost of capital, commonly referred to as the *cost of capital*. This represents the cost of funds used to acquire the firm's total assets and is found by averaging the rate of return expected to be received by all parties contributing to the firm's financial structure. Actual computation of the firm's cost of capital is discussed in Chapter 8. Application of the evaluative criteria to the discounted cash-flow procedures is discussed in the following chapter.

3. The firm's cost of capital is constant over time and is not affected by the amount of funds that is invested on capital projects. This assumption avoids the problems imposed by *capital rationing* and varying money and capital market rates.

There are two types of capital rationing: internal and external. *Internal capital rationing* involves the constraints resulting from the limitations of existing managerial ability in assuming any new project or expansion responsibilities. Some firms attempt to circumvent this constraint by expanding through the acquisition of ongoing companies and thereby purchasing the needed managerial expertise along with the physical assets. *External capital rationing* originally referred to a lack of capital available to finance desirable projects. While this aspect of external capital rationing remains a primary consideration in the capital acquisition process, other external constraints also require close attention. Such constraints include lack or potential inavailability of critical materials, skilled labor, water and sewer supplies, and government permits to carry out construction and operate facilities.

4. Investment opportunities are independent of each other. There are no interrelationships among projects under consideration (mutually exclusive, contingent, and complementary projects do not exist); furthermore, *there is no correlation between the cash flows of any pair of projects under consideration by the firm* or between the cash flows of any project and the ongoing operations of the firm. This assumption is necessary to avoid the potential conflicts that may arise in ranking projects falling into the several categories of dependent projects. We discuss these conflicts in Chapter 7.

5. Borrowing and lending rates are equal. This means that the rate that must be paid by the firm to obtain capital from the capital markets (borrowing) is equal to the rate the firm can earn if it purchases securities in the capital markets (lending). This assumption is necessary to assure that a firm will be able to re-invest the incremental cash flows resulting from the use of an asset at the *same rate* that is used to discount those incremental cash flows to their present value. As noted earlier, the use of the compound interest, annuity, and present value tables is predicated on reinvesting intermediate cash flows at a constant rate over the life of the investment. The reason that it may not be possible to reinvest intermediate cash inflows at the same rate used to discount the project is that the market level of interest rate varies (sometimes appreciably) over the period of the life of a project. A methodology for evaluating projects during periods when interest rates and reinvestment rates are expected to vary is included in Chapter 7.

6. Perfect capital markets exist. This means that (a) no lender or borrower in the markets possesses sufficient power to influence prices; (b) any participant in the markets can lend or borrow as much as desired without affecting security prices (i.e., there is not an upward-sloping supply curve for capital); (c) bankruptcy and transaction costs do not exist; (d) all participants in the markets have access to the same cost-free information, this information is interpreted in exactly the same way by all participants, and such information is immediately incorporated into all security prices; and (e) capital rationing does not exist.

Certainty, Risk and Uncertainty—An Introduction

We have assumed that the projects being evaluated would not change the risk complexion of the firm overall. That is, the projects being evaluated have the same degree of risk as the firm. In order to understand this assumption better, we will define the three states certainty, risk, and uncertainty and the different types of risk with which the decision maker must deal.

Certainty postulates that the decision-maker knows in advance the exact future values of all the parameters that may affect the decision.

Risk postulates that the decision-maker is (1) aware of all possible future states of the environment, including the economy and business, that may occur and thereby affect relevant decision parameters and (2) able to place a probability on the value each parameter given the occurrence of each of these states.

Uncertainty postulates that the decision-maker may or may not (1) be aware of all the possible states that affect the decision and (2) be able to place a probability distribution on the occurrence of each.

In Part IV we examine the problems inherent in project selection under conditions of changing risk and describe procedures that are useful in selecting portfolios of projects in order to minimize risk. At this juncture it is useful to review three kinds of risk faced by financial managers.

1. Business risk is the variability in earnings that is a function of the firm's normal operations (as impacted by the changing economic environment) and management's decisions with respect to capital intensification. The use of more capital equipment generally results in higher fixed costs and thereby increases the variability of earnings before interest and taxes (EBIT) with output. It should be noted that business risk considers only the variability in EBIT and does not consider the effect of debt or other financing on the firm's risk posture.

2. Cataclysmic risk is the variability in earnings that is a function of events beyond managerial control and anticipation. Such events would include expropriation, erratic changes in consumer preferences, severe energy shortages, and the like.

3. Financial risk is the variability in earnings that is a function of the financial structure and the necessity of meeting obligations on fixed-income securities. The use of more debt or preferred stock results in greater obligatory payments and thereby increases the variability of earnings after taxes and the earnings per share.

PAYBACK

Payback is actually a measure of a project's liquidity and capital recovery rate rather than its profitability. The payback period is defined as the number of years required to recover the investment in a project. If the anticipated after-tax cash inflows are *equal each year*, then the payback period may be obtained by dividing the after-tax outflows related to the cost of the project by the after-tax cash inflows expected to be derived from the project. If the cash inflows are uneven, the payback period may be found as shown in Example 1.

When payback is used, projects may be accepted or rejected based on the number of years required to recover their cost. Projects may also be ranked using payback; the shorter the payback period, the higher the ranking. However, payback is more commonly used as a constraint rather than as a method for deciding among or ranking projects.

☐ **EXAMPLE 1** *Payback*

A corporation plans to invest funds to purchase a new machine. The projected cash inflows and outflows are shown below. Determine the payback period.

Time	Expected Cash Flows
Present	− $10,000
1	− 4,000
2–6	+ 3,000
7–15	+ 6,000
15[a]	+ 2,000

[a] Recovery of working capital.

Solution: Since the cash flows are not constant over the life of the project, the payback period may be found using tabular form, as follows.

Time	Expected Cash Flow	Net Cash Outflow
Present	− $10,000	− $10,000
1	− 4,000	− 14,000
2	+ 3,000	− 11,000
3	+ 3,000	− 8,000
4	+ 3,000	− 5,000
5	+ 3,000	− 2,000
6	+ 3,000	+ 1,000

The total investment is recovered during the sixth year. Because $2,000 remains outstanding at the start of the sixth year and $3,000 is expected to be received during the sixth year, the total investment will be recovered two-thirds of the way through the sixth year. The payback period is thus 5 years and 8 months.   ☐

When payback is used as demonstrated in Example 1, cash flows are considered only up to the time that the initial investment is recovered. As a result, the only question answered concerns the length of time needed to recover the initial investment. Weingartner[1] notes: "Generally, the break-even point is a point of indifference—with qualifications—beyond which an accounting profit is expected to be generated by the operation under analysis, and below which loss is expected." If the net revenues are constant, the aggregate profit will be proportional to project's life after the payback period has elapsed. "Thus, a longer anticipated life yields a higher initial profit, other things remaining equal, because depreciation expense will be lower. Indeed, the life of the project may be overestimated by the proposer not only to enhance its total profitability, but also to reduce the payback period on the accounting profit basis. A bias countering this one may arise in the selection of the shortest project or asset life which the tax authorities permit to improve the actual after-tax cash flow profitability.

[1] H. Martin Weingartner, "Some New Views on the Payback Period and Capital Budgeting Decisions," *Management Science*, 15, No. 12 (August 1969), B-599.

Cash flow payback, the usual concept, is less affected since depreciation enters only as a tax shield."[2]

The use of payback, then, depends on the importance to management of knowing the capital recovery period. Merritt and Sykes[3] note that: "It [payback] causes assessors to concentrate on unimportant and often irrelevant characteristics of an investment project to the detriment of its significant characteristics. It has harshly, but not unfairly, been described as the 'fish bait' test, since effectively it concentrates on the recovery of the bait (the capital outlay) paying no attention to the size of the fish (the ultimate profitability), if any."

The payback method has been further discredited for at least five reasons:

1. It fails to consider the expected revenues beyond the payback period established by the firm. Frequently, such payback periods are set from 2 to 5 years. The time period established generally is not based on an economic measure that would attach a cost to the use of funds and to the application of managerial effort, but rather may depend to a great extent on the firm's risk preferences for liquidity. Thus, for example, if a firm established a 3-year payback period requirement, revenues generated after the third year would not be considered when applying this method.

2. It fails to consider the time value of money.

3. It does not differentiate between projects requiring different cash investments.

4. While it does measure a project's rate of capital recovery or liquidity, it does not consider the firm's liquidity position as a whole, which is a much more important question. As Weingartner points out:[4] "The usually designated speculative and/or precautionary motive of firms to hold liquid or near liquid funds in order to seize upon unexpected opportunities is a different motive from that which requires each new investment separately to recover its original cost within a short time."

5. It ignores the cost of funds used to support the investment, even during the payback period. By ignoring the cost of funds, a very important cost is overlooked. Reconciliation of this problem is considered below.

A somewhat different approach to the application of payback, which takes into consideration the cost of funds necessary to support an investment, is demonstrated in the following section.

Payback Including The Cost of Funds

The payback method described earlier may be modified to incorporate the cost of funds used to support the project.[5] This procedure overcomes the fifth

---

[2]Ibid., p. B-601.

[3]A. J. Merritt and A. Sykes, *The Finance and Analysis of Capital Projects* (London: Longmans Green and Co. Ltd., 1963).

[4]Weingartner, "Some New Views on the Payback Period" p. B-599.

[5]W. G. Lewellen, H. P. Lanser, and J. McConnell, "Payback Substitutes for Discounted Cash Flow," *Financial Management*, vol. II, no. 2 (Summer 1973), present a procedure for establishing a one-to-one conversion of zero-net-present-value conditions into counterpart payback maxima. This approach renders the two approaches of discounted cash flow and payback operationally equivalent.

shortcoming just given and also proves useful in dealing with certain classes of cataclysmic risk. The methodology of incorporating the cost of funds into the payback method is demonstrated in Example 2.

□ **EXAMPLE 2** *Payback*

A corporation requires a rate of return of 15%. Using the project with cash flows as shown in Example 1, determine the period necessary to recover both the capital expenditures and the cost of funds required to support those expenditures.

Solution: Construct a table showing cash flows and costs of capital to support those funds.

Time	Expected Cash Flow	Dollar Cost of Funds at 15%	Cumulative Net Cash Flow
Present	− $10,000	0	− $10,000
1	− 4,000	− $1,500	− 15,500
2	+ 3,000	− 2,325	− 14,825
3	+ 3,000	− 2,224	− 14,049
4	+ 3,000	− 2,107	− 13,156
5	+ 3,000	− 1,973	− 12,129
6	+ 3,000	− 1,819	− 10,948
7	+ 6,000	− 1,642	− 6,590
8	+ 6,000	− 939	− 1,579
9	+ 6,000	− 237	+ 4,184

The total investment will be recovered in 9 years, assuming that all cash flows are year-end.   □

When the payback is used as shown in Example 2, it provides the period of time for the project to provide a return just equal to the cost of capital. The reader may verify this by discounting the expected cash flows to their present value at 15% for the 9-year payback period. We can conclude that the project must remain in use 9 years in order for the firm to cover its cost of capital and recover the funds invested in the project.

Since the payback, when employed as demonstrated in Example 2, indicates the period for both capital recovery and for recovery of the associated cost of funds, it can be used to advantage for analysis of cataclysmic risks. Examples of such risks include the probability of major technological changes that render ongoing processes valueless and sudden plant takeovers by foreign governments. These are risks associated with the possibility of the business going on for a period and then collapsing entirely.

Thus, payback is an all-or-nothing risk indicator and may be used to advantage in assessing risks relative to the time period during which an investment is expected to remain in use. For example, suppose that a firm were considering a project in a foreign country having the cash flows in Example 2. Payback shows that if the project remains in use and delivers the expected cash flows for 9 years, the firm will not suffer because it will have met its cost of capital. If the project operates more than 9 years, it will yield a return in excess of the firm's cost of capital. If management could estimate the possibility of the project's expropriation in terms of time from implementation, then payback, as used in Example 2, would provide an excellent cutoff time for risk analysis.

Why Payback Is Used

Although payback suffers from some severe limitations, it is frequently used by many companies. Furthermore, in periods of tight money and high interest rates, the use of payback tends to increase since cash flows expected beyond a short time horizon are of limited importance during periods when capital is very expensive. Various other reasons attributed to its frequent use include:

1. It is very simple.

2. Many managers have severe reservations about the estimates of expected cash flows to be received beyond the next 2 to 5 years and feel from past experience that if they can recover their investment in, for instance, 3 years, they will make a profit.

3. Many firms have liquidity problems and are very concerned about how rapidly invested funds will be recovered.

4. Some firms have high costs of external financing and must look to internally generated funds to support their future ventures. Hence, they are especially interested in the rate at which their investment will be recovered.

5. It is a simple matter to compensate for the differences in risk associated with alternative proposed projects: projects having higher degrees of risk are evaluated using shorter payback periods.

6. Some firms are involved in areas where the risk of obsolescence as a result of technical changes and severe competition is great. Therefore, they are anxious to recover funds rapidly.

7. Some firms manufacture products that are subject to model period changes and therefore must recover their investment within the model life.

Automobile manufacturers exemplify such firms. While payback does have severe limitations and is not a measure of profitability, it has been widely accepted for the reasons just described.

We recommend that payback be used as a supplemental evaluation tool, in conjunction with a discounted-cash-flow procedure. When payback is employed as in Example 2, we recommended its use in the following situations:

1. As a measure of a project's liquidity if such liquidity is of particular importance to the firm. Project liquidity should not be confused with profitability or with the firm's overall liquidity preference, as discussed above.

2. For projects involving very uncertain returns, especially when those returns become increasingly more uncertain in future time periods.

3. During periods of very high external financing costs, making capital recovery very important.

4. For projects involving a high degree of cataclysmic risk.

5. For projects subject to model-year changes or obsolescence resulting from technological changes, changing consumer preferences, and the like.

TABLE 4–1   Return on Investment Computed by Four Different Methods

Proposal—Bench Lathe

Investment	$1,000.00
Estimated useful life	5 years
Income: Year 1	300.00
" 2	300.00
" 3	300.00
" 4	300.00
" 5	300.00
Total	$1,500.00

Return-on-Investment Computations

Method 1:   Annual return on investment:

$$\frac{\text{annual income}}{\text{original investment}} \times 100 = \frac{300}{1,000} \times 100 = 30\%$$

Method 2:   Annual return on average investment:

$$\frac{\text{annual income}}{\dfrac{\text{original investment}}{2}} \times 100 = \frac{300}{500} \times 100 = 60\%$$

Method 3:   Average return on average investment:

$$\frac{\text{total income} - \text{original investment}}{\dfrac{\text{original investment}}{2} \times \text{years}} \times 100 = \frac{500}{\dfrac{1,000}{2} \times 5 \text{ years}} \times 100 = 20\%$$

Method 4:   Average book return on investment:

$$\frac{\text{total income} - \text{original investment}}{\text{weighted average investment}^{a}}$$

$$= \frac{500}{\dfrac{1,000 + 800 + 600 + 400 + 200}{5} \times 5 \text{ years}} \times 100 = 16\tfrac{2}{3}\%$$

[a] Sum of book values of asset each year, straight-line depreciation over life of the project.
SOURCE: N. E. Pflomm, *Managing Capital Expenditures*. (New York: The Conference Board, 1963).

RETURN ON INVESTMENT

The return-on-investment method compares the yearly after-tax (or pretax) income with the investment in the asset. The underlying idea is to compare the return expected to be received from a project with some preestablished requirement. Pflomm notes four methods in common use (see Table 4–1).[6] The simplest is to divide the average annual income by the total investment, as shown. The three other methods noted by Pflomm are also shown in the table.

In each calculation, the income figure refers to additional after-tax profits and may include depreciation cash throw-offs or may be net of those throw-offs.

[6] N. E. Pflomm, *Managing Capital Expenditures* (New York: Conference Board, 1963).

It is important for management to be aware that the differences in the potential results depend upon the procedure used. The investment refers to the actual after-tax, out-of-pocket cash flow and may or may not include the required additional working capital.

The primary shortcoming of all the rate-of-return procedures is that they do not consider the timing of the expected profits. Thus, a project with low initial profitability and high future profitability would have the same average return as a project with higher initial profitability and lower future profitability. The former project would have much less value to the firm than the latter. The difference between the average rate of return and the project's internal rate of return becomes increasingly significant for projects with relatively large inflows in the later years of their lives.

A second fault is much more insidious and warrants special attention, as it demonstrates a very important aspect of capital expenditure management. The real value of any asset to a firm is a function of management's ability to employ the asset in a productive manner. The firm's balance sheet (which indicates the book value of assets) is only a listing of the investments that the firm has made and the sources of capital used to obtain and maintain those investments. The amounts listed on the balance sheet reflect accounting values, which may differ substantially from both market values and productive values.

Since the balance-sheet book values neither reflect the value of assets in terms of their earning ability nor their market value, the return-on-investment method may be extremely misleading. Consider, for example, an apartment house having an original cost of $1 million 10 years ago, currently producing cash inflows (after-tax profits plus depreciation cash throw-offs) of $250,000 per year, and having a book value of $500,000. Based on the book value, the rate of return would be 50%. However, experience indicates that apartment house values, in general, have doubled over the last 10 years, so that the fair market value is probably close to $2 million. A $250,000 return on a $2 million investment is only 12.5%. This simple example clearly demonstrates two important facts: The rate-of-return method may give very misleading results and, in any capital investment problem, it is the fair market value or the productive value of the asset to the firm, not the book value, that must be considered. The book value is not relevant because it merely represents sunk costs and comes into play only when computing the tax impact of investments.

The Conference Board's survey indicates that about one-fourth of the firms surveyed use the method, but generally only as a supplemental tool. While rate of return is still used by some firms, we do not recommend it. The results frequently are erroneous, as the rate of return seldom, if ever, indicates the real value or earning power of a project.

QUESTIONS/PROBLEMS

1. A corporation plans to invest funds in a new machine. The initial after-tax cash outflow amounts to $10,000 and yearly cash inflows over its 6-year life are $2,200. Determine the payback period for the machine.

2. A certain project has yearly after-tax cash outflows and inflows as follows:

Year	Outflow	Inflow
Present	− $10,000	0
1	− 5,000	$3,000
2	0	4,000
3-6	0	5,000

Determine the payback period.

3. A corporation has a policy of rejecting any investment that does not result in recovery of cost within 4 years. They are considering three projects:

Time	Project A	Project B	Project C
Present	− $10,000	− $12,000	− $3,000
1	4,000	0	500
2	4,000	5,000	500
3	2,000	4,000	500
4	2,000	3,000	2,000
5	2,000	3,000	2,000
6	2,000	3,000	2,000
7	2,000	3,000	2,000

Determine the acceptable projects and rank them by payback period.

4. If a corporation requires a 10% after-tax return on its investments, determine the payback period for each investment listed in Problem 3.

5. The Johnson Company is considering the acquisition of a small company that will fit nicely into their present distribution system and complement present operations. Senior management requires a maximum 9-year payback period. The acquisition cost of the company is $8 million and the company yielded after-tax cash flows of $750,000 in the past year. A 5% after-tax growth rate has been projected. Additionally, the Johnson Company can save $50,000 per year by combining the two distribution systems. Should the acquisition be made assuming that the Johnson Company has a cost of capital of 9%?

6. Obel International Corporation is considering manufacturing a new product line in one of its three plants. The plants are located in the United States, Canada, and Mexico and the cost of capital at each location is 8%, 9%, and 14%, respectively. Expected cash flows at each location are as follows:

Time	United States	Canada	Mexico
Present	− $25,000	− $28,000	− $32,000
1	− 9,000	− 12,000	− 16,000
2	− 6,000	+ 2,000	+ 1,000
3	+ 1,000	+ 8,000	+ 13,000
4	+ 8,000	+ 16,000	+ 18,000
5-10	+ 18,000	+ 18,000	+ 18,000

Provide a payback-period chart based on net cash flow from each country and indicate your choice of location for the management.

7. The Green Thumb Sod Company has a required rate of return of 12%. Pete Moss, the company's financial wizard, must decide between two different heavy-duty, sod-cutting machines. Sod cutter A will cost $8,000 to purchase this year, plus an additional

$2,000 next year for testing and tuning. After this period, Pete estimates cash inflow generated by the machine will be $3,000 for the next 4 years, $2,000 the next 3 years, and $1,000 per year to the end of its 12-year useful life. Sod cutter B will cost $15,000, with no additional costs, and is expected to generate an income of $4,000 for the first 3 years, $3,000 the next 6 years, and $900 per year to the end of its 10-year useful life. Which machine should Pete recommend purchasing, assuming that he wants to recover both the capital expenditures and the cost of funds required to support these funds as soon as possible? All cash flows are year-end.

8. A project will provide cash inflows of $1,000 for 10 years. What is the maximum amount that could be invested in the project if capital recovery can take no more than 5 years? The cost of capital is 12%.

9. A project that has a 10-year life costs $5,000. It is expected to generate income of $800 per year each year of its life. Determine the project's return on investment using the four methods of Table 4–1.

Discounted Cash–Flow Evaluation Techniques

The analytical methods of discounted cash flows are based on the concept of discounting cash inflows and outflows to their present values, thus fully considering the time value of money. In this chapter we describe four methods: net present value (NPV), profitability index (PI), internal rate of return (IRR), and equivalent annual charge.

NET PRESENT VALUE

The present-value criterion for evaluating proposed capital investments involves summing the present values of cash outflows required to support an investment with the present value of the cash inflows resulting from operations of the project. The inflows and outflows are discounted to present value using the firm's required rate of return. The *net present value* (NPV) is the difference in the present value of the inflows and outflows:

$$\text{NPV} = \sum_{t=0}^{n} \frac{S_t}{(1+k)^t} - A_0 \tag{1}$$

where A_0 = present value of the after-tax cost of the project
S_t = cash inflow to be received in period t
k = appropriate discount rate (hurdle rate)
t = time period
n = useful life of asset

If the project cost is incurred over a period of time, then A_0 represents the present value of those cash outflows and may be expressed as shown in Equation (2):

$$A_0 = \sum_{t=0}^{n} \frac{A_t}{\left(1+k\right)^t}. \tag{2}$$

where A_t = the cash outflow in period t

If the NPV is positive, it means the project is expected to yield a return in excess of the required rate; if the NPV is zero, the yield is expected to exactly equal the required rate; if the NPV is negative, the yield is expected to be less than the required rate. Hence, except in unusual circumstances, only those projects that have positive or zero NPV's meet the NPV criterion for acceptance.

It should be noted that the cash inflows (S_t), which are discounted in the NPV method according to Equation (1), result from two sources: (1) using the asset over its productive life and (2) disposing of the asset at the end of its life. The net salvage value obtained from the disposal of the asset is the final cash inflow generated by the asset and must be included in the determination of the asset's NPV.

The primary difficulty encountered with NPV is in deciding the appropriate rate of return (the hurdle rate) to use in discounting the cash flows. The accuracy of the forecasts of cash flows influences the selection of a hurdle rate, so the use of NPV also depends on the accuracy of those forecasts. While the firm's cost of capital may be used as the discount rate, there exist questions concerning how the cost of capital should be calculated. These are examined in Chapters 8 and 17. Also, there may be difficulty involved in obtaining the data needed to perform the calculations, even after the procedural questions are resolved.

□ **EXAMPLE 1** *Determination of Net Present Value*

ABC Company is evaluating project Z, which requires a present cash outflow of $10,000 and generates cash inflows of $4,000 each year over its 6-year useful life. The asset is projected to have no salvage value at the end of its life. The company has set its required rate of return at 16%. Determine the NPV for Project Z.

Solution: We can determine the NPV for project Z either by using Equation (1) directly or by constructing the equivalent table.

In equation form the solution is

$$NPV = \sum_{t=0}^{n} \frac{S_t}{\left(1+k\right)^t} - A_0$$

$$= \sum_{t=1}^{6} \frac{\$4,000}{\left(1+0.16\right)^t} - \$10,000$$

Since project Z has equal annual cash inflows, we can evaluate the first term on the right-hand side of this equation by using the annuity factors from Appendix B, Thus,

$$NPV = (\$4,000)(3.684736) - \$10,000 = \underline{\$4,739}$$

Using the tabular format, we find:

Time	Cash Flow	Discount Factors for 16%	Present Value
0	− $10,000	1.0000	− $10,000
1–6	+ 4,000	3.684736	+ 14,739
			NPV = $ 4,739

Of course, we arrive at the same result using either approach. Therefore, the reader can utilize whichever method is more easily understood. If the project under evaluation has cash inflows that differ year by year over its life, the process of determining the project's NPV is slightly more complicated. Under such conditions, we need a separate term in the equation method for each cash inflow or a separate line for each cash inflow in the table. In addition, single-payment discount factors from Appendix B, would be used rather than the annuity factor used here. We illustrate the treatment of this additional complexity in Example 3.   □

Two other factors about NPV deserve mention.

1. The NPV model implicitly assumes that the *incremental cash inflows* will be *reinvested* to earn the firm's required rate of return throughout the life of the project. For example, project Z in Example 1 had an NPV of $4,739 when the project's cash flows are discounted at the firm's required rate of return of 16%. This NPV value implicitly assumes that ABC Company can reinvest project Z's cash inflows to earn 16% compounded annually between the time that they occur and the end of the project's life.

In practice, the reinvestment rate frequently differs from the discount rate. This results from the fact that the general level of interest rates normally changes (and sometimes substantially) over the life of a project. We deal with this problem as a part of our discussion of terminal value in Chapter 7.

2. The NPV of a project reveals the amount by which the productive value (present value of the cash inflows) exceeds or is less than the cost. Naturally, if we have a choice (if discretionary projects are involved), we choose only those projects whose productive values exceed or at least equal their costs. If the NPV of a project is positive, the amount of the NPV is the amount by which the project will *increase the value of the firm making the investment.* Thus, selecting that group of projects with the highest total NPV, other things being equal, should *maximize* the market value of the firm.

NPV PROFILES

Recall that one difficulty with the NPV model is in the determination of the appropriate required rate of return, or hurdle rate, to use in discounting the project's cash flows. One helpful approach to addressing this difficulty is the construction of an *NPV profile* for any given project. An NPV profile is a graphic representation of a project's NPV as the hurdle, or discount, rate is allowed to take on various values. The NPV profile shows how much the firm's required rate of return could increase and still yield a project attractive to the firm.

We illustrate the construction of an NPV profile in Example 2.

☐ **EXAMPLE 2** *NPV Profile for Project Z*

For project Z (Example 1), compute the NPV at discount rates from 0% to 40% at 5% intervals. Then, graph the results by showing the NPV's on the vertical axis and the discount rates on the horizontal axis (join the plotted points with a smooth curve).

Solution: The table summarizes the results of the NPV calculations.

Discount Rate	Project Z's Annual Cash Inflows	Present Value Annuity Factor for 6 years at the Given Discount Rate	Discounted Cash Inflows	Project Z's Cost	NPV at the Given Discount Rate
0%	+ $4,000	6.000000	$24,000	$10,000	$14,000
5	+ 4,000	5.075692	20,303	10,000	10,303
10	+ 4,000	4.355261	17,421	10,000	7,421
15	+ 4,000	3.784483	15,138	10,000	5,138
20	+ 4,000	3.325510	13,302	10,000	3,302
25	+ 4,000	2.951424	11,806	10,000	1,806
30	+ 4,000	2.642746	10,571	10,000	571
35	+ 4,000	2.385157	9,541	10,000	− 459
40	+ 4,000	2.167974	8,672	10,000	− 1,328

The following figure shows the NPV profile for project Z.

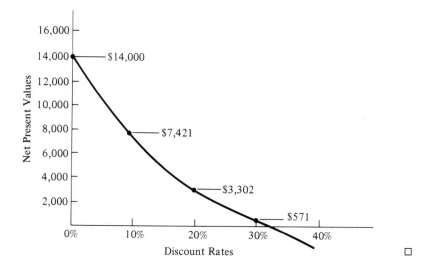

Several points about the NPV profile deserve mention. First, the profile for project Z shown in Example 2 is downward sloping. This will be the usual NPV profile for investments projects that have one or more cash outflows initially followed by an uninterrupted series of cash inflows over the project's life. We concentrate *exclusively* on such projects and their related profiles in this text. Second, the NPV profile intersects the vertical axis at a value representing the sum of the undiscounted cash flows for the project because the discount rate is zero. For project Z, this value is $14,000 (6 × $4,000 − $10,000). Third, the smooth NPV profile consists of the project's NPV's at all discount rates. Thus, for Project Z, the NPV found in Example 1 at the firm's 16% required rate of return—$4,739—is found on the profile at the 16% discount rate. Finally, we see that the profile crosses the horizontal axis at about 32.5%; NPV equals zero at this discount rate. Later in the chapter, we see that this rate is called the *internal rate of return*. The significance of this point is that as long as the ABC Company's required rate of return does not exceed 32.5%, project Z is a candidate for acceptance.

NPV FOR MORE-COMPLEX PROJECTS

We next turn to the determination of NPV for a project with a more-involved pattern of cash flows over its useful life.

□ **EXAMPLE 3**   *Net Present Value*

A certain investment is expected to take several years to develop and implement. If the costs and cash flows are as tabulated, determine the NPV at 14%.

Time	Amount	
Present	− $ 10,000	
1	− 60,000	
2	− 3,000,000	
3	− 350,000	
4	+ 550,000	
5–20	+ 800,000	
20	+ 300,000	Net salvage value

Solution: As mentioned in Example 1, we can determine a project's NPV utilizing either an equation or a table. Both methods are illustrated here.

Using Equations (1) and (2) for this project, we find:

$$
\begin{aligned}
\text{NPV} &= \sum_{t=0}^{n} \frac{S_t}{(1+k)^t} - \sum_{t=0}^{n} \frac{A_t}{(1+k)^t} \\[2mm]
&= \frac{\$550{,}000}{(1.14)^4} + \sum_{t=5}^{20} \frac{\$800{,}000}{(1.14)^t} + \frac{\$300{,}000}{(1.14)^{20}} \\[2mm]
&\quad -\$10{,}000 - \frac{\$60{,}000}{(1.14)^1} - \frac{\$3{,}000{,}000}{(1.14)^2} - \frac{\$350{,}000}{(1.14)^3} \\[2mm]
&= \$387{,}731
\end{aligned}
$$

Using a tabular form we find:

Solution Table for NPV Using 14% Discount Rate

Time	Cash Flow	Discount Factor	Present Value
Present	− $ 10,000	1.0	− $ 10,000
1	− 60,000	0.877193	− 52,632
2	− 3,000,000	0.769468	− 2,308,404
3	− 350,000	0.674972	− 236,240
4	+ 550,000	0.592080	+ 325,644
5–20	+ 800,000	3.309419	+ 2,647,534
20	+ 300,000	0.072762	+ 21,829
			NPV = $ 387,731

Since the NPV is positive, this project is a viable candidate for acceptance. Its acceptance is expected to increase the value of the firm by $387,731 in present-value terms. □

PROFITABILITY INDEX

The *profitability index* (PI) is the ratio of the present value of the after-tax cash inflows to the outflows. A ratio of 1 or greater indicates that the project in question has an expected yield equal to or greater than the discount rate. The profitability index is a measure of a project's profitability per dollar of investment. As a result, it may be used to rank projects of varying costs and expected economic lives in order of their profitability. But a word of caution is in order. If projects are ranked just by profitability index, the investment in a typewriter might appear better than one in a steel mill. The size of projects is ignored. And, as previously noted, the group of projects having the greatest combined net present value should be selected within the constraints of budget limitations, projects interdependency, mutual exclusivity, and the like.

$$PI = \frac{\text{present value of cash inflows}}{\text{present value of cash outflows}} \tag{3}$$

$$PI = \frac{\sum_{t=0}^{n} \frac{S_t}{(1+k)^t}}{A_0} \tag{4}$$

The relationship among net present value, profitability index, and the required rate of return is as follows:

Net Present Value	Profitability Index	Expected Returns
Negative	Less than 1	Less than required return
Zero	Equal to 1	Exactly equal to required return
Positive	Greater than 1	Greater than required return

□ **EXAMPLE 4**   *Ranking Projects Using the Profitability Index*

Three projects have been suggested to a corporation. The after-tax cash flows for each are tabulated below. If the corporation's cost of capital is 12%, rank them in order of profitability.

After-Tax Cash Flows

Time	Project A	Project B	Project C
Present	− $10,000	− $30,000	− $18,000
1	2,800	6,000	6,500
2	3,000	10,000	6,500
3	4,000	12,000	6,500
4	4,000	16,000	6,500

Solution: Each project must be evaluated to obtain the present value of the cash inflows and outflows. The present values of the inflows and outflows are as follows:

	Project A	Project B	Project C
PV of outflows	− $10,000	− $30,000	− $18,000
PV of inflows	10,281	32,040	19,743

The profitability indices are:

$$PI_A = \frac{\$10,281}{\$10,000} = 1.0281$$

$$PI_B = \frac{\$32,040}{\$30,000} = 1.068$$

$$PI_C = \frac{\$19,743}{\$18,000} = 1.0968$$

The projects would be ranked as follows: C, B, and A.   □

Note that the ranking using profitability indices measures return per dollar of investment. Thus, although project B in Example 4 has the highest NPV, it is not the most profitable per dollar of investment. Rather, project C is the most profitable per dollar of investment. Note further that all the projects have positive net present values, and hence all meet the 12% required rate of return.

INTERNAL RATE OF RETURN

By definition, the *internal rate of return* (IRR) is that rate which exactly equates the present value of the expected after-tax cash inflows with the present value of the after-tax cash outflows. This is expressed in Equation (5):

$$\sum_{t=0}^{n} \frac{S_t}{(1+r)^t} = \sum_{t=0}^{n} \frac{A_t}{(1+r)^t} \tag{5}$$

where r is the internal rate of return. Thus, at the internal rate of return, the NPV is zero.

The internal rate of return recognizes the time value of money and considers the anticipated revenues over the entire economic (useful) life of an investment.

☐ **EXAMPLE 5**   *Internal Rate of Return*

A new project has an after-tax cost of $10,000 and will result in after-tax cash inflows of $3,000 in year 1, $5,000 in year 2, and $6,000 in year 3. Determine the internal rate of return.

Solution: First, set up a solution table.

Time	Cash Flow		Discount Factor	Present Value
Present	− $10,000	×	1	− $10,000
1	3,000	×	Unknown	Unknown
2	5,000	×	Unknown	Unknown
3	6,000	×	Unknown	Unknown
			NPV = $	0.00

Since only the sum of the present values of the three cash inflows is known to be $10,000, there is no direct way of obtaining the answer. Therefore, it must be estimated and then checked. In order to make a first estimate of the answer, *it is possible to reconstruct the problem using an average cash inflow each year rather than the exact amounts given*. The average of $3,000, $5,000, and $6,000 is $4,666 per year. Based on the amount of $4,666, we can reconstruct a solution table.

Time	Cash Flow		Discount Factor	Present Value
Present	− $10,000	×	1	− $10,000
1–3	4,666	×	Unknown	10,000
			NPV = $	0.00

Now there is only one unknown, and this may be found as follows:

$$\$4,666 \times \text{d.f.} = \$10,000$$

$$\text{d.f.} = \frac{\$10,000}{\$\ 4,666} = 2.1431$$

The discount factor (d.f.) is 2.1431. To determine the corresponding internal rate of return, refer to Appendix B, fifth column. The closest factor is 2.139917, which corresponds to 19%. Thus, 19% is the estimate to be used in solving the problem. Refer back to the original solution table, and replace the unknown discount factors with the discount factors corresponding to 19%. Then multiply these by the cash inflows to determine the present values. The table is as follows:

Solution Table for NPV Using 19% Discount Rate

Time	Cash Flow		Discount Factor	Present Value
Present	− $10,000	×	1	− $10,000
1	3,000	×	0.840336	2,521
2	5,000	×	0.706165	3,531
3	6,000	×	0.593416	3,560
			NPV = − $	388

The NPV is negative. This means that the discount factors applied to the inflows are too small. Larger discount factors are obtained by using *lower* rates of return. The solution table for 17% is as follows:

Solution Table for NPV Using 17% Discount Rate

Time	Cash Flow		Discount Factor	Present Value
Present	− $10,000	×	1	− $10,000
1	3,000	×	0.854701	2,564
2	5,000	×	0.730514	3,652
3	6,000	×	0.624371	3,746
			NPV =	− $ 38

The NPV is much closer to zero, but still negative. Therefore, the rate of return must be lower than 17%. The solution table for 16% is as follows:

Solution Table for NPV Using 16% Discount Rate

Time	Cash Flow		Discount Factor	Present Value
Present	− $10,000	×	1	− $10,000
1	3,000	×	0.862069	2,586
2	5,000	×	0.743163	3,716
3	6,000	×	0.640658	3,844
			NPV =	$ 146

The NPV for 16% is positive. Therefore, we can conclude that the actual internal rate of return is between 16% and 17%; it may be found using linear interpolation, as demonstrated in Example 6. □

□ *EXAMPLE 6* Linear Interpolation

Refer to Example 5 and determine the internal rate of return. The answer lies between 16% and 17%. The NPV's corresponding to those rates are as follows:

Rate of Return	NPV
16%	$146
17%	− $ 38

Solution: The actual rate of return corresponds to NPV = 0. The situation is shown on the graph. The width of the lower scale is $146.00 + $38.00 = $184.00, as shown. The zero value is

$$\frac{\$38}{\$184} = 0.2$$

or 0.2 of the way below the 17% point. Therefore, the internal rate of return is 17% − 0.2% = 16.8%.

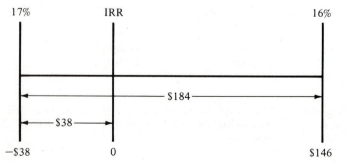

Once the IRR of a project has been determined, it is a simple matter to compare it with the required rate of return to decide whether or not the project is acceptable. If the IRR equals or exceeds the required rate, the project is acceptable. Ranking the projects is also a simple matter. Projects are ranked according to their IRR's: the project with the highest IRR is ranked first, and so on.

In Examples 5 and 6, the cash flows were conventional in nature—one or more outflows followed by a series of uninterrupted cash inflows. If there are changes in the signs of the cash flows over the asset's life, then there may be more than one internal rate of return. This is an unusual problem that demonstrates an anomaly of IRR. Since we recommend NPV as a more-useful evaluative method than IRR, we do not discuss the methods for determining multiple IRR's.

AGREEMENT BETWEEN NPV, PI, IRR

When a firm is evaluating a *single, independent, conventional* project, the three discounted cash-flow methods—NPV, PI, and IRR—*always* agree with respect to the attractiveness of the project. Notice the conditions we are placing on this statement. We must be evaluating only *one* project, whose cash flows or acceptance are not related to other projects under evaluation. Further, that project must have a conventional cash-flow pattern; that is, the project must have one or more cash outflows in the first years of its life and then have an uninterrupted series of cash inflows until the end of its useful life.

We can see that the three methods *must* agree by referring to the NPV profile. Consider again the NPV profile for project Z shown in Example 2. It is modified in Figure 5–1.

In Figure 5–1, we can see that project Z has a positive NPV and is therefore attractive at the 16% required rate of return. If a project's NPV is greater than 0 at the required rate of return, the project's IRR must exceed the required rate of return which signals that the project is attractive. This is true since the only way that the project's NPV can be reduced to zero, thereby obtaining the IRR, is to use a higher discount rate. Thus, IRR must exceed the firm's required rate of return. Figure 5–1 shows that the IRR of project Z is 32.5%, which exceeds the firm's 16% required rate of return.

To verify that the PI must also agree, recall the definitions of NPV and PI:

$$NPV = \text{discounted cash inflows} - \text{discounted cash outflows}$$

$$PI = \frac{\text{discounted cash inflows}}{\text{discounted cash outflows}}$$

If a project has a positive NPV, then its discounted cash inflows (DCI) necessarily exceed its discounted cash outflows (DCO). Furthermore, if NPV is greater than 0, then PI must be greater than 1 thereby signalling project attractiveness. For project Z, $NPV_{16\%} = \$4,739$ since DCI = \$14,739 and DCO = \$10,000; thus, PI = 1.4739, or \$14,739 ÷ \$10,000.

FIGURE 5–1   NPV Profile for Project Z

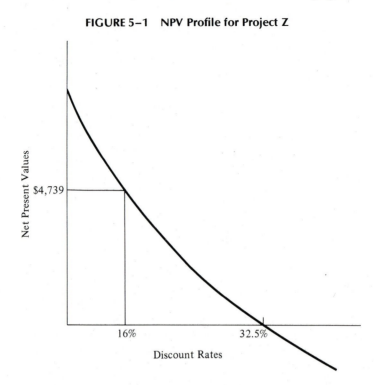

Therefore, if one of the three DCF models (NPV, PI, or IRR) determines that a single, independent, conventional capital project is a candidate for acceptance, *all three of these models will agree*. Conversely, if any of these three DCF models find that the project should be rejected, then *all three of these models will agree*.

However, if the firm is *ranking mutually exclusive projects, conflicts in project ranking can arise, depending on whether NPV, PI, or IRR is used*. Conditions under which such conflicts can arise and the resolution of these conflicts are treated in depth in Chapters 6 and 7.

At this juncture, we turn to the final DCF model, which has special applications for regulated industries.

EQUIVALENT ANNUAL CHARGE

The annual-capital-charge method involves discounting all the cash inflows and outflows to present value and determining the equivalent annual charge over the life of the project. The method is of particular importance in the areas of public price regulation such as for utilities. A utility may, for example, construct a power-generating station at great cost. The life and annual operating costs may also be projected. The annual-capital-charge method is used to find the equivalent annual charge that should be made to customers to cover the construction and operating costs, while also providing a required rate of return. The required rate of return may be the firm's cost of capital or another appropriate rate. The process is demonstrated in Example 7.

□ **EXAMPLE 7** *Equivalent Annual Charge*

A utility has spent $10,000,000 on a new facility. Operating costs are expected to be $800,000 per year over its 30-year life. If the utility requires a 9% return, determine the equivalent annual charge.

Solution: The equivalent annual charge consists of two parts: the $800,000 per year and the periodic payment needed to amortize $10,000,000 over 30 years at 9%. For the latter, refer to Appendix B, sixth column.

$$\text{annual charge} = 0.09733635 \times \$10,000,000$$

$$= \$973,363.50$$

The total equivalent annual charge is $973,363.50 + $800,000 = $1,773,363.50.   □

In many problems a salvage value or recovery of working capital will be involved. This may be handled easily by multiplying salvage value by the appropriate sinking-fund factor (Appendix B, third column). The product is then subtracted from the annual equivalent charge for the entire cost. The process is demonstrated in Example 8.

□ **EXAMPLE 8** *Equivalent Annual Charge with Salvage Value*

Suppose in Example 7 that the facility had a $1,000,000 salvage value. Recompute the equivalent annual charge.

Solution: First, find the present value of the salvage value:

$$PV = 0.075371 \times \$1,000,000 = \$75,371$$

Second, subtract the present value of the salvage value from the original cost:

$$\$10,000,000 - \$75,371 = \$9,924,629$$

Third, determine the equivalent annual charge:

$$\text{annual charge} = 0.09733635 \times \$9,924,629 = \$966,027.16$$

Last, add the equivalent annual charge to the $800,000 yearly operating cost to obtain the total annual charge:

$$\$800,000 + \$966,027.16 = \$1,766,027.16$$ □

The equivalent-annual-charge method is also useful for comparing alternatives that have unequal lives, as demonstrated in Example 9.

□ **EXAMPLE 9**   Equivalent Annual Charge

Two mutually exclusive projects have projected cash flows as shown:

Time	Project A	Project B
Present	− $10,000	− $8,000
1	− 2,000	− 2,500
2	− 2,000	− 2,500
3	− 2,000	− 2,500
4	− 2,500	− 3,800
5	− 2,500	− 3,800
6	− 2,500	− 3,800
7	− 3,000	
8	− 3,000	
9	− 3,000	
10	− 3,000	

In addition, project A will recover salvage value of $1,500 in year 10, while project B will recover $1,000 in year 6. Determine the equivalent annual charge for each project at 10% required rate of return.

Solution: Consider project A. The equivalent annual charge of the initial cost and salvage value are determined as in Examples 6 and 7.

$$\text{annual charge} = 0.16274539 \times \$10,000$$
$$= \$1,627.45$$
$$\text{equivalent payment} = 0.06274539 \times \$1,500$$
$$= \$94.12$$

The equivalent annual charge of the initial cost less salvage value is $1,533.33.

Next, find the present value of the outflows over the 10-year operating life:

$$\text{present value} = 2.48685 \times \$2,000 + 1.868409 \times \$2,500 + 1.789306 \times \$3,000$$
$$= \$4,973.70 + \$4,671.02 + \$5,367.92$$
$$= \$15,012.64$$

The present value of the outflows is $15,012.64. The equivalent annual charge is found in the same manner as that used for the initial investment:

$$\text{annual charge} = 0.16274539 \times \$15,012.64$$
$$= \$2,443.24$$

The total equivalent annual charge is, therefore, $1,533.33 + $2,443.24 = $3,976.57.

Consider project B. The equivalent annual charge of the initial cost and salvage values are determined in the same manner as for project A.

$$\text{annual charge} = 0.22960738 \times \$8,000$$
$$= \$1,836.86$$
$$\text{equivalent payment} = 0.12960738 \times \$1,000$$
$$= \$129.61$$

The equivalent annual charge of the initial cost less the salvage value is $1,707.25. The present value of the outflows is determined as follows:

$$\text{present value} = 2.486852 \times \$2,500 + 1.868409 \times \$3,800$$
$$= \$6,217.13 + \$7,099.95$$
$$= \$13,317.08$$

The present value of the outflows is \$13,317.08. The equivalent annual charge is:

$$\text{annual charge} = 0.22960738 \times \$13,317.08$$
$$= \$3,057.70$$

The total equivalent annual charge is therefore \$1,707.25 + \$3,057.70 = \$4,764.95. Project A is clearly superior to project B, as its equivalent annual cost is lower.   □

The annual-capital-charge method described above is a valuable managerial tool in that it does consider the time value of money and the flows over the entire asset life. Further, it is especially useful in serving as a baseline for setting rate structures as previously indicated, for evaluating nondiscretionary expenditure alternatives that are not profit producing, and for comparing projects having unequal lives. For example, to meet clean water requirements, a firm may have to install pollution-control equipment, but there may be choice as to the particular equipment to be installed and its associated operating costs. The annual-capital-charge method is ideal for comparing the costs of alternatives of this type.

CHANGING RESIDUAL VALUES OVER TIME— THE ABANDONMENT QUESTION

When a decision is made to accept a given project, it is implicitly assumed that the asset will generally decrease in value over its useful life. A discretionary project is accepted if it has a productive value to the firm that exceeds its cost. For most projects, the productive value continues to exceed the residual value of the asset throughout its useful life and abandonment never becomes an issue. There are two instances, however, when abandonment may be appropriate.

The first instance arises when costs and/or benefits change over the life of the project. An example of this is the rapid decrease in the productive values of automobile tooling as oil prices escalate. We deal with the question of capital abandonment under conditions of changing risk in Chapter 15. The second is when the market value of an asset is *expected* to rise during its life at a more rapid rate than the cash inflows resulting from the firm's use of the asset. Examples of the latter are easily found in both commercial and residential real estate. Depending upon the rate and method of depreciation permitted for a structure, the optimum abandonment time normally ranges from 7 to 12 years after acquisition, for example. The timing of such abandonments is of critical concern to the managers of limited real estate partnerships.

When investment opportunities are initially considered, key variables are identified and assumptions are made to arrive at some choice. As time passes, changes can occur that could affect these key variables. Assumptions made initially may prove incorrect, or perhaps some additional unforeseen new investment opportunities may arise. *Failure to abandon projects that are no longer desirable could be very costly. By the same reasoning, failure to abandon projects that could make funds available for substantially better investment opportunities might also be costly from an opportunity standpoint.* Therefore, the prudent financial manager must incorporate abandonment values (at various points throughout the life of the project) into the analysis for capital project evaluation and selection.

As a first approach to the abandonment problem, assume that the firm has the option to abandon the project at various points throughout its useful life. The methodology basically finds the maximum NPV of the project cash flows and the abandonment value considering all possible periods when the project can be abandoned.

In equation form, we want to determine the time period m that maximizes NPV^m:

$$NPV^m = \sum_{t=0}^{m} \frac{A_t}{(1+k)^t} + \frac{AV_m}{(1+k)^m} \qquad (6)$$

where A_t = operating cash flow of the project in period t
  k = firm's cost of capital
  AV_m = abandonment value in period m
  m = period when abandonment is being considered
  NPV^m = net present value of the cash flows from operating the project for m periods, as well as the abandonment value of the project at the end of the mth period

The use of Equation (6) is illustrated in Example 10.

□ **EXAMPLE 10**   *Abandonment Decision*

Consider that project Z has the following cash flows and abandonment values over its useful life:

Period	0	1	2	3	4	5
Cash Flows	− $7,500	$2,000	$2,000	$2,000	$2,000	$2,000
Abandonment Values	—	$6,200	$5,200	$4,000	$2,200	0

The firm's cost of capital is 10%. Determine the optimal time for project Z to be abandoned if it is accepted.

Solution: The analysis proceeds by preparing the following table:

Period	10% Discount Factor	Cash Flows	Abandonment After Period: 1	2	3	4	5
1	0.909	$2,000	$1,818	$1,818	$1,818	$1,818	$1,818
2	0.826	$2,000		1,652	1,652	1,652	1,652
3	0.751	$2,000			1,502	1,502	1,502
4	0.683	$2,000				1,366	1,366
5	0.621	$2,000					1,242
PV of operating cash flows			$1,818	$3,470	$4,972	$6,338	$7,580
PV of abandonment value			5,636	4,295	3,004	1,503	0
PV of total flows			$7,454	$7,765	$7,976	$7,841	$7,580
Investment outflow			7,500	7,500	7,500	7,500	7,500
NPV^m			($46)	$ 265	$ 476	$ 341	$ 80

As can be seen, the NPV is maximized by abandoning project Z at the end of period 3. It should also be noted that the abandonment option makes project Z considerably more attractive than if the firm had to hold the project until the end of its five-period useful life; that is, the NPV of the optimal holding period ($476 for three periods) is almost six times the NPV of the project if it is held to the end of its useful life ($80).   □

Example 10 demonstrates the importance of selecting the optimum time for the disposal of an asset. Naturally, the analysis must be ongoing because costs, revenues, and the market price of an asset will change from year to year. Consequently, it is necessary to recalculate the net present value and reconsider abandonment periodically throughout the life of an asset. The review of existing projects should take place at regular intervals and especially when events in the economy (for instance, changes in interest rates, changes in project replacement costs, or changes in projected revenues) dictate. Again, the primary objective is to maximize the present value of the firm's entire portfolio of assets.

QUESTIONS/PROBLEMS

1. The Fisher Beer Company is evaluating two brewing projects. The after-tax cash flows for the alternative proposals are summarized in the table.

Time	Project A	Project B
Present	− $20,000	− $28,000
1	5,000	8,000
2	5,000	8,000
3	6,000	8,000
4	6,000	8,000
5	6,000	8,000

Using a 10% rate, determine the NPV and PI for both projects.

2. Leisure Incorporated is evaluating two investment opportunities and will pick one. Project Fun requires an investment of $10,000, while Project Lazy requires an investment of $19,000. The after-tax cash flows are as follows:

	Cash Flows	
Year	Fun	Lazy
1	$2,000	$4,000
2	3,000	5,000
3	4,000	6,000
4	3,000	4,000
5	3,000	3,000

Determine the NPV and the profitability index associated with each given a hurdle rate of 10%.

3. A project costs $75 and will yield after-tax cash flows of $5 in years 1 and 2, $20 in years 3 and 4, and $25 in years 5 to 10. Find the IRR of the project.

4. Referring to Problem 3, determine the equivalent annual inflows which, when discounted at the IRR, will give a NPV of zero.

5. An investor paid $65,000 for a duplex that she intends to keep 5 years and then sell. In the first years she knows that she will have to spend a considerable amount for repairs. If she desires a 9% after-tax return and the cash flows are as tabulated below, will she achieve this return? Determine the net present value and profitability index.

Year	Cash Flows
1	− $ 100
2	4,900
3	5,300
4	4,800
5	74,500

6. A utility company is considering building a new generating facility for $50,000,000 with inflation-adjusted operating expenses of $1,000,000 annually for 30 years, the life of the installation after completion of construction. The salvage value is estimated at $1,500,000, and construction will take 2 years before the new facility can be brought on line. Consider the cost of construction to represent outflows of $25,000,000 each at the end of the first 2 years. Alternatively, the company can rebuild the present facility for $10,000,000 and reduce annual operating expenses from $2,000,000 to $1,500,000. If this alternative is chosen, power will have to be bought from a network grid for a year at a cost of $30,000,000 until the work is finished. Consider the costs of construction and purchase of power to be paid in equal installments at the start and end of the current year. This rebuilding project has an expected life of 15 years after rebuilding with no salvage value. Ignore investment tax credits and depreciation and determine the equivalent annual cost of each project based on a 7% return.

7. Inner City Memorial Hospital has been plagued with continuous operating deficits. Based on a study made by an outside consulting firm, it is decided that the deficits are due to the outdated structure of the current facility. The hospital's consultants have made the following recommendation. They indicated that they can update the current facility for $10,000,000. With these renovations the hospital's annual budget will be $8,000,000. They also state that they can build an entirely new facility for $15,000,000. This new facility would have an annual operating budget of $7,000,000. A state health care planner has been called in to decide which project would be less costly to the consumer. The planner has accumulated the following facts:

1. Both projects would have a useful life of 25 years with no salvage value.

2. Expenses are expected to increase equally over the years for both projects due to inflation.

3. A 10% discount rate is assumed.

Prepare an analysis that would indicate the least-costly alternative.

6

THE SUPERIORITY
OF THE NET–PRESENT–VALUE
TECHNIQUE

In the two previous chapters, we introduced the most widely used discounted cash flow (DCF) and non-DCF models used in capital budgeting. We argued that the DCF methods are superior to the non-DCF models because the former take the time value of money into account. In this chapter, we support our preference for the NPV model as the unique evaluation technique that consistently helps firms to maximize common shareholders' wealth positions. Whenever mutually exclusive projects are being evaluated, only the NPV model will consistently show the firm the project or set of projects that will maximize the value of the firm. The use of any other evaluation technique can lead the firm to select projects that leave the shareholders in inferior wealth positions.

We begin with a review of surveys that provide insight into the actual use of evaluation techniques in industry.

TRENDS IN THE USE OF PROJECT EVALUATION TECHNIQUES

Over the last 25 years, various surveys have provided information concerning the use of capital budgeting models. There has been a steady growth in the adoption of DCF techniques, at least among medium-sized and large firms. Robichek and MacDonald reported that in the mid-1950s, only 9% of Fortune 500 firms were using discounting techniques.[1] By 1975, Petry reported that 66% of his respondents were using DCF techniques.[2]

[1]A. A. Robichek, and J. G. MacDonald, "Financial Planning in Transition, Long Range Planning Service," Report No. 268, (Menlo Park, Calif.: Stanford Research Institute, January 1956).
[2]G. H. Petry, "Effective Use of Capital Budgeting Tools," *Business Horizons* 18, no. 5 (October, 1975), 57–65.

Also in 1975, Petty, Scott and Bird administered a questionnaire to all firms on the 1971 Fortune 500 list.[3] Table 6–1 shows how 109 firms responded to the following request: Rank the capital budgeting techniques used by your firm for projects related to new product lines.

It is interesting to note that 41% of their respondents use IRR as their primary evaluation technique and only 15% use NPV. Further, 58% of their respondents utilize DCF techniques as their primary evaluation method. As secondary evaluation techniques, payback and average rate of return score first and second with 37% and 24% of the respondents, respectively.

In a more recent survey, Gitman and Forrester selected a sample from the 600 firms experiencing the greatest stock price growth over the 1971–76 period.[4] The responses from 112 of those firms as to their primary and secondary capital budgeting techniques are given in Table 6–2.

Compared with the Petty, et. al., study cited earlier, the respondents in the current study show an even greater preference for IRR (53.6%) over NPV (9.8%) as a primary evaluation technique. Again, payback was found to be the most popular secondary technique.

In another study, Petry asked his sampled firms to indicate the reasons why various techniques were used.[5] The responses are shown in Table 6–3.

We want to draw attention to four of the reasons cited: recognizes the time value of money (17%), easy to use (12%), familiar to management (10%), and ease of comparison (7%). We applaud the first reason, but will argue that the latter three reasons are inconsistent with the results cited in Tables 6–1 and 6–2, which show that IRR is significantly more widely used than NPV. Namely, we show in this chapter that IRR does *not* show what most practitioners who use it *think* it shows. Further, we show that, in general, the ranking of two or more projects by their IRR's makes little sense because these figures are noncompara-

TABLE 6–1   Evaluation Techniques Used by 1971 Fortune 500 Companies

	\multicolumn{6}{c}{*Evaluation Techniques: New Product Lines Rank*}
Technique	*1*	*2*	*3*	*4*	*5*	*6*
Accounting return on investment	31%	24%	21%	12%	9%	0%
Payback period	11	37	38	15	16	0
Net present value	15	14	17	44	13	50
Internal rate of return	41	19	17	13	9	0
Profitability index	2	4	5	12	50	50
Other	0	2	2	4	3	0
Total	100%	100%	100%	100%	100%	100%

SOURCE: J. W. Petty, D. F. Scott, and M. M. Bird, "The Capital Expenditure Decision-Making Process of Large Corporations," *The Engineering Economist* 20 (1975), 162–63.

[3] J. W. Petty, D. F. Scott, and M. M. Bird, "The Capital Budgeting Decision Making Process of Large Corporations," *The Engineering Economist* 20, no. 3 (Spring 1975), 159–172.
[4] L. J. Gitman, and J. R. Forrester, Jr., "A Survey of Capital Budgeting Techniques Used by Major U.S. Firms," *Financial Management* 6, no. 3 (Fall 1977), 66–71.
[5] Petry, "Capital Budgeting Tools," p. 60.

ble unless the time patterns of the project cash flows are *identical* (in which case we would not need to rank the projects). Finally, we believe Chapter 5 shows that IRR is harder to use than NPV.

Our major goal in this chapter is to shed greater light on the shortcomings of IRR and its inability to contribute to the maximization of the shareholders'

TABLE 6–2   Evaluation Techniques Used by Firms Achieving Most Rapid Stock Price Growth Between 1971 and 1976

| | Capital Budgeting Techniques in Use | | | |
| | Primary | | Secondary | |
Technique	Number	Percent	Number	Percent
Internal (or discounted) rate of return	60	53.6	13	14.0
Rate of return (average rate of return)	28	25.0	13	14.0
Net present value	11	9.8	24	25.8
Payback period	10	8.9	41	44.0
Benefit/cost ratio (profitability index)	3	2.7	2	2.2
Total responses	112	100.0	93	100.0

Source: L. J. Gitman and J. R. Forrester, Jr., "A Survey of Capital Budgeting Techniques Used by Major U.S. Firms," *Financial Management* 6 (1977), 68.

TABLE 6–3   Reasons for Selecting a Given Capital Budgeting Technique

Reasons Cited	Number of Corporations Citing Reasons	Percentage of Total
1. Recognizes time value of money	37	17
2. Required for regulated business	27	12
3. Easy to use	26	12
4. Familiar to management	22	10
5. Accepted in our industry	20	9
6. Capital intensive industry	18	8
7. Ease of comparison	15	7
8. Long-lived investments	15	7
9. Appropriate	9	4
10. Other	9	4
11. High rate of equipment or merchandise obsolescence	8	4
12. High risks	5	2
13. Labor intensive industry	4	2
14. High cash flow in early years	3	1
15. Volatile product prices or demand	3	1
Total	221	100

Source: G. H. Petry, "Effective Use of Capital Budgeting Tools," *Business Horizons* (1975), 60.

wealth position. It is to be hoped that this chapter may play a part in a widespread rejection of the IRR approach in practice and its replacement by the far superior NPV technique.

DIFFERENCES AMONG THE DCF TECHNIQUES

Among the three DCF techniques—NPV, PI, and IRR—there are two *major* differences in the techniques that warrant discussion:

1. The *absolute* versus the *relative* measurement of project attractiveness.
2. The *reinvestment assumption*.

Each of these points is discussed in turn.

As we can tell by observing the three DCF models, the NPV model results in an *absolute* measure of the project's worth, while both PI and IRR are *relative* measures of project viability. Specifically, NPV shows the dollar amount by which the project's discounted cash inflows (DCI) exceed its discounted cash outflows (DCO). On the other hand, PI computes the ratio of DCI to DCO and IRR determines a percentage return figure. As you might expect, a model that ranks projects using an absolute figure of merit may very well arrive at a different ranking than the one obtained by a model that compares projects on a relative basis.

The major question that will be addressed in later sections of this chapter is: Can firms maximize shareholders' wealth (the primary objective of financial management) equally well with a relative or an absolute measure of project attractiveness? To remove some of the surprise element, the answer to this question is no! We show that NPV is *clearly superior* to either of the relative measures (PI and IRR) of project attractiveness in helping firms to maximize shareholders' wealth. Further, we recommend that the two relative models should be abandoned in favor of the NPV model.

Turning to the second major difference, we can state a general rule that is often overlooked by users of DCF models: All DCF models make the implicit assumption that the project's cash inflows can be reinvested to earn a return that is *equal to the rate used to discount the cash flows.* This reinvestment assumption is made for *each* cash inflow between the time it occurs and the end of the project's life. Thus, the NPV and PI models make the implicit assumption that the projects cash inflows can be reinvested at the firm's required rate of return. Analogously, the IRR model makes the implicit assumption that the cash inflows can be reinvested at the computed IRR rate.

In order to illustrate the implicit reinvestment assumptions, we introduce the concept of *terminal value.* The terminal value (TV) of a project is the value that would accumulate by the end of the project's life if the project's cash inflows were invested to earn a specified compounded return between the time the cash inflows occurred and the end of the project's life. The TV of a project is calculated using Equation (1).

$$\text{TV} = \sum_{t=0}^{n} S_t (1+i)^{n-t} \qquad (1)$$

where S_t = the cash inflow that occurs at the end of period t
  i = the reinvestment rate
  n = the useful life of the project

Example 1 demonstrates the respective reinvestment assumptions for NPV and IRR.

□ **EXAMPLE 1** *An Illustration of Reinvestment Assumptions*
A firm with an after-tax required rate of return of 14% is evaluating the following two projects:

	Project Cash Flows	
Year	A	B
0	− $10,000.00	− $10,000
1	+ 3,862.89	0
2	+ 3,862.89	0
3	+ 3,862.89	0
4	+ 3,862.89	+ 20,736

The firm has computed the NPV and IRR for each project:

	Project	
Model	A	B
$NPV_{14\%}$	$1,255	$2,277
IRR	20%	20%

(a) Show that project A will achieve a terminal value of $20,736 (which is exactly the final cash inflow for project B) when the reinvestment rate is 20% (which is exactly the IRR for both projects).
(b) Compute the TV for each project using a reinvestment rate of 14%.
(c) Show that each project's NPV is exactly the present value of the TV less its cash outflow.

Solution: (a) We determine the TV for project A using Equation (1):

$$TV_A = \sum_{t=0}^{n} S_t(1 + i)^{n-t}$$

$$= \$3,862.89(1.20)^{4-1} + 3,862.89(1.20)^{4-2}$$

$$+ 3,862.89(1.20)^{4-3} + 3,862.89(1.20)^{4-4}$$

$$= \$6,675.07 + 5,562.56 + 4,635.47 + 3,862.89$$

$$= \$20,736$$

This terminal value for project A exposes IRR's implicit reinvestment assumption that the entire cash inflow is reinvested to earn the IRR rate. Projects A and B are equivalent only if the terminal values are equivalent, and this only occurs if *project A's cash inflows are reinvested at the 20% IRR.*

(b) Turning to the NPV model, the TV for project A assuming a 14% reinvestment rate is:

$$TV_A = \$3{,}862.89(1.14)^{4-1} + 3{,}862.89(1.14)^{4-2}$$
$$+\, 3{,}862.89(1.14)^{4-3} + 3{,}862.89(1.14)^{4-4}$$
$$= \$19{,}010$$

The TV for project B is $20,736 because there are no intermediate cash inflows (i.e., those between the investment in the project and the end of its life) to reinvest.

(c) We compute the NPV of each project by discounting the TV using the firm's required rate of return and then subtracting the cost of the project, as shown in Equation (2):

$$NPV = \frac{TV}{(1+k)^n} - A_0 \tag{2}$$

where A_0 = the cash outflow
 k = the firm's required rate of return

For project A:

$$NPV_A = \frac{\$19{,}010}{(1.14)^4} - \$10{,}000$$
$$= \$11{,}255 - \$10{,}000 = \underline{\underline{\$1{,}255}}$$

This value equals the NPV for project A using the conventional NPV model introduced in Chapter 5. (To see that the NPV found using Equation (2) is equivalent to the NPV using Equation (1) from Chapter 5, see Problem 11 at the end of this chapter.)

For project B:

$$NPV_B = \frac{\$20{,}736}{(1.14)^4} - \$10{,}000$$
$$= \$12{,}277 - \$10{,}000 = \underline{\underline{\$2{,}277}}$$

Therefore, these two last computations show that the NPV model makes the implicit assumption that a project's cash inflows are reinvested at the firm's required rate of return. ☐

We now turn to a discussion of what the computed IRR value really conveys.

THE TRUE MEANING OF IRR

It is our contention that a majority of the users of the IRR model do not fully understand its implications. When we have asked users to describe the meaning of a computed IRR value, the almost unanimous response is IRR shows the compounded annual rate of return that is earned on the original investment in the asset over its entire life. This is *wrong*!

At this juncture, there are three definitions that can be offered for IRR:

1. It is the discount rate that equates a project's discounted cash inflows with its discounted cash outflows.

2. It is the return on investment that allows the project's cash inflows to reduce the value of the investment to zero at the end of the project's life.

3. It is the return earned on the funds that remain internally invested in the project.

The first definition is used and illustrated in Chapter 5 and probably requires no further elaboration. However, the second and third descriptions call for additional discussion.

The second and third definitions view a project or investment as analogous to a mortgage. That is, when an individual has a mortgage, the payments (cash inflows from the investment) go first toward interest (return from the investment); only after that do they reduce the outstanding principal (i.e., reduce the value of the investment). By the end of the life of the mortgage (investment) the outstanding principal (value of the investment) is reduced to zero. Over the life of the mortgage (investment) the lending party (the firm) has earned interest (a return) only on the outstanding principal (the amount of funds that remain invested in the investment).

An illustration should help clarify this discussion.

☐ **EXAMPLE 2** *A Project Viewed as a Mortgage*

For Project A shown in Example 1, which has an **IRR** = 20%, complete the following table, which views the project as a mortgage. Show that the project cash flows reduce the value of the investment to zero by the end of year 4.

Year	(1) Beginning Value of the Investment	(2) Cash Inflow	(3) 20% Return on Value of the Investment 20% × (1)	(4) Reduction in the Value of the Investment (2) − (3)	(5) Ending Value of the Investment (1) − (4)
1	$10,000	$3,862.89			
2		3,862.89			
3		3,862.89			
4		3,862.89			

The ending value of the investment in any year is the beginning value of the investment in the following year. Thus, the value from column (5) is carried back to column (1) for the next year.

Once the table is complete, explain Project A's IRR using the third definition above.

Solution: Carrying out the calculations, the completed table appears as follows:

Year	(1) Beginning Value of the Investment	(2) Cash Inflow	(3) 20% Return on Value of the Investment 20% × (1)	(4) Reduction in the Value of the Investment (2) − (3)	(5) Ending Value of the Investment (1) − (4)
1	$10,000.00	$3,862.89	$2,000.00	$1,862.89	$8,137.11
2	8,137.11	3,862.89	1,627.42	2,235.47	5,901.64
3	5,901.64	3,862.89	1,180.33	2,682.56	3,219.08
4	3,219.08	3,862.89	643.81	3,219.08	0

Looking at the above table we see that 20% is earned on $10,000 during year 1, 20% is earned on $8,137.11 during year 2, 20% is earned on $5,901.64 during year 3, and 20% is earned on $3,219.08 during year 4. Project A does not earn a 20% rate of return on $10,000 for the entire 4-year useful life; the return of 20% is earned only on funds that remain *internally invested in the project* (i.e., the value of the investment in each of the 4 years). Thus the IRR criterion makes the assumption that cash inflows are reinvested at the same rate, so that it can *claim a true compounded rate of return on the entire original investment for the entire useful life of the project*. However, it can be said that project A will generate a true compounded rate of return of 20% on $10,000 for 4 years if and only if the cash inflows of $3862.89 each year can be reinvested at a 20% return for the rest of the project's useful life. This was demonstrated in the computation of the terminal value for project A in Example 1.   □

As mentioned in Example 2, all that the computed IRR value shows is the rate of return on the funds that remain internally invested in the project. However, IRR users are under the misapprehension that IRR conveys the true compounded annual rate of return on the project. In reality, the true compounded rate of return on the project is related to IRR, as shown in Equation (3):

$$
\begin{array}{l}
\text{true rate} \\
\text{of return on} \\
\text{a project}
\end{array}
=
\begin{array}{l}
\text{weighted} \\
\text{average} \\
\text{of}
\end{array}
\left[
\text{IRR} \quad \text{and} \quad
\begin{array}{l}
\text{reinvestment} \\
\text{rate earned on} \\
\text{the project's} \\
\text{cash inflows}
\end{array}
\right]
\qquad (3)
$$

The weights used in Equation (3) are the cash inflows generated by the project. The *lower* the cash inflows early in the project's life, the longer the funds remain internally invested in the project; this dictates that IRR be the more heavily weighted factor in Equation (3). On the other hand, the *higher* the cash inflows early in the project's life, the earlier the funds have to be reinvested in other projects; this makes the reinvestment rate increasingly significant in the determination of the project's true rate of return.

Obviously, the true rate of return earned on a project is much more relevant than the project's IRR. However, even the project's true rate of return suffers from the limitation that rates of return are *relative* measures of project attractiveness that may or may not have anything to do with the maximization of shareholders' wealth. This is the topic explored in the final section of this chapter.

THE INABILITY OF IRR TO MAXIMIZE SHAREHOLDERS' WEALTH

When firms are evaluating mutually exclusive projects—two questions arise. First, can a conflict exist in ranking the projects using NPV, PI, and IRR? Second, if a conflict can and does arise, which technique should the firm utilize in order to maximize shareholders' wealth?

Fisher's Intersection

The answer to the first question is yes, it is possible for a conflict to arise in ranking mutually exclusive projects if the assets require different discounted cash outflows (a size disparity exists), if the projects have differing cash inflow patterns (a time disparity exists), or if the projects have unequal useful lives.

Notice that we said that a conflict *is possible*. That is, even if we have two or more mutually exclusive projects and even if one of the three disparities (size, time, or useful life) exists, there may or may not be a conflict between the rankings given the projects by NPV, PI, and IRR. Consider Figure 6-1.

Part (a) shows that project B dominates project C. This means that project B's NPV profile is everywhere above the NPV profile of project C. Thus, project B will have a greater NPV and PI than project C, regardless of the cost of capital; project B also has a higher IRR than project C. In part (b), the NPV profiles of projects D and E are tangent at only one point, but project D's profile is everywhere else above project E and project D has a higher IRR. Thus, there

FIGURE 6-1 **Examples of NPV Profiles for Three Sets of Two Mutually Exclusive Projects**

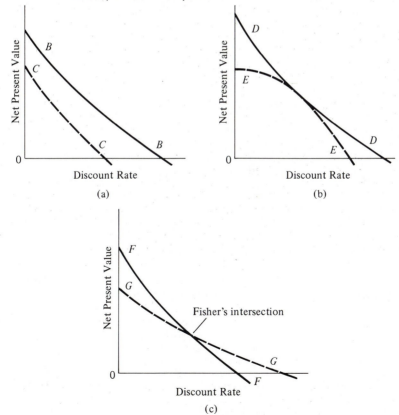

will again be no conflict between the rankings given D and E by the three techniques. In part (c), we see that: (1) the profiles for projects F and G have a single point of intersection; (2) the NPV for project F at a zero discount rate is greater than the NPV at a zero discount rate for project G; and (3) the IRR for project G is greater than the IRR for project F. Under these conditions, *there will be a conflict between NPV and IRR if the firm's cost of capital is less than the discount rate at which the intersection in NPV profiles occurs. Also, there may be a conflict between NPV and PI only if there is a size disparity between projects F and G, and there will be a conflict between PI and IRR only if NPV and PI agree in their rankings of the projects.*

The intersection shown in Figure 6–1(c) is of some importance. It is called *Fisher's intersection* after the great economist Irving Fisher, who was among the first to point out conflicts among NPV, PI, and IRR.[6] Fisher's intersection occurs at the interest rate where the NPV's of the two projects are equal; it is of significance because it is the *hurdle rate at which the preferred project using NPV changes from one project to the other.* In addition, as we mentioned before, at required rates of return less than Fisher's intersection, NPV and IRR conflict in their ranking of the two projects. On the other hand, if the required rate of return is greater than Fisher's intersection, no conflict between NPV and IRR exists.

We can determine the discount rate at which Fisher's intersection occurs between the NPV profiles for two projects (call them I and II) using Equation (4):

$$NPV_I = NPV_{II}$$

$$\sum_{t=0}^{n} \frac{(S_t)_I}{(1+f)^t} - (A_0)_I = \sum_{t=0}^{n} \frac{(S_t)_{II}}{(1+f)^t} - (A_0)_{II} \qquad (4)$$

where $(S_t)_I$, $(S_t)_{II}$ = the cash inflow in period t for project I and project II, respectively

$(A_0)_I$, $(A_0)_{II}$ = the cash outflow for project I and project II, respectively

f = the discount rate at which Fisher's intersection occurs

Notice that Equation (4) can be simplified by bringing all terms over to the left-hand side. Thus, the calculation of Fisher's rate (f) is similar to an IRR calculation. In addition, as with IRR, there can be zero, one, or multiple values for f. However, we limit our attention to cases in which there are zero or one intersection because these are the more usual cases. The reader interested in the problem of the existence and uniqueness of the Fisher's intersection is referred to that literature.[7]

The illustration of the calculation of Fisher's rate is the task of Example 3, which is adapted from an example originally presented by Hirshleifer.[8]

[6]See especially: Irving Fisher, *The Rate of Interest* (New York: Macmillan Publishing Co., Inc., 1907) and *The Theory of Interest* (New York: Macmillan Publishing Co., Inc., 1930).

[7]See J. C. T. Mao, "The Internal Rate of Return as a Ranking Criterion," *The Engineering Economist*, Summer 1966, pp. 1–13; J. C. T. Mao, *Quantitative Analysis of Financial Decisions* (New York: Macmillan Publishing Co., Inc., 1969), Chap. 7; W. H. Jean, *The Analytical Theory of Finance* (New York: Holt, Rinehart and Winston, Inc., 1970), Chap. 2; and E. F. Fama and M. H. Miller, *The Theory of Finance* (New York: Holt, Rinehart and Winston, Inc., 1972), Chap. 3.

[8]J. Hirshleifer, "On the Theory of Optimal Investment Decisions," *Journal of Political Economy*, 66 (August 1958), 329–352.

□ **EXAMPLE 3** *Fisher's Intersection*

A firm is evaluating the following two mutually exclusive, but quite profitable, projects:

	Project	
t	I	II
0	− $10,000	− $10,000
1	0	+ 20,000
2	+ 40,000	+ 10,000

As an aside, we can tell just by looking at the cash-flow patterns of the two projects which would be preferred by the NPV criterion at low-to-moderate discount rates and which project would have the higher IRR (see Problem 14 at the end of this chapter).

(a) As a review of Chapter 5, compute each project's IRR.

(b) Based on the cash-flow patterns for the two projects and the answer to part (a), can we determine if these two projects will have a Fisher's intersection? Explain.

(c) Using Equation (4), determine r' (the discount rate at Fisher's intersection) and the NPV at r' for both projects. Comment on the significance of r'.

(d) Using the above results, sketch the two NPV profiles.

Solution: (a) Computing the two IRR's, we find:

$$\text{IRR}_\text{I} \Rightarrow \frac{-\$10,000}{(1+r_\text{I})^0} + \frac{0}{(1+r_\text{I})^1} + \frac{\$40,000}{(1+r_\text{I})^2} = 0$$

Therefore,

$$r_\text{I} = 100\%$$

$$\text{IRR}_\text{II} \Rightarrow \frac{-\$10,000}{(1+r_\text{II})^0} + \frac{\$20,000}{(1+r_\text{II})^1} + \frac{\$10,000}{(1+r_\text{II})^2} = 0$$

Therefore,

$$r_\text{II} = 141.4\%$$

(b) By looking at the cash-flow patterns for the two projects, we can tell that project I has a higher NPV than project II at a zero discount rate. This can be seen by taking the undiscounted sum of the cash flows for the two projects: the NPV at 0% for project I is − $10,000 + 0 + $40,000 = $30,000; the NPV at 0% for project II is − $10,000 + $20,000 + $10,000 = $20,000. In addition, the results of part (a) show that project II has a greater IRR than project I. Therefore, we can conclude that the NPV profiles for these two projects must intersect at a discount rate somewhere to the left of the smaller IRR (i.e., somewhere less than 100%). We compute this rate, f, in part (c).

(c) Using Equation (4), we find:

$$\text{NPV}_\text{I} = \text{NPV}_\text{II}$$

$$\frac{-\$10,000}{(1+f)^0} + \frac{0}{(1+f)^1} + \frac{\$40,000}{(1+f)^2} = \frac{-\$10,000}{(1+f)^0} + \frac{\$20,000}{(1+f)^1} + \frac{\$10,000}{(1+f)^2}$$

$$\frac{-\$20,000}{(1+f)^1} + \frac{\$30,000}{(1+f)^2} = 0$$

Therefore,

$$f = 50\%$$

The NPV level achieved by both projects at $f = 50\%$ is determined by substituting 50% into the NPV equation for k using either project's cash flows:

$$NPV_I = -\$10,000 + \frac{0}{(1.50)^1} + \frac{\$40,000}{(1.50)^2}$$

$$= \underline{\underline{\$7,778}}$$

We would find the same NPV value at $k = 50\%$ for project II.

The significance of the f value is that for any required return less than 50%, the NPV model will prefer project I, while the IRR model will prefer project II. For required returns above 50%, both NPV and IRR will rank project II higher than project I. Thus, depending on the level of the required rate of return relative to 50%, there either will or will not be a conflict between NPV and IRR in ranking these two projects. In addition, the farther the firm's required rate of return is below 50%, the greater the NPV dominance of project I over project II.

(d) We now have sufficient data to plot the two NPV profiles.

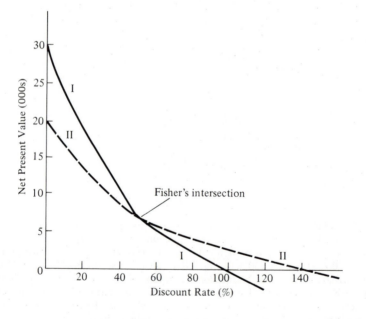

□

How IRR Selects the Wrong Project

Let's take a closer look at our results in Example 3. For required rates of return less than 50% (where a conflict in project ranking between NPV and IRR exists), one of the two models will clearly lead the firm to select the *wrong* project, which will result in the common shareholders being worse off than they would have been if the better project had been accepted.

It is important for us to determine whether it is the NPV model or the IRR model that has the inherent flaw that occasionally produces a conflict, and therefore an error, in project ranking. The answer to this question is the focus of Example 4.

□ **EXAMPLE 4**   *The Inability of IRR to Maximize Shareholders' Wealth*

For the two projects shown in Example 3, we want to show that one project clearly dominates the other. This will indicate which model leads the firm astray by showing a preference for an inferior project.

Consider the following tabulation of the project cash flows:

		Project	
t	*I*	*I Modified*	*II*
0	− $10,000		− $10,000
1	0		+ 20,000
2	+ 40,000		+ 10,000

Notice that the two projects have the same cash outflow in year 0. In addition, in year 2, the cash inflow of project I exceeds that of project II. One way of showing the dominant project is to modify the cash flows of one of the projects. We will demonstrate by modifying project I. First, equate the cash flows for project I in year 2 with those of project II. Then discount the remainder of the second year cash flow of project I ($40,000 − $10,000 = $30,000) back one year using the firm's required rate of return. Thus, project I modified and project II will have equal cash flows in year 0 and year 2 and we can determine the *dominant* project by comparing the year 1 cash inflows.

(a) For a firm with a 16% required rate of return, complete the given table.

(b) On the basis of part (a), which project dominates and will NPV or IRR lead the firm to accept the wrong project? Can you generalize the results found in part (a): Over what required rates of return will project I dominate II? Discuss.

(c) Some IRR proponents might argue that project II is preferred because it generates a $20,000 cash inflow in period 1, which can be used for reinvestment in attractive opportunities. However, if such attractive opportunities exist, the firm would still be able to accept project I and borrow $20,000 in period 1 at the cost of capital.

The loan can be repaid in period 2 with part of the $40,000 cash inflow. For this firm, with a 16% cost of capital, prepare a table similar to the one given, which has a column for the original project I cash flows, the loan cash flows just discussed, the total of these two sets of cash flows (which is actually a revised set of cash flows for project I), and the cash flows of project II. Which project dominates? Generalize your results.

Solution: (a) The completed table is as follows:

		Project	
t	*I*	*I Modified*	*II*
0	− $10,000	− $10,000	− $10,000
1	0	+ 25,860	+ 20,000
2	+ 40,000	+ 10,000	+ 10,000

We arrive at the value of $25,860 for the year 1 cash inflow of modified project I by multiplying the $30,000 of the cash inflow of year 2 ($30,000 remains after $10,000 of the original $40,000 is left in year 2) by the 1-year discount factor for 16% (0.862). This results in a modified, *but equivalent*, cash flow series for project I.

(b) We can thus see that project I dominates project II and that any rational decision-maker would prefer project I to II. The project preferred by the NPV criterion (project I) would leave the firm with greater wealth than the project preferred by the IRR criterion (project II). In fact, by examining the modified cash-flow series, we can see that the firm would be throwing away $5,860 of wealth in year-1 dollars if it followed the IRR criterion rather than the NPV criterion.

Recall from Example 3 that Fisher's intersection occurs at $r' = 50\%$. The NPV model would continue to prefer project I at all required rates of return up to 50%. Thus, the modified project I cash flows would continue to dominate project II for all required rates of return up to 50% (see Problem 12 at the end of this chapter for a demonstration of this). For required rates of return in excess of 50%, the cash flows of project II will dominate the cash flows of modified project I because at such required rates of return, the NPV criterion prefers project II (see Problem 13 for a further development of this). At discount rates greater than 50%, the IRR criterion is correct in ranking project II higher than project I; however, the IRR criterion is correct only because it agrees with the NPV criterion, not because it is a valid evaluation criterion. We saw that IRR was clearly wrong in ranking projects where it conflicted with NPV (i.e., at discount rates lower than 50%.)

(c) For a firm with a 16% cost of capital, we prepare a table comparing the two projects given that the firm can accept project I and take out a loan for $20,000 at the end of year 1:

| | | | *Project* | |
| | | | I and | |
t	*I*	*Loan*	*Loan Combined*	*II*
0	− $10,000		− $10,000	− $10,000
1	0	+ $20,000	+ 20,000	+ 20,000
2	+ 40,000	− 23,200[a]	+ 16,800	+ 10,000

[a] This value includes $3,200 in interest plus the principal of $20,000.

Again, we see that project I plus the loan clearly dominates project II. Under both alternatives, the firm has $20,000 to invest in those attractive opportunities at the end of year 1. The additional returns earned on the $20,000 are added to the returns on each project and project I will, of course, continue to dominate. Project I will continue this domination over project II even if the firm has an opportunity to invest more than $20,000 at the end of year 1 and given that loans are available if the firm accepts either project (see Problem 16 at the end of this chapter).

Consistent with our generalized results in part (b), project I with the loan continues to dominate project II as long as the firm can borrow funds at a rate less than 50%, the Fisher's rate for these two projects found in Example 3. □

As noted in Example 4, IRR can have a detrimental impact on shareholders' wealth. This fact can also be demonstrated by showing how much the shareholders' wealth would increase at the end of the life of the project as a result of accepting that project. This is done for two mutually exclusive projects in Example 5.

□ **EXAMPLE 5** Inability of IRR to Maximize Shareholders' Wealth, Revisited

A firm with a 10% cost of capital is evaluating projects A and B as follows:

t	A	B
0	− $200,000	− $200,000
1	+ 50,000	+ 102,500
2	+ 50,000	+ 102,500
3	+ 235,000	+ 102,500
$NPV_{10\%}$	$ 63,335.84	$ 54,902.33
$PI_{10\%}$	1.31668	1.2745
IRR	23.0%	25.03%

NPV and PI rank project A higher, while IRR prefers project B. Somewhat artificially, assume that the firm will obtain the $200,000 required at their cost of capital and that any amount can be repaid each year. Show the impact on shareholders' wealth at the end of the life of each project, where cash inflows over the life are used to pay interest and principal on the $200,000 required.

Solution: The analysis proceeds by preparing the following tables for each project:

Project A

Year	Beginning Balance	Interest at 10%	Cash Inflow	Retirement of Principal	Ending Balance	Increase in Shareholders' Wealth[a]
1	$200,000	$20,000	$50,000	$30,000	$170,000	
2	170,000	17,000	50,000	33,000	137,000	
3	137,000	13,700	235,000	137,000	0	$84,300

[a]Cash inflow in year 3 less the interest in year 3 less the beginning balance for year 3.

Project B

Year	Beginning Balance	Interest at 10%	Cash Inflow	Retirement of Principal	Ending Balance	Increase in Shareholders' Wealth[a]
1	$200,000	$20,000	$102,500	$82,500	$117,500	
2	117,500	11,750	102,500	90,750	26,750	
3	26,750	2,675	102,500	26,750	0	$73,075

[a]Cash inflow in year 3 less the interest in year 3 less the beginning balance for year 3.

Project A increases shareholders' wealth by $84,300, compared to $73,075 for Project B. So again, if the firm followed the IRR criterion and accepted project B, it would lead to a sacrifice of $11,225 in the shareholders' wealth position at the end of the 3-year life of both projects. IRR is clearly an inferior criterion compared to NPV in maximizing shareholders' wealth.

It is important to note the relationship between each project's increase in shareholders' wealth at the end of year 3 and its NPV; *namely, if we discount each project's increase in shareholders' wealth back to time zero at the firm's required rate of return, we get precisely the NPV for that project*. To illustrate,

$$\begin{pmatrix} \text{NPV for} \\ \text{project A} \end{pmatrix} = \begin{pmatrix} \text{increase in share-} \\ \text{holders wealth for} \\ \text{project A} \end{pmatrix} \times \begin{pmatrix} \text{present value} \\ \text{factor for 3} \\ \text{years and 10\%} \end{pmatrix}$$

$$= (\$84,300) \times (0.751315)$$
$$= \underline{\$63,335.84}$$

Parallel results can be found for project B.

If it is argued that there are attractive reinvestment opportunities in years 1 and 2 for the $102,500 cash inflows of project B, it can again easily be shown that project A is still superior when an additional loan is obtained (at the cost of capital) to have this amount of funds available in each year. The comparison is as follows:

Project A

Time	Original	Loan	Revised	Project B
0	− $200,000		− $200,000	− $200,000
1	+ 50,000	+ $ 52,500	+ 102,500	+ 102,500
2	+ 50,000	+ 52,500	+ 102,500	+ 102,500
3	+ 235,000	− 121,275[a]	+ 113,725	+ 102,500

[a]The loan repayment of $121,275 consists of $105,000 in principal, $5,250 in interest for the loan outstanding in period 2, and $11,025 in interest for the loan outstanding in period 3 of $110,250 ($52,500 + $52,500 + $5,250).

Again, project A clearly dominates project B, and any rational decision-maker would select A rather than B.   □

At this juncture we might question why such difficulties are experienced in the use of IRR. It could be said that IRR does a good job of measuring the *compounded rate of return over time on the funds that remain invested in an asset, but the problem is that this figure has nothing at all to do with maximizing shareholders' wealth*. A firm that attempted to *maximize IRR* could very well find that the highest IRR project had an original cost of $100 and a return next year of $150, leading to a 50% IRR; shareholders would be pleased over the $50 net return, but would raise more questions about how the remaining portion of the capital budget was invested. If management replied that they did not want to invest any more than $100 because to do so would deteriorate the IRR below the very attractive 50% level achieved, they would be looking for new jobs. *The NPV criterion shows clearly and unambiguously the impact of projects on shareholders' wealth or the present value of the firm. However, the same is obviously not true for IRR.*

If three projects have NPV's of $10,000, $14,000, and $16,000, these figures show the magnitudes of the increase in shareholders' wealth if the respective investments are accepted. On the other hand, if these same projects have IRR's of 40%, 30%, and 25% and PI's of 1.68, 1.22, and 1.53, respectively, we have no idea which of the three will lead to the greatest increase in shareholders' wealth by looking at their IRR's and PI's. In fact, as has been illustrated in many examples in this chapter, the increase in shareholders' wealth can be the opposite of the rankings indicated by either the IRR or PI criterion. In an informative and hard-hitting article, Keane points out:

> The internal rate of return, therefore, is invalid not because of any implicit reinvestment assumption or because of the possibility of producing multiple yields, but simply because a rate of return expressed in percentage terms is inappropriate for discriminating between projects of different sizes. All but *identical* projects have different sizes whatever their initial outlays or expected lives may suggest, and although the rate of return method might appear at times to give correct investment advice, it is *never* in fact correct in principle.[9]

Weingartner also has a number of uncomplimentary things to say about the profitability index.[10] He demonstrates that given a size disparity between two mutually exclusive projects, there will be a conflict between NPV and PI whenever

$$\frac{b_1}{b_2} < \frac{c_1}{c_2}$$

where b_j = net present value of project j
    c_j = cost of project j

Assume that $b_1 > b_2$, which means that the NPV criterion prefers project 1. Under the condition specified above, the PI will rank project 2 higher than 1, which is in conflict with NPV. This can be seen by noting that since all the b's and c's are positive, the following inequality exists.

$$\frac{b_1}{c_1} < \frac{b_2}{c_2}$$

The relationship between the PI's is as follows:

$$\text{PI}_1 = \frac{b_1 + c_1}{c_1} < \frac{b_2 + c_2}{c_2} = \text{PI}_2$$

To obtain this expression, we simply added unity to both sides of the inequality. In such circumstances, as Weingartner points out,[11] the PI criterion "would lead to selection of the project with the *lower net present value which would make a lower contribution to the wealth of the owners of the firm*" [emphasis added]. Finally, Weingartner concludes his article by stating:

> Our examples of mutually exclusive alternatives reinforce the conclusion that PI does not provide aid in the choice among such alternatives. In two examples,

[9]S. M. Keane, "Let's Scrap IRR Once and For All!," *Accountancy* (February 1974), pp. 78–82.
[10]H. Martin Weingartner, "The Excess Present Value Index—A Theoretical Basis and Critique," *Journal of Accounting Research* (Autumn 1963), pp. 213–224.
[11]Ibid., p. 220.

ranking by means of PI and by IRR led to the same *incorrect choice*. In the third example, these rankings were different, and the PI criterion resulted in the wrong choice. In all these instances, *the NPV criterion and Fisher's rate of return yield similar answers which are correct* in the absence of capital rationing or more complex interrelationships between investments [emphasis added].[12]

To conclude this section, the next example demonstrates in another way that utilizing the NPV criterion will lead to wealth maximization even when NPV conflicts with IRR and PI in the ranking of mutually exclusive projects. Irving Fisher was probably the first to use rigorously the type of analysis called upon in the demonstration, hence it is referred to as Fisherian analysis.

☐ **EXAMPLE 6**   *Inability of IRR and PI to Maximize Shareholders' Wealth (Second Revisit)*

A firm with a cost of capital of 10% has a current wealth position of $250,000. The accompanying graph shows combinations of consumption this year and consumption next year that can be obtained given the firm's current wealth position, the cost of capital (or market rate of interest), and the assumptions of equal borrowing and lending rates. Notice that one possible consumption pattern would be $250,000 this year and $0 next year; another would be $0 this year and $275,000 next year [$275,000 would be available for consumption next year since the $250,000 could be invested at the market rate of interest, 10%—$275,000 = $250,000(1.10)]. Consider that the firm has determined its desired consumption pattern and that is to consume $150,000 this year and $110,000 next year.

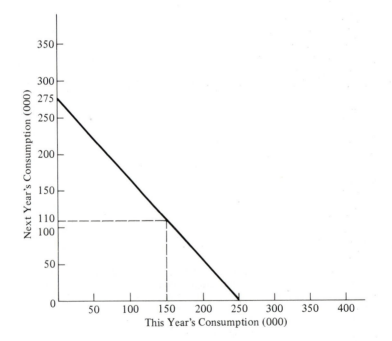

Notice, of course, that this consumption pattern, as is true for all others on the line, has a present value of $250,000 (using the market discount rate of 10%) and a future value next year of $275,000. The firm is evaluating two mutually exclusive projects:

Year	I	II
0	− $40,000	− $ 80,000
1	+ 80,000	+ 150,000
$NPV_{10\%}$	$32,727	$ 56,364
$PI_{10\%}$	1.82	1.70
IRR	100%	87.5%

Both PI and IRR rank project I above project II, whereas NPV reverses this order.

Using a graph similar to the one shown above, demonstrate that project II, if accepted by the firm, will place the firm in a superior wealth position than if project I were accepted (i.e., demonstrate that following the NPV criterion maximizes shareholders' wealth, whereas PI and IRR fail to).

Solution: The graph showing the original wealth position, that achieved by accepting project I (labeled I) and that achieved by accepting project II (labeled II), is as shown. Note in the figure that the lines for projects I and II are determined geometrically by two points: (1) the point found by first moving horizontally to the left along the line

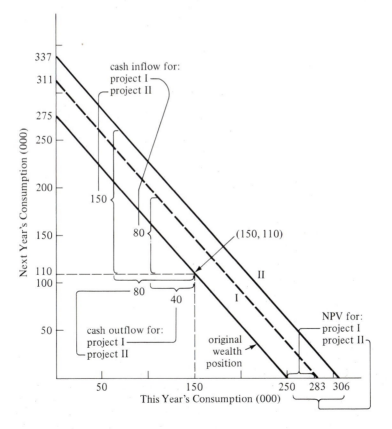

$110,000 of consumption next year in the amount of the investment for each project, and then moving vertically upward in the amount of the cash inflow in period 1; and (2) the point on the horizontal axis at $250,000 (the firm's original current wealth position) plus the NPV of the project.

The wealth position of the firm (in terms of current dollars) after accepting either project I or project II is equal to the firm's current level of wealth ($250,000) plus the NPV of either project. Thus, as we can clearly see, the wealth position of the firm after *accepting project II dominates* the wealth position of the firm if project I were accepted. The exhibit shows that the wealth line of project II is above and to the right of that of project I; therefore, the firm with project II can achieve any level of current and future consumption that could be achieved by accepting project I *and still have wealth left over*. A quantification of the level of the *dominance in current wealth position is the difference in the NPV's of the two projects*—$23,630 (NPV for project II is $56,360 minus the NPV for project I = $32,730). This difference shows the amount by which the firm is *wealthier* by following the NPV criterion rather than either PI or IRR. That is, if the firm used either PI or IRR, shareholders' wealth would be decreased by $23,630 compared with the selection of projects using the superior NPV criterion.

Hence, the *direct link* between the *NPV criterion and shareholder-wealth maximization has been established* using yet another type of analysis (two-period Fisherian analysis). The selection of the project or projects that *maximize NPV will lead to shareholder-wealth maximization*. This is obviously not the case for either PI or IRR.   □

In addition to the points discussed above, Example 6 demonstrates the inferiority of the basic rationale behind PI and IRR. We have discussed that these models rank projects using a *relative criterion*. These two relative evaluation techniques use the rate of change in the firm's wealth position (IRR) or the number of dollars of DCI per dollar of DCO (PI) to rank projects. Unfortunately though, both of these relative ranking techniques totally ignore the *number of dollars invested in competing projects* and, *more importantly, the resulting absolute change in the firm's wealth position after accepting either of the alternatives*. It is nice to have a rapid rate of change in wealth or a high number of dollars of DCI per dollar of DCO, but neither of these characteristics buys shareholders anything—only wealth can do that! Therefore, since the firm is trying to maximize shareholders' wealth position, we strongly recommend that the NPV criterion be used because it is the only model capable of helping the firm achieve this goal; both IRR and PI should be abandoned because they totally ignore shareholders' wealth.

SUMMARY

The several examples included in our analysis should convince even the skeptical reader that the NPV criterion is clearly superior in maximizing shareholders' wealth to either the IRR or PI criterion.

In the following chapter, we demonstrate how the NPV model is rich enough to handle the evaluation of mutually exclusive projects under a wide variety of conditions. We call solely upon the NPV model to select the preferred project from a mutually exclusive set because only this model leads to shareholder-wealth maximization.

QUESTIONS/PROBLEMS

1. Briefly discuss the difference between relative and absolute capital budgeting evaluation techniques. Classify NPV, PI, and IRR.
2. Discuss the general assumption that discounted cash flow (DCF) models make concerning the reinvestment of cash inflows. What reinvestment assumptions do NPV, PI, and IRR make?
3. Name two major reasons why the DCF models can conflict when ranking mutually exclusive projects. Could both of these reasons be an explanation for a conflict between NPV and PI in ranking mutually exclusive projects? Discuss.
4. Give four verbal definitions for the internal rate of return.
5. Where does the word *internal* in IRR come from? Is there any difference between a project's IRR and its true compounded annual rate of return? Discuss.
6. What is meant by *Fisher's intersection*? Why is it important in evaluating mutually exclusive investments?
7. True or false: There will always be a conflict between NPV and IRR for two mutually exclusive projects with NPV profiles with a Fisher's intersection. Justify.
8. True or false: By observing the NPV profiles for two mutually exclusive projects, we can determine whether there will be a conflict between NPV and PI. Justify.
9. Answer the following true-false questions based on the two-period Fisherian analysis shown in Example 6.
   (a) The original wealth position of the firm is 250 units of this year's consumption and 0 units of next year's consumption or 0 units of this year's consumption and 275 units of next year's consumption; this means that the market rate of interest is 10% and any other market rate of interest would lead to a different amount available for next year's consumption.
   (b) The desired consumption pattern of 150 this year and 110 next year has a present value of 250 units, which is also true of all other points on the line.
   (c) As can be seen from the graph, project I has an NPV of 283, while project II has an NPV of 306.
   (d) The wealth position of the firm after accepting project II dominates that after accepting project I because the firm could throw away 23 units of current consumption if it had accepted project II and still be as well off as if it had accepted project I.
   (e) Given these two projects, NPV and PI do conflict in their rankings because NPV prefers project II, while PI prefers project I.
   (f) In this type of analysis, the only time when PI could lead to an inferior wealth position in comparing mutually exclusive projects would be when a size disparity exists between the projects.
   (g) Similarly, in this type of analysis, the only time that IRR could lead to an inferior wealth position would be when a size disparity exists between the projects.
   (h) In this type of analysis, neither IRR nor PI can distinguish between different size investments because they are relative measures of project attractiveness.
   (i) Neither IRR nor PI has anything in particular to do with maximizing wealth position because they are both relative measures that ignore the absolute magnitude of the wealth generated by an investment.
   (j) A project with a negative NPV would be rejected by this type of analysis because the wealth line after accepting the investment would be lower and to the left of the current wealth line, which means that the former would be dominated.
   (k) In this type of analysis, the terminal value criterion would give rankings that are *always* consistent with the NPV criterion.

10. Two of the most widely used methods of evaluating capital investment projects are the net present value (NPV) technique and the internal rate of return (IRR) method. When two or more mutually exclusive investments are being evaluated, conflicts can arise between the rankings given the projects by NPV and IRR. The questions below point to potential difficulties that can arise.

Consider the following two mutually exclusive investment proposals,[13] which are graphed below:

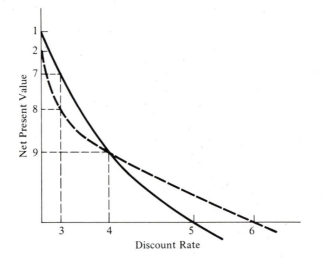

Project A

Year	Net Cash Flows	Discounted at:		
		6%	15.5%	28.5%
0	− $100			
1	+ 30	$28.29	$25.95	$23.34
2	+ 30	26.70	22.50	18.18
3	+ 70	58.80	45.36	32.97
4	+ 70	55.44	39.34	25.69
		$169.23	$133.15	$100.18

Project B

Year	Net Cash Flows	Discounted at:		
		6%	15.5%	34%
0	− $100			
1	+ 60	$56.58	$51.90	$44.82
2	+ 60	53.40	45.00	33.42
3	+ 30	25.20	19.44	12.48
4	+ 30	23.76	16.86	9.30
		$158.94	$133.20	$100.02

[13] The two projects used in this problem originally appeared in an example in R. Conrad Doenges, "The 'Reinvestment Problem' in A Practical Perspective," *Financial Management* (Spring 1972), pp. 85–91.

(a) The project whose discounted-cash-flow pattern is shown by the curve intersecting the axes at points 1 and 5 is:
   A. Project A
   B. Project B
(b) The dollar value that point 1 on the graph equals is:
   A. $169.23
   B. $158.94
   C. $200.00
   D. $100.00
   E. $69.23
(c) The dollar value that point 2 on the graph equals is:
   A. $158.94
   B. $169.23
   C. $58.94
   D. $180.00
   E. $80.00
(d) The discount rate that point 5 on the graph equals is:
   A. 0%
   B. 6%
   C. 15.5%
   D. 28.5%
   E. 34%
(e) The dollar amounts that points 7 and 8 equal, respectively, are:
   A. $200 and $180
   B. $169.23 and $158.94
   C. $100 and $80
   D. $69.23 and $58.94
   E. None of the above
(f) Using the NPV criterion, project B would be preferred to project A for all discount rates:
   A. Greater than 0%
   B. Less than 6%
   C. Less than 15.5%
   D. Greater than 15.5%
   E. Less than 28.5%
(g) Using the NPV criterion, *only one* project would be *acceptable* at the following rate:
   A. 6%
   B. 15.5%
   C. 28.5%
   D. 32%
   E. 40%
(h) Using the IRR criterion, project A would be preferable to project B when the discount rate is:
   A. Greater than 0%
   B. Greater than 15.5%
   C. Less than 15.5%
   D. Greater than 28.5%
   E. None of the above
(i) There would be a conflict between the rankings of the two projects using NPV vs. IRR when the discount rate is:
   A. Greater than 0%
   B. Greater than 6%
   C. Less than 15.5%
   D. Greater than 15.5%
   E. None of the above

(j) Using the IRR criterion, project B would be preferable to project A when the discount rate is:
  A. Greater than 0%
  B. Greater than 6%
  C. Less than 15.5%
  D. Greater than 15.5%
  E. Greater than 28.5%

(k) At a discount rate of 32%, there would be a conflict between the preferred investment using NPV vs. IRR:
  A. True
  B. False

(l) At a discount rate of 40%, there would be a conflict between the preferred investment using NPV vs. IRR:
  A. True
  B. False

(m) The value for point 9 on the graph would equal

  A. $\dfrac{-100}{(1+r)^0} + \dfrac{30}{(1+r)^1} + \dfrac{30}{(1+r)^2} + \dfrac{70}{(1+r)^3} + \dfrac{70}{(1+r)^4}$, where $r =$ #4

  B. $\dfrac{-100}{(1+r)^0} + \dfrac{60}{(1+r)^1} + \dfrac{60}{(1+r)^2} + \dfrac{30}{(1+r)^3} + \dfrac{30}{(1+r)^4}$, where $r =$ #4

  C. Expression A, where r will equate it to zero
  D. Expression B, where r will equate it to zero
  E. Both A and B
  F. None of the above

(n) Referring to question (m), the value for point 4 on the graph will be
  A. The value of r that will equate expression A with that of B
  B. The value of r that will equate expression A to zero
  C. The value of r that will equate expression B to zero
  D. Both B and C
  E. None of the above

11. Show that if NPV's reinvestment assumption is met (i.e., the reinvestment rate i equals the firm's required rate of return k), then Equation (2) in this chapter is equivalent to Equation (1) in Chapter 5.

12. For the two projects shown in Examples 3 and 4, show that the cash-flow series for project I modified as discussed and illustrated in Example 4 will continue to dominate project II for required rates of return of 20%, 30%, 40%, 45%, and 49%.

13. Consider two firms that have required rates of return of 60% and 70%. Compute the NPV for both project I and project II shown in Examples 3 and 4 using a 60% and a 70% required rate of return. For both of these rates, demonstrate that project II will dominate project I modified using the approach illustrated in Example 4.

14. For the two projects shown in Example 3, the NPV criterion will prefer project I at low and moderate discount rates, whereas project II has a higher IRR than project I. Discuss what project characteristics would lead the NPV model to prefer project I and why this is the case based on the way this model evaluates projects. Similarly, discuss the project characteristics that would lead the IRR model to prefer project II and why this is the case based on the way this model evaluates projects.

15. Part (a) of the solution to Example 4 shows that project I modified dominated project II in the amount of $5,860 (rounded) in cash-flow terms at the end of year 1. What is the relationship of this amount to the NPV's of the two projects? (*Hint*: Determine the present value of $5,860 using a 16% discount rate; next determine the NPV of each project using a 16% discount rate).

16. For the two projects shown in Examples 3 and 4, show that project I still dominates project II if the firm has the opportunity to invest $30,000 at the end of year 1 and a loan bearing interest at 16% can be obtained in conjunction with either project.

17. For the two projects shown in Examples 3 and 4, show that project I no longer dominates project II if a firm must pay 60% to obtain the $20,000 desired at the end of year 1 (if project I is accepted).

18. For the conditions described in Problem 17, show why project II dominates project I plus the loan in the amount of the answer to Problem 17.

19. For the two projects shown in Example 1, discuss the conditions under which each of the following occurs.

    (a) The true rate of return [as computed by Equation (3)] on project A will be *exactly equal* to the true rate of return on project B.

    (b) The true rate of return on project A will be *greater than* the true rate of return on project B.

    (c) The true rate of return on project A will be *less than* the true rate of return on project B.

20. Based on your discussion in problem 19, demonstrate by using terminal value [Equation (1)] that shareholders would: (a) be indifferent between projects A and B under the condition you specify in part (a) of your answer to Problem 19; (b) prefer project A to project B under the condition you specify in part (b) of your answer to Problem 19; and (c) prefer project B to project A under the condition you specify in part (c) of your answer to Problem 19.

21. Based on projects A and B in Example 1, is the 20% return on project B the true guaranteed rate of return, but is the 20% return on project A not guaranteed and is the true rate of return dependent upon the reinvestment rate which can be earned on the cash flows that take place at the end of years 1, 2, and 3? Discuss.

7

Capital Budgeting for Mutually Exclusive Projects

In Chapter 6, we demonstrated the superiority of the NPV criterion over the other DCF approaches, IRR and PI. In the current chapter, we illustrate how the NPV model effectively handles the evaluation of mutually exclusive projects. In addition, we demonstrate the enrichment of the NPV model to handle changing required rates of return in the future as well as changing reinvestment rates.

ELABORATIONS OF THE BASIC NPV MODEL

Chapter 5 introduces the basic NPV model, which assumes that the firm's required rate of return remains constant over the project's life. We reintroduce this model as Equation (1):

$$\text{NPV} = \sum_{t=0}^{n} \frac{S_t}{(1+k)^t} - \sum_{t=0}^{n} \frac{A_t}{(1+k)^t} \tag{1}$$

where S_t = the cash inflow in period t
A_t = the cash outflow in period t
n = the useful life of the project
k = the firm's required rate of return

Of course, the NPV model does not encounter any major difficulty if the firm estimates that its required rate of return will change in future years. In fact, the straightforward elaboration of Equation (1) merely calls upon the geometric sum to determine the appropriate discount factor. Equation (2) determines the NPV for a project under the assumption that the firm will have a changing required rate of return:

$$NPV = \sum_{t=0}^{n} \frac{S_t}{\prod_{j=1}^{t}(1+k_j)} - \sum_{t=0}^{n} \frac{A_t}{\prod_{j=1}^{t}(1+k_j)} \tag{2}$$

where k_j = the firm's required rate of return in period j

The perceptive reader has already suspected that Equation (1) is a special case of Equation (2). And this is the case. If all the values of k_j are equal, Equation (2) reduces to the simpler Equation (1).

As discussed in Chapter 6, both Equations (1) and (2) make the implicit assumption that the reinvestment rate (i) will equal or be a close approximation for the firm's required rate of return (k). If the firm's reinvestment rate is *not* approximately equal to its required rate of return, then the NPV model's calculations are based upon an erroneous assumption. The greater the deviation of the reinvestment rate from the firm's required rate of return, the greater the error that the basic NPV model makes in evaluating the attractiveness of a given project.

In order to overcome the error that the basic NPV model makes when i does not equal k, we must call upon the terminal value (TV) calculation introduced in Chapter 6. Recall that the TV calculation shows the total value of a project's cash inflows under the assumption that they are reinvested to earn a specific annual rate of return i. We repeat the TV model here for convenience as Equation (3):

$$TV = \sum_{t=0}^{n} S_t(1+i)^{n-t} \tag{3}$$

Equation (3) determines TV under the assumption that the reinvestment rate (i) remains constant over the life of the project.

Once the TV is computed using Equation (3), a modified NPV value (which we call NPV*) can be computed using Equation (4):

$$NPV^* = \frac{TV}{(1+k)^n} - \sum_{t=0}^{n} \frac{A_t}{(1+k)^t} \tag{4}$$

Two characteristics should be noted about Equation (4). First, we call equation (4) a modified NPV model (NPV*) because we are no longer assuming that the reinvestment rate equals the firm's required rate of return, as in Equations (1) and (2). In Equation (4), we are assuming the project's cash inflows can be reinvested at the annual rate of return i and the firm's required rate of return is k. Second, Equation (4) assumes the firm's required rate of return remains constant over the life of the project.

As we saw above, it is a straightforward extension of the NPV model to allow the required rate of return to change over the life of the project. Applying the same methodology to Equation (4) that we did to Equation (1) in order to arrive at Equation (2), we see that:

$$NPV^* = \frac{TV}{\prod_{j=1}^{n}(1+k_j)} - \sum_{t=0}^{n} \frac{A_t}{\prod_{j=1}^{t}(1+k_j)} \tag{5}$$

Equation (5) determines the modified NPV value (NPV*) under the assumption that the firm's required rate of return changes over the life of the project. Further—along the same lines as our earlier discussion about the relationship between Equations (1) and (2)—Equation (4) is just a special case of Equation (5) under the assumption that the firm's required rate of return is constant over the project's life.

Finally, the calculation of TV in Equation (3) makes the assumption that the reinvestment rate (i) remains constant over the project's life. Of course, this reinvestment rate could very well change over time. Under such conditions, a project's TV is computed using Equation (6):

$$\text{TV} = \sum_{t=0}^{n} S_t \left[\prod_{j=t+1}^{n} \left(1 + i_j \right) \right] \tag{6}$$

where i_j is the reinvestment rate that can be earned in period j. The compounding process shown by the geometric sum begins in period $t + 1$ because we are making the usual assumption that the cash flows S_t occur at the *end* of period t. Hence, each cash inflow can be reinvested starting in period $t + 1$. It should also be mentioned that Equation (6) reduces to Equation (3) if the reinvestment rate remains constant over the project's life.

Once TV has been computed using Equation (6), the modified NPV value can be computed using: (1) Equation (4), if the firm's required rate of return remains constant over the project's life; or (2) Equation (5), if the required rate of return changes over time.

With these elaborations of the basic NPV model, we can handle all possible conditions relative to the firm's expected future required rate of return, as well as its expected reinvestment rate. Although these values of k and i present forecasting difficulties, we must address the prospect that such values are not very likely to remain constant at their current levels over project lives of 5, 10, or 20 years.

The NPV and NPV* models presented can be applied to the evaluation of independent projects, as well as to sets of mutually exclusive projects. The evaluation of independent projects requires only the application of the decision rule: The project is a candidate for acceptance if NPV (or NPV*) is greater than or equal to zero because projects satisfying this condition will increase shareholders' wealth. The ranking of mutually exclusive projects using NPV and NPV* is the task of the next section.

EVALUATING MUTUALLY EXCLUSIVE PROJECTS

So that we can correctly evaluate mutually exclusive projects in order to select the one that will maximize shareholders' wealth, there are three major questions to be addressed. Over the lives of the mutually exclusive projects:

1. Is the firm's reinvestment rate (i) expected to *differ significantly* from the firm's required rate of return (k)?

2. Is the reinvestment rate (i) expected to *change* over the projects' lives or is it expected to *remain constant*?

3. Is the firm's required rate of return (k) expected to *change* over the projects' lives or is it expected to *remain constant?*

Depending on the answers to these three questions, the firm can select the appropriate version of the NPV model in order to choose the preferred project from a mutually exclusive set of projects.

In addition to these three questions, we have the preliminary question concerning whether the firm is subject to capital rationing or not. If the firm is subject to capital rationing, then all feasible *portfolios* of capital projects must be evaluated in order to select the one maximizing NPV or NPV* without violating any of the firm's resource limitations. Mathematical programming techniques provide an efficient mechanism by which feasible portfolios are evaluated. We explore mathematical programming approaches to capital budgeting in Chapters 20 and 28.

If capital rationing does not exist, then each set of mutually exclusive projects can be evaluated on its own merit. Where firms have conditions of *no capital rationing*, the only necessary decision is which project in each mutually exclusive set is best and whether it has a positive NPV or NPV*. All the best projects with positive NPV or NPV* values should be undertaken in order to maximize shareholders' wealth.

Figure 7–1 presents a flow chart, which guides the firm in the selection of the appropriate model to evaluate mutually exclusive projects.

As can be seen, the first question that must be answered in the flow chart is whether capital rationing exists. Once this question is handled, we next address the three major questions about the equality of i and k and whether each remains constant or changes over time. The appropriate version of the correct model to use (NPV or NPV*), as well as the choice of how TV is computed, depends upon the answers to these three major questions. Thus, the flow chart merely presents a map for the selection of Equations (1)–(6), depending on prevailing conditions.

Figure 7–1 is a *general* tool, which can be used to rank mutually exclusive projects that exhibit *any* of the three types of disparities—*size, time or useful life.* Each of these disparities imposes different difficulties on the project-ranking process; however, the flow chart properly handles the difficulties by selecting the appropriate model. In the next three sections, we apply the flow chart to mutually exclusive sets of projects that possess each of these disparities.

Projects With A Size Disparity

A size disparity is exhibited in a set of mutually exclusive projects if a difference exists in the original cash outflow required by the projects. Such projects are comparable and can be handled with the techniques presented in this chapter, as long as capital rationing does not exist (i.e., the first question posed in Figure 7–1). Where capital rationing does not exist, the firm can obtain *any amount* of capital funds at the same cost of capital. Thus, differences in cash outlays between (or among) mutually exclusive projects are irrelevant (because the firm can obtain sufficient funds to accept all attractive investments) and the

FIGURE 7–1   Flow Chart for Ranking Mutually Exclusive Projects

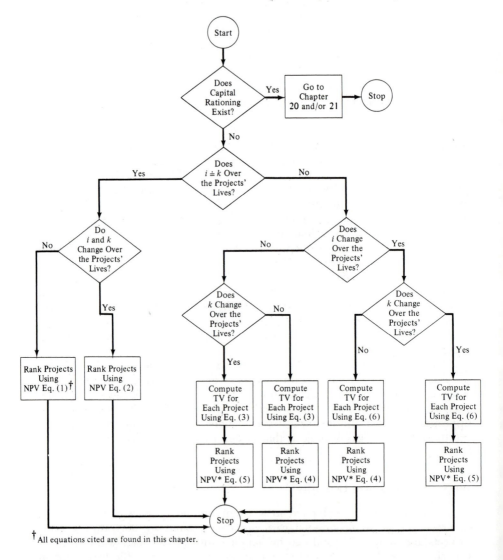

† All equations cited are found in this chapter.

one that generates the greatest increase in shareholders' wealth should be selected.

Consider the two projects shown in Example 1.

□ **EXAMPLE 1**   *Ranking Two Mutually Exclusive Investments Which Exhibit a Size Disparity*

Alpha Company is evaluating two projects:

	Project	
Characteristic	X	Y
Original investment	$240,000	$180,000
Annual cash inflows	80,000	62,000
Useful life	6 years	6 years

Given its 16% required rate of return, these values are computed by Alpha to rank the two projects:

	Project	
Criterion	X	Y
$NPV_{16\%}$	$54,779	$48,454
$PI_{16\%}$	1.23	1.27
IRR	24%	26%

Alpha Company sees that there is a conflict in the ranking of these two projects using NPV versus PI and IRR. The firm determines the discount rate at which Fisher's intersection occurs and finds $f = 20\%$. A sketch of the NPV profile for each project is shown in Figure 7–2.

Alpha Company estimates that its cost of capital will be closely approximated by the reinvestment rate it is able to earn over each of the next 10 years. In addition, the firm feels that the actual value for i and k would remain constant over the lives of projects X and Y and could range from a low of 12% to a high of 18%. Using Figures 7–1 and 7–2, help Alpha Company select the correct project.

Solution: Referring to Figure 7–1, we see that Alpha Company should use the basic NPV model shown in Equation (1) to rank projects X and Y because $i = k$ and both will remain constant over the lives of these two projects. Using Equation (1), the NPV of each project at each of the rates in the range 12% to 18% is:

	12%	*13%*	*14%*	*15%*	*16%*	*17%*	*18%*
NPV of Project X	$88,913	$79,804	$71,093	$62,759	$54,779	$47,135	$39,808
NPV of Project Y	74,907	67,848	61,097	54,638	48,454	42,529	36,851

We see that project X dominates project Y over the entire range 12% to 18%. The excess of NPV for project X over that for project Y is greater at the lower rates in the range. Notice also that the NPV's computed in the table correspond to the NPV profile for each project shown in Figure 7–2. The NPV profiles are relevant or exact for *only one branch shown in Figure 7–1—the branch where i = k and where they do not change over the lives of the projects.* These are the conditions that Alpha Company estimates will prevail for the two projects in question. Therefore, we can use Figure 7–2 or the given table to rank projects X and Y.

Thus, given the estimated future conditions, Alpha Company should select project X rather than project Y because the NPV of project X exceeds that of project Y for all rates between 12% and 18%. The shareholders of Alpha Company will be *wealthier* in the amount of the difference between the two NPV's if the firm selects project X rather than project Y. This is true *even though project Y has a higher IRR.* In addition, as Figure 7–2 shows, project X continues to dominate project Y for all values of *i = k* less than 20%. At rates in excess of Fisher's intersection, the preferred project shifts to project Y because at

FIGURE 7–2   NPV Profiles for Projects X and Y

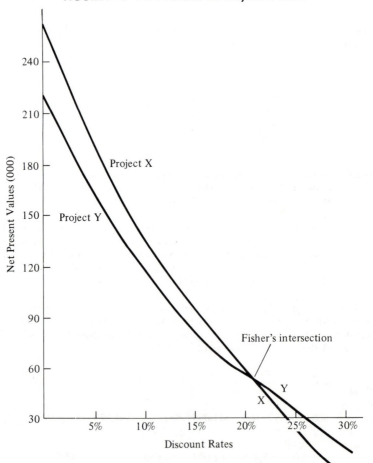

such rates for i and k, project Y has a greater NPV. This again shows the importance of Fisher's intersection and its utility in performing sensitivity analysis in ranking mutually exclusive projects. □

The ranking of the two projects in Example 1 was straightforward because the future conditions estimated by the firm enabled us to rank the projects using the basic NPV model. The firm could very well have envisioned a series of events that necessitated the computation of TV and NPV* in order to rank the projects under evaluation properly. For a slightly more complex problem setting, consider Example 2.

□ **EXAMPLE 2** *A Size Disparity with Changing Cost of Capital and Reinvestment Rates*

Alpha Company wants to rank the two projects under evaluation in Example 1 for the following conditions. First, the company estimates that i will equal k over the lives of the two projects. Second, rather than remaining constant at 16%, these two values (i and k) are estimated to be 16% for the first 2 years, 18% for the next 2 years, and 21% for the last 2 years of the projects' lives. Help Alpha Company select the correct evaluation technique and then rank projects X and Y.

Solution: Using Figure 7–1, we see that NPV computed with Equation (2) is appropriate where $i = k$ and the values are changing over time. Thus, for project X:

$$NPV_X = \sum_{t=0}^{n} \frac{S_t}{\prod_{j=1}^{t}(1+k_j)} - \sum_{t=0}^{n} \frac{A_t}{\prod_{j=1}^{t}(1+k_j)}$$

$$= \frac{\$80{,}000}{1.16} + \frac{80{,}000}{(1.16)^2} + \frac{80{,}000}{(1.16)^2(1.18)} + \frac{80{,}000}{(1.16)^2(1.18)^2} + \frac{80{,}000}{(1.16)^2(1.18)^2(1.21)}$$

$$+ \frac{80{,}000}{(1.16)^2(1.18)^2(1.21)^2} - \$240{,}000$$

$$= \$68{,}966 + 59{,}453 + 50{,}384 + 42{,}698 + 35{,}288 + 29{,}163 - \$240{,}000$$

$$= \underline{\$45{,}952}$$

This calculation is slightly more involved than the one in Example 1. Here, even with a constant cash inflow over the project's life, the discount factors for each year must be computed rather than found in tables of annuity discount factors. As we would expect, the NPV for project X here ($45,952) is less than that of Example 1 with a constant 16% rate ($54,779). This result occurs because the project contributes less to the value of the firm as the firm's cost of funds increases to 18% and 21% over the project's life.

For project Y:

$$NPV_Y = \frac{\$62{,}000}{1.16} + \frac{62{,}000}{(1.16)^2} + \frac{62{,}000}{(1.16)^2(1.18)}$$

$$+ \frac{62{,}000}{(1.16)^2(1.18)^2} + \frac{62{,}000}{(1.16)^2(1.18)^2(1.21)} + \frac{62{,}000}{(1.16)^2(1.18)^2(1.21)^2} - \$180{,}000$$

$$= \$53{,}448 + 46{,}076 + 39{,}048 + 33{,}091 + 27{,}348 + 22{,}602 - \$180{,}000$$

$$= \underline{\$41{,}613}$$

Given these calculations, we see that Alpha Company should rank project X first and project Y second. The difference of $4,339 in the NPV values again shows the amount by which the shareholders benefit by accepting project X rather than the project with the higher IRR (project Y). ☐

Projects With A Time Disparity

In addition to projects with differences in the original cash outflows, firms often encounter projects with the same cash outflow but differing patterns of cash inflows. In this latter case, the projects are called *mutually exclusive projects that exhibit a time disparity*. In order to rank such projects, we again use Figure 7–1 to arrive at the appropriate model.

☐ **EXAMPLE 3**   *Ranking Projects With A Time Disparity and Unequal (But Constant Over Time) Values of i and k*

Delta Company is evaluating Projects A and B:

	Project A	Project B
Cash outflow	$70,000	$70,000
Cash inflows		
Year 1	10,000	50,000
2	20,000	40,000
3	30,000	20,000
4	45,000	10,000
5	60,000	10,000

Delta Company has a cost of capital of 14% and has computed the NPV, PI, and IRR for the two projects:

Criterion	Project A	Project B
$NPV_{14\%}$	$32,219	$29,252
$PI_{14\%}$	1.46	1.42
IRR	27.2%	37.6%

Over the coming 5 years, Delta Company estimates that its cost of capital will remain constant at 14%, but that its reinvestment rate will be 20%. Recall that all three models cited earlier would be in error relative to the reinvestment rate that Delta expects to experience. In particular, the NPV and PI assume that the cash inflows of each project will be reinvested at 14%, while the IRR model assumes that the cash inflows of project A can be reinvested at 27.2% while those of B can be reinvested at 37.6%.

Provide assistance to Delta Company in selecting the right model and in ranking projects A and B.

Solution: Referring to Figure 7–1, we see that if $i \neq k$ and both i and k are constant over the lives of the projects, we should use Equation (3) and compute the TV for each project and Equation (4) to compute the NPV*.

The terminal value calculations would be as follows:

$$TV_A = \sum_{t=0}^{n} S_t (1+i)^{n-t}$$

$$= \$10,000(1.20)^{5-1} + 20,000(1.20)^{5-2}$$
$$+ 30,000(1.20)^{5-3} + 45,000(1.20)^{5-4}$$
$$+ 60,000(1.20)^{5-5}$$

This terminal value can either be computed directly or through the use of compound interest factors from column one on the 20% page in Appendix B,

$$TV_A = \$10,000(2.0736) + 20,000(1.7280) + 30,000(1.44)$$
$$+ 45,000(1.20) + \$60,000$$
$$= \$212,496$$

For project B:

$$TV_B = \$50,000(2.0736) + 40,000(1.7280) + 20,000(1.44)$$
$$+ 10,000(1.20) + \$10,000$$
$$= \$223,600$$

Ranking the projects, we find:

$$NPV^*_A = \frac{TV_A}{(1+k)^n} - A_0$$
$$= \frac{\$212,496}{(1.14)^5} - \$70,000$$
$$= \$40,364$$

$$NPV^*_B = \frac{\$223,600}{(1.14)^5} - \$70,000$$
$$= \$46,131$$

Thus, we see that Delta Company should prefer project B to project A since $NPV^*_B = \$46,131$ is greater than $NPV^*_A = \$40,364$. Given that the firm can reinvest cash inflows at 20% over the next 5 years, project B will result in a net increase in the value of the firm of $46,131, while project A will yield a net increase of only $40,364 (both these figures are based on the firm's cost of capital being 14% over the next 5 years).

□

In Example 3, we assumed that, although $i \neq k$, both values remained constant over the lives of the two projects. The more usual case is when both values vary in the future depending on economic conditions, the level of interest rates, the competitive environment faced by the firm, and the like. Figure 7–1 and Equations (1)–(6), on which Example 3 is based, provide substantial flexibility in the treatment of changing values for i and k, as well as the performance of sensitivity analysis. The next example illustrates this flexibility.

□ **EXAMPLE 4**   Time Disparity with Changing Cost of Capital and Reinvestment Rates

Gamma Company is evaluating two mutually exclusive projects:

t	C	D
0	− $1,000,000	− $1,000,000
1	+ 300,000	+ 600,000
2	+ 700,000	+ 700,000
3	+ 1,500,000	+ 1,000,000

Gamma estimates that these values for i and k will prevail during each of the next 3 years:

t	k_t	i_t
1	12%	15%
2	13%	18%
3	14%	20%

Using Figure 7–1, rank projects C and D for Gamma Company.

Solution: From Figure 7–1, we see that if $i \neq k$, and both i and k vary over the project lives, we should utilize Equation (6) to compute the TV of each project and then rank the projects using Equation (5) for NPV*.

Equation 6 is:

$$TV = \sum_{t=0}^{n} S_t \left[\prod_{j=t+1}^{n} (1 + i_j) \right]$$

Note again that the compounding process starts in the year following each cash inflow (S_t) because such flows take place at the end of each year t. Thus, in the given table of i- and k-values, the value for $i_1 = 15\%$ is extraneous information because the earliest that cash flows can be reinvested is during year 2, when $i_2 = 18\%$.

We find:

$$TV_C = \$300,000(1.18)(1.20) + 700,000(1.20) + \$1,500,000$$

$$= \$2,764,800$$

$$TV_D = \$600,000(1.18)(1.20) + 700,000(1.20) + \$1,000,000$$

$$= \$2,689,600$$

We next determine the NPV*:

$$NPV*_C = \frac{TV_C}{\prod_{j=1}^{n} (1 + k_j)} - A_0$$

$$= \frac{\$2,764,800}{(1.12)(1.13)(1.14)} - \$1,000,000$$

$$= \$916,295$$

$$NPV*_D = \frac{\$2,689,600}{(1.12)(1.13)(1.14)} - \$1,000,000$$

$$= \$864,174$$

Thus, we see that Gamma Company should rank project C higher than project D because $NPV^*_C = \$916,295$ is greater than $NPV^*_D = \$864,174$. In present-value terms, project C will increase shareholders' wealth by \$52,121 more than will project D.   □

We have dealt with the treatment of mutually exclusive projects that have had either a size disparity or a time disparity. The ranking of such projects has been illustrated under a variety of conditions relative to the firm's required rate of return (or cost of capital) and the estimated reinvestment rate. The final type of disparity is that of unequal useful lives. This type of disparity combines the first two, in that projects with unequal lives usually require different cash outflows and have varying cash-inflow patterns.

Projects With Unequal Useful Lives

It is sometimes argued that projects with unequal useful lives are inherently noncomparable because they have different durations of cash flows. Our position is that projects with unequal lives *are comparable* as long as the firm evaluating such projects can adequately address the critical question: *What will take place at the end of the shorter-lived project?* It can generally be assumed that at the end of the shorter-lived project, one of two types of reinvestment will occur: (1) The asset will be replaced with another possessing similar characteristics; or (2) the funds will be reinvested elsewhere by the firm at a specified reinvestment rate.

If the type of reinvestment can be pinpointed, we can rank mutually exclusive projects with unequal lives by calling upon the familiar approach outlined in Figure 7–1. In order to utilize the flow chart effectively, we must discuss several points.

First, we must compare the projects with a *common termination date*. This date can be *no earlier* than the *end of the longer-lived project* (if project abandonment is ruled out). If we assume that each project is replaced by another with similar characteristics, then the period over which the two *replacement chains*—the series of replacements of each asset by another of similar characteristics—must be compared is the *least common multiple of the lives of the two assets*. If we assume that at the end of the life of the shorter-lived asset the funds are reinvested elsewhere at a specified reinvestment rate, then the two assets should be compared over the period of the *longer-lived project*.

Second, the magnitude of the funds available for reinvestment elsewhere in the firm each year must be incorporated into the analysis through the TV calculation. This analysis will be demonstrated in Example 5.

Third, as we see in Figure 7–1, we must address three questions in order to appropriately discount the cash flows: (1) What is the firm's reinvestment rate? (2) What is the firm's cost of capital? (3) Will each of these values change over time?

We illustrate the application of this methodology in Example 5, which calls upon two projects originally cited by Solomon.[1]

---

[1] See Ezra Solomon, "The Arithmetic of Capital Budgeting Decisions," *The Journal of Business*, vol. 29, no. 2 (April 1956), 124–129.

□ **EXAMPLE 5**   *The Evaluation of Replacement Chains for Two Assets*
Mew Company is evaluating two projects:

	Project	
t	G	H
0	− $10,000	− $10,000
1	+ 12,000	0
2	0	0
3	0	0
4	0	+ 17,490

Mew computes these evaluation criteria based on its cost of capital of 12%:

	Project	
Criterion	G	H
$NPV_{12\%}$	$714	$1,115
$PI_{12\%}$	1.07	1.11
IRR	20%	15%

Based on the above analysis, it appears as though project H is more attractive on an NPV and a PI basis, and project G is more attractive using the IRR criterion.

However, this analysis ignores what takes place at the end of the life of project G. It is rather inequitable to compare project G, which has a 1-year life, with project H, which has a 4-year life; no consideration is given to the fact that the funds generated at the end of year 1 by project G can be reinvested until the end of year 4 (i.e., the end of project H's life).

When confronted with the above challenge, Mew states that if project G is implemented it will be replaced each year for four years with a similar machine by the same manufacturer. In addition, Mew states that excess cash flows generated by project G can be reinvested to earn 14% during year 2, 15% during year 3, and 16% during year 4.

Rank these two projects using the appropriate models.

Solution: Project H is unaffected by any of the factors given earlier since it is the longer-lived project and has no intermediate cash inflows. Thus, the terminal value of project H is $17,490 and its NPV* = $1,115.

On the other hand, in order to analyze project G we must perform three steps: (1) determine the net cash flows when considering the annual replacements; (2) determine the TV given the reinvestment of the net cash flows at the relevant rates stated above; and (3) compute NPV* based on the firm's cost of capital.

In order to determine the net cash flows for project G, this table is helpful:

Time	Replication of Project G				Overall Net Cash Flow
	1	2	3	4	
0	− $10,000				− $10,000
1	+ 12,000	− $10,000			+ 2,000
2		+ 12,000	− $10,000		+ 2,000
3			+ 12,000	− 10,000	+ 2,000
4				+ 12,000	+ 12,000

In order to determine the terminal value of project G, we utilize the overall net cash flows generated by project G and the estimated reinvestment rates. We do this as follows:

$$TV_G = \sum_{t=0}^{n} S_t \left[\prod_{j=t+1}^{n} (1 + i_j) \right]$$
$$= \$2{,}000(1.14)(1.15)(1.16)$$
$$+ 2{,}000(1.15)(1.16) + 2{,}000(1.16) + 12{,}000$$
$$= \underline{\$20{,}030}$$

Finally, we compute NPV* for project G:

$$NPV^*_G = \frac{TV_G}{(1+k)^n} - A_0$$
$$= \frac{\$20{,}030}{(1.12)^4} - \$10{,}000$$
$$= \underline{\$2{,}729}$$

Therefore, we see that $NPV^*_G = \$2{,}729$ and $NPV^*_H = \$1{,}115$. Clearly, the successive replacements of project G over four years dominates the performance of project H. Mew Company should select project G. □

Example 5 illustrates the treatment of unequal project lives, wherein it is assumed that the shorter-lived project is replaced at the end of its life with an asset with the same cost and benefits as the original asset.

The recommended methodology encounters no difficulties in handling any other pattern of costs and benefits associated with the replications of the shorter-lived project. In times of high rates of inflation, it is unlikely that future project-related costs and benefits will remain unchanged. Although we treat the problem of inflation in depth in Chapter 9, at this point it is sufficient to state the simple rule that one way to handle inflation is to discount the inflated costs and benefits at a rate that also incorporates the impact of inflation on the firm's cost of capital. Example 6 demonstrates how unequal, useful-lived projects are handled to incorporate the effects of inflation.

□ **EXAMPLE 6** *The Evaluation of Replacement Chains with Inflation Factored In*

The Sigma Company is evaluating two projects:

t	J	K
0	− $40,000	− $54,000
1	+ 30,000	+ 25,000
2	+ 33,000	+ 27,750
3		+ 30,802

Sigma needs the use of this type of asset for at least the next 6 years (which happens to be the least common multiple of the lives of these two assets); thus, each asset will be replaced with a similar one from the same manufacturer at the end of its life.

Sigma has observed purchase prices of these two assets over the last decade. Project J has had price increases that average 12% compounded annually, while project K has had compounded annual price increases of 14%. Sigma expects these trends to continue over the next 6 years.

In addition to the differing effects of inflation on the purchase prices of these two assets, inflation impacts the operating costs—and thus the cash inflows—of the two assets differently. Sigma estimates (as shown in the table given earlier) that the cash inflows for project J will grow at 10% compounded annually, while project K's cash inflows will grow at 11% compounded annually. Again, this pattern is expected to continue over the next 6 years.

Finally, Sigma estimates that its cost of capital after the impact of inflation and its reinvestment rates over the next 6 years will be as follows:

t	i_t	k_t
1	18%	12%
2	12%	13%
3	15%	14%
4	17%	16%
5	20%	17%
6	22%	19%

Use Figure 7–1 to help Sigma rank projects J and K.

Solution: We begin the analysis by preparing a table for each project that determines the overall net cash flow given the necessary number of replications in order to cover 6 years. Such a table was also prepared in Example 5.

For Project J:

	Replication of Project J			Overall Net
t	*1*	*2*	*3*	Cash Flow
0	− $40,000			− $40,000
1	+ 30,000			+ 30,000
2	+ 33,000	− $50,176		− 17,176
3		+ 36,300		+ 36,300
4		+ 39,930	− $62,941	− 23,011
5			+ 43,923	+ 43,923
6			+ 48,315	+ 48,315

For Project K:

	Replication of Project K		Overall Net
t	*1*	*2*	Cash Flow
0	− $54,000		− $54,000
1	+ 25,000		+ 25,000
2	+ 27,750		+ 27,750
3	+ 30,802	− $80,003	− 49,201
4		+ 34,191	+ 34,191
5		+ 37,952	+ 37,952
6		+ 42,126	+ 42,126

Using the final column in each of these tables, we can now compute the terminal value at the end of year 6. Referring to Figure 7–1, we see that Equation (6) should be used to compute these TV values due to the changing reinvestment rates over the next 6 years. In addition, recall that only the *cash inflows* will be compounded out in the TV calculation. Once computed, the TV will be used in Equation (5) for NPV*.

For Project J:

$$TV_J = \sum_{t=0}^{6} S_t \left[\prod_{j=t+1}^{6} (1 + i_j) \right]$$

$$= \$30,000(1.12)(1.15)(1.17)(1.2)(1.22)$$
$$+ 36,300(1.17)(1.2)(1.22) + 43,923(1.22)$$
$$+ 48,315$$
$$= \$66,186 + 62,178 + 53,586 + 48,315$$
$$= \$230,265$$

For Project K:

$$TV_K = \sum_{t=0}^{6} S_t \left[\prod_{j=t+1}^{6} (1 + i_j) \right]$$

$$= \$25,000(1.12)(1.15)(1.17)(1.20)(1.22)$$
$$+ 27,750(1.15)(1.17)(1.20)(1.22)$$
$$+ 34,191(1.20)(1.22) + 37,952(1.22) + 42,126$$
$$= \$55,155 + 54,662 + 50,056 + 46,301 + 42,126$$
$$= \$248,300$$

Finally, we are ready to compute NPV* for each project. Figure 7–1 indicates that Equation (5) is appropriate based on the changing *k*-values over the next 6 years.

$$NPV^* = \frac{TV}{\prod_{j=1}^{n}(1+k_j)} - \sum_{t=0}^{n} \frac{A_t}{\prod_{j=1}^{t}(1+k_j)}$$

Notice that both projects will require discounting the cash outflows using the second term on the right-hand side of the above equation—namely, any cash outflows shown in the table prepared for each project in the *overall net cash flow* column beyond year 0 must be discounted back to time zero.

$$NPV^*_J = \frac{\$230,265}{(1.12)(1.13)(1.14)(1.16)(1.17)(1.19)} - 40,000$$
$$- \frac{17,176}{(1.12)(1.13)} - \frac{23,011}{(1.12)(1.13)(1.14)(1.16)}$$
$$= \$98,818 - 67,321$$
$$= \$31,497$$

$$NPV^*_K = \frac{\$248,300}{(1.12)(1.13)(1.14)(1.16)(1.17)(1.19)} - 54,000$$
$$- \frac{49,201}{(1.12)(1.13)(1.14)}$$
$$= \$106,558 - 88,101$$
$$= \$18,457$$

Thus, we see that project J is significantly more attractive to Sigma than is project K, based on the NPV* values. The analysis that led to this conclusion has incorporated the effects of inflation, the sequence of replacements necessary to have 6 years of service from each asset, the varying reinvestment rates over time, and Sigma Company's changing cost of capital with inflation reflected.   □

The approach illustrated in Example 6 provides an appropriate methodology for ranking projects with unequal lives as long as the assumption that each project will be replaced by one of similar profitability until a common horizon date is valid. If this is not the case, we need to know the best estimate for the rate at which cash flows from each project can be reinvested up to a common horizon date (usually the end of the useful life of the longer-lived project). Given this estimate (which could vary from year to year), we can call upon the techniques of the previous section and find the terminal value (TV) and NPV*. As shown in Figure 7–1, the latter approach should be implemented any time that projects with unequal lives are analyzed and the reinvestment rate differs from the cost of capital.

□ **EXAMPLE 7**   *Unequal Useful Lives with Differing Reinvestment Rates*

The Tan Company, with a present cost of capital of 14%, is evaluating two mutually exclusive projects, which have different useful lives:

t	P	Q
0	− $10,000	− $12,000
1	+ 5,506	+ 4,991
2	+ 5,506	+ 4,991
3	+ 5,506	+ 4,991
4		+ 4,991
IRR	30%	24%
$NPV_{14\%}$	$ 2,783	$ 2,542
$PI_{14\%}$	1.278	1.212

Given the reinvestment assumptions of the models above, project P dominates project Q. However, management feels that during the next 4 years there will be changes in business conditions, which will result in the reinvestment rates and costs of capital shown in the following table:

t	i_t	k_t
1	6%	14%
2	8%	10%
3	9%	10%
4	10%	10%

Rank the two projects for Tan Company under the assumption that the cash inflows for each project will be reinvested at the rates shown above and that neither project will be replaced at the end of its life. Recall that a common terminal horizon (i.e., the life of the longer project) must be used to evaluate the projects.

Solution: Based on Figure 7–1, we use Equation (6) to compute the terminal value for each project:

$$TV = \sum_{t=0}^{n} S_t \left[\prod_{j=t+1}^{n} (1 + i_j) \right]$$

$$TV_P = \$5,506.27[(1.08)(1.09)(1.10)]$$
$$+ 5,506.27[(1.09)(1.10)] + 5,506,27(1.10)$$
$$= \$7,130.18 + 6,602.02 + 6,056.92$$
$$= \$19,789.10$$

$$TV_Q = \$4,991.11[(1.08)(1.09)(1.10)]$$
$$+ 4,991.11[(1.09)(1.10)] + 4,991.11(1.10)$$
$$+ 4,991.11$$
$$= \$6,463.09 + 5,984.34 + 5,490.22 + 4,991.11$$
$$= \$22,928.76$$

Finally, we rank the two projects with NPV* using Equation (5):

$$NPV^* = \frac{TV}{\prod_{j=1}^{n} (1 + k_j)} - \sum_{t=0}^{n} \frac{A_t}{\prod_{j=1}^{n} (1 + k_j)}$$

$$NPV^*_P = \frac{\$19,789.10}{(1.14)(1.10)(1.10)(1.10)} - \$10,000$$
$$= \$3,041.97$$

$$NPV^*_Q = \frac{\$22,928.76}{(1.14)(1.10)(1.10)(1.10)} - \$12,000$$
$$= \$3,111.16$$

Thus, we see that based on the new estimates for i_t and k_t, project Q is slightly more attractive than project P. □

This concludes our examination of mutually exclusive projects. We have shown how Figure 7–1 provides the financial analyst with the proper model to rank any set of mutually exclusive projects under any conditions relative to costs of capital and reinvestment rates.

SUMMARY

Preceding sections focus on the complications frequently encountered in practice when the financial manager grapples with formulation of the firm's capital budget. The issues presented really represent a set of alert signals suggesting further investigation. The financial manager should show caution whenever the following situations arise:

1. The projects analyzed are different in size.

2. The projects have different life spans.

3. The cash-flow patterns (increasing, decreasing, or uniform) vary from one project to the next.

4. The company's future reinvestment opportunities are expected to change significantly from the present set of investment options.

5. The firm's marginal cost of capital is expected to rise significantly over time.

6. There exist capital and/or labor constraints on the budget.

Under any of the above circumstances, the mechanical application of ranking techniques without regard to the underlying assumptions can trap the financial manager into manifestly wrong decisions. Therefore, we present Figure 7–1 to provide a framework for the correct analysis and ranking of mutually exclusive projects. The approach of Figure 7–1 is couched in NPV and NPV* terms because of the *uniquely consistent superiority of this approach in maximizing shareholders' wealth.*

The financial manager will devise the capital budget to maximize the present value of the firm; this suggests the acceptance of new capital projects as long as the project shows a positive NPV or NPV*. The preferred capital budget is that combination of projects which maximizes total NPV or NPV*. The admonition holds even if the firm must resort to new financing to absorb all viable projects. In reality, new financing may not be feasible for several reasons, such as delays entailed in marketing new securities, problems of corporate control created by new stockholders, and restrictive provisions in bond indentures.

More important perhaps than the limits imposed by financing arrangements is the ability of the firm to digest new projects due to labor bottlenecks and scarce management talent. A capital budget is not simply an exercise in applied finance, but comprises a host of technological and managerial problems. Consequently, for a variety of reasons, the firm may be pragmatically stopped from accepting more than a restricted number of projects in a given time period or over a longer span.

What principle should guide the preparation of a capital budget in the presence of such constraints? Within the limits imposed by the constraints, the firm should select that combination of projects which maximizes the NPV of the budget. To accomplish the objective, management might have to look beyond the present fiscal period to a longer planning horizon. These problems—the need to allocate resources to projects over several fiscal periods, limited financial and managerial resources, and technological uncertainties—become critically important in constructing a capital budget and modify the strict adherence to the NPV criterion also implied by Figure 7–1. The problem of maximizing NPV subject to such stated constraints is best described and resolved by mathematical programming techniques discussed in Chapters 20 and 21.

QUESTIONS/PROBLEMS

1. Discuss four aspects of the capital budgeting problem setting that must be addressed in order to select the appropriate model to rank mutually exclusive projects.
2. Discuss those characteristics of capital projects and the firm that warrant special attention when making capital investment decisions.
3. When projects have unequal useful lives, what are the two major alternatives that the firm has at the end of the life of the shorter project? How is each of these alternatives treated in ranking mutually exclusive projects with unequal lives?
4. If a firm estimates that $i = k$ over the life of the two mutually exclusive projects under evaluation, can the NPV profiles be used to rank the projects? Why or why not? If so, how would this be done?
5. Can NPV profiles be drawn when the firm feels that either i or k or both will change over the projects' lives? Why or why not?
6. State one approach for the treatment of capital investment evaluation under inflationary conditions.
7. The following two mutually exclusive projects are under evaluation:

Year	Project A	Project B
Present	− $25,000	− $25,000
1	10,000	0
2	10,000	5,000
3	10,000	10,000
4	10,000	30,000

(a) Determine the NPV of projects A and B. The firm's cost of capital is 10%.
(b) Determine the IRR of projects A and B.
(c) What is the reinvestment rate assumed under IRR?
(d) State *completely* the reasons for the conflict in ranking these two projects by NPV and IRR.
(e) Assume that the firm estimates that its cost of capital will remain at 10% but that the reinvestment rates faced over the next 4 years will be:

t	i_t
1	10%
2	12%
3	14%
4	16%

Rank the two projects.
8. XYZ Company is evaluating the following two mutually exclusive projects:

Year	Project A	Project B
Present	− $20,000	− $20,000
1	5,000	17,000
2	9,000	5,000
3	16,000	5,000

Over the coming 3 years, the firm estimates that the following reinvestment rates and costs of capital will be encountered:

t	i_t	k_t
1	10%	12%
2	14%	13%
3	18%	16%

Rank these two projects using the appropriate methodology.

9. The Rinky Dink Rickshaw Transport Company has a capital budget of $15,000. There are two alternative projects in which the entire sum may be invested: Graffiti Remover and a Roach Zapper. Each project has an initial cost of $15,000 and an estimated life of 4 years. The Roach Zapper will produce greater returns later in the project life, owing to the tenacious quality of Rickshaw roaches and the difficulty in extermination. The Graffiti Remover will produce greater returns at the beginning of the project, because the machine will become less efficient as it gets older.

	Roach Zapper		Graffiti Remover
Year	Cash Flows	Year	Cash Flows
0	− $15,000	0	− $15,000
1	3,500	1	8,000
2	5,000	2	6,500
3	6,000	3	4,000
4	8,000	4	2,000

Rinky Dink's cost of capital is 14% and the reinvestment rate is 17%. Rank these two projects using the appropriate methodology.

10. Mrs. Surekill, the administrator of Savelife Hospital, a small general-care hospital in the Appalachian Mountains, is in a quandary. She has alleviated all her capital budgeting problems for the coming fiscal year except for the electrocardiology and stress-testing departments.

EKG is an established department, which prefers to buy a new electrocardiograph machine every 4 years. They have two machines at present. The newest machine has been the primary machine for the past 4 years, with the older machine used as backup. Most of the income from a new machine, if purchased, would be in the first 4 years.

Stress Testing, on the other hand, is a new department that wants a treadmill device used to measure stress on the cardiovascular system. Since it is a new department, not yet in operation, it is estimated that its income would be low initially, but would increase as the availability of the new test became known to the house staff and was accepted by them.

The following table illustrates the expected after-tax cash flows by year for the two machines, each of which would cost $10,000:

Year	EKG	Stress Test
Present	− $10,000	− $10,000
1	4,000	1,000
2	4,000	1,000
3	4,000	1,000
4	4,000	3,000
5	1,000	3,000
6	1,000	3,000
7	1,000	7,000
8	1,000	7,000

Savelife faces an increasing reinvestment rate over the coming 8 years, starting at 12% and increasing by 2% per year. The hospital's cost of capital is 18% and will remain constant over the next 10 years. Rank these two projects for Mrs. Surekill.

11. Mr. I. M. Kool, a manager at the NoSweat Air Conditioning Company, is faced with the prospect of having to replace one of the large machines used in the plant. Two machines currently on the market will perform the job satisfactorily—the Hi-Grade and Superior machines. The expected after-tax cash flows for each machine are:

Year	Hi-Grade	Year	Superior
0	− $60,000	0	− $80,000
1	15,000	1	24,000
2	16,500	2	24,000
3	20,000	3	20,000
4	20,000	4	20,000
5	20,000	5	18,000
6	20,000	6	18,000

The firm's cost of capital is 16% and its reinvestment rate is 20%. Rank the two projects.

12. The Waltzer Company is evaluating the following two mutually exclusive projects:

Time	Project A	Project B
0	− $20,000	− $20,000
1	+ 5,000	+ 16,000
2	+ 8,000	+ 10,000
3	+ 10,000	+ 5,000
4	+ 20,000	+ 5,000

(a) Based only on observation, which project would you expect IRR to prefer? Which project would you expect NPV to prefer? Assuming $i = k = 15\%$.

(b) Compute the IRR and NPV of projects A and B.

(c) $k = 15\%$ over the life of the project and $i = 12\%$ over the life of the project. Which project is preferred?

13. For the two projects under evaluation by the Waltzer Company in Problem 12, assume the following changes in i and k over the life of the projects:

t	i_t	k_t
1	20%	25%
2	15%	20%
3	10%	15%
4	5%	10%

Which project is preferred? Show your work.

14. For the two projects under evaluation by the Waltzer Company in Problem 12, assume $i = 13\%$ over the life of the projects, but k varies as follows:

t	k_t
1	25%
2	20%
3	15%
4	10%

Which project is preferable?

15. For the two projects under evaluation by the Waltzer Company in Problem 12, assume $k = 18\%$ over the life of the project, but i varies as follows:

t	i_t
1	20%
2	15%
3	10%
4	5%

Which project is preferred?

16. For the two projects under evaluation by the Waltzer Company in Problem 12, assume the following changes in i and k over the life of the project:

t	i_t	k_t
1	20%	20%
2	15%	15%
3	10%	10%
4	5%	5%

Which project is preferred?

17. The Philly Bus Service wants to add to its fleet to improve its service. It has a choice of two models:

Model O: 3-year life, cost of $26,000, and cash inflow of $12,000 per year.
Model P: 4-year life, cost of $38,000, and cash inflows of $19,000 per year.

Assume that each bus will be replaced at the end of its life by a model with the same cost and future benefits. Assume further that Philly's cost of capital is 14% and its reinvestment rate is 18%. Rank the two projects.

18. For the two projects shown in Problem 17, assume that the cost of model O will increase by 12% per year, while model P will increase by 10% per year. In addition, assume that the benefits of model O are $12,000 in the first year and increase at 8% each year thereafter. Benefits of model P are $19,000 in the first year and increase at 11% each year thereafter. The firm's reinvestment rate remains at 18%, but its cost of capital starts at 14% and increases by 1% each year thereafter. Rank the two projects under these new conditions reflecting inflationary effects.

19. Edna Finn, restaurateur de premier classe, has $10,000 to invest in round lot purchases of French red wine. She may buy $10,000 shipments of freshly bottled Bordeaux or Beaujolais. Beaujolais matures quickly and must be consumed within the first several years of bottling. Bordeaux takes a longer time to mature and its value is greater in later years. The cash flows resulting from the two mutually exclusive purchases and subsequent sale are as follows:

Year	Beaujolais	Bordeaux
0	− $10,000	− $10,000
1	8,000	0
2	5,000	0
3	3,000	0
4	2,000	0
5	1,000	0
6	1,000	0
7		7,000
8		7,000
9		11,000
10		11,000
11		18,000
12		18,000

The restaurateur expects a reinvestment rate of 10% in the first 3 years, 12% in years 4–6, and 14% for the duration of the Bordeaux. Cost of capital is expected to be 12% for 6 years and 15% for the last 6 years. Rank the two projects.

20. For the two projects shown in Example 1 and for the values $i = k = 12\%$, 15%, and 18%, show: (a) the TV [using Equation (3)] for project X is greater than the TV for Project Y; and (b) the NPV* [using Equation (4)] for project X is greater than the NPV* for project Y. [The NPV* values will equal NPV for each project demonstrating that when $i = k$ and these values remain constant, Equation (1) is just a simplification of Equations (3) and (4).]

21. Show the following:
    (a) Equation (1) will result when all k_j are equal in Equation (2).
    (b) Equation (2) results when $i_j = k_j$ in Equation (5).
    (c) Equation (1) results when $i = k$ in Equation (4).

Cost of Capital

The four discounted-cash-flow procedures used to evaluate alternative investments (internal rate of return, net present value, profitability index, and annual capital charge) all measure cash flows in terms of a required rate of return (hurdle rate) to determine their acceptability. This hurdle rate was referred to earlier as the firm's cost of capital, and as noted in our discussion of risk analysis, the actual hurdle rate applied may be the cost of capital adjusted to compensate for project risk differing from that of the normal risk complexion of the firm. But what exactly is the cost of capital and how do we go about determining it? These are the questions that will be addressed in this chapter. This will necessitate an examination of the general problem of managing the financial structure and the valuation of the firm.

We shall confront the problems initially utilizing traditional methodology. Later (in Chapter 17), we examine the capital asset pricing model and discuss an alternative procedure for calculating the firm's cost of capital utilizing this model.

CONVENTIONAL WISDOM

The *cost of capital* refers to the rates of return expected by those parties contributing to the financial structure: preferred and common shareholders as well as creditors. It represents the cost of funds used to acquire the total assets of the firm. Thus, it is generally calculated as a weighted average of the costs associated with each type of capital included in the financial structure of the enterprise. Several factors merit additional comment and examination.

1. The cost of capital, considered as a rate of return, disaggregates into a risk-free rate plus a premium for risk. The risk premium covers the business and financial risk of the firm relative to available, alternative investments. Since the risk-free rate is common to all firms, differences in the cost of capital among firms originate in their riskiness. *The cost of capital embodies the average risk posture of the firm, that is, the composite risk of the firm as a portfolio of operational projects which makes up its risk complexion.*

2. Since the firm's capital cost is the security holders' income, *the cost of capital represents a rate of return that will maintain the market value of the outstanding securities within the context of overall market movements.* Investors have available to them a wide range of investment options, from risk-free government securities to common stocks of varying quality. Hence, in arranging their portfolios, they expect to receive a risk premium appropriate to the quality of a given investment. If the security concerned does not appear to promise such a yield at its current price, the price will drop until the yield equates with investor expectations.

3. The cost of capital is that rate which will enable the firm to sell new securities at current price levels. The firm must have the potential of using the new funds in ways that generate yields sufficient to cover the risk-free rate and the required premium for risk.

The reader will note that we have expressed the concept of the cost of capital in three different ways. But there is an underlying commonality: the firm must manage its assets and select capital projects with the goal of obtaining a yield at least sufficient to cover its cost of capital. If it fails in this objective, the market price of its outstanding securities will decline. If it achieves yields greater than the cost of capital, it is likely that the price of securities, especially the common stock, will be bid upward. Consequently, *the cost of capital is seen as an opportunity cost.* As an opportunity cost, it has dual aspects: from the investment standpoint, the firm competes against a variety of alternative uses of funds to attract investor capital, while internally the firm must select business projects with estimated yields that maintain the market value of its securities by promising returns commensurate with investor expectations (i.e., cover the required risk premium).

As a final note, a firm does not calculate the cost of capital and post it on the company bulletin board. Nor does the firm calculate it by picking up the annual report. Rather, it is a *dynamic concept: a synthesis of the costs of new equity and debt.* It conforms to the *marginal cost* of each; a weighted average cost for the next dollar of capital apportioned between debt and equity securities. Capital budgeting deals with future cash flows and calculates yields (or internal rates of return) on the next dollar of invested capital. The cost of capital stresses the cost of that dollar based upon market expectations. The theory of marginal cost pricing dictates, therefore, the acceptance of projects to the point of equality between the internal rate and the hurdle rate based upon the cost of capital.

The discussion of the cost of capital thus far has assumed some optimum balance of the financial mix, but the question is yet to be addressed. The following section examines those factors which affect the financial structure and indicates how we may go about selecting a financial structure. But again it is important to note that the firm's optimum financial structure is not fixed, but dynamic.

FINANCIAL STRUCTURE

The firm manages assets and selects capital projects to secure the maximum return appropriate to the level of acceptable risk. Conversely, it manages the financial structure to minimize the cost of capital (i.e., to obtain the lowest weighted average cost of capital). Assuming that both business risk and financial risk influence the weighted-average cost of capital, the introduction of debt into the financial structure up to some point lowers the weighted-average cost. Debt capital has cost advantages:

1. Owing to higher priority in the order of payment, the interest of debt is *normally* lower than the other types of capital.

2. Unlike payments to equity, interest qualifies as a tax deduction so that some portion of these charges is borne by Uncle Sam. Tax deductibility reduces the effective cost of debt capital.

3. Given a long-term upward trend in the price level, inflation makes debt cheaper in real terms if the rate of increase in the price level exceeds the anticipated inflation rate at the time of floatation.

Therefore, in managing the financial structure, the firm strives to achieve that combination of debt and equity that results in the lowest weighted-average cost of capital. This is the optimum financial structure. For any given level of earnings after taxes, it will also maximize the value of the firm. Thus, cost of capital is inextricably linked to the valuation of the firm and of capital projects.

To determine the optimum capital structure (i.e., debt/equity ratio) it is necessary to know investor preferences for risk, that is, their utility functions for risk versus return. This subject will be discussed at some length in Part IV. Assume that we know the investor risk preferences in terms of both the interest rates charged and the return on equity required for different financial mixes. Given this information, we may find the optimum financial mix by determining the weighted-average cost of capital for each possible mix and selecting that mix with the lowest cost. This procedure is demonstrated in Table 8–1.

In this table, the optimum financial structure is shown to consist of equal portions of debt and equity. In reality, the proportions vary from industry to industry based upon debt capacity and the variability of net-operating income. Therefore, in accepting a capital project, the manager should assess not only the NPV of the project but how it affects the variability of net operating income and whether it enhances or detracts from the debt capacity of the firm.

Before we enter into the discussion of those calculations required to compute the firm's cost of capital, we briefly discuss the impact of debt on the variability of earnings.

TABLE 8–1 Cost of Capital

(1) Percentage Debt	(2) Percentage Equity	(3)[a] Interest × (1 − t) where t = 50%	(4)[b] Required Return on Equity (%)	(5)[c] Weighted-Average Cost [(1) × (3) + (2) × (4) = (5)]	(6)[d] Value of Business EAT = $100,000 ÷ (5)
0	100	—	10.0	10.0	$1,000,000
10	90	4.0	10.1	9.5	1,052,631
20	80	4.0	10.2	9.0	1,111,111
30	70	4.0	10.3	8.4	1,190,476
40	60	4.5	10.5	8.1	1,234,567
50	50	5.0	11.0	→ 8.0	1,250,000
60	40	6.0	11.5	8.2	1,219,512
70	30	7.0	12.5	8.7	1,149,425
80	20	7.5	16.0	9.2	1,086,956

[a] t is the firm's marginal tax rate, 50%.

[b] The required return on common stock equity can be expected to increase as a function of risk. The greater the proportion of debt, the greater the financial risk.

[c] Optimum capital structure comprises 50% debt and equity with a weighted-average cost of capital (K) of 8%. At this point, the pretax, explicit cost of debt (10%) plus the implicit cost of debt represented by the rise in the cost of equity (1%), for the first time in the series exceeds the basic cost of all equity financing, which is 10%. In a continuous distribution, the lowest value of K coincides with the point at which the *total* cost of debt (K_D) equates to the cost of equity (K_e).

[d] The value of the business is the earnings after taxes, which is assumed to be constant at $100,000 divided by the cost of capital. Notice that the value is maximized at the point of optimum financial structure.

Debt and Variability of Earnings

Two kinds of risk influence the variability of earnings after taxes: business and financial. These two types of risk warrant further attention in terms of operating and financial leverage.

Business risk relates to the variability of net operating income, or *earnings before interest and taxes* (EBIT). It is measured by the *degree of operating leverage* (DOL). Operating leverage arises from the mix of fixed and variable costs in the manufacturing and administrative design of the firm. All things equal, the degree of operating leverage typically increases with the relative importance of fixed costs in total costs. Bear in mind: net operating income constitutes the funds available for distribution to creditors, stockholders, and tax collectors. After this point, the income statement describes the division among the shareholders. The degree of operating leverage at an output Q may be determined using Equation (1):

$$\text{DOL} = \frac{Q(P - \text{vc})}{Q(P - \text{vc}) - \text{FC}} = \frac{\% \text{ change in EBIT}}{\% \text{ change in output and sales}} \tag{1}$$

where $P =$ unit price
    vc = variable cost per unit
    FC = total fixed costs

Financial risk relates the variability of *earnings after taxes* (EAT) to the way the firm is financed, the *debt equity ratio*. Variability tends to increase as the proportion of fixed interest charges rises. The *degree of financial leverage* (DFL) measures financial risk and may be found using Equation (2):

$$\text{DFL} = \frac{\text{EBIT}}{\text{EBIT} - I} = \frac{\% \text{ change in EPS or EAT}}{\% \text{ change in EBIT}} \tag{2}$$

where I is the interest on debt.

How do we interpret the leverage measures? DOL and DFL are multipliers describing the effects of a percentage change in sales or operating income on the bottom line. For example, assuming a linear relationship between sales and variable costs and a constant tax rate, if the DOL were 5, a 10% change in sales would generate a 50% change in operating income. Or if the DFL were 3, a 10% change in EBIT would cause a 30% change in EAT. It follows that combined leverage (the product of DOL and DFL) measures the effect of a percentage change in sales on EAT. For example, in financial structure A of Table 8–2, a 10% increase in sales (from $100,000 to $110,000) creates a 43.3% increase (rounded) in both EBIT ($15,000 to $21,500) and EAT ($7,500 to $10,750). In financial structure E, the same 10% increase in sales generates a 43.3% increment in EBIT ($15,000 to $21,500), a 67.1% increase in both EBT ($9,600 to $16,100) and EAT ($4,800 to $8,050). In short, adding debt to the capital structure raises the variability of earnings before and after taxes. Financial structure E shows how financial risk adds to the firm's business risk (represented by operating leverage).

Yet the common shareholders may applaud leveraging. The reason is obvious from Table 8–2 where leveraging the financial structure has increased

TABLE 8–2 Leverage Effects: Total Variability

	Financial Structure A All Equity: 10,000 Shares	Financial Structure B Equity: 7,000 shares Debt: $30,000 at 6%	Financial Structure C Equity: 5,000 shares Debt: $50,000 at 6%	Financial Structure D Equity: 3,000 shares Debt: $70,000 at 6%	Financial Structure E Equity: 1,000 shares Debt: $90,000 at 6%
Net sales	$100,000	$100,000	$100,000	$100,000	$100,000
Less Cost of sales:					
Opening inventory	$ 5,000	$ 5,000	$ 5,000	$ 5,000	$ 5,000
Net purchases	40,000	40,000	40,000	40,000	40,000
Total	$45,000	$45,000	$45,000	$45,000	$45,000
Closing inventory	15,000 30,000	15,000 30,000	15,000 30,000	15,000 30,000	15,000 30,000
Gross operating income	$ 70,000	$ 70,000	$ 70,000	$ 70,000	$ 70,000
Less					
Selling expenses	$25,000	$25,000	$25,000	$25,000	$25,000
Administrative expenses	30,000 55,000	30,000 55,000	30,000 55,000	30,000 55,000	30,000 55,000
Net operating income (EBIT)	$15,000	$15,000	$15,000	$15,000	$15,000
Less					
Financial charges		1,800	3,000	4,200	5,400
Net income (EBT)	$15,000	$13,200	$12,000	$10,800	$9,600
Taxes (rate = 50%)	7,500	6,600	6,000	5,400	4,800
Net income (EAT)	$ 7,500	$ 6,600	$ 6,000	$ 5,400	$4,800
Earnings per share (EPS)	$ 0.75	$ 0.94	$ 1.20	$ 1.80	$ 4.80
Operating leverage (DOL) $\dfrac{Q(P-\text{vc})}{Q(P-\text{vc})-\text{FC}}$	$\dfrac{15,000}{15,000}=1$ 4.3	$\dfrac{15,000}{13,200}=1.14$ 4.3	$\dfrac{15,000}{12,000}=1.25$ 4.3	$\dfrac{15,000}{10,800}=1.39$ 4.3	$\dfrac{15,000}{9,600}=1.56$ 4.3
Financial leverage (DFL) $\dfrac{\text{EBIT}}{\text{EBIT}-F}$	$\dfrac{15,000}{15,000}=1$	$\dfrac{15,000}{13,200}=1.14$	$\dfrac{15,000}{12,000}=1.25$	$\dfrac{15,000}{10,800}=1.39$	$\dfrac{15,000}{9,600}=1.56$
Combined leverage DOL × DFL	$4.3 \times 1 = 4.3$	$4.3 \times 1.14 = 4.9$	$4.3 \times 1.25 = 5.38$	$4.3 \times 1.39 = 5.98$	$4.3 \times 1.56 = 6.71$

Operating leverage (DOL) for Financial Structure C:

$$\frac{Q(P-\text{vc})}{Q(P-\text{vc})-\text{FC}} = \frac{100,000(1.00-0.35)}{100,000(1.00-0.35)-50,000} = 4.3$$

Basic data:
Selling price (P) $1.00; Fixed operating costs (FC) $50,000; Variable costs (vc) $0.35/unit; Number of units (Q) 100,000 units

earnings per share from $0.75 to $4.80. As long as EPS increases in greater proportion than risk, the market price of the shares will rise. How far the process goes depends on the risk-return trade-offs of investors in assessing the prospects of the firm.

A Modifying Position

To this point, the discussion has assumed that both operating and financial risk influence the cost of capital. Thus, the way the company is financed—the debt/equity ratio—can raise or lower the cost of capital and, in turn, the market value of the common shares. Not everyone shares these views.

Some authorities look to business risk as the basic risk of the business which determines the cost of capital. All things equal, the cost of capital responds only to a change in business risk (i.e., the variability of net operating income). The segment of the income statement after net operating income deals simply with "financial packaging"; it cannot alter the amount of funds available or their variability. The position does not deny the reality of financial risk, but instead holds that it is discounted solely against the common stock and does not affect the valuation of the firm.

Both the modifying proposition and the conventional wisdom recognize that financial leverage affects the required yield on the common shares. The issue is whether a firm can lower its cost of capital by manipulating the financial structure; whether it can raise the market value (within limits) of the common shares by additions of debt to the financial structure. Probably the weight of practitioner opinion would answer yes, but the available research does not give a definitive response. The issue is of major importance in the evaluation of projects that involve revision of the financial structure (refunding projects or conglomerate mergers).

CALCULATING THE MARGINAL COST OF CAPITAL

The marginal cost of capital is determined by taking a weighted average of the marginal costs of each of the components in the firm's financial structure. Initially, we examine how the marginal costs of each of the components may be determined. Then we discuss the averaging process.

Throughout our discussion of the cost of capital, we use current market values, as opposed to historical book values, to represent the amounts of each component in the financial structure. Our choice is based on the fact that the book values represent only historical amounts. For example, the dollar amount of common stock reflected on the firm's balance sheet is not indicative of its current market value. Similarly, the market values of preferred stock and many forms of debt may change appreciably from their book values as market interest rates and money supplies fluctuate.

Common Stock Equity

Chapter 3 develops Equation (3), which relates the firm's cost of equity to the price of the common stock and its dividend, where it is assumed that the dividend will grow at the given rate g for the foreseeable future.

$$K_e = \frac{D_1}{P_0} + g \tag{3}$$

where K_e = cost of common stock equity
D_1 = expected dividend in the next period
P_0 = current market price
g = annual growth rate of the dividend

Because the marginal cost of capital represents the amount that the firm must earn on the net proceeds derived from new issues, it is necessary to consider floatation costs. Therefore, for new issues Equation (3) is rewritten as Equation (4):

$$_nK_e = \frac{D_1}{P_0(1 - F)} + g \tag{4}$$

where $_nK_e$ = cost of new equity capital
F = floatation cost expressed as a percentage of the market price

The value $_nK_e$ discounts the anticipated return on new common to equal the net proceeds of the issue. However, once new common is issued, there is no distinction on the security markets between the cost of new and old common. The earnings on the funds raised by the sale of additional shares must be sufficient to cover floatation costs and reward risk or the price of the common shares will decline.

As an alternative to Equation (4), the cost of common stock equity capital may be thought to consist of the return on a risk-free investment such as that available from Treasury Notes, plus premiums to compensate for the business and financial risks associated with the particular investment.

Retained Earnings

The market value of the common stock reflects the residual value of the firm as perceived by the investors. As such, it encompasses the total common equity portion and therefore includes the firm's retained earnings. Thus, we argue that retained earnings are not relevant to the calculation of the cost of capital since when using market weights, the value of the common stock includes the retained earnings. We are not interested in book values and rather argue that the market discounts retained earnings as a part of the value of common stock. Others take a differing view.

After-tax profits may either be retained in the firm or distributed as cash dividends. Retention of profits presumes the availability of sufficient investment opportunities (either internal or external) to make it more attractive to shareholders for the firm to retain rather than distribute the earnings. As a practical matter, there is generally an upper limit to the amount of earnings a firm may retain. This limit is predicated on the need for the firm to maintain a stable cash dividend policy.

If there are sufficient internal investment opportunities to use all the retained earnings, the question must be resolved as to how much return is required from the retained earnings. The opportunity cost from the shareholder's viewpoint is the dividend foregone. If the opportunity cost to investors is the dividend, we want to determine the magnitude of that opportunity cost. Assuming that shareholders must pay taxes on the dividends (albeit at varying rates) and that they desire a return on funds available for reinvestment at the same rate they are obtaining from existing investments (namely, K_e), then Equation (5) provides the cost of retained earnings:

$$R = K_e(1 - t_p)(1 - B) \tag{5}$$

where R = cost of retained earnings
K_e = cost of equity capital
t_p = average of all the shareholders' marginal tax rates
B = average brokerage fee

It is necessary to introduce brokerage costs into Equation (5) because it is almost never possible to achieve a return of K_e without the use of a broker.

The cost of retained earnings is also a meaningful factor in determining the firm's optimal capital structure. Its computation is principally significant for internal planning: choosing the proportion of new debt, new common, and retained earnings that will minimize the marginal cost of capital. Internally, the cost of *new* common will be greater than the cost of financing by retained earnings, since the funds raised from the new common must earn an amount sufficient to cover the floatation costs plus the yield required to maintain the market value of the common shares.

Cost of Preferred Stock

Most preferred stocks are perpetual in nature, and therefore their explicit costs may be viewed in the same terms as a perpetuity. However, in the same manner as debt, preferred affects financial risk. Accordingly, the true cost of preferred from the perspective of the common shareholders is the rate that must be earned on the assets acquired through preferred financing to cover the yield on the preferred plus the increased yield on the common. The cost of the firm's outstanding preferred is simply its dividend divided by its current market price.

$$K_p = \frac{D_p}{P_p} \tag{6}$$

where K_p = cost of preferred stock
D_p = preferred dividend
P_p = price of the preferred

As was the case for common stock, we must consider floatation costs for new issues of preferred. Thus, Equation (6) is modified as Equation (7):

$$_nK_p = \frac{_nD_p}{_nP_p(1 - F)} \qquad (7)$$

where $_nK_p$ = cost of new preferred equity capital
$\quad _nD_p$ = dividend on the new issue
$\quad F$ = floatation cost expressed as a percentage of the market price
$\quad _nP_p$ = sale price of the new preferred issue

Cost of Debt

Firms have both short- and long-term debts, and it is therefore necessary to consider all forms of debt financing as input to the cost of capital. Some authorities argue that certain short-term obligations are "free" (non-interest-bearing) and also that capital budgeting relates only to long-term commitments of invested capital. We reject that position. First, accounts payable and some accruals are only superficially free if the debts are discharged within a defined payment period. At times, firms make regular use of trade credit and choose not to accept the discount for prompt payment. Second, some firms consistently resort to commercial credit to finance current assets, and these finance charges must be covered by earnings just as interest on long-term debt. Third, many capital projects drain working capital and require additional short-term financing. Fourth, the financial structure has interchangeable components. The amount and cost of one type of capital depends upon the proportions raised from other sources. The combination, in turn, shapes the firm's financial risk and the cost of capital. Fifth, the accounts payable and accruals, while short-term in terms of payments, tend to roll over and thereby are a part of the firm's permanent financing.

The cost of debt represents an estimate of the yield required to raise designated amounts of short- and/or long-term financing. The firm's commercial banker or investment banker would provide the estimates based on market conditions. The projected yield is placed on an after-tax basis. *However, the total cost of debt involves two elements: the nominal yield based on the face amount of the securities issued when sold at par and the implicit cost or the yield increment on the common needed to maintain its market value in view of the added financial risk.* Note in Table 8–1 the increased return required of the common as debt is added to the capital structure. The required return on the common increases from 10% to 16% with implicit cost of debt, 6%. *Thus, from the viewpoint of the equity holders, the cost of debt is the rate that must be earned on debt-financed assets to cover the net cost of borrowed funds and the incremental yield on the common stock.*

Since we have already dealt with the question of optimum structure with respect to amounts of debt and equity, it is necessary to examine the overall debt structure to ascertain the marginal cost of debt at a given point in time. We assume that the firm has attempted to achieve an optimum debt structure consisting of varying amounts and types of long- and short-term obligations. The optimum structure will, of course, vary over time. The calculation of the explicit marginal cost of debt is demonstrated in Example 1.

□ **EXAMPLE 1**   Cost of Debt

A corporation has a debt structure shown on its balance sheet as follows:

Accounts payable	$ 3,000,000
Short-term debt	
(12% revolving credit)	2,000,000
Accrued expenses	3,000,000
Bonds Series A	
(5%, due in 12 years)	5,000,000
Bonds Series B	
(8%, due in 26 years)	7,000,000
Total	$20,000,000

Series A bonds are selling at $750, while Series B bonds are selling at $900. The corporation takes any available discounts for prompt payment and there is, therefore, no explicit cost to either the accounts payable or accrued expenses. Determine the marginal cost of debt.

Solution: First, determine the market financial structure using market amounts for the bonds. The market structure is as follows:

Accounts payable	$ 3,000,000
Short-term debt	
(12% revolving credit)	2,000,000
Accrued expenses	3,000,000
Bonds, Series A	
(5%, due in 12 years)	3,750,000
Bonds, Series B	
(8%, due in 26 years)	6,300,000
Total	$18,050,000

The sum disaggregates into short- and long-term debts amounting to $8,000,000 and $10,050,000 or 44.3% and 55.7%, respectively.

The explicit cost of the short-term debt amounts to only $240,000, or 3% based on the total $8,000,000 short-term debt. This represents the marginal cost of the short-term component. This conclusion is based on the fact that as the firm expands in terms of acquiring more fixed assets, the relative amounts of accounts payable and accruals will remain fixed, and that since the firm is currently paying 12% on its revolving credit, 12% is the marginal pretax rate for revolving credit.

The explicit cost of the long-term debt is, of course, the interest paid. But what we need to know is the marginal cost of the next dollar of long-term debt. This requires a consideration of the preference for capital gains versus ordinary income. For a person in the 40% marginal tax bracket (a reasonable position for a bondholder), we find that Series A has a 5.63% after-tax yield to maturity while Series B has only 5.18%.[1] To obtain

[1] Use the after-tax cash inflows (i.e., 60% of the yearly interest) and adjust for capital gains appropriately.

the marginal explicit cost of long-term debt, we must find the yield to maturity the composite group of current bondholders would require for new bonds sold at par (i.e., the coupon rate). Put another way, what yield would investors require on new bonds amounting to $10,050,000 (the market value of the outstanding issues) to be indifferent as to keeping their existing portfolio or trading it for the new?

The current portfolio has a weighted yield determined as follows:

Debt	Amount	Proportion	Yield	Weighted Yield
Series A	$ 3,750,000	0.373	0.0563	0.0210
Series B	6,300,000	0.627	0.0518	0.0325
	$10,050,000			0.0535

All the income from the new bonds will be ordinary income, so 5.35% is 60% of the total required yield (assuming the 40% investor marginal tax rate). The required yield is therefore 8.9%. The marginal explicit pretax cost of the outstanding bonds is 8.9%.

The marginal explicit cost of debt is the weighted-average cost of the short- and long-term debt and is calculated to be 6.3%.

Debt	Amount	Proportion	Cost	Weighted Cost
Short-term	$ 8,000,000	0.443	0.030	0.0133
Bonds	$10,050,000	0.557	0.089	0.0496
	$18,050,000			0.0629

The marginal *pretax* cost of debt is 0.0629. If the firm had a 50% marginal tax rate, the after-tax cost would be 3.15%.   □

When floatation costs are involved, the marginal costs of the various components of debt are determined using Equation (8):

$$K_i = \frac{I(1-t)}{P(1-F)} \tag{8}$$

where K_i = after-tax cost of the specific component of debt
I = dollar amount of interest
t = firm's marginal tax rate
P = sale price of the debt
F = floatation cost as a percentage of the sale price

Cost of Depreciation

Depreciation provides a source of funds if the firm generates sufficient sales to cover the costs of production and interest. This is usually the case, and in most instances depreciation is an important source of funds. Depreciation may be used as a source of funds to replace plant and equipment, improve liquidity, or returned to stockholders by means of the mechanism of stock repurchase or, if law permits, through dividends. Since there are a variety of uses for the funds generated through depreciation, they are certainly not free, but rather have an opportunity cost.

Central to the argument of the cost of funds generated through depreciation is the question of how the funds will be used. If the funds are not going to be used to replace assets, but rather to repay debts or distributed to shareholders, the whole process of determining the firm's cost of capital comes into question. The reason for determining the cost of capital is to use it as a benchmark in the evaluation of proposed capital investments. If the firm is not making capital investments, which includes external expansion, the important question is not how to obtain the cost of capital but rather how to otherwise use the funds to best increase shareholder wealth. This might be accomplished by means of reduction of debt (with concurrent reduction of interest expense and financial risk), improving liquidity balances (which also reduces financial risk), distributing funds as dividends (which automatically increases shareholder wealth), or repurchasing stock (which should result in an increase in the market price). All the choices enumerated above should increase shareholder wealth.

With respect to utilization of funds generated by means of depreciation, the question to be addressed is which use or combination of uses will result in the greatest increases in shareholder wealth. The question may be further expanded to deal with that portion of funds generated through profits but which is not normally distributed as dividends. In general, management who cannot find appropriate uses for funds as investment in capital equipment and the like must then develop plans for using the funds in some other manner to increase shareholder wealth. Since this text deals with capital investment, the subject of alternative uses for funds will not be discussed except as a part of the topic of capital abandonment.

Assuming that funds generated through depreciation are to be utilized as a part of the capital expenditure process, what is their cost? *Since the funds generated through depreciation are a return of investment and since the investment was composed of funds obtained from equity and debt, it is therefore reasonable to use the cost of capital as the cost of depreciation. If this line of reasoning is followed, it is not necessary to include depreciation in the calculation of the cost of capital.* With respect to obtaining the cost of capital, funds generated through depreciation may be ignored, but in making capital expenditures, we should require the same return on investments made using funds generated by means of depreciation as we do for all other funds.

The Marginal Cost of Capital

The marginal cost of capital is calculated by taking a weighted average of the marginal costs of each component in proportion to the respective amounts of each that the firm will raise. The process is demonstrated in Example 2.

□ **EXAMPLE 2**   *Marginal Cost of Capital*

A corporation plans to raise $400,000 of new capital as follows:

Current liabilities: $20,000 at 11% (assume no floatation or service charge)
Long-term debt: $50,000 at 9% (floatation costs, $\frac{1}{2}$ of 1%)
Preferred stock B: $30,000, floatation cost (F) estimated at 2%; sold at $42 per share with a stated dividend of $2.50
Common stock: $300,000, floatation cost (F) estimated at 10%, dividend $1 per share; market price $50 per share, anticipated growth rate of dividend, 10%

The firm's marginal tax rate is 50%. Determine the cost of each component and the marginal cost of capital.

Solution: Cost of long-term debt:

$$K_i = \frac{I(1-t)}{P(1-F)} = \frac{\$4,500(1-0.5)}{\$50,000(1-0.005)} = \frac{\$2,250}{\$49,750} = 0.0452$$

Cost of preferred:

$$_nK_p = \frac{_nD_p}{_nP_p(1-F)} = \frac{\$2.50}{\$42(1-0.02)} = \frac{\$2.50}{\$41.16} = 0.0607$$

Cost of new common:

$$_nK_e = \frac{D_1}{P_0(1-F)} + g = \frac{\$1.00}{\$50(1-0.10)} + 0.10 = \frac{\$1.00}{\$45} + 0.10 = 0.1222$$

Marginal Cost of Capital (K_{mc})

	Market Values	Market Weights	After-Tax Cost	Weighted After Tax
Current liabilities	$ 20,000	0.050	0.0550	0.00275
Long-term debt	50,000	0.125	0.0452	0.00565
Preferred stock B	30,000	0.075	0.0607	0.00455
New common	300,000	0.750	0.1222	0.09165
	$400,000	Marginal cost of capital =		0.10460

The marginal cost of capital is approximately 10.5%.   □

QUESTIONS/PROBLEMS

1. McLaughlin Industries has a debt structure shown on its balance sheet as follows:

Accounts payable	$ 7,200,000
Short-term debt	4,800,000
(12% revolving credit)	
Accrued expenses	7,200,000
Bonds, Series A	12,000,000
(5%, due in 12 years)	
Bonds, Series B	16,800,000
(8%, due in 26 years)	

The Series A bonds are selling at $80, while the Series B bonds are selling at $120. The firm takes advantage of prompt-payment discounts, so there is no explicit cost to either the accounts payable or accrued expenses. Determine the marginal cost of capital, assuming that the firm's tax rate is 46% and that the tax rate for the average investor is 40%.

2. The Trebelhorn Growth Corporation has the following debt structure:

Trade accounts payable	$5,000,000
Short-term debt (8%)	4,000,000
Accrued expenses	3,000,000
Bonds, Series A	7,000,000
(7%, due in 15 years)	
Bonds, Series B	7,000,000
(8%, due in 26 years)	

Series A bonds are presently selling for $800 and Series B bonds are presently selling for $900. Assume that the average tax bracket of the shareholders is 40%. Further assume that the corporation's marginal tax rate is 50%.

In a stepwise sequence, calculate the following:
(a) The market financial structure using the market amounts for the bond.
(b) The explicit cost of short-term debt (assume payments made within the discount period).
(c) The marginal pretax cost of outstanding bonds.
(d) The marginal after-tax cost of debt.

3. The Kay Manufacturing Corporation plans to raise $2,000,000 of new capital for a plant expansion. The debt structure it plans is as follows:

Current liabilities	$100,000 at 12%
Long-term debt	$550,000 at 9.25%, floatation costs 0.75%
Preferred stock	$350,000, floatation cost 2.5%; sold at $35 per share with $1.75 dividend
Common stock	$1,000,000, floatation cost estimated at 10%, dividend $1.25 per share, market price $47, anticipated growth in dividend, 8%

The firm's marginal tax rate is 46% and the average tax rate of its shareholders is 35%. Determine the cost of each component and the after-tax marginal cost of capital.

4. The Lemanski Corporation intends to raise $6,000,000 of new capital by the following methods:

Current liabilities	Increase by $600,000 at 13.46% financing
Long-term debt	$1,800,000 at 7.78% financing with a floatation cost of 9%
Preferred stock	$600,000 with a floatation cost of 15%; stock will be sold at $50 per share with a stated dividend of $4
Common stock	$3,000,000 with a floatation cost of 12%; stock will be sold at $50 per share; the expected EPS is $2.50, with a dividend growth rate of 12%

The corporation tax rate is 46%.

(a) Determine the cost of each component and calculate the marginal cost of capital.

(b) What is the marginal cost of capital if all floatation costs are reduced by one-third?

5. Apple Industries, Inc. has the balance sheet shown:

Dec. 31, 19XX (in millions)

Assets		*Liabilities and Owner's Equity*	
Cash	$ 6.0	Accounts Payable	$ 8.0
Accounts Receivable	8.0	Notes Payable (8%)	2.0
Inventory	12.0	Long-term Debt (9%)	14.0
Land	6.0	Preferred Stock (20,000	
		shares, par value $100)	2.0
Fixed Assets, Net	14.0	Common Stock (500,000	
		shares outstanding, par $6.)	3.0
Other	2.0	Paid-in Capital	5.0
		Retained Earnings	14.0
	$48.00		$48.0

The Common Stock has a market price of $20 per share, and will pay a dividend next year of $1.50 which has been growing at an annual rate of 8%. The preferred stock underwriting fee was 5% of the sale price on the stock ($98). It pays a $7 dividend. Their average shareholder has a marginal tax rate of 30%. Shareholder brokerage fees average 4%. Determine the following, if Apple has a 46% marginal tax rate.

(a) The cost of Common Stock.

(b) The cost of Preferred Stock.

(c) The after-tax cost of Debt.

(d) The cost of Retained Earnings.

(e) The weighted average cost of capital.

6. ABC has graphed the relationship between EPS and EBIT for the four financing plans as shown below:

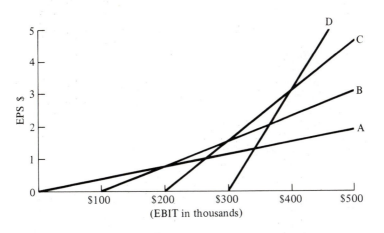

Answer the following:

(a) Which plan represents *all* equity financing? Circle one: A B C D

(b) What is the value of EBIT for which plans C and D both give the same EPS? What is the EPS?

   (c) Plan A yields higher values of EPS for all values of EBIT between _____ and _____ .

   (d) For values of EBIT less than _____ plan C will result in negative EPS.

   (e) Which plans represents the *greatest* use of financial leverage? Circle one: A   B   C   D.

   (f) If EBIT were expected to be $450,000 which plan would result in the highest EPS? Circle one: A   B   C   D.

   (g) The annual interest cost associated with plan C is _____ .

   (h) Which plan represents the *least* use of financial leverage? Circle one: A   B   C   D.

   (i) Three of the six intersections are of little importance. They are between lines: circle three: AB   AC   AD   BC   BD   CD.

   (j) If plan C was used and EBIT fell from $400,000 to $300,000, by how much would EPS decrease?

7. Three financing plans are available to Corporation which needs $2,500,000 for construction of a new plant. The EBIT resulting from the new plant is expected to be $500,000 per year. Corporation is in the 46% marginal tax bracket. Money can be borrowed as follows:

    First: $500,000 at 16%
    Next: $500,000 at 20%
    Over: $1,000,000 at 24%

   If funds in excess of $1,000,000 are borrowed, management expects to be able to sell stock for $38 per share. If *less* than $1,000,000 is borrowed, management expects that it will be able to obtain $42 per share.

   The three plans for financing the plant are listed below:

   1. All equity
   2. $800,000 debt, the remainder equity
   3. $1,400,000 debt, the remainder equity

   Calculate the EPS for each of the three plans

8. Corporation has computed various costs, as listed below.

   1. Fixed costs: $70,000
   2. Unit cost of production: labor $4.00, materials $3.00
   3. Selling cost per unit: $2.00
   4. Sale price per unit: $11.00

   (a) Determine the profit at 40,000 units output.

   (b) Determine the degree of operating leverage at 40,000 units.

   (c) Suppose the output increases by 10% to 44,000 units. Compute the profit at 44,000 units and check your answer with part (b).

9

The Management of Forecasting, Sensitivity Analysis, and Adjustment for Price Trends

This part of the book deals with computing the cash flows that form the basis of capital budgeting. During the first eight chapters we assumed that the cash flows were given and evaluated the attractiveness of given projects. But, computing cash flows is probably the most critical part of the entire capital budgeting process; if these estimates are not accurate, then any analysis, regardless of its detail and sophistication, will probably lead to less than optimal decisions.

In theory, computing cash flows is a reasonably simple and straightforward process consisting of two steps:

1. Forecast the costs, sales, and expenses as they relate to a particular project.

2. Include in these estimates depreciation and other tax factors, such as investment tax credits, and compute the after-tax cost (cash outflows) and revenues (cash inflows) expected to result from the implementation of the project over its useful life.

As a practical matter, the first step is more difficult and more critical. We discuss it in this chapter.[1] The second step (dealing with depreciation and the tax laws) is complicated, but can be accomplished by a good tax accountant or attorney. We discuss it in the following two chapters.

[1]The authors express their sincere appreciation to Dr. Oliver H. Winn, Director, Management Information Systems Center, Glassboro State College, for his assistance in preparing this chapter.

THE ROLE OF FORECASTING IN THE CAPITAL BUDGETING PROCESS

The entire capital budgeting process hinges on the accuracy of the forecasts of the cash outflows and inflows surrounding a project. Thus, it is important for the analyst to obtain accurate forecasts and have some measure of the *reliability of those forecasts* regardless of the fact he or she is seldom responsible for actually generating the forecasts. Rather, the analyst must do two things.

1. Identify all of the variables that factor into the cash flows and determine which of those variables are critical to the success of the project. The latter part of this process is called *sensitivity analysis*. As an example, we noted earlier that the sensitivity of a project's NPV to inaccurate estimates of salvage value decreases rapidly as increasingly higher discount rates are used. Consequently, in periods of high interest rates, we should not allocate much time or other resources to refining the forecasts of salvage value. Rather, *at the onset it is essential to identify those elements of a project which will have a pronounced effect on its success*. These are the elements that warrant the allocation of resources necessary to obtain accurate forecasts and these are the elements that warrant close monitoring both during the acquisition process and after the project's implementation.

2. Indicate to those generating the estimates the degree of forecasting accuracy required and plan to analyze the design of the forecasting systems used to produce the estimates.

In carrying out these two steps, the analyst must keep in mind that the "riskiness" surrounding any project may result from the *inherent riskiness of the project itself*, as in basic research and development (R and D), and/or from *the use of forecasting methods that yield erroneous estimates*. The replacement of an existing machine may turn out to be more risky than implementing an R and D project if the sales forecasts used to base the demand for the machine's output are poorly designed and lead to exaggerated estimates of cash inflows.

Thus, the goal of this chapter is to describe methods that may be used to identify those factors critical to a project's success or failure and to indicate how to evaluate forecasts in terms of their probable reliability with respect to the project being evaluated.

DETERMINING THE KEY VARIABLES—THE SENSITIVITY ANALYSIS

In order to start the process of determining key variables consider Example 1 which represents a typical industrial capital budgeting replacement decision including forecasts for inflation.

☐ *EXAMPLE 1*   *Replacement Investment Decision*

A corporation is considering the acquisition of a machine with an estimated cost of $30,000. The machine is to replace an existing machine, which has been fully depreciated and is estimated to have negligible salvage value but can be used for the foreseeable future. The new machine is expected to have a 10-year useful life. The rationale for the purchase of the new machine has been presented by the plant engineer, who anticipates two advantages:

1. Reduction in down-time and maintenance. Down-time for the existing machine is about 3 hours per week. This results in one worker sitting idle while repairs are made. It is expected that regular off-shift maintenance could keep the new machine operating a full 40 hours per week.

2. Increased output and reduced unit labor cost. Output could be increased to 12,800 units per year from the current 10,000, while dropping unit labor costs in current dollars to $1.40 from the current $2.30.

The internal cost accountants have provided the following cost analysis for the output currently produced:

	Per Unit		*Per Year (10,000 units)*
Sales		$10.00	$100,000
Cost of goods sold			
Labor	$2.30		$23,000
Materials	1.00		10,000
Utilities/fuel	0.80		8,000
Other	1.70		17,000
		− $5.80	− $58,000
Sales expenses		− 2.80	− 28,000
Depreciation[a]		− 0.10	− 1,000
Earnings before taxes		$1.30	$13,000
Taxes (46%)		− 0.60	− 6,000
Earnings after taxes		$0.70	$ 7,000

[a] Depreciation for other facilities is allocated at $0.10 per unit.

The sales department indicates that there have been some back orders for the product and that they could sell 10,500 units per year now with a 4% annual increase in unit sales volume until the capacity volume of 12,800 units per year is reached. They expect that the per-unit sales expense will be the same for any additional volume sold, before considering the impact of inflation.

The treasurer's office requires a 15% after-tax hurdle rate at present for projects of this type, but the treasurer expects both the hurdle rate and reinvestment rates to change over the 10-year project life as follows:

Year	*Hurdle Rate*	*Reinvestment Rate*
Present	15%	—
1	16	16%
2	15	16
3	14	15
4–10	13	14

The tax manager would plan for a 10% investment tax credit[2] and would depreciate the machine over a 5-year life to a zero salvage value for tax purposes using the following

[2] In this example, the investment tax credit is 10% and the depreciation is based on the full cost of the asset. Technically, based on current tax law (see Chapters 10 and 11), the depreciable base of the asset would be the cost of the asset less one half of the investment credit or else the credit percentage would have to be reduced from 10% to 8%. This complication is ignored until the following two chapters.

annual percentage cost recovery: 15%, 22%, 21%, 21%, and 21%. (Note that the machine is expected to last 10 years.)

The corporate economist has estimated the following average inflation rates for the next 10-year period:

Item	Average Annual Increase
Sale Price	8%
Labor	7
Materials	10
Utilities/Fuel	15
Other	7
Sales Expense	8
Depreciation	N/A
Taxes	N/A

Based on the information provided, develop pro forma income and cash flow statements with and without the new machine for the 10-year expected life. Compute the project's terminal value, net present value, and internal rate of return.

Solution: The solution is straightforward, but requires numerous tedious calculations; it is thus most appropriately solved using a computer. Pro forma profit and loss statements and cash-flow reports for years 1 and 10 are given, along with an income and cash-flow summary. On the income and cash-flow summary, the net present value was determined by subtracting $27,000 (purchase cost less $3,000 investment tax credit) from the present value of the difference in cash inflows between the new and old machines. The net present value is $30,779.30, indicating that the new machine is a viable candidate and should be considered for acceptance.

Income and Cash-Flow Summary

Period	Without Project		With Project	
	Net Income	Cash Flow	Net Income	Cash Flow
1	$7,020.00	$ 8,020.00	$10,044.00	$15,594.00
2	7,430.40	8,430.40	10,228.60	17,920.60
3	7,832.59	8,832.59	11,812.50	19,248.20
4	8,219.09	9,219.09	13,337.60	20,818.70
5	8,580.77	9,580.77	14,963.40	22,491.70
6	8,906.55	9,906.55	20,085.80	21,363.30
7	9,183.05	10,183.10	21,090.10	22,370.10
8	9,394.26	10,394.30	22,013.90	23,293.90
9	9,521.00	10,521.00	22,875.40	24,155.40
10	9,540.13	10,540.13	23,648.06	24,928.06

Terminal value	$210,379.00
Present value	$ 57,779.30
Net present value	$ 30,779.30
Internal rate of return	23%

Profit and Loss Statement
Period 1

	Without Project		With Project	
	Unit	*10,000 Units*	*Unit*	*10,500 Units*
Sales	$10.00	$100,000.00	$10.00	$105,000.00
Cost of goods sold				
Labor	2.30	$23,000.00	1.40	$14,700.00
Material	1.00	10,000.00	1.00	10,500.00
Utilities/fuel	0.80	8,000.00	0.80	8,400.00
Other	1.70	17,000.00	1.70	17,850.00
	−$5.80	−$58,000.00	−$4.90	−$51,450.00
Sales exp.	− 2.80	− 28,000.00	− 2.80	− 29,400.00
Depreciation	− 0.10	− 1,000.00	− 0.53	− 5,550.00
Earnings before taxes	$1.30	$13,000.00	$1.77	$18,600.00
Taxes (46%)	− 0.60	− 5,980.00	− 0.81	− 8,556.00
Earnings after taxes	$0.70	$ 7,020.00	$0.96	$10,044.00

Cash Flow Report for Period 1

	Without Project	*With Project*	*Difference*
Net income	$7,020.00	$10,044.00	$3,024.00
Depreciation	1,000.00	5,550.00	4,550.00
Cash flow	$8,020.00	$15,594.00	$7,574.00

Profit and Loss Statement
Period 10

	Without Project		With Project	
	Unit*	10,000 Units	Unit*	12,800 Units
Sales	$19.99	$199,900.00	$19.99	$255,872.00
Cost of goods sold				
Labor	4.23	$42,284.60	2.57	32,945.20
Material	2.36	23,579.50	2.36	30,181.70
Utilities/fuel	2.81	28,143.00	2.81	36,023.10
Other	3.13	31,253.00	3.13	40,004.90
	−$12.53	−$125,260.90	−$10.87	−$139,154.90
Sales exp.	− 5.60	− 55,972.20	− 5.60	− 71,644.40
Depreciation	− 0.10	− 1,000.00	− 0.10	− 1,280.00
Earnings before taxes	$ 1.76	$ 17,666.90	$ 3.42	$ 43,792.70
Taxes (46%)	− 0.81	− 8,126.77	− 1.57	− 20,144.64
Net income	$ 0.95	$ 9,540.13	$ 1.85	$ 23,648.06

Cash Flow Report for Period 10

	Without Project	With Project	Difference
Net income	$ 9,540.13	$23,648.06	$14,107.93
Depreciation	1,000.00	1,280.00	280.00
Cash flow	$10,540.13	$24,928.06	$14,387.93

□

*Unit values are rounded.

The next step is to determine which of the variables are critical to the success of the project. This requires a sensitivity analysis—asking how much the final outcome (net present value) would change as a result of errors in the estimates. In Example 2, we examine each variable to determine its sensitivity.

□ **EXAMPLE 2**   *Key Variable Determination—Sensitivity Analysis*

Recompute the net present value based on each of the following changes to original estimates. Tabulate the results showing the dollars and percentage change in net present value. Analyze the results and indicate the key variables.

1. Volume increases to 10,500 units and remains level (does not increase yearly to 12,800 units).

2. Unit labor cost decreases to $1.68 rather than to $1.40.

3. The hurdle rates and reinvestment rate are 2% higher than estimated in each of the 10 years.

4. The hurdle rates and reinvestment rates are as anticipated for years 1–3, but are 2% higher than estimated in each of the succeeding years.

5. The sale price increases only 6.4% annually rather than the estimated 8%.

6. Labor costs increase 8.4% annually rather than the estimated 7%.

7. Materials costs increase 12% annually rather than the estimated 10%.

8. Utilities and fuel costs increase 18% annually rather than the estimated 15%.

9. Other costs increase 8.4% annually rather than the estimated 7%.

10. Sales expenses increase 9.6% annually rather than the estimated 8%.

Solution: The results are tabulated as follows:

		Change in NPV	
Change	*Revised NPV*	*Dollar*	*Percentage*
1. Volume of 10,500	$20,507	$10,272	33%
2. Unit labor $1.68	19,319	11,460	37
3. Hurdle and reinvestment rates plus 2%	26,190	4,589	15
4. Hurdle and reinvestment rates plus 2%, years 4–10	29,224	1,555	5
5. Sale price increases 6.4% annually	22,500	8,279	27
6. Labor increases 8.4% annually	19,320	11,459	37
7. Materials increase 12% annually	29,489	1,290	4
8. Utilities and fuel increase 10% annually	29,511	1,268	4

The results of the sensitivity analysis indicate that the key variables are volume, labor cost, and annual changes in sale price and labor costs. If sales volume does not increase as anticipated, the project's NPV will decrease by 33%. A further sensitivity analysis might be advisable to determine the outcome if, for example, sales volume fell from the current 10,000 units to a "worst case." At this point, the analyst should suggest some possible volumes, such as 7,000 or 8,000, and ask the sales department to estimate the probability of such volumes. Corresponding NPV's will indicate to management the potential for downside risk resulting from reductions in volume.

The estimate in unit labor costs is another crucial factor. If unit labor decreases to $1.68 rather than $1.40, the NPV will decrease 37%. The remaining two most sensitive variables are annual increase in sales price and annual increase in labor costs. Twenty percent errors in these estimates will result in 27% and 37% reductions in NPV. Interestingly, increasing the hurdle rates and reinvestment rates by 2% for each year impacts NPV by only 15%. The analyst may want to consider increasing these by 4% for each year to further gauge the impact of potential high costs of money.   □

Example 2 clearly pinpoints the critical, or most sensitive, variables. Consequently, it is the estimates for these inputs that the analyst must check most carefully. In our discussion of risk we suggest obtaining a set of estimates for each sensitive variable and attaching corresponding probabilities to each. Then, using a computer, it is possible to consider alternative sets of potentially undesirable (and desirable) scenarios. In most instances management is concerned primarily with downside risk, so that appropriate contingency plans may be developed to deal with those possibilities. Certainly, the possibility of outcomes better than anticipated must be considered. But, the problems associated with higher-than-expected cash flows are generally easier to solve than those resulting from lower cash flows—thus, our interest lies primarily in potential downside risk. In Example 3 we consider two downside risk scenarios and their impact on the capital budgeting problem in Examples 1 and 2. The first is a recesssion model; the second an inflation model.

□ **EXAMPLE 3**   *Sensitivity Analyses of Several Variables*

Consider two possible economic scenarios: recession and inflation. In the recession case, hold volume constant at 10,500, increase sales price 6.4% yearly, and start with unit labor at $1.68. Determine the cash flow, terminal and net present values.

In the inflation case, allow volume to expand to 12,800, increase the hurdle rate and reinvestment rates by 4% for each year, use unit labor of $1.68, increase sales price 8% annually, and increase labor, materials, utilities and fuel, other, and sales expenses by 8.4%, 12%, 18%, 8.4%, and 9.6%, respectively. Determine the cash flows, terminal value, and net present value.

Solution: The results are tabulated as follows:

Recession Case
Income and Cash Flow Summary

Period	Without Project Net Income	Without Project Cash Flow	With Project Net Income	With Project Cash Flow
1	$7,020.00	$8,020.00	$ 8,456.40	$14,006.40
2	6,566.40	7,566.40	7,092.20	14,742.20
3	5,980.17	6,980.17	6,901.96	14,252.00
4	5,240.35	6,240.35	6,406.88	13,756.90
5	4,322.99	5,322.99	5,745.11	13,095.10
6	3,200.80	4,200.80	8,291.37	9,341.37
7	1,842.63	2,842.63	7,210.43	8,260.43
8	212.98	1,212.98	5,868.60	6,918.60
9	− 1,728.62	− 728.62	4,225.06	5,275.06
10	− 4,028.35	− 3,028.35	2,233.15	3,283.15

Terminal value	$119,103.00
Present value	$ 32,711.10
Net present value	$ 5,711.10
Internal rate of return	16%

Inflation Case
Income and Cash Flow Summary

	Without Project		With Project	
Period	*Net Income*	*Cash Flow*	*Net Income*	*Cash Flow*
1	$7,020.00	$8,020.00	$8,456.40	$14,006.40
2	6,648.48	7,648.48	7,659.26	15,351.30
3	6,113.08	7,113.08	8,008.37	15,444.10
4	5,380.74	6,380.74	7,990.13	15,471.20
5	4,412.61	5,412.61	7,696.62	15,225.00
6	3,163.02	4,163.02	10,442.30	11,719.80
7	1,578.39	2,578.39	8,973.31	10,253.30
8	− 404.18	595.82	7,019.68	8,299.68
9	− 2,858.46	− 1,858.46	4,511.32	5,791.32
10	− 5,870.97	− 4,870.97	1,341.59	2,621.59

Terminal value	$173,282.00
Present value	$ 33,688.50
Net present value	$ 6,688.50
Internal rate of return	20.4%

Note that the NPV's are still positive, but that profit and cash flows without the new machine become negative in the later periods of the analysis. Thus, the new machine looks good—but in comparison to a poor alternative.   □

Throughout our discussion of sensitivity analysis, we have assumed that inflation will impact each input by a different amount. Such is the situation in any company; to talk of *an* inflation rate is meaningless. Composite inflation rates, such as the CPI and PPI, are useful only if the inputs employed by the firm are the same and used in the same proportion as the inputs used to compute the composite index. Since this never happens, it is necessary to forecast inflation rates for each input. If there were several alternative projects available to accomplish the same goal, logic would argue toward selection of the project which, on the average, would tend to use less of those inputs with high expected inflation rates.

QUESTIONS/PROBLEMS

1. Differentiate between the risk inherent in a project and forecasting risk.
2. In Example 1 different values were used for the hurdle rate and the reinvestment rate. In general, would these values be the same or would they differ? Explain.
3. If the same values for the hurdle rate and the reinvestment rate were used, would the project's NPV be more or less sensitive to changes in those rates as compared to the situation in Example 2 where in they are assumed to be different?
4. The examples in this chapter provide for the computation of the project's internal rate of return based on assumed reinvestment rates. Explain the meaning of the calculated internal rate of return using these assumptions.
5. "Any project can be made to look attractive when compared to a sufficiently undesirable alternative." Such a statement could be applied to the "Inflation Case" in Example 3. When comparing the two mutually exclusive alternatives, "Without

Project" and "With Project," is it fair to compare the two as shown or would you abandon the "Without Project" alternative prior to the tenth period? Assume that if abandonment did take place any cash flows would be reinvested in other projects at the assumed reinvestment rates rather than replacing the project.

6. Visit with a financial officer of a local company and discuss the elements of this chapter. Obtain the forecasts for a project he/she is considering, develop a sensitivity analysis, identify the critical variables, and indicate how profit and cash flows would be effected by 20% errors in these estimates.

10

Taxation and Depreciation

Proposed capital expenditures are evaluated by comparing the expected after-tax costs with the estimated after-tax revenues they are expected to generate. In order to compare costs with revenues, it is necessary to establish a systematic managerial process for collecting, summarizing, and analyzing pertinent financial and nonfinancial data. Given the various types of requests for capital expenditures that management can anticipate, it is necessary to understand the depreciation and taxation procedures applicable in each instance, since both impact profits as well as cash inflows and outflows. Profits and (especially) cash flows are of particular importance to the process of evaluating capital expenditures.

In this chapter we discuss the methods used to determine depreciation and the effects of depreciation and taxation on profitability and cash flows.[1] The reader must be aware of the constantly changing tax structure: altered by revision to statute, IRS rulings, and tax court decisions. The material presented herein reflects the changes in the Economic Recovery Tax Act of 1981 (ERTA), and the Tax Equity and Fiscal Responsibility Act of 1982 (TEFRA) but forms only a base for analysis; the reader is cautioned to incorporate changes as they occur.

[1]The authors express their sincere appreciation to John C. Benstead, Tax Partner, Cherry Hill Office, Deloitte, Haskins and Sells for his review and for providing various tables in this chapter.

DEPRECIATION

When an asset is purchased, it is necessary to match the expenses with revenues during the period in which it is used. *Depreciation* is a systematic recognition of such expenses in an historical framework in order to match the expense with revenues while the asset is being used. Depreciation recognizes the eventual wasting of the asset through wear, obsolescence, or the like, and provides for the recognition of the expense before or no later than its retirement.

The federal tax laws permit inclusion of depreciation as a tax-deductible expense. To be eligible for depreciation, an asset must have a useful life of 1 or more years and be used in a trade or business or held for production of income. Since depreciation does not require a cash outlay, it is categorized as an *implicit* expense; other expenses requiring payment are explicit costs.

To determine the depreciation for an asset, it is necessary to know three things:

1. The depreciable value of the asset:

$$\text{depreciable value} = \text{total capitalized cost} - \text{salvage value} \qquad (1)$$

where the salvage value consists of the estimated resale value reduced by any costs of its removal or sale. For tax purposes under ERTA and TEFRA, salvage value is not considered when determining depreciable value.

2. The useful life of the asset. The useful life is the period over which that asset may reasonably be expected to function in a business.

For tax purposes, the useful life is defined in the ERTA by dividing all assets into four depreciable life categories, described below. This "categorization" represents a significant departure from past practices. Prior to the ERTA, each type of asset was depreciated for tax purposes over a period that reasonably approximated the actual period during which the asset would be used. The IRS published guidelines for thousands of assets providing an *asset depreciation range* (ADR) for each asset. The ADR specified a range of years from which the depreciable life for tax purposes could be chosen. For example, printing presses had a range from 9 to 13 years with an ADR *midpoint* of 11 years. The ADR is still very important because the ADR midpoint is now used to define some of the depreciation categories applicable to certain groups of assets.

The new depreciation categories really have little to do with an asset's useful life. Rather, they were established as a means of permitting businesses to depreciate assets over shorter periods of time. This permits the recovery of the asset's cost more rapidly and thereby makes the acquisition more attractive to a company.

3. The method of depreciation appropriate to the asset. There are specific methods of depreciation that may be used as part of the *accelerated cost recovery system* (ACRS), which is included in the ERTA. These are described later. In all cases, straight-line depreciation may be substituted at the option of the owner.

ACCELERATED COST RECOVERY SYSTEM (ACRS)[2]

The ERTA specifies rapidly accelerated depreciation methods as a means of increasing the level of investment in plant and equipment. The system results, for example, in fully depreciating an asset with a 12-year ADR midpoint in only 5 years.

1. Eligible property. Most tangible depreciable property will be eligible for ACRS. However, property depreciated by methods other than a term of years and amortized property will not be eligible for ACRS. Retirement-replacement-betterment (RRB) property of railroads is covered by ACRS and transitional rules are provided for the change from RRB to ACRS.

To prevent the "churning" of used property solely to obtain the benefits of the increased investment incentives, certain "churned" property will be excluded from ACRS. The statute provides for the exclusion of property used in 1980 from ACRS unless the owner and user change. The Treasury is also granted broad authority to issue regulations to disallow ACRS in inappropriate circumstances. Prior depreciation rules will continue to apply to such property.

2. Recovery periods. The following periods have been established:

3 years: Autos, light-duty trucks, R and D equipment and all personal property with an ADR midpoint life of 4 years or less.

5 years: Most other equipment, including public utility property with a current ADR life of 18 years or less, single-purpose agriculture structures, and petroleum-storage facilities designated as Section 1245 property.

10 years: Public utility property with an ADR midpoint life greater than 18 years but not greater than 25 years, railroad tank cars, and real property with an ADR midpoint life of 12.5 years or less.

15 years: Public utility property with an ADR midpoint life exceeding 25 years and real property with an ADR midpoint life of over 12.5 years.

Taxpayers will be allowed to elect the following *extended* recovery periods in lieu of the regular recovery period when straight-line depreciation is used.

Property Class	Optional Periods
3-year	5 or 12 years
5-year	12 or 25 years
10-year	25 or 35 years
15-year	35 or 45 years

3. Recovery methods. Personal Property (and 10-year real property): Tables are set forth in the law that approximate the following recovery method and

---

[2]Much of the material in this section was provided by Deloitte, Haskins, and Sells.

incorporate the half-year convention.[3] These rates are applied only to the regular recovery periods (3-5-10-15 years):

Year	Method
Commencing in 1981	150% declining balance, changing to straight-line

Table 10–1 is applicable for property placed in service commencing in 1985.[4]

TABLE 10–1   Rates for ACRS Personal Property and 10-year Real Property

Percentage by Property Class

Recovery Year	3-year	5-year	10-year
1	29	18	9
2	47	33	19
3	24	25	16
4		16	14
5		8	12
6			10
7			8
8			6
9			4
10			2

□ **EXAMPLE 1**   *ACRS Depreciation*

An asset having a depreciable value of $10,000 is to be depreciated under the ACRS system over 5 years. Determine the annual depreciation each year using Table 10–1.

Solution: Refer to the 5-year column in Table 10–1 and multiply the depreciable value by the percentages as shown:

Year	Base	Percentage	Depreciation
1	$10,000	18%	$1,800
2	10,000	33	3,300
3	10,000	25	2,500
4	10,000	16	1,600
5	10,000	8	800

    □

[3] The half-year convention specifies that one-half year's depreciation is to be taken in the first year of an asset's life, as opposed to computing the percentage based on the month of acquisition. Heretofore, for example, an asset purchased in March was depreciated 10 months, unless the ADR system was used.

[4] Table 10–1 incorporates the half-year convention and approximates 150% declining balance with a change to straight-line. If an asset is not fully depreciated before it is disposed, then depreciation will not be allowed in the year of its disposition. The astute reader will note a discrepancy in the table—it does not correspond exactly to 150% declining balance, but it must be used. If straight-line depreciation is used, one-half year depreciation is allowed in the first year; if the property is held for the entire period, one-half year is allowed in the last year. Thus, if an asset having a 5-year life is depreciated straight-line, the depreciation would be spread over 6 years with the following percentages each year: 10, 20, 20, 20, 20, 10.

For real property the half-year convention does not apply; real property will be recovered month to month in the years of acquisition and disposal. Also, composite depreciation for real property is now required. The prior law permitted various systems of a structure, such as plumbing and heating, to be depreciated using schedules differing from the bricks and mortar. This is no longer permitted. (See Table 10–2).

Depreciation is included as an accounting expense, but does not result in any outlay of cash. *The amount deducted for depreciation on the firm's income statement is added to any earnings after taxes to obtain the firm's cash flow from operations.* Profits are referred to as *return on investment*, while the funds generated by means of depreciation, amortization, and the like are referred to as *return of investment. The total of profits plus depreciation and similar cash throw-offs is the cash flow from operations.* While depreciation does not require an out-of-pocket expenditure, it does impact tax liability, profits, and cash flow. The greater the depreciation, the lower the profits before taxes (and thus the taxes), and therefore the higher the cash flow.

The primary consideration in using accelerated depreciation is that it tends to reduce earnings before taxes and, consequently, income taxes while increasing *cash flows* during the early years of the life of the asset. The reverse is true during the latter years. Since it is desirable to have both high profits and cash flows, firms frequently use two methods of depreciation: straight-line (which results in

TABLE 10–2   ACRS Cost Recovery Tables for Real Estate

All Real Estate (Except Low-Income Housing)
The applicable percentage is:

If the Recovery Year Is:	Month Placed in Service											
	1	2	3	4	5	6	7	8	9	10	11	12
1	12	11	10	9	8	7	6	5	4	3	2	1
2	10	10	11	11	11	11	11	11	11	11	11	12
3	9	9	9	9	10	10	10	10	10	10	10	10
4	8	8	8	8	8	8	9	9	9	9	9	9
5	7	7	7	7	7	7	8	8	8	8	8	8
6	6	6	6	6	7	7	7	7	7	7	7	7
7	6	6	6	6	6	6	6	6	6	6	6	6
8	6	6	6	6	6	6	5	6	6	6	6	6
9	6	6	6	6	5	6	5	5	5	6	6	6
10	5	6	5	6	5	5	5	5	5	5	6	5
11	5	5	5	5	5	5	5	5	5	5	5	5
12	5	5	5	5	5	5	5	5	5	5	5	5
13	5	5	5	5	5	5	5	5	5	5	5	5
14	5	5	5	5	5	5	5	5	5	5	5	5
15	5	5	5	5	5	5	5	5	5	5	5	5
16		1	1	2	2	3	3	4	4	4	5	

(NOTE: This table does not apply for short taxable years of less than 12 months.)

higher profits) for reporting income to shareholders, and an accelerated method (which results in lower taxable income and tax liability) for tax purposes. The difference in the results using the two methods is reconciled by establishing a deferred income tax liability account as a balance sheet line item.[5] *It should be noted that the total profitability and cash flows over the entire life of an asset are not affected by the choice of a method of depreciation. Only the timing of the profits and cash flows is changed.* Since it is generally considered desirable to receive cash flows from the use of an asset as early as possible in its life, accelerated depreciation methods are usually employed for tax computation.

TAXATION AND CAPITAL EXPENDITURES

In order to estimate the cash flows involved in purchasing assets and to estimate the cash inflows resulting from their use, taxes must be computed. In this section we are primarily concerned with federal taxes on operating income, taxes on capital gains and losses, recapture of depreciation, investment tax credits, and state taxes on operating income.

Federal Taxation on Ordinary Income

The corporate taxable income (earnings before taxes) is that portion of the total income remaining after all the operating and administrative expenses and interest are paid and depreciation deducted. The calculation of tax payable is a simple matter once the taxable income has been determined. All corporations bear federal income tax on ordinary income at the rates shown in Table 10–3.

If the corporation has a net operating loss, the loss may be carried back 3 years and forward 7 *or* carried forward 10 years for pre-1971 carryovers (and 15 years for losses after 1975). Thus, if a firm has had profits in the 3-year period prior to the loss and if these profits are still available to apply losses against, then the firm may enjoy a tax refund that will at least partially make up for the loss. If the loss is carried forward, then taxes will be reduced in future years. The firm also may elect not to carry losses back, but rather to carry them forward for 15 years.

TABLE 10–3   Corporate Federal Income Tax Rates

	1983 and Later Years
First $25,000 taxed at	15%
Next $25,000 taxed at	18%
Next $25,000 taxed at	30%
Next $25,000 taxed at	40%
Over $100,000 taxed at	46%

[5] For a discussion of deferred income taxes, see Charles T. Horngren, *Introduction to Management Accounting*, 4th ed. (Englewood Cliffs, N.J.: Prentice-Hall, Inc., 1978), pp. 652–655.

State Taxation on Ordinary Income

There is little uniformity to the taxation of corporate income by states, but it should be noted that the state income tax is included as an income statement expense for computing federal income taxes. As such, its impact on earnings after taxes depends to a great extent on the rate of federal tax being paid. For example, in a state that imposes a 5% tax, if a firm has a 46% marginal federal tax rate, the effective state tax rate would be only 2.7%. The reader should be cognizant of state taxes, but because of the large variation among states and the detailed computations involved, we do not include them in our cash-flow calculations.

Capital Gains and Losses[6]

Capital gains and losses take place when a firm buys and subsequently sells assets or securities that are not ordinarily purchased and sold in the business of the firm. Capital gains and losses may be either long- or short-term in nature. Short-term gains or losses occur when an asset is held for less than 1 year. In the evaluation of capital expenditures, we are primarily concerned with long-term capital gains and losses and recapture of depreciation (which is discussed below). Long-term capital gains are taxed at either the rate applied to ordinary income or 28%, whichever is lower. Short-term capital gains are always included as a part of ordinary income.

□ **EXAMPLE 2** *Tax on a Long-Term Capital Gain*

A corporation had a taxable income of $30,000 and a long-term capital gain of $30,000 in 1983. Determine its federal income tax liability.

Solution: The first $25,000 of ordinary income is taxed at 15%, the remaining $5,000 at 18%. Since $5,000 of ordinary income is to be taxed at 18%, only $20,000 of the capital gain may be taxed at 18%. The remaining $10,000 is taxed at 30%. The tax is

---

[6]In the study of capital gains and losses it is necessary to define capital assets and related property. A capital asset is any property except the following:

Inventories.
Property held primarily for sale to customers in the ordinary course of business.
Depreciable property used in a trade or business.
Real property used in a trade or business.
Short-term, non-interest-bearing government obligations issued at a discount basis.
Copyrights, literary, musical, or artistic composition, letters, or similar property.
Accounts or notes receivable received in the ordinary course of business for services rendered or from the sale of property.

Land and depreciable property used in business are not capital assets, but if they are sold or exchanged, in most instances they are treated as capital assets with respect to capital gains and losses and recapture of depreciation.

summarized as follows:

Ordinary income	$25,000 × 0.15 =	$ 3,750
Ordinary income	5,000 × 0.18 =	900
Capital gain	20,000 × 0.18 =	3,600
Capital gain	10,000 × 0.30 =	3,000
		$11,250

As an alternative, all of the capital gain could have been taxed at 28%.   □

Recapture of Depreciation

In some instances when property is depreciated and later sold for an amount in excess of its book value, recapture of depreciation will take place. Any recapture of depreciation on personal property (Section 1245) is taxed as ordinary income. Any time the book value is less than the sale price, the gain will be taxed as ordinary income up to the amount of the accumulated depreciation. If property is sold for an amount in excess of the purchase price, that excess is taxed as a capital gain. The gains and losses for the year are netted together to determine the actual gain or loss.

The tax on recapture of depreciation of real property (Section 1250) differs significantly from personal property. Since the portion of depreciation subject to recapture depends on date of asset acquisition, method of depreciation used, and type of property involved, the reader is referred to a tax service, such as that of the Commerce Clearing House or Prentice-Hall, for details in this area.

□ **EXAMPLE 3** *Determination of Recapture of Depreciation and Capital Gain*

A corporation purchased personal (Section 1245) property 10 years ago for $1,000,000 and subsequently depreciated it to a book value of $600,000. If the corporation sells the property for $1,200,000 and has a 46% marginal tax rate, determine the recapture of depreciation, the long-term capital gain, and the additional tax liability if it sells the property.

Solution: The capital gain is the difference between the *sale price* and the *purchase price*.

Sale price	$1,200,000
Less purchase price	− 1,000,000
Capital gain	$ 200,000

The recapture of depreciation is the difference between the *purchase price* and the *book value* in this example, since the asset was sold for *more* than its original cost.

Purchase price	$1,000,000
Less book value	− 600,000
Recapture of depreciation	$ 400,000

The tax is calculated as follows:

Recapture	$400,000 × 0.46 = $184,000
Long-term capital gain	200,000 × 0.28 = 56,000
	Additional tax $240,000

    □

□ **EXAMPLE 4** *Determination of Recapture of Depreciation and Capital Gain*

Use the facts in Example 3, except that the sale price of property is $800,000.

Solution: Since the sale price did not exceed the purchase price, there is no capital gain. However, there is a recapture of depreciation. The recapture of depreciation in this case is the difference between the *sale price* and the *book value* since the asset was sold for *more* than the book value but *for less* than its original cost.

Sale price	$800,000
Less book value	− 600,000
Recapture of depreciation	$200,000

The recapture would be taxed as ordinary income as follows:

$$\$200,000 \times 0.46 = \$92,000$$

Total tax $92,000   □

Section 1231 Assets

Section 1231 of the Internal Revenue Code provides that certain losses may be deducted from ordinary income. Several types of assets are included under the provisions of Section 1231. We are primarily concerned with the following:

1. Real property used in the taxpayer's business held for more than 1 year and not regularly for sale to customers.
2. Depreciable assets used in the taxpayer's business held for more than 1 year and not regularly for sale to customers.

Real and depreciable assets are those which are used in the business such as buildings, machinery, and the like. Land or precious metals purchased for speculative purposes and sold at a loss would not qualify for the liberal treatment offered under Section 1231.

The treatment of Section 1231 applies only when the total of Section 1231 losses exceeds all Section 1231 gains. If there is a net Section 1231 loss, then the net losses occurring from sale of Section 1231 assets may be deducted from ordinary income.

The special provision for deducting net long-term losses on Section 1231 property from ordinary income is of particular importance to financial managers with respect to the timing of the sale of assets. For example, suppose that a firm could sell two assets. The sale of the first would result in a $10,000 long-term capital gain, while the second would result in a $10,000 loss covered by Section 1231. If the firm sold both in the same year, the gain and loss would just offset each other, and there would not be any change in tax paid. However, if the gain were taken one year and the loss the next, a subsequential tax savings would be enjoyed. Assume that the firm's marginal tax rate is 46%. The tax savings on the Section 1231 loss would be $4,600. However, the additional tax payable on the gain would be only $2,800 since the tax rate is 28%.

A net tax savings of $1,800 would be obtained. Hence Section 1231 makes the timing of disposal of capital assets extremely important.

Capital Loss Carry-Back and Carry-Forward

If there is a net long-term capital loss in any year on the sale of assets not covered by Section 1231, *it may not be deducted from ordinary income of the same or any other year. It must be applied against long-term capital gains from the other years.* The loss must first be applied against long-term capital gains made 3 years prior to the loss, then 2 years prior, working forward to the fifth year after the loss has occurred. This permits the firm to apply a long-term capital loss in 1 year against gains in 8 years, starting 3 years prior to the loss and ending 5 years after the loss. Any loss remaining after the fifth year following the loss is no longer available to the corporation as a deduction.

EXPENSING DEPRECIABLE ASSETS

Commencing in 1982, capital expenditures up to a specified amount may be expensed rather than depreciated for tax purposes. This benefit, as shown in Table 10–4, is primarily for small businesses.

TABLE 10–4   Limitation on Expensing Depreciable Assets

Taxable Year Begins In	Limitation Amount
1982	$ 5,000
1983	5,000
1984	7,500
1985	7,500
1986 and later years	10,000

INVESTMENT TAX CREDIT

Investment tax credit (ITC) provides for the reduction of federal income tax liability by permitting part of the cost of certain types of assets to be deducted from the tax liability in the year the property is placed in service. Currently, investment tax credit is up to 10% of the purchase price of certain assets.

The purpose of the tax credit is to stimulate the purchase of certain types of property, meeting the following qualifications: the property must (1) be depreciable; (2) have a useful life of at least 3 years; (3) be tangible personal property or other tangible property[7] (except buildings and their structural components) used as an integral part of manufacturing, production, extraction, and so on; and (4) be placed in service in a trade or business or for the production of income during the year. Property is considered to be placed in service in the earlier of the following:[8]

1. The tax year in which, under your depreciation practice, the period for depreciation begins.

2. The tax year in which the property is placed in condition or state of readiness and availability for service.

Tangible personal property includes depreciable tangible property, except land and land improvements such as buildings. Machinery and equipment are the principal types of property that qualify as tangible personal property. Other types of property include accessories to a business, such as grocery counters and air conditioners, automobiles used for business, and livestock.

The amount of the investment tax credit allowed for qualifying property depends upon the property's useful life and whether it is new or used. Moreover, the amount of tax credit allowed in any one year is limited, but any excess may be carried back or forward in a manner similar to operating losses. Credit may be carried back 3 years and forward 15 years.

For the purpose of computing investment tax credit, the amount qualifying is the total purchase price less any deduction for old property traded in. This applies, in general, to the purchase of both new and used property. However, no more than $125,000 of the cost of qualifying used property may be counted toward investment tax credit.[9]

The amount of investment tax credit that may be taken is based on the asset's depreciable life as shown in Table 10–5.

TABLE 10–5   Investment Tax Credit

Property Class	Investment Tax Credit
3-year	6%
5-year	10%
10-year	10%
15-year	10%

[7]That is, Section 38 property. Included in the 1978 Revenue Act is a provision extending the ITC to expenditures incurred to rehabilitate nonresidential structures, such as factories, warehouses, hotels, and stores. Additional tax credits are also available for six categories of energy property. Such credits are normally in addition to regular ITC. The 1981 ERTA added petroleum-storage facilities used in connection with distribution activities and certain railroad rolling stock used within and without the United States.

[8]However, credits may be taken for certain qualifying expenditures, called *progress payments*, made in the building or acquiring of qualified investment property.

[9]Increases to $150,000 in 1985.

If property is disposed of before the end of its *property class life*, then all or a portion of the investment tax credit must be recaptured, as shown in Table 10–6.

TABLE 10–6   Investment Tax Credit Recapture

	Recapture Percentage	
Year of Disposition	*3-year Property*	*5-10-15-year Property*
1	100%	100%
2	66%	80%
3	33%	60%
4	0%	40%
5	0%	20%

At-risk rules now affect assets applicable to investment tax credit.[10] Credit is allowed only to the extent that capital is at risk. Twenty percent of the basis of the property on a recourse basis must be at risk at all times. When this 20% is maintained, the "safe-harbor" rule is met and the owner is allowed the full ITC. An example of the safe-harbor, at-risk rule is shown in Table 10–7.

TABLE 10–7   Example of Safe-Harbor, At-Risk Rule

	Safe-Harbor Rule Met	*Safe-Harbor Rule Not Met*
Cash	$20,000	$15,000
Bank financed nonrecourse note	80,000	85,000
Purchase price	$100,000	$100,000
At-Risk amount	100,000	15,000
ITC rate	10%	10%
Investment credit	$10,000	$1,500

The amount of investment tax credit taken in any one year is limited to the income tax liability shown on the tax return, or $25,000 plus 85% of the tax liability in excess of $25,000, whichever is less.

The ERTA added new credit for the rehabilitation of certain classes of buildings. In order to qualify, the rehabilitation must be substantial, costing

TABLE 10–8   ITC For Rehabilitation Expenditures

Property Class	*Investment Tax Credit*
30–39-year-old buildings[a]	15%
40-year-old or older buildings[a]	20%
Certified historic structure[b]	25%

[a]Applies to nonresidential buildings only.
[b]Applies to both residential and nonresidential buildings.

[10]At-risk rules apply to individuals, Subchapter S Corporations and certain closely held corporations.

$5,000 or more *and* equaling or exceeding the adjusted basis (book value) of the building. Straight-line depreciation must be used when depreciating rehabilitation expenditures that are subject to ITC. Rehabilitation credits by property age are provided in Table 10–8.

Special Consideration for Trade-ins

As noted in the section on investment tax credit, if an asset is traded in, the basis for the investment tax credit is the price paid in excess of the trade-in value. Thus, if a qualifying asset costs $10,000 and an old asset is traded in for $2,000, the investment tax credit would be calculated based on the $8,000 cash payment. At the 10% rate, the credit would be $800. Instead, if the old asset was sold outright, the total price of the new asset would receive the full benefit of the investment tax credit, that is, 10% of $10,000, or $1,000. There appears to be an obvious advantage to selling the old asset rather than trading it in. The advantage depends, however, on the amount allowed for trade-in versus the amount that could be realized by means of an outright sale. Frequently, a vendor will allow a higher trade-in because being a dealer places him at an advantage in terms of reselling the old asset.

But there are other considerations. If an asset is sold, a capital gain, loss, or recapture of depreciation may take place. If an asset is traded in at a value other than the book value, such gains or losses are not incurred for tax purposes but, rather, the price of the newly acquired asset is adjusted for purposes of depreciation. Suppose that the old asset, described above as having a trade-in value of $2,000, had a book value of only $1,000. A capital gain would not be recognized for tax purposes if the asset were traded in. Rather, the cost of the new asset, for purposes of tax depreciation, would be $9,000 (i.e., $1,000 book value plus $8,000 cash). The $1,000 gain would be amortized over the life of the new asset by reducing its depreciation. If the new asset had a 10-year life with no expected salvage value and is depreciated straight-line, the depreciation would be $900 per year rather than $1,000. If the old machine had a book value of $3,000, the new machine would be depreciated using $11,000 as the cost (i.e., $3,000 book value plus $8,000 cash), for $1,100 annual depreciation. Again, a loss for tax purposes would not be recognized at the time of the transaction.

INVESTMENT TAX CREDIT AND DEPRECIATION

TEFRA imposed a limit on the combined amounts of depreciation and investment tax credit which may be taken for an asset. If the full investment tax credit is taken, then the depreciable base must be reduced by half of the amount of the credit. For example, suppose an asset costs $100,000 and a 10% investment tax credit is taken ($10,000). Then the depreciable base would be reduced by $5,000 (half of the credit). As an alternative, the investment tax credit may be reduced by 2% and the depreciable base left unchanged.

SUMMARY

This chapter provides the primary information pertaining to the calculation of depreciation and taxation as it relates to capital expenditure decision. Both depreciation as it affects profits, taxation, and cash flow, and corporate and state taxes as they affect profits and cash flows, are very important to the evaluation of capital investments.

QUESTIONS/PROBLEMS

1. An asset has a total cost of $10,000. It has an expected useful life of 10 years but may be depreciated for tax purposes using ACRS with a 5-year life. Determine the depreciation using straight-line depreciation for 10 years and ACRS for 5 years. Recall that the half-year convention must be incorporated when using straight-line depreciation.

2. Using 150% declining balance depreciation and the half-year convention, develop a 5-year depreciation schedule giving the percentages of the property to be depreciated each year. Compare this with the figures provided in Table 10–1, 5-year column.

3. Suppose in Problem 1 above that a 10% investment tax credit was to be taken. Recompute the 5-year ACRS depreciation.

4. A company has ordinary income of $150,000, a recapture of depreciation of $30,000 and a $20,000 long-term capital gain. Determine its tax liability.

5. A company purchased a machine for $200,000, took 10% investment tax credit, and depreciated it using a 5-year ACRS life. After 3 years the company sold the machine for $100,000. Determine the tax liability on the sale.

6. A company that has ordinary income of $50,000 is considering the sale of a machine that originally was purchased for $150,000 and has a book value of $75,000. Determine the change in the firm's tax liability based on selling the machine for the following amounts.
   (a) $200,000
   (b) $100,000
   (c) $40,000

Determining Cash Flows

The analysis of capital expenditures is predicated on knowledge of the cash outflows needed to acquire assets and the cash inflows that are expected to result from their use.[1] It is the purpose of this chapter to indicate how these cash flows may be determined, based on sales and cost estimates combined with the relevant tax implications of the transactions that we are considering.

COST OF ACQUISITION AND DISPOSAL OF ASSETS

The total funding requirements for the acquisition of new assets are summarized below.

Total fund requirements equal:
Land purchased.
Equipment and facilities purchased.
Patents and processes purchased.
All costs relating to purchases (transportation, legal fees, installation, and so on).
Additional working capital required.
Tax liability on the sale of replaced assets.
Interest on construction loans and the like.
Property taxes on land and buildings before they are placed in use.

[1]The authors express their sincere appreciation to John C. Benstead, Tax Partner, Cherry Hill Office, Deloitte, Haskins and Sells for his review of this chapter.

less:

Funds realized from the sale of replaced assets.
Tax benefits arising from the sale of replaced assets.
Investment tax credits.
Tax benefits from payment of construction loan interest and property
    taxes.

All these items must be considered to obtain the *net cash outflow* required to acquire an asset.

The costs to purchase assets, whether they be equipment, land, or intangibles, are perhaps the easiest to estimate and, in general, may be estimated with the greatest degree of accuracy.

Tax law requires that all the costs relating to the acquisition of assets be capitalized and that the assets be depreciated over their useful lives, as described in Chapter 10. Thus, legal costs necessary to the purchase of real estate, for example, should be capitalized as a part of the total cost of acquisition. Also, costs such as shipping, receiving, and installing a machine would be capitalized. The question of capitalization actually varies appreciably according to the size of the firm making the acquisition. Consider the purchase of a new machine. The actual costs (in addition to the purchase price) could include the following: shipping, insurance during shipping, construction of a foundation, crane operation, plumbing, wiring, and final setup. If the firm had to pay outside contractors for each of these services, the costs would be capitalized. However, if the firm had a maintenance crew that did much of the work as a part of their normal duties, the costs would usually not be capitalized. Similarly, if a firm had its own legal staff, legal fees that would otherwise be capitalized would generally be included as a part of the ordinary expense of operating the business.

Working capital is the difference between current assets and current liabilities. In many instances when new assets are required, additional working capital is also needed. If a firm expanded its operations, it would likely need more cash and inventories. When the inventories are purchased, accounts payable will tend to increase. Similarly, when the product is sold, accounts receivable will be generated. Further, accruals for wages and taxes would tend to increase. In almost all instances, the increase in current assets will exceed the increase in current liabilities, and thus there will be a requirement for added working capital. Additional working capital needed to support the operation of a fixed asset is expected to be recovered when the asset is removed from service. *Thus, if it is necessary to increase working capital to support additions to fixed assets, the increase represents a use of funds only during the life of those assets. It is expected that all of the additional working capital will be recovered when the asset is retired and is noted as a cash inflow at that time.*

The tax liability or benefit arising from the sale of an existing asset which is discontinued from service may be appreciable and must be considered as a part of the total cash flow involved in the acquisition of a new asset. The implications of sale versus trade-in on capital gains and losses and investment credits make this decision very important in capital expenditure analysis.

When new plant and facilities are acquired, there is often an appreciable time between the initial cash outlays to purchase land and the time when the facility is put into operation. Frequently, construction loans are required. For tax purposes, interest on such loans must be capitalized along with property taxes during the period prior to the asset being placed in operation.

Investment tax credits are provided when certain types of assets are acquired. Since such credits are deducted directly from federal tax liability (and generally within the same calendar quarter as the acquisition is made), they represent a reduction in the cost of acquisition.

When an asset is retired from use, the firm may anticipate recovery of some salvage value and working capital. The net portion of salvage and working capital are noted as cash inflows at the time of asset retirement. Further, the firm may have to pay taxes if capital gains or recovery of depreciation is involved and may have to recapture some investment tax credit if the asset was not held for as long a period as was originally anticipated. If capital losses are involved, tax reductions may be enjoyed. While some assets, such as buildings, are depreciated for tax purposes, their actual fair market value may increase. If management anticipates an increase in value, the various taxes involved should be calculated and the amount, net of taxes, likely to be received when the asset is sold should be projected. In some instances a large portion of the profitability of an investment will be realized at the time of its sale. This is especially true for residential real estate.

The process of determining the out-of-pocket cash flow for a major project is demonstrated in the following examples.

□ **EXAMPLE 1**   *Funding Requirements*

A corporation is considering the construction of a new plant to replace its existing facilities. Pertinent information relating to the current plant is listed in the following table:

	Book Value	*Sale price*
Land	$100,000	$2,500,000
Buildings	275,000	− 60,000[a]
Machinery	500,000	375,000

[a] Cost to demolish old buildings.

Cost factors for the new plant are as follows:

	Purchase Price	*Related Costs*
Land	$2,000,000	$200,000 real estate fees
		50,000 property taxes during construction
		80,000 interest during construction
Buildings	3,600,000	$ 60,000 property taxes during construction
		100,000 interest during construction
Machinery and equipment	1,600,000	$400,000 installation
Additional working capital	250,000	

All equipment and machinery have an ACRS life of 5 years. Assume that the old property was held for a sufficient period of time so that no recapture of ITC is required. The corporation is in the 46% marginal tax bracket. Determine the net out-of-pocket cost to purchase the new plant.

Solution: First calculate the gross amount to be received from the sale of the old property.

	Sale Price
Land	$2,500,000
Buildings	(60,000)
Machinery	375,000
Total	$2,815,000

The net amount received will be the sale price less the applicable taxes. The Section 1231 gains are determined as follows and taxed as long-term capital gains:

	Capital Gains (Losses)
Land	
(sale price − book value)	
$2,500,000 − $100,000	$2,400,000
Building	
(book value + demolition costs)	
$275,000 + $60,000	(335,000)
Machinery	
(book value − sale price)	
$500,000 − $375,000	(125,000)
Net capital gain	$1,940,000

The tax on the capital gain would be $1,940,000 × 0.28 = $543,200, so the net amount received from the sale is as follows:

Sale price	$2,815,000
Capital gains tax	− 543,200
Net sale price	$2,271,800

The total cost of the new plant plus working capital is listed below. The interest on construction loans and property taxes incurred during construction are capitalized and amortized generally over a 10-year period. Amortization begins the year that the assets are placed in service. Full amortization may be taken for the first year regardless of the month that the property is placed in service.

Land	$2,330,000
Buildings	3,760,000
Machinery and equipment	2,000,000
Added working capital	250,000
Total cost	$8,340,000

Investment tax credit of 10% of the cost of the new machinery and equipment will be enjoyed. The investment tax credit is $2,000,000 × 0.10 = $200,000. The net out-of-pocket cost equals the total purchase price of the new plant less the net sale price of the old, and less investment tax credits.

Total cost new plant	$8,340,000
Net sale price of old	− 2,271,800
Investment tax credits	− 200,000
Out-of-pocket cost	$5,868,200

The corporation would have to pay $5,868,200 to purchase the new plant.   ☐

☐ **EXAMPLE 2** *Funding Requirements with Trade-in*

Suppose that the corporation in Example 1 was able to trade in the machinery for $600,000 rather than sell it for $375,000. Assuming that the purchase price of the new machinery and equipment remains unchanged, determine the difference in funding requirements.

Solution: First, calculate the gross amount to be received from the sale and trade-in of the old property.

	Sale Price and Trade-in Allowance
Land	$2,500,000
Buildings	(60,000)
Machinery	600,000
Total	$3,040,000

The net amount received is the sale price less capital gains taxes. The capital gains are determined as in Example 1, except that a gain is not recognized on the sale of the used machinery. Thus, the net capital gain includes the $2,400,000 gain on the land less the $335,000 loss on the buildings, or $2,065,000. The capital gain tax at the 28% rate is $578,200, so the net amount received is:

Sales price and trade-in	$3,040,000
Capital gains tax	− 578,200
Net sales price	$2,461,800

The total cost of the new plant plus working capital remains unchanged at $8,340,000. The investment tax credit on the machinery and equipment is reduced because the $600,000 trade-in value is subtracted from the $2,000,000 purchase price, leaving a $1,400,000 basis for the credit. The investment tax credit is $140,000. The net out-of-pocket cost for the new plant is as shown:

Total cost of new plant	$8,340,000
Net sale price of old	− 2,461,800
Investment tax credits	− 140,000
Out-of-pocket cost	$5,738,200

☐

Note that the reduction in the out-of-pocket cost resulting from the trade-in of $600,000 for the used machinery in Example 2 rather than the $375,000 sale price in Example 1 is only $130,000. The difference results from changes in the capital gains and investment tax credits. In the next section we examine the differences in cash inflows resulting from the two types of transactions so that their bearing on capital expenditure decisions may be fully appreciated.

TIMING OF CASH OUTFLOWS

Examples 1 and 2 did not include a time analysis of expenditures, which is also an integral part of the economic analysis of capital expenditures. In the analysis of a large project such as the one outlined in Example 1, the development of a time-flow chart such as the one shown is useful.

Time	Activity	Cash Flow
0	Purchase land	− $2,200,000
3 months	Start construction	− 900,000
6 months	Property taxes	− 20,000
1 year	Construction project	− 2,000,000
	Property taxes	− 25,000
	Loan interest	− 80,000
18 months	Complete construction	− 700,000
	Property taxes	− 30,000
	Purchase machinery	− 1,600,000
	Investment tax credit	+ 200,000
21 months	Install machinery	− 400,000
24 months	Sell old plant	+ 2,271,800
	Property taxes	− 35,000
	Interest	− 100,000
	Working capital	− 250,000
	Net cash outflow	− $5,868,200

CASH FLOWS FROM ASSET OPERATION

In order to evaluate proposed capital expenditures, it is necessary to estimate the after-tax cash flows which are likely to be received as a result of using the asset over its projected life. *After-tax cash flows* consist of the sum of the additional after-tax profits generated from the use of an asset plus the depreciation cash throw-offs. Determination of the cash flows is demonstrated in the following examples.

□ **EXAMPLE 3**   *Profitability and Cash Flow*

A machine costs $15,000. It has a life of 5 years and will be depreciated straight-line to zero salvage value. Use of the machine will result in an increase in income of $20,000 per year. Concurrently, operating expenses will rise by $16,000 per year. Assume that the firm considering the purchase of the machine has a 30% tax rate. Determine the profit and cash flow of the machine.

Solution: The profitability is calculated using the typical income statement method.

	Change in Income Statement	*Change in Cash Flow*
Income	$20,000	$20,000
Less operating expenses	− 16,000	− 16,000
Less depreciation	− 3,000	
Earnings before taxes	$ 1,000	
Less tax	− 300	− 300
Earnings after taxes	$ 700	
Increased cash flow		$ 3,700

The cash flow may also be determined by adding earnings after taxes to the depreciation. The depreciation expenses did not result in any outflow of cash, so at the end of the year, the firm would have $700 + $3,000 = $3,700 of increased cash inflow from operating the machine. □

□ **EXAMPLE 4** Profitability and Cash Flow

A machine purchased 5 years ago for $30,000 has been depreciated straight-line to a book value of $20,000. Its original projected life was 15 years with zero salvage value. Its current market value is $10,000 and, if sold, it would result in a Section 1231, long-term loss. A machine is available that has a purchase price of $45,000, including installation costs. The old machine could be sold for its market value. The new machine has a 15-year projected life, will be depreciated based on a 5-year ARCS life, has zero salvage value, and is expected to reduce operating costs by $7,000 per year. Compute the cash outflow needed to acquire the new machine and the inflows over its life. The firm has a 46% marginal tax rate.

Solution: The disposal of the old machine will result in a $10,000 loss under Section 1231. Since the marginal tax rate is 46%, the tax savings is $4,600. Thus, a total of $14,600 will be received. The cost of the new machine is $45,000, and the investment tax credit at 8% is $3,600. The out-of-pocket cost for the new machine is as follows:

New machine purchase price	$45,000
Recapture investment tax credit, old machine[2]	1,000
Investment tax credit at 8%	− 3,600
Sale of old machine	− 10,000
Section 1231 tax savings	− 4,600
Out-of-pocket cost	$27,800

The new machine costs $45,000 and has a 15-year projected life and zero salvage value. Depreciation is based on Table 10-1. The existing machine was being depreciated at the rate of $2,000 per year, so additional depreciation will result each year for the first 5 years of the new machine's life, while a loss in depreciation will be experienced in the second 5-year period. The 10-year period represents the remaining life of the old machine. The cash flows are determined in Table 11-1.

[2]Assuming the old machine was purchased in 1979, the law required a 7-year life for full investment tax credit. Keeping it only 5 years would require recapturing one-third of the original $3,000 ITC, or $1,000.

TABLE 11−1   Differential Cash Flows for Example 4

Year	Cost Reduction	Added Depreciation	EBT	Tax 46%	EAT	CF
1	$7,000	$ 6,100	$ 900	$ 414	$ 486	$6,586
2	7,000	12,850	− 5,850	− 2,691	− 3,159	9,691
3	7,000	9,250	− 2,250	− 1,035	− 1,215	8,035
4	7,000	5,200	1,800	828	972	6,172
5	7,000	1,600	5,400	2,484	2,916	4,516
6-10[a]	7,000	− 2,000	9,000	4,140	4,860	2,860
11-15	7,000	0	7,000	3,220	3,780	3,780

[a]Year 10 corresponds to the end of the expected life of the original machine   □

The examples used to develop cash flows are typical of the types of problems encountered in investment analysis. In the development of the examples, one important point should be underscored relative to sunk costs. *Sunk costs* represent cash outflows that were made in the past and are no longer recoverable. Thus, the economic significance of sunk costs within the context of capital investment decisions is limited to the impact which these costs may have on tax liabilities. For instance, in Example 4 the machine currently being used had a book value of $20,000 with a market value of only $10,000. The $10,000 difference represents a sunk cost, but part of it was recoverable so that the actual sunk cost was limited to only $5,400 since $4,600 was recoverable by means of tax reductions.

SALES VERSUS TRADE-IN: EFFECT ON CASH INFLOWS

Earlier in this chapter we demonstrated the impact on the cash outflows needed to acquire an asset resulting from the decision to trade in the asset versus selling it. Now we want to examine the impact of the same decision on the expected cash inflows. This will be accomplished in Example 5.

□ **EXAMPLE 5**   *Differential Cash Flows with Sale Versus Trade-in*

Refer to Examples 1 and 2 and assume a 5-year ACRS life for the new machinery and equipment, zero salvage value, a 46% marginal tax rate, $1,500,000 earnings before depreciation and taxes, and that the project is placed in operation on July 1. Determine the difference in cash inflows in Examples 1 and 2. Use Tables 10-1 and 10-2.

Solution: Consider Example 1 first. The new machines and equipment had a total cost of $2,000,000, less half of the ITC for a depreciable basis of $1,900,000. The financial statements for purposes of computing cash flows are shown at the top of the next page.

Next, consider Example 2. For purposes of depreciation, the cost of the machinery and equipment consists of the cash amount paid plus the book value of the old machinery less one-half of the ITC. The amount paid equals the purchase price of $2,000,000 less trade-in of $600,000, or $1,400,000. The book value was $500,000, so the depreciable value is $1,900,000 less $70,000, or $1,830,000. The financial statements for purposes of

	Changes in Income Statement	Changes in Cash Flows
Earnings before taxes and depreciation	$1,500,000	$1,500,000
Less depreciation on buildings	− 216,000	
Less depreciation on machinery and equipment	− 342,000	
Less amortization of interest and property tax	− 29,000	
Earnings before taxes	$ 913,000	
Less tax (46%)	− 419,980	− 419,980
Earnings after taxes	$ 493,020	
Increased cash flow		$1,080,020

value is $1,900,000 less $70,000, or $1,830,000. The financial statements for purposes of computing cash flows are as follows:

	Changes in Income Statement	Changes in Cash Flows
Earnings before taxes and depreciation	$1,500,000	$1,500,000
Less depreciation on buildings	− 216,000	
Less depreciation on machinery and equipment	− 329,400	
Less amortization of interest and property taxes	− 29,000	
Earnings before taxes	$ 925,600	
Less tax	425,776	− 425,776
Earnings after taxes	$ 499,824	
Increased cash flow		$1,074,224

The difference in cash flows between Examples 1 and 2 amounts to $5,796 per year in favor of Example 1 (sale rather than trade-in). Since the cash outflow of Example 1 exceeded that of Example 2 by $130,000, the increase in yearly cash flows of $5,796 would obviously not warrant the added expenditure. But the important point to recognize is that in many situations there are choices facing management that bear heavily on cash-flow projections, and each must be weighted. In Examples 1 and 2 the trade-in appears to be preferable.

FURTHER CONSIDERATIONS OF THE TIMING OF CASH FLOWS

Earlier in the chapter we included a time analysis showing the projected cash outflows for a 2-year plant construction. In many instances cash flows must be adjusted to reflect the actual time of receipt or payment. Consider a firm opening a new plant with projected yearly sales, operating expenses, and related costs. During the first year the lags in accounts receivable and payable, inventory buildups, and accruals warrant special attention. The first year and subsequent yearly cash flows are developed in Example 6.

□ **EXAMPLE 6**   *Operating Cash Flows*

A corporation anticipates additional sales of $1,000,000 per year resulting from its new plant. Cost and revenue projections are detailed below.

Revenues: All sales on credit with a 60-day average collection period.

Costs: Materials are 30% of sales with 2 months' safety stock; payment made 30 days after monthly deliveries. Labor costs are 25% of sales with payment two weeks after the end of salary period, which is monthly.

Utilities and fuels are 15% of sales with bills received at end of month and paid 30 days after receipt.

Administrative costs are 10% of sales and paid in month they occur.

Determine the pretax cash flows for the first and subsequent years, ignoring depreciation and taxes.

Solution: Consider the initial year first. Sales are projected at $1,000,000, but with a 60-day collection period, cash received can only be expected to be $833,333. Materials cost $25,000 per month and a 2-month safety stock is required. With payment in 30 days, the first year cost would be $50,000 plus $25,000 × 11 months, or $325,000. Monthly labor costs amount to $20,833. With a 2-week lag in payment, the first-year cost is $229,163, with the next salary payment due 2 weeks after the start of the second year of operation. Utilities and fuels cost $12,500 per month. A 30-day payment lag results in a first-year cost of $137,500. Administrative costs are paid in the month they occur, so the yearly cost is $100,000. The first year is summarized as follows:

Cash receipts	$833,333
Materials	− 325,000
Labor	− 229,163
Utilities and fuel	− 137,500
Administrative costs	− 100,000
Earnings before depreciation and taxes	$ 41,670

In subsequent years the cash flows would be as follows:

Cash receipts	$1,000,000
Materials	− 300,000
Labor	− 250,000
Utilities and fuel	− 150,000
Administrative costs	− 100,000
Earnings before depreciation and taxes	$ 200,000

□

Whenever a plant is expanded or a new operation undertaken, lower earnings and cash flow may result during the initial period of operation. In addition to the lags in collections and payments, start-up costs may also reduce profitability.

SUMMARY

Accurate estimates of cash flows, including all provisions for depreciation and taxation, are essential as inputs to the evaluation of proposed capital expenditures. In this chapter we have described how the cash flows are computed based on cost estimates. We further examined the implications of outright sale of used assets versus trade-ins and the lags in expenditures and receipts in new plant start-up.

Throughout the chapter we have emphasized that capital budgeting decisions are based upon the evaluation of relevant incremental benefits and costs affected by the project under consideration. In each instance, we estimate the costs and anticipated revenues relating to the project within the context of the firm as a whole.

QUESTIONS/PROBLEMS[3]

1. A corporation is considering replacing an older truck with a newer model, which, owing to more efficient operation, will reduce operative costs from $20,000 to $16,000 per year. Sales are $30,000 per year. The old truck cost $30,000 when purchased nearly 5 years ago, had an estimated useful life of 15 years, zero salvage value, and is being depreciated straight-line. At precent, its market value is estimated to be $20,000, if sold outright. The new truck costs $40,000 and would be depreciated straight-line to a zero salvage value over a 10-year life. The corporation has a 46% marginal tax rate. Determine the following.
   (a) The cash outflow required to acquire the new truck assuming the old truck is sold at the present time.
   (b) The yearly cash flows from operations resulting from the old truck and the new truck.
   (c) Summarize the cash flows and calculate the differential cash flows over the 10-year period.
2. Consider Problem 1 with the following changes: The old truck cost $40,000 and had a $10,000 projected salvage value. Determine (a), (b), and (c) as in Problem 1.
3. Consider Problem 1 with the following changes: The old truck has useful life of 10 years, but with increased maintenance of $1,000 per year could be operated for another 5 years. Determine (a), (b), and (c) as in Problem 1.
4. Consider Problem 1 with the following changes: The old truck has useful life of 10 years and could be sold for a projected salvage value of $10,000 at the end of its useful life, or $20,000 at present. Determine (a), (b), and (c) as in Problem 1.
5. Consider Problem 1 with the following changes: The old truck cost $30,000 and had an expected 10-year life with negligible salvage value. The old truck could be rebuilt at the end of its 10-year life to operate at its current level of efficiency for another 5 years. This would cost $10,000, which would be depreciated straight-line to zero salvage. The old truck could be sold at present for $15,000. The salvage value of the truck when 15 years old is also expected to be negligible. Determine (a), (b), and (c) as in Problem 1.
6. A corporation has decided to purchase a new machine for their business. The following are the facts relating to the disposal of the old machine and purchase of the new:
   1. The original cost of the old machinery was $2,000,000.
   2. The book value of the old machinery is $400,000 and it can be traded in for $900,000. It is fully depreciated.
   3. The cost to remove the old machinery is $30,000.

---

[3] Unless otherwise noted, be sure to consider the investment tax credit.

4. The cost for the new machine is $3,500,000.
5. Wiring by a contractor will cost $15,000.
6. The cost of installation by an outside contractor is $145,000.
7. The legal fees are $115,000.
8. The costs of wiring, installation, and legal fees will be capitalized.
9. The added working-capital requirements are $50,000.
10. The depreciation method used for financial and tax accounting is straight-line.
11. The marginal tax rate is 46%.
12. The expected useful life of the new machine is 20 years.
   Determine the out-of-pocket cost to purchase the new machine.

7. Suppose in Problem 6 that the old machine is sold for $750,000 rather than traded in. Determine the net cash outflow to purchase the new machine.

8. Referring to Problems 6 and 7, determine the depreciable base for the new machine, for tax purposes only, for both the trade-in and sale.

9. A corporation purchased new equipment costing $200,000 to support a new product line. The equipment has a 5-year life with negligible expected salvage value and will be depreciated based on an ACRS 3-year life. Additional first-year sales are expected to be $175,000 with fixed costs (not including depreciation) of $25,000 and variable costs of $35,000. General and administrative costs are estimated to be 15% of sales. Sales and variable and administrative costs are expected to increase at 10% per year. If the corporation's marginal tax rate is 46%, determine the after-tax profit and cash flow of each year, the cash outflow required to purchase the equipment, and the NPV based on a 14% discount rate and ACRS rates applicable to 1984.

10. A2Z Corporation is expanding its Hoboken, New Jersey, chemical cleaning-products plant in order to increase sales and market share. Construction will be completed in September and the plant will be in full operation October 1. A tabulation of projected incremental costs and revenue is shown below. Determine the incremental cash flows for the first 2 years (ignoring depreciation and taxes).

Item	$ / Year	Notes
Sales	$2,520,000	See collection experience.[a]
Raw material *A*	408,000	3 months initial stock (includes permanent 2 months safety stock), required payment net 30 (end of month).
Raw material *B*	144,000	2 months initial stock required (includes permanent 1 month safety stock), payment net 30 (end of month).
Miscellaneous raw materials	180,000	Average 1 month stock required, net 25.
Electricity	9,600	Net 25 (first billing Nov. 1).
Fuel oil	12,000	Net 30 (first billing Nov. 1).
Water	6,000	Net 30 (first billing Nov. 1).
Labor, hourly	144,000	Paid weekly, 1-week lag.
Salaried supervision	60,000	Paid monthly on last working day.
Packages, containers, and so on	210,000	2 months initial supply required (includes permanent 1 month safety stock) net 30 (end of month).

[a]Collection experience on sales: 1st month 20%, 2nd month 70%, 3rd month 10%.

11. ERTA permits expensing a limited amount of depreciable equipment each year. Suppose that $10,000 could be expensed this year or depreciated by ACRS over 5 years. Consider two discount rates, 8% and 10%, and determine the present value of the difference tax shields assuring a 46% marginal tax rate. Assume the investment tax credit will affect tax liabilities due presently.

12

Introduction to Risk Analysis

During the first part of our study of capital investments (in Part II of the text), we assumed that any decisions involving investments would not alter the risk complexion of the firm. This is not to say that we were operating under conditions of certainty, but rather that we held risk constant. However, it is a truism that it is frequently difficult to make either short- or long-term estimates of the cash flows for capital investments with a high degree of accuracy. As a consequence, in this and the following chapters, we examine capital investment decisions under conditions of risk and uncertainty. Initially, we direct our attention to individual projects and then to portfolios of projects.

CERTAINTY, RISK, AND UNCERTAINTY

Up to this point we have assumed that projects being considered have a risk posture consistent with that of the firm overall. This meant that the acceptance of projects would not change the firm's risk complexion (i.e., risk has been held constant). A decision-maker may be faced with conditions of certainty, risk, or uncertainty, these are differentiated below:

Certainty postulates that the decision maker knows in advance the precise values of all the parameters possibly affecting the decision.

Risk postulates that the decision-maker is (1) aware of all possible future states of the economy, business, and so on, which may occur and thereby affect relevant decision parameters and (2) able to place a probability on the value of the occurrence of each of these states.

Uncertainty postulates that the decision-maker (1) may not be aware of all the possible states that affect the decision, and/or (2) may not be able to place a probability on the occurrence of each.

We deal with conditions of certainty and risk, assuming for the present that it is possible to reduce problems under conditions of uncertainty to those of risk by collecting additional data (at some cost). We recognize that techniques such as adaptive and optimal control processes, heuristic programming, and artificial intelligence methods are currently being developed to deal with capital investment evaluation under conditions of uncertainty. Although we shall not deal with any of these, we expect, as they become more fully developed, that they will become an integral part of the risk analysis methodology.

At this juncture it is useful to review the general kinds of risk faced by financial managers. Although the types of risk tend to be interrelated, it is helpful in financial planning, decision making, and control to identify various categories. We shall refer to these in this and the following chapters as we examine the capital investment decision under conditions of risk.

1. Business risk is the variability in earnings that is a function of the firm's normal operations (as impacted by the changing economic environment) and management's decisions with respect to capital intensification. The use of more capital equipment (increasing operating leverage) generally results in higher fixed costs and thereby increases the variability of earnings before interest and taxes (EBIT) with output (as measured by the degree of operating leverage). It should be noted that business risk considers only the variability in EBIT, and does not consider the effect of debt or other financing on the firm's risk posture. Although business risk encompasses the variability in earnings due to economic changes and management investment policies, it is instructive to view these as investment and portfolio risk.

2. Investment risk is the variability in earnings due to variations in the cash inflows and outflows of capital investment projects undertaken. This risk is associated with forecasting errors made in market acceptance of products, future technological changes, degree of intertemporal relationship of cash flows, changes in costs related to projects, and other environmental risks discussed below.

3. Portfolio risk is the variability in the earnings due to the degree of efficient diversification that the firm has achieved in its operations and its overall portfolio of assets. The risk is reduced by the firm seeking out capital projects and merger candidates that have a low or negative correlation with their present operations. The full impact of portfolio effects is discussed in Chapter 14.

4. Cataclysmic risk is the variability in earnings that is a function of events beyond managerial control and anticipation. Such events would include expropriation, erratic changes in consumer preferences, severe energy shortages, and the like.

5. Financial risk is the variability in earnings that is a function of the financial structure and the necessity of meeting obligations on fixed-income securities. The use of more debt or preferred stock (increasing financial leverage) results in greater obligatory payments and thereby increases the variability of earnings after taxes (EAT) and earnings per share (EPS) (as measured by the degree of financial leverage).

Business and financial risk and the effects of operating and financial leverage were discussed in Chapter 8. Our next objective is to discuss methods of measuring expected return and the possible dispersion of return resulting from the various risks facing the firm.

RISK AND RETURN

Since risk is an inherent part of almost all capital investment decisions, it is necessary to consider it as well as the expected return associated with various decision alternatives. The probability distribution, which describes all possible outcomes, must be defined along with the mean or expected value of cash flows in order to evaluate alternative courses of action. The expected value of a probability distribution is defined in Equation (1):

$$\bar{R} = \sum_{i=1}^{N} (R_i P_i) \tag{1}$$

where $\bar{R}$ = expected value
R_i = return associated with the ith outcome
P_i = probability of occurrence of the ith outcome
N = number of possible outcomes

Calculation of the expected return for an investment is demonstrated in Example 1.

□ **EXAMPLE 1** *Expected Return*

A financial manager faces conditions of risk in terms of economic strength in the coming year. Three different states may occur: strong economy with probability 0.3; moderately strong economy, 0.5; and weak economy, 0.2. Three alternative 1-year investments are under consideration offering returns as follows:

State of Economy	Probability	Expected Investment Outcomes		
		A	B	C
Strong	0.3	$1,800	$1,600	$2,000
Moderately strong	0.5	1,500	1,200	1,600
Weak	0.2	800	1,000	900

Determine the expected return for project A.

Solution: For investment A:

$$\bar{R} = (0.3)(\$1{,}800) + (0.5)(\$1{,}500) + (0.2)(\$800)$$
$$= \$540 + \$750 + \$160$$
$$= \underline{\$1{,}450}$$

The mean return for investment A is $1,450. This return is determined by weighting the return for each state of the economy by its respective probability of occurrence. The expected return for investment B is $1,280 and for investment C is $1,580.   □

The amount of variability or dispersion that is present in the probability distribution of returns associated with a decision alternative is referred to as the risk of that decision alternative. There are several measures of risk that have been advocated for use by financial managers. Statisticians speak of both *absolute* and *relative measures of risk* (variability or dispersion). *Absolute measures of dispersion* include the range, mean absolute deviation, variance, standard deviation, and semivariance. The *relative measure of dispersion is the coefficient of variation.* Each of these measures is defined in equation form:

$$R_g = R_h - R_l \tag{2}$$

where R_g = range of the distribution
R_h = highest value in the distribution
R_l = lowest value in the distribution

$$\text{MAD} = \sum_{i=1}^{N} P_i \left(|R_i - \bar{R}| \right) \tag{3}$$

where MAD is the mean absolute deviation;

$$\sigma^2 = \sum_{i=1}^{N} P_i \left(R_i - \bar{R} \right)^2 \tag{4}$$

where σ^2 is the variance of the distribution;

$$\sigma = \sqrt{\sum_{i=1}^{N} P_i \left(R_i - \bar{R} \right)^2} \tag{5}$$

where σ is the standard deviation;

$$\text{SV} = \sum_{j=1}^{K} P_j \left(R_j - \bar{R} \right)^2 \tag{6}$$

where SV = semivariance
j = index set, which includes all values of the random variable that are less than the expected value
K = number of outcomes less than the expected value

$$\nu = \frac{\sigma}{\bar{R}} \tag{7}$$

where ν is the coefficient of variation.

The calculation of the various measures of risk or dispersion is demonstrated in Example 2.

□ **EXAMPLE 2** *Measurement of Risk*

Using the information in Example 1, determine the value for each measure of risk defined above for investment *A*.

Solution:

$$R_g = \text{range} = \$1{,}800 - \$800 = \$1{,}000$$

This value simply means that there is a $1,000 difference between the lowest return that could be earned with investment A and the highest possible return. The range for investment B is $600 and for investment C is $1,100.

$$MAD = (0.3)(|\$1,800 - \$1,450|) + (0.5)(|\$1,500 - \$1,450|) + (0.2)(|\$800 - \$1,450|)$$
$$= (0.3)(\$350) + (0.5)(\$50) + (0.2)(\$650)$$
$$= \$260$$

The MAD's for investments B and C are $192 and $272, respectively. MAD shows that average variability of the values of the distribution from the mean without regard to the sign of the deviation.

$$\sigma^2 = (0.2)(\$800 - \$1,450)^2 + (0.5)(\$1,500 - \$1,450)^2 + (0.3)(\$1,800 - \$1,450)^2$$
$$= (0.2)(-\$650)^2 + (0.5)(\$50)^2 + (0.3)(\$350)^2$$
$$= 122,500$$
$$\sigma = \sqrt{\sigma^2} = \$350$$

The standard deviation is a measure of how representative the expected return is of the entire distribution. The larger the standard deviation, the less representative the mean is because of the greater scatter around the mean. The variance and standard deviation for investment *B* are 49,600 and $222.71, respectively, and for investment C are 145,600 and $381.58.

The final absolute measure of dispersion is the semivariance, which is similar to the variance but looks only at deviations below the mean, since these are the unfavorable deviations that quantify the downside risk.

$$SV = (0.2)(\$800 - \$1,450)^2 = (0.2)(422,500)$$
$$= 84,500$$

Note that the downside risk as measured by the semivariance is about 70% of the total variability as measured by the variance for investment A (84,500 as compared to 122,500). The semivariance for investments B and C are 18,880 and 92,480, respectively. Finally,

$$\nu = \frac{\$350}{\$1,450} = 0.2414$$

The coefficient of variation is 0.2414 for investment A and 0.1742 and 0.2418 for investments B and C, respectively. The coefficient of variation shows the amount of risk (as measured by the standard deviation) per dollar of expected return. That is, the lower the coefficient of variation, the smaller is the amount of relative risk. When evaluating alternatives that have different expected returns, a relative measure of variability such as the coefficient of variation is required to accurately compare the riskiness of the alternatives. □

The expected value of return and measures of risk for all three investments are as follows:

Comparison of Expected Return and Risk
for Three Investment Alternatives

	Investment A	*Investment B*	*Investment C*
Expected return	$1,450	$1,280	$1,580
Range	$1,000	$600	$1,100
Mean absolute deviation	$260	$192	$272
Variance	122,500	49,600	145,600
Standard deviation	$350	$223	$382
Semivariance	84,500	18,880	92,480
Coefficient of variation	0.2414	0.1742	0.2418

Given the expected value and various measures of risk surrounding each investment, we now interpret the measures within the context of Example 2. The range simply measures the total variability in possible returns for each investment. It establishes the upper and lower limits of possible outcomes. It is rarely used in practice because it (1) considers only the extremal values (and, by default, ignores all the others) and (2) ignores the probabilities attached to any of the values within the distribution.

The variance, its counterpart the standard deviation, and MAD all measure dispersion in terms of the probabilities associated with each possible outcome. The variance and standard deviation are preferred in decision making under conditions of risk, since the value provided by MAD is distorted by disregard for the signs of the deviations of each value from the mean. As a practical matter, *the standard deviation is used most commonly as it has the same units as the original variable and is the measure of dispersion used with the expected value to characterize several distributions, including the normal distribution.* The semivariance is a special case of the variance, used to measure downside risk. Advocates of the semivariance say that deviations above the mean add to an investment's attractiveness, but since investors frequently tend to avoid downside risk, only deviations below the mean need be quantified. Risk aversion will be further addressed in the following sections.

Thus far, our discussion has been limited to measures of absolute dispersion. While these are statistically valid, their use in financial decision making requires evaluation of risk within the framework of the expected return. Therefore, it is necessary to simultaneously consider both risk and return by means of the measure of relative dispersion, the coefficient of variation. Refer to the preceding table and note that investments A and C have equal coefficients of variation, indicating equal risk per dollar of expected return, whereas investment B has a significantly lower coefficient of variation, indicating a lower risk per dollar of expected return.

Given all the above, which of the three alternatives should the financial manager select? In this problem setting, as in most under conditions of risk, the statistics provide additional information about the alternatives, but they do not specify which should be selected by all decision-makers. *None of the alternatives is dominant, which would mean that it simultaneously has a higher expected value and a lower level of risk.* The final decision would have to be made in terms of the decision-maker's utility function, that is, his or her specification of preferences considering all relevant aspects of the problem setting. We present a formal discussion of utility theory, after a brief introduction to tree diagrams and decision trees.

DECISION TREES

A technique that has been recommended to handle complex, sequential decisions over time involves the use of decision trees. A *decision tree* is a formal representation of available decision alternatives at various points through time which are followed by chance events that may occur with some probability. A ranking of the available decision alternatives is usually achieved by finding the expected returns of the alternatives, which merely requires multiplying the returns earned by each alternative for various chance events by the probability that the event will occur and summing over all possible events. To illustrate the use of decision trees in a very simple problem setting, consider Example 3.

□ **EXAMPLE 3**   *Decision Tree Example*

A firm is considering three alternative single-period investments, A, B, and C, whose returns are dependent upon the state of the economy in the coming period. The state of economy is known only by a probability distribution:

State of the Economy	Probability
Fair	0.25
Good	0.40
Very good	0.30
Super	0.05
	1.00

The returns for each alternative under each possible state of the economy are as follows:

	State of the Economy			
Alternative	Fair	Good	Very Good	Super
A	$10	$40	$ 70	$ 90
B	− 20	50	100	140
C	− 75	60	120	200

Use a decision tree to evaluate the three alternatives.

Solution: The decision tree for this problem is shown in the table. Notice that we have followed the somewhat standard convention of using a square node to represent decision alternatives and round nodes to show chance events. On the far right side of the tree, the returns for each state of the economy have been weighted by the probability that the state will occur. The sum of these values for all possible states of the economy is the expected return associated with each of the three decision alternatives. Thus, once the decision tree has been "folded back," the selection of the alternative that maximizes expected return is immediate.

Decision Alternative	Expected Return
A	$44.00
B	$52.00
C	$51.25

Alternative *B* maximizes the expected return, alternative *C* is a close second, and alternative *A* is a rather distant third.   □

Decision Alternative	State of the Economy	Probability of State of Economy	Return Earned	Weighted Return
	fair	0.25	$10	$ 2.50
	good	0.40	40	16.00
	very good	0.30	70	21.00
	super	0.05	90	4.50
A			$E(R_A)$ =	$44.00
	fair	0.25	−$20	−$ 5.00
B	good	0.40	50	20.00
	very good	0.30	100	30.00
	super	0.05	140	7.00
C			$E(R_B)$ =	$52.00
	fair	0.25	−$75	−$18.75
	good	0.40	60	24.00
	very good	0.30	120	36.00
	super	0.05	200	10.00
			$E(R_C)$ =	$51.25

The decision-tree analysis illustrated in Example 3 is an initial step in the evaluation of investments. Of course, several additional dimensions of the problems cry out for further analysis:

1. The degree of *risk* associated with each of the alternatives, as computed by one or more of the six measures illustrated in the previous section.

2. The requisite performance of *sensitivity analysis* by determining both of the following factors:

(a) the degree to which the estimated *probabilities* of the various states of the economy would have to change in order for the current "optimal" solution to be no longer optimal;

(b) the extent to which the estimated *returns* associated with the alternatives and the states of the economy would have to change in order for the current optimal solution to no longer be optimal.

3. The need to consider the multiperiod returns on capital projects with their resulting effects on the risk of the project over its life.

4. The need to consider the *utility* that the firm attaches to each of the alternatives based on the firm's goals, risk posture, risk-return preferences, and so on. (Again, the area of utility theory will be discussed momentarily.)

Later chapters will treat each of these four aspects in detail. However, as a preview of the later analysis and in order to illustrate the usefulness of decision trees, we present the following elaborations.

There is a technical difference between the problems handled with tree diagrams and those handled with decision trees. *Tree diagrams* are used to evaluate a *single project* over one or more periods, where returns on the project are based on chance events that can be conditioned on prior outcomes. *Decision trees* are used to select the *best project from among two or more projects* based on chance events.

Using either tree diagrams or decision trees enables the analyst to compute the mean and standard deviation of a project's discounted cash flows with models that have been recommended in the literature.[1] Namely, the expected discounted cash inflow ($\overline{A}$) for a project is determined using Equation (8):

$$\overline{A} = \sum_{s=1}^{M} A_s P_s \tag{8}$$

The standard deviation of the discounted cash inflows is determined using Equation (9):

$$\sigma_A = \sqrt{\sum_{s=1}^{M} \left(A_s - \overline{A} \right)^2 P_s} \tag{9}$$

where A_s = discounted cash inflow associated with series s in the distribution $\sum_{t=1}^{N} A_t^s$
A_t^s = discounted cash inflow which occurs in series s during period t
P_s = joint probability of a single-line series s, which equals:

$$P\{A_1^s\}\left[\prod_{t=2}^{N} P\{A_t^s|A_{t-1}^s\}\right]$$

s = given series in the distribution
t = given period in the life of the project
M = number of line series in the distribution
N = number of periods in the life of the project

It should be noticed that P_s is a joint probability, which is found by multiplying several conditional probabilities for successive chance events. Computation of these parameters is illustrated in Example 4.

□ **EXAMPLE 4**   *Tree Diagram for Three-Period Project*

Consider project P, which has a three-period useful life. The financial analyst feels that a tree diagram and Equations (8) and (9) are the most efficient and accurate ways to evaluate the project.

The possible cash inflows for each period (which are already discounted back to the present) and their associated probabilities are as follows:

[1]See J. F. Magee, "How to Use Decision Trees in Capital Investments," *Harvard Business Review* (September–October 1964), pp. 79–96; and R. D. Hespos and P. A. Strassmann, "Stochastic Decision Trees for the Analysis of Investment Decisions," *Management Science* (August 1965), pp. 244–259.

Period 1 $A_1^s P\{A_1^s\}$	Period 2 $A_2^s P\{A_2^s|A_1^s\}$	Period 3 $A_3^s P\{A_3^s|A_2^s\}$

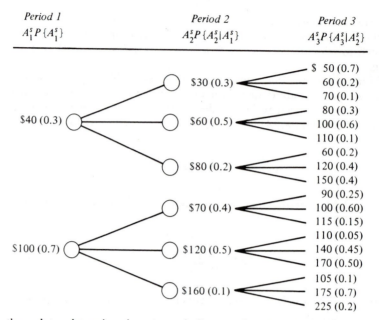

Using these data, determine the expected discounted cash inflow and its standard deviation.

Solution:

Series	Period 1		Period 2		Period 3		$A_s = \sum_{t=1}^{3} A_t^s$	P_s	$(A_s \times P_s)$
	A_1^s	$P\{A_1^s\}$	A_2^s	$P\{A_2^s|A_1^s\}$	A_3^s	$P\{A_3^s|A_2^s\}$			
1	$ 40	0.3	$ 30	0.3	$ 50	0.7	$120	0.063	$ 7.56
2	40	0.3	30	0.3	60	0.2	130	0.018	2.34
3	40	0.3	30	0.3	70	0.1	140	0.009	1.26
4	40	0.3	60	0.5	80	0.3	180	0.045	8.10
5	40	0.3	60	0.5	100	0.6	200	0.090	18.00
6	40	0.3	60	0.5	110	0.1	210	0.015	3.15
7	40	0.3	80	0.2	60	0.2	180	0.012	2.16
8	40	0.3	80	0.2	120	0.4	240	0.024	5.76
9	40	0.3	80	0.2	150	0.4	270	0.024	6.48
10	100	0.7	70	0.4	90	0.25	260	0.070	18.20
11	100	0.7	70	0.4	100	0.60	270	0.168	45.36
12	100	0.7	70	0.4	115	0.15	285	0.042	11.97
13	100	0.7	120	0.5	110	0.05	330	0.0175	5.775
14	100	0.7	120	0.5	140	0.45	360	0.1575	56.70
15	100	0.7	120	0.5	170	0.50	390	0.175	68.25
16	100	0.7	160	0.1	105	0.1	365	0.007	2.555
17	100	0.7	160	0.1	175	0.7	435	0.049	21.315
18	100	0.7	160	0.1	225	0.2	485	0.014	6.79
								1.000	$291.725

$$\bar{A} = \sum_{s=1}^{18} A_s P_s = \$291.725$$

It should be pointed out that in the first table, the A_s column is the sum of the three columns A_1^s, A_2^s, and A_3^s; furthermore, the P_s column is the product of the three probabilities $(P\{A_1^s\})(P\{A_2^s|A_1^s\})(P\{A_3^s|A_2^s\})$ and that the latter two probabilities are conditional on prior period outcomes.

The following table is helpful in computing σ_A:

Series	A_s	$A_s - \bar{A}$	$(A_s - \bar{A})^2$	P_s	$(A_s - \bar{A})^2 P_s$
1	$120	− $171.725	29,489.476	0.063	$1,857.837
2	130	− 161.725	26,154.976	0.018	470.790
3	140	− 151.725	23,030.476	0.009	207.184
4	180	− 111.725	12,482.476	0.045	561.711
5	200	− 91.725	8,413.476	0.090	757.213
6	210	− 81.725	6,678.976	0.015	100.185
7	180	− 111.725	12,482.476	0.012	149.790
8	240	− 51.725	2,675.476	0.024	64.211
9	270	− 21.725	471.976	0.024	11.327
10	260	− 31.725	1,006.476	0.070	70.453
11	270	− 21.725	471.976	0.168	79.292
12	285	− 6.725	45.226	0.042	1.899
13	330	38.275	1,464.976	0.0175	25.637
14	360	68.275	4,661.476	0.1575	734.182
15	390	98.275	9,657.976	0.175	1,690.146
16	365	73.275	5,369.226	0.007	37.585
17	435	143.275	20,527.726	0.049	1,005.859
18	485	193.275	37,355.226	0.014	522.973
				1.000	$8,348.274

Now,

$$\sigma_A = \sqrt{8,348.274}$$
$$= \$91.37$$

Thus, the expected discounted cash inflow for project P is $291.73, and the standard deviation of the cash inflows is $91.37. These values for $\bar{A}$ and σ_A are used to determine if this project is sufficiently attractive to be undertaken by the firm evaluating it.   □

Next, we turn to an introduction to utility theory, which is the premier criterion for decision-making under risk.

UTILITY THEORY

As discussed above, the relaxation of the certainty assumption necessitates consideration of both the expected return and risk criteria for evaluating decision alternatives. However, decision-makers will view varying degrees of risk and return differently, hence will select divergent decision alternatives. Utility theory is an attempt to formalize rational decision-making, wherein preferences among alternatives are specified by a given decision-maker. The utility value attached to various alternatives represents an integration of all aspects relevant to the decision.

In this section we provide an introduction to the theory of utility analysis. Our particular interest lies in its application to the trade-off between risk and return, which is developed further in Chapter 13 in our coverage of certainty equivalents. The treatment of utility theory contained herein is very brief. The reader should refer to Appendix A for a list of additional readings on this subject.

When faced with a decision, the decision maker must consider the following within the framework of personal preferences.

1. The opportunity set of all relevant goals and objectives.

2. The hierarchy of goals and acceptable trade-offs of goals within the hierarchy.

3. The perceptions of risk per se and risk-return preference (i.e., the incremental expected return required to justify acceptance of an additional unit of risk).

4. The preferences for current versus future consumption as affected by present wealth position, liquidity requirements, and so on.

In order to be able to specify and differentiate among various classes of risk preference (or aversion), it is useful to define the decision-maker's utility function with respect to required return and risk. This necessitates acceptance of the *axioms of coherence.*[2]

1. Given any two payoffs (which may involve nonmonetary, as well as monetary values), a decision-maker can specify preference of one over the other or indifference between the two.

2. If a given decision-maker prefers payoff P_1 to P_2 and P_2 to P_3, then necessarily P_1 is preferred to P_3 (*transitivity or consistency of preferences*).

3. If a decision-maker prefers P_1 to P_2 and P_2 to P_3, there is some probabilistic mixture of P_1 and P_3 that is preferred to P_2, some other probabilistic mixture of P_1 and P_3 that is inferior to P_2, and a third probabilistic mixture of P_1 and P_3 that will leave the decision-maker indifferent relative to P_2.

4. If a decision-maker prefers P_1 to P_2 and P_3 is some other payoff, a probabilistic mixture of P_1 and P_3 will be preferred to the same probabilistic mixture of P_2 and P_3.

5. If a decision-maker is indifferent between payoffs P_4 and P_5, they may be substituted for each other in any decision setting.

6. If a decision-maker prefers P_1 to P_2, two probabilistic mixtures of P_1 and P_2 will find the former preferred if and only if the former has a larger proportion of P_1.

If the decision-maker accepts the axioms of coherence, it is reasonable to assume that he or she will act to *maximize utility.* This means selection of those available decision alternatives that will lead to the greatest level of satisfaction. Since preferences are necessarily subjective, the exact specification of a decision-maker's utility function is fraught with operational difficulties. Further, individual utility preferences are likely to change over time. However, we can specify three general categories of decision-makers based on their risk preferences: risk-averse, risk-indifferent, and risk-taking. The utility functions for each category of decision-maker are shown in Figure 12–1.

---

[2]Robert L. Winkler, *Introduction to Bayesian Inference and Decision* (New York: Holt, Rinehart, and Winston, Inc., 1972), pp. 260–264.

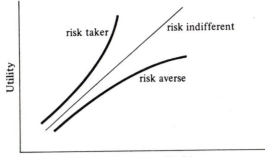

FIGURE 12–1   Relationship Between Income or Wealth and Utility

With respect to risk, decision-makers may be classified as follows:

1. Risk-averse decision-makers have decreasing marginal utilities for increases in wealth. For the risk-averse decision-maker, the chances to enjoy additional wealth are less attractive than the possibility of the pain associated with a decrease in wealth or income.

2. Risk-indifferent decision-makers have constant marginal utilities; hence, their utility curves are linear.

3. Risk-taking decision-makers have increasing marginal utilities for larger potential increases in wealth.

Within each of the three catagories, decision-makers demonstrate varying degrees of preference or aversion to risk. Thus, we can anticipate a different utility function for each individual decision-maker. Further, each decision maker has a whole family of nonintersecting utility curves, showing successively higher levels of satisfaction. To maximize expected utility, the decision-maker will strive to achieve the highest feasible curve within the available alternatives and constraints.

Within the arena of capital investment decision making, experience indicates that the great majority of managers are risk-averters, but again the specific degree of aversion varies over a wide spectrum. Figure 12–2 shows risk-return utility functions (indifference curves) for two managers. Manager A is less risk-averse than manager B. Both managers are willing to accept a 6% risk-free rate of return, but manager B requires increasingly greater returns as risk increases than does manager A. Thus, Figure 12–2 shows the risk-return preferences for two managers at one point in time.

As described above, each manager has a whole set of indifference curves, indicating successively higher levels of satisfaction. Such a family of indifference curves is shown in Figure 12—3. As we move up and to the left, each curve indicates a higher level of satisfaction.

Given the risk-return preferences, we are now in the position to discuss methods used to compensate for risk in the capital investment process. *There are three formal approaches commonly used to incorporate risk into the analysis: the risk-adjusted*

FIGURE 12–2   **Risk-Return Indifference Curves**

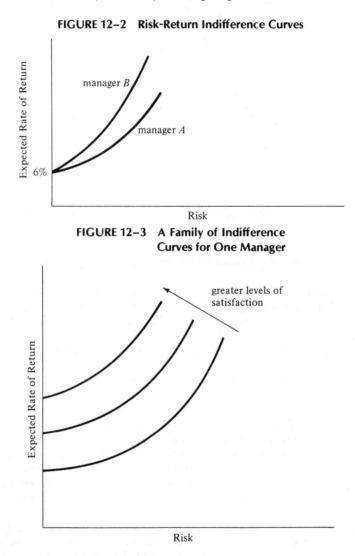

FIGURE 12–3   **A Family of Indifference Curves for One Manager**

discount rate technique, the certainty equivalent method, and the capital asset pricing model. The first two approaches are discussed in the next chapter and the third is treated in Chapter 17.

SUMMARY

This chapter provides an introduction to risk analysis. We first define conditions of certainty, risk, and uncertainty, as well as five major types of risk faced by financial managers. Next, we present several alternative measures that are helpful in quantifying risk. Following this, we illustrate the use of decision trees and tree diagrams in handling conditions of risk. Finally, we introduce the important area of utility theory. Although there are practical problems related to the use of utility theory, it provides a strong conceptual foundation for financial decision making under conditions of risk.

QUESTIONS/PROBLEMS

1. Contrast conditions of *certainty*, *risk*, and *uncertainty*.
2. Discuss the characteristics of the six major measures of risk introduced in this chapter.
3. Discuss the difference between the types of problems handled by decision trees and those handled by tree diagrams.
4. Discuss the strengths and weaknesses of utility theory in decision making under conditions of risk.
5. A petrochemical company had two investment proposals under the following states of the economy: normal, deep recession, mild recession, minor boom, and major boom. The probabilities of various states of the economy are as follows:

	Proposal A		*Proposal B*	
State	*Probability*	*Cash Flow*	*Probability*	*Cash Flow*
Deep recession	0.10	$3,000	0.10	$2,000
Mild recession	0.20	3,500	0.20	3,000
Normal	0.40	4,000	0.40	4,000
Minor boom	0.20	4,500	0.20	5,000
Major boom	0.10	5,000	0.10	6,000

Determine the following.
   (a) Expected return.
   (b) Mean absolute deviation.
   (c) Variance.
   (d) Standard deviation.
   (e) Semivariance.
   (f) Coefficient of variation.
   Interpret the measures.
6. A hospital administrator is faced with the problem of having a limited amount of funds available for capital projects. She has narrowed her choice down to two pieces of X-ray equipment, since the radiology department is the greatest producer of revenue. The first piece of equipment (project A) is a fairly standard piece of equipment that has gained wide acceptance and should provide a steady flow of income. The other piece of equipment (project B), although more risky, may provide a higher return. After deliberation with the radiologist and director of finance, the administrator has developed the following table:

Expected Cash Inflow per Year

Probability	*Project A*	*Probability*	*Project B*
0.6	$2,000	0.2	$4,000
0.3	1,800	0.5	1,200
0.1	1,000	0.3	900

Discovering that the Budget Director of the hospital is taking graduate courses in business, the hospital administrator has asked him to analyze the two projects and make his recommendations. Prepare an analysis that will aid the Budget Director in making his recommendation.

7. The Hatchet Company is evaluating four alternative single-period investment opportunities whose returns are based on the state of the economy. The possible states of the economy and the associated probability distribution is as follows:

State	Fair	Good	Great
Probability	0.2	0.5	0.3

The returns for each investment opportunity and each state of the economy are as follows:

	State of Economy		
Alternative	Fair	Good	Great
W	$1,000	$3,000	$6,000
X	500	4,500	6,800
Y	0	5,000	8,000
Z	− 4,000	6,000	8,500

(a) Using the decision-tree approach, determine the expected return for each alternative.

(b) As a method of performing sensitivity analysis on the decision tree drawn in part (a), it could be determined how much the probabilities of the various states of the economy would have to change in order for the best alternative currently to be replaced by one of the others. For this problem, consider the two alternatives with the highest expected returns (i.e., those ranked 1 and 2 by expected returns). Assume that the probability of a "great" economy will remain constant at 0.3. What would the probability of a "fair" and a "good" economy have to be in order for alternative 2 to become alternative 1?

8. For the three-period project shown below, compute the expected value and the standard deviation for the discounted cash inflow over the project's useful life.

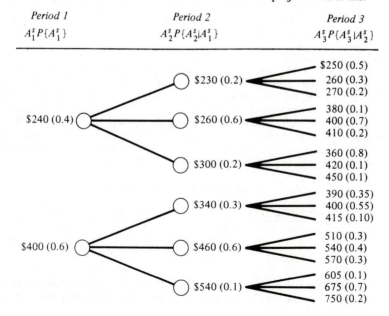

Period 1	Period 2	Period 3
$A_1^s P\{A_1^s\}$	$A_2^s P\{A_2^s|A_1^s\}$	$A_3^s P\{A_3^s|A_2^s\}$

9. The Wee Producem Company is deciding whether to introduce a new product on the market. At the present time they have two decisions to make: the overall decision of whether to introduce the product with additional production costs of $15,000,000 versus dropping the project and simply suffer the loss of the $2,500,000 already invested, or to do further market research at a cost of $1,500,000 and then make the introduction decision (with the same costs as above). Wee Producem estimates that the market research group will assign a probability of 0.7 that the product will be introduced. Because of the unusual nature of the product, only two final outcomes are possible: outcome A derives $40,000,000 profit while outcome B derives a $5,000,000 loss. The present estimated likelihood of outcome A is 0.6 and 0.4 for outcome B.

   Determine the optimal strategy by using a decision tree to compare the expected returns of the different possible strategies.

Project Selection
Under Conditions of Risk

In the previous chapter we provide the basics of measuring risk and decision-making under conditions of risk. We are now prepared to examine the evaluation of capital projects under conditions of risk. We illustrate the use of two models: the certainty equivalent method and the risk adjusted discount approach. As we shall see, each method requires the computation of the expected value and the standard deviation of the distribution that quantifies the returns of the project over its useful life.

CERTAINTY EQUIVALENT METHOD FOR RISK ADJUSTMENT

The certainty equivalent method permits adjustment for risk by incorporating the manager's utility preference for risk versus return directly into the capital investment process. The method is especially useful when management perceives different levels of risk associated with the estimated annual cash flows over the life of a project. Given the limitations of economic forecasting, it is reasonable to assume that the estimates of cash flows during the early periods in a project's life are likely to be more accurate than those corresponding to the latter years. It is just this reasoning that motivates many firms to rely on payback as a surrogate measure of risk to supplement the discounted-cash-flow methods. However, the formal methods discussed in this and the following sections overcome all the drawbacks associated with payback while permitting management to impute its risk preference directly into the capital budgeting decision.

When the certainty equivalent method is used, the estimated annual cash flows (which represent the expected value of a probability distribution of returns) are multiplied by a certainty equivalent coefficient (CEC), designated in equation form as α.

The CEC reflects management's perception of the degree of risk associated with the estimated cash-flow distribution as well as management's degree of aversion to perceived risk, as evidenced by their utility function. The product of the expected cash flow and the CEC represents the amount that management would be willing to accept for certain in each year of the project's life as opposed to accepting the cash-flow distribution and its associated risk. Hence, the name *certainty equivalent method.*

The CEC's range in value from zero to 1. The higher values indicate a lower penalty assigned by management to that cash-flow distribution. A value of 1 indicates that management does not associate any risk with the estimated cash flow and therefore is willing to accept the expected value of the cash-flow estimate as certain. *Since the certainty equivalent method compensates for risk in its entirety, it is therefore appropriate to discount all certainty equivalent adjusted cash flows at the risk-free rate of return as opposed to the firm's cost of capital.* The risk-free rate of return is that return normally associated with the return available from Treasury Bills, since these are short-term and have guaranteed return and principal repayment at maturity. The risk-free rate of return is an accurate representation of the time value of money given that the cash flows are not subject to variability.

In our discussion of the NPV technique, we employed a cost of capital as the discount rate. *The cost of capital reflected the normal risk posture of the firm and included the risk-free rate of return plus additional return requirements to compensate for the business and financial risk as defined above.* Conversely, the certainty equivalent method compensates for business and financial risk with the CEC and then discounts at the risk-free rate.

The certainty equivalent model is defined in Equation (1):

$$\overline{CE} = \sum_{t=0}^{n} \frac{\alpha_t \overline{R}_t}{(1+i)^t} \qquad (1)$$

where $\overline{CE}$ = expected certainty equivalent value over the life of the project
   $\overline{R}_t$ = expected cash flow in period t
   α_t = certainty equivalent factor which converts the expected risky cash flow $\overline{R}_t$ into its perceived certainty equivalent value
   i = risk-free rate which is assumed to remain constant over the life of the project
   n = number of years in the project's life

The value of the certainty equivalent coefficient is one only for risk-free investments, such as Treasury Bills. The values for the certainty equivalent coefficients corresponding to projects falling within the firm's normal risk posture are less than 1.

Note again that the NPV approach lumps together the discounting for time and the adjustment for risk, whereas the certainty equivalent method disaggregates the two by adjusting for risk with the α factor and discounting for the time value of money at the risk-free rate.

In utilizing the certainty equivalent method, it is important to have a valid approach for approximating the certainty equivalent coefficients. One procedure for ascertaining CEC values for different time periods is to undertake a historical review of project performance. Projects are first divided into general categories, such as normal replacement, expansion, and R and D. Then, within each category, on a year-by-year basis, the measures of risk and return are determined. The result is a probability distribution of cash flows by year of project life, from which the coefficient of variation may be obtained. The CEC for each year and each category of project would then be assigned according to the magnitude of the coefficient of variation weighted by managers' preference for risk aversion. An example of the result of dividing projects into categories, determining coefficients of variation based on historical preference, and assigning CEC's is shown in Table 13–1 for a 4-year period based on *the utility preferences for one firm at a point in time.* It should be noted that the logical choice for categories of investments is predicated on the historical values of the coefficient of variation. Thus, in Table 13–1, "Replacement investment—category I" groups all projects of that type that *normally* have a coefficient of variation in year 1 of less than 0.10. However, from year to year over a project's life, it is possible for the project to change categories. That is, its projected CEC is determined based on the expected coefficient of variation for each year of the project's life. Further, the factors are for a point in time given a risk-free rate of return and cost of capital. A change in the risk-free rate, cost of capital, or management's utility preferences will result in a revision of the CEC values. *The results of evaluating a project having the same risk complexion as the firm should be consistent when using either the firm's cost of capital or the risk-free rate with certainty equivalent adjustment.*

The change in a project's expected coefficient of variation from year to year depends on the intertemporal correlation (i.e., the degree of correlation that exists between the annual cash flow distributions over time) of expected cash flows. This leads to multiperiod and portfolio analyses, which are discussed in subsequent chapters. As a final note, the CEC value assigned to year 4 for "Research and development—category II" in our sample firm is zero. This implies that management is completely disregarding the cash flows for year 4,

TABLE 13–1   Certainty Equivalent Factors for Different Investment Groups Developed by XYZ Company

	Coefficient of Variation, v	Certainty Equivalent Coefficient			
		Year 1	*Year 2*	*Year 3*	*Year 4*
Replacement investments—category I	$v \leq 0.10$	0.95	0.92	0.89	0.85
Replacement investments—category II	$0.10 < v \leq 0.25$	0.90	0.86	0.82	0.77
Replacement investments—category III	$v > 0.25$	0.84	0.79	0.74	0.68
New investment—category I	$v \leq 0.10$	0.92	0.88	0.85	0.80
New investment—category II	$0.10 < v \leq 0.25$	0.86	0.82	0.78	0.73
New investment—category III	$v > 0.25$	0.80	0.75	0.70	0.64
Research and development—category I	$v \leq 0.20$	0.82	0.76	0.70	0.60
Research and development—category II	$v > 0.20$	0.70	0.60	0.50	0

and the analysis thereby approaches the payback method, wherein *all* cash flows are ignored after a stated period.

The procedure for using certainty equivalent coefficients is demonstrated in Example 1.

□ **EXAMPLE 1**   *Certainty Equivalent Method*

XYZ Company, which developed the CEC values shown in Table 13–1, is evaluating a *new investment* project with expected returns and standard deviations during its 4-year life as follows:

Year	Expected Return	Standard Deviation	Coefficient of Variation
1	$1,000	$200	0.20
2	1,200	216	0.18
3	1,200	168	0.14
4	1,800	144	0.08

The cash outflow is $3,000 and the risk-free rate of return is 6%. Find the certainty equivalent factors corresponding to the coefficient of variation listed above (see Table 13–1). Then, determine the expected certainty equivalent value, $\overline{CE}$.

Solution: The following table is helpful in computing $\overline{CE}$:

Time	$\overline{R}_t$	α_t	$\alpha_t \overline{R}_t$	Discount Factor at 6%	Discounted $\alpha_t \overline{R}_t$
Present	− $3,000	1.00	− $3,000	1.000	− $3,000
1	+ 1,000	0.86	860	0.943	811
2	+ 1,200	0.82	984	0.890	876
3	+ 1,200	0.78	936	0.840	786
4	+ 1,800	0.80	1,440	0.792	1,140
					$\overline{CE} = \$613$

The meaning of $\overline{CE}$ is discussed below.   □

The certainty equivalent value is analogous to the net present value in that the decision rule for both methods is to reject projects that have negative $\overline{CE}$'s or NPV's. In Example 1, since the project in question had a positive $\overline{CE}$ (i.e., $613), it represents a candidate for acceptance. However, further analysis is required.

In our earlier discussions, we pointed out that to maximize shareholders' wealth, the set of projects that maximized NPV should be accepted. If we limit our examination of certainty equivalents to $\overline{CE}$, we should select that set of projects having the largest total $\overline{CE}$. However, another powerful evaluation tool is available to us: *We may ascertain the probability distribution for the certainty equivalent of each project and then develop acceptance criteria in keeping with both risk aversion and maximization of shareholders' wealth.* For example, we might select a decision rule requiring rejection of any project that has a probability less than 90% of achieving a positive CE value. Then, from the remaining group, select the set of projects having the largest total $\overline{CE}$. We treat the probability distribution of certainty equivalents later in the chapter.

Thus far in our discussion, we have assumed that the risk-free rate remains constant over time. If this assumption is relaxed, Equation (1) may be rewritten in its more general form as Equation (2).

$$\overline{CE} = \sum_{t=0}^{n} \frac{\alpha_t \overline{R}_t}{\prod_{k=1}^{t} (1 + i_k)} \tag{2}$$

where i_k = risk-free rate in year k
$\prod$ = the product operator

The application of Equation (2) is demonstrated in Example 2.

□ **EXAMPLE 2**   *Certainty Equivalent Value for a Change in Risk-Free Rates*

Suppose that the estimated cash flows for a project, the risk-free rates of return, and the certainty equivalent coefficients are as follows:

Time	α_t	$\overline{R}_t$	Risk-Free Return
Present	1	− $3,000	—
1	0.95	1,000	0.05
2	0.92	1,500	0.06
3	0.89	1,700	0.07

Determine $\overline{CE}$.

Solution:

$$\overline{CE} = -\$3,000 + \frac{0.95(\$1,000)}{1 + 0.05} + \frac{0.92(\$1,500)}{(1 + 0.05)(1 + 0.06)}$$

$$+ \frac{0.89(\$1,700)}{(1 + 0.05)(1 + 0.06)(1 + 0.07)}$$

$$= -\$3,000 + \$905 + \$1,240 + \$1,270$$

$$= \$415 \qquad\qquad □$$

RISK-ADJUSTED DISCOUNT RATE

The rationale underlying the use of the risk-adjusted discount rate (RADR) technique is that projects which have greater variability in the probability distributions of their returns should have these returns discounted at a higher rate than projects having less variability or risk. A project that had no risk associated with it would be discounted at the risk-free rate, since this is the appropriate rate just to account for the time value of money. Any project that has risk associated with it has to be discounted at a rate in excess of the risk-free rate in order to discount both for futurity (the time value of money) and for the risk associated with the project (a risk premium). Projects that are of average riskiness vis-à-vis the firm's normal operations should be discounted at the firm's cost of capital, since this figure reflects the normal risk faced by the firm. Those projects having greater-than-normal risk should be discounted at a rate in excess of the cost of capital; conversely, projects that exhibit less risk than that associated with a firm's normal operations should be discounted at a rate between the risk-free rate and the cost of capital. The risk-adjusted rate is found by Equation (3):

$$r' = i + u + a \tag{3}$$

where r' = risk-adjusted discount rate
i = risk-free rate
u = adjustment for the firm's normal risk
a = adjustment for above (or below) the firm's normal risk

It should be noted that the sum of i and u is the firm's cost of capital, since that discount rate is appropriate for projects having average, or "normal," risk. Notice that the term for the abnormal risk adjustment could either be positive or negative, based on whether the project has more or less risk associated with it than the average project for the firm in question.

Equation (4) may be used to determine the expected present value when employing a risk-adjusted discount rate:

$$\overline{\text{RAR}} = \sum_{t=0}^{n} \frac{\overline{R}_t}{(1 + r')^t} \tag{4}$$

where $\overline{\text{RAR}}$ = expected value of the distribution of discounted cash flows over the life of the project (risk-adjusted net present value)
$\overline{R}_t$ = expected value of the distribution of cash flows in year t
r' = risk-adjusted discount rate based on the perceived riskiness of the project under consideration
n = number of years in the project's life

The amount of risk adjustment is based on management's utility preference for risk aversion, so that this adjustment reflects the management's perception of the risk associated with the project per se, its risk-return preferences, the firm's wealth position, and the impact of the project on the firm's other goals. Table 13–2 provides risk adjustments for the categories of investments defined in Table 13–1, reflecting the utility preferences for a particular firm (XYZ Company) at a particular time. Although all the project types shown in Table 13–2 are generally required to achieve the firm's cost of capital as a minimum return, there may be some categories of projects that have a risk sufficiently low to warrant their implementation, even though their projected return is below the firm's cost of capital.

Reference to Table 13–2 indicates that estimating a risk-free rate of 10% would apply a 16% hurdle rate to a project falling into "Replacement investment—category III." *It should also be noted that unlike the certainty equivalent method,*

**TABLE 13-2   Return Requirements for Various
Investment Groups Developed by XYZ Company**

Investment Grouping	*Required Return*
Replacement investments— category I	Risk-free rate plus 2%
Replacement investments— category II	Risk-free rate plus 4%
Replacement investments— category III	Risk-free rate plus 6%
New investment— category I	Risk-free rate plus 8%
New investment— category II	Risk-free rate plus 10%
New investment— category III	Risk-free rate plus 15%
Research and development— category I	Risk-free rate plus 10%
Research and development— category II	Risk-free rate plus 20%

*the RADR technique as it is generally used in practice applies the same discount rate to the
project throughout its useful life.*

The application of Equation (4) is demonstrated in Example 3.

□ **EXAMPLE 3**   *Calculation of* $\overline{RAR}$

A firm is considering the adoption of a "Replacement investment—category II"
project which has the cash flows as shown by the following distributions:

Original Cost		Cash Inflows Years 1–5		Years 6–10	
Probability	*Amount*	*Probability*	*Amount*	*Probability*	*Amount*
0.3	$13,000	0.2	$2,000	0.2	$2,600
0.4	14,000	0.4	2,400	0.6	3,200
0.3	15,000	0.3	2,800	0.1	3,400
		0.1	3,400	0.1	3,600

The risk-free rate is 10%. Determine the risk-adjusted net present value.

Solution: First, determine the mean value for each cash flow and incorporate into
Equation (4) as follows:

$$\overline{RAR} = -\$14,000 + \sum_{t=1}^{5} \frac{\$2,540}{(1.14)^t} + \sum_{t=6}^{10} \frac{\$3,140}{(1.14)^t}$$

$$= -\$14,000 + \$8,720 + \$5,599$$

$$= \$319$$

Since the $\overline{RAR}$ is positive, this project represents a candidate for acceptance.   □

In addition to the expected value of the return, we may also examine the probability distribution in a manner similar to that discussed above for the certainty equivalent method. This task will be addressed later in this chapter.

The following section compares the certainty equivalent and risk-adjusted methods and describes some conflicts that may arise when using the two methods.

COMPARING CERTAINTY EQUIVALENT AND ADJUSTMENT OF THE DISCOUNT RATE

Risk adjustment using the risk-adjusted discount rate method has been criticized primarily for two reasons.

1. The method does not examine the riskiness associated with each project or the changes in riskiness over its life, but rather groups projects into general risk categories. It applies the same discount-rate risk premium over the entire life of the project. Certainty equivalent requires individual examination of projects in each time period since riskiness associated with a given project may change over its life. In fact, investment uncertainty may be concentrated in only a few years of the project's life, and once this uncertainty is resolved, all future years have a much more moderate risk posture.

2. Risk adjustment combines the two parts of the discounting process: the risk-free return for time and the risk premium. The use of a high constant discount rate over a project's entire useful life implies that its riskiness is increasing over time. The implication results from the fact that discounting equates to an exponential decay of the value of cash as a function of time. The difference between the present value of cash flows discounted at the risk-free rate and the present value of those same cash flows when discounted at a risk-adjusted hurdle rate increases exponentially with the passage of time. The process is illustrated in Example 4.

☐ **EXAMPLE 4** *Risk-Adjusted Discount Rate and Certainty Equivalent*
A project costing $10,000 has a 12-year life and expected cash inflows of $1,800 each year. The risk-free rate of return is 7%, the firm's cost of capital is 10%, and the hurdle rate to be applied for this project is 15%. (The project is a "New investment—category I," as previously defined in Tables 13–1 and 13–2.) Management anticipates that the dispersion of earnings after the fifth year will be relatively constant given that all start-up problems will be resolved by that time. Therefore, they will apply the CEC's from Table 13–1 for the first four periods and 0.75 thereafter. Determine the project's NPV using the risk-adjusted discount rate and the certainty equivalent, and compare the two.

Solution: First consider the risk-adjusted discount method.

Time	$\overline{R}_t$	Discount Factor at 15%	Present Values
Present	−$10,000	1	−$10,000
1–12	1,800	5.420619	9,757
		RAR =	−$ 243

Next consider the certainty equivalent method.

Time	$\overline{R}$	α_t	$\alpha_t \overline{R}_t$	Discount Factor at 7%	Discounted $\alpha_t \overline{R}_t$
Present	−$10,000	1	−$10,000	1	−$10,000
1	1,800	0.92	1,656	0.934579	1,548
2	1,800	0.88	1,584	0.873439	1,384
3	1,800	0.85	1,530	0.816298	1,249
4	1,800	0.80	1,440	0.762895	1,099
5–12	1,800	0.75	1,350	4.555475	6,150
					$\overline{CE}$=$ 1,430

The two solutions demonstrate the contrasting results of using the two methods. The project would be rejected using the risk-adjusted method, but accepted using certainty equivalent. The difference can be highlighted by looking at the table below, which compares the discounted cash flows using the certainty equivalent method, the risk-adjusted discount rate (15%), and the cost of capital (10%).

Year	(1) Discounted $\alpha_t \overline{R}_t$	(2) $\overline{R}_t$ Discounted at 15%	(3) $\overline{R}_t$ Discounted at 10%
Present	−$10,000	−$10,000	−$10,000
1	1,548	1,565	1,636
2	1,384	1,361	1,488
3	1,249	1,184	1,352
4	1,099	1,029	1,229
5	963	895	1,118
6	900	778	1,016
7	841	677	924
8	786	588	840
9	734	512	763
10	686	445	694
11	641	387	631
12	599	336	574
	$\overline{CE}$=$1,430	$\overline{RAR}$= −$ 243	NPV =$2,265

The table shows the value of the cash flows using each of the three approaches. If the certainty equivalent factors are an accurate risk adjustment for this project, it can be seen that the use of a constant risk-adjusted rate of 15% overcompensates for the risk of the project in every year except the first (since the present value using a discount rate of 15% is less than the present values of the $\alpha_t \overline{R}_t$ values). Notice that the difference between these present values is as small as $23 in year 2 and as large as $263 in year 12. It should be stressed that RAR method, with a constant discount rate, assumes that the risk of the project grows over time; in fact, that it grows at an exponential rate over time, owing to the compounding process associated with the discount factors (since the discount factors are the reciprocals of compound interest factors). However, if the certainty equivalent factors are an accurate risk adjustment for this project, then risk is constant in years 5–12 (evidenced by the constant α_t factor of 0.75) rather than growing exponentially, as implicitly assumed by the RAR method. Finally, it should be noted by comparing columns (1) and (3) that for the first 10 years of the project's life, the project is more risky than the firm in general (since the present values using the cost of capital are higher than the discounted $\alpha_t \bar{R}_t$ values), but for the last 2 years the project is less rrisky than the firm overall (since in years 11 and 12 the discounted $\alpha_t \bar{R}_t$ values are higher than the present values using the cost capital). However, considering the entire life of the project, it is more risky than the firm overall, since $\overline{CE}$ is less than the NPV value found using the appropriate discount rate for projects of average riskiness to the firm (i.e., the 10% cost of capital). □

The concepts of correlation and covariance are used in the next section, as well as in the next two chapters. As will be seen, the variance of any portfolio or sum of random variables is dependent upon the covariance of all possible pairs of the components. The covariance, in turn, is a function of the correlation coefficient, which expresses the nature and strength of the relationship between components.

VARIABILITY IN THE RISK-ADJUSTED DISCOUNT RATE AND CERTAINTY EQUIVALENT PROBABILITY DISTRIBUTIONS

In previous sections we discuss the necessity for expressing cash inflows as probability distributions having both a mean and a standard deviation. Because each year's cash inflow is known only by means of a probability distribution, the composite picture of a project's attractiveness over its entire life will also be described by a probability distribution having these two statistics: a mean, $\overline{RAR}$ or $\overline{CE}$, and a standard deviation, σ_{RAR} or σ_{CE}. We have shown how the expected RAR and CE values are determined. It remains for us to show how the standard deviation is arrived at and how this measure is used to assess the project's attractiveness.

The standard deviation of the RAR or the CE distribution uses as data inputs the standard deviations of each year's cash-inflow distribution *and* the degree of correlation between the cash-flow distributions over the life of the project. This latter aspect (i.e., the intertemporal correlations between cash-flow distributions) plays an important part in determining the magnitude of σ_{RAR} and σ_{CE}, since the interrelationships can either intensify or reduce risk.

To begin our discussion of how to find σ_{RAR} or σ_{CE}, consider the general formula for finding the variance of the sum of three random variables $(\tilde{X}, \tilde{Y}, \tilde{Z})$, where each is multiplied by a constant $(a, b,$ and c, respectively).

$$\text{Var}(a\tilde{X} + b\tilde{Y} + c\tilde{Z}) = a^2\sigma_{\tilde{X}}^2 + b^2\sigma_{\tilde{Y}}^2 + c^2\sigma_{\tilde{Z}}^2$$
$$+ 2ab\rho_{\tilde{X},\tilde{Y}}\sigma_{\tilde{X}}\sigma_{\tilde{Y}} + 2ac\rho_{\tilde{X},\tilde{Z}}\sigma_{\tilde{X}}\sigma_{\tilde{Z}}$$
$$+ 2bc\rho_{\tilde{Y},\tilde{Z}}\sigma_{\tilde{Y}}\sigma_{\tilde{Z}} \qquad (5)$$

where $\sigma_{\tilde{X}}^2$ and $\sigma_{\tilde{X}}$ = the variance and the standard deviation of the random variable $\tilde{X}$, respectively

$\rho_{\tilde{X},\tilde{Y}}$ = correlation coefficient between the random variables $\tilde{X}$ and $\tilde{Y}$

Notice that the first three terms show the contribution of the three variances, and the last three terms show the contribution of the covariances between all pairs of the three random variables.

To derive the expressions for σ_{RAR} and σ_{CE}, consider that Equation (5) refers to a capital investment project that has a 3-year useful life. Thus, the random variables $\tilde{X}$, $\tilde{Y}$, and $\tilde{Z}$ are the cash-inflow distributions of years 1, 2, and 3, respectively; similarly, the constants a, b, and c refer to the discount factors in years 1, 2, and 3, which reflect the time value of money for a given risk-free rate. [These discount factors are, of course,

$$\frac{1}{1+i}, \quad \frac{1}{\left(1+i\right)^2}, \quad \text{and} \quad \frac{1}{\left(1+i\right)^3}$$

respectively, for the risk-free rate i.] At this point we consider only two types of cash-flow interdependencies: case I, independent cash flows; and case II, perfectly correlated cash flows.

Case I: Independent Cash Flows

Under this assumption, the cash flows over the life of the project are independent, meaning that successive years' cash flows are not related in any systematic way (i.e., there is a random relationship among cash flows). This condition probably occurs in highly competitive markets devoid of trade names, advertising, and so on, where exogenous forces shape the market demand. Thus, variability in cash flows over the life of the project will be reduced, owing to a canceling out of the cash flows above and below the expected values. If independence is assumed, the correlation ρ_{xy} for all pairs of years in Equation (5) are equal to zero. Hence, the last three covariance terms will drop out and we have

$$\mathrm{Var}\left(a\tilde{X} + b\tilde{Y} + c\tilde{Z} \right) = a^2\sigma_{\tilde{X}}^2 + b^2\sigma_{\tilde{Y}}^2 + c^2\sigma_{\tilde{Z}}^2$$

Recall that $\tilde{X}$, $\tilde{Y}$, and $\tilde{Z}$ refer to the cash-inflow distributions of years 1, 2, and 3 of a project and that a, b, and c are the discount factors in those three respective years. Hence, calling $\mathrm{Var}(a\tilde{X} + b\tilde{Y} + c\tilde{Z})$, σ_{RAR}^2 or σ_{CE}^2, we arrive at the desired general expression for case I:

$$\sigma_{RAR}^2 \quad \text{or} \quad \sigma_{CE}^2 = \sum_{t=0}^{n} \frac{\sigma_t^2}{\left(1+i\right)^{2t}} \tag{6}$$

It should be noted that the discount factor is raised to the $2t$ power because of the fact that the values of a, b, and c, which equaled the discount factors

$$\frac{1}{1+i}, \quad \frac{1}{\left(1+i\right)^2}, \quad \text{or} \quad \frac{1}{\left(1+i\right)^3}$$

were all squared in Equation (5); hence, each factor is raised to the $2t$ power. Of course, if the standard deviation σ_{RAR} or σ_{CE} is desired, we simply take the square root of Equation (6).

Case II: Perfectly Correlated Cash Flows

Under the assumption that cash flows are perfectly correlated, we are positing that given the outcome of year 1's cash inflow, all subsequent cash inflows are predetermined, since they will be as many standard deviations above or below their respective means as year 1's cash inflow was. Such a relationship among cash inflows would exist in monopolistically competitive markets, replete with brand names, high-pressure advertising, limited entry, and so on. The variability here will be greater than that found in case I. This is due to the risk-intensification tendencies of positive correlation, which results from the lack of counteracting variations above and below the means over the life of the project found in the independent cash-flow case.

If perfect correlation is assumed, the correlation coefficients $\rho_{\tilde{X}\tilde{Y}}$ for all pairs of years in Equation (5) are equal to $+1$. Hence, Equation (5) becomes

$$\mathrm{Var}(a\tilde{X} + b\tilde{Y} + c\tilde{Z}) = a^2\sigma_{\tilde{X}}^2 + b^2\sigma_{\tilde{Y}}^2 + c^2\sigma_{\tilde{Z}}^2$$
$$+ 2ab\sigma_{\tilde{X}}\sigma_{\tilde{Y}} + 2ac\sigma_{\tilde{X}}\sigma_{\tilde{Z}}$$
$$+ 2bc\sigma_{\tilde{Y}}\sigma_{\tilde{Z}}$$

where the right side can be factored as follows:

$$\mathrm{Var}(a\tilde{X} + b\tilde{Y} + c\tilde{Z}) = (a\sigma_{\tilde{X}} + b\sigma_{\tilde{Y}} + c\sigma_{\tilde{Z}})^2$$

Hence, again calling the left-hand side of this expression σ_{RAR}^2 or σ_{CE}^2 and substituting the usual values for the constants and standard deviations, we arrive at

$$\sigma_{\mathrm{RAR}}^2 \quad \text{or} \quad \sigma_{\mathrm{CE}}^2 = \left[\frac{\sigma_1}{1+i} + \frac{\sigma_2}{(1+i)^2} + \frac{\sigma_3}{(1+i)^3} \right]^2$$

For the general project with a useful life of n years, the expression above would become

$$\sigma_{\mathrm{RAR}}^2 \quad \text{or} \quad \sigma_{\mathrm{CE}}^2 = \left[\sum_{t=0}^{n} \frac{\sigma_t}{(1+i)^t} \right]^2 \tag{7}$$

The use of the two formulas for σ_{CE}^2 (i.e., both for independent cash flows and for perfectly correlated cash flows) is illustrated in Example 5.

□ **EXAMPLE 5** *Variance for Perfectly Correlated and*
Independent Cash Flows

Consider project Alpha, which has an original cost of $200, a 3-year useful life, and cash-inflow distributions as follows:

	Period 1		Period 2		Period 3	
Outcome	R_{A1}	P_{A1}	R_{A2}	P_{A2}	R_{A3}	P_{A3}
1	$100	0.10	$ 40	0.10	$ 10	0.10
2	120	0.20	80	0.25	60	0.30
3	140	0.40	120	0.30	100	0.30
4	160	0.20	160	0.25	160	0.20
5	180	0.10	200	0.10	270	0.10

The risk-free rate is 6%.

Compute σ_{CE}^2 under the assumption that (a) cash inflows are independent over Alpha's useful life; and (b) cash inflows are perfectly correlated over Alpha's useful life.

Solution: Computing the standard deviations for each of the 3 years above, we would find:

$$\sigma_1 = 21.91, \qquad \sigma_2 = 45.61, \qquad \sigma_3 = 69.54$$

These three standard deviations are now used to compute σ_{CE}^2.

(a) Assuming independent cash inflows,

$$\sigma_{CE}^2 = \sum_{t=0}^{n} \frac{\sigma_t^2}{(1+i)^{2t}}$$

$$= \frac{(21.91)^2}{(1.06)^2} + \frac{(45.61)^2}{(1.06)^4} + \frac{(69.54)^2}{(1.06)^6}$$

$$= \underline{\underline{5,484.07}}$$

or

$$\sigma_{CE} = \underline{\underline{\$74.05}}$$

(b) Assuming perfectly correlated cash inflows,

$$\sigma_{CE}^2 = \left[\sum_{t=0}^{n} \frac{\sigma_t}{(1+i)^t} \right]^2$$

$$= \left[\frac{21.91}{1.06} + \frac{45.61}{(1.06)^2} + \frac{69.54}{(1.06)^3} \right]^2$$

$$= (20.67 + 40.59 + 58.39)^2$$

$$= (119.65)^2 = \underline{\underline{14,316.1225}}$$

or

$$\sigma_{CE} = \underline{\underline{\$119.65}}$$

Of course, it can be seen that σ_{CE} assuming perfectly correlated cash inflows is significantly greater than σ_{CE} where cash inflows are assumed to be independent. This is due to the risk-intensifying result produced by high positive correlation among the cash flows over the life of the project rather than the canceling-out effect of independent (zero-correlation) cash inflows over the project's life. □

The natural reactions of the financial manager to the computation of σ_{CE} under various assumptions might be:

1. How can the degree of intertemporal correlation among the cash flows be accurately determined?

2. How can σ_{CE} be used to help evaluate capital projects?

These questions will be examined in turn.

We admit that the degree of intertemporal correlation among the cash-inflow distributions over the life of the project is indeed difficult to estimate. However, some comfort can be taken in the fact that σ_{CE} *will take on its maximum value when perfect correlation exists among cash-inflow distributions. Further, a somewhat moderate value of σ_{CE} is arrived at when it is assumed that cash inflows are independent. It should be noted that σ_{CE} would get smaller as the degree of correlation were allowed to take on negative values and that σ_{CE} would equal zero if it were assumed that the cash inflows were perfectly negatively correlated over the life of the project.* Hence, it is suggested that σ_{CE} be used to evaluate capital projects along the lines of sensitivity analysis, following three steps:

1. σ_{CE} should be computed under the two assumptions of independence and perfect correlation, as demonstrated in the Example 5.
2. The risk-return characteristics of the project should be evaluated under the extreme assumption of perfect correlation and the more moderate assumption of independence.
3. The firm, based on its utility curve and its best estimate of the intertemporal correlation, should either reject the proposal or let it stand as a candidate for possible adoption.

The latter two steps in the approach above point to the answer to the second question posed: How can σ_{CE} be used to help evaluate capital projects? The argument would proceed as follows: If it can be reasonably assumed that each year's cash-inflow distribution is normal or approximately normal, the central limit theorem would tell us that the certainty equivalent distribution will be normal or approximately normal with mean $\overline{CE}$ and standard deviation σ_{CE}. The latter distribution can then be used to make probability statements about the certainty equivalent value, taking on any value of interest using the familiar standardized Z-value and tables of the normal distribution (see Appendix C): $Z = (X - \overline{X})/\sigma$. Such probability values are helpful for the firm to evaluate a single project in isolation or to compare several projects. The ultimate decision about project acceptance is determined by the firm's utility function ranking of the project attractiveness based on the relevant risk-return information given above. An illustration of this situation follows.

□ **EXAMPLE 6**   *Comparison of Two Projects Using the Certainty Equivalent Method*

The firm in Example 5 is also evaluating project Delta, which costs $300 and whose cash-inflow distributions are as follows:

Outcome	Period 1		Period 2		Period 3	
	R_{D1}	P_{D1}	R_{D2}	P_{D2}	R_{D3}	P_{D3}
1	$ 80	0.10	$ 80	0.05	$ 80	0.01
2	100	0.20	100	0.10	100	0.04
3	120	0.40	120	0.15	120	0.10
4	140	0.20	140	0.60	140	0.70
5	160	0.10	160	0.10	160	0.15

The firm assigns the following certainty equivalent factors for the two projects based on their variability in cash flows over their useful lives:

Project Alpha	Project Delta
$\alpha_1 = 0.92$	$\alpha_1 = 0.95$
$\alpha_2 = 0.80$	$\alpha_2 = 0.92$
$\alpha_3 = 0.65$	$\alpha_3 = 0.90$

(a) Compute $\overline{CE}$ for both projects.

(b) Compute σ_{CE} for project Delta based on the following assumptions:
   (1) Cash inflows are independent.
   (2) Cash inflows are perfectly correlated.

(c) Compute and explain the coefficient of variation for the certainty equivalent distributions for both projects under both correlation assumptions.

(d) Compute the probability that both projects will have positive certainty equivalent values, where σ_{CE} is computed under both assumptions of independence and perfect correlation, where the CE distributions are normal.

Solution: (a) To compute $\overline{CE}$ for each project, we need the expected cash inflow for each of the 3 years.

Project Alpha:

$$\overline{R}_1 = \$100(0.1) + \$120(0.2) + \$140(0.4) + \$160(0.2) + \$180(0.1) = \underline{\underline{\$140}}$$

$$\overline{R}_2 = \$40(0.1) + \$80(0.25) + \$120(0.3) + \$160(0.25) + \$200(0.1) = \underline{\underline{\$120}}$$

$$\overline{R}_3 = \$10(0.1) + \$60(0.3) + \$100(0.3) + \$160(0.2) + \$270(0.1) = \underline{\underline{\$108}}$$

Now, to determine $\overline{CE}$, we multiply the expected cash inflows by their respective certainty equivalent factors and discount at the risk-free rate. Finally, the original cost of projects A and D of \$200 and \$300, respectively, were substituted.

$$\overline{CE}_A = \frac{(0.92)(\$140)}{1.06} + \frac{(0.80)(\$120)}{(1.06)^2} + \frac{(0.65)(\$108)}{(1.06)^3} - \$200$$

$$= \$265.89 - \$200.00 = \underline{\underline{\$65.89}}$$

Project Delta:

$$\overline{R}_1 = \$80(0.1) + \$100(0.2) + \$120(0.4) + \$140(0.2) + \$160(0.1) = \underline{\underline{\$120}}$$

$$\overline{R}_2 = \$80(0.05) + \$100(0.1) + \$120(0.15) + \$140(0.6) + \$160(0.1) = \underline{\underline{\$132}}$$

$$\overline{R}_3 = \$80(0.01) + \$100(0.04) + \$120(0.10) + \$140(0.7) + \$160(0.15) = \underline{\underline{\$138.80}}$$

$$\overline{CE}_D = \frac{(0.95)(\$120)}{1.06} + \frac{(0.92)(\$132)}{(1.06)^2} + \frac{(0.90)(\$138.80)}{(1.06)^3} - \$300$$

$$= \$107.55 + \$108.08 + \$104.89 - \$300 = \underline{\underline{\$20.52}}$$

(b) Computing σ_{CE} for project Delta:

(1) For independent cash flows:

$$\sigma_1 = 21.90, \qquad \sigma_2 = 19.39, \qquad \sigma_3 = 14.09$$

The reader should verify these values.

$$\sigma_{CE}^2 = \frac{(21.90)^2}{(1.06)^2} + \frac{(19.39)^2}{(1.06)^4} + \frac{(14.09)^2}{(1.06)^6}$$

$$= 864.61$$

or

$$\sigma_{CE} = \$29.40$$

(2) For perfectly correlated cash flows:

$$\sigma_{CE}^2 = \left[\frac{21.90}{(1.06)^1} + \frac{19.39}{(1.06)^2} + \frac{14.09}{(1.06)^3} \right]^2$$

$$= (20.66 + 17.26 + 11.83)^2$$

$$= 2475.06$$

or

$$\sigma_{CE} = \$49.75$$

(c) The coefficient of variation can now be computed for the two projects, which is a relevant method of comparison because of the size disparity between the two projects:
(1) For independent cash flows:

Project Alpha	*Project Delta*
$\nu = \dfrac{\sigma_{CE}}{CE}$	$\nu = \dfrac{\sigma_{CE}}{CE}$
$= \dfrac{\$74.05}{\$65.89}$	$= \dfrac{\$29.40}{\$20.52}$
$= 1.12$	$= 1.43$

This means that for project Alpha there is 1.12 times as much risk as there is expected return, *or* that for every dollar of expected return there is $1.12 of risk, as measured by the standard deviation. For project Delta, the standard deviation is 143% of the expected certainty equivalent return, *or* there is $1.43 of risk for each dollar of expected return. Further, because the two coefficients of variation can be directly compared, project Delta has about 1.3 times as much risk per dollar of expected return as project Alpha.
(2) For perfectly correlated cash flows:

Project Alpha	*Project Delta*
$\nu = \dfrac{\sigma_{CE}}{CE}$	$\nu = \dfrac{\sigma_{CE}}{CE}$
$= \dfrac{\$119.65}{\$65.89}$	$= \dfrac{\$49.75}{\$20.52}$
$= 1.82$	$= 2.42$

Similar interpretations can be attached to these values, as was given above. Notice that the relative variability of the two projects has increased proportionately compared with independent cash flows; project Delta's coefficient of variation is still about 1.3 times as great as project Alpha's.

(d) Finally, the probability that each project achieves a positive certainty equivalent factor is determined as follows:

(1) For independent cash flows:

Project Alpha:

$$Z = \frac{0 - \$65.89}{\$74.05} = -0.89 \Rightarrow 0.3133$$

This means that 31.33% of the area under the curve falls between a CE-value of 0 and $\overline{CE} = 65.89$. Thus, the probability that project Alpha achieves a positive certainty equivalent value is 0.8133 (0.5000 + 0.3133). It should be noted that the above probability exceeded 0.5000 because $\overline{CE}$ was positive; if $\overline{CE}$ was negative, the probability that the CE value would take on a value greater than zero would be less than 0.5000 and is quantified by the area in the upper tail of the distribution.

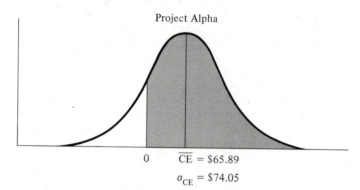

Project Alpha

$$\overline{CE} = \$65.89$$
$$\sigma_{CE} = \$74.05$$

Project Delta:

$$Z = \frac{0 - \$20.52}{\$29.40} = -0.698 \Rightarrow 0.2574$$

Thus, the probability that project Delta achieves a positive CE-value is 0.7574. Project Delta has almost a 75% chance of achieving a positive CE value, whereas project Alpha has about an 80% chance of doing this *under the assumption that cash flows of the two projects are independent over time.*

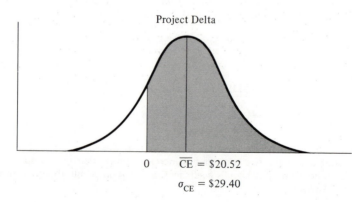

Project Delta

$$\overline{CE} = \$20.52$$
$$\sigma_{CE} = \$29.40$$

(2) For perfectly correlated cash flows:
Project Alpha:

$$Z = \frac{0 - \$65.89}{\$119.65} = -0.551 \Rightarrow 0.2092$$

$$P\{CE \geq 0 \text{ for project Alpha}\} = \underline{\underline{0.7092}}$$

Project Delta:

$$Z = \frac{0 - \$20.52}{\$49.75} = -0.412 \Rightarrow 0.1598$$

$$P\{CE \geq 0 \text{ for project Delta}\} = \underline{\underline{0.6598}}$$

Under the assumption of perfectly correlated cash flows, the probability of the two projects achieving positive CE-values is rather close: 0.7092 for Alpha versus 0.6598 for Delta. Which of these two projects (if either) would meet the firm's criteria for acceptance and what ranking would be assigned to each depends upon the firm's utility function, which quantifies its hierarchy of goals, risk preferences, and attitudes toward risk-return trade-offs. Neither project dominates the other by simultaneously offering a higher expected CE value and a lower σ_{CE}. The measures computed in part (c) of this example plus the probabilities computed in part (d) under the two intertemporal correlation assumptions provide data inputs that help the financial manager rank the two projects and decide which, if either, should be accepted. The ultimate decision depends upon the firm's utility function. □

SUMMARY

This chapter discusses the important area of risk analysis in capital budgeting. When the certainty assumption is relaxed, the need arises to examine both a measure of central tendency (i.e., expected return) and a measure of the variability in the distribution of returns (e.g., the standard deviation, coefficient of variation, etc.) Further, because of the importance of other goals, trade-offs between them, and risk preferences of decision makers, the "maximize expected utility criterion" is suggested as being appropriate for decision making under conditions of risk.

The two conventional models to evaluate single projects under conditions of risk—the risk-adjusted discount rate technique and the certainty equivalent method—are introduced and examined in some depth. Both the expected values for these two models and their standard deviations (computed under different assumptions about intertemporal correlations among cash-inflow distributions) are computed. Finally, under the assumption that the component cash-flow distributions are normal, it is demonstrated how probability statements can be made concerning the likelihood that various values are taken on by the random variable measuring certainty equivalent values.

This chapter concentrates on the evaluation of a single project. Chapter 14 looks at the area of portfolio effects wherein the risk of a combination of projects can be reduced by careful selection to minimize the covariance among all pairs of projects. After that, capital asset pricing theory is examined as a way of integrating this chapter and the following one, which deals with portfolio effects.

QUESTIONS/PROBLEMS

1. A machine with a 4-year life is being replaced with a modern, more efficient piece of equipment with a longer expected life. The equipment will require a payment of $55,000 in the first 30 days of its operation. The expected returns and standard deviation are as follows:

Year	Expected Returns	Standard Deviation
1	$14,000	$1,200
2	16,000	1,800
3	18,000	2,000
4	20,000	1,950
5	22,000	3,000

The risk-free rate of return is 5%. The CEC values and the coefficient of variation are as follows for the 5-year period:

Coefficient of Variation	Certainty Equivalent Coefficient				
	Year 1	Year 2	Year 3	Year 4	Year 5
$v \leq 0.10$	0.92	0.88	0.85	0.80	0.74
$0.10 \leq v \leq 0.25$	0.86	0.82	0.78	0.73	0.69

Determine the expected certainty equivalent value.

2. A boiler manufacturing company uses a certainty equivalent approach in its evaluation of risky investments. Currently, the company is faced with two alternative projects. Project A is replacement investment—category II; project B is new investment—category II, according to Table 13–1. The expected values of net cash flows for each project and risk-free returns are as follows:

Year	A	B	Risk-Free Return
Present	− $40,000	− $50,000	—
1	20,000	20,000	0.05
2	20,000	25,000	0.06
3	20,000	30,000	0.07

Which of the alternatives should be selected?

3. A corporation is considering two projects and will choose one or the other based upon their RAR. The corporation's cost of capital is 14% and the firm estimates that the risk-free rate will be 10%. Project A is a replacement investment—category II. Project B is a new investment—category II. Project A's projected cash-flow distribution is as follows:

Original Cost		Cash Flows for Years 1–6	
Probability	Amount	Probability	Amount
0.3	$100,000	0.15	$20,000
0.3	110,000	0.25	25,000
0.4	120,000	0.25	30,000
		0.15	35,000
		0.10	45,000
		0.10	45,000

Project B's projected cash-flow distribution is as follows:

Original Cost		Cash Flows for Years 1–6	
Probability	*Amount*	*Probability*	*Amount*
0.5	$225,000	0.25	$50,000
0.2	210,000	0.25	60,000
0.3	200,000	0.15	70,000
		0.15	75,000
		0.10	80,000
		0.10	85,000

Determine the RAR for each project using Table 13–2 for return requirements for investment groups.

4. A company is considering an investment costing $8,000. The investment is such that the size of the inflows will be correlated with the state of the economy. Economists can reliably estimate the following probabilities for the next 3 years.

State	Probabilities for Years 1–3
Recession	0.3
Normal	0.6
Boom	0.1

Company officials can reliably predict the inflows associated with each state of the economy.

State	Net Cash Inflows
Recession	$2,000
Normal	$5,000
Boom	$8,000

Assume a cost of capital of 11% and a risk premium of 9%. Compute the risk adjusted NPV.

5. A corporation has a cost of capital of 12%, a risk-free rate of return of 6%, and is considering project replacement, which has a 8-year expected life. The project will cost approximately $50,000 and will generate cash inflows of $10,000 each year.

   This project is a category II investment (Table 13–1) and the corporation has a hurdle rate of 15%. The corporation also expects that the dispersion of cash flows after year 4 will be relatively constant and that the CEC's from the table will be used during the initial period and 0.77 thereafter. Determine the project's NPV using the risk-adjusted discount rate and the certainty equivalent and evaluate the results.

6. The Hothouse Corporation is considering project "Woody," the construction of a wood-pruning machine that has the ability to turn entire forests into bundled cords of firewood ready to be delivered to customers.

   The project is anticipated to have an initial cost of $30,000,000 a 3-year useful life, and cash-inflow distributions as follows:

	Cash Inflow per Year (in millions)		
Probability	RW_1	RW_2	RW_3
0.2	$15	$ 8	$20
0.3	20	25	25
0.4	30	40	30
0.1	40	50	35
1.0			

Compute σ_{CE} under the assumption that cash inflows are independent over Woody's useful life and under the assumption that cash inflows are perfectly correlated over Woody's useful life. Assume that the risk-free rate of return is 6%.

7. A manufacturing company is evaluating two alternative projects. Project A consists of an expansion of the same business by building a new facility at the same location. The total project cost is estimated to be $30,000. Project B consists of an acquisition of another firm selling products unrelated to the company's primary business. The total cost of the project is $40,000. The following table shows the cash-inflows distribution.

	Project A (cash flow, $000)							Project B (cash flow, $000)					
Outcome	RA_1	PA_1	RA_2	PA_2	RA_3	PA_3	Outcome	RA_1	PA_1	RA_2	PA_2	RA_3	PA_3
1	10	0.3	15	0.2	10	0.3	1	15	0.2	20	0.3	15	0.2
2	15	0.5	20	0.6	25	0.6	2	20	0.6	25	0.5	30	0.6
3	20	0.2	25	0.2	30	0.1	3	25	0.2	30	0.2	40	0.2

(a) Compute $\overline{CE}$ for both projects.
(b) Compute σ_{CE} for both projects based on the assumption that cash flows are independent and cash flows are perfectly correlated.
(c) Compute and explain the coefficient of variation of the certainty equivalent distributions for both correlation assumptions.

Assume that the risk-free rate is 6%, constant over the life of projects, and that the company considers cash flows for the first 3-year period.

8. The Energystics Corporation is evaluating two projects. One is the installation of a load shedder, which costs $5,000, including peripheral sensing equipment, and the other, the installation of a 5-ton, high-efficiency air conditioning unit at a cost of $8,000 installed. The energy savings from these two projects are listed below. Distributions are based on the probabilities of future rate increases as set by a local electric company. The risk-free rate in this area is 6%.

Load Shedder

	Period 1		Period 2		Period 3	
Rate Inc. (%)	R_{ls}	P_{ls}	R_{ls}	P_{ls}	R_{ls}	P_{ls}
4%	$2,000	0.50	$3,000	0.25	$4,000	0.25
8%	4,000	0.25	5,000	0.50	6,000	0.25
12%	6,000	0.25	7,000	0.25	8,000	0.50

Air Conditioner

	Period 1		Period 2		Period 3	
Rate Inc. (%)	R_{ac}	P_{ac}	R_{ac}	P_{ac}	R_{ac}	P_{ac}
4%	$3,000	0.50	$4,000	0.25	$5,000	0.25
8%	6,000	0.25	7,000	0.50	8,000	0.25
12%	9,000	0.25	10,000	0.25	11,000	0.50

Energystics assigns the following certainty equivalent factors for the two projects under consideration based on their variability over the three time periods.

Load Shedder	Air Conditioner
$\alpha = 0.95$	$\alpha = 0.95$
$\alpha = 0.85$	$\alpha = 0.75$
$\alpha = 0.75$	$\alpha = 0.60$

(a) Compute $\overline{\text{CE}}$ for both projects.
(b) Compute σ_{CE} based on independent and perfectly correlated cash flows.
(c) Compute the coefficient of variation for the CE distributions for both projects under both correlation assumptions.
(d) Compute the probability that both projects will have positive certainty equivalent values when σ_{CE} is computed under both assumptions of independence and perfect correlation.

14

Portfolio Effects

Chapter 12 provides an overview of decision-making under conditions of risk and the importance of utility theory. Chapter 13 illustrates capital project evaluation for single projects under conditions of risk. As you recall, we determined the risk-adjusted NPV and its standard deviation over the useful life of the project. This chapter shifts the focus of evaluation from individual projects to combinations of projects. Projects that may not be acceptable when considered in isolation might merit acceptance when an optimum *combination* of new and existing projects is sought. This result may occur due to favorable *interaction or portfolio effects* between projects. Thus, we recommend that the firm be viewed as an amalgam of previously accepted projects.

The chapter initially concentrates on portfolios of securities and later applies the principles and techniques to portfolios of capital projects. The chapter draws heavily on the work of Dr. Harry Markowitz, who has been called the father of modern portfolio theory. Every student and practitioner of finance should be familiar with Markowitz' classic works as they have a significant impact on financial decision-making under conditions of risk.[1]

The chapter begins by introducing the covariance between a given pair of investments. Next, we present tools for determining the risk and return on portfolios of investments. Finally, we discuss the determination of optimal portfolio of investments, which provides a preview of Part V, *Capital Asset Pricing*.

---

[1]See H. Markowitz, "Portfolio Selection," *Journal of Finance*, (March 1952) and *Portfolio Selection: Efficient Diversification of Investment* (New York: John Wiley & Sons, Inc., 1959).

PORTFOLIO EFFECTS

Suppose that we consider combinations of possible investments as portfolios. Each investment in the combination has an expected return and risk, the latter measured by its standard deviation. To evaluate different combinations (or budgets) we need an expected return and standard deviation on *each combination*. The expected return, $E(R_p)$, on the combination may be computed using Equation (1):

$$E(R_p) = \sum_{j=1}^{N} X_j E(R_j) \tag{1}$$

where X_j = proportion of the total budget allocated to the jth project
$\quad E(R_j)$ = expected rate of return on the jth project

The standard deviation of the budget (σ_p), however, is not simply a weighted averaged of the project sigmas (σ_j), although these represent one component. Rather, the risk of the budget (σ_p), in addition, reflects the covariances among projects in combination. *Covariance measures the impact that a pair of securities will have on the portfolio variance due to their interactive effects (i.e., correlation) and their respective standard deviations.* The covariance between two projects (or securities) is the product of three terms: the correlation coefficient and the standard deviations of the two projects, as expressed in Equation (2):

$$\text{Cov}_{ij} = \rho_{ij}\sigma_i\sigma_j \tag{2}$$

The reader should recall that the correlation coefficient (ρ_{ij}) measures the nature and strength of the relationship between two securities or two projects. The correlation coefficient can take on values in the following range:

$$-1.0 \le \rho_{ij} \le +1.0$$

Note that the covariance will take on the sign of the correlation coefficient (ρ_{ij}) since both standard deviations must be greater than or equal to zero. Thus, the covariance can be positive, negative, or zero, depending on whether the correlation coefficient is positive, negative, or zero, respectively. (The covariance could also be zero if either standard deviation were zero, which would be the case for a risk-free asset.)

1. Positive covariance implies that if the cash flows of one project exceed their expected value, the cash flows of the other project in turn are likely to exceed their expected value, and vice versa. Positive covariance intensifies the risk of the combination of assets.

2. Negative covariance, by contrast, suggests that if the cash flows of one project exceed their expected value, the cash flows of the other will tend to fall below their expected value, and vice versa. Negative covariance, accordingly, tends to significantly reduce risk in the budget combination.

3. Zero covariance (when it results from $\rho_{ij} = 0$) means that the cash flows of the two projects move independently of each other; if the cash flows of one project exceed their expected value, the other project's cash flows are just as likely to exceed as to fall below their expected value. Zero covariance reduces risk in the portfolio.

The standard deviation of the combination is expressed in Equation (3):

$$\sigma_p = \sqrt{\sum_{j=1}^{N} X_j^2 \sigma_j^2 + 2 \sum_{j=1}^{N-1} \sum_{i=j+1}^{N} X_i X_j \text{Cov}_{ij}} \qquad (3)$$

where i and j represent all projects in the budget, *paired off* for purposes of computing covariance.

The covariance term may be plus (positive covariance), minus (negative covariance), or zero. Obviously, in constructing a portfolio, one would strive *in theory* for a negative covariance sufficient to offset the first term and produce $\sigma_p = 0$. In practice, the returns on capital projects and securities tend to move with the general economy so that negative covariance is seldom obtainable. Generally, the crux of portfolio construction lies in minimizing the degree of positive covariance.

CALCULATING THE COVARIANCE

One approach to computing the covariance considers pairs of observations for the returns on two projects. Deviations of these returns from the respective expected values are multiplied by each other, and then by the joint probability that this pair of returns will occur as shown in Equation (4):

$$\text{Cov}_{ij} = \sum_{t=1}^{N} [R_{it} - E(R_i)][R_{jt} - E(R_j)] P_t \qquad (4)$$

where Cov_{ij} = covariance between the ith and jth projects
$\quad P_t$ = joint probability of the paired cash flows for project i and project j
$\quad R_{it}$ = return on the ith project in period t (an element in the probability distribution of returns in project i)
$\quad R_{jt}$ = return on the jth project in period t (an element in the probability distribution of returns in project j)

It should be pointed out that the joint probability, P_t, in Equation (4) can be based on historical experience, an informed subjective estimation, or a simulation of possible outcomes for the two projects under evaluation. Example 1 illustrates the computation of the covariance using Equation (4).

☐ **EXAMPLE 1**   *Expected Value, Standard Deviation, and*
Portfolio Covariance

Assume that a corporation is evaluating two projects, X and Y. After performing 400 simulation runs showing the interaction of the cash flows generated by the two projects, the following table was prepared to summarize the results. This table presents the data necessary to determine the probabilities of various cash flows for each project, as well as the ways in which the two projects interact.

Table of Cash Flows Generated in 400 Simulation Runs

	Project Y			
Project X	$100,000	$250,000	$400,000	Total
$100,000	50	20	5	75
$200,000	72	155	3	230
$300,000	28	25	42	95
Total	150	200	50	400

Compute the following:

(a) A table of joint and marginal probabilities based on the table of simulation results given above.

(b) The expected value and the standard deviation of the cash-flow distribution for each of the two projects.

(c) The covariance between the cash flows of projects X and Y using Equation (4) and a contingency-table format.

Solution: (a) To facilitate the computations, the contingency table of the number of observations is first converted into joint and marginal probabilities:

	Project Y			
Project X	$100,000	$250,000	$400,000	Total
$100,000	0.125	0.05	0.0125	0.1875
$200,000	0.180	0.3875	0.0075	0.5750
$300,000	0.070	0.0625	0.1050	0.2375
Total	0.375	0.5000	0.1250	1.0000

(b) To compute the expected cash inflow and the standard deviation for each project, we use the marginal probabilities of each of the three possible outcomes:

Project X:

$$E(R_x) = \$100,000(0.1875) + \$200,000(0.5750) + \$300,000(0.2375)$$
$$= \$18,750 + \$115,000 + \$71,250$$
$$= \$205,000$$

$$\sigma_x = \sqrt{\begin{array}{c}(100,000 - 205,000)^2(0.1875) + (200,000 - 205,000)^2(0.5750) \\ + (300,000 - 205,000)^2(0.2375)\end{array}}$$

$$= \sqrt{2,067,187,500 + 14,375,000 + 2,143,437,500}$$
$$= \$65,000$$

Project Y:

$$E(R_y) = \$100,000(0.375) + \$250,000(0.500) + \$400,000(0.125)$$
$$= \$37,500 + \$125,000 + \$50,000$$
$$= \$212,500$$

$$\sigma_y = \sqrt{\begin{array}{c}(100,000 - 212,500)^2(0.375) + (250,000 - 212,500)^2(0.5) \\ + (400,000 - 212,500)^2(0.125)\end{array}}$$

$$= \sqrt{4,746,093,750 + 703,125,000 + 4,394,531,250}$$
$$= \$99,216$$

(c) Next, we compute the covariance between projects X and Y. We use the joint probabilities in the body of the table and restate the table in a form consistent with Equation (4) by showing each cash flow as a deviation from its respective mean (i.e., subtract $205,000 from each cash flow for project X and $212,500 from each of project Y's cash flows):

Project X	Project Y		
	$-\$112,500$	$+\$37,500$	$+\$187,500$
$-\$105,000$	0.1250	0.0500	0.0125
$-\$\ \ 5,000$	0.1800	0.3875	0.0075
$+\$\ 95,000$	0.0700	0.0625	0.1050

The covariance is computed by multiplying the respective values for each row and column by the corresponding joint probability, with due regard to the signs.

$$
\begin{aligned}
\text{Cov}_{xy} = & \ (-105,000)(-112,500)(0.1250) + (-5,000)(-112,500)(0.18) \\
& + (+95,000)(-112,500)(0.07) + (+37,500)(-105,000)(0.05) \\
& + (+37,500)(-5,000)(0.3875) + (+37,500)(+95,000)(0.0625) \\
& + (+187,500)(-105,000)(0.0125) + (+187,500)(-5,000)(0.0075) \\
& + (+187,500)(+95,000)(0.1050) \\
= & \ + (1,476,562,500) + (101,250,000) + (-748,125,000) \\
& + (-196,875,000) + (-72,656,250) + (222,656,250) \\
& + (-246,093,750) + (-7,031,250) + (1,870,312,500) \\
= & \ 3,670,781,250 - 1,270,781,250 \\
= & \ +2,400,000,000
\end{aligned}
$$

The above calculation shows that the covariance between these two projects is 2.4 billion. This result quantifies the contribution of the interaction between the two projects to the risk of a portfolio of the two projects. We realize that this result is not intuitive so we'll try to bring it into focus.

The contribution of each project to the risk of a portfolio of the two projects is quantified by the variance of the project in question. Thus, project X contributes 4.225 billion ($65,000^2$) to the portfolio risk and project Y would contributes 9.844 billion ($99,216^2$) to the portfolio risk. As mentioned before, the portfolio effects between the two projects are quantified by the covariance. In addition, as mentioned, the covariance takes on its maximum value when the correlation coefficient equals $+1$. Had this been the case here, the covariance by Equation (2) would equal:

$$
\text{maximum Cov}_{xy} = \rho_{xy}\sigma_x\sigma_y
$$

$$
= (+1)(\$65,000)(\$99,216)
$$

$$
= +6,449,040,000
$$

Therefore, we see that the actual covariance of 2.4 billion is far below (only about 37% of) the maximum covariance that could have resulted for these two assets. This "moderate" actual covariance resulted from the fact that the correlation between the two assets is only $+0.372$. Finally, the contribution of the interaction effect between the two assets to the portfolio risk is far below the contribution of either project X (4.225 billion) or project Y (9.844 billion) singly.

Throughout subsequent examples in this chapter, we try to add to your intuitive understanding of the covariance.

A more convenient method of calculating the covariance between two projects makes use of Equation (2):

$$\text{Cov}_{ij} = \rho_{ij}\sigma_i\sigma_j \tag{2}$$

This requires that the correlation coefficient ρ_{ij} be computed directly by regressing the paired cash flows of the two projects under consideration. Since the covariance can be computed using Equation (2), Equation (2) can be substituted directly into Equation (3) as shown in Equation (5):

$$\sigma_p = \sqrt{\sum_{j=1}^{N} X_j^2\sigma_j^2 + 2\sum_{j=1}^{N-1}\sum_{i=j+1}^{N} X_i X_j \rho_{ij}\sigma_i\sigma_j} \tag{5}$$

Note in Equation (5) that the standard deviation on a portfolio or combination of assets is the square root of the sum of the weighted variances plus twice the sum of the weighted covariances between all possible pairs of securities or projects. Thus, the covariance plays a critical role in determining the size of the portfolio standard deviation.

To see this computational approach for both Cov_{ij} and σ_p, consider Example 2.

□ **EXAMPLE 2** *Portfolio Expected Value and Standard Deviation*

A firm desires to evaluate the combination of two projects having the following characteristics as a portfolio.

	R_1	R_2
$E(R_j)$	32%	35%
σ_j	7%	10.7%
X_j	0.5	0.5
ρ_{ij}	-0.32	

Compute $E(R_p)$ and σ_p.

Solution:

$$E(R_p) = \sum_{j=1}^{N} X_j E(R_j)$$

$$= (0.5)(0.32) + (0.5)(0.35)$$

$$= 0.335 \quad \text{or} \quad 33.5\%$$

and

$$\sigma_p = \sqrt{\sum_{j=1}^{N} X_j^2\sigma_j^2 + 2\sum_{j=1}^{N-1}\sum_{i=j+1}^{N} (X_i)(X_j)(\rho_{ij})(\sigma_j)(\sigma_i)}$$

$$= \sqrt{(0.5)^2(0.07)^2 + (0.5)^2(0.107)^2 + 2(0.5)(0.5)(-0.32)(0.07)(0.107)}$$

$$= \sqrt{0.001225 + 0.0028623 - 0.0011984}$$

$$= 0.0537, \quad \text{or} \quad 5.37\% \qquad \qquad \Box$$

It should be noted that the slightly negative correlation between projects R_1 and R_2 in Example 2 substantially reduces the risk on R_2 through pooling. Hence, while R_2 considered in isolation might be rejected, the combination of R_1 with R_2 could become a more attractive alternative than other combinations.

To summarize the key points in terms of building a portfolio of assets, the crux of the problem lies in balancing σ_j, X_j, and Cov_{ij} to minimize risk for a desired level of return. Since σ_i, σ_j, and ρ_{ij} are fixed for a given pair of projects i and j, finding X_i and X_j to minimize risk becomes of interest to the financial manager building a portfolio of assets.

MINIMUM RISK PORTFOLIOS

Considering two projects i and j, σ_p is minimized if the proportion invested in project i is determined as shown in Equation (6):

$$X_i = \frac{\sigma_j^2 - \text{Cov}_{ij}}{\sigma_i^2 + \sigma_j^2 - 2\,\text{Cov}_{ij}} \tag{6}$$

Equation (6) is derived by differentiating Equation (5) with respect to X_i, setting the derivative equal to zero, and solving for X_i.

Based on our discussion, the following observations (decision rules) should provide the financial manager with insight and strategies for diversification in building a portfolio or capital budget. We consider two assets, i and j, but the results can be generalized for a large number of projects.

1. If $\rho_{ij} = 0$, the covariance term in Equation (5) for σ_p drops out and the portfolio's standard deviation is the square root of the weighted sum of the project variances:

$$\sigma_p = \sqrt{\sum_{j=1}^{N} X_j^2 \sigma_j^2}$$

Further, the proportion of project i that should be selected to minimize risk under these conditions (i.e., $\rho_{ij} = 0$) is found using Equation (6), modified as follows:

$$X_i = \frac{\sigma_j^2}{\sigma_i^2 + \sigma_j^2}$$

That is, to minimize risk in the combination, X_i should equal the ratio of the variance of j to the sum of the variances of i and j.

2. If $0 < \rho_{ij} < \sigma_i/\sigma_j$ (where σ_i is the smaller of the two standard deviations), the portfolio standard deviation will be determined using Equation (5), where both the sum of the weighted variances and the weighted positive covariance plays a part. However, diversification is still attractive, since σ_p will be smaller than either σ_i or σ_j individually if the proportion invested in X_i is determined using Equation (6).

3. If $\rho_{ij} > \sigma_i/\sigma_j$, diversification will not be attractive, since the positive correlation and covariance are too great to reduce σ_p below the smaller standard deviation, σ_i. Hence, to minimize risk, X_i should equal 1.

4. If $\rho_{ij} < 0$, σ_p will be less than the square root of the sum of the weighted variances, owing to the negative weighted covariance. σ_p and X_i are then determined using Equations (5) and (6), respectively.

5. If $\rho_{ij} = -1$, σ_p can be driven to zero by selecting the proper proportions of the two securities or projects whereby the weighted covariance in Equation (5) is equal to the sum of the weighted variances. This proper proportion is found by simplifying Equation (6) for the $\rho_{ij} = -1$ case, as follows:

$$X_i = \frac{\sigma_j}{\sigma_i + \sigma_j}$$

The observations are illustrated in Example 3.

□ **EXAMPLE 3** *Portfolio Expected Return and Standard Deviation*
Two projects have the following risk-return characteristics:

	P_1	P_2
$E(R_j)$	15%	20%
σ_j	12%	16%

Determine $E(R_p)$ and σ_p for the minimum risk portfolio, where the correlation coefficient between the two projects is: (a) 0; (b) 0.20; (c) 0.90; (d) -1.

Solution: (a) Given that $\rho_{ij} = 0$, the optimal proportion is determined as follows:

$$X_i = \frac{\sigma_j^2}{\sigma_i^2 + \sigma_j^2}$$

$$X_1 = \frac{(0.16)^2}{(0.12)^2 + (0.16)^2}$$

$$= \frac{0.0256}{0.0144 + 0.0256}$$

$$= 0.64$$

Thus, the minimum-risk combination is to invest 0.64 of the portfolio in P_1 and 0.36 in P_2.

Now the expected value and standard deviation of the portfolio may be computed.

$$E(R_p) = 0.64(0.15) + 0.36(0.20)$$

$$= 0.096 + 0.072$$

$$= 0.168, \quad \text{or} \quad 16.8\%$$

$$\sigma_p = \sqrt{(0.64)^2(0.12)^2 + (0.36)^2(0.16)^2}$$

$$= \sqrt{0.00589824 + 0.00331776}$$

$$= 0.0960, \quad \text{or} \quad 9.60\%$$

Notice that σ_p is significantly lower than either σ_{p_1} or σ_{p_2}.

(b) Given that $\rho_{ij} = +0.20$, the optimal proportion is determined as follows:

$$X_i = \frac{\sigma_j^2 - \text{Cov}_{ij}}{\sigma_i^2 + \sigma_j^2 - 2\,\text{Cov}_{ij}}$$

$$X_1 = \frac{(0.16)^2 - (0.2)(0.12)(0.16)}{(0.12)^2 + (0.16)^2 - 2(+0.2)(0.12)(0.16)}$$

$$= \frac{0.02176}{0.03232}$$

$$= 0.673$$

$$E(R_p) = (0.673)(0.15) + (0.327)(0.20)$$

$$= 0.10095 + 0.0654$$

$$= 0.16635, \quad \text{or} \quad 16.6\%$$

$$\sigma_p = \sqrt{(0.673)^2(0.12)^2 + (0.327)^2(0.16)^2 + 2(0.673)(0.327)(0.2)(0.12)(0.16)}$$

$$= \sqrt{0.0065221776 + 0.0027373824 + 0.0016901452}$$

$$= 0.10464, \quad \text{or} \quad 10.5\%$$

Notice that σ_p is still lower than the smaller standard deviation, but that we are investing a greater percent of funds (0.673 vs. 0.64) in P_1 than when $\rho_{ij} = 0$. In general, as the correlation becomes more highly positive, more of the funds will be invested in the less-risky project. This continues until $\rho_{ij} = \sigma_1/\sigma_2$ (where $\sigma_1 < \sigma_2$), at which point 100% of the available funds are invested in the less-risky project.

(c) Given that $\rho_{ij} = +0.90$, by rule 3 we see that $\rho_{ij} = +0.90 > 12\%/16\% = +0.75$, diversification will not be beneficial, and 100% of the funds should be invested in P_1. Given this degree of correlation, we can demonstrate that even a high percentage invested in P_1 (say 85% in P_1 and 15% in P_2) will not reduce σ_p below $\sigma_{p_1} = 12\%$:

$$\sigma_p = \sqrt{(0.85)^2(0.12)^2 + (0.15)^2(0.16)^2 + 2(0.85)(0.15)(0.90)(0.12)(0.16)}$$

$$= \sqrt{0.010404 + 0.000576 + 0.0044064}$$

$$= 0.12404, \quad \text{or} \quad 12.4\%$$

As X_1 increases from 0.85 to 1.00, the σ_p value would continually get smaller, decreasing from 12.404% to 12%.

(d) Given that $\rho_{ij} = -1.0$, we see by rule 5 that the proportion to invest in P_1 is just over 57%:

$$X_1 = \frac{\sigma_2}{\sigma_1 + \sigma_2} = \frac{0.16}{0.12 + 0.16} = 0.571429$$

Having this percent invested in P_1 should drive σ_p to zero.

$$E(R_p) = (0.571429)(0.15) + (0.428571)(0.20)$$

$$= 0.08571435 + 0.0857142$$

$$= 0.17142855 \text{ or } 17.1\%$$

$$\sigma_p = \sqrt{ \begin{array}{l} (0.571429)^2(0.12)^2 + (0.428571)^2(0.16)^2 \\ + 2(-1)(0.12)(0.16)(0.571429)(0.428571) \end{array} }$$

$$= \sqrt{0.0047020478 + 0.0047020314 - 0.0094040792}$$

$$= 0$$ □

FIGURE 14–1   Portfolio Standard Deviations (σ_p) as the Correlation Coefficient (ρ_{ij}) Varies from +1 to −1

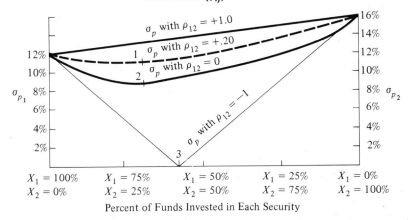

Percent of Funds Invested in Each Security

Based on the results of Example 3, we may draw the following conclusions:

1. As ρ_{ij} decreases from +1.0 through σ_1/σ_2 ($\sigma_1 < \sigma_2$), 100% of the funds will be invested in the less-risky project.

2. As ρ_{ij} gets smaller, eventually decreasing to −1.0, a smaller and smaller percentage will be invested in the less-risky security, since the interaction between ρ_{ij}, σ_i, σ_j, X_i, and X_j causes σ_p to be minimized as X_i is decreased and X_j increased to capitalize on the favorable covariance effects between the two projects or securities. Figure 14-1 illustrates these facts. As shown in Figure 14–1, the minimum-risk percentages invested in P_1 go from 0.673 (point 1 in Figure 14–1) when $\rho_{12} = +0.20$, to 0.64 (point 2 in Figure 14–1) when $\rho_{12} = 0$, to 0.571 (point 3 in Figure 14–1) when $\rho_{12} = -1.0$.

EFFICIENT PORTFOLIOS OR BUDGETS

In earlier chapters, individual projects were ranked by net present value. Since the objective of capital budgeting is to increase the present value of the firm, "rational" management accepted all projects with a positive NPV, within the constraints of available capital, and the like. However, this decision rule for individual projects suggests that there does not exist a combination of projects that would be superior to a single investment meeting the criterion. The single project standard ignores the advantage of diversification to improve the quality of earnings through reduction of risk.

When the firm must choose among several capital proposals, a wiser decision rule seeks the combination of projects that maximizes expected present value and minimizes the variance or standard deviation. But experience attests that expected present value and standard deviation generally vary directly, and management can trade off additional risk against additional income. The better decision rule, therefore, stresses the concept of efficient portfolios: those combinations that for any given expected value have a minimum standard deviation (risk); or for any chosen level of risk (standard deviation), the highest expected return.

Assume that management has a fixed sum to invest and can choose from a number of possible combinations, as illustrated in Figure 14–2. Out of all the combinations obtainable, only some will be efficient. *A combination is inefficient if there exists another portfolio with a higher expected value and a lower standard deviation, a higher expected return and the same standard deviation, or the same expected return and a lower standard deviation.* Eliminating the inefficient portfolios from the set of all possible combinations, the array of efficient portfolios may be plotted as line *AF* in Figure 14—3. Combinations falling below this *efficient frontier* are inefficient: a better return or lower risk or both can always be secured by moving to the frontier. The portfolios above the efficient frontier are unobtainable with the funds and projects available for investment.

Among the efficient set we want to select that combination representing the optimum portfolio (i.e., the combination of risk and return preferred by the investor). The solution lies in the application of utility theory. Figure 14–4 depicts a set of utility isoquants (1, 2, and 3) for a risk-averse decision-maker. *Each isoquant plots a series of combinations with different risks and returns which have the same total utility for the investor. On higher utility curves, total utility increases, so that total utility $U_3 > U_2 > U_1$.* All combinations of risk and return on curve 2 have the same total utility, but this quantum is larger than the total utility of the combinations on curve 1. *Accordingly, the optimal portfolio for a given investor is found at the tangency point between the efficient frontier and utility isoquant.* This tangency point (*B*), as shown in Figure 14–5, marks the highest level of satisfaction the investor can attain with the funds available for investment. Other decision-makers with unique utility functions would locate their maximum satisfaction at other points

FIGURE 14–2   Attainable Portfolios

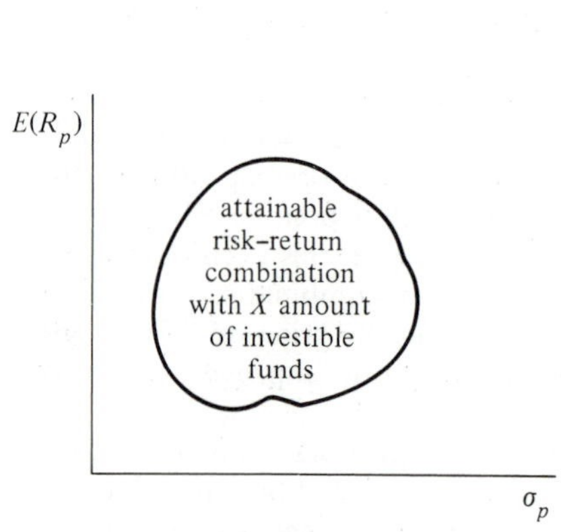

FIGURE 14–3   Efficient Frontier

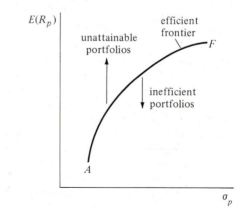

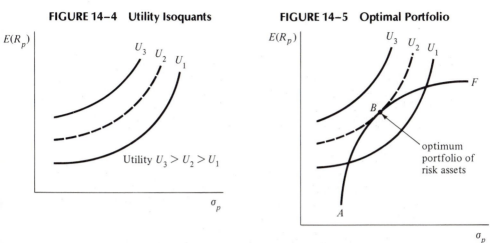

FIGURE 14–4 Utility Isoquants

Utility $U_3 > U_2 > U_1$

FIGURE 14–5 Optimal Portfolio

optimum portfolio of risk assets

of tangency. Each decision-maker has his or her own preferred combinations of risky assets (projects or securities).

Let income connote utility and risk, disutility. At the point of equilibrium (B),

$$\frac{\Delta_{\text{utility}}}{\Delta_{\text{disutility}}} = \frac{\Delta E(R_p)}{\Delta \sigma_p}$$

The equilibrium point is important to the subsequent discussion. Since all portfolios in the efficient set comprise risky assets, the equilibrium defines the decision-maker's preferred combination of risky assets—that combination which dominates all other risky asset packages.

We now address the problem of actually determining the efficient frontier.

DETERMINING THE EFFICIENT FRONTIER

As shown in Figure 14–3, the efficient frontier is a plot of desirable portfolios in risk (σ_p) versus return [$E(R_p)$] space. As you might expect, the efficient frontier is determined by computing σ_p and $E(R_p)$ for a given set of securities as the percentage invested in each security is allowed to vary. By definition, *each portfolio on the efficient frontier has the maximum return for a given level of risk or the minimum risk for a given level of return*. The values for the portfolio risk and return are computed using Equations (3) and (1), respectively.

The shape of the efficient frontier and its location relative to the risk-return axes will vary depending upon the candidate investments under evaluation or changes in the degree of correlation that exists between the investments under evaluation. Example 4 examines the calculation of the risk-return coordinates that yield the plot of the efficient frontier.

□ **EXAMPLE 4**   *Determination of the Efficient Frontier*

Use the following two investments, originally introduced in Example 3:

	P_1	P_2
$E(R_j)$	15%	20%
σ_j	12%	16%

Determine the values for $E(R_p)$ and σ_p for the following values of X_1 and X_2:

X_1	X_2
1.00	0
0.75	0.25
0.50	0.50
0.25	0.75
0	1.00

The following values for ρ_{12} should be used to determine separate efficient frontiers:

$$\rho_{12} = +1.0; \qquad \rho_{12} = +.20; \qquad \rho_{12} = 0; \quad \text{and} \quad \rho_{12} = -1.0$$

Use a tabular format to present the values for $E(R_p)$ and σ_p for the five values of X_1 and X_2 and the four values of ρ_{12}. Finally, plot the four efficient frontiers (one for each value of ρ_{12}) in risk-return space.

FIGURE 14–6   **Efficient Frontiers for P_1 and P_2**

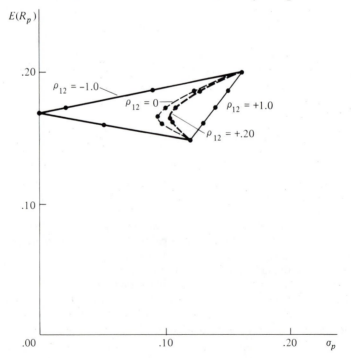

Solution: The table of values for $E(R_p)$ and σ_p is as follows:

		$\rho_{12} = +1.0$		$\rho_{12} = +.20$		$\rho_{12} = 0$		$\rho_{12} = -1.0$	
X_1	X_2	$E(R_p)$	σ_p	$E(R_p)$	σ_p	$E(R_p)$	σ_p	$E(R_p)$	σ_p
1.0	0	0.15	0.12	0.15	0.12	0.15	0.12	0.15	0.12
0.75	0.25	0.1625	0.13	0.1625	0.1055	0.1625	0.0985	0.1625	0.05
0.50	0.50	0.1750	0.14	0.1750	0.1092	0.1750	0.10	0.1750	0.02
0.25	0.75	0.1875	0.15	0.1875	0.1294	0.1875	0.1237	0.1875	0.09
0	1.0	0.20	0.16	0.20	0.16	0.20	0.16	0.20	0.16

It is instructive to examine this table before we plot the four efficient frontiers. Notice that the values of $E(R_p)$ do not change as ρ_{12} changes. Further, notice that σ_p is an increasing *linear* function only when $\rho_{12} = +1.0$. In the other three cases (i.e., $\rho_{12} = +0.20$, $\rho_{12} = 0$, and $\rho_{12} = -1.0$), σ_p is a nonlinear function of X_1 and X_2. The values shown in the given table plus the values for $E(R_p)$ and σ_p computed for the minimum-risk portfolios computed in Example 3 enable us to plot the efficient frontiers, as shown in Figure 14–6.

Notice that each of the efficient frontiers starts at the minimum-risk portfolio (which was one of the reasons why the minimum-risk portfolio is significant) and ends at the maximum risk/maximum return portfolio. Of course, it can be observed pictorially in Figure 14–6 that as ρ_{12} decreases, the value of σ_p decreases, which results in the efficient frontier coming closer to the σ_p-axis.   □

PORTFOLIO THEORY AND CAPITAL BUDGETING

Application of the portfolio model to capital budgeting is not without some difficulty. An investment in common stocks is *divisible*; the purchaser acquires units (or shares) each with the same expected return and standard deviation. The efficient frontier is thus a continuous line and the weighting system reflects the percentage of the total investment allocated to one asset or to the amounts of risk and risk-free assets.

Few capital projects divide into homogeneous units with the same expected return and standard deviation. Most projects are lumpy, or *indivisible*. Acceptance means taking the entire project: the whole return and whole standard deviation. The firm cannot buy fractions. It cannot acquire 60% of the return and standard deviation of a project. The continuity of the line between portfolios in Figure 14–3 or 14–6 is due to variations in fractional holdings in a group of divisible projects. For *indivisible projects*, it would not be realistic to join the efficient projects with a continuous line, since fractional projects are not permitted. In constructing portfolios of indivisible projects, therefore, the weighting system is either 0 or 1. The solution in terms of optimum expected return and standard deviation for a portfolio of indivisible projects is most easily reached using integer programming, as illustrated in Chapter 21.

Lower-Confidence-Limit Criterion

If the number of projects considered is large, the efficient set might involve a substantial number of combinations from which to choose. The use of the lower confidence limit model can reduce the problem to a manageable size. The approach assumes that the investor can state his preference in terms of a minimum acceptable return (the lower confidence limit) as opposed to minimizing risk for a given specified return. The lower confidence limit (L) is found using Equation (7):

$$L = E(R_p) - K\sigma_p \qquad (7)$$

where K is a constant chosen by the investor and refers to the number of standard deviations in the normal distribution. Thus, the investor (or manager) establishes a floor below which the return on the budget should not fall. Depending on the minimum return stipulated, K may represent 1, 1.5, 2,... standard deviations below the expected return. In other words, the investor, by putting a value on K, establishes a minimum acceptable return on the budget and/or the amount of downside risk she or he willingly bears. If $K = 2$, this means that the manager is willing to accept only a 2.28% probability of the return falling below the minimum acceptable amount.

As the minimum acceptable return (L) increases for a given budget, there will be fewer efficient combinations from which to choose. The efficient frontier shrinks as previously efficient portfolios are now considered inefficient. To illustrate the concept, consider Example 5.

□ **EXAMPLE 5** *Application of Lower-Confidence-Limit Criterion*

An investor is evaluating the following three portfolios:

Portfolio	$E(R_p)$	σ_p
A	0.22	0.10
B	0.28	0.12
C	0.38	0.14

All three of these portfolios are efficient. Depending upon his or her utility function, the investor might choose any one of the three portfolios. Assume that she or he is only willing to accept a 0.0228 chance of the return falling below L. Determine the value of K that would be assigned and the minimum acceptable returns on the portfolios.

Solution: Assuming a normal distribution, a value of $K = 2$ would include about 95% of the cases. Hence, a K equaling 2 would find only 2.28% of the cases falling below L. (More risk-averse investors would increase the value of K since they would require fewer cases falling below L.) The minimum acceptable returns on the portfolios now become:

Portfolio	$E(R_p)$	—	$K(\sigma_p)$	=	L
A	0.22	—	2(0.10)	=	0.02
B	0.28	—	2(0.12)	=	0.04
C	0.38	—	2(0.14)	=	0.10

Portfolio C now dominates based on the following rule: Specify the value of K and choose the portfolio with the highest minimum return, L.   □

SUMMARY

This chapter explores the important area of portfolio effects in which the focus of the capital investment process shifts from the individual project to that of combinations of projects. The discussion centers around the concept of covariance between pairs of candidate projects that might be included in the capital budget. The computation of the covariance is considered, as well as the determination of the expected return and standard deviation on the portfolio of assets. The area of efficient portfolios is introduced, as is that of selecting the optimal efficient portfolio when either exclusively risk assets or a combination of risk and risk-free assets are available for the investor. This chapter serves as a bridge to introduce Chapter 16, which deals with capital asset pricing theory.

QUESTIONS/PROBLEMS

1. Empirical studies have derived the following probabilities of the specific outcomes for two projects.

Project A	Project B			Total
	$250,000	$300,000	$400,000	
$50,000	0.1254	0.1073	0.0764	0.3091
$75,000	0.0909	0.0673	0.1691	0.3273
$90,000	0.1654	0.0618	0.1364	0.3636
Total	0.3817	0.2364	0.3819	

Compute the mean and standard deviation of each project as well as the covariance between the two projects, using the contingency-table format.

2. Consider the returns for these four securities:

OBS	Sec 1	Sec 2	Sec 3	Sec 4
1	$ 9	$25	$30	$5
2	10	23	31	6
3	12	22	31	5
4	15	20	32	4
5	16	19	30	2

The correlation coefficients for all combinations of securities are shown below, along with the standard deviations of each security:

$$\rho_{12} = -0.98 \qquad \sigma_1 = 3.05$$
$$\rho_{13} = 0.24 \qquad \sigma_2 = 2.39$$
$$\rho_{14} = -0.85 \qquad \sigma_3 = .84$$
$$\rho_{23} = -0.28 \qquad \sigma_4 = 1.52$$
$$\rho_{24} = 0.79$$
$$\rho_{34} = 0.28$$

(a) Compute the covariances for all possible pairs of securities.
(b) Compute the variance of the six two-security portfolios assuming a 50%–50% allocation.

3. Given $\rho_{xy} = 0$ and the incomplete joint and marginal probability table below, calculate the variance of the portfolio of the two securities X and Y in equal proportions. Use the completed table to show that the covariance of the two securities is equal to 0.

Joint and Marginal Probabilities of Cash Flow Generated in 500 Simulation Runs

Project X	$100	$200	$300	Total
		Project Y		
$150	0.20			
$200			0.05	0.20
$250				
Total	0.50			1.00

(*Hint:* Recall that if two events A and B are independent of each other, $P(A \cap B) = P(A) \cdot P(B)$. Use this hint to fill in all the joint probabilities in the table and then proceed with the solution.

4. RCA is evaluating two securities, which have the following means and standard deviations:

$$E(R_A) = 20\% \qquad E(R_B) = 28\%$$
$$\sigma_A = 10\% \qquad \sigma_B = 14\%$$

RCA feels that the following correlation coefficients could exist between the two securities: (a) +0.85; (b) +0.40; (c) 0; (d) −1.0. Determine the minimum-risk portfolios for each of these correlation coefficients, as well as the portfolio return and standard deviation. Selling short is not permitted.

5. For securities A and B and each of the correlation coefficients shown in Problem 4, compute the expected portfolio return and the portfolio standard deviation for the following mixtures:

% in A	% in B
100	0
75	25
50	50
25	75
0	100

Also, sketch the four efficient frontiers that are generated on the same graph.

6. A firm is evaluating the following four efficient portfolios:

Portfolio	$E(R_p)$	σ_p
1	0.12	0.04
2	0.24	0.06
3	0.30	0.10
4	0.32	0.12

Determine the optimal portfolio if the firm is willing to accept only a 5% chance that the portfolio return falls below the lower confidence level (L).

15

Monitoring and Controlling the Capital Budgeting Process

We have stressed the quantitative formulation of the capital budget and supporting theoretical concepts. However, the budgeting process is not an abstraction from reality; it takes place in an organization with all its attendant problems of human relations, ambitions, and political maneuvering. Some individuals may have pet projects—attachments resulting perhaps from many hard hours of detailed analysis. Others may oppose a proposal out of fear that it will shift the corporate power structure to their discomfort or evoke unemployment. The cynical quickly learn that any project can be made to look good or bad by comparing it against a sufficiently poor or strong alternative. It is for top management to monitor the process to assure that all possible alternatives have been arrayed so that a reasonably sound budget may be constructed. This chapter touches on a few of the cautionary points in the management of the capital budget. These include the following important truths:

1. Capital budgeting necessitates forecasting.
2. It is vitally important to review and control implemented projects.
3. Not all capital projects succeed.
4. The process of evaluating proposed capital projects must be cost-justified.

CAPITAL BUDGETING NECESSITATES FORECASTING

Capital budgeting speaks of *future revenues* and *expenses*, yet textbooks usually ignore the process of how these estimates are derived. Capital budgets are forecasts of varying duration and uncertainty usually based on significant assumptions.

In theory, an assumption is an explicit statement about the expected performance of the economy, industry, or the firm; the likelihood of disruptive events
(strikes, new technology, or other unusual occurrences); and the consistency of or
changes in accounting policy. Typically omitted from assumptions such as those
stated in Table 15–1 are those implicit in the choice of a forecast methodology.
All forecasting techniques specify a distinctive link between future revenues and
various determining factors. These are *technical* assumptions that relate to the
statistical model used in projecting the future.

Few companies employ a purely quantitative model to forecast revenues and
expenses, but a growing number of companies make some use of quantitative
projection methods. The choice of methodology is decidedly a matter of judgment and involves assumptions concerning the relevant variables and their
interrelationships. Different statistical techniques, applied to the same data base,
can yield different forecasts. The same technique may yield divergent results for
different time spans or if other explanatory variables are included (Table 15–2).
Naturally, management will modify its forecasting procedures to obtain estimates with a reliability appropriate to the circumstances of the business.

Statistical models are not perfect predictors and the variance from actual
sales will in part be attributable to the particular assumptions of the model. Too
often these assumptions lack explicit statement; more often, they would not be

TABLE 15–1   Quality of Published Assumptions: Recent U.S. Examples

1. Sales are based on the average monthly sales for the 17-month period ended
September 30, 19—, and have been adjusted to reflect anticipated increases in demand as
expected by the company.

2. Cost of sales... reflect unit cost changes in relation to increased sales volume and
other factors anticipated by the company.

3. Operating expenses... assume no changes for inflation or otherwise during the life
of the project. General operating expenses for... and... are based on assumptions of
partial occupancy.

4. Cross revenues... are based on past trends and current charges adjusted for
managerial policies contemplated for the proposed expanded facilities and anticipated
price-level changes in the future.

5. Historically the... rates have been increased to absorb the rising costs of health-care
services and accordingly have maintained a satisfactory margin of income over expenses.
It is the opinion of... management that this trend will continue.

6. The mix of furniture to be rented has been assumed and a weighted average
computed. This resulting theoretical set costs $509.40 and rents for $41.20 per month.

7. Although salaries and other costs will increase in the future, advertising costs
should decrease at the assumed level of activity per store. For this reason, total expenses
are assumed to remain constant.

8. Our outlook for continued rapid growth... is based on expansion of the boat and
motorcycle trailer market, increasing market penetration, expanded geographical distribution, the introduction of new products, and, of course, the past record of the company.

9. We expect... to have another good year in 19—, but operating projections are
less reliable than in some other... operations.... This projection is based on the expecta-
tion that a new labor agreement will be successfully negotiated... and that appropriate
rate increases will be granted.

Source: Published annual reports of various U.S. corporations.

TABLE 15-2 Some Assumptions Underlying Forecasting Models

1. The conditions in the past which generated the observed data will persist into the future. In the concept of stationarity, the future becomes an extension of the past, and historical simulation is the standard method for validation of the model. Yet many of the changes affecting business activity spring from discontinuities and by definition are either unpredicted or unpredictable.

2. As a corollary, models generally respond to novel circumstances slowly. Rates of change are often too rapid for models to accommodate—the reaction time of the model is too slow. However, even in a stable situation, the time required to collect data, process data, and provide output to the decision maker may conflict with the time schedule of budget formulation.

3. A further corollary, if the data base is flawed—if it contains inadequate, inaccurate, or irrelevant historical information—the past may be as obscure as the future. The model cannot rise above the quality of the input data.

4. In the case of noncausal models, the variable is a function of time.

5. The evolution of the variables is completely systematic and hence predictable.

6. Except where qualified by the introduction of weights, all previous observations yield the same amount of information about the likely value of the next observation.

7. Causal models assume that the average relationship calculated between dependent and independent variable(s) will hold for the future. The task of defining these relationships is a formidable one during period of accelerated change. Models of simple static systems are easy to construct, but their naivete will likely trap the user. On the other hand, models of complex and dynamic systems require painstaking efforts and *may* improve the precision of the projections—albeit with a higher price tag for the information.

8. Unless sales and cost data are considered to be random and normally distributed, the models do not provide a statistical basis for establishing the probability of error or confidence interval estimates. In the absence of the normality presumption above, practice resorts to establishing ranges based upon past deviations between actual and project results such that one can be reasonably certain the next period's projection will fall within the established limits. Statistically speaking, however, the assumption that future deviations will fall within the defined range is at best tenuous.

understood by top management even if stated in elementary terms. The truth we seek here is that the technical assumptions combined with the effects of leverage can convert a small variance in gross revenues into an acceptable variance in net operating revenues of the project.

Planning assumptions relate to market and production strategies as well as erratic events (for example: outcome of litigation) and, perhaps, the intuitive adjustments of top officers. In this respect, production strategies merit special comment. The bridge that leads from project revenues to net operating revenues in a given period is distinct from the external link of revenues (or savings) to the market. Revenue projections only initiate the analysis of the project, for management has considerable latitude in responding to the market environment. It may, for example, alter the product mix, adjust production schedules, modify inventory policies, regulate discretionary expenditures, and so on. Consequently, any single projected (or most probable) revenue level can translate into a broad range of net operating cash flows.

Prime cost projections assume reliable estimates of factor prices and efficiencies in production; variable overheads may be allocated to product lines by statistical formulas and management judgment; discretionary fixed costs may actually be revised throughout the budget period; programmed fixed costs (such as supervisory salaries or financial charges) share the uncertainties of interest-rate changes and similar variations in specific price levels. Other illustrations could be introduced, but the list is sufficient to emphasize the uncertainties of projecting project earnings and stresses the variety of assumptions, environmental and internal, buttressing net cash flow estimates.

There exists a group of standard assumptions, akin to the "going concern" principle in financial accounting, which are vital to appraisal of the forecast, yet merit explicit mention only by exception. Unless alerted to the contrary, the reader of a financial forecast (or capital budget) properly assumes that the firm's accounting statements are prepared in a manner consistent with the applicable accounting principles adopted by the firm in the annual report.[1] Similarly, the composition of top corporate management, the continuing availability of normal sources of supply, reasonable stability of the tax environment, and so on, are implied unless the user is informed to the contrary.

Each forecasting and budgeting system should be uniquely designed to meet the objectives of the company. Successful forecasting commences with close collaboration among executives, other internal users of forecasted data, and systems consultants. Collaboration begins with three basic questions:

1. What is the purpose of the forecast? How is it to be used? The desired accuracy and power of the techniques chosen will largely hinge on the answers.

2. What are the staff requirements to implement the forecasting system? For example, personnel capacities vary according to the detail and accuracy required. For primarily quantitative approaches, forecasters should be competent in research techniques, in application of mathematical-statistical models, and in computer usage. On the other hand, judgmental methods call upon personnel in marketing who have long association with the industry. Best results require a blending of both types.

3. What, if any, additional facilities or services are needed to inaugurate the forecasting-budgeting space and equipment, access to computer capability, library resources, and subscriptions to external data sources?

Because information, personnel, and facilities have price tags attached, the forecast-budget system must relate to the realistic needs of the business and balance the tangible values of better information against the costs of acquiring the data. In some situations, simple techniques and few organizational shifts may well accomplish the purpose.

Viewed as an integrated system, the forecast of project cash benefits and costs represents the first step in the preparation of a comprehensive capital

---

[1]Although capital budgeting is on a cash-flow basis, as we note, management must consider the impact of the capital budget on the firm's conventional accounting statements (see Chapters 20–22). A capital budget that may pass muster on an NPV basis may have severe adverse effects in the short term on the accounting statements, and this management may not choose to accept.

budget. The budget will be no better than the soundness of the forecasting techniques employed. Business forecasting, short- or long-term, is a field unto itself. However, the astute financial manager will always inquire as to how the budget estimates were prepared.

REVIEW AND CONTROL OF CAPITAL INVESTMENT PROJECTS

The capital budgeting process does not terminate with the selection of a set of projects that the firm believes will provide maximum benefits without violating any of the firm's resource constraints. Rather, sound financial management demands that the firm carefully monitor project implementation as well as perform postcompletion audits on major projects.

The review and control of capital expenditures can be divided into two major categories:

1. The review and control of projects in the process of being implemented. These are called *in-progress* projects. This review and control entails auditing the cash outflows related to the acquisition of the project. This process results in information of cost underruns or overruns.

2. The review and control of projects as they are used in the firm's operations. This entails auditing the benefits generated by the project, as well as the operating expenses incurred as the project is used. The goal is to determine the cash flows being generated over the life of the project.

Much effort is expended in evaluating capital projects in order to select those projects that *should be* most beneficial in helping the organization to achieve its goals. Once a set of projects has been selected, management may assume that the projects will be implemented in an optimal fashion. Of course, this is rarely the case. Witness the constantly recurring cost overruns, as well as timing delays, in the efforts to carry out any large-scale capital project. Thus, it is necessary to exert strict control on in-progress projects.

There are two parts to the process of controlling in-progress capital projects. First is the establishment of internal accounting control procedures to accumulate all relevant project-related costs. Second is the use of periodic progress reports that gauge actual expenditures against estimates and provide explanations for significant variances that occur. The timing of the reports may be on a regular calendar basis (such as monthly) and/or keyed to critical events in the acquisition process. The latter would be especially useful if network methods for project scheduling such as PERT or CPM are employed.

The first step specified usually sees the establishment of control accounts for each in-progress capital project. These control accounts are charged with all relevant expenditures, which are further categorized into those items that will be capitalized and those that will be expensed in the current year. These accounts reflect both out-of-pocket payments for materials, labor, overhead, outside purchases, and subcontracts, as well as relevant allocated expenses.

The segregation of costs on a project-by-project basis facilitates the control process because appropriate attention can be given projects as they approach various completion points and/or a cost-overrun status. Further, the use of *responsibility accounting procedures* is also beneficial since control centers that are held accountable for any given project must be notified when cost overruns are imminent so that proper control measures can be implemented.

The use of regular progress reports as projects are being implemented provides several benefits for an organization. First, such timely information presents advance warning to management of potential future difficulties in time for corrective action to be taken. Second, these reports provide a basis for data input to the cash-budgeting process. Third, these reports provide insight to management on projects that could require additional expenditures due to inflation and other unforeseen causes. Fourth, as part of the control process, these reports provide the basis for comparing cumulative actual expenditures with budgeted amounts so that variances can be computed and explanations provided for significant unfavorable variances.

Such procedures should provide valuable assistance to firms in the control of in-progress capital projects. Next, we turn to the postcompletion audit of capital projects.

POSTCOMPLETION AUDITS OF CAPITAL PROJECTS

It is essential for firms to review and control capital projects once they are in use. This is necessary in order to compare their actual benefits with their forecasted benefits, to compare actual operating costs with forecasted operating costs, and to take timely corrective action, if necessary.

In addition, several additional benefits accrue to firms that use postcompletion audits. First, the audits provide an on-the-scene verification of the profitability or savings generated by the project. The audit attempts to isolate the effects of the project under study as far as possible. The auditor, as part of his or her investigation, should seek out reasons why projects turned out either significantly more or significantly less profitable than projected on either an absolute dollar or a percentage basis. In arriving at these results, as much detail as practicable should be provided rather than arbitrarily aggregating different cost or benefit categories; the latter technique could obscure relevant offsetting changes.

Second, divisions and managers are more likely to act in their own (as well as the organization's) best interests relative to the implementation and operation of new capital projects if they realize that postcompletion audits will be performed and that they will be held accountable for the results. The feedback provided to responsible managers should help them to improve their future estimation of costs and benefits, as well as to provide insight about effective operating strategies for new capital projects. Organizations should stress that postcompletion audits are not designed to censure managers, but rather to help them improve their forecasting and operating activities.

Next, the postcompletion audit is beneficial in identifying the causes of difficulties in project implementation and/or operation. The variances of actual results from projected results raise questions that demand explanation and point to possible areas where breakdowns may have occurred. The insight provided here will often suggest corrective action that should be taken or point to alternative courses of action (including the possibility of project abandonment) that should be explored.

Finally, the results obtained through postcompletion audits provide managers of divisions—as well as the members of the capital budgeting review committee —with information that should be helpful in evaluating similar projects in the future. Audits enable organizations to learn from past successes and difficulties so that their operations will be more effective and efficient in the future.

Given these benefits, questions arise concerning who should perform and review postcompletion audits, which projects should be the subject of such audits, and how the process should be carried out.

Ideally, the postcompletion audit should be performed by an independent and unbiased individual, preferably from the internal audit staff or the corporate controller's staff. This will increase the chances that an objective evaluation will be performed.

The postcompletion audit should be reviewed by the manager of the department or division that proposed the project so that he or she can see the results and obtain helpful feedback for operating decisions and future proposals. The manager who recommended the project will usually be one of the major resource persons that the auditor utilizes in preparing the postcompletion audit since the manager will be one of the more informed individuals concerning the reasons for variances of actual results from projections.

The postcompletion audit should also be reviewed by everyone in the project-approval process, including the group or individual that actually approved the project in question. This will facilitate the learning process among key individuals in terms of future proposals.

Clearly, not all capital projects deserve the time, resources, and effort required to perform a postcompletion audit. Most firms perform audits on very large outlay projects or those of special significance to management. In addition, corporate and division managers can often select projects for audit that are of interest or concern in order to gauge results and/or locate difficulties. Finally, a number of projects may be selected randomly at each division in order to provide feedback to local and corporate management.

Pflomm derived an extensive list of data frequently included on postcompletion audits by the 346 manufacturing firms that participated in his Conference Board study.[2]

The following information was usually included:

Number of the approved appropriation request.
Location that requested the appropriation.
Description of the item(s) purchased.
Purpose of the project.
Amount authorized.
Amount actually expended.

[2] Norman E. Pflomm, *Managing Capital Expenditures*, (New York: The Conference Board, 1963), pp. 83–84.

Estimated savings and/or return on investment.
Actual savings or return.
Reasons for variations.
Signatures of those who prepared and/or reviewed the postaudit.

In addition, Pflomm identified the following supplemental information that he often found included in the postcompletion audit:[3]

Estimated versus actual project completion dates with explanations of delays.
Explanation of project cost overruns.
Action taken to correct deficiencies.
Future prospects for currently failing projects.
Details of equipment performance.
Comments on the adequacy of local accounting records needed for making a postaudit.

We view the review and control of accepted projects as a vitally important link in the overall management of capital expenditures. All too often, organizations downplay or disregard entirely this essential step in obtaining feedback and taking corrective action. In order to facilitate the initiation of postcompletion audits in organizations, we include Figure 15–1, which shows a comprehensive checklist and evaluation form developed by a food projects firm to use with their standard postcompletion audit form (Figure 15–2). These exhibits were originally published in the Conference Board report by Pflomm and are reprinted with permission.[4] It is to be hoped that these exhibits will provide guidance for firms seeking to implement or modify their postcompletion audit systems.

THE ABANDONMENT DECISION UNDER CONDITIONS OF RISK

The abandonment option is initially explored in Chapter 5. In intervening chapters we discuss various factors that create uncertainty relative to a project's actual costs and benefits. The following list is indicative of some of these major factors: problems in forecasting future cash flows, problems in estimating inflation rates, interest rates, and future tax rates, difficulties in estimating variability in the project's returns over its life, and difficulties in accurately assessing portfolio effects among projects. This chapter examines the necessity of monitoring accepted projects to see if they are "on track." The abandonment option constitutes one of the alternatives open to management in constructing the capital budget.

Managing the capital budget of a corporation must be a dynamic process. Capital investments cannot be viewed as a commitment to the end. Since changes in the attractiveness of projects or even entire divisions or subsidiaries can occur, regular periodic reappraisals of investments must be undertaken to determine whether the value of continuing the endeavor exceeds abandoning it.

[3]*Ibid.*
[4]*Ibid.*, pp. 90–94.

FIGURE 15–1

CAPITAL PROJECT FINANCIAL EVALUATION AUDIT CHECKLIST

Division -
Project -

	Payback Years	Return on Funds Employed		Total New Funds	
		5 Years	10 Years	5-Yr. Average	10-Yr. Average

Original Request -

Latest Estimate/Actual -

General Comments -

Audit Performed by -
Date of Audit -

Item	Points To Be Checked	Yes Sat.	No Un- sat.	Un- nec.	Remarks/ Reference
Funds Employed					
1. Cash	A. Was total computed according to formula?		_____		
2. Receivables	A. Compare Latest Estimate or Actual to total reported in original submission for:				
	1. Reasonableness of absolute amount.		_____		
	2. Relationship to Net Sales.		_____		
	3. Obtain reason for significant differences.		_____		
	B. Compare relationship to Net Sales for this project to the relationship for the division in total.		_____		
	C. Check Distribution Sales and Service allocations.		_____		
3. Inventories	A. Compare Latest Estimate or Actual to total reported in original submission for:				
	1. Reasonableness of absolute amount.		_____		
	2. Inventory turnover (cost of goods sold + inventory). (a) Also compare to Divisional Turnover.		_____ _____		
	3. Obtain reason for significant differences.		_____		
	B. Is total shown incremental to this project?		_____		
	1. Check division's allocation of inventory to this project.		_____		
	2. Check levels of inventory for this product both before and after this project.		_____		
4. Prepaid and Deferred Expense	A. Compare Latest Estimate or Actual to total reported in original submission for:				
	1. Reasonableness of absolute amount.		_____		
	2. Relationship to expense items in Profit and Loss (marketing, etc.).		_____		
	3. Obtain reasons for significant differences.		_____		

FIGURE 15–1 *(continued)*

Item	Points To Be Checked	Yes Sat.	No Un-sat.	Un-nec.	Remarks/Reference
	B. Check division's computations.	_____			
	C. Check books of account for years where actual figures are available.	_____			
5. Current Liabilities	A. Compare Latest Estimate or Actual to total reported in original submission for:				
	1. Reasonableness of absolute amount.	_____			
	2. Obtain reason for significant differences.	_____			
	B. Check division's computation.	_____			
	1. Has 50% of tax expense been included?	_____			
6. Total Working Funds	A. Verify arithmetical accuracy of total (lines 1 through 4, less line 5).	_____			
7. Land	A. Compare Latest Estimate or Actual to total reported in original submission for:				
	1. Reasonableness of absolute amount.	_____			
	2. Obtain reasons for significant variation.	_____			
	B. Trace amount capitalized to:				
	1. Original purchase records.	_____			
	2. Engineering reports.	_____			
	3. Check year-end workpapers.	_____			
8. Buildings	A. Compare Latest Estimate or Actual to total reported in original submission for:				
	1. Reasonableness of absolute amount.	_____			
	2. Obtain reasons for significant variation.	_____			
	B. Trace amount capitalized from Construction Work in Progress into fixed asset account.	_____			
	1. Spot check invoices in vendor's files.	_____			
	2. Check engineering final close-out report.	_____			
	3. Check year-end workpapers.	_____			
	C. Does total shown in first year plus first-year depreciation equal amount in original request?	_____			
	D. Verify reasonableness of depreciation method:				
	1. Is method used acceptable?	_____			
	2. Is estimated life of asset reasonable?	_____			

FIGURE 15–1 *(continued)*

Item	Points To Be Checked	Yes Sat.	No Un- sat.	Un- nec.	Remarks/ Reference
9. Manufacturing and Engineering	A. Compare Latest Estimate or Actual to total reported in original submission for:				
	1. Reasonableness of absolute amount.		_____		
	2. Obtain reasons for significant variation.		_____		
	B. Trace amount capitalized.		_____		
	1. Check engineering reports.		_____		
	2. Check vendors' invoices.		_____		
	3. Check year-end workpapers.		_____		
	C. Does total shown in first year plus first-year depreciation equal amount in original request?		_____		
	D. Verify reasonableness of depreciation method:		_____		
	1. Is method used acceptable?		_____		
	2. Is estimated life of asset reasonable?		_____		
10. Total Engr'g.	A. Compare Latest Estimate or Actual to total reported in original submission for:				
	1. Reasonableness of absolute amount.		_____		
	2. Obtain reasons for significant variation.		_____		
	B. Check total to Engineering Report on Project.		_____		
11. Other (Explain)	A. Compare Latest Estimate or Actual to total reported in original submission for:				
	1. Reasonableness of absolute amount.		_____		
	2. Obtain reasons for significant variation.		_____		
12. Expense (After Taxes)	A. Compare Latest Estimate or Actual to total reported in original submission for:	_____			
	1. Reasonableness of absolute amount.		_____		
	2. Check to total expense amount included on Appropriation Request.		_____		
	3. Obtain reasons for significant differences.		_____		
	B. Verify that total has been repeated for all years.		_____		
13. Total Capital Funds	A. Verify arithmetical accuracy of total (add lines 7 through 12).		_____		
14. Tot. New Funds	A. Verify arithmetical accuracy of total (lines 6 plus 13).		_____		
15. Cumulative Depreciation	A. Determine that line 15 equals cumulative annual depreciation shown on line 32. (The accuracy of line 32 will be determined later.)		_____		

FIGURE 15–1 *(continued)*

Item	Points To Be Checked	Yes Sat.	No Un-sat.	Un-nec.	Remarks/ Reference
16. Cum. Net Profit & Depreciation	A. Determine that this line is identical to line 34. (The accuracy of line 34 will be determined later.)	_____			
17. New Funds to Repay	A. Determine that this line equals line 14 plus line 15 minus line 16 for each year.	_____			
	B. Verify accuracy of payback calculation (shown on top of form).				
	1. Determine the number of years with a figure on line 17. This is the number of full years to repay that is to be listed on the first line in payback calculation above.	_____			
	2. Determine the part year (second line above) by dividing the figure on line 17 in the last full year to repay column, by the total on line 33 in the succeeding year.	_____			
	3. The sum of these items will determine the total years to repay.	_____			
Profit and Loss Projection					
18. Gross Sales	A. Compare Latest Estimate or Actual to total reported in original submission for:				
	1. Reasonableness of absolute amount.	_____			
	2. Obtain reasons for differences.	_____			
	B. Determine whether sales were incremental to this project:				
	1. Check reasonableness and accuracy of division's calculations.	_____			
	(a) Where appropriate, check production records and convert output to sales dollars.	_____			
	2. If not a new product, determine capacity of previously existing facilities and subtract this from total sales for product, which should give incremental sales.	_____			
19. Deductions	A. Compare Deductions from Gross Sales in this Profit and Loss projection to the historical and planned rate for:				
	1. The total division, and	_____			
	2. The total product Profit and Loss, and	_____			
	3. Obtain reasons for any significant variations.	_____			
	4. Check divisional allocation to this project.	_____			

FIGURE 15–1   *(continued)*

Item	Points To Be Checked	Yes Sat.	No Un-sat.	Un-nec.	Remarks/Reference
20. Net Sales	A. Verify arithmetical accuracy (line 18 less line 19).	_____			
21. Cost of Goods Sold	A. Check division's computation.	_____			
& & 22. Gross Profit	1. Review cost records before and after capital project, thereby ascertaining savings.	_____			
	B. Compare the Gross Profit rate in this Profit and Loss projection to the historical and planned rate for:				
	1. The original submission, and	_____			
	2. The total division, and	_____			
	3. The total product Profit and Loss, and	_____			
	4. If a new product, to any similar products.	_____			
	5. Obtain explanations of significant variations.	_____			
23. Advertising	A. Check division's computation.	_____			
	B. Compare as a % of Net Sales to the historical and planned rate for:				
	1. The original submission, and	_____			
	2. The total division, and	_____			
	3. The total product Profit and Loss, and	_____			
	4. If a new product, compare to similar products when possible, and	_____			
	5. Observe trends in rate and absolute amounts,	_____			
	6. Obtain explanations of any significant variations.	_____			
24. Selling	A. Check division's computation.	_____			
	B. Compare as a % of Net Sales to the historical and planned rate for:				
	1. The original submission, and	_____			
	2. The total division, and	_____			
	3. The total product Profit and Loss, and	_____			
	4. If a new product, compare to similar products when possible, and	_____			
	5. Observe trends in rate and absolute amounts,	_____			
	6. Obtain explanations of any significant variations.	_____			

FIGURE 15–1 *(continued)*

Item	Points To Be Checked	Yes Sat.	No Un- sat.	Un- nec.	Remarks/ Reference
25. General and Administrative	A. Check division's computation.	————		————	
	B. Compare as a % of Net Sales to the historical and planned rate for:				
	1. The original submission, and	————		————	
	2. The total division, and	————		————	
	3. The total product Profit and Loss, and	————		————	
	4. If a new product, compare to similar products when possible, and	————		————	
	5. Observe trends in rate and absolute amounts,	————		————	
	6. Obtain explanations of any significant variations.	————		————	
26. Research	A. Check division's computation.	————		————	
	B. Compare as a % of Net Sales to the historical and planned rate for:				
	1. The original submission, and	————		————	
	2. The total division, and	————		————	
	3. The total product Profit and Loss, and	————		————	
	4. If a new product, compare to similar products when possible, and	————		————	
	5. Observe trends in rate and absolute amounts,	————		————	
	6. Obtain explanations of any significant variations.	————		————	
27. Other	A. Division should satisfactorily explain totals included on this line. Auditor should take steps necessary to satisfy himself of reasonableness and accuracy of these totals.	————		————	
28. Adjustment	A. Division should satisfactorily explain totals included on this line. Auditor should take steps necessary to satisfy himself of reasonableness and accuracy of these totals.	————		————	
29. Profit Before Taxes	A. Verify arithmetical accuracy.	————		————	
30. Taxes	A. Verify that proper tax rate has been used.	————		————	
31. Net Profit	A. Verify arithmetical accuracy.	————		————	
32. Annual Depreciation	A. Determine reasonableness of totals (see Items 8D and 9D).	————		————	
33. Annual Net Profit & Depreciation	A. Verify arithmetical accuracy (lines 31 plus 32).	————		————	

FIGURE 15–1   *(continued)*

Item	Points To Be Checked	Yes Sat.	No Un- sat.	Un- nec.	Remarks/ Reference
34. Cumulative Net Profit and Depreciation	A. Verify arithmetical accuracy (should equal the cumulative total of line 33).				
5- and 10-Year Averages	A. Verify arithmetical accuracy of all 5- and 10-year average figures shown.				
Return on Funds	A. Verify that correct 5- and 10-year average figures have been brought up to Return on Funds section in the upper right-hand corner of the form.				
	B. Confirm Return on Funds calculations for both the 5- and 10-year periods.				

Since managing the capital budget is usually a rationing problem, a company cannot afford to tie up funds in investments that are below acceptable standards. Managing the capital budget must be viewed as a continuing process of optimally allocating available funds. Thus, this process must include the reevaluation of projects already undertaken.

When investment opportunities are initially considered, key variables are identified and assumptions are made to arrive at some choice. As time passes, changes can occur that could affect these key variables. Assumptions made initially may prove incorrect, or perhaps some additional unforeseen new investment opportunities may arise. *Failure to abandon projects that are no longer desirable could be very costly. By the same reasoning, failure to abandon projects that could make funds available for substantially better investment opportunities might also be costly from an opportunity standpoint.* Therefore, the prudent financial manager must incorporate abandonment values (at various points throughout the life of the project) into the analysis for capital project evaluation and selection.

The most widely cited work in the abandonment area under conditions of changing risk posture is that due to Robichek and Van Horne,[5] in which they recommend the use of decision trees and simulation to handle abandonment values. To illustrate the use of decision trees, consider Figure 15–3, which shows the cash flows for project A over its 3-year useful life.[6] Note that Figure 15–3 has the same design as the tree diagrams for single projects, which are discussed in Chapter 12. However, the presence of the abandonment option (which is shown at the bottom of the figure) necessitates that a decision-tree approach be taken to evaluate whether the project should be abandoned or not at each point in time where this option exists. Figure 15–4 shows a small part of the decision tree that

---

[5]A. A. Robichek and J. C. Van Horne, "Abandonment Value and Capital Budgeting," *Journal of Finance,* 22, no. 4 (December 1967), 577–590.

[6]This example originally appeared in Robichek and Van Horne, "Abandonment Value," pp. 579–582.

FIGURE 15–2 Postcompletion Audit Form for Capital Projects

FUNDS EMPLOYED AND PROFIT AND LOSS PROJECTIONS

XYZ / DIVISION	CHICAGO, ILLINOIS / LOCATION	Project "A" / PROJECT TITLE	PROJECT NO. 11	SUPPLEMENT NO. —

RETURN OF NEW FUNDS EMPLOYED	PAY BACK YEARS FROM DATE OF COMPLETION		RETURN ON NEW FUNDS EMPLOYED	A—Average Funds Employed—Line 14			
	Number Of Full Years To Pay Back	4.0 YEARS		B—Profit Before Taxes—Line 32			
	Part Year Calculation	.5 YEARS		C—Calculated Return—B ÷ A			
	Total Years To Pay Back	4.5 YEARS					

		A	B	C
Five-Yr. Average		$ 2,902	$ 1,228	42.3 %
Ten-Yr. Average		$ 2,447	$ 1,828	74.7 %

Funds Employed	1st Yr.	2nd Yr.	3rd Yr.	4th Yr.	5th Yr.	5-Yr. Avg.	6th Year	7th Year	8th Year	9th Year	10th Year	10-Yr. Avg.
1 Cash	290	222	209	215	221	232	233	239	251	263	276	242
2 Receivables	338	287	296	304	312	307	329	338	355	372	388	332
3 Inventories	766	651	670	689	709	697	747	766	804	843	881	753
4 Prepaid and Deferred Expenses	12	10	11	11	11	11	12	12	13	13	14	12
5 Current Liabilities	(121)	191	502	520	543	327	581	603	643	682	721	487
6 Total Working Funds (1 thru 4-5)	1,527	979	684	699	710	920	740	752	780	809	838	852
7 Land Gross Cost 100	100	100	100	100	100	100	100	100	100	100	100	100
8 Buildings 1,000	976	928	881	835	790	882	747	705	664	624	586	774
9 Machinery & Equipment 1,240	1,166	1,024	891	768	655	900	552	459	376	302	238	643
10 Engineering 100	94	82	71	61	51	72	42	34	27	21	16	50
11 Other (Explain)	—	—	—	—	—	—	—	—	—	—	—	—
12 Expense (After Taxes) 60	28	28	28	28	28	28	28	28	28	28	28	28
13 Total Capital Funds (7 Thru 12)	2,364	2,162	1,971	1,792	1,624	1,982	1,469	1,326	1,195	1,075	968	1,595
14 Total New Funds (6 + 13)	3,891	3,141	2,655	2,491	2,334	2,902	2,209	2,078	1,975	1,884	1,806	2,447
15 Cum. Depreciation On 8 Thru 11	104	306	497	676	844		999	1,142	1,273	1,393	1,500	
16 Cum. Net Profit & Deprec. (Line 37)	(108)	430	1,503	2,597	3,718		4,895	6,099	7,360	8,679	10,053	
17 New Funds To Repay (14 + 15-16)	4,103	3,017	1,649	570	—		—	—	—	—	—	

Profit and Loss Projection	1st Yr.	2nd Yr.	3rd Yr.	4th Yr.	5th Yr.	5-Yr. Avg.	6th Year	7th Year	8th Year	9th Year	10th Year	10-Yr. Avg.
18 Unit Volume	2,000	1,700	1,750	1,800	1,850	1,820	1,950	2,000	2,100	2,200	2,300	1,965
19 Gross Sales	7,426	6,312	6,498	6,683	6,869	6,758	7,240	7,426	7,797	8,169	8,540	7,296
20 Deductions	670	570	586	603	620	610	653	670	704	737	771	658
21 Net Sales	6,756	5,742	5,912	6,080	6,249	6,148	6,587	6,756	7,093	7,432	7,769	6,638
22 Cost of Goods Sold	3,210	2,901	2,957	3,011	3,066	3,029	3,196	3,251	3,382	3,512	3,642	3,213
23 Gross Profit	3,546	2,841	2,955	3,069	3,183	3,119	3,391	3,505	3,711	3,920	4,127	3,425
24 G.P. % Net Sales	52.5	49.5	50.0	50.5	50.9	50.7	51.5	51.9	52.3	52.7	53.1	51.6
25 Advertising	3,358	1,725	649	661	669	1,413	719	747	799	838	887	1,105
26 Selling	300	300	300	300	300	300	320	320	320	340	350	315
27 General & Administrative	65	65	65	75	80	70	80	80	85	85	85	77
28 Research	130	20	20	20	20	42	10	10	10	10	10	26
29 Start-up Costs	135					27						14
30 Other (Explain)	2	1	1	3	1	2	1	2	1	1	2	1
31 Adjustment (Explain)	10	12	35	55	75	37	77	79	81	83	85	59
32 Profit Before Taxes	(454)	718	1,885	1,955	2,038	1,228	2,184	2,267	2,415	2,563	2,708	1,828
33 Taxes—Federal & State Income	(242)	382	1,003	1,040	1,085	653	1,162	1,206	1,285	1,364	1,441	973
34 Net Profit	(212)	336	882	915	953	575	1,022	1,061	1,130	1,199	1,267	855
35 Annual Depreciation	104	202	191	179	168	169	155	143	131	120	107	150
36 An. Net Profit & Deprec. (34 + 35)	(108)	538	1,073	1,094	1,121	744	1,177	1,204	1,261	1,319	1,374	1,005
37 Cum. Net Profit & Depreciation	(108)	430	1,503	2,597	3,718		4,895	6,099	7,360	8,679	10,053	

FIGURE 15–3 Expected Future Cash Flows for Project A

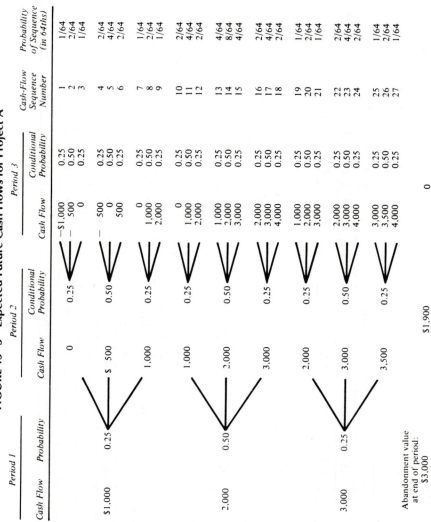

Period 1		Period 2		Period 3		Cash-Flow Sequence Number	Probability of Sequence (in 64ths)
Cash Flow	Probability	Cash Flow	Conditional Probability	Cash Flow	Conditional Probability		
$1,000	0.25	0	0.25	−$1,000	0.25	1	1/64
				− 500	0.50	2	2/64
				0	0.25	3	1/64
		$ 500	0.50	− 500	0.25	4	2/64
				0	0.50	5	4/64
				500	0.25	6	2/64
		1,000	0.25	0	0.25	7	1/64
				1,000	0.50	8	2/64
				2,000	0.25	9	1/64
2,000	0.50	1,000	0.25	0	0.25	10	2/64
				1,000	0.50	11	4/64
				2,000	0.25	12	2/64
		2,000	0.50	1,000	0.25	13	4/64
				2,000	0.50	14	8/64
				3,000	0.25	15	4/64
		3,000	0.25	2,000	0.25	16	2/64
				3,000	0.50	17	4/64
				4,000	0.25	18	2/64
3,000	0.25	2,000	0.25	1,000	0.25	19	1/64
				2,000	0.50	20	2/64
				3,000	0.25	21	1/64
		3,000	0.50	2,000	0.25	22	2/64
				3,000	0.50	23	4/64
				4,000	0.25	24	2/64
		3,500	0.25	3,000	0.25	25	1/64
				3,500	0.50	26	2/64
				4,000	0.25	27	1/64

Abandonment value at end of period:
$3,000 $1,900   0

232

FIGURE 15-4 Partial Decision Tree for Project A

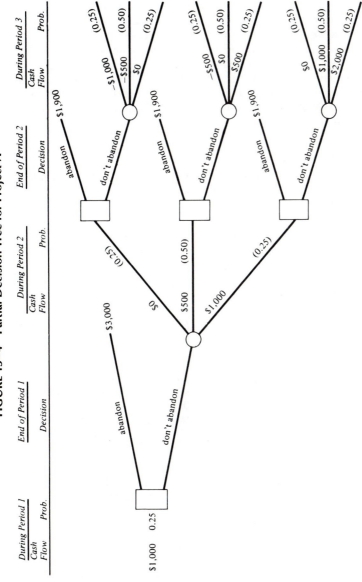

would be necessary to evaluate abandoning project A. If the cash flow in period 1 was $1,000, in order to decide whether the project should be abandoned at the end of period 1, the entire tree in the exhibit must be folded back. We know that the value of the project if abandoned at the end of period 1 is $3,000, but we must compute the value of the decision alternative "don't abandon." This necessitates evaluation of all subsequent states of nature and decision alternatives which emanate from this branch, in order to compare the expected values of these two alternatives. The procedure then is to select the alternative at each decision node which maximizes the expected present value of future benefits. For the abandon alternative, the expected present value is merely the expected value of the abandonment value probability distribution; whereas for the don't abandon alternative, we would have to compute the present value of all future cash flows whether they be from keeping the project or abandoning it later. This process is illustrated in Example 1.

□ **EXAMPLE 1**   Abandonment Values at End of Period 2

For each of the cash-flow sequences shown in Figure 15–3 determine whether it would be better to abandon or retain at the end of year 2. Assume that all cash flows have already been discounted for time.

Solution: For each of the branches shown in the decision tree, the value of not abandoning is found by summing the product of the year 3 cash flows multiplied by their respective probability of occurrence. The decision is made by comparing this value to the abandonment value of $1,900.

Period 1 Flow	Period 2 Flow	Value of Not Abandoning at End of Period 2	Decision
$1,000	$ 0	−$ 500	Abandon
1,000	500	0	Abandon
1,000	1,000	1,000	Abandon
2,000	1,000	1,000	Abandon
2,000	2,000	2,000	Don't abandon
2,000	3,000	3,000	Don't abandon
3,000	2,000	2,000	Don't abandon
3,000	3,000	3,000	Don't abandon
3,000	3,500	3,500	Don't abandon

Thus, the partially folded back decision tree would appear as in Figure 15–5. Note that the branch of the less desirable alternative at the end of period 2 has been marked with a pair of parallel lines.   □

Example 1 is continued in Example 2, where we evaluate abandonment at the end of period 1. To evaluate the alternative of abandoning or not at the end of period 1, we would fold back the tree to the end of period 1. The value of not abandoning is determined by adding the value of the optimal decision at the end of period 2 (found in Example 1) to the cash flows in period 2 and then multiplying by the respective probability of occurrence and summing over all events. This is shown in Example 2 on page 236.

FIGURE 15–5

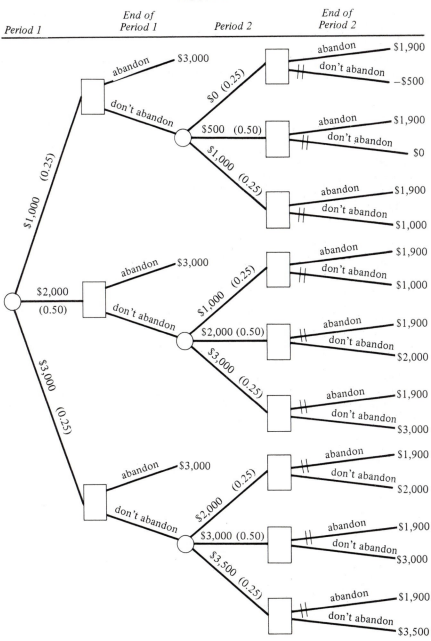

☐ **EXAMPLE 2**   *Abandonment Decisions at the End of Period 1*

For each of the possible cash flows of project A that can occur in period 1, compute the expected value of not abandoning and determine the optimal decision (abandon or not) at that point in time.

Solution: For each of the three possible cash flows in period 1, the value of not abandoning project A is found by multiplying column 4 by column 5 in the following table:

(1)	(2)	(3)	(4)	(5)	(6)
					Value of
					Not Abandoning
		Value of			*at the*
Period 1	*Period 2*	*Optimal Decision*	*Sum of*	*Probability*	*End of Period*
Cash Flow	*Cash Flow*	*at End of Period 2*	*(2) and (3)*	*of Event*	*1*
	$ 0	$1,900	$1,900	0.25	$ 475
$1,000	500	1,900	2,400	0.50	1,200
	1,000	1,900	2,900	0.25	725
					$2,400
	$1,000	$1,900	$2,900	0.25	$ 725
2,000	2,000	2,000	4,000	0.50	2,000
	3,000	3,000	6,000	0.25	1,500
					$4,225
	$2,000	$2,000	$4,000	0.25	$1,000
3,000	3,000	3,000	6,000	0.50	3,000
	3,500	3,500	7,000	0.25	1,750
					$5,750

The decision tree folded back to the end of period 2 is shown in Figure 15–6. Thus, the optimal decision at the end of period 1 would be to abandon project A if the cash flow in period 1 was $1,000; however, if the cash flow in period 1 was either $2,000 or $3,000, the optimal decision would be to continue to hold project A (i.e., do not abandon).

FIGURE 15–6

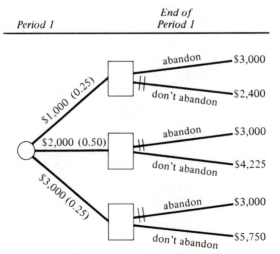

Summarizing the results of Examples 1 and 2 by referring back to the two decision trees drawn, we see that (1) if the period 1 cash flow was $1,000, project A should be abandoned at the end of period 1; (2) if the period 1 cash flow was $2,000, the project should be held for the second period and abandoned at the end of the second period *only if* the period 2 cash flow was $1,000 (if the period 2 cash flow is either $2,000 or $3,000, the project should be held for period 3); (3) if the period 1 cash flow is $3,000, the project should be held for its entire useful life. Following these decision rules, the firm will optimally hold or abandoned project A over its life.   □

The examples demonstrate that the abandonment option increases the expected NPV of the project compared with the same project without the alternative of abandoning at various points throughout its useful life. In addition, the abandonment option also has a desirable impact on both the absolute and relative risk of the project, as well as on the skewness in the distribution of the NPV values over the project's useful life. These characteristics are demonstrated in Example 3.

□ **EXAMPLE 3**   *Impact of Abandonment on Project Risk*

Consider project B, which has a 2-year useful life, an original cost of $400,000, and possible cash inflows (in thousands of dollars) as follows:

Period 1		Period 2		
Cash Flow	Probability	Cash Flow	Conditional Probability	Cash-Flow Sequence
$300	0.3	$250	0.30	1
		300	0.50	2
		350	0.20	3
$400	0.4	$300	0.30	4
		400	0.50	5
		500	0.20	6
$500	0.3	$400	0.30	7
		500	0.40	8
		600	0.30	9

The firm's cost of capital is 12% and the undiscounted cash flows tabulated above would lead to an expected NPV of $271,000 as follows:

Cash-Flow Sequence	Total Present Value of Cash Flow (thousands)	Sequence Probability	Expected Value (thousands)
1	$467	0.09	$ 42
2	507	0.15	76
3	547	0.06	33
4	596	0.12	72
5	676	0.20	135
6	756	0.08	60
7	765	0.09	69
8	845	0.12	101
9	925	0.09	83
		1.00	$671

$$\text{Expected present value} = \$671,000$$
$$\text{Initial investment} = \underline{\ 400,000}$$
$$\text{Expected net present value} = \$271,000$$

In addition, the calculation of the variance, semivariance, measure of skewness, and coefficient of variation for project B shown below uses the techniques developed in Chapters 12 and 13.

Cash-Flow Sequence	NPV of Sequence	Expected NPV	Sequence Deviation	Sequence^2 Deviation	$\times$	Sequence Probability	$=$	Result
1	$ 67	$271	$- \$204$	41,616		0.09		3,745
2	107	271	$-$ 164	26,896		0.15		4,034
3	147	271	$-$ 124	15,376		0.06		923
4	196	271	$-$ 75	5,625		0.12		675
5	276	271	$+$ 5	25		0.20		5
6	356	271	$+$ 85	7,225		0.08		578
7	365	271	$+$ 94	8,836		0.09		795
8	445	271	$+$ 174	30,276		0.12		3,633
9	525	271	$+$ 254	64,516		0.09		5,806
						$\overline{1.00}$		$\overline{20,194}$

$$\text{Variance} = V_B = 20,194$$
$$\text{Standard deviation} = \sigma_B = \sqrt{20,194} = \$142$$
$$\text{Semivariance} = SV_B = 9,377$$
$$\text{Measure of skewness} = \frac{V_B}{2SV_B} = 1.077$$
$$\text{Coefficient of variation} = \frac{\sigma_B}{E(X_B)} = 0.524$$

Now, consider that the firm has the option to abandon project B at the end of year 1 for $280,000. Compute the expected NPV, the standard deviation, variance, semivariance, measure of skewness, and coefficient of variation given the abandonment option and show that these measures dominate their counterparts given that the abandonment option did not exist.

Solution: Given the possible cash inflows in periods 1 and 2 and their associated probabilities as shown in the first table above, the expected present values of the second period's cash inflows are computed in the following table:

Cash-Flow Sequence	Cash Flow	Present[a] Value	Conditional Probability	Expected Present Value
1	$250	$199	0.3	$ 60
2	300	239	0.5	120
3	350	279	0.2	56
			Branch total	$\overline{\$236}$
4	$300	$239	0.3	72
5	400	319	0.5	160
6	500	399	0.2	80
			Branch total	$\overline{\$312}$
7	$400	$319	0.3	96
8	500	399	0.4	160
9	600	478	0.3	143
			Branch total	$\overline{\$399}$

Present value of salvage (0.8929)($280) = $250

---

[a] PV factor = 0.7972.

If a cash inflow of $300 occurs in period 1, project B is expected to be abandoned for $280 at the end of period 1. Cash-flow sequences 1 to 3 are reduced to one sequence with a present value of $518 (i.e., $300 + $280)(0.8929). In all other cases, the project is held for year 2 rather than abandoned. The following table computes the expected NPV with the abandonment option:

Cash-Flow Sequence	Total Present Value of Cash Flow	Sequence Probability	Expected Value
1-3	$518	0.3	$155
4	596	0.12	72
5	676	0.20	135
6	756	0.08	60
7	765	0.09	69
8	845	0.12	101
9	925	0.09	83
		$\overline{1.00}$	$\overline{\$675}$

$$\text{Expected present value} = \$675$$
$$\text{Initial investment} = \underline{\ \ 400}$$
$$\text{Expected net present value} = \$275$$

Given these calculations, we now compute the measures of risk and skewness for the abandonment option.

Cash-Flow Sequence	NPV of Sequence	Expected NPV	Sequence Deviation	Sequence² Deviation	×	Sequence Probability	=	Result
1-3	$118	$275	− $157	24,649		0.3		7,395
4	196	275	− 79	6,241		0.12		749
5	276	275	+ 1	1		0.20		0
6	356	275	+ 81	6,561		0.08		525
7	365	275	+ 10	8,100		0.09		729
8	445	275	+ 170	28,900		0.12		3,468
9	525	275	+ 250	62,500		0.09		5,625
						$\overline{1.00}$		$\overline{18,491}$

$$\text{Variance} = V_B = 18{,}491$$
$$\text{Standard deviation} = \sigma_B = \sqrt{18{,}491} = \$136$$
$$\text{Semivariance} = SV_B = 8{,}144$$
$$\text{Measure of skewness} = V_B/2SV_B = 1.135$$
$$\text{Coefficient of variation} = \frac{\sigma_B}{E(X_B)} = 0.495$$

Finally, the following table compares project B with and without the abandonment option, as well as the percent changes in each of the computed statistics.

Net Present Value	Without Abandonment	With Abandonment	Percent Change
Expected value	$ 271	$ 275	+1.5
Standard deviation	$ 142	$ 136	−4.2
Skewness	1.077	1.135	+5.4
Coefficient of variation	0.524	0.495	−5.5

As shown, all the measures of risk and skewness moved in a favorable direction as the abandonment option was included. Notice that the standard deviation has decreased by 4.2% and the relative size of the standard deviation to the expected return has decreased by a significant 5.5%. Further, the measure of skewness has increased 5.4%, to 1.135. Since the skewness value is greater than 1 and larger than before, the distribution is more skewed to the right than previously. A distribution more skewed to the right has a lower downside risk. Thus, the risk of *cash flows below the expected value is reduced*.   □

Reflecting on the results of Example 3, it should be stressed that the abandonment option will not always have the impact on project risk and return obtained in that problem (i.e., project risk was reduced and project return was increased). On the contrary, project risk could increase if the expected abandonment values are sufficiently large and/or project return could decrease if abandonment variances are sufficiently small. Thus, the abandonment option in its most general form should be handled by using the utility maximization criterion based upon the investor's risk-return preferences.[7]

As can clearly be seen from Examples 1, 2, and 3, the calculations can quickly become tedious as the number of periods increase, or the number of possible cash flows each period increase, or if the abandonment value is known only by a probability distribution. Thus, Robichek and Van Horne recommended and illustrated the use of the Monte Carlo simulation under such conditions.[8] The simulation model to handle the abandonment problem is a straightforward extension of the models discussed in Chapter 22. In addition, the interested reader is referred to the appendix in the Robichek and Van Horne article,[9] where the authors give a brief description of the simulation model they used.

Finally, Bonini formulated a dynamic programming model that finds the optimal abandonment strategy under both conditions of certainty and uncertainty.[10] The approach can also be viewed as an analytic extension of the Hillier formulation for quantifying project risk[11] where the abandonment option exists. The interested reader should consult this reference.

This section should be closed with a word of caution. Capital budgeting projects should be monitored, and it may become advantageous to terminate some. However, the abandonment decision must stand the test of maximizing shareholders' wealth. It is often extremely difficult to estimate the costs and benefits of abandoning large capital projects which may necessitate closing down or selling off a product line or division. Such changes involve disentangling accounting and tax effects, managerial reassignments, work-force dislocations, customer relations problems, community and societal impacts, and so on. Thus, the process can entail very long lead times, perhaps spanning a decade. The proper timing of abandonment and the attendant dislocations affect the ultimate decision and modify the structures of theory.

---

[7]The authors thank Dr. Arthur C. M. Clarke for pointing out these aspects in a book review on the first edition of this text which was published in *The Engineering Economist*.

[8]Robichek and Van Horne, "Abandonment Value," pp. 582–584.

[9]Ibid., pp. 588–589.

[10]C. P. Bonini, "Capital Investment Under Uncertainty with Abandonment Options," *Journal of Financial and Quantitative Analysis*, 12, no. 1 (March 1977), 39–54.

[11]F. S. Hillier, "The Derivation of Probabilistic Information for the Evaluation of Risky Investment," *Management Science*, 9, no. 3 (April 1963), 443–457.

COST-JUSTIFYING CAPITAL BUDGETING

Capital budgeting must be monitored by management for yet another reason: it can be expensive in manpower, time, and facilities. The sophistication of the process naturally varies with the size of the firm and the importance of the projects under consideration. Also, the techniques we have discussed can be applied to a wide variety of project types: plant and equipment; lease versus buy analysis; refunding proposals; advertising expenditures; research and development projects; and abandonment issues. So many and varied are the applications that at the outset, management must establish a cutoff point; that is, spending proposals below a certain amount will be treated as simple expenditure items. Above this amount, the budgeting process will take over.

The objective is to establish a cost-effective budgeting procedure. This is fostered by following up on projects to assure that the desired return is realized, abandoning projects that fail the test, and limiting the budgeting process to projects of a size appropriate to the analytical techniques applied. The latter, it should be noted, is not the most common sin of the U.S. financial management; rather the converse—spending large sums without appropriate analysis.

Nonetheless, one can appropriately raise the question of whether firms using the more sophisticated discounted-cash-flow methods show enhanced profitability compared to those which adhere to older rules of thumb. The evidence is uncertain on the point and the analysis difficult, owing to the presence of so many variables intruding on the firm's profitability other than the capital budgeting decision. Yet we can cite some research on the topic. George A. Christy, for example, matched earnings per share of his surveyed companies against the capital budgeting techniques employed. Christy found no significant relationship between profitability and the methodology of long-range asset management.[12]

By contrast, Suk H. Kim at the University of Detroit surveyed 114 machinery companies and related their average earnings per share to several variables: the degree of sophistication in capital budgeting, size of the firm, capital intensity, degree of risk, and debt ratio. Kim found a positive relationship between profitability and the budgeting technique when the latter is considered as a broad process involving the added variables ignored in the Christy study.[13]

SUMMARY

In this chapter we stress the importance of financial forecasting (both short-run and long-run) in the capital budgeting decision-making process. An overview of major assumptions and strategies in financial forecasting is presented.

---

[12] George A. Christy, *Capital Budgeting: Current Practices and Their Efficiency* (Eugene, Ore.: Bureau of Economic Research, University of Oregon, 1966).

[13] "Capital Budgeting Practices in Large Corporations and Their Impact on Overall Profitability," *Baylor Business Studies* (January 1979), pp. 49–66.

Next, the very important area of the review and evaluation of previously accepted capital projects is addressed. The impact of the abandonment option on the attractiveness of investment proposals is measured and illustrated by examples. The optimal time to abandon a project is that period which leads to a maximization of the NPV considering both the present value of project cash inflows and the present value of the abandonment value. Under conditions of changing risk, it is shown that the abandonment option can increase the expected NPV, decrease both the absolute and relative risk of the project, and increase the positive skewness of the project (which reduces the downside risk of the project).

Finally, the importance of cost-effective capital project evaluation is stressed so that firms avoid committing major dollar amounts without appropriate analysis.

QUESTIONS/PROBLEMS

1. Discuss the importance of capital budgeting to a firm's overall strategic planning and the interrelationships between capital budgeting and the functional areas of finance, production, personnel, marketing, and accounting.
2. Discuss the importance of forecasting to capital budgeting and the importance of taking cognizance of the assumptions underlying forecasting models in use.
3. List at least three reasons why capital investment projects may have to be abandoned before the end of their useful lives in order to maximize shareholders' wealth.
4. The Ridgway Company is evaluating a capital project that it feels has quite a bit of uncertainty associated with it. Namely, the firm feels that the following probabilities should be assigned to various cash flows and abandonment values (which are all considered to be independent):

		Period				
		0	1	2	3	4
Cash flows	Pr = 0.2	− $14,000	+ $10,000	+ $ 9,000	+ $ 8,000	+ $ 7,000
	Pr = 0.5	− 20,000	+ 12,000	+ 14,000	+ 15,000	+ 16,000
	Pr = 0.3	− 22,000	+ 13,000	+ 15,000	+ 17,000	+ 19,000
Abandonment values	Pr = 0.3		+ 10,000	+ 7,000	+ 6,000	+ 4,000
	Pr = 0.6		+ 11,000	+ 9,000	+ 7,000	+ 5,000
	Pr = 0.1		+ 12,000	+ 11,000	+ 8,000	+ 6,000

The firm's cost of capital is 12%, and this project is considered to be of average riskiness to the firm. Because of the independence between successive years' cash flows and between these flows and the abandonment values, expected values can be used to determine the NPV and the optimal time to abandon. Compute the following.
   (a) The expected NPV if the project is held to the end of its useful life.
   (b) The optimal time to abandon the project, which is determined by maximizing the expected value of NPV^m.
5. Jones Brothers, Inc., is considering investing in a new machine to package cough drops. The machine has a potential useful life of 3 years, with a possibility of abandonment at the end of year 1 or 2. The possible cash flows, abandonment values,

and their associated probabilities are as follows:

Year 1		Year 2		Year 3	
Cash Flow	*Prob.*	*Cash Flow*	*Prob.*	*Cash Flow*	*Prob.*
				$ 8,000	0.3
		$ 6,000	0.2	10,000	0.3
$4,000	0.4	7,000	0.4	12,000	0.4
		8,000	0.4	13,000	0.3
				15,000	0.3
				10,000	0.2
		8,000	0.2	11,000	0.4
9,000	0.6	11,000	0.6	13,000	0.4
		12,000	0.2	15,000	0.2
				16,000	0.4

At the end of year 1:		At the end of year 2:	
Value	*Probability*	*Value*	*Probability*
$16,000	0.2	$10,000	0.3
18,000	0.7	12,000	0.6
19,000	0.1	14,000	0.1

Jones Brothers' required rate of return for this project is 14%.

(a) Draw the complete decision tree, which represents the decision alternatives available to the firm at various points through time.

(b) For each of the possible cash flows during year 2, determine whether the project should be abandoned at the end of year 2.

(c) For each of the cash flows during year 1, determine whether the project should be abandoned at the end of year 1.

(d) Summarize your results in parts (b) and (c) concerning what the firm should do in both years for all possible cash flows that could occur (i.e., make a recommendation to Jones Brothers about whether it should hold or abandon the asset for each possible cash flow).

(e) Assuming that the project cost is $20,000, compute the expected NPV, σ_{NPV}, semivariance, measure of skewness, and coefficient of variation for the project without the abandonment option.

(f) Compute all of the measures mentioned in part (e) but this time with the abandonment option.

16

INTRODUCTION TO CAPITAL ASSET PRICING

In our discussion of portfolio effects, we measured portfolio risk by determining the covariance of each project (or security) with all other projects (or securities) in the combination. The calculations (variances and covariances) for even a small number of projects quickly become voluminous. The number of inputs for a portfolio of N projects equals $N(N+3)/2$, since we need to consider the expected return and standard deviation for each security and the covariance between all possible pairs of securities. If management were evaluating 12 projects, this approach entails 90 calculations. As N increases in size, the input requirements grow geometrically; witness, that 100 projects would require 5,150 inputs and 200 projects would require 20,300 inputs! In addition, the problem of estimating probabilities and joint probabilities of the cash flows further complicates the application of the portfolio model to capital budgeting. Theoreticians can point to conceptual devices for estimating probabilities, but at this stage of their development, they do not enjoy wide currency among managers.

An alternative approach, employing techniques familiar to financial managers and corporate economists, uses the capital asset pricing model (CAPM).[1] This relates the return of a project (or security) to a broad-based economic indicator of returns on risky assets such as Standard & Poor's 500 Index of Stocks, industry profitability ratios, and so on. The model posits a linear correlation between the returns on the risky asset and the index.

---

[1] For purposes of study of capital asset pricing, we define capital asset as one with a life of more than 1 year, expected to earn an income sufficient to cover the amortization of its acquisition cost and operation expenses plus a net yield commensurate to the time value of money and risk. The term includes long-lived physical assets (plant and equipment) plus claims on such assets (common stocks, bonds, and other securities).

In contrast to the number of calculations demanded by the full variance-covariance portfolio model, the new input requirement is simply $3N + 2$ when using Sharpe's single-index model, expressed as Equation (1) in the next section. For 12 projects, this totals 38 inputs, a reduction of 52; for 100 projects, 302 inputs are required; for 200 projects, 602, which are reductions of 94% and 97%, respectively, compared to the full variance-covariance model. Moreover, simple linear correlation is a rudimentary technique in statistical analysis and sales forecasting. Thus, business managers and staff specialists have at least a nodding acquaintance with the idea involved. In sum, we shall pursue the same objective —constructing and evaluating portfolios by their expected return and standard deviation—but use market-based data rather than direct comparison of project cash flows. This has the added advantage of stressing the link between the financial manager and the investor. How the investor values the decisions of management determines the present worth of the enterprise.

CAPM has a potential significance in capital budgeting in that:

1. It provides a method of determining the expected or required return of a capital project or security, if it can be related to a broad-based economic indicator.

2. It provides an alternative calculation for the cost of capital as discussed in Chapter 17.

3. It can be used in the valuation of the firm and to determine the firm's incremental debt capacity if a project is accepted. Thus, it ties together the investment and financing decisions as well as the valuation process. This application of CAPM is illustrated in Chapter 17.

THE SINGLE-INDEX MODEL

To start the study of CAPM, consider the single-index model developed by Sharpe:[2]

$$\tilde{R}_{jt} = \alpha_j + \mathrm{B}_j\left(\tilde{R}_{mt}\right) + \tilde{e}_{jt} \tag{1}$$

where $\tilde{R}_{jt}$ = random variable showing the return on asset j (a project or security) in period t

$\tilde{R}_{mt}$ = random variable showing the return on a broad-based market index in period t

α_j, B_j = parameters for asset j (which are developed by regression analysis) which best describe the *average relationship* between the returns $\tilde{R}_{jt}$ and $\tilde{R}_{mt}$

$\tilde{e}_{jt}$ = random-error term for asset j in period t

This simple linear regression model determines the parameters α_j and B_j so that returns on individual projects (or securities) can be estimated using the

[2] William F. Sharpe, "A Simplified Model for Portfolio Analysis," *Management Science* (January 1963), pp. 277–293.

equation plus an estimate for the value of the market index. It should be pointed out that because $\tilde{R}_{jt}$ and $\tilde{R}_{mt}$ are both random variables, the simple linear relationship will not be 100% accurate; thus, the random-error term $\tilde{e}_{jt}$ measures the difference between the actual returns on project j in period t and those predicted using the regression equation. In regression analysis, the parameters α_j and B_j are determined by the method of least squares, which necessitates that the random-error term $\tilde{e}_{jt}$ will have an expected value of zero and a variance that is a positive, finite constant, Q_j^2, for all values of t (the time variable). In addition to the assumptions above, the following three assumptions are also made in order to arrive at the significant simplifications discussed above:

1. The random-error term is uncorrelated with the market index: $\mathrm{Cov}(\tilde{e}_{jt}, \tilde{R}_{mt}) = 0$.

2. The random-error terms are not serially correlated over time: $\mathrm{Cov}(\tilde{e}_{jt}, \tilde{e}_{j,\,t+n}) = 0$ for any value of n.

3. The random-error term for project j is not correlated with any other project's random-error term: $\mathrm{Cov}(\tilde{e}_{jt}, \tilde{e}_{it}) = 0$.

Given the assumptions above, we can determine the expected value and the variance of Equation (1). These values will be discussed in turn.

$$E(\tilde{R}_{jt}) = E\left(\alpha_j + B_j(\tilde{R}_{mt}) + \tilde{e}_{jt}\right)$$
$$= \alpha_j + B_j\left(E(\tilde{R}_{mt})\right) + E(\tilde{e}_{jt})$$
$$= \alpha_j + B_j\left(E(\tilde{R}_{mt})\right) \qquad (2)$$

where $E(\tilde{R}_j)$ and $E(\tilde{R}_m)$ are, respectively, the expected value of the return on project j and the expected value of the return on the market index.

Examining Equation (2) we see that the expected return on project j can be divided into two independent components:

$\alpha_j =$ return on project j due exclusively to its own merits

$B_j\left(E(\tilde{R}_{mt})\right) =$ return on project j associated with the response of project j to changes in the broad-based index of economic activity $\tilde{R}_{mt}$

In ordinary regression analysis, these two components are, respectively, the y-intercept and the slope of the regression line. Both values (α_j, B_j) can be determined using the usual least-squares equations. Figure 16–1 shows the relationships. Equations (3) and (4) are the least-squares equations for α_j and B_j:

$$B_j = \frac{n \sum_{t=1}^{n} \tilde{R}_{mt}\tilde{R}_{jt} - \left(\sum_{t=1}^{n} \tilde{R}_{mt}\right)\left(\sum_{t=1}^{n} \tilde{R}_{jt}\right)}{n \sum_{t=1}^{n} \tilde{R}_{mt}^2 - \left(\sum_{t=1}^{n} \tilde{R}_{mt}\right)^2} \qquad (3)$$

$$\alpha_j = E(\tilde{R}_j) - B_j\left(E(\tilde{R}_m)\right) \qquad (4)$$

Example 1 demonstrates the use of Equations (3) and (4).

□ **EXAMPLE 1**   *Regression Model*

A new project is under consideration. This project is very similar to the project whose returns over a 10-period horizon are shown in the table. The returns on the appropriate market index are also shown.

Period (t)	Similar Project $\tilde{R}_{jt}$	Market Index $\tilde{R}_{mt}$
1	.09	.07
2	.10	.09
3	.10	.10
4	.11	.12
5	.10	.11
6	.11	.10
7	.11	.10
8	.10	.09
9	.09	.08
10	.07	.07

(a) Compute the values for α_j and B_j.
(b) Write and explain the regression equation.

Solution: The following table will be helpful in computing α_j and B_j:

t	$\tilde{R}_{jt}$	$\tilde{R}_{mt}$	$\tilde{R}_{jt}\tilde{R}_{mt}$	$\tilde{R}_{mt}^2$
1	0.09	0.07	0.0063	0.0049
2	0.10	0.09	0.0090	0.0081
3	0.10	0.10	0.0100	0.0100
4	0.11	0.12	0.0132	0.0144
5	0.10	0.11	0.0110	0.0121
6	0.11	0.10	0.0110	0.0100
7	0.11	0.10	0.0110	0.0100
8	0.10	0.09	0.0090	0.0081
9	0.09	0.08	0.0072	0.0064
10	0.07	0.07	0.0049	0.0049
Total	$\Sigma \tilde{R}_{jt} = 0.98$	$\Sigma \tilde{R}_{mt} = 0.93$	$\Sigma \tilde{R}_{jt}\tilde{R}_{mt} = 0.0926$	$\Sigma \tilde{R}_{mt}^2 = 0.0889$

$$B_j = \frac{n\Sigma \tilde{R}_{mt}\tilde{R}_{jt} - (\Sigma \tilde{R}_{mt})(\Sigma \tilde{R}_{jt})}{n\Sigma \tilde{R}_{mt}^2 - (\Sigma \tilde{R}_{mt})^2}$$

$$= \frac{10(0.0926) - (0.93)(0.98)}{10(0.0889) - (0.93)^2}$$

$$= \frac{0.9260 - 0.9114}{0.8890 - 0.8649}$$

$$= 0.6058$$

$$\alpha_j = E(\tilde{R}_j) - B_j(E(\tilde{R}_m))$$

$$= 0.098 - (0.6058)(0.093)$$

$$= 0.0417$$

FIGURE 16–1   Simple Linear Regression Equation Relating $\tilde{R}_j$ to $\tilde{R}_m$

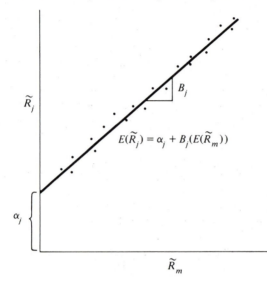

Thus, the regression equation is

$$E\left(\tilde{R}_j\right) = \alpha_j + \text{B}_j\left(E\left(\tilde{R}_m\right)\right)$$

$$= 0.0417 + 0.6058\left[E\left(\tilde{R}_m\right)\right]$$

The regression equation states that the expected return on the project $(E(\tilde{R}_j))$ comprises a basic yield of 4.17% (α_j) plus 60.58% (B_j) of the expected return on the market index $(E(\tilde{R}_m))$.   □

To complete our discussion of the single-index model, we now turn to Equation (5), which derives the variance of the returns on project j:

$$\text{Var}\left(\tilde{R}_{jt}\right) = \text{Var}\left(\alpha_j + \text{B}_j\left(\tilde{R}_{mt}\right) + \tilde{e}_{jt}\right) \qquad \text{from Equation (1)}$$

$$= \text{Var}(\alpha_j) + \text{Var}\left(\text{B}_j\left(\tilde{R}_{mt}\right)\right) + \text{Var}(\tilde{e}_{jt})$$

$$= \text{B}_j^2\sigma_m^2 + Q_j^2 \qquad\qquad\qquad (5)$$

where σ_m^2 and Q_j^2 are, respectively, the variance on the market index and the variance on the random-error term $\tilde{e}_{jt}$.

Notice that the variance shown in Equation (5) stresses the fact that the total risk on project j can be attributed to two distinct types of risk:

1. The risk associated with project j's response to the market index multiplied by the variability in the market index itself: $\text{B}_j^2\sigma_m^2$.

2. The risk associated with the random-error term of project j (i.e., due to unexplained causes other than the market index), Q_j^2.

The first of these has come to be known as *systematic risk*. This risk cannot be diversified away since it is the result of variability in the market of risky assets. The latter is known as *unsystematic risk*. It can be diversified away through the selection of other risky assets that are lowly or negatively correlated with the asset in question. Thus, we can speak of partitioning the total risk associated with the returns on project j into its two components:

$$
\begin{array}{lll}
\text{total risk} & = \text{systematic risk} & + \text{unsystematic risk} \\
\text{on project } j & \text{(nondiversifiable)} & \text{(diversifiable)} \\
\sigma_{R_j}^2 & = B_j^2 \sigma_m^2 & + Q_j^2
\end{array}
$$

Several interrelationships are worthy of note. The unsystematic risk on a given project, Q_j^2, is the square of a familiar measure in regression analysis, the standard error of estimate. The *standard error of estimate* is the average amount of error that is made in predicting returns on project j using the regression equation:

$$
Q_j = \sqrt{\frac{\text{variation due to error}}{n-2}}
$$

To more fully explain the numerator of this expression, we will partition the variance in returns on project j in a slightly different way than we did above. In regression analysis, the partitioning is as follows:

$$
\begin{array}{lll}
\text{total variation} & \text{variation} & \text{variation} \\
\text{in returns of} & = \text{explained by} & + \text{due to error} \\
\text{project } j & \text{the regression} & \text{(unexplained} \\
& \text{equation} & \text{variation)}
\end{array}
$$

$$
\sum_{t=1}^{n} \left(\tilde{R}_{jt} - \bar{R}_j \right)^2 = \sum_{t=1}^{n} \left(E(\tilde{R}_{jt}) - \bar{R}_j \right)^2 + \sum_{t=1}^{n} \left(\tilde{R}_{jt} - E(\tilde{R}_{jt}) \right)^2 \quad (6)
$$

It should be noted that $\tilde{R}_{jt}$ refers to the actual return on project j; $E(\tilde{R}_{jt})$ is the expected value of the return on project j in period t using the regression equation. $\bar{R}_j$ is the expected value for the return on project j. The standard error of estimate is stated more formally as

$$
Q_j = \sqrt{\frac{\Sigma \left(\tilde{R}_{jt} - E(\tilde{R}_{jt}) \right)^2}{n-2}} \quad (7)
$$

Further, there are two final regression statistics of interest. The *coefficient of determination* shows the percentage of the total variation in the dependent variable that is explained by variations in the independent variable. The *coefficient of nondetermination* shows the percentage of the total variation that is left unexplained by the independent variable being used. Of course, the sum of these two coefficients must be 100%. By examining Equation (6), we see that these two statistics may be expressed as shown in Equations (8) and (9):

$$\text{coefficient of determination} = \rho^2 = \frac{\Sigma\left(E\left(\tilde{R}_{jt}\right) - \bar{R}_j\right)^2}{\Sigma\left(\tilde{R}_{jt} - \bar{R}_j\right)^2} \tag{8}$$

$$\text{coefficient of nondetermination} = 1 - \rho^2 = \frac{\Sigma\left(\tilde{R}_{jt} - E\left(\tilde{R}_{jt}\right)\right)^2}{\Sigma\left(\tilde{R}_{jt} - \bar{R}_j\right)^2} \tag{9}$$

The coefficient of determination is the square of the correlation coefficient. Thus, this value is also related to the amount of covariance between the project returns and the returns on the market index. The computation of these statistics and their precise interpretation in the terms of our problem are illustrated in Example 2.

□ **EXAMPLE 2**   *Calculation of Relevant Statistics*
     For the data shown in Example 1, compute the following.
(a) The standard error of estimate.
(b) The coefficient of determination.
(c) The coefficient of nondetermination.
(d) The variance in the market index.
(e) The variance of the returns on project j.
(f) The correlation coefficient and the covariance between $\tilde{R}_{jt}$ and $\tilde{R}_{mt}$.

     Solution: The following table will be helpful in computing the desired statistics above:

	(1) $\tilde{R}_{jt}$	(2) $\tilde{R}_{mt}$	(3) $E(\tilde{R}_{jt})$	(4) $(\tilde{R}_{jt} - \bar{R}_j)^2$	(5) $(\tilde{R}_{jt} - E(\tilde{R}_{jt}))^2$	(6) $(E(\tilde{R}_{jt}) - \bar{R}_j)^2$	(7) $(\tilde{R}_{mt} - \bar{R}_m)^2$
t							
1	0.09	0.07	0.0841	0.000064	0.00003481	0.00019321	0.000529
2	0.10	0.09	0.0962	0.000004	0.00001444	0.00000324	0.000009
3	0.10	0.10	0.1023	0.000004	0.00000529	0.00001849	0.000049
4	0.11	0.12	0.1144	0.000144	0.00001936	0.00026896	0.000729
5	0.10	0.11	0.1083	0.000004	0.00006889	0.00010609	0.000289
6	0.11	0.10	0.1023	0.000144	0.00005929	0.00001849	0.000049
7	0.11	0.10	0.1023	0.000144	0.00005929	0.00001849	0.000049
8	0.10	0.09	0.0962	0.000004	0.00001444	0.00000324	0.000009
9	0.09	0.08	0.0902	0.000064	0.00000004	0.00006084	0.000169
10	0.07	0.07	0.0841	0.000784	0.00019881	0.00019321	0.000529
	$\Sigma\tilde{R}_{jt}$	$\Sigma\tilde{R}_{mt}$	$\Sigma E(\tilde{R}_{jt})$	$\Sigma(\tilde{R}_{jt} - \bar{R}_j)^2$	$\Sigma(\tilde{R}_{jt} - E(\tilde{R}_{jt}))^2$	$\Sigma(E(\tilde{R}_{jt}) - \bar{R}_j)^2$	$\Sigma(\tilde{R}_{mt} - \bar{R}_m)^2$
Total	0.98	0.93	0.9804	0.001360	0.00047466	0.00088426	0.00241

     Columns (1) and (2) in the table are the historical observations of $\tilde{R}_{jt}$ and $\tilde{R}_{mt}$, respectively, for the last 10 periods, as shown in Example 1. Column (3) shows the values computed by substituting the values of $\tilde{R}_{mt}$ into the regression equation. Column (4) shows the values for the square of the quantity of the actual $\tilde{R}_{jt}$ minus $\bar{R}_j$ (where $\bar{R}_j = \Sigma\tilde{R}_{jt}/10 = 0.098$). Column (5) is the square of the difference between the actual $\tilde{R}_{jt}$ [column (1)] and the predicted value using the regression equation $E(\tilde{R}_{jt})$ [column (3)]. Column (6) is the square of the difference between column (3) and $\bar{R}_j = 0.098$. Column (7) is the square of the difference between column (2) and $\bar{R}_m = \Sigma\tilde{R}_{mt}/10 = 0.093$. Thus, we see that the

total variation or total sum of squares = 0.00136

variation explained by the regression equation = 0.00088426

variation unexplained by the regression equation = 0.00047466

total variation = explained variation + unexplained variation

0.00136 = 0.00088426 + 0.00047466

0.00136 ≅ 0.00135892

(a) Standard error of estimate:

$$Q_j = \sqrt{\frac{0.00047466}{10-2}} = \sqrt{0.0000593325}$$

$$= 0.007703, \quad \text{or} \quad 0.7703\%$$

This measure shows that the average amount of error made in predicting the return on project j using the return on the market index and our regression equation $E(\tilde{R}_j) = 0.0417 + 0.6058(E(\tilde{R}_m))$ is 0.7703%. Further, assuming that the variability around the regression line approximates a normal distribution, ±2 standard errors would include approximately 95% of the variations. Thus, we could be 95% certain that the return on project j would lie within an interval described by the expected return $(E(R_j))$ plus and minus 1.5406% (2 × 0.7703%).

(b) and (c) Coefficients of determination and nondetermination:

$$\rho^2 = \frac{0.00088426}{0.001360} = \underline{\underline{65\%}}$$

$$1 - \rho^2 = \frac{0.00047466}{0.001360} = \underline{\underline{35\%}}$$

These two measures show that 65% of the variation in returns on project j is explained by the variation in the market index, while 35% of the variation in returns on project j is due to factors other than the variation in the market index used in the regression equation.

(d) Variance in the market index: This measure is computed using the usual formula for variance:

$$\sigma_m^2 = \frac{\Sigma\left(\tilde{R}_{mt} - \bar{R}_m\right)^2}{n-1} = \frac{0.00241}{10-1}$$

$$= 0.0002677 \text{ or } 0.02677\%$$

The variance in the market index is the average variability in the return on the market index around the mean return.

(e) Variance in returns on project j: This measure can be computed using either the general formula for the variance shown in part (d) or Equation (3):

$$\sigma_{R_j}^2 = \frac{\Sigma\left(\tilde{R}_{jt} - \bar{R}_j\right)^2}{n-1} = \frac{0.001360}{10-1}$$

$$= 0.0001511 \text{ or } 0.01511\%$$

Using Equation (3), we have the following:

$$\text{Var}\left(\tilde{R}_j\right) = \sigma_{R_j}^2 = B_j^2\sigma_m^2 + Q_j^2$$

$$= (0.6058)^2(0.0002677) + 0.0000593325$$

$$\sigma_{R_j}^2 = 0.0000982441 + 0.0000593325$$

$$= 0.0001576, \quad \text{or} \quad 0.01576\%$$

The difference between these two figures is due to rounding.

(f) Finally, the correlation coefficient and the covariance between the returns on project j and the market are of interest.

$$\rho = \sqrt{\rho^2} = \text{coefficient of determination} = \sqrt{0.6501911765}$$

$$\rho_{\tilde{R}_j,\,\tilde{R}_m} = +0.806$$

The covariance is found in the usual manner:

$$\text{Cov}\left(\tilde{R}_j, \tilde{R}_m\right) = \left(\rho_{\tilde{R}_j,\,\tilde{R}_m}\right)\left(\sigma_{\tilde{R}_j}\right)\left(\sigma_m\right)$$

$$= (+0.806)(0.0126)(0.0164) = 0.0001666$$

Last, it can be shown that B_j has an alternative definition of interest:

$$B_j = \frac{\text{Cov}\left(\tilde{R}_j, \tilde{R}_m\right)}{\sigma_m^2}$$

$$= \frac{0.0001666}{0.0002677}$$

$$= \underline{0.622} \approx 0.6058 \qquad \text{as computed in Example 1}$$

This definition underscores the nature of B_j; it monitors the sensitivity of the project returns to changes in the market index. □

To conclude this section, note that the capital asset pricing model, subject to qualification, produces the same information on the project, an expected return, $E(R_j)$, and sigma, σ_j, as that developed from the probability distributions of period cash flows. However, by contrast, the $E(R_j)$ and σ_j from the CAPM model use market data (i.e., the relationship of project returns to a broad-based index). In this regard, the illustrations in Examples 1 and 2 assume that the relationship between the risky asset returns and the appropriate market index described by the beta value will hold for the future or at least the life of the asset. Hence, if the analyst has the expected return on the index over the relevant period, he or she can forecast the expected return, $E(R_j)$, based upon the regression equation. The expected return should also be thought of as a required return given the relationship with the market index of risky asset returns. In the capital budgeting situation, this required return can be compared to an expected return calculated by conventional means (i.e., the expected internal rate of return) and a decision made on the acceptability of the project. Our discussion of the cost of capital in Chapter 17 picks up this theme.

PORTFOLIO PARAMETERS

An important application of CAPM is its use to calculate the risk-return characteristics of portfolios. The portfolio return $E(R_p)$ offers no special problems: a simple weighted average of the expected returns on the individual projects (or securities), as shown in Equation (10):

$$E(R_p) = \sum_{j=1}^{N} X_j E(R_j) \tag{10}$$

where X_j denotes the proportion of the total budget or portfolio invested in the jth project (or security).

In the same manner, the beta value of the portfolio,[3] (B_p), is given by Equation (11):

$$B_p = \sum_{j=1}^{N} X_j B_j \tag{11}$$

However, the measurement of portfolio risk by the CAPM approach provides interesting insights into the construction of portfolios. Recall from Chapter 14 that the Markowitz formulation described portfolio risk as the weighted variance of the individual projects plus twice the sum of the weighted covariances:

$$\sigma_p = \sqrt{\sum_{j=1}^{N} X_j^2 \sigma_j^2 + 2 \sum_{j=1}^{N-1} \sum_{i=j+1}^{N} X_i X_j (\rho_{ij})(\sigma_i)(\sigma_j)}$$

Under CAPM, σ_p, based upon market data, becomes

$$\sigma_p = \sqrt{B_p^2 \sigma_m^2 + \sum_{j=1}^{N} X_j^2 Q_j^2} \tag{12}$$

Equation (12) recognizes two kinds of risk in a similar vein to that for individual securities discussed above:

1. Systematic risk ($B_p^2 \sigma_m^2$) is that portion of total risk (σ_p) based upon the relationship with the market index ($\tilde{R}_m$). Since all risky assets in the portfolio correlate to some degree with the index of risky assets, the systematic risk is nondiversifiable. No combination of risky assets can eliminate the market risk.

2. Unsystematic risk ($\sum X_j^2 Q_j^2$) is that element of total risk (σ_p) responding to forces beyond the market index. If the market discounts all that is known about the risky asset's values, the unsystematic risk measures the variability in the returns due to unanticipated, or random factors. For example, the market may discount all that is known about the production, marketing, and financial strategies of General Motors, yet the price and yield on GM stock will still vary because of new, unforeseen, randomly occurring events (the energy crisis, technological innovation, political turns, etc.). This is diversifiable risk and in a properly diversified portfolio, $\sum_{j=1}^{N} X_j^2 Q_j^2$ will *tend to zero*. The reason is as follows: Q_j^2 is the square of the standard error of the estimate or the unexplained variance. As N is increased in the summation above, the values of X_j^2 become proportionately smaller, so that in the limit the summation approaches zero. Since the limit is never actually reached, the diversifiable risk will only approach zero.

---

[3] The reader should note that the portfolio beta value is also the beta for the firm as a whole, since the firm is an aggregate of all existing projects.

FIGURE 16-2   Effects of Diversification on Systematic, Unsystematic, and Total Risk

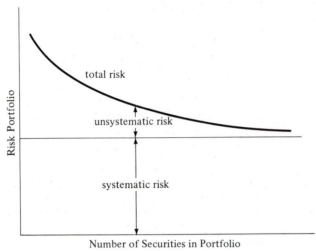

Number of Securities in Portfolio

Figure 16-2 shows how the two risks change as randomly selected securities are added to a portfolio. Empirical studies have shown that with as few as 10 to 15 securities in a portfolio, total risk can be reduced to almost the systematic level.[4]

Example 3 illustrates the calculation of portfolio parameters under CAPM.

□ **EXAMPLE 3**   *Calculation of Portfolio Parameters Using CAPM*

Consider a firm desiring to combine projects Zeta and Delta into a portfolio in the proportions shown in the table below. The procedures described in the previous section have already been applied and the regression equations developed with the market index also shown:

	Project Zeta	*Project Delta*
α_j	0.05	0.02
B_j	0.5	1.5
X_j	0.6	0.4
Q_j	0.0088	0.007

Market index statistics:

$$E\left(\tilde{R}_m\right) = 0.093, \qquad \sigma_{R_m} = 0.016$$

Compute $E(R_p)$, B_p, and σ_p.

[4]See J. Evans and S. H. Archer, "Diversification and the Reduction of Dispersion: An Empirical Analysis," *Journal of Finance* (December 1968), pp. 761–767; and K. H. Johnson and D. S. Shannon, "A Note on Diversification and the Reduction of Dispersion," *Journal of Financial Economics* (December 1974), pp. 365–372.

Solution: To compute $E(R_p)$, we must first compute the expected return on each project, using Equation (2).

Project Zeta:

$$E(R_Z) = \alpha_Z + B_Z\big(E(\tilde{R}_m)\big)$$
$$= 0.05 + 0.5(0.093)$$
$$= 0.097$$

Project Delta:

$$E(R_D) = \alpha_D + B_D\big(E(\tilde{R}_m)\big)$$
$$= 0.02 + 1.5(0.093)$$
$$= 0.16$$

Portfolio expected return:

$$E(R_p) = \Sigma X_j E(R_j)$$
$$= 0.6(0.097) + 0.4(0.16)$$
$$= 0.1222$$

Portfolio beta:

$$B_p = \Sigma X_j B_j$$
$$= 0.6(0.5) + 0.4(1.5)$$
$$= 0.9$$

Portfolio standard deviation:

$$\sigma_p = \sqrt{(B_p)^2 (\sigma_{R_m})^2 + \Sigma X_j^2 Q_j^2}$$
$$= \sqrt{(0.9)^2 (0.016)^2 + (0.6)^2 (0.0088)^2 + (0.4)^2 (0.007)^2}$$
$$= \sqrt{0.00020736 + 0.0000278 + 0.00000784}$$
$$= \sqrt{0.000243}$$
$$= 0.0156 \qquad\qquad \square$$

EFFICIENT FRONTIER UNDER CAPM

CAPM assumes a linear relationship between project returns and the market index. The random-error term, Q_j, is assumed to be independent of the index and independent of the random terms for all other projects. As a result of these assumptions, which are not true in general, some part of the true variability of $E(R_j)$ is lost. Hence, portfolios constructed by CAPM are less efficient compared to those constructed using the more elaborate covariance technique. Figure 16–3 compares the approximate character of the index frontier to the true efficient frontier.

The proximity of the index frontier to the true efficient set derived from the covariances of the cash flows depends on two related considerations:

1. Whether a linear function best describes the dependence of the projects (or securities) on the index. This advises experimentation with higher degree polynomials and transformations.

FIGURE 16-3   Comparison of Efficient Frontiers CAPM versus Covariance Technique

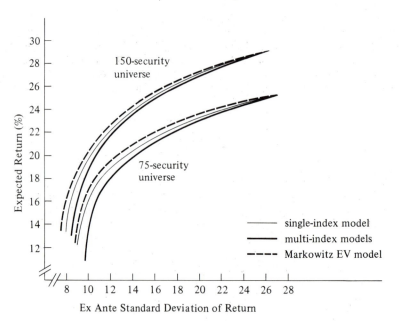

SOURCE: Kalman J. Cohen and Jerry A. Pogue, "An Empirical Evaluation of Alternative Portfolio-Selection Models," *The Journal of Business*, 40, no. 2 (April 1967), 179.

2. Whether the index selected is the best predictor of changes in the dependent variable *j*. In turn, this recommends the selection of an index after experimentation with a number of possible choices or the use of multi-index models.

Capital Market Line

For a given investor, the optimum portfolio locates at the tangency between his or her indifference map and the efficient frontier (Figure 14–5) common to all investors. But investors are a diverse group, their utility maps differ, and each might prefer a different point (optimum portfolio) along the common efficient frontier. *The aggregate of these individual investor preferences is represented by the capital market line, as shown in Figure 16–4. For the market to be in equilibrium, the portfolio at M must contain every risky asset in the exact proportion to that asset's fraction of the total market value of all risky assets.* That is, if all investors are holding a part of the same portfolio as their risky asset commitment, this portfolio would have to consist of all risky assets available in the marketplace. The portfolio at *M*, therefore, with each risky asset weighted by its market value relative to the total market value of

FIGURE 16–4   Capital Market Line

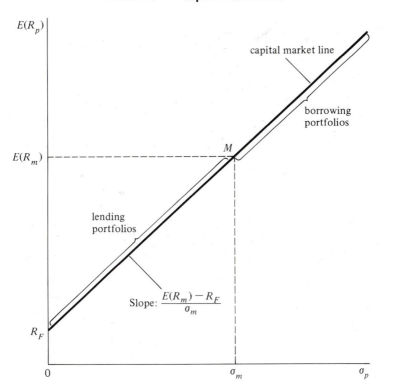

all risky assets is termed the *market portfolio*. The formula for the capital market line (CML) is given by Equation (13):

$$E(R_p) = R_F + \frac{E(R_m) - R_F}{\sigma_m} \sigma_p \tag{13}$$

where $E(R_p)$ = expected return on an efficient portfolio
σ_p = standard deviation of returns on portfolio p
R_F = risk-free rate
$E(R_m)$ = expected return on the market portfolio of risky assets
σ_m = standard deviation of the market portfolio

Point R_F on the capital market line describes the return on portfolios composed of risk-free assets (for example, Treasury bills). Moving up the market line, the investor allocates available funds to portfolios with larger proportions of risky assets. The increased commitment to risky assets increases portfolio returns $[E(R_p)]$. At point M, the investor has all available funds invested in risky assets (the market basket of risky assets). Between points R_F and M, the investor is in a creditor position (i.e., giving up funds in exchange for claims on assets). Beyond point M, the investor begins to leverage his or her portfolio by borrowing at the risk-free rate (R_F) and investing the proceeds to build larger holdings of the market basket of risky securities. Several conclusions follow:

1. The expected return on an efficient portfolio is a linear function of its risk.

2. All efficient portfolios would have to be on the capital market line.

3. The slope of the line, $[E(R_m) - R_F]/\sigma_m$, is called the *market price of risk* or the *price of risk reduction.*

4. The intercept of the line, R_F, is the *market price of time*, or the time value of money.

5. The relationship does not apply to individual securities or portfolios that are imperfectly diversified. This implies that there is no reward for assuming risk that could be eliminated by proper diversification.

6. All investors *with the market in equilibrium* elect to hold the same portfolio of risk assets (the market portfolio). If, for example, General Motors stock comprised 3% of the total value of all publicly traded stocks, the risk segment of each investor's portfolio should allocate 3% to GM. The dollar size of an investor's portfolio depends on his or her wealth, but the profile of risky assets will be proportionately the same for each investor. Individual risk preferences affect only the allocation of funds within individual portfolios between risky and riskless assets.

7. Because all rational investors share in the market portfolio, each will perceive the riskiness of any given security in terms of its contribution to the riskiness of a fully diversified portfolio (i.e., the market portfolio). Hence, the financial manager needs to define risk in terms of the market portfolio if he or she is to be consistent with the criteria used by investors in valuing securities.

8. Investors increase their returns by changing the proportions of their portfolio (X_j) invested in risky and risk-free securities. Higher risk and return result from increasing the proportion invested in risky assets.

Security Market Line

The capital market line dealt with required return on a portfolio. The security market line (SML) shows the required return on each security in relation to risk. Termed the *market-price-of-risk line*, every security in the market portfolio of risky assets will be priced so that its expected return may be calculated using Equation (14):

$$E(R_j) = R_F + [E(R_m) - R_F]\frac{\text{Cov}(R_j, R_m)}{\sigma_m^2} \qquad (14)$$

where $E(R_j)$ designates the required return on a given security.

The required return demanded by investors on a security, therefore, depends on the following four factors:

1. The risk-free rate.

2. The expected return on the market portfolio.

3. The variance on the market portfolio.

4. The covariance of the security's returns with the market portfolio.

The equation for the security market line is graphed in Figure 16–5.

FIGURE 16–5   Security Market Line

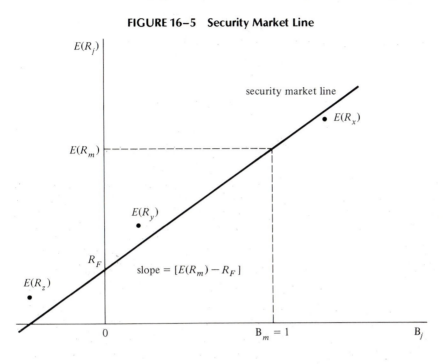

The SML differs from the CML in two major respects:

1. For the individual security, the risk measure is the covariance instead of the standard deviation. The substitution underscores that the risk of an individual security or firm depends upon its contribution to the risk of the portfolio in which it is placed.

2. The risk of the market portfolio is measured by its variance, not the standard deviation.

If a security had a beta value of 2 [recall that $B_j = \text{Cov}(R_j, R_m)/\sigma_m^2$] and $R_F = 0.06$ and $E(R_m) = 0.10$, then

$$E(R_j) = 0.06 + 2(0.10 - 0.06)$$

$$= 0.14, \quad \text{or} \quad 14\%$$

A rational, risk-averse investor would not acquire the risky asset unless it promised a return at least equal to 14%. In Figure 16–5, therefore, security X earns a return in excess of the market portfolio ($E(R_m)$) but is not a desirable investment, owing to its strong covariance with market returns; Y has a lower expected return but may be a worthwhile investment, owing to its low correlation with the market portfolio; Z, a risky asset, correlates negatively with the market portfolio and hence $E(R_Z)$ is less than the risk-free rate and therefore may also be worthy of consideration. *Generally, with the SML drawn as shown in Figure 16–5, returns above the SML are acceptable (i.e., securities Y and Z); below the SML, the amount of risk assumed is not justified by the expected return (i.e., security X).* An extensive example of CAPM applied to the selection of capital budgeting projects is included in Chapter 17.

SUMMARY

This chapter examines the capital asset pricing model, a new approach that can be beneficially applied to the valuation of risky assets, whether they be securities or capital projects. Accordingly, this chapter calls upon several concepts and statistics developed in previous chapters on risk analysis and portfolio effects. Examples are used to illustrate the calculations of important new CAPM parameters.

However, financial management is not an abstract science cultivating abstruse mathematical models for self-edification. It survives by its ability to function. No matter how sophisticated the mathematical construct, a financial model must ultimately stand or fall on its contribution to the decision-making process. Contribution may take the form of a new insight on some aspect of financial management and/or the provision of a methodology to optimize results. We must now turn to the applicability of CAPM to the strategic decisions involved in long-term asset management.

QUESTIONS/PROBLEMS

1. For the data given below for project j and the market index, compute the values for α_j, B_j, and write the regression equation:

Period, t	Project, $R_{jt}(\%)$	Market Index, $R_{mt}(\%)$
1	9	10
2	8	9
3	8	8
4	10	8
5	11	10

2. For the data given in Problem 1, compute and explain the following.
   (a) The $E(R_{jt})$ value for each R_{mt}.
   (b) The covariance between $\tilde{R}_{jt}$ and $\tilde{R}_{mt}$.
   (c) The correlation coefficient between $\tilde{R}_{jt}$ and $\tilde{R}_{mt}$ and explain its meaning.
   (d) The standard error of estimate.
   (e) The coefficient of determination.
   (f) The coefficient of nondetermination.
3. For the data given in Problem 1, compute and explain the following:
   (a) The variance of the returns on the market index.
   (b) The variance of the returns on project j.

(c) The systematic risk on project j.

(d) The unsystematic risk on project j.

4. The Notos Company is analyzing a project shown below. To facilitate the computation of relevant statistics, the firm has prepared the following tables.

Year	$\tilde{R}_{jt}$	$\tilde{R}_{mt}$	$\tilde{R}_{jt}\tilde{R}_{mt}$	$\tilde{R}_{mt}^2$	$E(\tilde{R}_{jt})$
1	0.11	0.10	0.0110	0.0100	0.1086
2	0.12	0.11	0.0132	0.0121	0.1179
3	0.12	0.12	0.0144	0.0144	0.1271
4	0.13	0.11	0.0143	0.0121	0.1179
5	0.10	0.10	0.0100	0.0100	0.1086
Total	0.58	0.54	0.0629	0.0586	0.5801

Year	$\tilde{R}_{jt} - \bar{R}_j$	$(\tilde{R}_{jt} - \bar{R}_j)^2$	$\tilde{R}_{jt} - E(\tilde{R}_{jt})$
1	$0.11 - 0.116 = -0.006$	0.000036	$0.11 - 0.1086 = 0.0014$
2	$0.12 - 0.116 = 0.004$	0.000016	$0.12 - 0.1179 = 0.0021$
3	$0.12 - 0.116 = 0.004$	0.000016	$0.12 - 0.1271 = -0.0071$
4	$0.13 - 0.116 = 0.014$	0.000196	$0.13 - 0.1179 = 0.0121$
5	$0.10 - 0.116 = -0.016$	0.000256	$0.10 - 0.1086 = -0.0086$
Total		0.000520	

Year	$[\tilde{R}_{jt} - E(\tilde{R}_{jt})]^2$	$E(\tilde{R}_{jt}) - \bar{R}_j$	$[E(\tilde{R}_{jt}) - \bar{R}_j]^2$
1	0.0000020	$0.1086 - 0.116 = -0.0074$	0.00005476
2	0.0000044	$0.1179 - 0.116 = 0.0019$	0.00000361
3	0.0000504	$0.1271 - 0.116 = 0.0111$	0.00012320
4	0.0001464	$0.1179 - 0.116 = 0.0019$	0.00000361
5	0.00007396	$0.1086 - 0.116 = -0.0074$	0.00005476
Total	0.00027716		0.00023994

Compute the following.

(a) α, B.

(b) The covariance between $\tilde{R}_{jt}$ and $\tilde{R}_{mt}$.

(c) The correlation coefficient.

(d) The total risk on $\tilde{R}_{jt}$.

(e) The systematic risk.

(f) The unsystematic risk.

(g) The standard error of estimate.

(h) The coefficient of determination.

5. In 1967, a security of the Dru-White Corporation yielded a return of 4%. For the next 6 years it returned a steady 2% above the prime rate, which was 5% in 1968, 1969, and 1970, and 6% in 1971, 1972, and 1973. In the past 3 years, the stock returned 11%, 12%, and 13%. Our analysts have charted a regression line using the single index model. They tell us that their line explains three-fourths of the total variation in returns of the Dru-White security. If we want 90% certainty, within what limits of the predicted value will the true value lie?

6. Random Investments Corporation is planning to combine these two projects into a portfolio. The various statistics are listed for each security and the market index.

Compute the expected return on the portfolio, the beta of the portfolio, and the portfolio standard deviation.

	Security A	Security B
α_j	−0.03	0.04
B_j	+0.75	+0.95
X_j	0.33	0.67
Q_j	0.0075	0.0025

$E(\tilde{R}_m) = 0.095$
$\sigma_{R_m} = 0.012$

7. Consider the following four portfolios and market parameters:

Portfolio	$E(R_p)$	σ_p
1	0.12	0.04
2	0.13	0.06
3	0.16	0.10
4	0.22	0.12

$R_F = 0.06$
$E(R_m) = 0.12$
$\sigma_m = 0.05$

Using the capital asset pricing model, determine which of these portfolios have expected rates of return that exceed the required rate of return and thus are underpriced, and those which are overpriced.

8. Starting with the equation for the security market line:

$$E(R_j) = R_F + [E(R_m) - R_F]\frac{\text{Cov}_{jm}}{\sigma_m^2}$$

Derive the equation for the capital market line by recalling that in equilibrium, an efficient portfolio is perfectly correlated with the market (i.e., $\rho_{jm} = +1.0$).

9. A firm is evaluating the following three securities.

j	$E(R_j)$	ρ_{jm}	σ_j
1	0.075	+0.3	0.04
2	0.14	+0.9	0.09
3	0.12	+0.2	0.14

The market parameters are: $R_F = 0.07$, $E(R_m) = 0.13$, and $\sigma_m = 0.05$.

(a) Compute the beta coefficients for each of these three securities and explain both the absolute risk of each security and the relative riskiness or volatility of each of the securities compared to the market.

(b) Using the equation for the security market line, determine whether each of these securities falls above or below the security market line (i.e., whether each is overpriced or underpriced).

(c) Briefly discuss why each security is overpriced or underpriced (be precise) and various ways that each could become priced appropriately.

17

Capital Asset Pricing, Project Selection, and the Cost of Capital

Chapter 8 describes the marginal cost of capital as a weighted average cost of the next dollar of debt and equity for the *firm*. It reflects the risk posture of the firm or the average risk implicit in all previously accepted capital projects. Consequently, the marginal cost of capital would not be likely to represent the risk associated with the future capital projects and would have to be adjusted before being used in estimating the net present value of a proposed project. Our previous discussion notes several methods of risk adjustment. The capital asset pricing model (CAPM) constitutes yet another technique of project evaluation.

CAPM IN PROJECT EVALUATION

One potential difficulty that may be encountered with the application of conventional methods for risk adjustment is increasing, or ratcheting upward, the firm's cost of capital. This could come about by accepting projects having risk postures in excess of the firm's risk complexion and thereby increasing the firm's risk posture. If this were to happen, the firm's marginal cost of capital would increase to reflect the firm's new risk structure. If, however, the conventional methods are correctly applied, the firm will also accept projects having a lower risk complexion than the firm overall, and the ratcheting effect should not take place. Put another way, the average cost of capital represents a strategic rate that management strives to earn on the totality of the operation; management accepts some projects with higher and others with lower risk-return levels, but the average risk-return posture approximates that embodied in the marginal cost of capital.

The capital asset pricing model can also be used to calculate a market-based hurdle rate, risk-adjusted to the project under evaluation. The methodology relates a project's expected returns to an index representing a broad-based measure of economic activity. In Table 17–1, a project's expected return, $E(R_j)$, and the expected return on the index, $E(R_m)$, are computed based upon different states of the economy and their respective probability of occurrence.

In Table A of Table 17–1, the returns from the index, R_m, and four projects (a, b, c, and d) are shown for four possible states of the economy. The probability of each state of the economy is denoted by P_s. All of the forecasted returns (R_m, R_a, R_b, R_c, and R_d) and probabilities in Table A represent estimates for single periods for each of the projects and the market index. Estimates may be the result of projections from historical data or simulation. The data in Table A are the results of economic forecasts.

Table B is a summary of the calculations needed to obtain the expected return, variance, and standard deviation for the market index. Note that the estimated returns for the market index, R_m, are expressed in decimal form in Table B rather than as percentages as in Table A. The results show that the expected return on the market index is 20.2%, with a standard deviation of 11.36%.

Table C derives the necessary inputs to determine the required return from investment a, consistent with its risk characteristics. The results for all four projects are shown in Table D. The required return as determined using Equation (1) is compared with the project's expected return. The project's expected return is the weighted average of the estimated returns of each of the possible states of the economy. If the expected return equals or exceeds the required return, the project is accepted; otherwise, it is rejected.

$$R_j^0 = R_F + \left[E(R_m) - R_F \right] B_j \tag{1}$$

where R_j^0 = required return from project j
R_F = risk-free rate of return
$E(R_m)$ = expected return on the market index
B_j = beta factor for project j, which is defined in Equation (2)

$$B_j = \frac{\mathrm{Cov}(R_j, R_m)}{\sigma_m^2} \tag{2}$$

where $\mathrm{Cov}(R_j, R_m)$ = covariance between the returns on project j and the returns on the market index
σ_c^2 = variance of the market index

Based on the inputs of Table D, it is possible to compute the required return for each project, R_j^0, employing Equation (1). In our computation we will assume that the risk-free rate of return, R_F, is 8%:

		R_j^0	$E(R_j)$
$R_a^0 =$	$0.08 + (0.202 - 0.08)0.421$	$= 13.14\%$	15.9%
$R_b^0 =$	$0.08 + (0.202 - 0.08)1.596$	$= 27.47\%$	20%
$R_c^0 =$	$0.08 + (0.202 - 0.08)1.513$	$= 26.46\%$	23%
$R_d^0 =$	$0.08 + (0.202 - 0.08)0.745$	$= 17.09\%$	8%

TABLE 17–1   Illustration of Project Evaluation Using CAPM

Table A

State of the Economy	P_s	R_m	R_a	R_b	R_c	R_d
Revival (S_1)	0.20	20%	15%	40%	15%	10%
Prosperity (S_2)	0.50	30%	20%	30%	40%	15%
Recession (S_3)	0.20	6%	13%	00%	00%	−6%
Depression (S_4)	0.10	0%	3%	−30%	00%	−3%
	1.00					

Table B

State of the Economy	P_s	R_m	$P_s \times R_m$	$[R_m - E(R_m)]$	$[R_m - E(R_m)]^2$	$[R_m - E(R_m)]^2 P_s$
S_1	0.20	0.20	0.040	−0.002	0.000004	0.0000008
S_2	0.50	0.30	0.150	+0.098	0.009604	0.0048020
S_3	0.20	0.06	0.012	−0.142	0.020164	0.0040328
S_4	0.10	0.00	0.000	−0.202	0.040804	0.0040804
		$E(R_m)$	=0.202		σ_m^2	=0.0129160
					σ_m	=0.1136485

Table C[a]

State of the Economy	P_s	R_a	$P_s \times R_a$	d_a / $R_a - E(R_a)$	d_m / $R_m - E(R_m)$	$d_a d_m$	$d_a d_m P_s$
S_1	0.20	0.15	0.030	−0.009	−0.002	+0.000018	+0.0000036
S_2	0.50	0.20	0.100	+0.041	+0.098	+0.004018	+0.0020090
S_3	0.20	0.13	0.026	−0.029	−0.142	+0.004118	+0.0008236
S_4	0.10	0.03	0.003	−0.129	−0.202	+0.026058	+0.0026058
		$E(R_a)$	=0.159			$\mathrm{Cov}(R_a, R_m)$	= +0.005442

$$B_a = \frac{\mathrm{Cov}(R_a, R_m)}{\sigma_m^2} = \frac{+0.005442}{0.012916} = 0.421$$

Table D

$E(R_a) = 0.159$	$\mathrm{Cov}(R_a, R_m) = +0.005442$	$B_a = 0.421$
$E(R_b) = 0.20$	$\mathrm{Cov}(R_b, R_m) = +0.020620$	$B_b = 1.596$
$E(R_c) = 0.23$	$\mathrm{Cov}(R_c, R_m) = +0.019543$	$B_c = 1.513$
$E(R_d) = 0.08$	$\mathrm{Cov}(R_d, R_m) = +0.009620$	$B_d = 0.745$

[a] The notation d_a and d_m is used to represent the deviation of the return for each state of the economy from the expected return of project a and the market, respectively. Mathematically, $d_a = R_a - E(R_a)$ and $d_m = R_m - E(R_m)$, as shown in columns (4) and (5) of Table C.

Using the CAPM approach, only project A would be accepted, since its expected return exceeds its required return.

Figure 17–1 shows where each project falls relative to the market price of risk line [i.e., the security market line (SML)]. Only project A falls above the SML, indicating that it offers a rate of return sufficient to compensate for its risk. The other three projects fall below the SML, since their returns are not sufficient to cover the market-related risk.

Several aspects of the capital asset pricing approach illustrated above warrant attention.

1. The possible states of the economy over the life span of the projects must be forecasted. It should be noted that intermediate and long-term forecasting as commonly practiced by business firms have larger variances than do short-term projections.

2. The probabilities related to different states of the economy can be derived from historical data on cyclical behavior and/or by simulation.

3. Based upon these variables, the forecaster can project returns on the broad-based market index. It will suffice that the market index consists of assets

FIGURE 17–1   Project Selection Using Capital Asset Pricing

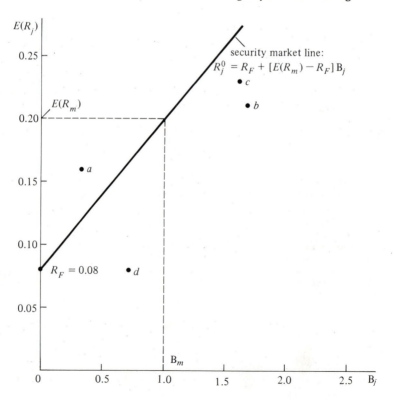

comparable or meaningfully related to the projects studied. Alternatively, the analysis could have employed historical data on the relationship between similar projects and the market index to calculate beta.

4. The forecasted returns of the index and the projects are correlated to derive the beta on each project. Managers seek projects such as project A, with returns in excess of the levels required by the risk-return market relation illustrated in Figure 17–1. When such projects are added to the firm's portfolio, the expected returns on the firm's common stock (at its previous existing price) will be higher than those required by the market line.

5. In practical implementation, the success of the method hinges on the stability of beta. Empirical evidence points to instability when only a few time periods are utilized in the calculation, but the variance in beta tends to decrease as the number of time periods increases. This raises the issue of whether beta is a viable statistic in the evaluation of shorter-term capital projects.

6. Myers and Turnbull suggest the real determinants of beta are more complicated than the above illustration would imply.[1] Beta, they stress, depends on the link between forecast errors for cash flow and those for the market return, the growth trend in cash flows, asset life, the pattern of expected cash flows over time, and the procedure by which investors forecast asset cash flows. Given the Myers-Turnbull caveats, beta becomes extremely difficult to measure accurately. Moreover, the calculated beta will generally lead to biased hurdle rates in the presence of strong growth opportunities for the firm.

7. CAPM provides an alternative approach for estimating the firm's cost-of-equity capital. If we know the beta of the firm, B_p, then the cost-of-common stock equity capital can be defined using Equation (3):

$$K_e = R_F + \left[E(R_m) - R_F \right] B_p \tag{3}$$

Equation (3) may be used to determine the firm's cost of equity capital in place of the dividend-valuation model derived in Chapter 3 and discussed in Chapter 8.

8. The project's acceptance or rejection is a function of the investment's own systematic risk. Thus, since the contribution of the project to the firm's variance of equity rate does not affect the accept or reject decision given by the security market line, diversification can be ignored in capital budgeting decisions. Each project is evaluated on its own merits without reference to the firm's existing investments.

COST OF CAPITAL AND VALUATION OF THE FIRM

The CAPM, in a capital budgeting context, provides the decision-maker with a risk-adjusted hurdle rate peculiar to the project evaluated and an alternative methodology for computing the cost of capital. It follows that CAPM relates immediately to the valuation process discussed earlier in this chapter.

---

[1]S. C. Myers and S. M. Turnbull, "Capital Budgeting and Asset Pricing Model: Good News and Bad News," *The Journal of Finance* (May 1977) pp. 321–333. Also see comments on this article by R. S. Hamada, "Discussion," *The Journal of Finance* (May 1977) pp. 333–336.

Hence, in looking at a project, it is pertinent to assess the value of the project based upon systematic risk and—with that knowledge—to estimate the debt-carrying capacity of the proposed acquisitions. Martin and Scott make a valuable contribution to the analysis of these questions.[2]

Based upon the work of Modigliani and Miller,[3] Martin and Scott define the value of the firm, as well as any asset to comprise the present value of an uncertain income stream (EBIT) plus the present value of a certain stream of tax savings generated by debt, as shown in Equation (4):

$$V = \frac{\text{EBIT}(1-t)}{K_e} + \frac{D(K_d)(t)}{K_d} \tag{4}$$

where t = marginal tax rate on the firm or the project

D = market value of debt in firm's capital structure

K_d = rate at which the market capitalizes a certain stream of tax savings generated by debt

K_e = rate at which the market capitalizes the expected after-tax returns of an unlevered (debt-free) company with the same EBIT and risk posture

V = value of the firm (V_F) or value of the project (V_P), depending on the purpose of the analysis

Equation (4) facilitates the incorporation of added information bearing on the acceptance of the project.

Also, K_e is calculated using Equation (3), as modified by substituting B_0 for B_p in Equation (5):

$$K_e = R_F + \left[E(R_m) - R_F\right]B_0 \tag{5}$$

The value B_0 represents the beta coefficient of an unlevered stream of income (EBIT) of the same size and risk level. It is *approximated* using Equation (6):

$$B_0 = B_p \frac{S}{S_0 - \text{MTS}} \tag{6}$$

where B_p = beta of the firm's common stock assuming its current levered position

S = market value of the firm's equity shares in period $t = 1$

S_0 = market value of the firm's equity, debt and preferred in period $t = 1$

MTS = market value of the tax shelter on the outstanding debt for the preceding period as defined in Equation (7), below.

For example, assume the following information relative to a firm before the acceptance of a capital project:[4]

EBIT = $95,000	$K_d = 0.10$	$S = $23,800
$D = $17,000	$t = 0.5$	$S_0 = $40,800
$E(R_m) = 0.15$	$R_F = 0.06$	$B_p = 2.41$

---

[2] See John D. Martin and David F. Scott, Jr., "Debt Capacity and the Capital Budgeting Decision," *Financial Management* (Summer 1976), pp. 7–14.

[3] Franco Modigliani and Merton Miller, "Corporate Income Taxes and the Cost of Capital: A Correction," *The American Economic Review* (June 1963), pp. 433–443.

[4] The following example is adapted from Martin and Scott, "Debt Capacity."

Then we may determine the following:

1. *Market value of tax shelter*:

$$\text{MTS} = \frac{D(K_d)(t)}{K_d} \tag{7}$$

where D=current amount of outstanding debt
K_d=pretax average cost of outstanding debt

$$\text{MTS} = \frac{\$17,000(0.10)(0.5)}{0.10} = \$8,500$$

2. *Beta value of the unencumbered cash flow*:

$$B_0 = B_p \frac{S}{S_0 - \text{MTS}}$$

$$= 2.41 \frac{\$23,800}{\$40,800 - \$8,500} = 2.41 \frac{\$23,800}{\$32,300} = 1.78$$

3. *Unlevered cost of equity*:

$$K_e = R_F + \left[E(R_m) - R_F \right] B_0$$
$$= 0.06 + (0.15 - 0.06)1.78$$
$$= 0.22 \quad \text{or} \quad 22\%$$

4. *Value of firm before acceptance of the project* (V_F):

$$V_F = \frac{\text{EBIT}(1 - t)}{K_e} + \frac{D(K_d)(t)}{K_d}$$

$$= \frac{\$95,000(1 - 0.5)}{0.22} + \frac{17,000(0.10)(0.5)}{0.10}$$

$$= \$215,909.09 + \$8,500$$
$$= \$224,409.09$$

5. *Firm's average cost of capital before acceptance of the project*:

$$K = \frac{\text{EBIT}(1 - t)}{V_F} \tag{8}$$

where K=firm's average cost of capital before acceptance of the project
t=firm's marginal tax rate
V_F=value of the firm before acceptance of the project

Applying Equation (8), we have the following:

$$K = \frac{\$95,000(1 - 0.5)}{\$224,409.09} = 0.21 \quad \text{or} \quad 21\%$$

Debt capacity is here defined as the risk of insolvency resulting from the use of financial leverage; that is, the risk that the unencumbered cash flows will be less than or equal to zero. The unencumbered cash flows may be found using Equation (9):

$$C = \text{EBIT} + \text{depreciation} - \left(I + \frac{SF}{1 - t} \right) \tag{9}$$

where C=unencumbered cash flow prior to the acceptance of the project
 I=annual interest expense prior to the acceptance of the project
 SF=sinking-fund payments or principal payments required under existing debt agreements

If C is assumed to be normally distributed with an expected value of $E(C)$ and standard deviation σ_C, the risk of insolvency is defined by the probability statement, Equation (10):

$$P(C \le 0) = P[E(C) - Z\sigma_C \le 0] \tag{10}$$

where Z is the ratio of $E(C)/\sigma_C$ corresponding to the number of standard deviations that the firm's expected unencumbered cash flow $E(C)$ lies away from zero. In short, we have a probability distribution of unencumbered cash flows. Assume for the firm in our illustration that $E(C) = \$100,000$ and $\sigma_C = \$78,125$; then the Z-value is determined as follows:

$$Z = \frac{\$100,000}{\$78,125} = 1.28$$

Reading from the normal table, Appendix C, 1.28 corresponds to approximately a 10% risk of insolvency.

Shifting the focus to the capital project that the firm is considering, assume that the project has an unencumbered cash flow $E(P)$ of \$10,000 and a σ_P of \$7,800. The coefficient of correlation between the cash flows of the firm and the project is 0.80. What does acceptance of the project add to the debt capacity of the firm? Using the Markowitz portfolio model described in Chapter 14, standard deviation of the firm's unencumbered cash flows after acceptance of the project is determined using Equation (11):

$$\sigma_{FC} = \left[\sigma_C^2 + \sigma_P^2 + 2(\rho)(\sigma_C)(\sigma_P)\right]^{1/2} \tag{11}$$

where σ_{FC}=standard deviation of the firm's unencumbered cash flows after the acceptance of the project
 σ_C^2=variance of the firm's unencumbered cash flows prior to acceptance of the project
 σ_P^2=variance of project's unencumbered cash flows
 ρ=correlation coefficient between the firm's unencumbered cash flows and those of the new project

Using the information for the firm and project discussed above and applying Equation (11) results in the following:

$$\sigma_{FC} = \left[(78,125)^2 + (7,800)^2 + 2(0.80)(78,125)(7,800)\right]^{1/2}$$

$$= \$84,495$$

The expected unencumbered cash flows of the firm now total \$110,000 (\$100,000 originally plus \$10,000 on the new project). To find the risk of insolvency we again employ the normal distribution.

$$Z = \frac{\$110,000}{\$84,495} = 1.3$$

A Z-value of 1.3 corresponds to a probability of 0.0968; that is, acceptance of the project has reduced the risk of insolvency from 10% to 9.68%.

6. *Computation of additional debt capacity*: The acceptance of a new project may affect the capacity of the firm to utilize additional debt while retaining its original risk of insolvency. To determine the *debt service* that may be added, we employ Equation (12):

$$Z = \frac{E(C') - d}{\sigma_{FC}} \tag{12}$$

where $E(C')$ = expected unencumbered cash flow after acceptance of the project
d = added debt service that can be carried at the 10% risk level

Applying Equation (12) to our example, where $Z = 1.28$, yields the following:

$$1.28 = \frac{\$110,000 - d}{\$84,495}$$

$$d = \$1,846$$

Since $K_d = 10\%$, \$1,846 of added *debt service* translates to an \$18,460 increment in debt capacity (\$1,846/0.10).

7. *Value of firm after acceptance of the project* (V_{FC}): To compute the value of the firm after acceptance of the project, we use Equation (4), where the EBIT value is the new $E(C')$ value less depreciation on the new project, and the value of D is the original debt plus the incremental debt capacity determined in step 6. For our example, the calculations are as follows, assuming a new value for EBIT of \$105,000 after acceptance of the project.

$$V_{FC} = \frac{EBIT(1 - t)}{K_e} + \frac{D(K_d)(t)}{K_d}$$

$$= \frac{\$105,000(1 - 0.5)}{0.22} + \frac{\$35,460(0.10)(0.5)}{0.10}$$

$$= \$238,636.36 + \$17,730$$

$$= \$256,366.36 \tag{4}$$

The increase in the value of the firm is \$31,957.27 (\$256,366.36 less the value of the firm before acceptance, \$224,409.09).

8. *Average cost of capital after acceptance of the project*:

$$K_{FC} = \frac{EBIT(1 - t)}{V_{FC}} \tag{13}$$

where K_{FC} = firm's average cost of capital after acceptance of the project
V_{FC} = value of the firm after acceptance of the project

Applying Equation (13) results in the following:

$$K_{FC} = \frac{\$105,000(1 - 0.5)}{\$256,366.36}$$

$$= 0.20$$

We have now come full cycle with CAPM, using it as follows:

1. As an alternative in the computation of the cost of equity.

2. As a hurdle rate in the selection of capital projects.

3. In combination with the Modigliani-Miller tax model, as a technique for valuing the firm and determining its debt capacity.

4. To determine the firm's average cost of capital.

The Martin-Scott formulation, to recapitulate, defines debt capacity by the level-of-insolvency risk. They demonstrate how the risk of insolvency might be reduced by the acceptance of *one additional capital project*. Whenever the risk of insolvency is reduced, the firm increases its absolute debt capacity. If the project is accepted and the incremental debt capacity implemented, the value of the firm is enhanced.

The Martin-Scott model states that the impact of a project on the firm's expected level of cash flow is *additive*; that is, equal to the level of annual before tax cash flows expected from the acceptance of the project. However, the crucial point is that the impact of the project on the *variability* of the firm's cash flow is not additive. Variability depends upon the correlation between the expected cash flows of the firm and the project—the portfolio effect. The portfolio effect, in turn, depends upon the characteristics of the firm and the project. Consequently, the same project can affect the valuations of two firms in different ways.

We should also take note of the practical difficulties in applying the Martin-Scott model. One obstacle centers on the calculation of B_0 (the beta coefficient of a debt-free stream of income) derived from the estimate of the market of the firm's capital structure less the market value of the tax shelter, as in Equations (6) and (7). The problem is one of homogeneity in firm characteristics over the period used in estimating B_0. A period long enough to attain stability in the value of B_0 will likely involve capital budgeting decisions, which affect changes in the capital structure and risk posture of the firm.

On this note, others have added further caveats to the application of the Martin-Scott model. Conine, for example, asserts that the integration of the Modigliani-Miller tax model and CAPM implicitly assumes the firm issues riskless debt and is not compatible with the issuance of risky corporate debt. He presents a methodology to correct this inconsistency between theory and practice.[5] Gahlon and Stover, on the other hand, stress the restrictiveness of illustrating the theory by assuming only one project is acceptable. A capital budget generally comprises several projects of different size and variability. In this case, the model must consider the correlation of cash flows *between* the firm and the individual projects, as well as the sizes and correlation *among* the project cash flows. The objective lies in selecting that combination of projects which maximizes the increase in the value of the firm while keeping the probability of insolvency at some target level. Otherwise, it is possible that two projects might win acceptance when analyzed independently but in combination could actually decrease the value of the firm.[6]

[5]Thomas E. Conine, Jr., "Debt Capacity and the Capital Budgeting Decision: A Comment," *Financial Management* (Spring 1980), pp. 20–22.

[6]James M. Gahlon and Roger D. Stover, "Debt Capacity and the Capital Budgeting Decision: A Caveat," *Financial Management* (Winter 1979), pp. 55–59.

SUMMARY

In this chapter we take the theoretical conceptions of capital asset pricing developed in Chapter 16 and apply them to financial management considerations, such as the evaluation of capital projects, the value of the firm before and after the acceptance of a capital project(s), the impact of the capital budget on the firm's debt capacity, determination of the firm's cost of equity capital and its average cost of capital. Few would disagree this constitutes a substantial array of topics—all revolving around the calculation of essentially a single statistic: beta. Manifestly, the application of CAPM to financial management has profound implications for the practice of corporate finance and the supporting securities industry. But capital asset pricing is not without its critics and it is to these arguments we must now turn.

QUESTIONS/PROBLEMS

1. The Capital Asset Pricing Corporation is evaluating the three projects shown below, which have various returns based on the states of nature shown:

State of Nature	Probability	Market Returns	Project Returns		
			P_1	P_2	P_3
1	0.1	−0.10	−0.30	−0.15	0.00
2	0.2	0	−0.10	−0.05	0.04
3	0.3	0.05	0.15	0.04	0.08
4	0.2	0.09	0.25	0.10	0.09
5	0.2	0.12	0.35	0.15	0.10

(a) Compute the expected returns for each project, as well as the expected return and standard deviation for the market, based on the probability distributions above.
(b) Compute the covariance between each project and the market.
(c) Compute the beta for each project.
(d) Compute the required rate of return for each project based on the capital asset pricing model, assuming that the risk-free rate is 6%.
(e) Discuss which of the projects are candidates for acceptance and why.

2. If the CAP Corporation's average marginal cost of capital were 12% and it evaluated the projects by the internal rate of return method, how would its project selections differ?

3. Safetynet, Inc., management is risk-averse and sets the return required on capital projects as

$$R_j = R_F + b \times \sigma(R_j)$$

where R_F is the risk-free interest rate and b is a penalty per unit of risk; management defines risk in terms of standard deviation of returns. The following two projects are under consideration:

Project	$E(R_i)$	$\sigma(R_i)$	Cost	Life
X	0.12	0.025	2,000	∞
Y	0.20	0.070	2,000	∞

The risk-free rate is 8%, and b is 2.0
(a) Evaluate projects X and Y individually, and decide whether to accept or reject.
(b) Assume the projects are independent (i.e., uncorrelated) and evaluate the portfolio combination of X plus Y. Is the portfolio acceptable? Explain.
(c) Assume the firm already possesses a single capital project, X, and will evaluate Y as an additional investment. Is Y acceptable? Explain.

4. Cavaliere Company has joined the "beta revolution," and believes capital projects ought to be evaluated using measures of systematic risk, as defined by modern portfolio theory. The security market line is estimated as:

$$R_j = R_f + B_j(R_m - R_f)$$
$$= 0.08 + B_j(0.16 - 0.08)$$
$$= 0.08 + 0.08B_j$$

where R_f is the risk-free rate, R_m is the return expected on the general market index, and B_j is a measure of the nondiversifiable risk of a project's cash flows. Two 1-year projects, S and T, are described below:

Project	B_i	$E(R_i)$	$\sigma(R_i)$
S	0.4	0.12	0.025
T	1.6	0.20	0.070

(a) Evaluate projects S and T individually, and decide whether to accept or reject.
(b) Evaluate the portfolio combination of S plus T. Is the combination acceptable? Explain.
(c) Assume the firm already possesses a single capital project and will evaluate T as an additional investment. Is T acceptable? Explain.

5. Locklow Aircraft is considering the introduction of a new fuel-efficient airliner. The present financial condition of Locklow shows the following:

EBIT = \$190,000	$K_d = 0.15$	$S = \$23,800$
$D = \$ 34,000$	$t = 0.52$	$S_0 = 40,800$
$E(R_m) = 0.30$	$R_f = 0.10$	$B_p = 2.00$
$E(C) = \$500,000$	$\sigma = \$78,125$	$\sigma_p = \$7,800$

The project has an unencumbered cash flow of \$50,000 with a standard deviation of \$5,000. The coefficient of correlation between the cash flows of the firm and the project is 0.60, and debt is carried at a 10% risk level.
(a) Before acceptance of the project, determine:
    (i) Market value of the tax shelter;
    (ii) Beta value of the unencumbered cash flow;
    (iii) Unlevered cost of equity;
    (iv) Value of the firm before acceptance of the project;
    (v) Average cost of capital before acceptance of the project.
(b) After acceptance of the project, determine:
    (i) The firm's additional debt capacity;
    (ii) Value of the firm after acceptance of the project;
    (iii) Average cost of capital after acceptance of the project.

18

A Critique of the Capital Asset Pricing Model

The Capital Asset Pricing Model (CAPM) provides a comprehensive theory of finance linking the decisions of financial managers to the risk-return expectations of investors. Although it amplifies Markowitz's seminal work on portfolio selection and traces its roots to the economist's theory of choice, CAPM takes the ultimate step in the progress of finance from a descriptive-institutional discipline to the deductive-empirical scientific method.

All the same, the scientific method is a restless device. Each advance in knowledge unearths new insights and opens the door to refinements and/or new theoretical constructs. Application ineluctably lags behind the output of research, making the latter prone to the perils of faddism.[1] Happily, in finance, the penalties of unfettered inquiry are self-limiting, for theory ultimately must be validated by better decision-making in firms and on security markets. Such caveats condition our critique of the CAPM.

ASSUMPTIONS OF CAPITAL ASSET PRICING

It is trite but essential to observe that no theory is any better than the assumptions upon which it rests. These should bear some relevance, albeit imperfect, to the realities of the phenomenon explained. CAPM rests upon two sets of assumptions:

[1]Victor L. Andrews, "Sterile Promises in Corporate Capital Theory, *Financial Management*, 8, no. 4 (Winter 1979), pp. 7–11.

1. *Assumptions about investor behavior*:

(a) Investors are risk-averse. They expect to be rewarded for assuming risk.

(b) Acting rationally, investors choose only efficient portfolios: the largest return, $E(R_p)$, for a given level of risk, σ_p; or the lowest risk, σ_p, for a specified return, $E(R_p)$.

(c) As a corollary, investors optimize their portfolio combinations by efficient diversification.

(d) Investors have the same time horizon regarding the risk-return payoff on risk assets. They strive to maximize the single period expected utility of terminal wealth.

(e) All investors share the same estimates of the expected return and risk $[E(R_p), \sigma_p,$ and $\text{Cov}(R_p, R_m)]$ for all risk assets traded.

2. *Assumptions about the market*:

(a) All investors can borrow or lend in unlimited amounts at the risk-free rate (R_F).

(b) There are no taxes or transaction costs.

(c) Information is freely available to all investors.

(d) All assets are perfectly divisible and perfectly liquid (i.e., marketable at the going price).

(e) The cost of insolvency or bankruptcy is zero.

CAPM, in effect, says that the market is efficient, that it quickly discounts all publicly available information. Some proponents go further and affirm that the market has discounted all information, public and otherwise, on a security. This, in turn, leads to the *random-walk hypothesis*, stating that changes in stock prices cannot be predicted on the basis of past price movements. Hence, historical data on market-price changes will not enable the trader to earn above-normal, risk-adjusted returns. The best strategy then lies in buying into the market portfolio and sitting tight. The strategy assures that the investor always does as well as the market, and he or she cannot beat the market in any event.

In this respect, when CAPM is applied to the problem of evaluating capital projects, the user must bear in mind that investments in securities versus plant and equipment are not completely analogous. Securities are *divisible* assets; fractional shares can be rounded to integer amounts in constructing a portfolio. Each share of a given stock has the same expected return and systematic risk. On the other hand, capital projects are generally indivisible—accepted or rejected in toto. The choice is all or nothing. Fractional acceptance is not a viable alternative. The efficient frontier for a set of capital projects consequently becomes a sequence of corner points, which can be connected only artificially to form a continuous frontier (Figure 18–1).

The assumption of zero bankruptcy or insolvency cost is manifestly suspect. Under real-world conditions, assets of a bankrupt firm are sold at distress prices and accompanied by selling cost, legal fees, and other opportunity costs of a cumbersome legal system. Reality tells us the assets of the bankrupt will not be

FIGURE 18-1   Efficient Frontier: Capital Projects

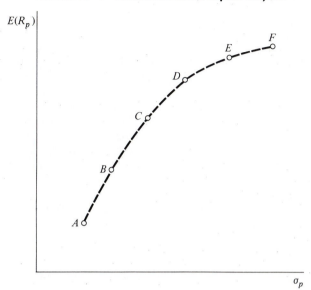

sold at their economic values with any residual value distributed to the share-holders. Under these circumstances, investors are not able to diversify their risks as CAPM presumes.

Moreover, the probability of a firm's financial collapse depends upon total risk (defined by Markowitz), not on systematic risk per se. Accordingly, when bankruptcy costs are significant and potential, the financial manager may be well advised to formulate the capital budget with an eye on total risks and not to focus simply on systematic risk. This implies a degree of risk aversion greater than that which would maximize shareholders' wealth under CAPM.[2] In short, the manager should be confident that the risk of insolvency is sufficiently low before evaluating investment alternatives on the basis of systematic risk alone.

Similarly, if investors in fact have different borrowing or lending rates or different expectations and time horizons and if transaction costs do exist and information is not available without cost, then there will not be a single capital market line nor one best market portfolio. This, too, imparts added significance to residual risk.

Finally, when we affirm that the stock market discounts all available information, we must bear in mind the market does not record information in the manner of a computer. Rather, it registers the reactions of the participants to the received news. These reactions may be rational in terms of the participants' perspectives, but rationality does not equate with infallibility. Judged by hindsight, the security markets have not been outstandingly successful as indicators of economic activity or of industry and company performance.

[2] James C. Van Horne, *Financial Management and Policy* (Englewood Cliffs, NJ: Prentice-Hall, Inc. 1983), pp. 208–209.

SOME OPERATIONAL PROBLEMS

Stability of Beta

Alpha (α_j) and beta (B_j) describe an average relationship between the behavior of the security and market index existing in some prior period and *assumed to hold for the future.* Although the parametric values can be updated annually or quarterly, the model fundamentally relies on past performances, capturing the influences on the market at the time of calculation. Is the beta computed from historical data a good surrogate for the true beta reflecting investors' estimates of the stock's future volatility? If so, the financial manager has a significant new tool to assist his or her deliberations aimed at maximizing shareholders' wealth or the present value of the enterprise.

Some recent surveys indicate that the historically computed beta closely approximates the true, contemporary beta. Blume, for example, showed that the beta of a firm:[3]

1. Is fairly stable over time.

2. Can be forecast accurately from historical data.

3. Generally tends over a long time span, 1926–1968, to unity, the beta of the market as a whole.

Logue and Merville found that beta values bear a significant correlation to the firm's financial policies expressed in liquidity ratios, leverage measures, dividend payments, and profitability.[4]

Not all the evidence is affirmative. In another investigation, Levy examined the weekly returns for over 500 stocks on the New York Stock Exchange over the period December 30, 1960, through December 18, 1970 (520 weeks) to establish stationary data for betas over 52-week, 26-week, and 13-week forecast periods for stock portfolios ranging from 1, 5, 10, 25, and 50 stocks per portfolio.[5] Levy concluded:

1. Average betas are reasonably predictable for large portfolios, less predictable for smaller portfolios, and quite unpredictable for individual securities.

2. Forecasts are clearly better over longer periods than over shorter periods.

3. Although predictability improves as the forecast period lengthens, the relative improvement tends to be less for larger portfolios.

4. For portfolios of 25 stocks or more over forecast intervals of 26 weeks and longer, historical betas seem to be fairly good and stable indicators of future risk.

Levitz's study supported Levy's conclusions.[6] He showed that for individual stocks the correlation of historical and actual betas was extremely poor (i.e., 0.55 for the test period). However, for portfolios—even with as few as 10 stocks—sta-

---

[3] Marshall E. Blume, "On the Assessment of Risk," *Journal of Finance*, 26 (March 1971), pp. 1–10.
[4] Dennis E. Logue and Larry J. Merville, "Financial Policy and Market Expectations," *Financial Management* (Summer 1972), pp. 37–44.
[5] R. A. Levy, "On the Short-term Stationarity of Beta Coefficients," *Financial Analysts Journal* (November-December 1971), pp. 55–62.
[6] G. D. Levitz, *A Study of the Usefulness of Beta Analysis in the Management of Common Stock Portfolios* (New York: Brown Brothers, Harriman & Co., 1972).

tistically significant correlations were obtained, in some instances up to 0.90. He states:

> For individual stocks the historical beta coefficient is not an accurate predictor of future relative volatility, although it may provide a "best-guess" estimate.

There is doubt, too, about the interpretation of alpha. Alpha, the *y*-intercept of the regression line, indicates the rate of return produced, on the average, by the investment independent of the market. Stocks with high alphas tend to have lower betas, and vice versa. Wells notes that one means of obtaining above-average performance lies in selecting a stock with a positive alpha.[7] When one stock has a higher (lower) return than another stock with the same beta, it has done better (worse) against the market than its beta would have predicted and this is said to be due to its alpha factor or the residual, nonmarket influences unique to each stock. Alpha mirrors influences from the industry, such as technological breakthroughs, management shifts, merger prospects, and so on. However, more research is needed to assess the full significance of alpha.

Identifying the Market Portfolio

Addressing himself to the problems of application in CAPM, Roll shows that the operational equations are not testable unless the exact composition of the true market portfolio is known and used. Furthermore, if the true market portfolio were indeed known, the only hypothesis that could be tested by the Security Market Line is the efficiency of the market portfolio.

Using proxies—such as the Standard & Poor's 500 Index or the New York Stock Exchange Index—does not solve the problem. If the proxy index is not efficient, the CAPM relationship does not hold. Conversely, if the proxy index is efficient, this does not establish that the true market portfolio is also efficient since the composition of the true market portfolio is unknown.[8]

It is likely, of course, that most feasible proxy portfolios are highly correlated with one another and the true market portfolio. The correlation may exist whether or not the portfolios are mean-variance efficient. The condition would seemingly support the viewpoint of some CAPM advocates that the exact composition of the true market portfolio and its surrogates is unimportant in practice. However, Weston notes:

> Small differences from the true market portfolios, however, can cause substantial biases in the measurement of risk and expected return.... Until the total market portfolio containing all assets is known and measured, ambiguities in the tests of the asset pricing models and of security investment performance will remain.[9]

[7]C. Wells, "The Beta Revolution: Learning to Live with Risk," *Institutional Investor* (September 1971), pp. 21–64.

[8]Richard Roll, "Ambiguity When Performance Is Measured by the Securities Market Line," *The Journal of Finance*, (September 1978), pp. 1051–1069.

[9]J. Fred Weston, "Developments in Finance Theory," *Financial Management*, 10, no. 2 (Summer, 1981) 5–22.

The validation problem is further complicated by allowing for different borrowing and lending rates, different expectations and time horizons, the presence of transactions cost, and other lapses from the assumptions of CAPM that abort the possibility of a single-security market line and a single market portfolio. But tests for efficiency presuppose identification of the relevant market portfolio, as well as its composition. In short, not only have we not identified the composition of the true market portfolio, we do not know whether such a portfolio can operationally exist at all.

Market Efficiency

When security market performance is compared against the criteria of efficiency, troublesome anomalies surface. For example, common stocks constitute claims on real assets. Ex ante, we should reasonably expect stocks to provide a hedge against inflation. Investigation indicates otherwise. Bodie found that in the United States during the period 1953–1972, common stocks failed to serve as hedges against either anticipated or unanticipated inflation.[10]

In an attempt to explain the failure of common stocks to perform as inflation hedges, Modigliani and Cohn hypothesized that inflation had a negative effect on value due to its impact on accounting determined profits. The market, in turn, committed two basic valuation errors:

1. It failed to realize that in a period of inflation part of the interest expense is not truly an interest expense but rather a repayment of real principal.

2. It tended to capitalize long-run profits not at a real rate of interest but at a rate that varied with the nominal interest rate.[11] Cohn and Lessard demonstrated this phenomenon was not restricted to U.S. markets.[12]

Another anomaly appears when portfolios are formed on the basis of firm size. Banz, and later Reinganum, demonstrated that small firms systematically experienced average rates of return nearly 20% per year greater than those of large firms, even after accounting for differences in estimated betas. An adequately specified model of equilibrium should eliminate persistent abnormal returns.[13]

In evaluating the market's performance against the criteria of efficiency, several caveats must be borne in mind. First, the statistical tests of efficiency are essentially tests of the *joint* hypothesis of the validity of the regression model (CAPM) *and* of market efficiency. Whenever the assumptions of the model do not accord with reality, the "lapses" of the market may be traceable to the model and not to market inefficiency per se. Second, the notion of efficiency has evolved

---

[10]Z. Bodie, "Common Stocks as a Hedge Against Inflation," *The Journal of Finance*, 31, no. 2 (May 1976), 459–470.

[11]F. Modigliani and R. Cohn, "Inflation, Rational Valuation and the Market" *Financial Analysts Journal*, 35, no. 2, (March-April 1979), 24–44.

[12]Richard A. Cohn and Donald R. Lessard, "The Effect of Inflation on Stock Prices: International Evidence," *The Journal of Finance*, XXXVI, no. 2 (May 1981), 277–289.

[13]Cited in Marc R. Reinganum, "The Arbitrage Pricing Theory: Some Empirical Results," *The Journal of Finance*, XXXVI, no. 2 (May 1981), 313–321.

from stronger and more rigid notions of efficiency to weaker specifications since the introduction of CAPM. It is vital to define the level of efficiency expected from the market before assessing market performance. Third, the market prices of securities (common stocks) respond to the risk-return calculations of traders. How is return measured: by accounting numbers or cash flow? Accounting earnings are subject to a variety of options (regarding depreciation, inventory valuation, bad debt allowances, and so on), which significantly affect earnings after taxes. Furthermore, accounting returns represent a mixture of present and past values because the firm's balance sheet comprises a heterogeneous conglomeration of assets and liabilities acquired or incurred at different price levels. Cash flow is the better statistic to employ in measuring return, but it is complicated to measure given the information available to investors. Nor are cash-flow ambiguities diminished by resorting to the device of adding depreciation back to accounting earnings—a shorthand method frequently favored by security analysts and finance researchers. The conclusion is manifest: If the measurement of earnings is flawed, then the calculations of the required return (R_j) and the beta (B_j) are misleading. Market efficiency cannot be tested by the use of flawed data, no matter how sophisticated the mathematical construct.

Multiperiod Investments

In common stock investment, CAPM relates the cash flows of the investment to the returns on the market portfolio of risky assets:

$$R_j^0 = R_F + B_j \left[E(R_m) - R_F \right] \tag{1}$$

where R_j^0 = required return on the investment

R_F = risk-free rate of return

$E(R_m)$ = expected return on the market portfolio

Return is defined as the price at the end of the period less the price at the beginning of the period plus dividends received divided by the price at the beginning of the period. The returns on the stock and on the market portfolio are both single-period returns—monthly, quarterly, or annually—are identical in content, and are directly comparable.

However, the use of CAPM in a capital budgeting context raises questions on the comparability of the measured returns. Capital projects are evaluated using an (internal rate of return) IRR or NPV (net-present value). Each involves the discounting of cash flows over several time periods. Therefore, the return on the market portfolio in CAPM (a single-period return) is not comparable to IRR (a multiperiod measurement). Also, the content of the two returns differ. The return on the market portfolio (R_m) combines dividend inflows and changes in the market price of securities for the period involved. Cash flows of a capital project do not incorporate changes in the market price of the initial investment, but may include a final residual value.[14]

---

[14] Richard S. Bower and Donald R. Lessard, "An Operational Approach to Risk-Screening," *The Journal of Finance*, XXVIII, no. 2 (May 1973), 321–337.

In Chapter 17, we partially address the problem of multiperiod returns in CAPM for capital budgeting utilizing a basic model proposed by Weston.[15] This allows for the computation of returns on the project and the market portfolio period by period. If we go a step further and include the residual values of the initial investment at the end of each period, the criterion of comparable returns is met.

This can be done in either of two ways. First, the firm could take an already accepted project similar to the one under consideration and compare its rate of return (R_{jt}) with the return on the market portfolio (R_{mt}) for the same time frame. From this historical data, a beta value can be calculated and applied to the new project. The approach assumes that the future will repeat the past—i.e., the project and market portfolio cash flow patterns will be substantially unchanged. There is here an implicit forecast of no change—a robust assumption to put forth in a dynamic economy. Second, the firm could face the forecasting problem directly and compute an expected return on the project $[E(R_{jt})]$ and the market $[E(R_{mt})]$. From these projections, the firm can calculate beta (B_j) in order to determine the required return $[R_j^0]$ on the capital expenditure proposed. The approach requires the application of long-term forecasting techniques to project cash flows, to the market portfolio of risk securities, and to the risk-free rate of return. The forecast problem is made explicit, but the task is not eased. Suffice to say, the error factor in business forecasting tends to increase with the passage of time, and it is particularly difficult to forecast interest rates or the performance of the security markets over an extended time frame. On the other hand, the beta obtained is future-oriented rather than being the product of historical relationships.

□ **EXAMPLE 1**

Assume a 10-year project with the following data:

(1) Period (t)	(2) Investment	(3) Expected Residual Value, $E(S_t)$	(4) Expected Cash Flow, $E(C_t)$	(5) Expected Return on Market Portfolio, $E(R_{mt})$
0	$200,000			
1		$180,000	$40,000	0.20
2		160,000	30,000	0.15
3		140,000	35,000	0.10
4		120,000	45,000	0.20
5		100,000	50,000	0.22
6		80,000	45,000	0.25
7		70,000	40,000	0.20
8		50,000	35,000	0.18
9		25,000	30,000	0.17
10		5,000	25,000	0.15
				$E(R_m) = \underline{\underline{0.182}}$

The risk-free rate of return is $R_F = 12\%$. Should the project be accepted?

[15] J. Fred Weston, "Investment Decisions Using the Capital Asset Pricing Model," *Financial Management*, 2, no. 1, (Spring 1973), 25–33.

Solution:

TABLE 18-1 Multiperiod Analysis of Projected Expected Returns $[E(R_{jt})]$

(1)	(2)	(3)	(4)	(5)
		Expected Residual Value at End of	*Expected Cash*	*Expected Returns,* $E(R_{jt}) = \dfrac{E(S_t) + E(C_t) - E(S_{t-1})}{E(S_{t-1})}$
Period	*Investment*	*Each Period, $E(S_t)$*	*Flow, $E(C_t)$*	
0	$200,000			
1		$180,000	$40,000	0.100
2		160,000	30,000	0.056.
3		140,000	35,000	0.094
4		120,000	45,000	0.178
5		100,000	50,000	0.250
6		80,000	45,000	0.250
7		70,000	40,000	0.375
8		50,000	35,000	0.215
9		25,000	30,000	0.100
10		5,000	25,000	0.200
				$E(R_j) = 0.182$

Part I:
The expected return for the project each period is calculated using Equation (2):

$$E(R_{jt}) = \frac{(S_t - S_{t-1}) + E(C_t)}{S_{t-1}} \tag{2}$$

For period 1, this becomes:

$$E(R_{j1}) = \frac{(\$180,000 - \$200,000) + \$40,000}{\$200,000}$$

$$= \frac{-\$20,000 + \$40,000}{\$200,000} = 0.10$$

We calculate $E(R_{jt})$ in this way in order to make it comparable to the return on the market portfolio,

$$E(R_{mt}) = \frac{(P_t - P_{t-1}) + D_t}{P_{t-1}} \tag{3}$$

where P_t = value of portfolio at the end of the period
P_{t-1} = value of portfolio at the beginning of the period
D_t = dividends for period t

Part II:
Determine the beta value of the project in relation to expected return on the market portfolio by linear-regression analysis:

$$E(R_j) = \alpha_j + B_j(E(R_m)) \tag{4}$$

Using the least-squares method, the value of beta is calculated to be 1.24. Therefore, for the project under consideration, the required return—using Equation (1)—becomes

$$R_j^0 = R_F + B_j[E(R_m) - R_F] = 0.12 + 1.24(0.182 - 0.12) \tag{5}$$
$$= 0.197, \quad \text{or} \quad 19.7\%$$

The required return on the project, R_j^0 can be used in either of two ways:

1. Comparison with the expected return on the project $E(R_j)$. If the project's required return exceeds the expected returns $R_j^0 > E(R_j)$), then the project is rejected. The return on the project is not commensurate with the risk accepted. Conversely, if $R_j^0 < E(R_j)$, the project merits favorable consideration inasmuch as the return compensates for the risk. In our illustration, because $R_j^0 > E(R_j)$ (0.197 > 0.182), the firm should reject the project.

   2. Use of the required return as the discount rate in computing the NPV for the project.

(1) Period (t)	(2) Cash Flow	(3) Discount Factor at 19.7%[a]	(4) Present Value (2 × 3)
1	$40,000	0.8354	$33,416
2	30,000	0.6979	20,937
3	35,000	0.5831	20,408
4	45,000	0.4871	21,920
5	50,000	0.4069	20,345
6	45,000	0.3399	15,296
7	40,000	0.2840	11,360
8	35,000	0.2373	8,305
9	30,000	0.1983	5,949
10	25,000	0.1656	4,140
		Total present value	$162,076
		Investment (t_o)	200,000
		Net present value	($37,924)

[a] Discount factor computed using calculator $(1/(1 + R)^t)$ since the rate falls between table intervals.

The project has a negative net present value and would normally be rejected. □

SUMMARY

   It is the nature of hypothesis testing in finance that the jury is always out. More research has to be done on CAPM, as well as on arbitrage pricing theory (APT) and other multivariable models. CAPM, an inheritance from economic theory, must concentrate on the composition of the market portfolio. Until the question of the composition of the market portfolio is resolved, it will not be possible to test the efficiency of the market or of investor portfolios. There is also the problem of circular reasoning, in that the CAPM assumes the market is efficient and then proceeds to employ the CAPM construct in testing the efficiency of the market. We cannot have it both ways.

   The time element presents another complicating factor in the real-world application of CAPM. CAPM, conceived by Sharpe, is a single-period, single-factor equilibrium model in the tradition of static economic analysis. Intertemporal analysis (dynamic analysis), as we have seen, is handled more by expediency than by conformity with the full array of restrictive assumptions underlying CAPM. Perhaps the way out of this particular conundrum is to look at the disequilibria models prevalent in modern economic theory.

   On the other hand, APT has a long road to run before it will enter the discussions of corporate management. If multifactor models are per se more desirable, the APT adherents have yet to specify the multifactors.

   This returns us to our starting point that CAPM remains the only comprehensive theory of finance that does enjoy some real-world application. Such limited acceptance is perhaps traceable to the capability of the model to describe tendencies—albeit imperfectly—that apparently hold up even when the assumptions are not fully met. As in scientific investigation, it is sometimes possible to predict results without fully knowing all the causes.

QUESTIONS/PROBLEMS

1. What does the assumption of rationality mean?
2. Is information freely available to all investors? Does it really matter that all investors have equal access to security information for the market to be efficient?
3. Why are capital projects generally indivisible?
4. Summarize the problem of intertemporal cash flows when CAPM is applied to capital budgeting. How does the CAPM model in Chapter 17 (Equations 1 and 2) differ from the model in this chapter?
5. The Avant Garde Corporation is evaluating three projects:

	Cash Flows		
Period (t)	P_1	P_2	P_3
0	−$1,000	−$1,000	−$1,000
1	600	250	100
2	300	200	140
3	150	140	180
4	250	150	100
5	350	200	100

The residual values for each project by period are:

	Residual Values		
Period (t)	P_1	P_2	P_3
0	−$1,000	−$1,000	−$1,000
1	500	700	900
2	300	300	800
3	100	300	850
4	100	300	1,000
5	100	300	1,200

(a) Compute the expected cash flow and the expected return for each project.
(b) Compute the beta for each project. The market returns, $E(R_{mt})$, are:

Period	$E(R_{mt})$
1	0.20
2	0.13
3	0.18
4	0.25
5	0.20

(c) Compute the required return R_j^0 on each project assuming a risk-free rate (R_F) of 0.12.
(d) Which projects would be accepted and why?

INTRODUCTION TO MATHEMATICAL PROGRAMMING

Throughout the text we have examined various types of financial decisions, all of which have the following characteristics:

1. Scarce resources had to be allocated among competing decision alternatives.

2. The decision-maker was striving to achieve an overriding goal or objective.

3. Various restrictions and requirements were imposed on the decision maker.

The decision-making process becomes more complex as the number of alternatives increases, as these alternatives become interdependent, and as the number of constraints on the decision-maker increases. Given the decision-making setting described above, a natural and powerful set of tools referred to as *mathematical programming models* can be utilized to facilitate the evaluation of decision alternatives. This chapter surveys the area of mathematical programming as an introduction to the following three chapters, where these models are applied to the capital budgeting problem setting, first under conditions of certainty and then under conditions of risk.

MATHEMATICAL PROGRAMMING MODELS

Mathematical programming (MP) models are a set of techniques in the broader fields of operations research or management science. These fields utilize quantitative models to describe various business, industrial, or governmental problem settings to gather information, obtain greater insight, or evaluate various decision alternatives. In our definition of mathematical programming, we used the term "quantitative models," which deserves further elaboration. Quantitative models are descriptive representations of a real problem setting using mathematical equations. Such models are constructed to obtain information and insight about a problem setting more quickly and in a less costly and less disruptive way than by experimenting directly on the actual system. These models are, therefore, "abstractions" of the real system; that is, they try to capture only the most critical elements and relationships that exist in the real system; otherwise, it would be as difficult, time-consuming, and costly to analyze the model as the real system. Because quantitative models can be rather involved, a "solution algorithm" must generally be used to solve the model. A solution algorithm is merely a step-by-step process that guarantees reaching the correct solution to the model formulation.

The complexity of real systems, as well as hidden interrelationships among system components, makes it advantageous for the analyst to perform "sensitivity analysis" on the solution obtained. Sensitivity analysis is a process whereby the analyst determines how significantly the solution to the problem will change if various assumptions about the system are modified in the model. This process points to the characteristics of the system that are most critical and that require most attention in the management control area. Sensitivity analysis generally leads to changes in the model representation that may require re-solving the model to obtain information on the new solution. The results of the sensitivity analysis become inputs to the decision-making process wherein additional quantitative and qualitative factors (not reflected in the original model) which differentiate the various alternatives are taken into account before the "best" alternative is selected for implementation into the real system. Periodically after this implementation, feedback is obtained to determine how well the system is functioning, so that timely corrective action can be taken, if necessary. This model-building and decision-making process is summarized in Figure 19-1.

To begin our discussion of MP models, we must define a number of terms. There are two major categories of equations that are used in MP models:

1. The objective function describes the goal or objective the decision-maker desires to achieve.

2. Constraint equations describe any limitations on resources, restrictions imposed by the environment within which the system functions, or managerial policies that the firm desires to observe.

The basic approach of MP models is to optimize the objective function while simultaneously satisfying all the constraint equations that limit the activities of the decision maker. In formulating both the objective function and the constraint equations used in MP models, two types of variables are used:

1. Input parameters are values specified by the decision-maker to describe characteristics of the system.

2. Decision variables will be determined by the model as a part of achieving the optimal solution.

FIGURE 19–1   Model-Building and Decision-Making Process

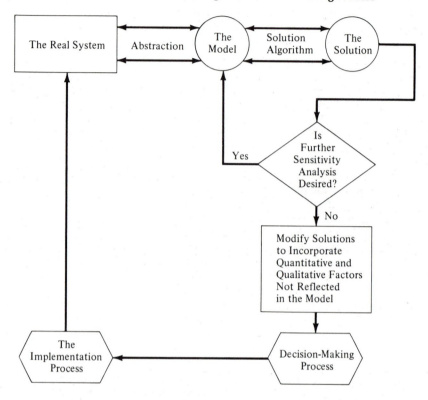

As a brief illustration of these definitions, consider a firm manufacturing and selling two products (X and Y) and desiring to determine that product mix that will maximize total dollar profit. The firm estimates that the unit profit figures are $6 and $18, respectively. The objective function to maximize profit for this firm would therefore be expressed as follows:

$$\text{maximize profit} = \$6X + \$18Y$$

In this objective function the two values $6 and $18 are the *input parameters* since management had to specify these values pertaining to their two products. The variables X and Y, which designate the number of units of product X and the number of units of product Y that should be produced, are *decision variables* since the model will determine their values to maximize profits.

CATEGORIES OF MATHEMATICAL PROGRAMMING MODELS

Within the general class of models referred to as *mathematical programming*, there are several specific models that can be applied to problem settings, depending on the assumptions made about the problem being analyzed and the

TABLE 19–1   Categories of Mathematical Programming Models

Conditions of Certainty	*Conditions of Risk*[a]
1. Linear programming (LP)	1. Stochastic LP (SLP) LP under uncertainty (LPUU) Chance-constrained programming (CCP)
2. Integer programming (IP)	2. IP under uncertainty (IPUU)
3. Goal programming (GP)	3. Stochastic GP (SGP)
4. Nonlinear programming (NLP) Quadratic programming (QP)	4. NLP under uncertainty (NLPUU) QP under uncertainty (QPUU)
5. Dynamic programming (DP)	5. DP under uncertainty (DPUU)

[a] Based on our definitions of risk and uncertainty in Chapter 12, the models listed technically assume conditions of risk, while in the literature they are frequently referred to in terms of *uncertainty*.

interrelationships among system components. Several categories of mathematical programming models are shown in Table 19–1. Each utilizes different types of equations in the objective function or constraint equations and/or permits different assumptions about the input parameters: either these values are assumed to be known with certainty or they are assumed to be known only by means of a probability distribution (i.e., conditions of risk exist). *Herein lie the major strengths of mathematical programming models: they are optimization models (i.e., they find the best possible solution for a given problem representation), and they can accurately describe virtually any real-world system assuming that either conditions of certainty or risk exist.* Hence, MP models provide a powerful tool for the decision-maker.

The use of the basic *linear programming* (LP) model, which we will discuss in more detail in the following section, requires three assumptions:

1. The input parameters are known with certainty.

2. Both the objective function and the constraint equations can be accurately described using linear equations.

3. The decision variables are continuous (i.e., they can take on any value).

Linear programming is the most widely known and used MP model because it represents problems with reasonable accuracy utilizing linear equations that may be solved easily with computerized solution algorithms.

If the assumption of certainty is relaxed, the decision-maker may select among three alternative models available for handling conditions of risk in a linear programming setting:

1. Stochastic LP is a two-stage decision process wherein stage 1 decisions are fixed and random events are generated; then the stage 2 decisions are determined in order to optimize the objective function given the stage 1 decisions and the random events.

2. LP under uncertainty is also a two-stage decision process wherein stage 1 decisions are fixed and random events are generated; then stage 2 decisions are determined to minimize the penalty assessed for violation of any of the constraints caused by the random events that were encountered.

3. Chance-constrained programming attempts to maximize the expected return or minimize the variance of returns, where, owing to the stochastic nature of the input parameters, the constraint equations are required to hold only with some probability less than 1.

Integer programming (IP) relaxes the third assumption required by the LP model, namely, that the decision variables must be continuous. IP allows the decision variables to take on integer values. This seemingly small change in the LP model greatly increases solution time as compared to the corresponding LP problem but permits the solution of large classes of problems wherein the decision variables must take on integer values. IP under uncertainty is analogous to LP under uncertainty.

Goal programming (GP) is a powerful and interesting extension of LP, wherein a hierarchy of multiple objectives is incorporated into the model; thus, the objective function becomes multidimensional. GP provides an effective operational methodology to maximize expected utility as discussed in Chapter 12. Stochastic GP is analogous to stochastic LP and is treated in a similar manner.

Nonlinear programming (NLP) is an MP model wherein either or both the objective function and the constraint equations must be described using nonlinear equations. NLP is frequently used to solve problems involving curvilinear cost functions.

Quadratic programming is a special type of nonlinear programming model wherein the only nonlinearity is in the objective function. QP models are significantly easier to solve than NLP models because there is no general way to solve the latter type of problem. Again, the "risk" setting merely necessitates incorporating the probability distributions of the input parameters, which may also be incorporated into the QP model.

Dynamic programming (DP) is a useful method of optimizing a system over time. In addition, DP may be used to divide large decision problems into a sequence of smaller, interrelated decision problems wherein recursive equations are used to describe the flow of decisions and the state of the system. Recursive equations relate adjacently indexed variables of a set so that if we know the value of one variable, we can determine the value of the next one; and so on. DP under uncertainty assumes that new information is acquired as the decision-maker moves through time and that this information is used to update system parameters and to aid in the sequential decision process.

This brief introduction to the various MP models is designed to give an overview rather than specific details of each model. Several of the models will be examined in more depth in this and the following chapters. Extensive research has been undertaken in the area of mathematical programming applied to various problem areas in finance, as evidenced by the entries cited in the selected bibliography. The interested reader is encouraged to seek out such references.

LINEAR PROGRAMMING

Because of the widespread use and importance of linear programming (LP), it is examined in greater detail in this section. In our initial discussion of LP, three major assumptions underlying its use were cited. These assumptions imply various other aspects of LP models, which are delineated in Table 19-2. In our discussion of other MP models, we noted that several of the assumptions required for LP can be relaxed in order to establish models that more closely describe the real-world decision settings faced by the analyst. For example, the LP assumption of certainty can be relaxed by utilizing SLP, LPUU, or CCP; the limitation of a single objective function can be overcome by using GP; and the need for continuous rather than discrete variables may be relaxed by using IP. Of course, each of these enrichments to the basic LP model necessitates greater input requirements, as well as more computer time and memory to solve the model. It should be stressed that the LP model, although it has shortcomings, is a reasonable starting point for many practical decision problems. Thus, the methodology of LP problem-solving deserves study.

The basic approach to LP problem-solving proceeds through the following stages:

Stage 1: Formulate the problem in the LP framework. This requires specification of input parameters and decision variables, the objective function, and all relevant constraint equations. The latter two sets of equations must all be linear in nature.

Stage 2: Solve the problem using either a graphical approach, the simplex method, or a computer-based solution algorithm.

Stage 3: Interpret the optimal solution which is expressed in terms of an alternative decision point within the feasible solution domain.

TABLE 19-2   Assumptions of Linear Programming Models

The major assumptions of linear programming models are as follows:

1. The objective of the system under analysis and all its relevant resource limitations, restrictions, and requirements can be accurately described using *linear equations.* That is, the objective function and all constraint equations must be linear.

2. Conditions of *certainty* exist. All the model's parameters (i.e., the objective function coefficients, the technical coefficients in the constraints, and the right-hand-side values in the constraints) are known precisely and are not subject to variation.

3. All decision variables are restricted to *nonnegative* values.

4. Only a *single objective* is optimized.

5. The decision variables are considered to be continuous rather than discrete. This is known as the *divisibility* assumption.

6. Resources available are *homogenous.* Example: if 10 hours of direct labor are available, each of these hours is just as productive as any other and can be used equally well on any activity that requires direct labor.

7. Proportionality exists. This means that if it is desired to increase the activity level of any decision variable, proportionately greater amounts of each resource are required. The linearity assumption implies proportionality.

8. All parameters of the model are *unaffected* by changes in methods used, level of utilization, economics of scale, and so on. Again, the linearity assumption implies this.

9. The system is *additive* in nature: the whole is equal to the sum of the parts. The effectiveness of the system equals the sum of each system component's effectiveness. The total resources utilized equal the sum of the resources used on each activity variable.

10. Independence exists throughout the system. This means there is no interaction among decision variables, resources available, or different operations performed.

Stage 4: Perform a detailed sensitivity analysis on the optimal solution to determine ranges for each of the input parameters wherein the optimal solution remains valid.

In order to illustrate stages 1 and 2, consider the graphical LP solution demonstrated in Example 1.

□ **EXAMPLE 1**   *Graphical Solution to LP Problem*

A firm manufactures and sells two grades of leather wallets, standard and deluxe. Two resources are constrained for the coming week: production time (80 hours are available) and process and shipping time (1,000 wallets can be shipped during the coming week regardless of which of the two types of wallets make up the order). The firm has sufficient raw materials, working capital, and so on, to support any desired product mix. Further, the firm can sell any number of units of either type of wallet at the going market price. However, the firm wants to produce a minimum of 400 units of its deluxe wallet in order to satisfy the demands of its prime customers for this type of wallet. Management has been provided with the following financial and production data:

Model	Production Time (hr.)	Sale Price
Standard	0.05	$ 7.00
Deluxe	0.1	$10.00

Production time is estimated to cost the firm $40 per hour. Shipping and processing costs are estimated to be $3 per unit. Management desires to select the product mix that will maximize the total dollar contribution needed to cover fixed costs and generate profits. Formulate this problem using the LP model and solve it graphically.

Solution: To formulate this problem using the LP model, the following decision variables must be defined:

X_1 = number of units of the *standard* wallet to be produced

X_2 = number of units of the *deluxe* wallet to be produced

To specify the objective function, variable cost per unit must be determined for each product so that this amount can be subtracted from selling price per unit to determine the contribution margin per unit:

	Standard	Deluxe
Sale price per unit	$7.00	$10.00
Variable production cost per unit	− 2.00	− 4.00
Variable shipping cost per unit	− 3.00	− 3.00
Contribution margin per unit	$2.00	$ 3.00

The LP formulation is as follows:

$$\text{maximize total dollar contribution} = \$2X_1 + \$3X_2$$

subject to

production capacity:	$0.05X_1 + 0.10X_2 \leq 80$ hours
shipping capacity:	$1X_1 + 1X_2 \leq 1000$ units
minimum requirements:	$X_2 \geq 400$ units
nonnegativity condition:	$X_1, X_2 \geq 0$

The graphical solution is shown in Figure 19–2 and the method of arriving at the optimal solution is described below.

As shown in Figure 19–2, the area labeled *feasible region* consists of all possible X_1- and X_2-values that simultaneously satisfy all the constraint equations. Not all these possible combinations must be evaluated to determine the optimal solution because we have a helpful theorem in LP which states that the optimal solution can only occur at an *extreme point* to the feasible region (i.e., at the intersection of two or more constraints or a constraint and either axis) or possibly along a boundary between two extreme points. There are two methods of determining the optimal solution in the graphical approach:

1. The objective function could be graphed at successively higher values moving farther away from the origin; the optimal solution is reached when the objective function line is as far away from the origin but still touching the feasible region—the point or boundary where the objective function is tangent is the optimal solution.

FIGURE 19–2

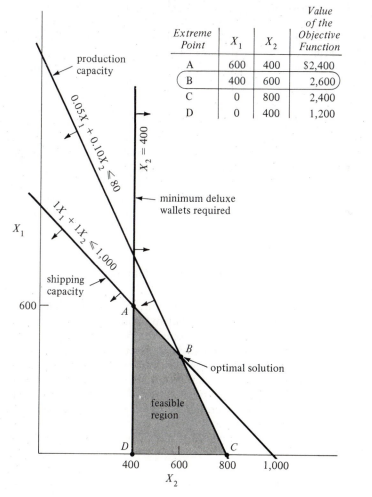

Extreme Point	X_1	X_2	Value of the Objective Function
A	600	400	$2,400
B	400	600	2,600
C	0	800	2,400
D	0	400	1,200

2. The coordinates for each extreme point are determined either graphically or algebraically and these values are substituted into the objective function, with the results being tabulated as shown in the insert to Figure 19–2; the extreme point with the largest value of the objective function is the optimal solution.

As shown in Figure 19–2, the objective function is maximized at point B (400 standard and 600 deluxe wallets), where it equals $2,600. Since the objective function decreases as we move toward either point A or C, the optimal solution is only at point B rather than along either boundary. If the value of the objective function at *either* point A or C had also been $2,600, then any combination of X_1 and X_2 along the relevant boundary AB or BC would represent an optimal solution to the problem.   □

Whenever there are more than two decision variables, or if there are numerous constraint equations, the graphical LP method is of limited value. Hence, it becomes necessary to resort to an algebraic technique to arrive at the optimal solution. One of the most widely used techniques of solving LP problems is the *simplex method,* developed by George B. Dantzig[1] in the 1940s.

Several new definitions are necessary in order to understand the simplex method. First, the approach requires that all the constraint equations be converted to strict equalities if they are less-than-or-equal-to ($\leq$) or greater-than-or-equal-to ($\geq$) constraints in the original formulation of the problem. This requires that a unique *slack variable* be added to each "less than or equal to constraint" to convert it into a strict equality. Similarly, a unique *surplus variable* must be subtracted from each "greater than or equal to constraint" to convert it into a strict equality.

As mentioned, packaged computer algorithms can be used to perform all the LP problem calculations. An LP package available to users of IBM computers is referred to as the MPSX software package. Similar LP packages are available to users of other computers. Such packaged programs facilitate a capitalization on the speed and accuracy of the computer to handle the tedious calculations required by the simplex method. The reader can obtain documentation detailing the use and interpretation of any such software package.

INTERPRETATION OF THE OPTIMAL LP SOLUTION

At this juncture, we assume readers are able to formulate and solve LP problems (the first two stages in the problem solution listed above are complete). The last two stages will be illustrated using computer printouts from the MPSX packaged LP program. Stage 3 entails a complete interpretation of the optimal solution, including the *shadow prices. Shadow prices show how much the decision-maker would be willing to pay to acquire 1 unit of each resource that is constrained in the problem.* Stage 4 is the sensitivity analysis of the optimal solution, which determines by how much each input parameter could change and leave the optimal solution unchanged in any significant way.

Interpretation of the optimal solution and the discussion of shadow prices is demonstrated in Example 2.

[1]George B. Dantzig, *Linear Programming and Extensions* (Princeton, N.J.: Princeton University Press, 1963).

□ **EXAMPLE 2** *Interpretation of the Optimal Solution: Shadow Prices*

Using the information provided in Example 1 and the optimal solution given below, completely interpret the optimal solution.

Solution: We are given the following optimal solution:

Basic Variables	X_1	X_2	S_1	S_2	R_1	RHS
X_1	1	0	-20	2	0	400
X_2	0	1	20	-1	0	600
R_1	0	0	20	-1	1	200
Objective function	0	0	20	1	0	$2,600

As can be seen, the basic variables are X_1, X_2, and R_1. These variables have a value of 1 in one of the rows and zeros everywhere else in the column for that variable. These variables are basic in the row where the 1 appears, which means that they take on the value shown on the right-hand side (RHS) in the table. Thus, $X_1 = 400$, $X_2 = 600$, and $R_1 = 200$. The value of the objective function is shown in the objective function row on the right-hand side ($2,600).

The two variables whose columns do not have a 1 in one row and zeros everywhere else in the column (i.e., S_1 and S_2) are nonbasic variables and hence take on values of zero in the optimal solution.

It is easy to demonstrate that these values satisfy the original constraints by substituting the values into the constraint equations.

production capacity
$$\begin{cases} 0.05X_1 & + 0.10X_2 & + S_1 = 80 \\ 0.05(400) & + 0.10(600) + 0 & = 80 \\ 20 & + 60 & + 0 = 80 \end{cases}$$

shipping capacity
$$\begin{cases} 1X_1 & + 1X_2 & + S_2 = 1,000 \\ 400 & + 600 & + 0 = 1,000 \end{cases}$$

minimum requirement for X_2
$$\begin{cases} X_2 - R_1 & = 400 \\ 600 - 200 & = 400 \end{cases}$$

The values shown in the objective function row under the slack and surplus variables have special significance. They are the *shadow prices* and *for slack variables, show the amount by which the value of the objective function would increase* (in a maximization problem) *if the original right-hand-side value associated with the slack variable were increased by 1 unit. For surplus variables, the shadow prices show the amount by which the objective function would increase if the original right-hand side associated with the surplus variable were decreased by 1 unit.* Thus, the shadow prices show the maximum amount that the decision-maker would be willing to pay to acquire 1 additional unit of a resource (for slack variables) or to have a requirement relaxed by 1 unit (for surplus variables). In this example, the shadow price for $S_1 = 20.00, for $S_2 = 1.00, while it is $0 for R_1. This means that the firm would be willing to pay up to a maximum of $20.00 (in addition to the current variable production cost of $40.00 per hour) to acquire 1 hour of added production time and $1.00 (in addition to the variable shipping cost of $3 per unit) to acquire 1 unit of added shipping capacity. To verify that these shadow prices are correct, consider a customer's order for 10 additional deluxe wallets. If the shadow prices are paid in addition to the current variables costs, the marginal revenue will just equal the marginal cost and the marginal profit will be zero. If the variable inputs can be obtained at a cost less than the shadow prices, profit will increase.

incremental contribution margin from the new order	=	incremental cost of filling new order if maximum shadow prices are paid to acquire additional resources
		production capacity:
		10 units $\times$ 0.10 hr./unit $\times$ $20/hr. = $20
10 units at $3 = $30		shipping capacity:
		10 units $\times$ $1/unit = $10
$30	=	$30

It should be stressed that shadow prices are incremental in nature—that is, they indicate the maximum additional amount that the firm would be willing to pay over and above the current prices paid for needed resources. To demonstrate this for this example, refer back to Example 1 to get the selling price per unit of the deluxe wallet and the variable cost per hour of production capacity as well as the variable cost per unit of shipping capacity. These values are respectively $10 per unit, $40 per hour, and $3 per unit. It is now shown that marginal revenue equals marginal cost for the new order of 10 wallets:

marginal revenue	=	marginal cost of filling new order if maximum shadow prices are paid (in addition to current cost) to acquire additional resources
		production capacity:
		10 units $\times$ 0.10 hr./unit $\times$ $60/hr. = $ 60.00
10 units at $10		shipping capacity:
		10 units $\times$ $4/unit = $ 40.00
$100.00	=	$100.00

Notice that the variable costs of $60 per hour and $4 per unit for production capacity and shipping capacity, respectively, are the sum of current costs (i.e., $40 per hour and $3 per unit, respectively) and the incremental shadow prices (i.e., $20 per hour and $1 per unit, respectively).

The shadow price for R_1 is zero because R_1 is a basic variable in the optimal solution which means that this constraint was not binding. That is, we exceeded the 400-unit minimum requirement for deluxe wallets by 200 units, so we would not be willing to pay anything to get this minimum requirement reduced. A similar interpretation would be given to a slack variable that was basic in the optimal solution. That is, since the constraint was not binding, not all of the amount of the resource originally available was utilized in the optimal solution. Thus, the firm would not be willing to pay anything to obtain additional units of the resource, because these units would just add to the already existing excess in the optimal solution.   □

The shadow prices discussed in Example 2 remain valid only within the specific range of additional units that the firm could acquire. In addition, questions often arise concerning the impact of changes in original values of input parameters on the optimal solution. Both of these areas may be addressed using the important tool referred to as *sensitivity analysis*.

SENSITIVITY ANALYSIS

Prudent financial management requires a determination of how sensitive the preferred alternative is to forecasting errors for the model's data inputs. The LP model is no exception. As mentioned earlier, sensitivity analysis in LP modeling ascertains how much of a change would be required in the input parameters in order for there to be a significant change in the optimal solution found by the model.

Sensitivity analysis can be performed either on the original right-hand-side values for each of the constraint equations or on the objective function coefficients for each decision variable. *In sensitivity analysis, on the right-hand side, Δ^+ and Δ^- are the amounts by which the original right-hand-side value could increase or decrease, respectively, without changing the basic variables in the optimal solution. In sensitivity analysis, on the objective function coefficients, Δ^+ and Δ^- are the amounts by which the objective function coefficient could increase or decrease, respectively, without changing the optimal solution.* Notice the difference in the statements made concerning the two types of sensitivity analysis. With respect to the right-hand-side values, we talked about leaving the same basic variables in the optimal solution but that the optimal values for each basic variable would change with any change of a right-hand-side value of a binding constraint. For objective function coefficients, we talked about the range within which the *optimal solution* (both the basic variables and their specific values) would remain unchanged. For all these input parameters, a range can be determined as specified in Equations (1) and (2):

$$\text{upper limit} = \text{original value plus } \Delta^+ \qquad (1)$$

$$\text{lower limit} = \text{original value less } \Delta^- \qquad (2)$$

We first undertake a sensitivity analysis of the right-hand-side values.

For slack variables that are basic variables in the optimal solution:

$$\Delta^+_{S_j} = \infty \qquad (3)$$

and

$$\Delta^-_{S_j} = \text{amount of this resource still available in the optimal solution} \qquad (4)$$

These two values are consistent with the discussion presented above. If there is some quantity of a resource still available in the optimal solution (i.e., the definition of slack variable being basic in the optimal solution), then if we had more of it originally, we would merely have more of it left over in the optimal solution. This would be true for any increase in the original amount available; hence, the value of Δ^+ is infinite. On the other hand, we could only decrease the original amount available by the amount left over in the optimal solution, since to decrease it by an amount greater than this would lead to a different optimal solution.

For surplus variables that are basic variables in the optimal solution:

$$\Delta^+_{R_j} = \text{value of this basic variable in the optimal solution} \qquad (5)$$

$$\Delta^-_{R_j} = \infty \qquad (6)$$

These values should be clear based on the discussion presented above relating to the complements of surplus variables (i.e., slack variables).

The same values for nonbasic variables in the optimal solution require computations based on the tableau from the optimal solution. *Thus, for slack or surplus variables that are nonbasic in the optimal solution:*

$$\Delta^+_{R_j} \quad \text{or} \quad \Delta^+_{S_j} = \min \left| \frac{b_i}{a_{ij} < 0} \right| \qquad (7)$$

$$\Delta^-_{R_j} \quad \text{or} \quad \Delta^-_{S_j} = \min \left\{ \frac{b_i}{a_{ij} > 0} \right\} \qquad (8)$$

where b_i = right-hand-side value in row i of the optimal solution

a_{ij} = coefficient in column j (i.e., the column of slack or surplus variable j) and row i

S_j = slack variable in column j which is associated with the original resource that we are interested in changing.

R_j = surplus variable in column j which is associated with the original resource that we are interested in changing

To perform sensitivity analysis on, for example, slack variable S_1, which is nonbasic in the optimal solution, we look up and down in column S_1 for values that are negative. For each that is found, divide its corresponding right-hand-side value by the a_{ij} value and take the absolute value. Among the resulting values, select the smallest: This value is Δ^+. Repeat the process looking for positive values in the column S_1 in order to compute Δ^-.

Finally, we look at sensitivity analysis on the objective function coefficients for a maximization problem. Of course, we perform this analysis on decision variables in the problem which again can either be basic or nonbasic in the optimal solution.

For decision variables that are nonbasic in the optimal solution:

$$\Delta^+_{X_k} = \text{value of the shadow price for this decision variable} \atop \text{in the optimal solution} \qquad (9)$$

$$\Delta^-_{X_k} = \infty \qquad (10)$$

If a decision variable is nonbasic in the optimal solution, the values found using Equations (9) and (10) should indicate that the decision variable was not attractive enough to enter the solution. Hence, it will remain unattractive if its objective function coefficient is decreased by any amount (i.e., $\Delta^- = \infty$). Furthermore, as pointed out above, the shadow price in the optimal solution shows the amount by which the objective function would decrease if a nonbasic variable were forced into solution; thus, the objective function coefficient would have to increase by more than its shadow price in order to make the nonbasic variable in question attractive (i.e., $\Delta^+ =$ shadow price in the optimal solution).

For decision variables that are basic in the optimal solution:

$$\Delta^{+}_{X_k} = \min \left| \frac{C_j}{a_{ij} < 0} \right| \tag{11}$$

$$\Delta^{-}_{X_k} = \min \left\{ \frac{C_j}{a_{ij} > 0} \right\} \tag{12}$$

where C_j = value in the objective row of the optimal tableau in column j
a_{ij} = coefficient in row i (i.e., the row in the optimal tableau where X_k is basic) and column j
X_k = decision variable k of interest which is basic in row i of the optimal tableau

To perform sensitivity analysis on, for example, decision variable X_2, which is basic in row 4 of the optimal tableau, we would look across row 4 for negative a_{ij} values. For each one that is found, divide the C_j value (i.e., the value in the objective function row of the tableau) for that column by the a_{ij} value and take the absolute value. Among the resulting values, select the smallest: this is $\Delta^{+}_{X_2}$. The process would then be repeated looking for positive a_{ij} values in row 4 in order to compute $\Delta^{-}_{X_2}$.

All the computations above were for *maximization problems*. In order to compute the Δ^{+} and Δ^{-} values for a *minimization problem*, the identities of the two values are interchanged; that is, Equations (9) and (11) became the appropriate formulas for Δ^{-} and Equations (10) and (12) are used to compute Δ^{+}.

Example 3 illustrates the computation of Δ^{+} and Δ^{-} values.

□ **EXAMPLE 3**   *Sensitivity Analysis*

Perform a complete sensitivity analysis on the following optimal solution:

Basic Variables	X_1	X_2	S_1	S_2	R_1	RHS
X_1	1	0	−20	2	0	400
X_2	0	1	20	−1	0	600
R_1	0	0	20	−1	1	200
Objective function	0	0	20	1	0	$2,600

Solution: Sensitivity analysis will first be performed on the original right-hand-side values. Recall that in the original problem we had the following resources available and minimum requirements:

production capacity ≤ 80 hours

shipping and processing capacity ≤ 1,000 units

minimum requirement for deluxe wallets ≥ 400 units

Slack variables S_1 and S_2 correspond to the production and shipping capacity constraints, respectively; surplus variable R_1 corresponds to the minimum requirement for deluxe wallets. Thus, these columns in the tableau are relevant for sensitivity analysis on the original right-hand-side values for rows 1, 2, and 3, respectively.

Since R_1 is a basic variable in the optimal solution, we examine it first. R_1 is a surplus variable that is basic in the optimal solution, so its Δ^+ and Δ^- values are found using Equations (5) and (6).

$$\Delta_{R_1}^+ = 200, \text{ the value of } R_1 \text{ in the optimal solution}$$

$$\Delta_{R_2}^- = \infty$$

The range of possible values that the minimum requirement for deluxe wallets could take on using Equations (1) and (2) is as follows:

$$\text{range} \begin{cases} \text{upper limit} = \text{original amount plus } \Delta^+ = 400 + 200 = 600 \\ \text{lower limit} = \text{original amount minus } \Delta^- = 400 - \infty = -\infty \end{cases}$$

Hence, if our minimum requirement were any value less than 600 units of the deluxe wallet, we would have the same optimal basis that we presently have.

The two capacity constraints have slack variables that are nonbasic. Therefore, performance of a sensitivity analysis using Equations (7) and (8) yields the following results:

$$\Delta_{S_1}^+ = \min \left| \frac{400}{-20} \right| = 20 \text{ hours}$$

$$\Delta_{S_1}^- = \min \left\{ \frac{600}{20}, \frac{200}{20} \right\} = \min(30, 10) = 10 \text{ hours}$$

Thus, if the actual production capacity falls anywhere in the range of 70 hours $(80 - 10$ hours) to 100 hours $(80 + 20$ hours), we have the same optimal basis as currently (X_1, X_2, R_1), and their new optimal values can be determined by performing calculations on the optimal tableau.

In addition, the shadow price of $20 per hour of production capacity remains valid as long as the firm does not attempt to purchase more than 20 additional hours $(\Delta_{S_1}^+)$ of production capacity or to sell more than 10 hours $(\Delta_{S_1}^-)$ at that price. Outside this range there is a new shadow price, indicating the value of each production hour to the firm. Thus, there is a close and important relationship between shadow prices and the values of Δ^+ and Δ^- determined in sensitivity analysis.

For S_2, the sensitivity analysis yields the following results:

$$\Delta_{S_2}^+ = \min \left| \frac{600}{-1}, \frac{200}{-1} \right| = 200 \text{ units}$$

$$\Delta_{S_2}^- = \min \left\{ \frac{400}{2} \right\} = 200 \text{ units}$$

Thus, if the actual shipping capacity falls anywhere in the range 800 units $(1,000 - 200)$ to 1,200 units $(1,000 + 200)$, we again have the same optimal basis and do not have to re-solve the problem in order to determine the optimal solution. The same comments as above hold true for the shadow price of $1 for each unit of shipping capacity remaining valid only within the range 800 to 1,200 units of shipping capacity.

To perform sensitivity analysis on the original objective function coefficients for the two decision variables, which are both basic in the optimal solution, we use Equations (11) and (12):

$$\Delta_{X_1}^+ = \min \left| \frac{20}{-20} \right| = \$1.00$$

$$\Delta_{X_1}^- = \min \left\{ \frac{1}{2} \right\} = \$.50$$

Thus, if the profit coefficient for standard wallets falls anywhere between $3.00 ($2.00 + $1.00) and $1.50 ($2.00 − $.50), we have the same optimal solution. Similarly, for deluxe wallets:

$$\Delta^+_{X_2} = \min \left| \frac{1}{-1} \right| = \$1.00$$

$$\Delta^-_{X_2} = \min \left\{ \frac{20}{20} \right\} = \$1.00$$

Thus, if the profit coefficient for deluxe wallets falls anywhere between $4.00 ($3.00 + $1.00) and $2.00 ($3.00 − $1.00), we have the same optimal solution as before.   □

Up to this point we have been saying that within the ranges for right-hand-side values which are determined by means of sensitivity analysis, the optimal basis would remain unchanged. Further, it was mentioned that the new optimal values for each of the basic variables could be determined by looking at the optimal tableau rather than having to re-solve the complete problem. We now explore how this is done.

Whenever a specific right-hand-side value in the original problem is changed to take on some other value within its sensitivity-range limits, the column of its slack variable becomes the relevant column to use in the optimal tableau in order to determine the new optimal value for each basic variable. The new optimal values are computed using Equation (13):

$$\begin{pmatrix} \text{new optimal value} \\ \text{of basic variable } i \end{pmatrix} = \begin{pmatrix} \text{current optimal} \\ \text{value of basic} \\ \text{variable } i \end{pmatrix} + (a_{ij}) \begin{pmatrix} \text{change in original} \\ \text{right-hand-side value} \end{pmatrix} \quad (13)$$

where a_{ij} is the value in the current optimal tableau in row i and in column j which is the column of the slack or surplus variable associated with the right-hand-side value that is being changed. Note that the "change in original right-hand-side value" shown in Equation (13) has *both* a magnitude (numerical value) and a direction (sign) that must be incorporated into the calculations.

Example 4 illustrates the use of Equation (13).

□ **EXAMPLE 4**   *Optimal Solution Using Sensitivity Range Limits*

Find the new optimal solution in our example problem if the number of *production hours* is actually: (a) 105 hours; (b) 72 hours.

Solution: (a) If the actual number of production hours is 105 hours, the problem has to be re-solved to obtain the new optimal solution because the value 105 hours falls outside the range 70 to 100 hours determined by sensitivity analysis in Example 3.

It should be noted that if we attempt to use Equation (13) to find the value of X_1 for the change up to 105 hours, the result is

$$X_1 = 400 \text{ units} + (-20)(+25 \text{ hr}) = -100 \text{ units}$$

which is of course *infeasible* since the nonnegativity constraint would be violated.

(b) Since 72 hours does fall within the range 70 to 100 hours, we can proceed with calculations as follows:

$$\begin{pmatrix} \text{new optimal} \\ \text{value of basic variable} \end{pmatrix} = \begin{pmatrix} \text{current} \\ \text{optimal value} \end{pmatrix} + \begin{pmatrix} a_{ij} \\ \text{value} \end{pmatrix} \begin{pmatrix} \text{change in} \\ \text{production capacity} \end{pmatrix}$$

$$X_1 = 400 \text{ units} + (-20)(-8 \text{ hr}) = 560 \text{ units}$$

$$X_2 = 600 \text{ units} + (+20)(-8 \text{ hr}) = 440 \text{ units}$$

$$R_1 = 200 \text{ units} + (+20)(-8 \text{ hr}) = 40 \text{ units}$$

$$\text{new profit} = \text{original profit} + (\text{shadow price}) \begin{pmatrix} \text{change in} \\ \text{production capacity} \end{pmatrix}$$

$$= \$2{,}600 + (+\$20)(-8 \text{ hr})$$

$$= \$2{,}440$$

The new profit can also be computed by multiplying the number of units of each product by its respective contribution margin and totaling. □

DUALITY THEORY

Another important area related to linear programming problem formulation and solution is referred to as *duality theory*. Corresponding to every maximization LP problem, usually called the *primal problem*, there is a closely related minimization problem called the *dual problem*. From our point of view, the major attractiveness of duality theory lies in the interesting economic interpretation of the dual problem and the insight that the dual problem provides for extensions of LP, mainly to integer linear programming.

The following properties of duality are the most important:

1. The primal problem is generally a maximization problem, which has less-than-or-equal-to constraint equations.

2. The dual problem is generally a minimization problem, which has greater-than-or-equal-to constraint equations.

3. The dual of the dual is the primal.

4. The decision variables in the dual correspond to constraint equations in the primal, and vice versa. Thus, if there are n decision variables and m constraint equations in the primal problem, there will be m decision variables and n constraint equations in the dual.

5. An optimal solution to the dual exists only when the primal has an optimal solution, and vice versa. Further, the optimal value of the objective function must be the same for the primal and the dual.

6. By examining the optimal tableau of the primal problem we can also determine the optimal values for the dual variables, since they are the shadow prices associated with each of the slack and surplus variables.

Formulation of the dual problem for the example problem that has been used throughout the chapter is demonstrated in Example 5.

□ **EXAMPLE 5** *Formulation of the Dual*

Formulate the dual for the problem in Example 1.

Solution: Recall the primal problem formulated in Example 1:

$$\text{Maximize } \$2X_1 + \$3X_2$$

subject to the following constraints:

$$0.05X_1 + 0.10X_2 \leq 80 \text{ hours production capacity}$$
$$1X_1 + 1X_2 \leq 1000 \text{ units shipping capacity}$$
$$1X_2 \geq 400 \text{ units minimum requirements for deluxe wallets}$$
$$X_1, X_2 \geq 0$$

where X_1 = the number of standard wallets to be produced
X_2 = the number of deluxe wallets to be produced
The dual problem is as follows:

$$\min(80u_1 + 1000u_2 - 400u_3)$$

subject to the following constraints:

$$0.05u_1 + 1u_2 + 0u_3 \geq \$2 \text{ profit for } X_1$$
$$0.10u_1 + 1u_2 - 1u_3 \geq \$3 \text{ profit for } X_2$$
$$u_1, u_2, u_3 \geq 0$$

where u_1 = the imputed price that the firm would be willing to pay per hour of production capacity
u_2 = the imputed price that the firm would be willing to pay per unit of shipping capacity
u_3 = the imputed price that the firm would be willing to pay per unit of minimum requirement for the deluxe wallet   □

The primal and dual forms in Example 5 are closely related to each other as originally stated. The dual problem seeks to find the *smallest imputed prices* (u_1, u_2, and u_3) *that should be associated with the firm's resources available or requirements on activities* (80 hours of production capacity, 1000 units of shipping capacity, and a minimum requirement to produce 400 units of the deluxe wallet) *subject to the requirement that these prices completely account for the profit generated per unit of each product.*

It should also be pointed out that the *decision variables* in the primal problem refer to the number of units of each product that should be produced while the slack variables refer to the quantity of excess resources available. In the dual problem, the decision variables are the imputed prices (or accounting values) associated with each of the resources that will be used to produce the various products, and the surplus variables show the excess of the imputed costs of a unit of output of a given product over its profit per unit. These interpretations of the description, based on the characteristics of duality, are expanded below:

1. The optimal production, which is found in the primal problem, determines the total profits generated and the quantity of excess resources still available.

2. The optimal price per unit for each resource is found in the dual, which generates the same total dollar value as was found in the primal.

3. The optimal price (found in the dual) for any resource of which there is an excess amount still available given the optimal production (found in the primal) will be zero.

4. Given the optimal prices found in the dual, any product whose profit does not equal the opportunity cost of the resources required to produce one unit will not be produced in the optimal product mix found in the primal problem.

In the next chapter, we demonstrate that the dual problem has a very important interpretation in the capital budgeting problem setting.

The optimal solution to the dual is closely related to the optimal solution of the primal problem. This is shown in Example 6.

□ **EXAMPLE 6** *Solution of the Dual*

Find the optimal solution to the dual problem formulated in Example 5 and compare it with the optimal primal solution.

Solution: The optimal primal solution, as developed in Example 2, is reproduced below:

Basic Variable	X_1	X_2	S_1	S_2	R_1	RHS
X_1	1	0	-20	2	0	400
X_2	0	1	20	-1	0	600
R_1	0	0	20	-1	1	200
Objective function	0	0	20	1	0	2600

The optimal solution to the dual is:

Basic Variables	u_1	u_2	u_3	R_2	R_3	RHS
u_2	0	1	1.	$-2.$	1.	1.
u_1	1	0	$-20.$	20.	$-20.$	20.
Objective function	0	0	200	400	600	2600

The optimal primal solution indicates that 400 standard and 600 deluxe wallets should be produced. This is 200 units over the minimum requirement of 400 deluxe wallets and generates $2,600 of profit. All of the production capacity originally available (80 hours), as well as the shipping capacity (1000 units) originally available, has been consumed by the optimal production plan. The shadow prices for these two resources show that the firm would be willing to pay up to a maximum of $20 to acquire one additional hour of production capacity and up to $1.00 to purchase one additional unit of shipping capacity.

The optimal dual solution shows that the optimal prices (u_1, u_2, and u_3) for the three resources or activities (production capacity, shipping capacity, and minimum production requirement of deluxe wallets) are $20, $1, and 0, respectively. Of course, these optimal values are exactly the shadow prices associated with the corresponding slack and surplus variables in the primal due to the interrelationships between the primal and dual formulations discussed earlier. The optimal value of the objective function for the dual is also $2600. The two surplus variables R_2 and R_3 are *nonbasic* in the optimal solution. This means that, given the optimal values to be paid for the resources needed (u_1, u_2, and u_3)

to produce products X_1 and X_2, the dollar profit generated by these two products is exactly accounted for.

The shadow prices in the optimal dual solution indicate the following:

1. The objective function would increase by $200 if u_3 were forced into solution at a value of 1.

2. The objective function would increase by $400 ($R_2$) if the right-hand-side value for constraint 1 were increased by 1 unit (i.e., if the dollar profit for product X_1 were increased from $2 to $3).

3. The objective function would increase by $600 ($R_3$) if the right-hand-side value for constraint 2 were increased by 1 unit (i.e., if the dollar profit for product X_2 were increased from $3 to $4). Sensitivity analysis would be performed on the dual in exactly the same way as it was done on the primal. □

SUMMARY

This chapter surveys the rather broad field of mathematical programming with an eye toward the use of this powerful class of management science models in the capital budgeting area. Model building is discussed in general, as well as in the specific area of mathematical programming. Various mathematical programming models are introduced to handle problems under the assumption that either conditions of certainty or risk were present in the decision setting.

Linear programming (LP) is treated in depth because of the importance of this technique, its widespread use, and the reliance of more advanced techniques on the LP formulation and solution. Problem formulation, graphical and computerized solution approaches, and sensitivity analysis are all discussed and illustrated with examples. Finally, the important area of duality is examined to show the interesting interrelationships and important economic interpretations of the primal-dual LP problems.

The material in this chapter forms a basis for the following two chapters. The strengths of mathematical programming techniques are examined as tools to assist the financial manager in evaluating capital investment alternatives and to integrate investment decisions with financing and dividend decisions.

QUESTIONS/PROBLEMS

1. The Datamax Company has recently become enthralled with linear programming and wants to utilize it in determining the optimal product mix for its two product lines. The relevant information about its products is as follows:

	Product X	*Product Y*
Selling price	$16.00	$23.00
Standard material cost	1.50	2.25
Standard labor cost	6.00	8.00
Standard machine time cost	4.50	5.25
Standard shipping cost	1.00	1.00
Maximum demand	None	500 units
Minimum requirements	100 units	None

In addition, Datamax has several resource constraints that cannot be violated:

raw-material constraint	1,000 units at $1.50 standard cost
labor-hours constraint	1,200 hours at $4.00 standard cost
machine-hours constraint	2,800 hours at $1.50 standard cost
shipping capacity constraint	650 units at $1.00 standard cost

Formulate this linear-programming problem and solve it using the graphical technique.

2. Find the optimal solution to Problem 1 using the simplex method or a packaged LP algorithm.

3. Perform a sensitivity analysis on the right-hand-side values for the solution arrived at in Problem 2.

4. Perform a sensitivity analysis on the objective function coefficients for the solution arrived at in Problem 2.

5. Formulate the dual LP problem for Problem 1. Solve it using the simplex method or a packaged LP algorithm.

6. A sophisticated farmer uses LP to determine the amount of various crops to plant. She has 1,000 acres of land on which she can grow corn, wheat, or soybeans. Each acre of corn costs $100 for preparation, requires 7 worker-days of labor, and yields a profit of $30. Each acre of wheat costs $120 for preparation, requires 10 worker-days of labor, and yields $40 in profit. Finally, soybeans cost $70 to prepare the land, require 8 worker-days, and yield a $20 profit. If the farmer has $100,000 available for preparation expenses, has 8,000 worker-days of labor available, and wants to maximize profit, her LP formulation would be:

$$\text{maximize } 30X_1 + 40X_2 + 20X_3$$

subject to

$$100X_1 + 120X_2 + 70X_3 + S_1 = 100,000$$
$$7X_1 + 10X_2 + 8X_3 + S_2 = 8,000$$
$$X_1 + X_2 + X_3 + S_3 = 1,000$$

$$X_i, S_i \geq 0 \qquad i = 1, 2, 3$$

Solve this problem using the simplex method or a packaged LP algorithm.

7. The optimal LP solution to Problem 6 is as follows:

	X_1	X_2	X_3	S_1	S_2	S_3	RHS
	0	1	1.9375	−0.04375	0.625	0	625
	1	0	−1.625	0.0625	−0.75	0	250
	0	0	0.6875	−0.01875	0.125	1	125
Z	0	0	8.75	0.1250	2.50	0	32,500

Answer the following questions about the optimal solution.

(a) What is the optimal amount of each of the three crops that should be planted?

(b) What is the dollar profit generated by the optimal planting? Show a proof that this figure is correct.

(c) Are there any excess resources given the optimal planting? Demonstrate that this is correct by plugging the optimal values for X_1, X_2, and X_3 into the constraint equations.

(d) How much would the farmer be willing to pay for an additional dollar of capital? An additional worker-day of labor? An additional acre of land?

(e) Demonstrate that the answers given for part (d) are correct assuming that the farmer wanted to plant 10 more acres of wheat.

(f) What is the meaning of the value in row Z and column X_3?

(g) Demonstrate that the value mentioned in part (f) is correct by computing the cost of planting an acre of X_3 using the shadow prices shown in the optimal tableau.

8. For the optimal solution given in Problem 7, perform a sensitivity analysis on the right-hand-side values.

9. For the optimal solution given in Problem 7, perform a sensitivity analysis on the objective function coefficients.

10. For the optimal solution given in Problem 7, find the new optimal solution if the original labor availability was 8,100 worker-days (i.e., what would be the new values for each of the basic variables if there were originally 8,100 worker-days of labor available?).

11. For the optimal solution shown in Problem 7, find the new optimal solution if the original amount of capital available was $104,000.

Multiperiod Analysis
Under Conditions of Certainty:
Linear Programming

Throughout the first seven chapters of the book, several assumptions are made that are at variance from the practical problem setting faced by decision-makers relative to capital investment decisions. Namely, it is assumed that capital investment projects are independent of each other and that the firm can obtain as much capital as is desired at the market rate of interest. These two assumptions, plus the assumption that conditions of certainty existed (the last of which was relaxed in Chapter 13), enable the decision-maker to consider each project individually to determine whether it should be accepted or rejected. However, when the former two assumptions are relaxed, a number of complexities arise in the decision setting. This chapter and the following two chapters explore the important tools of mathematical programming that are available to financial managers as they endeavor to handle these new complexities.

HISTORICAL PERSPECTIVE

In 1955, Lorie and Savage discussed the shortcomings of various methods of analysis, especially the internal-rate-of-return method, when capital is rationed.[1] They presented examples demonstrating:

1. Problems that develop because multiple projects under consideration are not independent.

2. Problems that develop when capital is rationed in more than a single time period.

---

[1]J. H. Lorie and L. J. Savage, "Three Problems in Rationing Capital," *The Journal of Business*, (October 1955), pp. 229–239.

3. Problems that develop when analyzing projects that have both cash inflows and outflows dispersed over their lives.

They overcame the first and third problems by utilizing the net present value approach rather than the internal rate of return. They *attempted* to overcome the second problem. However, the breakdown of their approach opened the way for the subsequent research that applied mathematical programming to the capital rationing problem area.

Charnes, Cooper, and Miller[2] and Weingartner[3] were the pioneers who concentrated on Lorie and Savage's second problem of capital rationing and its resolution. These authors demonstrated that Lorie and Savage's generalized multipliers do not exist for all types of capital rationing problems, that an optimal solution is not guaranteed using the multipliers, and that the transformed problem using the approach may not be equivalent to the original problem. Charnes, Cooper, and Miller formulated a LP (linear programming) model to assist the firm in allocating funds among competing uses considering both operating decisions and financial planning. Weingartner's outstanding work formulates the capital rationing problem first as an LP then as an IP (integer programming) model. His work also provided valuable insights concerning the shadow prices and dual variables for the integer programming formulation.

Since these pioneering works, there have been many advances in the area of mathematical programming applied to the capital budgeting problem. The major extensions have either sought to integrate other financial decision areas with the capital budgeting decision, relaxed the single goal assumption of LP and IP, or have attempted to handle the capital rationing problem under conditions of risk. The focus of Chapters 20 and 21 will be to survey the important areas of linear, integer, and goal programming as they apply to the capital rationing problem. Example problems will be formulated in the necessary framework and the optimal solutions interpreted for the reader.

MOTIVATION FOR THE USE OF MATHEMATICAL PROGRAMMING

As we have pointed out above, it can be demonstrated that (under the assumptions enumerated in Chapter 4) the selection of that set of projects which maximizes the net present value will simultaneously maximize shareholders' wealth or shareholders' utility. However, as argued in Chapter 7, when capital is rationed in one or more periods, no longer should we merely rank projects according to their net present values (or profitability indexes) and just continue to select them in order until the budget(s) are exhausted. This is true due to disparities in the original costs of projects under consideration, which may find that several projects with smaller original costs have a greater combined net present value than one larger project. Hence, what must be done is to find the

[2]A. Charnes, W. W. Cooper, and M. H. Miller, "An Application of Linear Programming to Financial Budgeting and the Cost of Funds," *The Journal of Business* (January 1959), pp. 20–46.
[3]H. Martin Weingartner, *Mathematical Programming and the Analysis of Capital Budgeting Problems* (Englewood Cliffs, N.J.: Prentice-Hall, Inc., 1963).

combination of *projects that will maximize net present value while not violating any relevant constraint.* As the number of projects and/or the number of years in the planning horizon increase, the number of feasible combinations of projects grows exponentially. Thus, it becomes advantageous to call upon a set of models such as mathematical programming, which does not require the explicit evaluation of each feasible combination and which can be solved within modest computer time and memory requirements (even for rather large problems). Mathematical programming models are powerful in that they are optimization techniques (i.e., they find the best possible solution to a given problem representation) and they can be used to accurately describe virtually any real-world problem setting. Numerous computerized solution algorithms are available through every computer manufacturer; thus, even small firms can afford to call upon mathematical programming techniques to facilitate the decision-making process in the capital budgeting area as well as other problem areas.

LINEAR PROGRAMMING REPRESENTATION

Based on the introduction to linear programming provided by Chapter 19, we can proceed directly to the formulation of the capital rationing problem using the LP model:

$$\text{Maximize NPV} = \sum_{j=1}^{N} b_j X_j \tag{1}$$

subject to

$$\sum_{j=1}^{N} C_{jt} X_j \le K_t \qquad t = 1, 2, \ldots, T \tag{2}$$

$$0 \le X_j \le 1 \tag{3}$$

where X_j = percent of project j that is accepted

b_j = net present value of project j over its useful life

C_{jt} = cash outflow required by project j in year t

K_t = budget availability in year t

N = the number of projects under evaluation

The above formulation merely states that the firm wants to select the set of projects that maximizes the net present value without violating any of the budget constraints.

In addition, the following aspects of the LP formulation for the capital rationing problem should be noted after referring back to the general assumptions of LP models listed in Table 19–2:

1. The X_j decision variables are assumed to be continuous—that is, partial projects are allowed in the LP formulation.

2. The usual nonnegativity constraint of LP is modified as shown in Equation (3) to also show an upper limit for each project—that is, it is required that each project have a maximum value of 1.00 or that it is accepted 100% (there is only one project of each type available). This upper limit does not create problems under conditions where multiple projects of the same type can be accepted. In such cases, we just define a new decision variable for each time that the project could be accepted.

3. It is assumed that all the input parameters—b_j, C_{jt}, K_t—are known with certainty.

4. The b_j parameter shows the net present value of project j over its useful life, where all cash flows are discounted at the cost of capital, which is known with certainty.

5. The values of C_{jt} in the budget constraints are not discounted back to year 0 since the budget funds available (K_t) are expressed in year t's dollars.

To illustrate the general approach, consider the following classic example.

□ **EXAMPLE 1**   *Lorie-Savage Nine-Project Problem*

The following nine-project, two-period problem was originally considered by Lorie and Savage. Later, it was used by Weingartner to illustrate the use of LP to represent the capital rationing problem:

Project	NPV_j	C_{1j} = Cash Outflow in Period 1	C_{2j} = Cash Outflow in Period 2
1	$14	$12	$ 3
2	17	54	7
3	17	6	6
4	15	6	2
5	40	30	35
6	12	6	6
7	14	48	4
8	10	36	3
9	12	18	3

Budget available: $\Sigma C_{1j} X_j \le \$50$; $\Sigma C_{2j} X_j \le \$20$

Formulate this problem as an LP and solve it using a packaged solution algorithm.

Solution: The LP formulation is as follows:

$$\text{Maximize NPV} = 14 X_1 + 17 X_2 + 17 X_3 + 15 X_4 + 40 X_5$$
$$+ 12 X_6 + 14 X_7 + 10 X_8 + 12 X_9$$

subject to

$$12 X_1 + 54 X_2 + 6 X_3 + 6 X_4 + 30 X_5 + 6 X_6 + 48 X_7$$
$$+ 36 X_8 + 18 X_9 + S_1 = 50 \quad \text{budget constraint year 1}$$
$$3 X_1 + 7 X_2 + 6 X_3 + 2 X_4 + 35 X_5 + 6 X_6 + 4 X_7$$
$$+ 3 X_8 + 3 X_9 + S_2 = 20 \quad \text{budget constraint year 2}$$

$$\left.\begin{array}{lll} X_1 + S_3 = 1 & X_4 + S_6 = 1 & X_7 + S_9 = 1 \\ X_2 + S_4 = 1 & X_5 + S_7 = 1 & X_8 + S_{10} = 1 \\ X_3 + S_5 = 1 & X_6 + S_8 = 1 & X_9 + S_{11} = 1 \end{array}\right\} \begin{array}{l}\text{upper limits on} \\ \text{project acceptance}\end{array}$$

$$X_j, S_i \ge 0 \quad i = 1, 2, \dots, 11; \quad j = 1, 2, \dots, 9 \quad \text{nonnegativity constraint}$$

The following aspects should be pointed out concerning this formulation.

The general approach taken in this example is similar to that shown in Equations (1)–(3). However, slack variables have been added to each less-than constraint so that a fuller interpretation can be given to the optimal solution. Slack variables S_1 and S_2 represent, respectively, the number of budget dollars in years 1 and 2 that remain unallocated to any of the nine projects under evaluation. Slack variables S_3 through S_{11} represent the percent of projects 1 through 9, respectively, that are not accepted by the firm—the sum of X_j and its corresponding slack variable S_{j+2} must equal 1.00 or 100% since the entire project must be either accepted or not accepted. The optimal LP solution, obtained from IBM's MPSX package, is shown in Table 20–1.

Interpreting the optimal solution, we see that the basic variables, that is, the variables that are equal to a positive value in the optimal solution, are X_1, X_3, X_4, X_6, X_7, X_9, S_4, S_7, S_8, S_9, S_{10}, which are equal to their corresponding values on the right-hand side of the optimal tableau (i.e., $X_1 = 1.0$, $X_3 = 1.0$, $X_4 = 1.0$, $X_6 = 0.969697$, and so on). Any of the variables in the problem that are not listed as basic variables are, in fact, nonbasic variables in the optimal solution, which means that they are equal to zero. Thus, $X_2 = X_5 = X_8 = 0$, which shows that these three projects should be completely rejected; in addition, $S_1 = S_2 = 0$, shows that the entire budget allotment of \$50 in year 1 and \$20 in year 2 has been spent on the six projects that have been designated for acceptance; further, $S_3 = S_5 = S_6 = S_{11} = 0$, since the projects corresponding to these slack variables (i.e., X_1, X_3, X_4, X_9) have been 100% accepted. To summarize, projects 1, 3, 4, and 9 have been fully accepted; 97% of project 6 is accepted; and only 4.5% of project 7 is accepted. These projects require the use of the entire budget in both years and generate the maximum objective function value of \$70.273, which is the net present value of the accepted projects. □

Examples shown below interpret the shadow prices in row Z of the optimal tableau, as well as perform sensitivity analysis on the optimal solution.

Of course, it could be asked: Do the partial projects in our LP solution to Example 1 really make sense? The answer is maybe. The LP solution above, which was arrived at using only tenths of a second of computer time, does provide considerable insight about the nine projects under evaluation. The fully accepted projects (1, 3, 4, and 9) are clearly very attractive to the firm. On the other hand, the partially accepted projects (6 and 7) were the last two to be brought into the firm's portfolio. These partial projects would be feasible only if the firm could find a partner or the other party interested in entering a joint venture to undertake the project in question. Recall that the use of LP to handle the capital rationing problem means that partial projects cannot be excluded from the optimal solution.

The LP formulation of the capital rationing problem above is significantly easier to solve than the integer programming formulation (discussed in Chapter 21), wherein no partial projects are allowed. Integer programming problems can take up to 100 times longer to solve on the computer than the equivalent LP formulation. Furthermore, Weingartner points out that the *number of partial projects accepted in an LP cannot exceed the number of years in which there is a budget constraint.*[4] Thus, if a firm were evaluating 100 projects over a 3-year planning horizon using LP, it is assured that there will be no more than three projects that are accepted only partially. This fact, plus the much more rapid solution time, makes it definitely advantageous to utilize the LP formulation.

[4]Weingartner, *Mathematical Programming*, Appendix A to Chapter 3.

TABLE 20–1 Optimal Tableau for LP Formulation of Lorie-Savage Nine-Project Problem

Basic Variables	X_1	X_2	X_3	X_4	X_5	X_6	X_7	X_8	X_9	S_1	S_2	S_3	S_4	S_5	S_6	S_7	S_8	S_9	S_{10}	S_{11}	RHS
X_1	1.0											1.0									1.00
X_3			1.0											1.0							1.00
X_4				1.0											1.0						1.00
X_6		0.455			5.91	1.0				−0.015	0.1818	−0.364		−1.0	−0.273					−0.273	0.969697
X_7		1.068			−0.114		1.0			0.023	−0.023	−0.205			−0.091					−0.341	0.045455
X_9								0.75	1.0											1.0	1.00
S_4		1.0											1.0								1.00
S_7					1.0											1.0					1.00
S_8		−0.455			−5.91			−0.75		0.015	−0.1818	0.364		1.0	0.273		1.0			0.273	0.030303
S_9		−1.068			0.114					−0.023	0.023	0.205			0.091			1.0		0.341	0.954545
S_{10}								1.0											1.0		1.00
Z		3.41			29.32			0.50		0.1364	1.864	6.77		5.0	10.45					3.95	70.273

OTHER CONSTRAINED RESOURCES

Example 1 included as less-than constraints only the budget limitation in 2 years and the upper limit on the acceptance of any project. Linear programming models can incorporate numerous other constraints which show other constrained resources, legal requirements, managerial policies, and requirements imposed by the environment. Example 2 illustrates several of these constraints.

□ **EXAMPLE 2**   *Modified Lorie-Savage Problem*

Consider a firm that is evaluating the same nine projects as in Example 1, but with limitations imposed on working-capital requirements for all projects ($25) over their useful lives, managerial supervision of the projects (120 hours), and a legal requirement for water purity control. (The firm feels that EPA will not bother it if it achieves at least 10 water purity control points in the projects it accepts.)

Project	NPV_j	C_{1j} = Cash Outflow in Period 1	C_{2j} = Cash Outflow in Period 2
1	$14	$12	$ 3
2	17	54	7
3	17	6	6
4	15	6	2
5	40	30	35
6	12	6	6
7	14	48	4
8	10	36	3
9	12	18	3

Budget available: $\Sigma C_{1j} X_j \leq \$50$; $\Sigma C_{2j} X_j \leq \$20$

Project	W_j = Working-Capital Requirement	M_j = Managerial Supervision in Hours	P_j = Water-Purity Control in Points
1	$ 5	20	1.2
2	11	80	6.3
3	7	18	2.7
4	4	14	2.2
5	8	88	8.8
6	5	16	2.0
7	12	74	5.7
8	9	60	5.9
9	6	28	3.2

Other constraints: $\Sigma X_j W_j \leq \$25$; $\Sigma X_j M_j \leq 120$; $\Sigma X_j P_j \geq 10$

Formulate and solve this problem as an LP and interpret the optimal solution.

Solution: The formulation is as follows:

Maximize NPV $= 14X_1 + 17X_2 + 17X_3 + 15X_4 + 40X_5 + 12X_6 + 14X_7 + 10X_8 + 12X_9$

subject to

$$12X_1 + 54X_2 + 6X_3 + 6X_4 + 30X_5 + 6X_6$$
$$+ 48X_7 + 36X_8 + 18X_9 + S_1 = 50 \quad \text{budget year 1}$$
$$3X_1 + 7X_2 + 6X_3 + 2X_4 + 35X_5 + 6X_6$$
$$+ 4X_7 + 3X_8 + 3X_9 + S_2 = 20 \quad \text{budget year 2}$$

$$\left. \begin{array}{lll} X_1 + S_3 = 1 & X_4 + S_6 = 1 & X_7 + S_9 = 1 \\ X_2 + S_4 = 1 & X_5 + S_7 = 1 & X_8 + S_{10} = 1 \\ X_3 + S_5 = 1 & X_6 + S_8 = 1 & X_9 + S_{11} = 1 \end{array} \right\} \begin{array}{l} \text{upper limits} \\ \text{on project} \\ \text{acceptance} \end{array}$$

$$5X_1 + 11X_2 + 7X_3 + 4X_4 + 8X_5 + 5X_6$$
$$+ 12X_7 + 9X_8 + 6X_9 + S_{12} = 25 \quad \text{working capital}$$
$$20X_1 + 80X_2 + 18X_3 + 14X_4 + 88X_5 + 16X_6$$
$$+ 74X_7 + 60X_8 + 28X_9 + S_{13} = 120 \quad \text{management supervision}$$
$$1.2X_1 + 6.3X_2 + 2.7X_3 + 2.2X_4 + 8.8X_5 + 2.0X_6$$
$$+ 5.7X_7 + 5.9X_8 + 3.2X_9 - R_1 = 10 \quad \text{water purity control}$$
$$X_j, S_i, R_1 \geq 0 \quad j = 1, \ldots, 9; \quad i = 1, 2, \ldots, 13$$

Notice that this formulation is exactly the same as the formulation in Example 1 except for the last three constraints, which show the new limited resources (working capital and management supervision) and a restriction imposed by legal authorities outside the firm (water pollution control). The new slack variables S_{12} and S_{13} show, respectively, the number of unused working capital dollars of the 25 originally available and the number of unallocated hours of management supervision among the 120 hours originally available. There is another new variable (R_1) in the last constraint, which is a "surplus variable," showing the number of water purity control points that accepted projects score above the minimum level of 10 specified by management. The optimal solution to this formulation is shown in Table 20–2.

The optimal solution shows a number of changes resulting from the additional constraints. As can be noticed from the tableau, projects 1, 3, 4, and 9 are fully accepted. Two projects are partially accepted—5 and 6—and are accepted 9.45% and 44.88%, respectively. There are excess budget dollars in year 1 (slack variable S_1) in the amount of $2.472, as well as excess hours of management supervision (slack variable S_{13}) in the amount of 24.5 hours. The accepted projects used the entire budget in year 2 and the entire working capital availability (slack variables S_2 and S_{12} are not among the basic variables and hence are equal to zero), while they generated an excess number of water purity points (1.029) over the minimum level of 10 as shown by the surplus variable R_1 being basic in the optimal solution. The new value of the objective function is $67.165, which is down from $70.273 in Example 1 because the current problem has additional constraints that must be met. □

Next, we consider the shadow prices and sensitivity analysis.

TABLE 20–2 Optimal Solution to Modified Lorie-Savage Nine-Project Problem

Basic Variables	X_1	X_2	X_3	X_4	X_5	X_6	X_7	X_8	X_9	S_1	S_2	S_3	S_4	S_5	S_6	S_7	S_8	S_9	S_{10}	S_{11}	S_{12}	S_{13}	R_1	RHS
X_1	1.0																							1.00
X_3			1.0																					1.00
X_4				1.0																				1.00
X_5		−0.244			1.0		−0.409	−0.307			0.0394	0.118		0.0945	0.110					0.165	−0.0472			0.094488
X_6		2.59				1.0	3.055	2.291			−0.063	−1.189		−1.55	−0.976					−1.46	0.276			0.448819
X_9									1.0															1.00
S_1		45.78					41.95	31.46		1.0	−0.803	−8.41		0.472	−3.45					−14.17	−0.236			2.472441
S_4													1.0											1.00
S_7		0.244					0.409	0.307			−0.0394	−0.118		−0.0945	−0.110	1.0				−0.165	0.0472			0.905512
S_8		−2.59					−3.055	−2.291			0.063	1.189		1.55	0.976		1.0			1.46	−0.276			0.551181
S_9																		1.0						1.00
S_{10}																			1.0					1.00
S_{13}		60.03					61.15	50.36			−2.46	−11.37		−1.496	−8.08					−19.12	−0.252	1.0		24.50394
R_1		−3.27					−3.19	−4.02			0.220	−0.139		0.429	1.22					1.73	0.135		1.0	1.029134
Z		4.323					6.283	5.213			0.819	4.46		2.165	7.693					1.039	1.417			67.165

SHADOW PRICES AND SENSITIVITY ANALYSIS

As pointed out in Chapter 19, sensitivity analysis is a critically important aspect of problem solving using mathematical programming models. Recall that *sensitivity analysis allows an interpretation of the shadow prices associated with each constraint equation, as well as determining the range of possible values that each of the model's input parameters could take on without changing the basic variables in the optimal solution to the problem.* Sensitivity analysis is important from the viewpoint of marginal analysis. Furthermore, it provides valuable insight to the decision-maker concerning the impact that LP's assumption, that each input parameter is known precisely and with certainty, has on the flexibility of the optimal solution. Of course, precious few factors in the capital budgeting problem setting are known precisely and with certainty. Hence, the decision-maker should be aware of how sensitive the optimal solution is to changes in each of the input parameters (i.e., objective function coefficients, right-hand-side values for the constraints, and coefficients of each decision variable in the constraints). The more critical parameters should receive more attention from management to make sure that control measures keep these parameters within acceptable limits.

In the LP formulation of the capital budgeting problem, *there are shadow prices associated with both accepted and rejected projects. These values enable the decision-maker to rank all projects according to their relative attractiveness* (as will be demonstrated in the next example). For accepted projects, the shadow prices are found under the slack variables (S_k) for the following constraints:

$$X_j + S_k = 1$$

The shadow prices are computed using the following expression:

$$\gamma_j = b_j - \sum_{t=1}^{T} \rho_t^* C_{jt} \tag{4}$$

where $\gamma_j =$ shadow price associated with accepted project j (shown under the slack variable associated with project j)

$b_j =$ net present value for project j shown in the objective function

$\rho_t^* =$ shadow price in the optimal solution associated with each resource t which is required to accept a project (shown under the slack variable associated with the corresponding resource)

$C_{jt} =$ quantity of resource of type t required by project j

The shadow prices γ_j may very well give a ranking for the projects which differs from that given by any of the simple models such as payback, NPV, IRR, or the profitability index. Such differences in ranking will exist because the latter models look at the projects independently and without any resource limitations. On the other hand, *the LP shadow prices show interrelationships among projects by means of the budget constraints; they evaluate the projects at the implicit cost (ρ_t^*) that is implied by the optimal use of resources of type t.*

In addition to the shadow prices for accepted projects discussed above, the rejected projects have shadow prices that are computed in an analogous way:

$$\mu_j = \sum_{t=1}^{T} \rho_t^* C_{jt} - b_j \tag{5}$$

where μ_j is the shadow price associated with rejected project j (shown in the objective function row in the column for X_j). *The μ_j value shows the amount by which the objective function would decrease if the firm were forced to accept the unattractive project j.* If such projects were accepted, this would mean that the scarce capital budget dollars would be used in a suboptimal way, since the opportunity cost associated with the cash outflows $(\Sigma\rho_t^*C_{jt})$ exceeds the present value of the benefits generated by the project. It should be mentioned that the μ_j values must be zero *for all projects that are accepted (including partially accepted projects) because the benefits of these projects must justify the cash outlays in the various periods of the planning horizon (C_{jt}) when they are evaluated at the implied cost of capital (ρ_t^*) when the budgets each year are used in an optimal way.*

The next example illustrates the computation of these shadow prices and explains their significance.

☐ **EXAMPLE 3** *Interpretation of Shadow Prices*

For Example 2, interpret all shadow prices shown in Table 20–2.

Solution: We start with the shadow prices for the slack and surplus variables S_1, S_2, S_{12}, S_{13}, and R_1, which are the slack and surplus variables associated with the resources that were originally available for our capital investment program—namely, the budget for years 1 and 2 (S_1 and S_2), working-capital funds (S_{12}), managerial supervision (S_{13}), and minimum requirement for water purity control (R_1). As the reader will notice, slack variables S_1, S_{13}, and surplus variable R_1 are basic variables in the optimal solution, since there are \$2.472 of the first year's capital budget (S_1) still remaining, 24.5 hours of management supervision time (S_{13}) available, and the desired level of 10 water purity control points established by management has been exceeded by 1.029 points (R_1).

Hence, the shadow prices for all of these variables are zero, since the firm would be unwilling to purchase any additional units of these resources (first year's capital budget or hours for supervision of projects by management) or to pay anything to reduce the original 10-unit lower limit for the desired level of water purity control points of accepted projects. If any of these corresponding right-hand-side values were changed (resources increased or minimum requirements decreased), the objective function would not increase, since the other constraints are binding on the optimal solution. They are the ones that would have to be altered. Since the objective function would not increase, the firm would not be willing to pay anything for any of these changes because the end result would only be that more of these resources would be left over in the optimal solution.

On the other hand, variables S_2 and S_{12} are nonbasic variables in the optimal solution, which means that their corresponding resources (budget dollars in year 2 and working capital funds, respectively) are completely exhausted in the optimal solution. The shadow price for S_2 is 0.819, which means that we would be willing to pay up to a maximum of 81.9% interest on new capital that we could raise in year 2 (a somewhat significant cost of capital) because the objective function would increase by this amount (0.819) for each dollar of additional budget that we could obtain. Naturally, we would not borrow unlimited amounts at 81.9%, but rather would limit the amount to a sum consistent with the other constraints within the problem. The exact amount is determined by the Δ^+ and Δ^- values. We now demonstrate that the 81.9% is correct. The two projects that would be affected are partial projects X_5 and X_6; if we had additional funds in year 2, we could purchase additional portions of one or both of these projects.

Currently, the contribution of these two projects to the objective function is the percent accepted of each multiplied by the objective function coefficients for the respective project:

	% Accepted		NPV Objective Function Coefficient		Contribution to Value of Objective Function
Project 5	(0.094488)	×	$40	=	$ 3.77952
Project 6	(0.448819)	×	$12	=	5.385828
					$9.165348

Consider now that we could obtain $2 of additional budget in year 2. The way that we determine the impact that this would have on each basic variable in the optimal solution is by looking up the column for S_2 in the optimal tableau. Notice that the coefficients in the row for X_5 and X_6 are 0.0394 and -0.063, respectively. This means that additional dollars in year 2 would *increase the percentage purchased of project 5* (by 3.94% for each dollar) and *decrease the percentage of project 6 purchased* (by 6.3% for each dollar). Thus, the new percentage of each project accepted if we had $2 additional in year 2 would be:

	Current Percent Accepted		Change per Dollar	Change in Dollars		New Percent Accepted		NPV Objective Function Coefficient		Contribution to Value of Objective Function
Project 5	0.094488	+	(0.0394)	× (+$2)	=	0.173288	×	$40	=	$ 6.93152
Project 6	0.448819	+	(−0.063)	× (+$2)	=	0.322819	×	12	=	3.873828
										$10.805348
				Less current contribution to value of objective function						9.165348
				Increase in value of objective function						$1.640000
				Divided by change in $ in year 2						÷ 2
				Increase in objective function value per dollar change						= $0.82 ≈ $0.819 Shadow price

In a similar fashion we can demonstrate that the shadow price for additional working capital dollars of $1.417 means that the objective function would increase by this amount for each dollar of such funds that could be raised over the original amount of $25. *Shadow prices are valid only within given ranges of change for each original resource, as demonstrated in the next example.*

As was pointed out above, each rejected project also has a shadow price, which can be interpreted and verified. The shadow prices under X_2, X_7, and X_8 (the three rejected projects) show the amount by which the objective function would decrease if we were forced to accept one of these three projects. Thus, these values give a ranking of the rejected projects; the smaller the shadow price, the less objectionable it would be to be forced to accept the project.

Project	Shadow Price
2	$4.323
8	$5.213
7	$6.283

Using Equation (5), we can show how each of these shadow prices was determined. The shadow price for project 8 is verified as follows:

$$\mu_8 = \sum_{t=1}^{T} \rho_t^* C_{8t} - b_8$$

$$= \underbrace{(0)(36)}_{\text{budget 1}} + \underbrace{(0.819)(3)}_{\text{budget 2}} + \underbrace{(1.417)(9)}_{\substack{\text{working} \\ \text{capital}}} + \underbrace{(0)(60)}_{\substack{\text{management} \\ \text{supervision}}} + \underbrace{(0)(5.9)}_{\substack{\text{water purity} \\ \text{control}}} - \underset{b_8}{10}$$

$$= 0 + 2.457 + 12.753 + 0 + 0 - 10 = \underline{\$5.21}$$

Similarly, using expression (4), we can verify any or all of the following shadow prices, which show the rank order of accepted projects:

$$\gamma_4 = 7.693$$

$$\gamma_1 = 4.46$$

$$\gamma_3 = 2.165$$

$$\gamma_9 = 1.039$$

$$\left.\begin{array}{c} \gamma_5 = 0 \\ \gamma_6 = 0 \end{array}\right\} \quad \text{partially accepted—marginal projects}$$

The shadow price for project 1 is verified as follows:

$$\gamma_1 = b_1 - \sum_{t=1}^{T} \rho_t^* C_{1t}$$

$$= 14 - \left[\underbrace{(0)(12)}_{\text{budget 1}} + \underbrace{(0.819)(3)}_{\text{budget 2}} + \underbrace{(1.417)(5)}_{\substack{\text{working} \\ \text{capital}}} + \underbrace{(0)(20)}_{\substack{\text{management} \\ \text{supervision}}} + \underbrace{(0)(1.2)}_{\substack{\text{water purity} \\ \text{control}}} \right]$$

$$= 14 - (2.457 + 7.085) = \underline{\underline{4.458}}$$ □

The shadow prices determined from the optimal solution are valid only within a given relevant range that each of the input parameters can take on. This area was discussed in Chapter 19, wherein we computed Δ^+ and Δ^- for each original right-hand-side value and each objective function coefficient. For instance, Example 3 mentions that the shadow price for budget dollars in year 2 is 0.819 or that we are willing to pay a rate of interest of 81.9% to obtain additional budget dollars in year 2. However, we would not be willing to pay this rate indefinitely. In fact, we would only be willing to pay such a high rate until:

1. One of the other resources still available (i.e., budget dollars in year 1, or managerial supervision time) became exhausted because of the acquisition of an additional portion of a partial project enabled by the new budget dollars obtained for year 2.

2. A partially accepted project became completely accepted through the new budget dollars obtained for year 2.

3: A partially accepted project became completely rejected since funds were removed from it as new budget dollars were obtained for year 2.

Notice that the occurrence of any of these conditions would change the basis of the optimal solution or make it infeasible. Thus, the values of Δ^+ and Δ^- for each input parameter will be the smallest of 1, 2, or 3. Sensitivity analysis is now completed in Example 4 by means of the computation of all Δ^+ and Δ^- values.

□ **EXAMPLE 4** *Sensitivity Analysis*
Compute and interpret all Δ^+ and Δ^- values for the optimal solution shown in Example 2.

Solution: Start with the right-hand-side values. Again, we notice that slack variables S_1 and S_{13}, as well as surplus variable R_1, are basic variables in the optimal solution. Hence, using the approach shown in Chapter 19, we find that

$$\Delta^+_{S_1} = \infty \qquad \Delta^+_{S_{13}} = \infty \qquad \Delta^+_{R_1} = 1.029$$
$$\Delta^-_{S_1} = 2.472 \qquad \Delta^-_{S_{13}} = 24.504 \qquad \Delta^-_{R_1} = \infty$$

The values above imply that we would have the same basis in the optimal solution (i.e., the same set of optimal projects will be accepted and the same resources will still be available) as long as each of the following resources takes on values within the respective ranges:

$$\begin{array}{ll} \text{budget} & \left\{ \begin{array}{l} \text{upper limit} = \infty = 50 + \infty \\ \text{lower limit} = \$47.528 = 50 - 2.472 \end{array} \right. \\[2ex] \text{management} & \left\{ \begin{array}{l} \text{upper limit} = \infty = 120 + \infty \\ \text{lower limit} = 95.496 \text{ hr} = 120 - 24.504 \end{array} \right. \\[2ex] \text{water-purity} & \left\{ \begin{array}{l} \text{upper limit} = 11.029 = 10 + 1.029 \\ \text{lower limit} = -\infty = 10 - \infty \end{array} \right. \end{array}$$

with labels: budget **in year 1**, management **supervision**, water-purity **control**.

The other two slack variables of interest are the nonbasic variables associated with the budget dollars in year 2 (S_2) and working capital (S_{12}). Using the approach shown in Chapter 19 to compute Δ^+ and Δ^- for nonbasic variables:

$$\Delta^+ = \min\left|\frac{b_i}{a_{ij} < 0}\right| \qquad \Delta^- = \min\left\{\frac{b_i}{a_{ij} > 0}\right\}$$

we find

$$\Delta_{S_2}^+ = \min\left(\left|\frac{0.448819}{-0.063}\right|, \left|\frac{2.472441}{-0.803}\right|, \left|\frac{0.905512}{-0.039}\right|, \left|\frac{24.50394}{-2.46}\right|\right)$$

$$= \min(7.124, 3.079, 23.218, 9.96)$$

$$= \underline{\underline{3.079}}$$

$$\Delta_{S_2}^- = \min\left(\frac{0.094488}{0.0394}, \frac{0.551181}{0.063}, \frac{1.029134}{0.220}\right)$$

$$= \min(2.398, 8.749, 4.678)$$

$$= \underline{\underline{2.398}}$$

$$\Delta_{S_{12}}^+ = \min\left(\left|\frac{0.094488}{-0.0472}\right|, \left|\frac{2.472441}{-0.236}\right|, \left|\frac{0.551181}{-0.276}\right|, \left|\frac{24.50394}{-0.252}\right|\right)$$

$$= \underline{\underline{1.997}}$$

$$\Delta_{S_{12}}^- = \min\left(\frac{0.448819}{0.276}, \frac{0.905512}{0.047}, \frac{1.029134}{0.135}\right)$$

$$= \underline{\underline{1.626}}$$

Thus, the ranges wherein the optimal basis will remain unchanged are:

$$\text{budget in}\atop\text{year 2} \quad \left\{\begin{matrix}\text{upper limit} = \$23.079 = \$20 + 3.079 \\ \text{lower limit} = \$17.602 = \$20 - 2.398\end{matrix}\right.$$

$$\text{working}\atop\text{capital} \quad \left\{\begin{matrix}\text{upper limit} = \$26.997 = \$25 + 1.997 \\ \text{lower limit} = \$23.374 = \$25 - 1.626\end{matrix}\right.$$

Again, the ranges above show the possible changes wherein the shadow prices would remain valid. For example, we would only be willing to pay the interest cost of 81.9% for additional budget dollars in year 2 until we acquired $3.079. Beyond that level the problem would have to be completely re-solved, because we would get a new optimal set of projects. A similar interpretation can be put on each of the other shadow prices and ranges.

Finally, we compute Δ^+ and Δ^- for each of the objective function coefficients (i.e., for the nine projects under consideration). For the rejected projects (i.e., nonbasic variables in the optimal solution), the determination is immediate:

$$\Delta_{X_2}^+ = 4.323 \qquad \Delta_{X_7}^+ = 6.283 \qquad \Delta_{X_8}^+ = 5.213$$

$$\Delta_{X_2}^- = \infty \qquad \Delta_{X_7}^- = \infty \qquad \Delta_{X_8}^- = \infty$$

These values show that if the objective function coefficient for any rejected project were reduced by any amount, the project would still be rejected. Further, the objective function coefficients would have to be increased by the amount of their shadow prices to make the rejected projects start to become attractive.

For any of the completely accepted projects (i.e., $X_j = 1.00$), the computations for Δ^+ and Δ^- are again straightforward:

	X_1	X_3	X_4	X_9
$\Delta^+_{X_j}$	∞	∞	∞	∞
$\Delta^-_{X_j}$	4.46	2.165	7.693	1.039

This table shows that the objective function coefficient for any completely accepted project j could be increased by any amount or decreased up to the value of the shadow price γ_j and the project would still be attractive enough to accept.

The partially accepted projects require computations covered in Chapter 19 to arrive at Δ^+ and Δ^-:

$$\Delta^+ = \min \left| \frac{C_j}{a_{ij} < 0} \right|$$

$$\Delta^- = \min \left(\frac{C_j}{a_{ij} > 0} \right)$$

$$\Delta^+_{X_5} = \min \left(\left| \frac{4.323}{-0.244} \right|, \left| \frac{6.283}{-0.409} \right|, \left| \frac{5.213}{-0.307} \right|, \left| \frac{1.417}{-0.0472} \right| \right)$$

$$= \min(17.717, 15.362, 16.980, 30.02)$$

$$= \underline{\underline{15.362}}$$

$$\Delta^-_{X_5} = \min \left(\frac{0.819}{0.0394}, \frac{4.46}{0.118}, \frac{2.165}{0.0945}, \frac{7.693}{0.110}, \frac{1.039}{0.165} \right)$$

$$= \min(20.787, 37.797, 22.91, 69.936, 6.297)$$

$$= \underline{\underline{6.297}}$$

$$\Delta^+_{X_6} = \min \left(\left| \frac{0.819}{-0.063} \right|, \left| \frac{4.46}{-1.189} \right|, \left| \frac{2.165}{-1.55} \right|, \left| \frac{7.693}{-0.976} \right|, \left| \frac{1.039}{-1.46} \right| \right)$$

$$= \min(13.000, 3.751, 1.397, 7.882, 0.712)$$

$$= \underline{\underline{0.712}}$$

$$\Delta^-_{X_6} = \min \left(\frac{4.323}{2.59}, \frac{6.283}{3.055}, \frac{5.213}{2.291}, \frac{1.417}{0.276} \right)$$

$$= \min(1.669, 2.057, 2.275, 5.134)$$

$$= \underline{\underline{1.669}}$$

Management can now see how sensitive the acceptance of each project is to its objective function coefficient. As can be seen, projects 3, 6, and 9 are rather sensitive to downside changes in their objective function coefficients. Management may very well take a close look at the estimates for cash flows associated with these projects to make sure they are realistic in that minor changes could make these projects unattractive. □

In concluding this section on sensitivity analysis, it should be stressed that the Δ^+ and Δ^- values for the objective function coefficients are critically important in that these coefficients may have significant biases because of the assumptions of LP and the capital budgeting problem setting. That is, the objective function coefficients are arrived at by discounting both cash inflows and outflows that are assumed to be known with certainty where the discounting is done at a rate that is assumed to be known with certainty. Thus, even small percentage changes in these inputs can cause large changes in the objective function coefficients, which could easily throw them outside the range wherein the optimal set of projects would remain unaffected. These facts have noteworthy managerial implications for accuracy in forecasting cash flows, accuracy in estimating future costs of capital, optimal project selection, and managerial control activities.

THE DUAL LP FORMULATION FOR THE CAPITAL BUDGETING PROBLEM

As discussed in Chapter 19, the dual LP formulation has important implications for the financial manager. Namely, the dual formulation and its optimal solution provide valuable information for both planning and control functions in the capital budgeting decision process; the solution contributes to both coordination of activities and motivation of decision-makers in decentralized organizations.

The dual formulation of the capital budgeting problem is constructed in the same manner, as discussed in Chapter 19. That is, there will be a dual decision variable associated with each constraint in the primal problem and there will be a constraint equation associated with each project in the primal problem. Further, these dual variables will be found in exactly the way that the shadow prices in the primal problem were computed (as illustrated in the previous section).

The general dual formulation that corresponds to the primal formulation in Equations (1), (2), and (3) is:

$$\text{minimize} \sum_{t=1}^{T} \rho_t K_t + \sum_{j=1}^{N} \gamma_j \tag{6}$$

subject to

$$\sum_{t=1}^{T} \rho_t C_{jt} + \gamma_j \geq b_j \qquad j = 1, 2, \ldots, N \tag{7}$$

$$\rho_t, \gamma_j \geq 0 \qquad t = 1, 2, \ldots, T; \quad j = 1, 2, \ldots, N \tag{8}$$

where ρ_t = dual decision variable which represents the cost associated with each resource of type t

γ_j = dual decision variable associated with project j which shows the excess of its net present value (b_j) over its required use of resources (C_{jt}) when the latter are "costed out" at the appropriate rate ρ_t for each resource t

It should be noted that constraint equation (7) is used in rearranged fashion to compute the values of the shadow prices γ_j and μ_j in the optimal primal solution as shown by Equations (4) and (5). Of course, this is another illustration of our discussion in Chapter 19 concerning the close relationship between the primal and dual LP problems and their optimal solutions.

It is only necessary to solve *either* the primal or the dual problem because the optimal solution for either contains all the information that is in the other. The only difference is the economic interpretation that is given the optimal values of the variables. The correspondence is interesting and helpful in arriving at a complete interpretation and can lend assistance in solving problems more efficiently.

PROGRAMMING AND THE COST OF CAPITAL: A CONTROVERSY

Before we leave the area of linear programming to look at two interesting and powerful extensions (integer programming and goal programming), a noteworthy controversy relative to the appropriate LP formulation should be mentioned. Weingartner's[5] pioneering work, which saw him formulate the primal and the dual LP capital budgeting problem along the lines that we have illustrated above, was not without its detractors. Baumol and Quandt[6] contend that the primal problem as formulated by Weingartner runs afoul due to the "Hirshleifer paradox."[7] A simple statement of the paradox is: Under capital rationing, *the appropriate discount* rate to use in determining the net present values of projects under consideration cannot be determined until the optimal set of projects is determined, so that the size of the capital budget is ascertained as well as the sources of the subsequent financing and hence the cost of capital (or the appropriate discount rate to use in calculating NPVs). However, the authors of the text contend that this is *not* a paradox at all, but rather a simultaneous problem wherein the firm should concurrently determine, through an iterative mathematical programming process, *both the optimal set of capital projects and the optimal financing package, using its associated marginal cost of capital in the discounting process.*

Nevertheless, Baumol and Quandt suggest a formulation that maximizes the utility of the dollars withdrawn from the firm by the owners for their consumption over the planning horizon. Weingartner[8] counters that this is not an operational approach; it assumes that all shareholders have the same linear utility preferences for consumption, it requires the assignment of utility values in advance of information about withdrawal possibilities, and it makes the period-by-period utilities independent of one another. He then proposes a more opera-

[5] Weingartner, *Mathematical Programming*.
[6] W. J. Baumol and R. E. Quandt, "Investment and Discount Rates Under Capital Rationing—A Programming Approach," *The Economic Journal* (June 1965), pp. 317–329.
[7] J. Hirshleifer, "On the Theory of Optimal Investment Decisions," *The Journal of Political Economy* (August 1958), pp. 329–352.
[8] H. Martin Weingartner, "Criteria for Programming Investment Project Selection," *Journal of Industrial Economics* (November 1966), pp. 65–76.

tional model, which maximizes the dividends to be paid in a terminal year, where throughout the planning horizon dividends are nondecreasing and can be required to achieve a specified annual growth rate. Over the past decade, several other authors have jumped into the controversy, each suggesting his own reformulation. The interested reader should consult the appropriate references in Appendix A.

SUMMARY

This chapter examines the application of linear programming to the capital rationing problem. The optimal solution indicates the portfolio of projects that maximizes NPV. In addition, the optimal tableau provides valuable information for financial managers in the form of shadow prices and for the performance of sensitivity analysis. Currently, LP is becoming more and more widely used in capital budgeting applications even by medium-size and small firms. The increasing availability of LP software packages and minicomputers or microcomputers should bring about even greater use of the powerful LP model in capital investment decisions.

The following chapter examines two extensions of LP—integer programming and goal programming. These models enable direct incorporation of additional practical considerations of the capital rationing problem.

QUESTIONS/PROBLEMS

1. The LP Company is considering the adoption of 10 projects that require varied budget commitments over the next 3 years. In addition, the projects have different manpower, managerial supervision, and machine-hour requirements. The table shows the relevant data:

Projects	NPV	Manpower Requirements	Management Supervision	Machine Hours	Budget Year 1	Year 2	Year 3
X_1	$10	5	1	50	$2	$1	$3
X_2	20	2	1	20	3	2	4
X_3	35	20	1	10	5	4	2
X_4	45	25	3	30	1	3	2
X_5	60	10	1	15	6	2	5
X_6	75	7	2	16	3	1	2
X_7	15	12	1	18	4	5	1
X_8	50	15	1	22	5	3	3
X_9	90	30	4	35	7	4	2
X_{10}	55	3	1	45	2	1	1
Constraints:		$K_1 \le 70$	$K_2 \le 8$	$K_3 \le 150$	$K_4 \le 20$	$K_5 \le 15$	$K_6 \le 20$

Formulate this as an LP problem and solve it using the simplex method or a packaged LP algorithm.

2. The Hyperspace Company is evaluating 12 projects which have cash outflow requirements and NPV's as shown in the following table:

		Cash Outflows		
Projects	NPV	Year 1	Year 2	Year 3
X_1	$19.31	$100	$ 0	$ 0
X_2	52.68	100	0	0
X_3	43.21	100	0	0
X_4	32.29	100	0	0
X_5	57.50	100	60	60
X_6	112.82	200	0	0
X_7	7.30	150	0	0
X_8	13.71	100	0	0
X_9	47.90	150	75	75
X_{10}	57.35	50	100	175
X_{11}	204.06	100	150	100
X_{12}	18.26	0	100	0
Constraints:		$K_1 \leq 1000$	$K_2 \leq 400$	$K_3 \leq 300$

Formulate this as an LP problem to maximize NPV and solve it using the simplex method or a packaged LP algorithm.

3. Formulate the Hyperspace Company problem (Problem 2) as an LP to maximize the present value of the cash inflows and solve it using the simplex method or a packaged LP algorithm. Hyperspace's cost of capital is 6%.

4. For the optimal solution to Problem 1:
   (a) Completely interpret the optimal solution by enumerating projects to be accepted and rejected, ranking of all projects, and the shadow prices.
   (b) Perform a complete sensitivity analysis.

5. For the optimal solution to Problem 2:
   (a) Completely interpret the optimal solution by enumerating projects to be accepted and rejected, ranking of all projects, and the shadow prices for budget constraints.
   (b) Is the ranking of the accepted projects the same as a simple ranking of the projects by their NPV's? If these rankings differ, why do they, and which ranking is more relevant?
   (c) Perform a complete sensitivity analysis.

6. The optimal solution to Problem 3 is shown on the following pages.
   For this optimal solution:
   (a) Completely interpret the optimal solution by enumerating projects to be accepted and rejected, ranking of all projects, and the shadow prices for budget constraints. (*Caution*: Be careful in interpreting the shadow prices.)
   (b) Is the ranking of the accepted projects the same as a simple ranking by their present value of cash inflows or by their NPV's? If these rankings differ, why do they, and which ranking is more relevant to the Hyperspace Company?
   (c) Perform a complete sensitivity analysis.

Optimal Solution

Basic Variables	X_1	X_2	X_3	X_4	X_5	X_6	X_7	X_8	X_9	X_{10}	X_{11}	X_{12}	S_1	S_2	S_3
X_1	1.0														
X_2		1.0													
X_3			1.0												
X_4				1.0											
X_6						1.0									
X_7							1.0		0.857					0.0067	−0.0019
X_8								1.0							
X_{10}									0.429	1.0					0.0057
X_{11}											1.0				
X_{12}												1.0			
X_5					1.0										
S_2									32.14					1.0	−0.571
S_{10}									−0.857					−0.0067	0.0019
S_{12}									1.0						
S_{13}									−0.429						−0.0057
Objective function									92.625					1.0467	1.7467

for Problem 3

S_4	S_5	S_6	S_7	S_8	S_9	S_{10}	S_{11}	S_{12}	S_{13}	S_{14}	S_{15}	RHS
1.0												1.0000
	1.0											1.0000
		1.0										1.0000
			1.0									1.0000
					1.0							1.0000
−0.667	−0.667	−0.667	−0.667	−0.552	−1.33		−0.667			−0.476		0.4000
							1.0					1.0000
				−0.343						−0.571		0.8000
										1.0		1.0000
											1.0	1.0000
				1.0								1.0000
				−25.71						−92.86	−100.	10.0000
0.667	0.667	0.667	0.667	0.552	1.33	1.0	0.667			0.476		0.6000
								1.0				1.0000
				0.343					1.0	0.571		0.2000
14.44	47.81	38.34	27.42	58.35	103.09		8.843			255.38	112.56	2237.71

21

Multiperiod Analysis Under Conditions of Certainty: Integer and Goal Programming

The previous chapter examines the use of LP (linear programming) to represent the capital budgeting problem under capital rationing. This chapter presents two powerful extensions of LP that provide financial managers with additional flexibility in handling the complexities often encountered in practice. Specifically, this chapter explores the use of integer programming (IP) and goal programming (GP) to determine optimal portfolios of capital projects.

Parallel to the development in the previous chapter, the present chapter guides the reader through the following major stages in using IP and GP models for the capital rationing problem:

Stage 1: Formulate the problem in the correct format by specifying the input parameters, the decision variables, the objective function, and all relevant constraint equations (including goal constraints in GP).

Stage 2: Solve the problem by using a computer software package appropriate for the model under study.

Stage 3: Completely interpret the economic meaning of the optimal solution for management so that effective financial decision making is facilitated.

Stage 4: Perform a complete sensitivity analysis on the optimal solution so that additional insights can be provided to management.

All four stages are vitally important in order to capitalize on the capabilities of the IP and GP models to the fullest extent. The advances in computer technology should enable more widespread use of the powerful and flexible models examined in this chapter. However, careful financial analysis, correct model formulation and interpretation, and overall informed use of the models is necessary in order to help prevent *meaningless results*.

INTEGER PROGRAMMING APPLIED
TO THE CAPITAL BUDGETING PROBLEM

In his pioneering work, Weingartner also suggested an integer programming approach to the capital budgeting problem in addition to the LP models discussed above. The main reasons for the use of IP in the capital budgeting setting are as follows:

1. Difficulties imposed by the acceptance of partial projects in LP are eliminated, since IP requires that projects either be completely accepted or rejected.

2. All the project interdependencies discussed in Chapter 7 can be formally included in the constraints of the IP, while the same is not true for LP due to the possibility of accepting partial projects.

The general IP formulation for the capital budgeting problem is shown below:

$$\text{maximize NPV} = \sum_{j=1}^{N} b_j X_j \qquad (1)$$

subject to

$$\sum_{j=1}^{N} C_{jt} X_j \le K_t \qquad t = 1, 2, \ldots, T \qquad (2)$$

$$X_j = \{0, 1\} \qquad j = 1, 2, \ldots, N \qquad (3)$$

Notice that the only change in the formulation above compared to the primal LP formulation shown in Equations (1), (2), and (3) in Chapter 20 is that Equation (3), which is the zero-one condition of IP, guarantees that each project is either completely accepted ($X_j = 1$) or that it is rejected ($X_j = 0$).

The second attractive feature of IP mentioned above deserves elaboration. In using the simple capital budgeting models (NPV, IRR, PI), it is assumed that all the investment projects are independent of each other (i.e., that project cash flows are not related to each other and do not influence or change one another if various projects are accepted). In using IP, virtually any project dependencies can be incorporated into the model by means of the special constraints discussed below.

Project Interrelationships

The three types of project dependencies defined in Chapter 7—mutually exclusive, prerequisite, and complementary projects—can be handled in a straightforward manner. Each will be discussed in turn.

Recall that *mutually exclusive* projects are defined as a set of projects wherein the acceptance of one project in the set precludes the simultaneous acceptance of any other project in the set. The existence of such a set of projects is incorporated in an IP model by the following constraint:

$$\sum_{j \in J} X_j \leq 1 \tag{4}$$

where J = set of mutually exclusive projects under consideration
   $j \in J$ = that project j is an element of the set of mutually exclusive projects J.

Note that the constraint states that *at most* one project from set J can be accepted; this means that the firm can choose not to accept any project from set J. On the other hand, if it is necessary to select one project from the set, constraint (4) would appear as a strict equality:

$$\sum_{j \in J} X_j = 1 \tag{5}$$

   Another important application of this constraint is the situation wherein a firm is considering the possibility of delaying a project for one or more years. For example, consider project X, which has the following characteristics:

Time	Cash Flows Project X
0	$-\$100$
1	$+\ \ 75$
2	$+\ \ 75$
3	$+\ \ 75$

The NPV of this project at 10% is $86.51. If the firm wants to determine whether it is desirable to delay project X either 1 or 2 years, the following two new projects, X' and X'', respectively, can be defined:

	Cash Flows	
Time	Project X'	Project X''
0	$\$\ \ 0$	$\$\ \ 0$
1	$-\ \ 100$	0
2	$+\ \ 75$	$-\ \ 100$
3	$+\ \ 75$	$+\ \ 75$
4	$+\ \ 75$	$+\ \ 75$
5		$+\ \ 75$

The NPV's (with a cost of capital of 10%) that would be included in the objective function for projects X' and X'', respectively, are $78.66 and $71.50. These values differ from the NPV of project X because of the 1- and 2-year delays, respectively, in the cash flows, which necessitate multiplying project X's NPV by $1/1.10$ to arrive at the NPV for X' and by $1/(1.10)^2$ to arrive at the NPV for X''. Of course, the $100 cash outflow would be shown in the budget constraint for year 0 for project X, year 1 for project X', and year 2 for project X''. Finally, to show that at most one of these three versions of project X can be accepted, the following constraint is included in the IP formulation:

$$X + X' + X'' \leq 1$$

Prerequisite (*or contingent*) projects are two or more projects wherein the acceptance of one project necessitates the prior acceptance of some other project(s). For example, if project A cannot be accepted unless project Z is accepted, we would say that project Z is a prerequisite project for acceptance of project A; alternatively, we could also say that acceptance of project A is contingent upon the acceptance of project Z. Again, the representation of this contingency relationship in IP is immediate:

$$X_A \leq X_Z \tag{6}$$

where X_A and X_Z are decision variables denoting projects A and Z. Note in Equation (6) that if project A is accepted (i.e., $X_A = 1$), then, necessarily, project Z must be accepted also. However, project Z can be accepted on its own and project A rejected. Of course, there are many possible variations to constraints (4), (5), and (6), as shown in Example 1.

□ **EXAMPLE 1**   *Project Interrelationship Constraints in IP*

Formulate the appropriate IP constraints for each of the following cases:

(a) Two projects (6 and 8) are mutually exclusive and a third project (16) is contingent upon the acceptance of *either* project 6 or 8.

(b) Project 10 cannot be accepted unless both project 7 and project 9 are accepted.

(c) In the set of projects 1, 2, 3, 4, and 5, at most three can be accepted; furthermore, for project 11 to be accepted, at least two projects from the set above must be accepted, and for project 14 to be accepted, three projects from the set above must be undertaken.

Solution:

(a) Two constraints are required to capture the conditions specified; one for the mutually exclusive relationship between projects 6 and 8 and the second for the contingency relationship between 16 and the two projects above:

$$X_6 + X_8 \leq 1$$
$$X_{16} \leq X_6 + X_8$$

(b) Only one constraint similar to Equation (6) is required to express this contingency:

$$2X_{10} \leq X_7 + X_9$$

We see that the only way project 10 can be accepted is for the constraint above to hold as an equality, which means that both sides will equal 2, which necessitates the acceptance of both $X_7 + X_9$.

(c) Three constraints are necessary to relate these conditions: one for the acceptance of at most three projects from the first set, and one each for the contingency between projects 11 and 14 and the first set:

$$X_1 + X_2 + X_3 + X_4 + X_5 \leq 3$$
$$2X_{11} \leq X_1 + X_2 + X_3 + X_4 + X_5$$
$$3X_{14} \leq X_1 + X_2 + X_3 + X_4 + X_5 \qquad \qquad □$$

The final type of project interrelationship is that of *complementary projects*, wherein the acceptance of one project enhances the cash flows of one or more other projects. This synergistic effect is reflected in an IP formulation by using the strategy outlined below.

Step 1: Define a new decision variable which represents the acceptance of the complementary project.

Step 2: Incorporate the new decision variable for the complementary project into the objective function and all relevant constraints. The coefficients for the new decision variable in the objective function and the constraints will be determined by the facts of the situation at hand (i.e., the magnitude of the cost savings and other benefits associated with the acceptance of the combined project).

Step 3: Write a constraint similar to Equation (4) for mutually exclusive projects that precludes the acceptance of either or both of the individual projects and the complementary project.

A brief illustration will be helpful. Consider that we have two complementary projects, 7 and 8. Either of these projects can be accepted in isolation. However, if both are accepted simultaneously:

1. The cost will be reduced by, say, 10%.
2. The net cash inflow will be increased by, for example, 15%.

To handle the problem, a new project (call it 78) would be constructed having a cost equal to 90% of the cost of project 7 plus project 8 and net cash inflows equal to 115% of those of project 7 plus project 8. In addition, we would need the following constraint to preclude acceptance of both projects 7 and 8 as well as 78, because the latter is the composite project consisting of the two former projects:

$$X_7 + X_8 + X_{78} \leq 1$$

To conclude this section, we turn to a comprehensive example of the flexibility of IP in representing the capital budgeting problem.

☐ **EXAMPLE 2**   *Complete IP Formulation*

Consider the following 15 projects:

Project	Cash Outflows			NPV
	C_{1j}	C_{2j}	C_{3j}	
1	40	80	0	24
2	50	65	5	38
3	45	55	10	40
4	60	48	8	44
5	68	42	0	20
6	75	52	20	64
7	38	90	14	27
8	24	40	70	48
9	12	66	20	18
10	6	88	17	29
11	0	72	60	32
12	0	50	80	38
13	0	34	56	25
14	0	22	76	18
15	0	12	104	28

Budget constraints: $\Sigma C_{1j} X_j \leq \$300$; $\Sigma C_{2j} X_j \leq \$540$; $\Sigma C_{3j} X_j \leq \$380$

The following project interrelationships exist:

1. Of the set of projects 3, 4, and 8, at most two can be accepted.
2. Projects 5 and 9 are mutually exclusive, but one of the two must be accepted.
3. Project 6 cannot be accepted unless both projects 1 and 14 are accepted.
4. Project 1 can be delayed 1 year—the same cash outflows will be required, but the NPV will drop to $22.
5. Projects 2 and 3 and projects 10 and 13 can be combined into complementary or composite projects wherein total cash outflows will be reduced by 10% and NPV increased by 12% compared to the total of the separate projects.
6. *At least one* of the two composite projects above must be accepted.
Required:

(a) Define the new decision variables needed for the problem above.
(b) Formulate the problem as an IP.

Solution:
(a) The required new decision variables, in addition to X_1 through X_{15} for the original 15 projects described above, are as follows:

X_{16} is a decision variable to denote the delay of project 1 for 1 year
X_{17} is a decision variable to denote the acceptance of the composite of projects 2 and 3
X_{18} is a decision variable to denote the acceptance of the composite of projects 10 and 13

(b) The IP formulation for this problem is as follows:

Maximize NPV =

$$
\begin{aligned}
& 24X_1 + 38X_2 + 40X_3 + 44X_4 + 20X_5 \\
& + 64X_6 + 27X_7 + 48X_8 + 18X_9 + 29X_{10} \\
& + 32X_{11} + 38X_{12} + 25X_{13} + 18X_{14} + 28X_{15} \\
& + 22X_{16} + 87.36X_{17} + 60.48X_{18}
\end{aligned}
\qquad \text{(a)}
$$

subject to

$$
\begin{aligned}
& 40X_1 + 50X_2 + 45X_3 + 60X_4 + 68X_5 \\
& + 75X_6 + 38X_7 + 24X_8 + 12X_9 + 6X_{10} \\
& + 85.5X_{17} + 5.4X_{18} \qquad\qquad \le 300 \qquad \text{(b)}
\end{aligned}
$$

$$
\begin{aligned}
& 80X_1 + 65X_2 + 55X_3 + 48X_4 + 42X_5 \\
& + 52X_6 + 90X_7 + 40X_8 + 66X_9 + 88X_{10} \\
& + 72X_{11} + 50X_{12} + 34X_{13} + 22X_{14} + 12X_{15} \\
& + 40X_{16} + 108X_{17} + 109.8X_{18} \qquad \le 540 \qquad \text{(c)}
\end{aligned}
$$

$$
\begin{aligned}
& 5X_2 + 10X_3 + 8X_4 + 20X_6 + 14X_7 \\
& + 70X_8 + 20X_9 + 17X_{10} + 60X_{11} + 80X_{12} \\
& + 56X_{13} + 76X_{14} + 104X_{15} + 80X_{16} + 13.5X_{17} \\
& + 65.7X_{18} \qquad\qquad\qquad \le 380 \qquad \text{(d)}
\end{aligned}
$$

$$
X_3 + X_4 + X_8 \le 2 \qquad \text{(e)}
$$

$$
X_5 + X_9 = 1 \qquad \text{(f)}
$$

$$
\left.
\begin{aligned}
2X_6 &\le X_1 + X_{14} \\
2X_6 &\le X_{16} + X_{14}
\end{aligned}
\right\}
\begin{aligned}
&\text{either constraint (g) or} \qquad \text{(g)} \\
&\text{(h) must be satisfied} \qquad \text{(h)}
\end{aligned}
$$

$$X_1 + X_{16} \leq 1 \tag{i}$$

$$X_2 + X_3 + X_{17} \leq 1 \tag{j}$$

$$X_{10} + X_{13} + X_{18} \leq 1 \tag{k}$$

$$X_{17} + X_{18} \geq 1 \tag{l}$$

$$X_i = \{0,1\} \qquad i = 1,2,\ldots,18 \tag{m}$$

A few comments should be made concerning this formulation. In expression (a), the objective function, the coefficients for X_1–X_{16} were given in the problem description, the coefficient for X_{17} equals 1.12 times (38 + 40), or 87.36, in order to show the 12% increase in NPV over the benefits generated by projects 2 and 3 separately. The coefficient for X_{18} is arrived at in a similar fashion. Equations (b), (c), and (d) are the budget constraints for years 1, 2, and 3, respectively. The coefficients for projects 1–15 are straightforward; the coefficients for X_{16} are those of X_1 delayed by 1 year; for X_{17} and X_{18} the coefficients are 90% of the sum of the coefficients for the respective pairs of projects.

Equation (e) shows that no more than two of projects 3, 4, and 8 can be accepted. Equation (f) shows that either project 5 or project 9 must be accepted but that both cannot be accepted, because they are mutually exclusive; the strict equality sign conveys that one of the two must be accepted (i.e., either $X_5 = 1$ or $X_9 = 1$). Equations (g) and (h) show that for project 6 to be accepted, *either* project 1 and project 14 must be accepted [Equation (g)] or project 1 delayed by 1 year (i.e., project 16) and project 14 must be accepted [Equation (h)]; it is assumed here that project 1 delayed by 1 year still satisfies the requirement that both project 1 and project 14 are accepted. Notice also that even if one of these combinations of projects 1 and 14 is accepted, project 6 can either be accepted or rejected because of the $\leq$ inequality. Further, if desired, equations (g) and (h) can be combined to arrive at a single constraint which must be satisfied: $2X_6 \leq X_1 + X_{14} + X_{16}$.

Equation (i) shows that *only one* of the two projects 1 or 16 (i.e., project 1 delayed by 1 year) *can be accepted*; if we wanted to force acceptance of one of these two, a strict equality would replace the $\leq$ sign. Equations (j) and (k) convey that with the two composite projects, at most one of the individual projects or the composite project can be accepted. Equation (l) indicates that either one or both of the composite projects must be accepted. Equation (m) states IP's usual (0, 1) requirement. □

Before this section is concluded, two significant shortcomings of the IP methodology must be discussed.

Clearly, the ability to include the various types of constraints for project interrelationships adds to the realism of the problem representation using IP as compared to LP (which encounters difficulty handling such constraints). Furthermore, the existence of partial projects in the optimal LP solution raises questions about how realistic the problem representation is. However, the question arises whether the price that has to be paid in moving to IP is worth the benefits gained, considering the difference in solution time and the lack of meaningful shadow prices in IP compared to LP.

As mentioned earlier, the seemingly innocent change in the IP formulation has a significant impact on the time it takes to solve the problem. For example, Pettway reported in his 1972 study on an IP formulation with 15 budget constraints and 28 projects that four of the six solution algorithms he tested failed to arrive at the optimal solution in 5 minutes of CPU time on an IBM 360-65; the two algorithms that did locate the optimal solution took 118 seconds and 181 seconds.[1] The solution time on the same problem formulated as an LP would be on the order of 1 to 2 seconds. Furthermore, the solution time for IP problems grows exponentially with the number of projects, owing to the combinatorial nature of the problem. One baffling aspect of IP solution times is their variability. Often, smaller problems (in terms of number of constraints and number of decision variables) can take longer to solve than larger problems. Further, very minor changes in the problem (even with the same number of constraints and decision variables) can significantly increase solution times. No single solution approach works best on all types of IP problems. However, given this somewhat bleak picture, Geoffrion and Nauss cite progress that is being made on several fronts in developing more efficient solution algorithms.[2]

The second shortcoming of IP formulations and solutions is perhaps more devastating: meaningful shadow prices (which show the marginal change in the value of the objective function for an incremental change in the right-hand sides of various constraints) are not available in IP. That is, many of the constraints on IP problems that are not binding on the optimal integer solution will be assigned shadow prices of zero, which indicates that these resources are "free goods." In reality, this is not true since the objective function would clearly decrease if the availability of such resources were decreased. Furthermore Baumol, who was one of the pioneers in the area of dual variables in IP (see his article with Gomory[3]), summarizes the problem of shadow prices in IP quite well:

> However, we must be careful here—the preceding interpretation amounts to our thinking of these dual prices as the marginal revenue of these inputs. In the integer programming case, this concept runs into difficulties. In integer programming, inputs clearly must be thought of as coming in *indivisible units*. For that reason we cannot speak, e.g., of the marginal profit contribution of a small change in input, i.e., we must deal with $\Delta R/\Delta X$ rather than dR/dX (as we do in LP) where ΔX is an indivisible unit of input X and R is total profit. But a dual price represents dR/dX, which may change over the range of a *unit change in X*, and hence it may well give an *incorrect evaluation* of the marginal revenue of input X [emphasis added].[4]

Thus, the IP model, in trying to handle the problem of indivisibilities, runs into problems itself because the feasible region consists only of points that have integer values for all decision variables. This same problem of "gaps in the

[1] Richard H. Pettway, "Integer Programming in Capital Budgeting: A Note on Computational Experience," *Journal of Financial and Quantitative Analysis* (September 1973), pp. 665–672.
[2] A. M. Geoffrion and R. Nauss, "Parametric and Post-Optimality Analysis in Integer Linear Programming," *Management Science* (January 1977), pp. 453–466.
[3] R. E. Gomory and W. J. Baumol, "Integer Programming and Pricing," *Econometrica* (September 1960), pp. 521–550.
[4] W. J. Baumol, *Economic Theory and Operations Analysis*, 2nd ed. (Englewood Cliffs, N.J.: Prentice-Hall, Inc., 1965), pp. 165–166.

feasible region" is the culprit in creating both of the problems cited above: computer time required to solve IP problems and difficulties in interpreting the shadow prices in IP. On the brighter side of things, Geoffrion and Nauss cite progress also on this latter problem area in their exceptional paper on parametric and postoptimality analysis in IP.[5]

This concludes our discussion of IP. We now turn to goal programming, which is another powerful extension of LP in handling the capital budgeting problem.

GOAL PROGRAMMING APPLIED TO THE CAPITAL BUDGETING PROBLEM[6]

Throughout the text, we point out that the primary goal of financial management is the maximization of shareholders' wealth. Given the ever-present complexities, this is a rather tall order, since it is not always obvious how to maximize shareholders' wealth in an operational manner. Thus, it seems logical that progress toward this global goal will be facilitated if it is disaggregated into various subgoals; the rationale being that as the subgoals are achieved, definite strides will be made in the direction of shareholder wealth maximization. It was demonstrated in Chapter 7 that under conditions of certainty and perfect capital markets, the selection of the set of capital projects that maximizes NPV will guarantee maximization of shareholders' wealth or utility.[7]

However, if capital market imperfections exist (such as capital rationing, differences in lending and borrowing rates, and so on), then the maximization of NPV *may very well not* lead to the maximization of shareholders' wealth. In addition, observation plus empirical studies have demonstrated that investors and managers are interested in and motivated by several objectives. The following are representative of the more significant: growth and stability of earnings and dividends per share; growth in sales, market share and total assets; growth and stability of reported earnings or accounting profit (as argued by the Lerner and Rappaport article[8]); favorable use of financial leverage; diversification to reduce variability in earnings; and return on sales, equity, and operating assets. Thus, only a model that incorporates multiple criteria or objectives can be a robust, yet operational, representation of the pluralistic decision environment found in real-world capital budgeting problem setting. Goal programming (GP) is such a multi-criteria model, in that it allows the establishment of a hierarchy of multiple objectives with diverse penalties associated with deviations from different goals. A brief survey of GP is presented prior to its application to the capital budgeting problem.

---

[5] Geoffrion and Nauss, "Parametric and Post-Optimality Analysis."

[6] This section draws on the paper by A. Fourcans and T. J. Hindelang, "The Incorporation of Multiple Goals in the Selection of Capital Investments," presented at the 1973 Financial Management Association Convention, Atlanta, Ga., October 1973.

[7] See also I. Fisher, *The Theory of Interest* (New York: Macmillan Publishing Co., Inc., 1930), and Hirshleifer, "On the Theory of Optimal Investment Decisions," *The Journal of Political Economy* (August, 1958), pp. 329–352.

[8] E. M. Lerner and A. Rappaport, "Limit DCF in Capital Budgeting," *Harvard Business Review*, (September-October 1968), pp. 133–138. See also Chapter 7, pp. 99–103.

Goal programming (GP) was originally proposed in 1961 by Charnes and Cooper.[9] The technique has been expanded and popularized by the more recent works of Ijiri,[10] Lee,[11] and Ignizio.[12] The approach is an extension of linear programming (LP) wherein the usual "unidimensional" objective function (i.e., the optimization of a single measure of effectiveness) is transformed into a "multidimensional" criterion (i.e., the deviations from several goals are minimized according to a priority ranking scheme). The priority structure specifies a hierarchy of multiple goals wherein the highest-order goals are strived for first. Only after the optimal level of priority 1 goals has been achieved will priority 2 goals be considered, and so on. In addition, the relative importance of two or more goals at any priority level is shown by the weights assigned to each. The model is flexible enough to handle conflicting objectives, situations wherein only underachievement or overachievement of a goal is penalized, and conditions where the decision-maker seeks to come as close as possible to a desired target. Thus, GP offers an operational method of approximating a decision-maker's utility curve that does not require the derivation of a family of utility functions in a multidimensional space. GP requires the assignment of ordinal priorities to the respective goals with relative weights required by any goals placed on the same priority level. The optimal trade-off among goals on the same or different priority levels can be established through various interactive approaches or through sensitivity analysis, which is discussed below.[13]

In formulating decision problems using the goal programming format, three major components are required:

1. The usual *economic constraints* of LP, which are also called *hard constraints*, in that they cannot be violated since they represent resource limitations or restrictions imposed by the decision environment.

2. The *goal constraints*, which are also called *soft constraints* because they represent managerial policies and desired levels of various objectives which are being sought by the decision-maker.

3. The *objective function*, which minimizes the weighted deviations from the desired levels of the various objectives according to a specified priority ranking.

Each of these components deserves elaboration. The economic constraints in GP are exactly like the constraints in LP problems. Thus, such constraints still require the usual slack or surplus variables. On the other hand, goal constraints are most conveniently specified as strict equalities that contain *two deviational variables*, represented as d_i^+ and d_i^-, which indicate that the desired level of goal i is either overachieved or underachieved, respectively. Of course, one of the two

[9]A. Charnes and W. W. Cooper, *Management Models and Industrial Applications of Linear Programming*, Vols. I and II (New York: John Wiley & Sons, Inc., 1961).

[10]Y. Ijiri, *Management Goals and Accounting for Control* (Amsterdam: North-Holland Publishing Co., 1965).

[11]S. M. Lee, *Goal Programming for Decision Analysis* (Philadelphia: Auerbach Publishing Co., 1972).

[12]J. P. Ignizio, *Goal Programming and Extensions* (Lexington, Mass.: Lexington Books, 1976).

[13]See J. S. Dyer, "Interactive Goal Programming," *Management Science*, 19, no. 1 (September 1972), 62–70; J. S. Dyer, "A Time-Sharing Computer Program for the Solution of the Multiple Criteria Problem," *Management Science*, 19, no. 12 (August 1973), 1379–1383; and A. Geoffrion, J. S. Dyer, and A. Feinberg, "An Interactive Approach for Multi-Criterion Optimization with an Application to the Operation of an Academic Department," *Management Science*, 19, no. 3 (November 1972), 357–368.

deviational variables will always be zero and the other will equal the magnitude of the deviation from the desired goal level; if the desired goal level is exactly met, both deviational variables will equal zero. The deviational variables are the mechanism that is used to tie the goal constraints into the objective function. That is, for each goal the appropriate deviational variable(s) is (are) placed in the objective function, depending upon the desired action for that goal. For example, if it is desired to achieve a minimum level of net income, the only deviational variable required in the objective function is d^-; on the other hand, if the decision-maker does not want to exceed a cost goal, the only deviational variable required in the objective function is d^+, since only exceeding the cost goal should be penalized.

More-complex actions relative to goals require the use of both deviational variables. If the decision-maker wants to come as close as possible to some goal level, then both overachieving and undershooting the goal is penalized; hence, the objective function term is minimize $(d^+ + d^-)$. If the decision-maker desires to maximize net income and has established an achievable minimum level of net income as referred to above, the maximization is carried out in two steps—first achieving the minimum level and then overshooting the minimum by the greatest possible amount; hence, the objective function term is minimize $(d^- - d^+)$; it should be noted that we want to maximize d^+ but recall that the overall objective function is being minimized, which means that we minimize $-d^+$ to obtain the same result. Finally, if the decision-maker wants to minimize the cost referred to above and has established a maximum level, the appropriate objective function term is minimize $(d^+ - d^-)$ using the same logic traced out for the maximization case. This discussion is summarized in Table 21–1 for convenient reference.

To formally represent the objective function in a GP problem, the following three aspects must be specified:

1. The *priority level* that the goal is placed on, which indicates the ordinal ranking scheme whereby the goals will be optimized.

2. The *relative weight* assigned to each goal when there are two or more goals on the same priority level; this weighting indicates the relative importance of the goals.

3. The *relevant deviational variable(s)*, which should be penalized with respect to each goal and is dependent upon the desired action as just discussed.

The priority level is shown by P_i, where the subscript i designates the level—the smaller the value of i, the more important is the goal. Further, it should be noted that there is an *absolute dominance* among the priority levels; that

TABLE 21–1   Appropriate Objective Function Terms in Goal Programming

Desired Action	*Objective Function Term*
Achieve a minimum level of some goal	minimize d^-
Do not exceed a specified level of some goal	minimize d^+
Come as close as possible to a specified goal level	minimize $(d^+ + d^-)$
Maximize the value achieved relative to a given goal level	minimize $(d^- - d^+)$
Minimize the value achieved relative to a given goal level	minimize $(d^+ - d^-)$

is, priority 2 will be considered only after all the goals on priority 1 are optimized and nothing on priority 2 can act to the detriment of the goals on priority 1, and similarly for all lower-priority levels. The relative weights are shown as coefficients of the various goals, with the higher weights representing the more important goals.

Goal programming formulations can be used to optimize over a planning horizon consisting of many time periods. Goals can be established for the entire horizon or for various subperiods within the horizon. GP can handle deterministic or stochastic problem settings. The GP model discussed in this chapter is a multiperiod goal program where conditions of certainty are assumed.

It should be mentioned that GP models in their fullest context should be viewed as an *iterative process*. A set of priorities and relative weights are assigned to the various goals and the optimal solution is obtained. Next, based on the degree of consensus of the original priorities and weights as well as to gain insight into trade-offs among goals, a *sensitivity analysis* should be performed to see the impact that varying priorities and weights has on the optimal values of decision variables. The less significant the impact on the decision variables, the less effort management has to expend in arriving at a consensus to specify the precise priority structure. Using the sensitivity information, the trade-off question can also be addressed based on management perceptions, risk posture, and preferences.

GP models are solved in the same fashion as LP models. Very simple problems with only two decision variables can be solved by a graphical procedure. More complex problems can be solved using the simplex method of GP[14] or, more preferably, using computerized algorithms.[15] The solution of GP problems can be visualized as follows. The original feasible region of the problem is bounded by the economic (hard) constraints, which cannot be violated. The highest-priority goal(s) is (are) examined first; we try to drive the appropriate deviational variables for all priority 1 goals to zero.

This results in a reduction in the size of the feasible region as we move on to priority 2 goals. Thus, each lower-priority level will have a successively smaller feasible region in as much as any portion of the region previously eliminated cannot be reexamined, owing to the absolute dominance relationship of higher priority levels over all successively lower priority levels. As we move from one priority level to the next lower one, the relevant feasible region can be a region, a plane, a line, or a single point in *n*-dimensional space, where *n* is the number of decision variables in the problem. Of course, the priority structure assigned to the goals will determine the order in which various regions will be cut off from the feasible region, and hence the optimal solution can differ significantly as different priority structures are utilized (including relative weights) for any given problem. This is why we stressed the importance of the iterative approach to GP problems through sensitivity analysis. Of course, once the feasible solution consists of only a single point, there is no way that we can move from that point on any lower priority level; thus, it must be the optimal solution. For this reason it is recommended that high-priority goals be stated as *achieving minimum levels* of

---

[14] See Lee, *Goal Programming*, Chap. 5; S. M. Lee, *Linear Optimization for Management* (New York: Petrocelli/Charter Publishers, Inc., 1976), Chap. 7; and Ignizio, *Goal Programming*, Chap 4.

[15] See Ignizio, *Goal Programming*, Chaps. 3, 5, and 6, where FORTRAN programs are presented for integer GP and nonlinear GP problems.

various goals or *not exceeding a maximum level*, rather than to maximize or minimize, because the latter alternatives will drive the decision-maker to a single point in the feasible region. Maximization or minimization operations can be carried out on low priority levels once all other relevant goals have been achieved.

We now illustrate the formulation and graphical solution of a simple two-project capital budgeting problem using a GP model.

☐ **EXAMPLE 3**   *Two-Project GP Formulation*

Consider that a firm is evaluating two projects with the following characteristics:

Project	Economic Constraints			Managerial Goals			
	Cash Outflow Year 1	Cash Outflow Year 2	Management Supervision	NPV	Net Income Year 1	Net Income Year 2	Net Income Year 3
1	25	20	5	14	10	11	12
2	40	15	16	60	4	7	11
Amount available	30	20	10 units				
Desired goals levels				Maximum	6	8	10

This firm has a strict limitation on the funds that can be utilized for capital expenditures in years 1 and 2, as well as on the amount of time available for the management supervision of new projects (the amount of each of these resources available is shown above); hence, there are three economic or hard constraints. Furthermore, partial projects can be accepted, but only one complete project of each type is available; cash outflows occur at the beginning of the period, while the subsequent cash inflows that generate net income cannot be used to finance the current year's or any later year's cash outflows. Four managerial goals have been established: to achieve minimum levels of net income in the first 3 years of the asset's life and to maximize NPV over the entire useful life of the asset. Management has assigned the net income goals in years 1, 2, and 3 to priority levels 1, 2, and 3, respectively, and the NPV goal to priority 4.

Formulate this problem as a GP and solve it using the graphical method.

Solution: First, the problem is formulated as a GP. The objective function shown below will be optimized subject to the economic and goal constraints shown first:

Economic constraints:

$$25X_1 + 40X_2 \le 30 \qquad \text{budget in year 1}$$
$$20X_1 + 15X_2 \le 20 \qquad \text{budget in year 2}$$
$$5X_1 + 16X_2 \le 10 \qquad \text{management supervision}$$
$$X_1 \qquad\quad \le 1 \qquad \text{upper limits on}$$
$$X_2 \le 1 \qquad\qquad\quad \text{project acceptance}$$
$$X_i, d_j^+, d_j^- \ge 0 \quad i = 1,2; j = 1,2,3,4 \qquad \text{nonnegativity}$$
$$P_k \gg P_{k+1} \quad \text{for all } k \qquad \text{absolute dominance between priority levels}$$

Goal constraints:

$$10X_1 + 4X_2 + d_1^- - d_1^+ = 6 \qquad \text{net income year 1}$$
$$11X_1 + 7X_2 + d_2^- - d_2^+ = 8 \qquad \text{net income year 2}$$
$$12X_1 + 11X_2 + d_3^- - d_3^+ = 10 \qquad \text{net income year 3}$$
$$14X_1 + 60X_2 + d_4^- - d_4^+ = 10 \qquad \text{NPV}$$

Objective function:

Minimum weighted deviations $= P_1 d_1^- + P_2 d_2^- + P_3 d_3^- + P_4 \left(d_4^- - d_4^+ \right)$

Note in this formulation that the goal level for the NPV goal (i.e., 10) was selected simply because it is an achievable value for the NPV of accepted projects given the economic constraints. Recall that the firm wants to maximize NPV. Further, as discussed above, we maximize in GP by first achieving a given goal level and then overachieving it by as much as possible.

The problem above is solved using the graphical method by drawing the lines representing all the economic constraints; these boundaries form the initial feasible region shown:

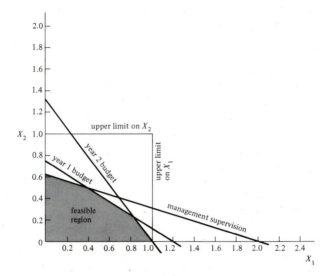

In diagrams (a) through (d), the four goal constraints are plotted and the region representing the deviation to be penalized has been eliminated as we move to the next lower priority level.

(a) Priority 1:

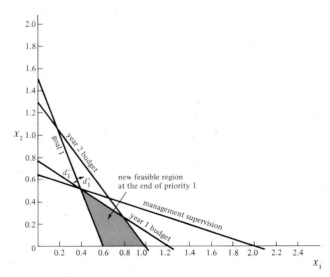

(b) Priority 2:

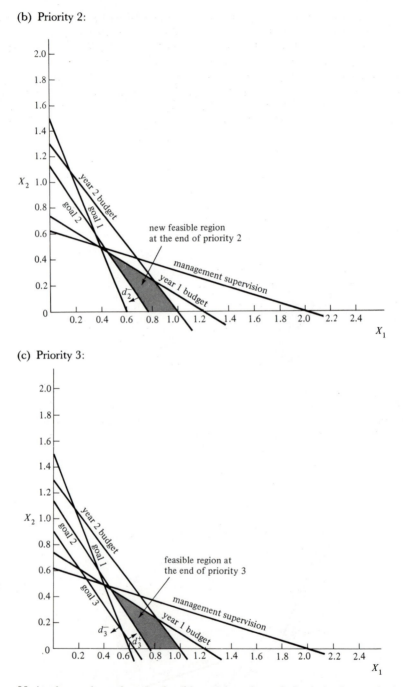

(c) Priority 3:

Notice that we have the same feasible region at the end of priority 3 as we had at the end of priority 2, since goal 3 is dominated by goal 2.

(d) Priority 4: Here we maximize NPV by first graphing goal 4, which has an NPV value of $10 and then moving as far above the line for the NPV goal as possible, which leads to the optimal solution of $X_1 = 0.415$ and $X_2 = 0.49$.

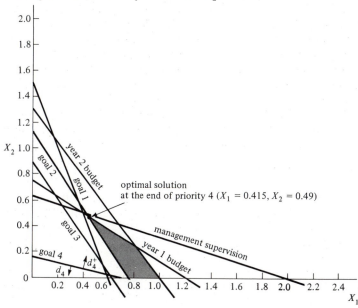

This optimal solution is quite different from the optimal solution if we just maximized NPV, which would have been to accept 0.625 of project 2 and nothing of project 1. The table summarizes the goal levels achieved by the LP and GP optimal solutions:

Goal	Optimal LP Solution $X_1 = 0$ and $X_2 = 0.625$	Optimal GP Solution $X_1 = 0.415$ and $X_2 = 0.49$
Net income year 1	2.5	6.11
Net income year 2	4.375	8.00
Net income year 3	6.875	10.37
NPV	37.5	35.21

As can be seen, the GP optimal solution generates a net income level in year 1 that is 2.4 times that generated by the optimal LP solution. In years 2 and 3, the optimal GP solution generates net income levels that are 1.8 and 1.5 times the respective net income levels for the optimal LP solution. The price paid for the achievement of these three short-run goals is 2.29 units of NPV. Most financial managers would be willing to sacrifice such a small amount of long-run profitability to achieve the more stable and consistent short-run growth in profitability provided by the GP optimal solution. These results demonstrate the power of a multiobjective model such as GP. ☐

Our next illustration of the use of GP in the capital budgeting setting will show how sensitivity analysis provides valuable information for management in addressing issues concerning trade-offs among their goals. In order to also be able to compare the results obtained here with the LP solution, we refer back to the Lorie-Savage problem shown in Example 1, Chapter 20.

□ **EXAMPLE 4**   *GP Formulation and Solution of the Lorie-Savage Problem*

The same firm that was evaluating the nine projects under the conditions described in Example 1, Chapter 20, now feels that the NPV objective should be supplemented with four other goals which reflect the short-run attractiveness of the projects. Specifically, the firm feels that stability and growth in sales as well as net income are very important vehicles to assist the firm in maximizing shareholders' wealth.[16]

The table shows the contribution that each of the projects will make to net income and sales growth in the next 2 years.

	Net Income		*Sales Growth*	
Project	*Year 1*	*Year 2*	*Year 1*	*Year 2*
1	2.0	4	0.02	0.03
2	2.0	4.2	0.01	0.03
3	1.6	2.5	0.02	0.02
4	1.2	2.8	0.01	0.02
5	3.0	5.0	0.03	0.04
6	1.1	1.4	0.01	0.01
7	1.5	3.0	0.01	0.02
8	1.2	1.8	0.01	0.015
9	1.3	2.4	0.01	0.018

The firm wants to achieve net income levels of 8 and 16, respectively, in years 1 and 2, and sales growth of 0.08 in each year, as well as to maximize NPV.

(a) Besides the information just presented, use the basic data on the nine projects from Example 1 to formulate all the economic and goal constraints for this problem.

(b) The firm is interested in evaluating two objective functions in order to determine the impact on the optimal set of projects:

1. Placing the net income goals on priority 1, the sales goals on priority 2, and the NPV goal on priority 3; on the first two priority levels the year 1 goals should be weighted twice as importantly as the year 2 goals.

2. All five goals placed on priority level 1 but with relative weights of 10 for net income in year 1, 2 for net income in year 2, 5 for sales growth in year 1, and 2 for sales growth in year 2, and 1 for NPV.

Formulate these two objective functions.

(c) After setting the target levels for net income and sales growth mentioned above, the firm feels it may be overoptimistic. Thus, the levels are revised to 7 and 12 in years 1 and 2, respectively, for net income and 0.07 in each year for sales growth. How will this affect the formulation in part (a)?

(d) If a computerized GP algorithm is available, obtain the optimal solutions for the two objective functions in part (b) and for the changes in the target levels mentioned in part (c). Briefly discuss differences in the optimal sets of projects. If a computerized algorithm is not available using the optimal solutions shown, briefly discuss the differences in the optimal sets of projects.

[16]A similar type of analysis was performed by C. A. Hawkins and R. A. Adams, "A Goal Programming Model for Capital Budgeting," *Financial Management* (Spring 1974), pp. 52–57.

Solution:
(a) The GP formulation is as follows:
Economic constraints:

$$12X_1 + 54X_2 + 6X_3 + 6X_4 + 30X_5$$
$$+6X_6 + 48X_7 + 36X_8 + 18X_9 + S_1 \qquad = 50 \qquad \text{budget constraint year 1}$$
$$3X_1 + 7X_2 + 6X_3 + 2X_4 + 35X_5$$
$$+6X_6 + 4X_7 + 3X_8 + 3X_9 + S_2 \qquad = 20 \qquad \text{budget constraint year 2}$$

$$\left.\begin{array}{ccc} X_1 + S_3 = 1 & X_4 + S_6 = 1 & X_7 + S_9 = 1 \\ X_2 + S_4 = 1 & X_5 + S_7 = 1 & X_8 + S_{10} = 1 \\ X_3 + S_5 = 1 & X_6 + S_8 = 1 & X_9 + S_{11} = 1 \end{array}\right\} \quad \begin{array}{l}\text{upper limits on} \\ \text{project acceptance}\end{array}$$

$$X_j, S_i, d_h^+, d_h^- \geq 0 \quad \left.\begin{array}{l} j = 1,2,\ldots,9 \\ i = 1,2,\ldots,11 \\ h = 1,2,\ldots,5 \end{array}\right\} \quad \text{nonnegativity constraint}$$

$$P_k \gg P_{k+1} \qquad \text{for all } k \qquad \begin{array}{l}\text{absolute dominance} \\ \text{between priority} \\ \text{levels}\end{array}$$

Goal constraints:

$$2X_1 + 2X_2 + 1.6X_3 + 1.2X_4 + 3X_5 + 1.1X_6$$
$$+1.5X_7 + 1.2X_8 + 1.3X_9 + d_1^- - d_1^+ = 8 \qquad \text{net income year 1}$$
$$4X_1 + 4.2X_2 + 2.5X_3 + 2.8X_4 + 5X_5 + 1.4X_6$$
$$+3X_7 + 1.8X_8 + 2.4X_9 + d_2^- - d_2^+ = 16 \qquad \text{net income year 2}$$
$$0.02X_1 + 0.01X_2 + 0.02X_3 + 0.01X_4 + 0.03X_5 + 0.01X_6$$
$$+0.01X_7 + 0.01X_8 + 0.01X_9 + d_3^- - d_3^+ = 0.08 \qquad \text{sales growth year 1}$$
$$0.03X_1 + 0.03X_2 + 0.02X_3 + 0.02X_4 + 0.04X_5 + 0.01X_6$$
$$+0.02X_7 + 0.015X_8 + 0.018X_9 + d_4^- - d_4^+ = 0.08 \qquad \text{sales growth year 2}$$
$$14X_1 + 17X_2 + 17X_3 + 15X_4 + 40X_5 + 12X_6$$
$$+14X_7 + 10X_8 + 12X_9 + d_5^- - d_5^+ = 40 \qquad \text{NPV}$$

Notice again that the goal level for the NPV goal is an arbitrary achievable value.
(b) The two objective functions are as follows:

1. Minimize weighted deviations $= P_1(2d_1^- + d_2^-) + P_2(2d_3^- + d_4^-) + P_3(d_5^- - d_5^+)$
2. Minimize weighted deviations $= P_1(10d_1^- + 2d_2^- + 5d_3^- + 2d_4^- + d_5^- - d_5^+)$

(c) The only changes that will be necessitated by the desired changes in the target goal levels is that the right-hand sides of goals one through four become 7, 12, 0.07, and 0.07, respectively.
(d) The optimal solutions for the two objective functions and the two different sets of goal levels are shown below:
Objective function 1 and goal values of 8, 16, 0.08, and 0.08:

Project Acceptance	Goal Levels Achieved	
$X_1 = 1.0000$	7.231	Net income year 1
$X_2 = 0.0426$		
$X_3 = 1.0000$	13.209	Net income year 2
$X_4 = 1.0000$		
$X_5 = 0.0000$	0.0699	Sales growth year 1
$X_6 = 0.9504$		
$X_7 = 0.0000$	0.0988	Sales growth year 2
$X_8 = 0.0000$		
$X_9 = 1.0000$	70.129	NPV

Objective function 2 and goal values 8, 16, 0.08, and 0.08:

Project Acceptance	Goal Levels Achieved	
$X_1 = 1.0000$	7.235	Net income year 1
$X_2 = 0.0000$		
$X_3 = 1.0000$	13.194	Net income year 2
$X_4 = 1.0000$		
$X_5 = 0.0000$	0.0702	Sales growth year 1
$X_6 = 0.9697$		
$X_7 = 0.0455$	0.0986	Sales growth year 2
$X_8 = 0.0000$		
$X_9 = 1.0000$	70.273	NPV

Objective function 1 and goal values 7, 12, 0.07, and 0.07:

Project Acceptance	Goal Levels Achieved	
$X_1 = 1.0000$	7.252	Net income year 1
$X_2 = 0.0000$		
$X_3 = 1.0000$	13.215	Net income year 2
$X_4 = 1.0000$		
$X_5 = 0.0000$	0.0703	Sales growth year 1
$X_6 = 0.9858$		
$X_7 = 0.0451$	0.0988	Sales growth year 2
$X_8 = 0.0000$		
$X_9 = 1.0000$	70.273	NPV

Objective function 2 and goal values 7, 12, 0.07, and 0.07:

Project Acceptance	Goal Levels Achieved	
$X_1 = 1.0000$	7.252	Net income year 1
$X_2 = 0.0000$		
$X_3 = 1.0000$	13.215	Net income year 2
$X_4 = 1.0000$		
$X_5 = 0.0000$	0.0703	Sales growth year 1
$X_6 = 0.9858$		
$X_7 = 0.0451$	0.0988	Sales growth year 2
$X_8 = 0.0000$		
$X_9 = 1.0000$	70.273	NPV

The optimal solutions above were obtained using the GP algorithm from Ignizio.[17]

As will be recalled, the optimal LP solution showed 100% acceptance of projects 1, 3, 4, and 9 as well as 97% acceptance of project 6 and 4.5% acceptance of project 7, which generated an NPV level of 70.273. All of the GP solutions above also accept 100% of projects 1, 3, 4, and 9. The only difference among the solutions is in the area of the partially accepted projects. With the original goal levels and priority structure, we find that projects 2 and 6 were partially accepted. Project 2 enters into the solution because of its contribution to the achievement of the new goals in the GP formulation. The other three GP solutions are virtually the same as the LP optimal solution. Greater variation in

[17]Ignizio, *Goal Programming*.

the optimal solutions would probably have been found if more projects were under evaluation and/or a greater diversity of goals were included in the formulation.   □

Our final illustration is a GP model; it is a global capital investment model that considers both replacement alternatives and new investment projects wherein multiple goals are sought after and conditions of capital rationing exist. The model is comprehensive in that it integrates the capital investment, financing, and dividend decisions of firms into a single optimization approach. New financing for the firm, which can take the form of either debt or equity, is incorporated into the model. In addition, cash inflows generated during the planning horizon by projects that are accepted as well as replacements that are made are taken into consideration. This comprehensive GP formulation and the accompanying example represent a more-typical capital investment problem faced by medium-sized firms. The GP model and existing computerized algo-rithms can easily handle such awesome-looking problems.

A COMPREHENSIVE GP MODEL

The Goals

The GP model illustrated below includes six goals which are of significant importance to firms in evaluating the selection of new capital projects, the optimal timing of equipment replacements, and the best way to finance such capital commitments:

1. Attainment of a minimum yearly level of net income generated by the new investments (both new projects and replacements).

2. Achievement of a minimum desired annual growth in the productivity of operating assets (both for new projects and equipment replacement decisions).

3. Achievement of a minimum desired level of earnings per dollar of stockholder's equity each year (a surrogate goal for earnings per share).

4. Minimization of the deviation from a financial leverage goal at the end of the planning horizon.

5. Attainment of a minimum desired growth rate in total assets over the planning horizon.

6. Maximization of the net present value of accepted projects given the budget constraints and that the goals above are satisfied as far as possible.

Other goals could be added to the list, but it is felt that these six represent the most important criteria that firms use in evaluating new capital investment and replacement decisions.

Table 21–2 gives the mathematical representation of the six goals men-tioned above, using the symbols defined in Table 21–3. A brief rationale will now be presented for the inclusion of each of the goals in the model.

The net-income goal was included in the model because both investors and managers have an objective of stable and steadily rising earnings. Such earnings are achieved only through judicious capital investments and equipment-replace-

TABLE 21–2   Goal Constraints of the Model

Net income: $e_j + \sum\limits_{i \in n_1} a_{ij} X_{ij} + \sum\limits_{i \in n_2} \bar{a}_{ij} Y_{ij} - (1 - t)I_j - d_{1j}^+ + d_{1j}^- = p_j$

$$j = 1, 2, \ldots, T$$

Productivity: $\sum\limits_{j=1}^{T} \sum\limits_{i \in n_1} r_{ij} X_{ij} + \sum\limits_{j=1}^{T} \sum\limits_{i \in n_2} \bar{r}_{ij} Y_{ij} - d_2^+ + d_2^- = U$

Earnings/dollar equity: $e_j + \sum\limits_{i \in n_1} a_{ij} X_{ij} + \sum\limits_{i \in n_2} \bar{a}_{ij} Y_{ij} - (1 - t)I_j - q_j \left(E_0 + \sum\limits_{k=1}^{j-1} E_k \right)$

$$- d_{3j}^+ + d_{3j}^- = 0 \qquad j = 1, 2, \ldots, T$$

Leverage: $E_0 + \sum\limits_{j=1}^{T} E_j + \sum\limits_{j=1}^{T} e_j + \sum\limits_{j=1}^{T} \sum\limits_{i \in n_1} a_{ij} X_{ij} + \sum\limits_{j=1}^{T} \sum\limits_{i \in n_2} \bar{a}_{ij} Y_{ij} - \sum\limits_{j=1}^{T} (1 - t)I_j$

$$- \sum\limits_{j=1}^{T} V_j \left(E_0 + \sum\limits_{k=1}^{j-1} E_k \right) - S\left(D_0 + \sum\limits_{j=1}^{T} D_j \right) - d_4^+ + d_4^- = 0$$

Growth rate in assets: $\sum\limits_{j=1}^{T} \sum\limits_{i \in n_1} BV_{ij}^T X_{ij} + \sum\limits_{j=1}^{T} \sum\limits_{i \in n_2} \overline{BV}_{ij}^T Y_{ij} - gA_0 - d_5^+ + d_5^- = 0$

Net present value: $\sum\limits_{j=0}^{T} \sum\limits_{i \in n_1} \dfrac{1}{(1 + k)^j} (b_{ij} X_{ij} - C_{ij} X_{ij} + W_T)$

$$+ \sum\limits_{j=0}^{T} \sum\limits_{i \in n_2} \dfrac{1}{(1 + k)^j} (\bar{b}_{ij} Y_{ij} - \overline{C}_{ij} Y_{ij} + \overline{W}_T) - d_6^+ + d_6^- = 0$$

ment decisions over time. Thus, this goal for each year of the planning horizon can be summarized as follows:

Net Income from on-going operations	+	Net Income generated by new investment projects	+	Net Income generated by equipment replacement projects	−	After-tax interest cost	=	Management's net income goal each year

Productivity increases over the planning horizon are another relevant area of concern in making new capital commitments, especially equipment-replacement decisions. Hence, how attractive a particular capital investment is can be measured in part by how much it increases productivity compared with current operations. The goal of achieving the minimum productivity increase established by management merely adds together the productivity growth per dollar invested in equipment replacements and new capital projects.

Earnings per share is one of the most closely watched statistics by investors and managers. Of course, this figure is based directly upon the level of net income (discussed in the first goal above) but also implicitly reflects the way that new capital investments (both new projects and equipment replacements) are financed (debt versus equity) and the dividend policy utilized by the firm. Thus, the next two goals—earnings per dollar of equity and leverage—incorporate two important dimensions used to judge how well a firm is doing in its profitability

TABLE 21–3   Glossary of Symbols in Alphabetical Order

A_0 = book value of total operating assets at time zero

a_{ij} = net income generated by project i in year j

$\bar{a}_{ij}$ = net income generated by the replacement of machine i in period j

b_{ij} = net cash inflow generated by project i in year j

$\bar{b}_{ij}$ = net cash inflow generated by replacement of machine i in period j

BV_{ij}^T = book value in year T of project i acquired in year j

$\overline{BV}_{ij}^T$ = book value in year T of replacement of machine i in period j

C_{ij} = cash outflow required for project i in year j

$\bar{C}_{ij}$ = cash outflow required to replace machine i in period j

D_0 = dollar amount of long-term debt outstanding at time zero

D_j = dollar amount of long-term debt acquired during year j

D_j^* = upper limit of the dollar amount of debt funds that can be acquired in year j

E_0 = dollar amount of equity outstanding at time zero

E_j = dollar amount of equity acquired during year j

E_j^* = upper limit of the dollar amount of equity funds that can be acquired in year j

e_j = dollar amount of net income generated by ongoing operations in year j

g = desired growth rate in assets over the planning horizon

I_0 = dollar amount of interest paid on long-term debt outstanding in year zero

I_j = dollar amount of interest paid on long-term debt outstanding in year j

i_j = percent interest rate paid on long-term debt in year j

k = firm's cost of capital to be used in discounting cash flows

n_1 = class of accepted projects in year j

n_2 = class of machine replacements undertaken in year j

n_1^* = class of accepted projects that have cash flows beyond the end of the planning horizon T

n_2^* = class of machine replacements that have cash flows beyond the end of the planning horizon T

p_j = net income goal in year j

q_j = earnings per dollar of equity goal in year j

r_{ij} = productivity growth per dollar invested achieved by accepting project i in year j

$\bar{r}_{ij}$ = productivity growth per dollar invested achieved by replacing machine i in year j

S = leverage goal to be achieved by the end of the planning horizon

t = corporate tax rate

U = productivity growth goal to be achieved by the end of the planning horizon

V_j = percent of dividends per dollar of equity to be paid in year j

X_{ij} = decision variable representing project i in period j

Y_{ij} = decision variable representing the replacement of machine i in period j

endeavors and its search for an optimal capital structure. The earnings per dollar of equity goal (which is a surrogate for earnings per share) adds net income of ongoing operations to the net income generated by new capital investments (after deducting interest charges on debt). This result is compared to management's target return per dollar of stockholders' equity to determine the quality of capital investment alternatives undertaken.

The financial leverage goal can be expressed as follows:

$$\frac{\text{total equity issued} + \begin{array}{c}\text{net income generated} \\ \text{by the firm's new} \\ \text{investments and} \\ \text{replacement projects}\end{array} - \text{dividends paid}}{\text{total debt incurred}} = \begin{array}{c}\text{management's} \\ \text{leverage goal}\end{array}$$

Therefore, through these two goals the model integrates the important investment, financing, and dividend policy dimensions of the capital budgeting and equipment-replacement decisions.

Growth rate in assets is a natural consideration in allocating capital among competing alternatives, because such growth contributes to the intrinsic value of the firm and its potential for stable and rising earnings. This goal is simply:

$$\frac{\begin{array}{c}\text{book value of} \\ \text{new capital investments} \\ \text{at end of planning horizon}\end{array} + \begin{array}{c}\text{book value of} \\ \text{equipment replacements} \\ \text{at end of planning horizon}\end{array}}{\begin{array}{c}\text{book value of initial assets at the} \\ \text{beginning of the planning horizon}\end{array}} = \begin{array}{c}\text{management's} \\ \text{desired growth} \\ \text{rate in assets} \\ \text{over the plan-} \\ \text{ning horizon}\end{array}$$

Finally, the introduction of capital-market imperfections weakens the validity of NPV as a *unique* criterion of investment evaluation. However, in conjunction with the goals above, definite strides are taken toward the maximization of shareholder's wealth. Hence, new investments and replacement decisions will be evaluated in terms of the first five goals. Then the feasible set of capital commitments that maximizes NPV will be undertaken. This goal adds the NPV of new investment projects to the NPV of equipment-replacement alternatives.

The Economic Constraints

Table 21–4 shows the economic constraints of the model. The interest expense constraint states that the dollar interest will be the amount of interest on debt outstanding at the beginning of the planning horizon plus the interest on new debt issued. It is assumed that no long-term debt matures or is retired during the planning horizon. The next constraint is the all-important budget constraint, which states that new funds committed to projects in any year cannot exceed the amount of new debt issued plus the amount of new equity issued plus the internally generated funds (i.e., ongoing operations of the firm plus cash inflows generated by new projects and replacements undertaken to date) less interest and dividend payments. These first two economic constraints are tied into the net income, leverage, and earnings per dollar of equity goals. Such interrelationships are needed to achieve the following important aspects: (1) the integration of the investment, financing, and dividend policy aspects of the

TABLE 21–4   Economic Constraints of the Model

Interest expense: $\quad I_j = I_0 + \displaystyle\sum_{k=1}^{j-1} i_k D_k \qquad j = 1, 2, \ldots, T$

Budget: $\quad \displaystyle\sum_{i \in n_1} C_{ij} X_{ij} + \sum_{i \in n_2} \bar{C}_{ij} Y_{ij} \le D_j + E_j + e_j + \sum_{k=1}^{j-1} \sum_{i \in n_1} a_{ik} X_{ik}$

$$+ \sum_{k=1}^{j-1} \sum_{i \in n_2} \bar{a}_{ik} Y_{ik} - (1-t) I_j - V_j (E_0 + \sum_{k=1}^{j-1} E_k) \qquad j = 1, 2, \ldots, T$$

Horizon value: $\quad W_T = \displaystyle\sum_{j=T+1}^{J} \sum_{i \in n_1^*} \frac{1}{(1-k)^{j-T}} (b_{ij} X_{ij} - C_{ij} X_{ij});$

$$\overline{W}_T = \sum_{j=T+1}^{J} \sum_{i \in n_2^*} \frac{1}{(1+k)^{j-T}} (\bar{b}_{ij} Y_{ij} - \bar{C}_{ij} Y_{ij})$$

Upper limits: $\quad D_j \le D_j^* \qquad E_j \le E_j^* \qquad j = 1, 2, \ldots, T$

Mutually exclusive
replacements:

$$\sum_{j=1}^{T} Y_{ij} \le 1 \qquad i = 1, 2, \ldots, N$$

Mutually exclusive
projects:

$\displaystyle\sum_{i \in C} X_{ij} \le 1 \qquad$ where C is a class of mutually exclusive projects in any year j

Decision variables: $\quad X_{ij} = \begin{cases} 1 & \text{if project is accepted in year } j \\ 0 & \text{otherwise} \end{cases}$

$$Y_{ij} = \begin{cases} 1 & \text{if machine } i \text{ is replaced in year } j \\ 0 & \text{otherwise} \end{cases}$$

Nonnegativity: $\quad d_{ij}^+, d_{ij}^-, D_j, E_j \ge 0 \qquad j = 1, 2, \ldots, T \qquad i = 1, 2, \ldots, 6$

capital budgeting and equipment-replacement decision areas; and (2) the optimal timing of changes in the firm's capital structure based on the cost and availability of funds in the capital markets, the firm's leverage goal, the attractiveness of new projects and replacements, and the portfolio of assets accepted to date in the planning horizon.

The next two constraints show the values of the discounted cash inflows less outflows for all accepted projects and replacements, respectively, which occur beyond the end of the planning horizon. These two values are used in the net present value goal. Upper limits are shown for the amount of new debt and new equity that can be issued each year to reflect market or self-imposed limits on the amount of external financing that the firm can undertake.

Finally, two constraints are shown which incorporate the fact that replacements of existing assets are mutually exclusive (i.e., if a given asset is replaced in year 1, the same original asset cannot be replaced in any other year of the planning horizon) and that new capital projects can be mutually exclusive (i.e., if one project is accepted, then any other project in the mutually exclusive set may not be accepted). Other project interdependencies discussed in the section on integer programming could also be incorporated in the model. The usual zero-one conditions are imposed both on the decision variables for new projects and for replacements. The nonnegativity requirement is placed on deviational variables and the debt and equity decision variables.

The Objective Function

The model's objective function consists of minimizing the appropriate deviations (d^+, d^-, or both) from the multiple goals according to the priority scheme established by the firm. Thus, for the first three goals and goal 5, only the d^- deviation will be penalized, since a minimum level of these goals is sought; for goal 4, both the d^+ and d^- deviations are important, because we seek to come as close as possible to the leverage goal that is established; and finally, we penalize ($d^- - d^+$) for goal 6 because we are seeking to maximize the NPV of accepted investments. For each of the six goals a priority level must be specified which shows its ordinal importance in the firm's hierarchy of objectives.

Owing to the flexibility of goal programming discussed above, a firm can tailor the model to its own hierarchy of goals and its own circumstances. For illustrative purposes, suppose that a corporation under consideration is concerned about the market price of its stock, since it finds equity issues a favorable way to obtain new financing for capital acquisitions. It also maintains that its image as a growth firm is very important. Given these conditions, the firm finds the following priority structure appropriate:

Priority 1 (P_1) The achievement of a minimum earnings per dollar of equity and the achievement of a minimum level of annual net income.

Priority 2 (P_2) The attainment of a specified growth in productivity of operating assets and a desired growth rate in assets over the planning horizon.

Priority 3 (P_3) Coming as close as possible to the firm's desired leverage goal at the end of the planning horizon.

Priority 4 (P_4) The maximization of the NPV of all accepted projects and replacements.

In addition, the firm decides that on the first priority level the earnings per dollar of equity goal is three times as important as the net income goal; on the second priority level, the growth rate in assets is thought to be twice as important as the productivity growth goal.

The hierarchy above is expressed mathematically by the following objective function:

$$\text{minimize weighted deviations} = 3P_1 \sum_{j=1}^{T} d_{3j}^- + P_1 \sum_{j=1}^{T} d_{1j}^- + 2P_2 d_5^- + P_2 d_2^-$$

$$+ P_3\left(d_4^+ + d_4^-\right) + P_4\left(d_6^- - d_6^+\right)$$

We now illustrate this comprehensive formulation with a numerical example.

□ **EXAMPLE 5**   *Comprehensive 28-Project Example*

The table on pages 356–57 presents cash flow data for 28 investment proposals. The data are adapted from test problems originally presented by Weingartner.[18] The projects have varying initial investments, cash flow patterns, and useful lives from 7 to 26 years. The planning horizon of interest was 10 years. To slightly simplify matters, the productivity goal will not be considered nor will the integer requirements on project acceptance or project interrelationship constraints. The desired levels of the various goals are also given at the bottom of the table, together with other input parameters for the model. The optimal solution and goal achievements are presented and discussed below.

Solution: The following table shows the optimal solution and goal achievements.

Model Solution

Goal Attainment

Year	Earnings per Dollar of Equity	Profit p		Amount Borrowed	Amount of Stock Issued
1				$200.00	$500.00
2	Achieved	Achieved,	p = $404		500.00
3	Achieved	Not achieved,	p = 333.75		183.18
4	Achieved	Achieved,	p = 572.27		
5	Achieved	Achieved,	p = 513.33		
6	Achieved	Achieved,	p = 454		
7	Achieved	Not achieved,	p = 336.71		
8	Achieved	Not achieved,	p = 248.60		
9	Achieved	Not achieved,	p = 206.33		
10	Achieved	Not achieved,	p = 106.66	200.00	

Leverage at the end of the planning horizon	Growth rate in assets	Net present value of accepted projects (at 6%)
$\dfrac{\text{Common stock}}{\text{Debt}} = 283\%$	111%	$381.30

Accepted Projects

Project	Proportion Accepted	Project	Proportion Accepted
1	1.00	17	1.00
2	1.00	18	1.00
3	1.00	19	1.00
4	1.00	20	1.00
5	0.092	21	1.00
6	1.00	22	1.00
7	0.948	23	1.00
13	0.559	25	1.00
15	1.00	28	1.00

[18] Weingartner, H. Martin, *Mathematical Programming and the Analysis of Capital Budgeting Problems* (Englewood Cliffs, NJ: Prentice-Hall, Inc., 1963) pp. 180–181.

Input Values

Project Number	1	2	3	4	5	6	7	8	9	10
					Cash Flows (dollars)					
1	−100	20	20	20	19	19	18	16	14	11
2	−100	20	18	18	18	18	14	14	14	14
3	−100	15	15	15	15	15	13	13	13	13
4	−100	20	6	11	7	16	5	14	18	3
5	−100	−60	−60	80	74	66	56	44	30	14
6	−200	25	25	25	25	25	25	25	25	25
7	−150	20	20	20	20	20	20	20	20	20
8	−100	20	18	16	14	12	10	4	−20	20
9	−150	−75	−75	60	60	55	50	44	38	36
10	−50	−100	−175	50	55	60	65	60	50	40
11	−100	−150	−100	10	20	30	40	60	60	60
12	−250	45	45	40	30	25	20	15	10	−40
13	−75	−75	−40	40	40	40	35	35	30	25
14	−180	20	12	16	13	11	19	17	12	15
15	−275	40	45	45	40	35	30	25	20	15
16	−140	20	20	18	16	14	11	8	−25	18
17		−100	18	17	15	12	8	−10	18	17
18		−85	20	20	16	15	13	10	7	3
19		−270	−100	125	115	105	80	60	35	25
20		−200	60	40	30	15	−25	−25	50	40
21		−355	60	70	80	70	55	40	25	15
22			−150	25	25	30	35	30	25	20
23							−80	20	20	20
24								−95	−60	47
25								−50	10	10
26									−60	−30
27										−175
28										−40

		1	2	3	4	5	6	7	8	9	10
Net Income generated by existing assets (e_j)	$400	360		320	280	240	200	160	120	80	40
Profit targets (p_j) (3% increase per year)	$404			416	428	441	454	468	482	496	511
Earnings per dollar of equity goal (q_j)	3%			3%	3%	4%	4%	4%	5%	5%	5%

Growth rate in assets
goal (G)   90 % over the planning horizon

Leverage
goal (S) $\dfrac{\text{equity}}{\text{debt}} = 250\%$ over the planning horizon

Upper bound on
borrowing $200 every year

Upper bound on
equity issue $500 every year

Cost of borrowing   5% every year

Depreciation
method   Straight line over the life of
                         each project

Existing assets $2000

Existing debt $300

Existing equity $800

Tax rate   50% every year

and Goals

								Years								
11	12	13	14	15	16	17	18	19	20	21	22	23	24	25	26	NPV of Projects at $k = 6\%$
								Cash Flows (dollars)								
6	-8															19.31
14	10	10	10	10	10	6	6	6	6	6						52.68
13	11	11	11	11	11	9	9	9	9	9						43.21
20	2	22	8	10	18	6	9	14	24							32.29
																57.50
25	25	25	25	25	25	25	25	25	25	25	25	25	25	25	25	112.82
20	20															7.30
18	16	14	12	10	4											13.71
35	34	33	30	25	17	9										47.90
30	20	10	-25	50	41	35	25	15	5							57.35
60	60	60	60	60	60	60	60	60	60	60	60	60	60	60	60	204.06
40	32	25	19	14	10	7	5									-8.77
15	5															6.02
19	13	14	17	20	14	11	15	17	12							-9.90
-75	35	30	25	20	15	10	5									-17.27
18	16	13	10	6	-25	16	16	14	11	8	5	2				-9.33
15	12	8	-10	18	17	15	12	8								18.26
																0.25
15	10															73.10
30	20	10														-12.90
5																-13.52
15	10	5														42.16
19	17	14	10	6	2											15.08
42	37	31	24	18	13	9	6	4	3							17.12
9	7	4	-14	9	9	8	6	3	-16	8	8	4				-1.97
-10	45	34	25	16	12	8	-20	21	16	12	9	7	5	3		20.92
50	45	35	25	10	-60	45	35	25	10							-0.64
15	13	9	7	5	2											2.22

It is interesting to analyze the achievement of the various goals. The earnings per dollar of equity goal is achieved each year in the planning horizon, while the profit targets exhibit a more erratic behavior. These goals are generally attained in the first 6 years (except in year 3), but the low magnitude of the cash throw-offs generated by existing operations prevents their achievement in the final years of the planning horizon.

Borrowing occurs in the very first and the last year of the planning period. Of course, the large outlays at the beginning of the horizon triggers the $200 borrowing in year 1. The bond issue of the last year, however, takes place so as to bring the leverage ratio closer to the desired target. In spite of this final borrowing, the leverage goal is overshot by a nonnegligible amount (283% for equity/debt).

The limit on the new stock issued is operative for the first 2 years, whereas only $183.18 is raised in the third year. Again, the firm would enter the stock market in order to meet the charges associated with the capital outlays of the first periods.

The accepted projects allow the firm to maintain a very comfortable growth in assets (111%), somewhat over the 90% desired level. Finally, the net present value of the portfolio of accepted projects is equal to $381.30.

It is also instructive to analyze the values of the deviational variables—d^+ and d^-—for each goal. Since the earnings per dollar of equity goal was achieved in each year, d_{3j}^- was equal to zero for each year, and d_{3j}^+ would equal the excess of the percent returns over the goals shown in the table of input values and goals. Similarly, for each year that the net income goal was achieved, the d_{1j}^- term would equal zero, which means that there would be no penalty in the objective function and that d_{1j}^+ would equal the excess of actual profits over the goal established. For example, in year 4, the net income goal was 428 and the actual level was 572.27; thus, the goal was achieved, $d_{14}^- = 0$, and $d_{14}^+ = 144.27$ (572.27 − 428.00). An analogous interpretation can be provided for the deviational variables for the other three goals. As in the previous example, sensitivity analysis could be performed to determine the impact on the optimal projects and goal achievement as the priority structure is changed.   □

SUMMARY

This chapter explores in depth the advanced models of mathematical programming applied to the capital budgeting problem under conditions of certainty. We examine the areas of integer linear programming, and goal programming. Both approaches provide a powerful methodology to determine the optimal set of projects under various conditions and consider several types of constraints or restrictions. Chapter 22 explores mathematical programming models under conditions of risk.

QUESTIONS/PROBLEMS

1. Firm XYZ has 10 projects with the following characteristics. Projects 1, 3, and 5 are mutually exclusive. For project 6 to be accepted, project 3 must also be accepted. Of projects 2, 4, 7, and 10, at least two must be accepted; however, project 7 cannot be accepted unless projects 8 and 9 are also accepted. If projects 5 and 9 are accepted together, their cost in combination is only 90% of the cost of the two individual projects. Finally, the firm feels that it must undertake at least 5 of the 10 proposed projects to maintain stable employment levels.

Formulate the appropriate IP constraints for Firm XYZ.

2. Firm TUB is evaluating the following 10 projects:

| Project | Cash Outflows | | | NPV |
	Year 1	Year 2	Year 3	
X_1	250	200	100	60
X_2	300	250	150	80
X_3	275	250	175	55
X_4	225	225	50	50
X_5	150	250	150	25
X_6	400	150	0	100
X_7	200	150	100	90
X_8	350	50	25	40
X_9	250	100	150	75
X_{10}	175	175	175	75
Constraints:	$K_1 \leq 2{,}000$	$K_2 \leq 1{,}500$	$K_3 \leq 1{,}000$	

The following interrelationships exist between the projects:
1. Only X_6 or X_7 can be accepted; not both.
2. If X_6 is accepted, X_2 cannot be accepted.
3. If X_7 is accepted, X_8 must be accepted.
4. X_9 and X_{10} are mutually exclusive, but one must be accepted.
5. If projects 2 and 4 are accepted in combination, 120% of the NPV will be generated and the cost will only be 85% of the combined cash outflows for the two projects separately.

Completely formulate this problem as an integer LP.

3. Acme Market is considering five new supermarkets, which have the following characteristics:

Project Characteristics	1	2	3	4	5
Cash outflow year 1	$10,000	0	$14,000	$30,000	$12,000
Cash outflow year 2	20,000	$18,000	10,000	15,000	0
Cash inflow year 1	8,000	0	5,000	3,000	4,000
Cash inflow year 2	12,000	8,000	6,000	18,000	20,000
Net income year 1	5,000	12,000	3,000	2,500	− 2,000
Net income year 2	10,000	6,000	5,000	14,000	16,000
Profitability index	1.4	1.8	0.6	1.2	0.9
Salvage value year 10	4,000	0	3,000	2,000	1,000

Acme has a budget constraint of $50,000 in year 1 and $40,000 in year 2. Any unused funds in year 1 can be invested in Treasury Bills at 6% and carried over into year 2. In addition, of the benefits received from accepted projects, 60% will be required for operating expenses or dividends; the remainder can be used for reinvestment in other projects. Acme's cost of capital is 10%. The projects noted above require cash outflows only in year 1 or 2 or both.

Among the five supermarkets, several interrelationships must be taken into account:
1. Either project 1 or project 4 *must* be accepted.
2. If project 2 is accepted, project 3 must also be accepted.
3. Project 1 cannot be accepted unless project 5 is also accepted.
4. Of the set of projects 1, 2, and 4, at most two may be accepted.
   The firm has established the following goals:
   Priority 1: Achieve a *minimum* net income of $15,000 in year 1.
   Priority 2: Weight 2—maximize NPV of accepted projects,
   weight 1—come *as close as possible* to a net income goal of $20,000 in year 2.

Multiperiod Analysis
Under Conditions of Risk

In Chapters 20 and 21 we explore the important models in the area of mathematical programming under conditions of certainty. Such models enable the decision-maker to select the set of projects that maximize net present value or (in the case of goal programming), endeavor to simultaneously achieve a hierarchy of multiple goals. Such models also enable the decision-maker to consider more realistic and complex problem settings than those handled by the simple models covered in Chapters 4–7. This chapter parallels the two previous chapters in that it introduces sophisticated approaches for handling conditions of risk in the capital budgeting problem. The new models surveyed here will enrich the simple risk models handled in Chapters 12, 13, and 14 by determining the set of projects that will maximize expected shareholder utility under the complex conditions of multiperiod uncertainty. The important area of Monte Carlo simulation is surveyed first and then applied to the capital budgeting problem. Next, the most helpful mathematical programming models under conditions of risk are discussed and their applications in capital budgeting are illustrated.

MONTE CARLO SIMULATION

Monte Carlo simulation is a flexible and useful operations research technique than can handle any finite problem whose structure and logic can be specified. *Simulation* is the imitation of a real-world system by using a mathematical model which captures the critical operating characteristics of the system as it moves through time encountering random events. Groff and Muth identify three major

FIGURE 22-1   Schematic of a Simulation Model

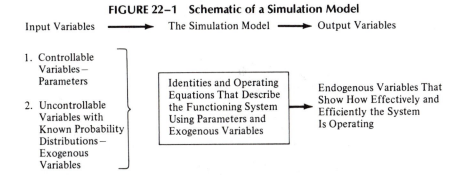

uses for simulation models:[1]

1. To determine improved operating conditions (i.e., systems design).

2. To demonstrate how a proposed change in policy will work and/or how the new policy compares with existing policies (i.e., systems analysis or sensitivity analysis).

3. To train operating personnel to make better decisions, to react to emergencies in a more efficient and effective manner, and to utilize different kinds of information (i.e., simulation games and heuristic programming).

Figure 22-1 shows a schematic of a simulation model composed of the following four major elements:

1. Parameters, which are input variables specified by the decision-maker which will be held constant over all simulation runs.

2. Exogenous variables, which are input variables outside the control of the decision-maker which are subject to random variation—hence, the decision-maker must specify a probability distribution which describes possible events that may occur and their associated likelihood of occurrence.

3. Endogenous variables, which are output or performance variables describing the operations of the system and how effectively the system achieved various goals as it encountered the random events mentioned above.

4. Identities and operating equations, which are mathematical expressions making up the heart of the simulation model by showing how the endogenous variables are functionally related to the parameters and exogenous variables.

A flow chart for a general simulation model is shown in Figure 22-2. The focus of the simulation is to develop empirical distributions for each endogenous variable in order to describe how efficiently and effectively the system operated during the 500 or 1,000 sampling trials that represent various combinations of random events encountered. As shown in Figure 22-2, the simulation progresses as follows. The parameters of the model are initialized and the probability distributions for each exogenous variable are read in; the simulation itself

[1]G. K. Groff and J. F. Muth, *Operations Management: Analysis for Decisions* (Homewood, Ill.: Richard D. Irwin, Inc., 1972), pp. 369–370.

FIGURE 22–2 General Flow Chart of a Simulation

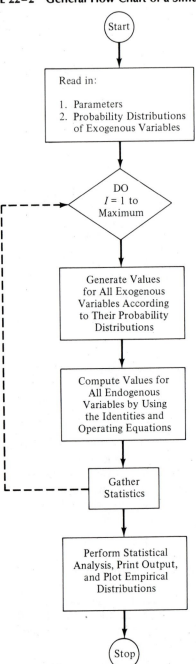

consists of the DO-LOOP, which will be executed the number of times the user specified (i.e., MAX is a parameter set by the decision-maker to show how many trials are desired wherein system behavior will be studied); on each simulation run, a value is generated for each exogenous variable by randomly selecting from its input probability distribution; based on these randomly generated values and the values of the parameters, a value is computed for each endogenous variable using the appropriate identity or operating equation; each simulation run provides one sampling observation for each endogenous variable, and when these observations are aggregated for all simulation runs, the analyst has an empirical distribution from which the usual statistics can be computed and probability statements made about the likelihood of the endogenous variable taking on a value within any given range; based on the empirical distributions and their statistics which are printed out after the completion of all simulation runs (as well as other such distributions arrived at through prior simulations performed using other values for the parameters, etc.), decisions are made.

A very good survey of the simulation technique appears in Groff and Muth.[2] In addition, Naylor et al. and Shannon[3] provide an extensive treatment of simulation studies, as well as an in-depth discussion of several applications.

Monte Carlo simulation has a number of significant advantages over comparable analytic techniques for handling conditions of risk. First, simulation can handle problems that may have the following characteristics:

1. Numerous exogenous random variables that are each described by unique probability distribution.
2. Any number of system interrelationships among variables.
3. Identities or operating equations taking on nonlinear, differential, or integral equation forms.

Virtually any analytic or optimization technique would have severe difficulties in handling such problems, if they could be handled at all. Second, sensitivity analysis can be performed in a straightforward manner so that the impact on the system can be pinpointed as parameters or the probability distribution for any combination of exogenous variables is varied. Third, even though simulation models are powerful and flexible, the cost of carrying out simulation runs is relatively small and simulation programs can be modified easily to reflect new structure and relationships in the system under study. However, simulation models (like any decision facilitating model) have their limitations:

1. Input requirements can often put great demands on the decision-maker.
2. Valid specification of system variables and interrelationships in the simulation model require a rather extensive understanding of the logical and mathematical properties (many of which can be hidden or nonobvious) of the real system under analysis.

[2] Ibid., Chap. 12.
[3] T. H. Naylor, J. L. Balintfy, D. S. Burdick, and K. Chu, *Computer Simulation Techniques* (New York: John Wiley & Sons, Inc., 1966); and R. E. Shannon, *System Simulation: The Art and Science* (Englewood Cliffs, N.J.: Prentice-Hall, Inc., 1975).

3. Experimental design requires careful attention by the analyst so that the simulation model can be verified and so that it provides output that is as free of error and as informative as possible.

SIMULATION APPLIED TO CAPITAL BUDGETING

One of the first authors to recommend that simulation be used in evaluating capital expenditures was David B. Hertz in his famous 1964 *Harvard Business Review* article.[4] Hertz, a consultant with McKinsey and Co., Inc., described the approach that his firm utilized to assist an industrial chemical producer who was evaluating a $10 million expansion of its processing plant which would have a 10-year service life. The simulation approach that was used had nine input variables:

Variables for investment cost analysis:

1. Original investment required.
2. Useful life of the facility.
3. Residual value of the investment.

Variables related to revenue generated by the investment:

4. Selling price of the product.
5. Size of the market.
6. Annual growth rate in the size of the market.
7. Share of the market captured by the firm.

Variables related to the operating costs associated with the investment:

8. Variable operating costs per unit of output.
9. Fixed operating costs per year.

The flow chart used by Hertz is shown in Figure 22–3. As can be seen, simulation encounters no difficulties in handling exogenous variables with any desired shape or moments (i.e., mean, variance, skewness, or kurtosis—the first four moments of the probability distribution). It is important to note that the probability distributions must be assessed by management so that they reflect the statistical dependence that exists between various combinations of variables: selling price and size of the market, size of the market and market growth rate, the trade-off between fixed and variable operating costs, and so on. Hertz does not discuss the exact methodology he used to accomplish the task but, as indicated, building interrelationships between variables into the model is one of the rather important aspects of simulation and requires careful attention by management and staff experts involved in building the simulation model.

Interpretation of the information about endogenous variables which is printed out and/or plotted by the computer at the end of the desired number of simulation runs is another essential phase of the overall simulation process. Of course, this output information usually provides valuable data that management uses to compare the risk-return characteristics of investment alternatives under

---

[4] David B. Hertz, "Risk Analysis in Capital Investment," *Harvard Business Review* (January–February 1964), pp. 95–106.

FIGURE 22–3

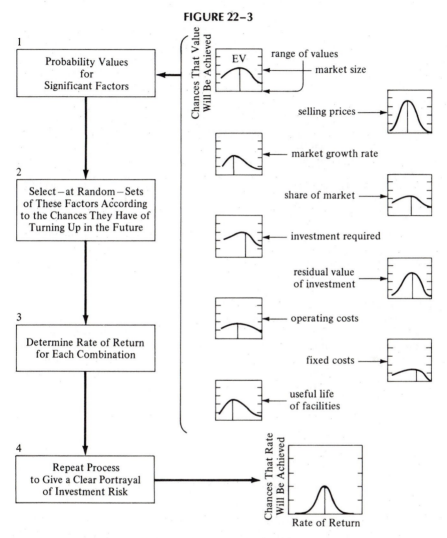

Simulation for investment planning. EV = expected value =average, or the "one best estimate."

SOURCE: David B. Hertz, "Risk Analysis in Capital Investment," *Harvard Business Review* (January–February 1964), p. 102. Copyright © 1963 by the President and Fellows of Harvard College; all rights reserved.

consideration and then to select the alternative that offers the maximum expected utility. To illustrate the ideas described above, consider Figure 22–4, again from the Hertz article. The figure shows the rate of return on two hypothetical alternatives (A versus B) that could be competing designs for the new plant addition in the chemical firm mentioned earlier. The differences are based on the degree of automation. The latter alternative has a higher intensity of capital equipment. The former requires the same dollar investment because more and better facilities to accommodate greater numbers of workers are necessitated by the nature of the less-automated plant. As can be seen, alternative B has both a higher expected return and a greater risk, owing to the increased variability in its returns as compared with alternative A. Management should use this information as well as similar results on other endogenous variables, in order to select the alternative that is preferred given the firm's utility function.

To summarize our discussion and illustrate the components of a simulation model, introduced in the previous section, we will now formally define the parameters, exogenous variables, endogenous variables, and the identities and operating equations for the capital budgeting problem setting using Example 1.

□ **EXAMPLE 1** *Formulation of Simulation Model for Capital Budgeting Problem*

For the general capital budgeting problem discussed in this section, formulate a simulation model by specifying the parameters, exogenous variables, endogenous variables, identities, and operating equations. A flow chart should also be drawn. It can be assumed that the selling price of the product is controlled by the firm and thus is not subject to uncertainty and that the risk-free rate will remain constant over the life of the project. Further, the firm will evaluate any projects under consideration by determining its net income after taxes each year, net cash flows each year, net present value over the life of the project, internal rate of return, and payback period.

Solution: The simulation model with the required components is presented in the table:

General Capital Budgeting Simulation Model

Parameters:

$$SP_t = \text{unit selling price in year } t$$
$$DR_t = \text{depreciation rate for year } t$$
$$i = \text{risk-free rate}$$
$$MAX = \text{total number of simulation runs to be performed}$$

Exogenous variables:

Stochastic variables with known probability distributions:

$$MG_t = \text{market growth rate during year } t$$
$$MS_t = \text{market size in number of units in year } t$$
$$SM_t = \text{share of the market in year } t$$
$$INV = \text{initial investment required by the project}$$
$$N = \text{useful life of the investment}$$
$$FC_t = \text{total operating fixed costs in year } t$$

FIGURE 22-4 Comparison of Two Investment Opportunities

Selected Statistics

	Investment A	Investment B
Amount of investment	$10,000,000	$10,000,000
Life of investment (years)	10	10
Expected annual net cash inflow	$1,300,000	$1,400,000
Variability of cash inflow		
1 chance in 50 of		
being *greater* than	$1,700,000	$3,400,000
1 chance in 50 of		
being *less than*[a]	$900,000	($600,000)
Expected return on investment	5.0%	6.8%
Variability of return		
on investment		
1 chance in 50 of		
being *greater* than	7.0%	5.5%
1 chance in 50 of		
being *less than*[a]	3.0%	(4.0%)
Risk of investment		
Chances of a loss		1 in 10
Expected size of loss	Negligible	$200,000

[a] In the case of negative figures (indicated by parentheses), *less than* means *worse than*.

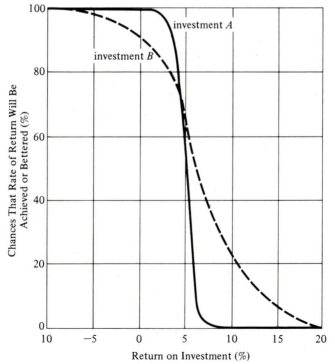

Source: David B. Hertz, "Risk Analysis in Capital Investment," *Harvard Business Review* (January–February 1964), p. 105. Copyright © 1963 by the President and Fellows of Harvard College; all rights reserved.

VC_t = variable operating costs per unit in year t

OC_t = other project related costs in year t

TR_t = tax rate in year t

Endogenous variables:

Performance variables computed by using identities and operating equations:

$USAL_t$ = unit sales generated by the project in year t

REV_t = total revenue generated by the project in year t

DEP_t = depreciation on the project in period t

TVC_t = total variable costs associated with the project in year t

TC_t = total costs associated with the project in year t

$NIAT_t$ = net income after tax generated by the project in year t

NCI_t = net cash inflow generated by the project in year t

BV_t = book value of the project at the end of year t

NPV_m = net present value for the investment on the mth simulation run

IRR_m = internal rate of return for the investment on the mth simulation run

$PAYB_m$ = payback period for the investment on the mth simulation run

Identities and operating equations:

$$BV_0 = INV$$
$$DEP_t = (DR_t)(BV_{t-1})$$
$$BV_t = BV_{t-1} - DEP_t$$
$$MS_t = (MS_{t-1})(1 + MG_{t-1}) \text{ for } t = 2,3,4,\ldots$$
$$USAL_t = (MS_t)(SM_t)$$
$$REV_t = (USAL_t)(SP_t)$$
$$TVC_t = (VC_t)(USAL_t)$$
$$TC_t = TVC_t + FC_t + OC_t + DEP_t$$
$$TAX_t = TR_t(REV_t - TC_t)$$
$$NIAT_t = REV_t - TC_t - TAX_t$$
$$NCI_t = NIAT_t + DEP_t$$
$$NPV_m = \sum_{t=1}^{N} \frac{NCI_t}{(1+i)^t} + \frac{BV_n}{(1+i)^n} - INV$$

IRR_m = rate r such that

$$\sum_{t=1}^{N} \frac{NCI_t}{(1+r)^t} + \frac{BV_n}{(1+r)^n} - INV = 0$$

$PAYB_m$ = payback period is the value K such that

$$\sum_{t=1}^{K} NCI_t = INV$$

A flowchart showing how the foregoing model would operate is as follows:

FIGURE 22–5

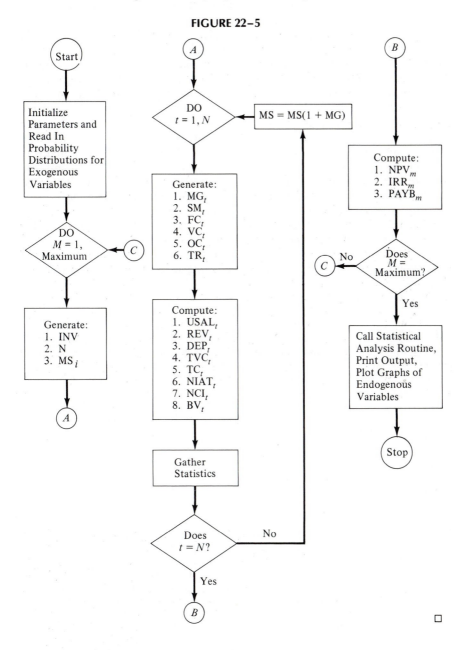

The general model can be enriched or reduced in terms of the number of variables based on the firm's needs. The approach used in Example 1 is straightforward and conventional except for the computation of NPV on each simulation run. It should be noticed that the risk-free rate (rather than the cost of capital or a risk-adjusted discount rate) is used to compute NPV, since the discounting process within a simulation model must only reflect discounting for futurity or the time value of money and not for the specific riskiness of the project under consideration. The degree of risk of the investment project is ascertained in the simulation runs themselves and will be reflected in all the empirical distributions of the endogenous variables. To discount the cash flows of the project at a rate in excess of the risk-free rate would burden the project with an improper double adjustment for uncertainty.[5] Thus, all that is required is to discount the cash flows at the risk-free rate in order to arrive at an empirical NPV distribution that contains valuable information regarding both the expected value and the risk associated with the project under consideration.

Any large-scale simulation would, of course, be performed on a computer since a minimum of 500 to 1,000 simulation runs are required to achieve stability in the results, and because there are usually many factors to monitor, as can be seen in Example 1. However, to provide insight concerning the operation of the simulation technique, the next example demonstrates a very simple hand simulation.

☐ **EXAMPLE 2**   Capital Budgeting Simulation Experiment

The Monte Carlo Company is evaluating an investment proposal which has uncertainty associated with the three important aspects: the original cost, the useful life, and the annual net cash inflows. The three probability distributions for these variables are shown below:

Original Cost		Useful Life		Annual Net Cash Inflows	
Value	Probability	Value	Probability	Value	Probability
$60,000	0.3	5 yr	0.4	$10,000	0.1
70,000	0.6	6 yr	0.4	15,000	0.3
90,000	0.1	7 yr	0.2	20,000	0.4
				25,000	0.2

The firm wants to perform five simulation runs of this project's life. The firm's cost of capital is 15% and the risk-free rate is 6%; for simplicity it is assumed that these two values are known for certain and will remain constant over the life of the project.

Determine the NPV, IRR, and payback period for each of the five simulation runs.

Solution: In order to perform the desired simulation runs by hand, a random-number table would be required. An excerpt from the RAND table which shows random numbers uniformly distributed between zero and 1 is shown below. From this table we can randomly generate values from each of the three discrete probability distributions shown above.

---

[5]See W. G. Lewellen and M. S. Long, "Simulation vs. Single-Value Estimates in Capital Expenditure Analysis," *Decision Sciences*, 3, no. 4 (October 1972), 22ff.

Table of Random Digits

09656	96657	64842	49222	49506	10145	48455	23505	90430	04180
24712	55799	60857	73479	33581	17360	30406	05842	72044	90764
07202	96341	23699	76171	79126	04512	15426	15980	88898	09658
84575	46820	54083	43918	46989	05379	70682	43081	66171	38942
38144	87037	46626	70529	27918	34191	98668	33482	43998	75733
48048	56349	01986	29814	69800	91609	65374	22928	09704	59343
41936	58566	31276	19952	01352	18834	99596	09302	20087	19063
73391	94006	03822	81845	76158	41352	40596	14325	27020	17546
57580	08954	73554	28698	29022	11568	35668	59906	39557	27217
92646	41113	91411	56215	69302	86419	61224	41936	56939	27816
07118	12707	35622	81485	73354	49800	60805	05648	28898	60933
57842	57831	24130	75408	83784	64307	91620	40810	06539	70387
65078	44981	81009	33697	98324	46928	34198	96032	98426	77488
04294	96120	67629	55265	26248	40602	25566	12520	89785	93932
48381	06807	43775	09708	73199	53406	02910	83292	59249	18597
00459	62045	19249	67095	22752	24636	16965	91836	00582	46721
38824	81681	33323	64086	55970	04849	24819	20749	51711	86173
91465	22232	02907	01050	07121	53536	71070	26916	47620	01619
50874	00807	77751	73952	03073	69063	16894	85570	81746	07568
26644	75871	15618	50310	72610	66205	82640	86205	73453	90232

The simulation process is now undertaken. In order to generate random numbers from the table, we would just start anywhere at random in the table, reading any pair of adjacent columns, since we need a two-digit random number and read either down the column or across the row. For this example we simply use the first two columns in the table and start at the top with the number 09 and then read down the column. In addition, the above three probability distributions should be cumulated to facilitate running the simulation.

	Original Cost			Useful Life			Annual Net Cash Inflows	
Value	Prob.	Cum. Prob.	Value	Prob.	Cum. Prob.	Value	Prob.	Cum. Prob.
$60,000	0.3	0.30	5 yr	0.4	0.40	$10,000	0.1	0.10
70,000	0.6	0.90	6 yr	0.4	0.80	15,000	0.3	0.40
90,000	0.1	1.00	7 yr	0.2	1.00	20,000	0.4	0.80
						25,000	0.2	1.00

Thus, we can immediately see that the original cost of the project will be $60,000 if the two-digit random number generated is between 00 but less than 30; the cost will be $70,000 if the random number generated is between 30 but less than 90; the cost will be $90,000 if the random number generated is between 90 and 99. This methodology carries over to the other two distributions.

The five simulations are now performed and the results are tabulated:

Simulation Results

	Original Cost		Useful Life		Annual Cash Flows				
Run	R.N.	Value	R.N.	Value	R.N.	Value	NPV	IRR	Payback
1	09	$60,000	24	5 yr	07	$10,000	−$17,876.36	Negative	None
2	84	70,000	38	5 yr	48	20,000	14,247.28	13.12%	3.5 yr
3	41	70,000	73	6 yr	57	20,000	28,346.48	18.00%	3.5 yr
4	92	90,000	07	5 yr	57	20,000	5,752.72	3.55%	4.5 yr
5	65	70,000	04	5 yr	48	20,000	14,247.28	13.12%	3.5 yr

Recall that the NPV is computed using the risk-free rate of 6%. Of course, this simulation is greatly simplified, but it should provide the general flavor of the approach. Notice that there is substantial variability in the results due to the small number of exogenous variables, their discrete distributions, and the small number of simulation runs performed.

$\square$

The basic simulation approach has been extended in several directions. Some of the more interesting are now discussed briefly with references given so that the interested reader can explore them further.

Kryzanowski, Lusztig, and Schwab discuss the application of a Hertz-type simulation model to a plant-expansion decision by a natural-resource firm.[6] Thuesen describes the use of simulation by the Georgia Power Company in performing risk analysis in the evaluation of nuclear vs. fossil-fuel power plants.[7] Philippatos and Mastai present a model designed to assist a wholesaler of nondurable goods in evaluating a proposed computer-controlled automated warehouse.[8] Chambers and Mullick present a simulation model that they designed and used at Corning Glass Works to evaluate five alternative manufacturing facilities in various foreign countries for one of their major product lines.[9] Fourcans and Hindelang formulate a general two-stage simulation model wherein both the subsidiary and the parent company of a multinational firm can evaluate and rank investment opportunities considering both project-related and critical international variables as well as various interrelationships among these variables.[10]

Cohen and Elton suggest that simulation is an efficient way of determining the elements of the variance-covariance matrix required to evaluate joint returns on a portfolio of capital budgeting projects under evaluation.[11] Salazar and Sen develop a simulation model which they combined with Weingartner's linear programming model; their simulation incorporates two types of uncertainty: environmental uncertainty based on what future economic, social, and competitive conditions may be; and cash flow uncertainty, wherein only the shape and parameters of a probability distribution are specified.[12] Their approach generates efficient portfolios of projects which are ranked as a function of differing environmental conditions and/or managerial preferences toward risk and return.

[6] L. Kryzanowski, P. Lusztig, and B. Schwab, "Monte Carlo Simulation and Capital Expenditure Decisions—A Case Study," *The Engineering Economist*, 18 (Fall 1972), 31–48.

[7] G. J. Thuesen, "Nuclear vs. Fossil Power Plants: Evolution of Economic Evaluation Techniques," *The Engineering Economist*, (Fall 1975), 21–38.

[8] G. C. Philippatos, and A. J. Mastai, "Investment in an Automated Warehouse: A Monte Carlo Simulation and Post-Optimality Analysis," *Proceedings of the 1971 Conference on Systems, Networks and Computers*, January 1971, Mexico City; also see G. C. Philippatos, *Financial Management: Theory and Techniques* (San Francisco: Holden-Day, Inc., 1973), Chap. 21.

[9] J. C. Chambers and S. K. Mullick, "Investment Decision Making in a Multinational Enterprise," *Management Accounting* (August 1971).

[10] A. Fourcans and T. J. Hindelang, "A Simulation Approach to Capital Budgeting for the Multinational Firm," presented to the *1976 Financial Management Association Conference*, October 1976, Montreal, Canada; also see Appendix 25A of this text.

[11] K. J. Cohen and E. J. Elton, "Intertemporal Portfolio Analysis Based on Simulation of Joint Returns," *Management Science*, 14 (September 1967), 5–18.

[12] R. C. Salazar and S. K. Sen, "A Simulation Model of Capital Budgeting Under Uncertainty," *Management Science*, 15 (December 1968), 161–179.

Finally, Carter suggests an interactive simulation model wherein all projects under consideration are simulated jointly in order to derive covariances among the projects.[13] Based on this simulation, the expected return and variance of various portfolios are computed and managers can obtain further information on any desired portfolio in order to make the final selection.

Our overview of the simulation methodology, plus the survey of the direction of simulation research, will be helpful in the following section, which introduces the complex area of mathematical programming under conditions of risk.

MATHEMATICAL PROGRAMMING UNDER RISK

This section surveys the application of mathematical programming models under conditions of risk to the capital budgeting problem. Table 19–1 identified the five categories of mathematical programming models under conditions of risk:

1. Stochastic linear programming (SLP)
Linear programming under uncertainty (LPUU)
Chance-constrained programming (CCP)
2. Integer programming under uncertainty (IPUU)
3. Stochastic goal programming (SGP)
4. Nonlinear programming under uncertainty (NLPUU)
Quadratic programming under uncertainty (QPUU)
5. Dynamic programming under uncertainty (DPUU)

Among these approaches, the major applications in the capital budgeting area have been in stochastic LP, chance-constrained programming, and quadratic programming under uncertainty. A brief overview of each of these models, as well as the significance of their application within the field of capital investment will be presented.

Stochastic Linear Programming

Stochastic LP (SLP) is a method of handling conditions of risk similar to Monte Carlo simulation already discussed. In SLP, a linear programming model replaces the identities and operating equations of the simulation model and the two-stage process proceeds as follows. In stage 1, we first set a number of decision variables and consider that they will be fixed (just like parameters in a simulation model) for all subsequent observations of random events. In stage 2, random events are generated and these values plus the parameters from stage 1 are substituted into the LP model. The LP is solved which provides one empirical observation of the optimal value of the LP objective function and the optimal values of the decision variables. Next, we go back and repeat the process

---

[13] E. E. Carter, *Portfolio Aspects of Corporate Capital Budgeting* (Lexington, Mass.: Lexington Books, 1974).

of generating random events and solving LP problems some desired number of times, thereby deriving a complete empirical distribution for the LP objective function. Finally, we compare this empirical distribution with other empirical distributions arrived at using different stage 1 decisions in order to ascertain that set of stage 1 decisions which optimizes the decision-maker's utility function.

The major SLP approach to capital budgeting is attributed to Salazar and Sen.[14] To provide greater insight into their approach and to further describe SLP, several figures from their article are presented. Salazar and Sen incorporate two kinds of uncertainty into their model: uncertainty related to significant economic and competitive variables which are likely to affect project cash flows and uncertainty related to the cash flows of the projects under consideration based on these variables. Salazar and Sen handle the first type of uncertainty by a tree diagram (similar to that introduced in Chapter 12) shown in Figure 22–6. Notice that there are 12 branches in the tree diagram with their respective joint probabilities of occurrence shown on the far right of the tree; the derivation of those probabilities is based on the table below the tree. In the SLP framework, the 12 branches in this tree diagram are considered as stage 1 decisions to be fixed; for each branch in the tree, cash flows for each project under consideration are randomly generated and then plugged into the LP model. To elaborate, consider the flow chart used by Salazar and Sen, which is shown in Figure 22–7. The first processing box in the flow chart randomly selects a branch from the tree shown in Figure 22–6. Next, the time counter, t, is set to 1 and then the project counter, j, is also set to 1. The two DO-LOOPS randomly generate the cash flows for all projects (up to $j = 15$—all 15 projects under consideration) over all time periods (up to $t = 21$—the planning horizon of the model). These random cash flows are plugged into the model's LP algorithm (which would be similar to the models discussed in Chapter 20) and the optimal set of projects, and the optimal objective function value is obtained. We then check to see if we have performed the desired number of simulations (S^*). If not, we go back and randomly select another branch from the tree diagram in Figure 22–6 and repeat the simulation and LP solution again. When all simulation runs have been performed, the empirical LP objective function results are plotted on the risk-return axes.[15] Given this summary of the results, management can decide which portfolio of assets optimizes its utility function. This approach is a flexible and powerful combination of mathematical programming and the simulation technique.

Chance-Constrained Programming

The next major category which has seen capital budgeting applications is that of *chance-constrained programming* (CCP). The approach of CCP is to maximize the expected value of the objective function subject to economic constraints that are allowed to be violated some given percentage of the time due to random variations in the system. Chance constraints are arrived at as follows. Consider

[14] Salazar and Sen, "A Simulation Model."
[15] Ibid., p. 173.

FIGURE 22–6 Tree Diagram Used by Salazar and Sen

Structure of the Model

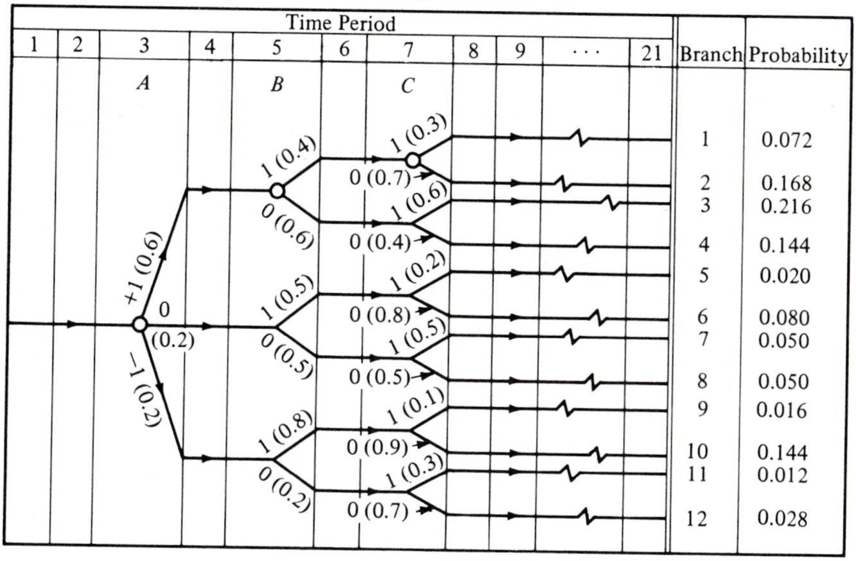
Time Period
1
2
3
4
5
6
7
8
9
. . .
21
Branch
Probability
A
B
C
+1 (0.6)
0
(0.2)
−1 (0.2)
1 (0.4)
0 (0.6)
1 (0.5)
0 (0.5)
1 (0.8)
0 (0.2)
1 (0.3)
0 (0.7)
1 (0.6)
0 (0.4)
1 (0.2)
0 (0.8)
1 (0.5)
0 (0.5)
1 (0.1)
0 (0.9)
1 (0.3)
0 (0.7)
1 0.072
2 0.168
3 0.216
4 0.144
5 0.020
6 0.080
7 0.050
8 0.050
9 0.016
10 0.144
11 0.012
12 0.028

Interpretation of Chance Nodes

Variable			*Environmental State*		*Probability of Occurrence*
Name	*Symbol*	*Time Period*	*Name*	*Symbol*	
GNP	A	3	Rises	+1	0.6
			No change	0	0.2
			Falls	−1	0.2
(Competitor's price— our price)	B	5	(0 or +)	1	0.4
			(−)	0	0.6
Introduction of new product by competitor	C	7	Yes	1	0.3
			No	0	0.7

Structure of the Model Interpretation of Chance Nodes

Variable			*Environmental State*		*Probability of Occurrence*
Name	*Symbol*	*Time Period*	*Name*	*Symbol*	
GNP	A	3	Rises	+1	0.6
			No change	0	0.2
			Falls	−1	0.2
(Competitor's price— our price)	B	5	(0 or +)	1	0.4
			(−)	0	0.6
Introduction of new product by competitor	C	7	Yes	1	0.3
			No	0	0.7

SOURCE: R. C. Salazar and S. K. Sen, "A Simulation Model of Capital Budgeting Under Uncertainty," *Management Science*, 15 (December 1968), 165.

FIGURE 22–7   Macro Flow Chart of System Program

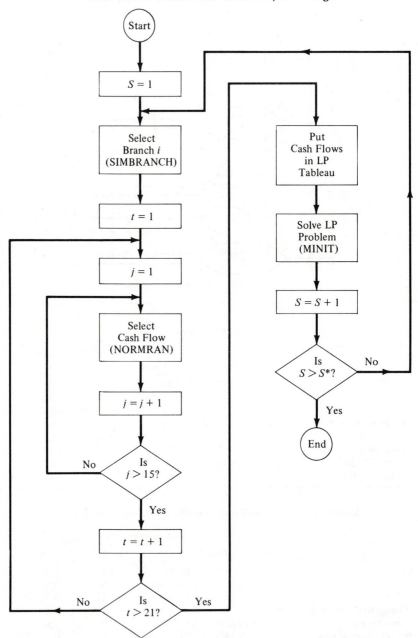

Source: R. C. Salazar and S. K. Sen, "A Simulation Model of Capital Budgeting Under Uncertainty," *Management Science*, 15 (December 1968), 169.

the usual constraints of LP:

$$\sum_{j=1}^{N} a_{ij}X_j \le b_i$$

Owing to randomness in either the a_{ij} coefficients or the b_i right-hand-side values, we show that the economic constraints do not have to be satisfied all the time by associating a probability or chance constraint statement with each economic constraint:

$$P\left\{ \sum_{j=1}^{N} a_{ij}X_j \le b_i \right\} \ge \alpha_i$$

where P = probability

α_i = minimum probability that the decision-maker is willing to accept that a given constraint is satisfied.

If $\alpha_i = 0.90$, for example, this would mean that the decision-maker requires that the economic constraint be satisfied at least 90% of the time and that he is willing to allow $\Sigma a_{ij}X_j$ to exceed b_i up to 10% of the time.

The solution methodology for CCP problems requires that the *deterministic equivalent* be derived for all chance constraints by taking into account the shape and parameters of the probability distributions for all random variables, as well as the degree of correlation between all pairs of random variables. This derivation usually results in nonlinear equations, which greatly threatens the feasibility of solving all but the smallest problems. Difficulties in problem solution escalate rapidly as the size of the problem grows or as the distributions of random variables describing the system depart from normality. The finding of these "deterministic equivalents" is beyond our scope, but the interested reader is referred to Charnes and Cooper[16] or Taha.[17]

Three significant contributions have been made in the area of CCP applied to capital budgeting. The earliest work was due to Naslund.[18] The expected horizon value of the firm was maximized subject to probabilistic constraints on financing alternatives that could be violated some fraction of the time. He considered both perfect and imperfect capital markets. Naslund's work extended Weingartner's (covered extensively in Chapter 20) to the risk area.

The second contribution was an article in 1967 by Byrne, Charnes, Cooper, and Kortenek.[19] Their model incorporates probabilistic payback and liquidity constraints as well as requirements for the firm's posture at the end of the planning horizon. Using the deterministic equivalents, the authors are able to derive a numerical solution for a small three-period, four-project example. They also present strategies for doing sensitivity analysis on the results. Because of the unresolved difficulty of solving large CCP problems, the same four authors

---

[16]A. Charnes and W. W. Cooper, "Deterministic Equivalents for Optimizing and Satisficing Under Chance Constraints," *Operations Research*, 11 (January 1963), 18–39.

[17]H. A. Taha, *Operations Research: An Introduction* (New York: Macmillan Publishing Co., Inc., 1971), pp. 649–653.

[18]B. Naslund, "A Model for Capital Budgeting Under Risk," *Journal of Business*, 39 (April 1966), 257–271.

[19]R. Byrne, A. Charnes, W. W. Cooper, and K. Kortenek, "A Chance-Constrained Programming Approach to Capital Budgeting," *Journal of Financial and Quantitative Analysis*, 2 (December 1967), 339–364.

recommended two alternative solution techniques based on assumptions that project cash flows could be closely approximated by discrete probability distributions.[20] The second article of the pair develops an integer LP model to approximate the nonlinear CCP model (for which no efficient solution technique exists).

The final major model was formulated by Hillier when he maximized the expected utility of the shareholders at the end of the planning horizon subject to probabilistic constraints on the net cash flows in each period, as well as cumulative net cash flows in each period over the planning horizon.[21] The author suggests two solution techniques:

1. An approximate LP model based on the deterministic equivalents for the chance constraints.
2. An exact branch-and-bound algorithm that he developed for handling continuous zero-one chance-constrained programming problems.[22]

To illustrate the CCP formulations and the results of finding the deterministic equivalent for chance constraints, consider the model suggested by Naslund.[23] His model consisted of the objective function plus the chance constraints shown below:

$$\text{Maximize } E\left(\sum_{j=1}^{N} A_j X_j + V_T - W_T \right)$$

subject to

$$P\left(\sum_{j=1}^{N} a_{1j} X_j + V_1 - W_1 \leq D_1 \right) \geq \alpha_1$$

$$P\left(\sum_{i=1}^{t} \sum_{j=1}^{N} a_{ij} X_j - \sum_{i=1}^{t-1} V_i r + \sum_{i=1}^{t-1} W_i r + V_t - W_t \leq \sum_{i=1}^{t} D_i \right) \geq \alpha_t$$

$$t = 2, 3, \ldots, T$$

$$0 \leq X_j \leq 1 \qquad V_t, W_t \geq 0$$

where $E =$ expected value operator
$P =$ probability of the expression within the parentheses
$A_j =$ horizon value at time T of all cash flows subsequent to the horizon associated with project j
$X_j =$ fraction of project j accepted
$V_t =$ amount of money lent in period t at interest rate r
$W_t =$ amount of money borrowed in period t at interest rate r

[20] R. Byrne, A. Charnes, W. W. Cooper, and K. Kortenek, "A Discrete Probability Chance Constrained Capital Budgeting Model—I and II," *Opsearch*, 6 (December 1969), 171–198, 226–261.

[21] F. S. Hillier, *The Evaluation of Risky Interrelated Investments* (Amsterdam: North-Holland Publishing Co., 1969); also F. S. Hillier, "A Basic Model for Capital Budgeting of Risky Interrelated Investments," *The Engineering Economist*, 17, no. 1, 1–30.

[22] F. S. Hillier, "Chance-Constrained Programming with Zero-One or Bounded Continuous Decision Variables," *Management Science*, 14, (September 1967), 34–57.

[23] Naslund, "A Model for Capital Budgeting," pp. 258–261.

a_{tj} = cash flows associated with project j in time period t —positive signs for this variable are associated with cash outflows while negative signs are associated with cash inflows

D_t = cash flow generated by other activities than the investment projects that we are going to consider

α_t = probability with which we require that the constraint within the parentheses hold

In the formulation, the following variables can be considered random: a_{tj}, A_j, D_i. Owing to this randomness, the constraints within the parentheses may not always be satisfied, but the decision-maker requires that they be satisfied at least α_t percent of time. Thus, the formulation maximizes the expected value of the horizon value of all accepted projects plus money lent, minus money borrowed at the horizon date, T. This maximization is carried out subject to a budget limitation expressed as a chance constraint in each period over the planning horizon. The constraint for period 1 states that the amount spent on new projects $(\Sigma a_{ij} X_j)$ plus the amount of funds lent (V_1) less the amount of funds borrowed (W_1) cannot exceed the cash flows generated by operations (D_1). The probabilistic constraint in each subsequent period considers cumulative cash inflows and outflows on all projects $(\Sigma\Sigma a_{ij} X_j)$, the cumulative amount of interest received on funds lent up to the present period $(\Sigma V_i r)$, the cumulative amount of interest paid on borrowed funds up to the present period $(\Sigma W_i r)$, and the cumulative cash inflow from operations (ΣD_i). The constraint states that cumulative net cash outflows for all projects up to the period minus cumulative interest earned plus cumulative interest paid plus amount lent less amount borrowed cannot exceed cumulative cash inflow from operations. Finally, we have the nonnegativity constraint and the upper limit on project acceptance. As indicated, to solve this problem the deterministic equivalent must be taken considering the random variables that are present. Naslund[24] assumed that the only random variables were the a_{tj}, which he further assumed were normally distributed with means U_{tj} and variances σ_{tj}^2 and further that all these variables were independent of one another. Given these assumptions, the deterministic equivalent that Naslund derived is:

$$\text{maximize } \sum_{j=1}^{N} A_j X_j + V_T - W_T$$

subject to

$$\sum_{j=1}^{N} U_{1j} X_j + V_1 - W_1 + \sqrt{\sum_{j=1}^{N} \sigma_{1j}^2 X_j^2}\, F^{-1}(\alpha_1) \le D_1$$

$$\sum_{i=1}^{t} \sum_{j=1}^{N} U_{ij} X_j - \sum_{i=1}^{t-1} V_i r + \sum_{i=1}^{t-1} W_i r + V_t - W_t$$

$$+ \sqrt{\sum_{j=1}^{N} \sigma_{tj}^2 X_j^2}\, F^{-1}(\alpha_t) \le \sum_{i=1}^{t} D_i \qquad t = 2, 3, \ldots, T$$

$$0 \le X_j \le 1 \qquad V_t, W_t \ge 0$$

[24] Ibid., p. 261.

where F^{-1} is the inverse cumulative density function associated with the random variables a_{tj}. As can be seen, all the constraints are nonlinear in the decision variables X_j because of the square root of the sum of the variances times X_j squared. Of course, these nonlinearities in the constraints cause significant problems in solving the formulation, since there is no general way of solving nonlinear programming problems. The approximation methods discussed above provide assistance in solving CCP problems. We now turn to a discussion of one final mathematical programming model under risk.

Quadratic Programming

Quadratic programming (QP) is the mathematical programming model wherein a nonlinear objective function is optimized subject to linear constraints. This model is far easier to solve than the nonlinear programming model, because the feasible region is convex. The convexity assures that a local optimal solution is also the global optimal solution. This greatly facilitates the optimization process, since the feasible region for a nonlinear model is not necessarily convex.

The earliest QP model in the capital budgeting area is attributed to Farrar,[25] who in 1962 extended the work of Markowitz (who used QP in portfolio selection) and Weingartner (who did pioneering work in the capital budgeting area) by reflecting both the project's expected net present value (NPV) and the variance of the NPV's in the objective function. The general QP formulation recommended by Farrar is as follows:

$$\text{maximize } Z = \sum_{j=1}^{N} X_j U_j - A \sum_{i=1}^{N} \sum_{j=1}^{N} X_i X_j \sigma_{ij}$$

subject to

$$\sum_{j=1}^{N} X_j = 1$$

$$X_j \geq 0$$

where X_j = proportion of the total budget invested in project j
U_j = expected NPV of project j
A = stockholders' average coefficient of risk aversion
σ_{ij} = covariance between the NPV of project i and project j —when $i = j$, this is the variance of project j

Note that the objective function seeks to maximize shareholders' expected utility, since it reflects both the mean and variance of all possible portfolios of projects plus the average coefficient of risk aversion. Thus, the trade-offs between risk and return are incorporated, as are the interactions between all possible pairs of investments projects.

One problem with this formulation was that the decision variables are continuous (i.e., $X_j \geq 0$) and that the decision variables are stated in the portfolio convention of percent of the budget availability (in a single period) to be invested in each project. To overcome these difficulties it was necessary to arrive

[25] D. F. Farrar, *The Investment Decision Under Uncertainty* (Englewood Cliffs, N.J.: Prentice-Hall, Inc., 1962).

at an integer quadratic programming algorithm that could efficiently handle realistic-size problems. Such a development was forthcoming when Mao and Wallingford[26] extended a previous integer LP branch-and-bound algorithm developed by Lawler and Bell.[27] They reported promising computational results showing that problems with 15 projects and 15 constraints were solved in less than 1 second of computer time. Of course, the variance-covariance matrix grows exponentially with the number of projects under evaluation.

The most recent quadratic programming capital budgeting model was developed by Thompson in a capital asset pricing context.[28] He formulated a single-period model which handles competitive and complementary projects where the market value is determined by the capital asset pricing model. However, he concluded his article with a word of caution:[29]

> The programming approach has been shown to deal effectively with multiperiod problems. Its credentials are strong. The capital asset pricing model, however, deals with a single period. Developing a multiperiod approach to capital budgeting using a multiperiod capital asset pricing model appears more formidable.

This concludes the discussion of QP, which provides the decision-maker with assistance in capturing the covariance between projects and between projects and the ongoing operations of the firm.

SUMMARY

This chapter presents an overview of sophisticated approaches for handling conditions of risk in a multiperiod setting. The first approach introduced is that of Monte Carlo simulation—a powerful and flexible approach to handling the capital budgeting problem. Next, the mathematical programming models under risk of stochastic LP, chance-constrained programming, and quadratic programming are surveyed and illustrated. These techniques provide valuable assistance to financial managers as they wrestle with capital budgeting problems under conditions of risk.

QUESTIONS/PROBLEMS

1. Discuss the strengths and weaknesses of Monte Carlo simulation in decision making under conditions of risk.
2. Discuss the major components of a Monte Carlo simulation model and illustrate these in the capital budgeting problem setting.

[26] J. C. T. Mao and B. A. Wallingford, "An Extension of Lawler and Bell's Method of Discrete Optimization," *Management Science* (October 1968), pp. 51–61.
[27] E. E. Lawler and M. D. Bell, "A Method for Solving Discrete Optimization Problems," *Operations Research* (November–December 1966), pp. 1098–1112.
[28] H. E. Thompson, "Mathematical Programming, The Capital Asset Pricing Model, and Capital Budgeting of Interrelated Projects," *The Journal of Finance*, 31, no. 1 (March 1976), 125–131.
[29] Ibid., p. 130.

3. Discuss the strengths and weaknesses of stochastic LP, chance-constrained programming, and quadratic programming for handling the capital budgeting problem under conditions of risk.

4. For the Monte Carlo Company shown in Example 2:
   (a) Using the probability distributions shown in Example 2 and assuming independence in the cash flows over time, compute the expected NPV and the standard deviation for this distribution over the life of the project.
   (b) Assuming normality, compute the probability that the NPV will be positive as well as the probability that it will exceed $10,000.
   (c) Perform 10 simulation runs for the project shown in Example 2 and compute the mean NPV and the standard deviation of this distribution.
   (d) Assuming normality, compute the probability that the NPV will be positive as well as the probability that it will exceed $10,000, based on the results of your 10 simulation runs in part (c). Compare these results with those obtained in part (b) and comment on any differences (i.e., Why do the differences arise? Which probabilities are more reliable? etc.).

5. The Wee Producem Company is deciding whether to introduce a new product on the market. At the present time they have two decisions to make: the overall decision of whether to introduce the product with additional production costs of $15,000,000 versus dropping the project and simply suffer the loss of the $2,500,000 already invested, or to do further market research at a cost of $1,500,000 and then make the introduction decision (with the same costs as above). Wee Producem estimates that the market research group will assign a probability of 0.7 that the product will be introduced. Because of the unusual nature of the product, only two final outcomes are possible: outcome A derives $40,000,000 profit while outcome B derives a $5,000,000 loss. The present estimated likelihood of outcome A is 0.6 and 0.4 for outcome B.

   Determine the optimal strategy by using a decision tree to compare the expected returns of the different possible strategies.

LEASE ANALYSIS: THE LESSEE'S PERSPECTIVE

Leasing is a process whereby the owner of a particular asset (lessor) enters into an agreement (lease) with the user (lessee) so that the latter can use the asset for a specified period of time. The lessee pays a certain amount (lease payment) to the lessor for the use of the asset.

Real estate still constitutes the largest single category of leased items, but numerous types of equipment, such as airplanes, railroad cars, ships, specialized equipment for farming, textile and oil industries, and computers, are being leased. Almost without exception, any type of equipment that a business can purchase, it can also lease. Within the consumer sector, leasing of durable goods, such as automobiles, washers, dryers, refrigerators, televisions, furniture, and the like, has also been increasing rapidly. The leasing industry is experiencing a dynamic growth period and is becoming increasingly important as a means of financing for business, consumers, and to some extent, government operations.

ADVANTAGES OF LEASING

From the viewpoint of the lessee, there may be many advantages to leasing versus purchasing. Naturally, a primary consideration is cost. The cost of a lease may be more or less than the cost to purchase and may differ among lessees. For example, if a firm has been running at a very low profit, it might not be able to enjoy the tax benefits of investment tax credit and accelerated depreciation which are associated with the purchase of some assets. A lessor could, however, take full advantage of the tax benefits and pass them along to the lessee by means of reduced lease payments.

Aside from the financial question, many other considerations become important in deciding whether to lease or purchase. The general advantages, inherent to all leases, are described below.

1. Leases provide an alternative source of obtaining facilities and equipment for firms that have limited capital budgets. In fact, capital projects can be analyzed on the basis of ownership or leasing and the respective NPV or IRR calculated for each alternative. Such a listing would provide wide visibility with respect to alternative capital acquisition plans. Some may be purchased and others leased, with the goal of selecting the most-profitable combination.

2. Frequently, equipment may be leased over a longer period than would be available through conventional financing. Usually, equipment loans run for a period that is substantially shorter than the economic life of the asset, whereas leases can be obtained for nearly the total length of the asset's life. This spreads the cost over a longer time period.

3. Leases are normally quoted at fixed rates or may be tailored to meet the cash budgets of the lessee. This avoids the risks associated with short- or intermediate-term financing and refinancing. Recall that many intermediate-term loans have balloon repayment features, in which the bulk of the principal is due at the end of the loan and, if the firm maintains its credit rating, forms the basis for a new loan. Such refinancing exposes the firm to added risk, as interest rates may change.

4. Leasing may conserve existing sources of credit for other uses and usually does not restrict a firm's borrowing capacity. Many loan indentures do restrict additional borrowing. Further, some firms which cannot raise the needed capital to purchase an asset due to marginal credit standings may be able to lease.

5. Leasing generally provides 100% financing, since a down payment is not required.

6. Leasing is quick and flexible as opposed to raising funds and making capital expenditures. The restrictive covenants usually found in loan indenture agreements are generally not included in lease agreements. Further, lease terms and options can be tailored to the specific need of the lessee. For example, lease payment schedules may be arranged to meet the seasonal cash flows of the lessee.

7. The total acquisition cost, including sales taxes, delivery and installation charges, and so on, may all be included in the lease payments. These front-end costs may be substantial and thereby result in heavy initial cash outflows if assets are purchased. This can be avoided through leasing.

8. Leasing can assist the process of cash budgeting by permitting accurate prediction of cash needs. This would be a desirable feature over short-term loans but less so over bond financing, which is long-term.

9. The entire lease payment is tax-deductible to the lessee. If land is involved in the lease, this is especially important, because land may not be depreciated.

10. Leasing avoids the costs of underwriting and floating new issues of stocks and bonds. Also, the public disclosure surrounding such offerings is avoided when a firm does not have to go to the capital markets to secure funds.

11. Leasing may avoid the risk of obsolescence. In fields that are changing rapidly, such as computer technology, ownership may be a distinct disadvantage when new products are introduced. But, risk avoidance has a price, which will be factored into the cost of the lease by the lessor.

LEASE VERSUS PURCHASE: SOME KEY VARIABLES

The preceding discussion on the merits of leasing versus ownership must culminate in the analysis of a specific decision to lease or buy. The criterion for this decision is the same as that for all capital budgeting proposals: namely, choose the alternative that maximizes the present worth of the enterprise. As in so many other instances, however, each business firm will have its own method of applying basic principles of financial analysis. Yet there are variables common to all leasing situations, and these must be identified and measured whatever the particular framework of analysis. The key variables in lease analysis, the focus of any lease negotiation, include the following:

1. Depreciation: The tax effects of depreciation represent an advantage of ownership that is lost under leasing. Since lease analysis is carried through on a cash-flow basis, depreciation represents a tax savings, and accelerated depreciation, all things equal, tends to swing the decision in the direction of ownership by increasing cash flows in the early years. The terminology of accelerated depreciation has been changed by the Economic Recovery Act of 1981 to Accelerated Cost Recovery System (ACRS) as described in Chapter 10.

2. Obsolescence: High rates of obsolescence (for instance, in computers and calculating equipment) increase the risks of ownership. This tends to make leasing a more attractive alternative.

3. Operating and maintenance charges: These represent an expense of ownership, although the gross charge is reduced by tax shields. If the lessor assumes these expenses as part of the lease agreement, the situation may make leasing a more-attractive alternative and may reduce the overall cost of acquiring the use of the asset. This will occur if the lessor can more cheaply maintain and/or operate the asset by reason of the economies of scale.

4. Salvage or residual values: After allowance for tax effects, residual values are an advantage of ownership lost under leasing. But salvage value is a highly uncertain value. High salvage values lower the costs of ownership. The problem is to forecast salvage within a reasonable range 5 or 10 years in the future. This is not an easy assignment. On the side of the lessor, salvage value reduces the cost of leasing. Under the pressure of negotiation, the lessor may transfer some of his or her uncertainties to the future; that is, the lessor might hopefully anticipate a higher residual to keep the lease payments down and win the contract. In fact, many leases depend on a significantly higher actual residual asset value than the amount established for purposes of depreciation to make their profit.

5. Discount rate: This is perhaps one of the most controversial features in lease evaluation. It can swing the decision one way or the other. Leasing analysis uses cash flows, and these extend over several fiscal periods. The cash flows, therefore, have to be discounted for the time value of money and for risk. But the risk associated with each of the cash flows of ownership may differ significantly. There are differing degrees of risk associated with sales, operating expenses, interest charges, and residuals. By contrast, once agreed upon, lease payments are usually fixed and certain. We would, therefore, not use the same discount rate on each cash flow. How, for example, should we discount the after-tax operating costs or the tax savings of depreciation? We discuss this problem later in the chapter.

   6. *Length of lease*: The length of time for which the lessee is committed to the lease payments and the extent of the penalties for premature cancellation greatly affect the flexibility of the firm and the risk associated with the acceptance of the lease.

   7. *Timing of lease payments*: Since the analysis uses a discounted-cash-flow approach, the timing of the lease payments (payable annually, semiannually, quarterly, or monthly) may, in a close situation, affect the decision. Similarly, the timing of lease payments, whether they are payable in advance or at the end of a designated period, must be considered.

   8. *Tax effects*: In Chapters 10 and 11 we discuss the implications of taxation on the cash flows derived from capital investments. With respect to leasing, it is important to note that lease payments are fully tax deductible by the lessee, while the lessor enjoys the advantages of depreciation. Any investment tax credits may be taken by the lessor or be passed on to the lessee. Naturally, the size of the lease payments will reflect who takes these credits. But another factor must be considered. Can a lessee fully utilize investment tax credits, accelerated depreciation, and finance charges? That is, does the firm have sufficient levels of income to make the deductions worthwhile? For example, in recent years capital-intensive industries, such as railroads, airlines, maritime shipping, steel, aluminum, and public utilities, already deferred a large portion of their taxes and stood to lose permanently the tax benefits of investment and accelerated depreciation on new projects. In like manner, oil and mining companies frequently resorted to leasing simply because depletion allowances held their effective tax rates below those of the lessor, the difference being used to reduce the lessee's net cost.

   There are two caveats to the preceding enumeration of key variables in leasing. First, the variables express the dollar benefits and costs of leasing, while ignoring the convenience factor of the arrangement. Because lease analysis is frequently a "sharp-pencil" calculation, convenience could swing the decision in favor of leasing. Second, the key variables isolated above do not constitute a definitive list of the significant clauses typifying most leases. For example, the lease may require a pledge of collateral and contain express or implied warranties, restrictions on the use of the equipment, and/or provisions relating to such factors as redelivery, default, bankruptcy, damages, and insurance. These clauses, largely contingent, can have monetary implications as circumstances change. The lessee may find it advisable, therefore, to allow for other variables in his or her financial analysis as judgment dictates.

   The question of leasing versus ownership represents a long-run financial planning decision and must be considered together with both capital budgeting and financial structure decisions. In some cases the asset to be leased or purchased will represent a mandatory investment; the project must be accepted, and the only decision is whether to acquire the asset by purchase or by lease. In such cases, lease analysis is essentially a financing decision, and we attempt to evaluate the lease against alternative ways of financing the asset. In other cases the lease arrangement itself is important in deciding whether to accept or reject a capital project. For example, some capital projects may only be available by lease; in other cases, it may not be sound financially to buy an asset, but leasing the same asset may be quite attractive. In this situation, lease proposals are incorporated in the capital budget as discrete projects, and the evaluation process should permit management to properly rank all proposed capital expenditures (including lease projects) in order of desirability.

LEASE VERSUS PURCHASE AS A FINANCING DECISION

The lessee desires to maximize present value. In our initial analysis, we make three assumptions relative to the lessee:

1. The project being considered is either mandatory or the decision has been made to acquire the asset, so all that remains is the question of how to finance the project. The lessee needs to know which method of financing (lease or purchase) is least costly.

2. Since leasing is a form of financing comparable to indebtedness, the asset if purchased will be financed by a bank loan. The underlying reasoning states that the borrowing capacity and cost of capital to a firm will be affected in about the same way by lease or debt financing.

3. The cash flows attributable to the project (except for residual value) will be discounted at the firm's after-tax cost of debt. This assumption will be discussed in greater detail later.

For the lessee, the financial analysis of lease versus purchase is quite simple: determine the yearly cost of each, discount to present value, and make the selection based on minimizing the present value of the cash outflows. But a word of caution is necessary. We have assumed the project is mandatory and must be included as an acquisition, whether it be purchased or leased. The decision we are presently examining is therefore one of financing rather than of capital expenditure. Thus, we ignore cash inflows from operations and rather seek to minimize the present value of the outflows over the project's life. The methodology for comparison is demonstrated in Example 1.

□ *EXAMPLE 1* *Lease Versus Purchase (Financing Decision)*
Assume a machine may be purchased by a lessee for $60,000, financed through a 12% bank loan, and depreciated using ACRS rates over its 3-year economic life. The loan would be paid back in *three* annual installments. The firm's cost of capital is 18%, a 20% rate is used to discount the residual value, and the marginal tax rate is 48% (federal and state). If leased, the rental would be $21,510 (if paid in advance) or $28,000 (if paid at the end of each period). At the end of its economic life, the asset has a residual value of

$2,000, and the tax rate applied to the residual is also 48%. Determine the NPV's of the three alternatives: lease with start-of-year payments, lease with end-of-year payments, and purchase, assuming that operating costs are the same whether the machine is leased or purchased.

Solution: First, consider the lease with start-of-year payments. The NPV is found as shown, using a 6.24% discount rate and a 48% tax rate. The 6.24% represents the after-tax interest cost of debt $[0.12(1 - 0.48)]$.

$$NPV = \$21,510(1 - 0.48) + \$21,510(1 - 0.48)(1.827303)$$
$$= 11,185 + \$20,439$$
$$= \$31,624$$

Next, consider the lease with end-of-year payments using the same 6.24% discount rate.

$$NPV = \$28,000(1 - 0.48)(2.661325)$$
$$= \$38,749$$

Last, consider the purchase. Based on a depreciable value of $60,000 the annual depreciation is as follows:

(1) *Period*	*(2)* *Cost of Asset*	*(3)* *ACRS Rates*[a]	*(4)* *Cost of Recovery* *(2) × (3)*
1	$60,000	.25	$15,000
2	60,000	.38	22,800
3	60,000	.37	22,200
Total		1.00	$60,000

[a]See Chapter 10, Table 10–1.

The loan schedule is the amount needed to amortize the $60,000 over a 3-year period at 12% (Appendix C, column 6):

$$\text{loan repayment} = \$60,000(0.416348)$$
$$= \$24,981$$

The loan schedule appears in tabular form as follows:

Period	*Repayment*	*Interest*	*Principal*	*Balance*
1	$24,981	$ 7,200	$17,781	$42,219
2	24,981	5,066	19,915	22,304
3	24,981	2,676	22,305	0
Total		$14,942	$60,000	

The loan interest payments and depreciation represent tax-deductible expenses (as would operating costs, which are not considered in this example). The yearly cash outflows are determined in tabular form as follows:

Period	*(1)* *Principal Payment*	*(2)* *Interest*	*(3)* *Cost Recovery*	*(4)* *Tax Shield* *(2) + (3) × 0.48*
1	$17,781	$7,200	$15,000	$10,656
2	19,915	5,066	22,800	13,376
3	22,305	2,676	22,200	11,940

(5) Cash Outflow (1) + (2) − (4)	(6) Discount Factor, 6.24%	(7) Present Value (5) × (6)
$14,325	0.941280	$13,484
11,605	0.886022	10,282
13,041	0.834022	10,876
		NPV = $34,642

The present value of the outflow is $34,642; the PV of the salvage is $602 [$2000(1 − 0.48) × 0.578704], so the PV of the net cash outflow is $34,040 if the machine is purchased. In this case, purchasing is superior to a lease contract calling for end of year payments but less appealing than the lease contract with start-of-year payments.   □

The discount rate used in lease versus purchase analysis is a very controversial issue. How do we justify the use of the after-tax cost of debt capital as the appropriate discount rate? The choice depends upon the assessment of risk. The following considerations weigh heavily in our choice:

1. In this particular problem, the capital budgeting question has already been decided. The project is required. The expenditure is nondiscretionary. As such, the question is one of financing.

2. If the firm as a whole reasonably expects to generate sufficient taxable income from its overall operations to use all tax deductions, tax shields are to be discounted at a low rate, since they are virtually risk-free.

3. The lease would enable management to avoid uncertain (risky) operating expenses; these amounts should also be discounted at a lower rate. In fact, the idea that a lease enables a firm to avoid risk leads some authorities to suggest a discount rate even lower than the risk-free rate, but, as a practical matter, debt cost is a reasonable approximation.

4. Some lease arrangements include lease payments that are contingent on future performance or other events; other leases are readily cancelable at the option of one or the other party. These types of situations also impact the choice of a discount rate. For example, a cancelable lease may actually be less burdensome than debt, since the face amount may be an upper limit with the lessee able, if necessary, to cancel and avoid losses. Here, the after-tax cost of debt might be too high a rate of discount.

5. The salvage value proceeds are generally a very uncertain amount, and if so, we logically discount them at a higher rate than the firm's average cost of capital. The rate reflects the firm's judgment about the estimate of the amount that can probably be recovered from the asset.

In Example 1, we ignore potential differences in operating costs with leasing versus purchasing. Frequently, because of economies of scale, such operating costs may differ, depending on whether an asset is leased or purchased. If differences do exist, they must be considered as a part of the decision process. The methodology is shown in Example 2.

□ **EXAMPLE 2** *Lease Versus Purchase (Financing Decision)*

Assume the same conditions as Example 1, except assume there is a $1,000 yearly operating cost associated with ownership, but not with leasing. Consider lease payments made at the start and at the end of each year and determine the advantage of lease versus purchasing.

Solution: The solution is shown in tabular form below. Note that the figures used in column (10) for Case I (after-tax lease cost) are found by multiplying the lease payment of $21,510 by 1 minus the marginal tax rate; similarly, the figures in column (8) for Case II result when $28,000 is multiplied by 1 minus the tax rate. Note also that when lease payments are made in advance, there is an advantage to leasing in this example, whereas if the payments are made at the end of the year, the advantage is in ownership.

Case 1: Lease Payment Made in Advance

Period	(1) Loan Payment	(2) Interest	(3) Principal	(4) Balance	(5) Cost Recovery	(6) Operating Cost
0	—	—	—	—	—	—
1	$24,981	$7,200	$17,781	$42,219	$15,000	$1,000
2	24,981	5,066	19,915	22,304	22,800	1,000
3	24,981	2,676	22,305	—	22,200	1,000

(7) Tax Deduction (2) + (5) + (6)	(8) Tax Shield 48% of (7)	(9) Net Ownership Cost (1) + (6) − (8)	(10) After-Tax Lease Cost
—	—	—	$11,185
$23,200	$11,136	$14,845	11,185
28,866	13,856	12,125	11,185
25,876	12,420	13,561	—

(11) Advantage to Ownership (10) − (9)	(12) Discount Factor ($K_d = 6.24\%$)	(13) PV to Own (11) × (12)
$11,185	—	$11,185
− 3,660	0.941280	− 3,445
− 940	0.886022	− 833
− 13,561	0.834022	− 11,310
2,000 salvage × (1 − 0.48)	0.578704 ($K_s = 20\%$)	602
	Advantage to leasing	− $3,801

Case II: Lease Payment Made at End of the Period

Period	(1) Loan Payment	(2) Interest	(3) Principal	(4) Balance	(5) Cost Recovery
1	$24,981	$7,200	$17,781	$42,219	$15,000
2	24,981	5,066	19,915	22,304	22,800
3	24,981	2,676	22,305	—	22,200

(6) Operating Costs	(7) Tax Deduction (2) + (5) + (6)	(8) Tax Shield 48% of (7)	(9) Net Ownership Cost (1) + (6) − (8)
$1,000	$23,200	$11,136	$14,845
1,000	28,866	13,856	12,125
1,000	25,876	12,420	13,561

(10) *After-Tax Lease Cost*	*(11)* *Advantage to Ownership* *(10) − (9)*	*(12)* *Discount Factor ($K_d = 6.24\%$)*
$14,560	− $285	0.941280
14,560	2,435	0.886022
14,560	999	0.834022
	2,000 salvage × (1 − 0.48)	0.578704 ($K_s = 20\%$)

	(13) *PV to Own* *(11) × (12)*
	− $268
	2,157
	833
	602
Advantage to ownership	$3,324

In Case I, since the NPV of ownership is negative, the leasing alternative represents the less costly method of financing, whereas in Case II, the reverse is true.　　□

The solution methodology demonstrated in Example 2 may be reduced to equation form by noting that the cost of the borrow-and-purchase alternative is the sum of the loan payments for each period plus operating expenses less interest, depreciation, and operating-expense tax shields, less the after-tax salvage value discounted to present value at a discount rate appropriate to the cash flows.[1] The cost of borrowing and purchasing is expressed in Equation (1):

$$\text{cost to purchase} = \sum_{t=1}^{N} \frac{P + O_t - (I_t + D_t + O_t)t_c}{(1 + K_d)^t} - \frac{S_N - (S_N - B)t_g}{(1 + K_s)^N} \quad (1)$$

where P = loan payment: interest and amortization of principal
　　L_t = lease payment in period t
　　I_t = interest payment in period t
　　D_t = cost recovery in period t
　　O_t = incremental operating costs of ownership in period t
　　t_c = firm's marginal tax rate on ordinary income
　　t_g = tax rate applicable to the disposal of assets (see Chapter 10, Examples
　　　　3 and 4)
　　S_N = expected cash value of asset in period N
　　B = book value of asset in period N
　　K_d = explicit after-tax cost of new debt capital
　　K_s = discount rate applied to residual value of the asset

Similarly, the cost to lease is the sum of the after-tax lease payments discounted

---

[1]The next section, including Equations (1) through (3), is based upon the article by R. W. Johnson and W. G. Lewellen, "Analysis of the Lease or Buy Decision," *Journal of Finance*, 27 (September 1972), 815–823.

by the after-tax cost of debt capital, as expressed in Equation (2):

$$\begin{array}{c} \text{cost to lease} \\ \text{with end-of-} \\ \text{period payments} \end{array} = \sum_{t=1}^{N} \frac{L_t(1 - t_c)}{(1 + K_d)^t} \tag{2}$$

If lease payments were made at the start of each period, we would sum from $t = 0$ to $t = N - 1$. This would have the effect of reducing the lease payment, as was demonstrated in Examples 1 and 2.

In many instances the question of lease versus purchase is not limited to a financial decision as was the case in this section. Rather, all alternatives must be examined to ascertain whether the project is acceptable based on its merits, and then the most advantageous method of securing it determined.

LEASE VERSUS PURCHASING AS A CAPITAL BUDGETING DECISION

In our discussion of lease versus purchase as a financing decision, we indicated that the capital budgeting decision had been made or the acquisition was mandatory and our concern lay in selecting the optimum mode for financing. Thus, we presumed conditions of certainty as to the financing and lease payment cash flows, and discounted them at the after-tax cost of debt. By contrast, *if the firm were considering the lease proposal as a distinct capital project to be ranked against all other projects, the cash flows would not be considered certain. Sales and operating costs change, tax rates and the like change frequently with business conditions, and sometimes lease payments also vary with business conditions. In this case, the financial manager would discount the separate cash flows of ownership or leasing at a rate appropriate to the level of risk.*

Moreover, it is axiomatic in capital budgeting that the return on investment be computed independently of the cost of financing. Yet in Example 1, interest charges were explicitly included in the ownership calculations. *The reason for including interest in the calculations was the need to find the difference in the after-tax cash flows between the leasing and borrowing alternatives. The project had already been accepted, and that decision was made independently of financing.* We had to look directly to those cash flows which would affect the financing decision. By contrast, in Example 2, we view the question of purchase or lease as two distinct, independent, and mutually exclusive projects. Further, it is not necessary to make any assumption of borrowing to meet the purchase price of the asset. These modifications change the structure of the calculations in three ways:

1. It is necessary to calculate the difference between net present value of ownership and the net present value of leasing as a basis for the decision.

2. The approach follows the general rule in capital budgeting of separating the return on a project from the cost of financing: specifically, we delete the interest charges from the costs of ownership in determining net present value.

3. Allowance is made for the uncertainties of the operating cash flows, tax shields, and residuals by discounting the first two by the firm's cost of capital and the latter by a rate appropriate to the risk level.[2]

---

[2]The cost of capital would be applied for projects having the same degree of risk as the firm overall. For projects of differing risk, adjustment would be made as indicated in Part IV.

The net present value anticipated from purchase of the asset, then, is the sum of the present value of the net after-tax operating profits (revenues less operating costs) plus the discounted after-tax cash proceeds from salvage less the cost of the asset. Similarly, the net present value of the leasing project would be the present value of the revenues less the lease payments and other costs, if any, associated with leasing. In comparing the net present values of the two alternatives, the revenues are assumed to be the same in both cases, which allows their deletion from the analysis.

In practice, two steps are required. We first determine whether the project is acceptable if purchased using the methodology outlined in Chapter 6. Then we compare the net present values of ownership versus leasing using Equation (3):

$$\Delta NPV = NPV(\text{purchase}) - NPV(\text{lease})$$

$$= \sum_{t=1}^{N} \frac{t_c(D_t) - O_t(1 - t_c)}{(1 + K)^t} + \frac{S_N - (S_N - B)t_g}{(1 + K_s)^N} \tag{3}$$

$$- C + \sum_{t=1}^{N} \frac{L_t(1 - t_c)}{(1 + K_d)^t}$$

where ΔNPV = difference between NPV (purchase) and NPV (lease)
   K = firm's marginal cost of capital

Excluding revenues from both NPV calculations, the net present value of ownership is the sum of depreciation tax shield, $t_c(D_t)$, less the after-tax operating costs, $O_t(1 - t_c)$, for each period discounted at the firm's cost of capital (K) plus the after-tax salvage, $S_N - (S_N - B)t_g$, discounted at some higher rate (K_s) less the cost of the equipment (C). The present value of leasing in the comparison (again excluding revenues) is the sum of after-tax rental for each period, $L_t(1 - t_c)$, discounted at the cost of debt capital (K_d). This amount is added to the present value of ownership, since it represents a negative NPV because the lease involves exclusively cash outflows. If ΔNPV is positive, purchasing is preferred, while if ΔNPV is negative, leasing is preferred.

The process of deciding between purchasing and leasing is demonstrated in Examples 3 and 4. In Example 3 we examine only the purchase, while in Example 4 we determine the difference in the purchase and lease costs using Equation (3) to determine which is preferable.

□ **EXAMPLE 3** *Purchase Decision*

A corporation may purchase or lease equipment costing $60,000 and having a salvage value of $2,000. If purchased, the cost of the equipment would be recovered using the ACRS rates over its 3-year life. If leased, the lease payment would be made at year's end and the cost would be $28,000. In either case, operating revenues would be increased by $30,000 per year and, if the equipment is purchased, operating costs would increase by $5,000 per year. The corporation's marginal tax rate is 48% (combined federal and state); its cost of capital, 20%; its after-tax cost of debt, 10%; and the risk-adjusted discount rate for salvage, 25%. The marginal tax rate also applies to the residual value. Assume, for sake of sake of simplicity, that the investment tax credit is not applicable. Determine the NPV of the purchase.

Solution: The changes in the corporations income statement and cash flows are tabulated:

Changes in Corporation's Income Statement

	Period 1	Period 2	Period 3
Revenues	$30,000	$30,000	$30,000
Operating expenses	− 5,000	− 5,000	− 5,000
Cost Recovery	− 15,000	− 22,800	− 22,200
Earnings before taxes	$10,000	$ 2,200	$ 2,800
Taxes at 48%	$ 4,800	1,056	1,344
Earnings after taxes	$ 5,200	$ 1,144	$ 1,456

Change in Corporation's Cash Flows

	Period 1	Period 2	Period 3
Cost Recovery	$15,000	$22,800	$22,200
Earnings after taxes	5,200	1,144	1,456
Cash flow	$20,200	$23,944	$23,656

The cash flows are shown discounted to present value below. The 20% rate is applied to the operating cash flows, while 25% is applied to salvage value.

Time	Amount	Discount Factor	Present Value
Present	− $60,000	1.000000	− $60,000
1	20,200	0.833333	16,833
2	23,944	0.694444	16,628
3	23,656	0.578704	13,690
3	Salvage 2,000 (1 − 0.48)	0.512000 (at 25%)	532
	•		NPV = − $12,317

Since the NPV of purchase is negative, the purchase is unacceptable. However, the lease may be acceptable. This determination is made using Equation (3). □

□ **EXAMPLE 4** *Lease Versus Purchase Comparison*

Using the information provided in Example 3, determine the ΔNPV of the lease and purchase employing Equation (3).

Solution: Employing Equation (3) in a sequential manner, we have the following:

$$\sum_{t=1}^{3} \frac{t_c(D_t) - O_t(1 - t_c)}{(1 + K)^t} = (\$7,200 - \$2,600)(0.833333)$$
$$+ (\$10,944 - \$2,600)(0.694444)$$
$$+ (\$10,656 - \$2,600)(0.578704)$$
$$= \$14,290$$

$$\frac{S_N(1 - t_g)}{(1 + K_S)^N} = \$2,000 \times (1 - 0.48) \times 0.512 = \$532$$

$$C = \$60,000$$

$$\sum_{t=1}^{3} \frac{L_t(1-t_c)}{(1+K_d)^t} = \$28{,}000(1-0.48)(0.909091) + 28{,}000(1-0.48)(0.826446)$$
$$+ 28{,}000(1-0.48)(0.751315)$$
$$= \$13{,}236 + \$12{,}033 + \$10{,}939$$
$$= \underline{\underline{\$36{,}208}}$$

$$\Delta NPV = \$14{,}290 + \$532 - \$60{,}000 + \$36{,}208$$
$$= -\$8{,}970$$

The negative Δ NPV means that leasing is preferable to purchase. □

The analysis illustrates the impact of choosing discount rates unique to the cash flows of ownership and leasing. A higher degree of risk surrounds the cash flows associated with ownership; therefore, these are discounted at the firm's cost of capital and at higher rates for salvage values. The lease cash flows, supported by contractual agreements, are discounted at the after-tax cost of debt capital.

In summary, if management has determined to acquire a project or if it is mandatory, the essential problem is to determine the lowest cost of financing. This problem was examined in the previous section. If, however, there is no presumption, the analysis looks at two mutually independent projects: one to purchase, the other to lease. Then, these projects are evaluated with all other projects being considered using the techniques detailed in Examples 3 and 4.

However, Equation (3) must be interpreted with care. It is possible that the asset acquisition may have a negative NPV whether purchased or leased. It may not be desirable to management on any grounds. Nonetheless, Equation (3) is valuable because it will always indicate the least undesirable alternative.

CALCULATING THE MAXIMUM LEASE PAYMENT

Before entering upon the negotiation of a lease, the prospective lessee should estimate the maximum lease payment he or she can economically afford, above which purchase becomes the more viable alternative. With this sum in mind, the key variables discussed earlier may be negotiated.

As a general rule, the maximum lease payment is that charge which has a present value equal to the present value of the ownership cost. Example 5 illustrates the specific analysis.

□ **EXAMPLE 5** *Calculation of Maximum Lease Payment*

Assume a lessee has the following data available for consideration:

Cost of the equipment (C)	$60,000
Salvage value (S)	$2,000
Asset cost recovery	ACRS rates
Operating costs of ownership (O)	$1,000

Assumed equivalent bank loan, $60,000 at 12% for 3 years, *before tax*

Equipment life	3 years
Cost of capital (K), *after tax*	10%
Discount factor applied to residual (K_s), *after tax*	20%
Marginal ordinary tax rate (t_c)	0.50 (combined federal and state)

Determine the pretax lease payments that will equate the present value of leasing and the present value of ownership.

Solution: The cost of ownership in each period is the loan payment plus the operating expenses *less* the tax shield provided by the interest, depreciation, and operating-expense tax deductions and in the final period *less* the after-tax residual value recovered.

Each period's net-ownership cost is then discounted at the firm's after-tax cost of debt and the residual is discounted at the given rate. The sum of these positive and negative flows is the *present value of the cost of ownership*.

	(1)	*(2)*	*(3)*	*(4)*
Period (t)	*Loan Payment (L)*	*Interest (I)*	*Cost Recovery (D)*	*Operating Cost (O)*
1	$24,981	$7,200	$15,000	$1,000
2	24,981	5,066	22,800	1,000
3	24,981	2,676	22,200	1,000

(5)	*(6)*	*(7)*	*(8)*
Tax Deduction	*Tax Shield*	*Net Ownership Cost*	*Discount Factor $[K_d(1 - t_c)]$*
(2) + (3) + (4)	*0.50 × (5)*	*(1) + (4) − (6)*	
$23,200	$11,600	$14,381	0.943396
28,866	14,433	11,548	0.889996
25,876	12,938	13,043	0.839619

(9)
Present Value of Ownership
(7) × (8)
$13,567
10,278
10,951
Total $34,796

Less:
Present value of
residual =
$2,000 × (1 − 0.50) × 0.578704   578
Present value of ownership $34,218

The after-tax lease payment of *each period* (R) is multiplied by the interest factor for the after-tax cost of debt (K_d). The sum of the products is a discounted divisor representing the equivalent present value of leasing. Dividing this figure into the present value of ownership gives the after-tax lease payment. Dividing this payment by one minus the marginal tax rate yields the pretax rental, which constitutes the leasing alternative with the same present value as ownership, or the *equivalent present value of leasing*. This is the maximum lease payment the lessee should be willing to pay. A higher lease payment makes ownership more attractive. As a corollary, the lessee should bargain for a lower rental.

Year	(1) *After-Tax Rental*	(2) *Discount Factor*	(3) *Present Value of Leasing* *(1) × (2)*
1	R	0.943396	0.943396R
2	R	0.889996	0.889996R
3	R	0.839619	0.839619R
			2.673011R

$$\text{present value of ownership} = \text{present value of leasing}$$
$$\$34{,}218 = 2.673011R$$
$$\$12{,}801 = R\,(\text{after-tax lease payment})$$
$$\text{pretax lease payment} = \frac{\text{after-tax lease payment}}{(1 - t_c)} = \frac{\$12{,}801}{(1 - 0.50)}$$
$$= \frac{\$12{,}801}{0.50}$$
$$= \$25{,}602$$

The lessee should attempt to negotiate down from the maximum lease payment of $25,602. □

SUMMARY

The use of leasing has grown extensively in recent years and for many firms it offers a viable alternative to purchasing. As such, it is necessary to examine leasing as an important part of the capital budgeting decision process.

In this chapter we examined the various advantages of leasing, types of leases, and legal aspects of leasing. Then we analyzed the lease-versus-purchase decision, first as a financing decision when the assets involved represented mandatory expenditures, and later as a capital budgeting decision involving discretionary expenditures.

QUESTIONS/PROBLEMS

1. The Mather Construction Company is considering purchasing or leasing a new crane whose purchase price is $75,000. The lease would run 10 years, the estimated life of the crane. If the company purchases the crane, they have projected its salvage value to be $7,500. Because of the high risk of the assigned salvage value, a 20% discount will be applied. The company's cost of borrowing is 12% and is in a 50% marginal tax bracket. The company uses ACRS rates.

If the company leases or buys, operating costs will be the same for the company.

The lease agreement offers two plans of 10 equal payments: (1) payment at the start of each year for $10,000 per year; (2) payment at the end of each year for $11,000 per year.

Determine the NPV's of the three alternatives: lease with start-of-the-year payments, lease with end-of-the-year payments, and purchase using 10 equal annual installments.

2. The Castaway Corporation makes disposable diapers in northeastern Pennsylvania and markets them locally. Recently, the market for Castaway Diapers has expanded so that they now need a fleet of 15 trucks for distribution purposes. The president is very traditional and believes in ownership of all equipment necessary to production and distribution; however, the finance department recommends an evaluation of leasing. Castaway will retain all drivers of the trucks regardless of the decision, and this will in no way affect the outcome of the decision.

   Castaway knows that if they purchase the trucks at $36,000 each, they can finance it through the First National Bank of Smalltown at 9% interest paid in five equal annual installments of the purchase price. They can depreciate the trucks using ACRS rates. The firm's cost of capital is 12%. Salvage on the trucks is calculated on the basis of low mileage in the neighborhood of 80,000 miles, which will be $9,000 at the end of 5 years. As Castaway is uncertain as to what the mileage will actually be, they will assign the salvage a slightly higher discount rate at 15%. Maintenance on the truck will be 5¢ per mile, with an additional $606 per year for licensing fees.

   Penske Leasing has offered Castaway an operating lease for the 15 trucks at $169,594.35 if paid in arrears for their 5-year life or $162,358.50 per year if paid in advance. The terms of the lease cover all services, including tires and towing charges and licensing.

   All calculations are made on the basis of a 52-week year and 80,000 miles on the total 15 trucks. Castaway is in the 48% tax bracket (combined federal and state).

   Determine which alternative would be the wisest choice. Show all work in tabular form. If leasing appears to be a viable alternative, explain why that is true.

3. The I-GOT-YA Company is considering purchasing a computer for $500,000. If they purchase the computer, a 14% loan must be taken out with the WE-GRAB-YOUR-MONEY Bank. Loan payments are required at the end of each year. I-GOT-YA Company uses ACRS rates for assets having a 5-year life. The computer is estimated to have a 5-year useful life with a salvage value of $20,000. I-GOT-YA anticipates some risk in the assigned salvage value, so a 20% discount factor is utilized in their lease vs. purchase analysis. Concurrently, the WE-LEASE-IT-ALL Company has offered to lease the same equipment to I-GOT-YA for 5 years, with the following terms and conditions:

   1. No maintenance expense required by I-GOT-YA.

   2. Annual rental of $117,523 if paid at the beginning of each year.

   3. Annual rental of $130,276 if paid at the end of each year.

   If I-GOT-YA purchases the computer, they must incur an additional $1,000 of maintenance expense in addition to depreciation. The marginal tax rate for I-GOT-YA is 48%.

   (a) Calculate I-GOT-YA Company's depreciation tables for years 1–5.

   (b) Set up a loan schedule for I-GOT-YA's $500,000 loan.

   (c) Determine the advantage/disadvantage of lease versus purchase considering rental payments at both the end and the beginning of each year.

4. Garrbadge Corporation is about to acquire a new piece of production equipment costing $100,000. The firm has the choice of borrowing the $100,000 at 10%, to be repaid in 10 annual installments of $16,273 each, or of leasing the machine for $16,500 per year, with payments at year-end. (Under the lease arrangement the firm is paying a 10% implicit interest rate; this is the rate the lessor is earning.) The machine will be used for 10 years, at the end of which time its estimated salvage value will be $10,000. If the firm leases the equipment, maintenance cost is included in the lease payment; but if it purchases the machine, it must spend an estimated $2,000 a year on

maintenance. (*Note*: The decision to acquire the production equipment was made previously as part of the capital budgeting process.) Determine whether the equipment should be leased or purchased if the effective income tax rate for the firm is 35%. The average after-tax cost of capital for Garrbadge Corporation is 10%, and the firm uses ACRS depreciation.

5. U.S. Motors is considering the acquisition of retooling equipment to regain its share of the market. Before entering upon lease negotiations, the vice president and treasurer wish to know the maximum rental U.S. Motors can afford to pay. The facts of the case are: cost of the equipment, $200,000; salvage, $6,667; operating cost of ownership, $10,000 per year; term of lease, 10 years; discount factor applied to salvage, 20% after tax; cost of new debt, 12% before tax; marginal tax rate, 48%. What is the maximum lease payment U.S. Motors will pay if rents are payable at the end of the period?

6. Assume a manufacturer has an order to produce 400,000 units on a certain type of equipment. The order represents the limit of his production capacity. The equipment can be produced on one or any combination of three machines which the firm can rent. The data on each machine is as follows:

	Machine A	Machine B	Machine C
Present value of contribution margin	$200,000	$195,000	$190,000
Production capacity	45,000	40,000	30,000
Annual rental cost	60,000	50,000	55,000
Annual maintenance	2,000	3,500	1,000
Labor requirements	3	4	1
Plant capacity	160	200	240

The firm has approximately $500,000 of working capital to cover annual rental charges. Thirty workers can be trained to operate the leased equipment. Annual maintenance costs are budgeted at $30,000. The available plant capacity is set at 2,000.

(a) Set up the objective function and constraints to obtain an LP solution indicating the number of units of one or a combination of machines to be leased.

(b) Run your program to determine optimal solution.

(c) Run a sensitivity analysis to determine the impact of lifting each constraint to the next highest total: for example, 400,000 units to 500,000 or 30 to 40.

(d) Using shadow prices, determine the needed increment in the contribution margin of the inferior lease agreements to make them attractive alternatives.

LEASE ANALYSIS: THE LESSOR'S PERSPECTIVE

Finance and accounting literature on leasing predominantly treats the position of the lessee. Professional journals mostly argue the merits of one particular financial model and the accounting presentation of leases in terms of the lessee's objectives. On the other hand, the lessor must address a more-complicated set of issues under a greater variety of circumstances. From the perspective of the lessor, the lease may be unleveraged or leveraged and/or offered by a lessor-dealer or lessor-manufacturer. The number of parties involved may range from two to seven. The methods of lease evaluation are similarly more diverse, although the same key variables (described in Chapter 23) form the substance of the analysis. Yet, whatever the nature of the lease transaction, the essential question for analysis remains constant: What lease payment should the lessor charge to accomplish the firm's objective of maximizing net present value?

UNLEVERED LEASES — THE LESSOR-VENDOR

Lessor-Dealer

The lessor-dealer acquires an asset with the intention of leasing it. Rent-a-car agencies come readily to mind. The lessor does not manufacture the asset, although the firm may maintain the asset in operating condition.

The lessor-dealer sets a minimum rental such that the present value of the after-tax rental cash inflows (R_t) equals or exceeds the cost of the asset (C) less the present value of the investment tax credit (PV_{ITC}) less the present value of the salvage (PV_S) less the present value of the depreciation tax shield (PV_{DT})

plus the present value of the after-tax operating expenses (PV$_O$) related to the lease. Consistent with capital budgeting conventions, cash flows are displayed on an after-tax basis.

The expression becomes:

$$C - \text{PV}_{\text{ITC}} - \text{PV}_{\text{S}} - \text{PV}_{\text{DT}} + \text{PV}_O = \sum_{t=1}^{N} \frac{R_t}{(1 + K_{\text{MC}})^t} \tag{1}$$

□ **EXAMPLE 1**   *Determining a Lease Payment— Lessor-Dealer*

A lessor of construction equipment is writing a lease contract based upon the following data:

Lease term (N)	8 years
Asset life	10 years
Asset cost (C)	$2,000,000
Residual value (S)	$400,000 (at the end of the lease)
Investment tax credit (ITC)	$200,000 (received at end of first period)
Lessor's marginal tax rate (t_c)	50% (combined federal and state)
Lessor's marginal cost of capital (K_{MC})	15% (after tax)
Discount rate on salvage (K_S)	20% (after tax)
Operating expense (O)	$2,000 (paid at end of each period)
Depreciation method:	Straight-line

What should the lease charge be in each case?
(a) It is paid at end of each period.
(b) It is paid at beginning of each period.

Solution: Based on Equation (1), we develop each of the necessary terms below. Present value of investment tax credit:

$$\text{PV}_{\text{ITC}} = \text{ITC} \times \frac{1}{(1 + K_{\text{MC}})^1} \tag{2}$$

$$= \$200,000 \times \frac{1}{(1 + 0.15)^1}$$

$$= \$200,000 \times 0.86957$$

$$= \$173,914$$

Present value of salvage or residual:[1]

$$\text{PV}_{\text{S}} = S \times \frac{1}{(1 + K_S)^N} \tag{3}$$

$$= \$400,000 \times \frac{1}{(1 + 0.20)^8}$$

$$= \$400,000 \times 0.23257$$

$$= \$93,028$$

---

[1] The economic life of the asset is 10 years. The term of the lease is 8 years. Depreciation is on a straight-line basis. Therefore, the residual value is $400,000 at the end of the eighth year, which represents the remaining depreciation of $200,000 per year over the 10-year life of the asset. At the end of the tenth year there is no residual value.

Present value of operating expenses after tax:

$$\text{PV}_\text{O} = O(1 - t_c) \times \sum_{t=1}^{N} \frac{1}{(1 + K_\text{MC})^t} \tag{4}$$

$$= \$2000(1 - 0.50) \times \sum_{t=1}^{8} \frac{1}{(1 + 0.15)^t}$$

$$= \$1000 \times 4.487322$$

$$= \underline{\$4,487}$$

Present Value of Depreciation Tax Savings:

The asset is depreciated on a straight-line basis over the 10-year life stipulated in the problem data. The problem assumes the book value of $400,000 is the same as the estimated market value at the end of the 8-year lease. Therefore, at the end of the tenth year, the asset has no book value and no salvage.

$$\text{annual depreciation} = \frac{\$2,000,000}{10} = \$200,000 \tag{5}$$

$$\text{PV}_\text{DT} = (Dt_c) \times \sum_{t=1}^{N} \frac{1}{(1 + K_\text{MC})^t}$$

$$= (\$200,000 \times 0.50) \times \sum_{t=1}^{8} \frac{1}{(1 + 0.15)^t}$$

$$= \$100,000 \times 4.487322$$

$$= \$448,732$$

Lease payment—if paid at the end of each period:

Referring to Equation (1),

$$C - \text{PV}_\text{ITC} - \text{PV}_\text{S} - \text{PV}_\text{DT} + \text{PV}_\text{O} = \sum_{t=1}^{N} \frac{R_t}{(1 + K_\text{MC})^t}$$

$$\$2,000,000 - \$173,914 - \$93,028 - \$448,732 + \$4,487 = R_t \times 4.487322$$

$$\$1,288,813 = 4.487322 R_t$$

$$\$287,212 = R_t$$

The $287,212 is an after-tax lease payment. This must now be converted to the pretax lease payment, which will be paid by the lessee:

$$\text{pretax lease payment} = \frac{R_t \, (\text{after-tax})}{(1 - t_c)} \tag{6}$$

$$\frac{\$287,212}{(1 - 0.50)} = \$574,424 \qquad \text{pretax rental}$$

Rent if paid at the beginning of each period:

We assume that all cash flows *except salvage and depreciation tax savings* are payable at the beginning of the period. Accordingly, Equation (1) is revised to allow for the new time sequence:

$$C - \text{ITC} - \text{PV}_\text{S} - \text{PV}_\text{DT} + \text{PV}_\text{O} = R_t \left[1.0 + \sum_{t=1}^{N-1} \frac{1}{(1 + K_\text{MC})^t} \right] \tag{7}$$

We revise the present value of operating expenses as follows:

$$PV_O = O(1 - t_c)\left[1.0 + \sum_{t=1}^{N-1} \frac{1}{(1 + K_{MC})^t}\right] \tag{8}$$

$$= \$2,000(1 - 0.50)\left[1.0 + \sum_{t=1}^{7} \frac{1}{(1 + 0.15)^t}\right]$$

$$= \$1,000[1.0 + 4.160420]$$

$$= \$1,000 \times 5.160420$$

$$= \$5160$$

Then we complete Equation (7) to obtain the after-tax lease payment:

$$\$2,000,000 - \$200,000 - \$93,028 - \$448,732 + \$5,160 = R_t\left[1.0 + \sum_{t=1}^{7} \frac{1}{(1 + 0.15)^t}\right]$$

$$\$1,263,400 = 1.0 + 4.160420R_t$$

$$\$1,263,400 = 5.160420R_t$$

$$\$244,825 = R_t$$

Finally, we convert to obtain the pretax lease payment:

$$\frac{R_t(\text{after-tax})}{(1 - t_c)} = \frac{\$244,825}{(1 - 0.50)} = \$489,650$$

In summary, the lessor-dealer would post a rental of \$574,424 if the cash flows were payable at the end of the period or \$489,650 if the cash flows, except as noted, were payable at the beginning of the period. □

UNLEVERED LEASES — THE LESSOR-MANUFACTURER

Lessor-Manufacturer

As a manufacturer of the product, the lessor has the option of selling or leasing the equipment. Boeing may sell or lease aircraft. IBM and Xerox offer similar options. The lessor-manufacturer, furthermore, may decide to emphasize one or the other of the available options. He or she might, for example, stress the sell option by lowering selling price, increasing trade allowances, or lowering the cost of full-service maintenance agreements. Alternately, the lessor-manufacturer might induce leasing by offering longer-term lease plans or lower lease payments. The decision to stress one or the other option depends upon the lessor-manufacturer's financial and tax position in relation to the state of the economy and the lessee trade. In any event, the lessor-manufacturer must determine the *minimum lease payment that would give him or her the same net present value as an outright sale.* Armed with this analysis, the company has the basis for a policy decision.

It is interesting to compare the lessor-manufacturer's posture with that of the lessor-dealer described earlier. The major differences emanate from the tax laws and include the following:

1. Depreciation tax shield: The lessor-manufacturer who elects to lease includes only the manufacturing cost in calculating the tax shield. The anticipated profit on sale of the asset does not form a part of his or her depreciable base. On the other hand, a dealer who purchases the equipment for subsequent lease capitalizes the manufacturer's profit included in the purchase price. The lessor-dealer's depreciable base consists of the purchase price plus work-up costs. The same holds for a conventional lessee making a decision to lease or purchase.

2. Investment tax credit: The investment tax credit equals 10% if the asset is held for 5 years. The lessor-manufacturer applies the rate only against the manufacturing cost. Conversely, any purchaser enjoys a higher investment tax credit because the rate is applied against the manufacturer's cost plus profit.

3. Gain or loss on sale of asset: If the equipment is sold above its book value before its economic life is terminated, the IRS regards the excess as ordinary income for tax purposes. Since the depreciable tax base differs between the lessor-manufacturer and the purchaser, the tax obligations of the two parties also differ.

Financial analysis of the lessor-manufacturer's decision proceeds through three steps:

1. Determine the net present value of outright sale. This is the selling price less the cost of producing the asset multiplied by one minus the firm's marginal income tax rate.

2. Determine the net present value of the cost of leasing. The NPV of the leasing cost will equal the negative outflow of the asset cost to the manufacturer plus the present value of the investment tax credit inflow plus the present value of the depreciation tax savings plus the present value of the after-tax salvage value inflow.

3. Determine the annual lease payment that will give the same net present value as selling the asset. The NPV of outright sales will equal the net present value of lease cost plus the net present value of the annual lease payments.

□ **EXAMPLE 2**   Determining a Lease Payment—Manufacturer-Lessor

Assume the following data for a manufacturer who has the option to sell or lease a product.

Selling price of asset (S)	$500,000
Manufacturer's cost (C)	200,000
Marginal tax rate (t_c)	0.50 (combined federal and state)
Cost of capital (K_{MC}), *after tax*	14%
Manufacturer's cost of new debt (K_d), *after tax*	6%
Investment tax credit (ITC) (payable at end of period 1)	0.10
Depreciation: ACRS	
Length of lease	8 years
ACRS write-off period	10 years

Determine the net present value of pretax lease rental that will have the same net present value as outright sale.

Solution: The *net present value* (*NPV*) *of an outright sale* equals the net selling price (*S*) less the cost of manufacturing the asset (*C*) times one minus the firm's marginal tax rate $(1 - t_c)$ and then discounted back one period under the assumption that all cash flows take place at the end of year 1.

$$\text{NPV} = \frac{(S - C)(1 - t_c)}{(1 + K_{\text{MC}})^1} \qquad (9)$$

$$= \frac{(\$500,000 - \$200,000)(1 - 0.50)}{(1 + 0.14)^1}$$

$$= \frac{\$150,000}{1.14}$$

$$= \$131,579$$

The *NPV of the leasing cost* equals the cost outflow of the asset to the manufacturer (*C*) plus the present value of the investment tax credit (PV_{ITC}) plus the present value of the depreciation tax savings (PV_{DT}) plus the present value of the after-tax salvage value (PV_{S}).[2]

$$\text{NPV of lease cost} = -C + \frac{\text{ITC}}{(1 + K_d)^1} + \sum_{t=1}^{N} \frac{D_t t_c}{(1 + K_d)^t} + \frac{(S - B)(1 - t_c)}{(1 + K_{\text{MC}})^N} \qquad (10)$$

Calculating the components, we have:

$$\text{ITC} = \$200,000 \times 0.10 = \$20,000$$

and, under the assumption that the benefits of the ITC will be received at the end of 1 year,

$$\text{PV}_{\text{ITC}} = \frac{\text{ITC}}{(1 + K_d)^1} = \frac{\$20,000}{(1 + 0.06)^1}$$

$$= \$18,868$$

and the cost recovery tax shield:

$$\text{PV}_{\text{DT}_{\text{MC}}} = \sum_{t=1}^{N} \frac{D_t t_c}{(1 + K_d)^t} \qquad (11)$$

Then, we have the following:

(1) Period	(2) Cost	(3) ACRS Percentage	(4) Cost Recovery	(5) Tax Deduction (4) × 0.50	
1	$200,000	0.09	$ 18,000	$ 9,000	
2	200,000	0.19	38,000	19,000	
3	200,000	0.16	32,000	16,000	
4	200,000	0.14	28,000	14,000	
5	200,000	0.12	24,000	12,000	
6	200,000	0.10	20,000	10,000	
7	200,000	0.08	16,000	8,000	
8	200,000	0.06	12,000	6,000	
9	200,000	0.04	8,000	4,000	end of
10	200,000	0.02	4,000	2,000	lease
			$200,000	$100,000	

[2] The after-tax cost of debt capital (K_d) is applied against the investment tax credit and depreciation tax savings due to the higher level of certainty surrounding these cash flows.

(6) Discount Factor	(7) PV of Tax Savings (5) × (6)	
0.943396	$ 8,491	
0.889996	16,910	
0.839619	13,434	
0.792094	11,089	
0.747258	8,968	
0.704961	7,050	
0.665057	5,320	
0.627412	3,764	(lease ends)
	$75,026	

NPV of lease cost = − $200,000 + $18,868 + $75,026
= − $106,106

Minimum lease payment with the same net present value of outright sale:

NPV of outright sale = NPV of lease cost + NPV of annual lease payments

If NPV of annual lease payments equals

$$R(1 - t_c) \sum_{t=1}^{N} \frac{1}{(1 + K_d)^t}$$

then,

$$\$131,579 = -\$106,106 + R(1 - 0.50)(6.209794)$$
$$\$131,579 = -\$106,106 + 3.1048974R$$
$$\$131,579 + \$106,106 = 3.104897R$$
$$\$76,552 = R \quad \text{(pre-tax rental)}$$

An annual lease payment of $76,552 on the proposed lease would yield the same NPV as an outright sale of the asset to the lessor-manufacturer. The lease payment represents an indifference point between the policy of leasing or selling. Armed with this insight, the manufacturer can work toward an optimal mix of sales and leases to achieve particular financial objectives. If the firm wishes to encourage leasing and charge a lease payment of $76,552, the manufacturer might increase the sales price of the asset. Should the manufacturer take the opposite tack, the firm might encourage sales by raising the rental above $76,552. □

BARGAINING AREA BETWEEN THE LESSOR AND LESSEE

In Chapter 23, we discussed the maximum lease payment the lessee should pay, above which ownership becomes the preferred alternative. In this chapter, we treat the minimum lease payment acceptable to the lessor. The two extremes define a bargaining area within which trade-offs can be negotiated on specific terms of the lease and/or the quality of the estimates of key variables tested. The lessee will bargain for a lease payment lower than the estimated maximum; the lessor, for a lease payment above the estimated minimum.

But what are the limits to bargaining on any specific variable, such as depreciation, operating expenses, or residual value? Consider Example 3.

□ **EXAMPLE 3** *Determination of Bargaining Area*

W. T. Poor Company has substantial operating-loss carry-overs and expects no income tax liability for the next 10 years. The capital budget committee recently approved the acquisition of certain equipment: cost $1,000,000, with an estimated 10-year life and no salvage value.

(a) What is the present value of the income tax benefits to a potential lessor, Lots-a-Lease Company, having a 20% cost of capital; a 48% tax rate (state and federal); ACRS write-off; and 10% investment tax credit.

(b) What is the annual lease payment equivalent of the present value of tax benefits calculated in part (a) (or what is the maximum amount of annual lease payment reduction to be expected as a result of the lessor utilizing the tax benefits)?

Solution: (a) Present value of tax benefits:

To W. T. Poor Company	$ 0	
To Lots-a-Lease Company	338,100	(Schedule A)
Difference	$338,100	
Annual lease equivalent (R)	$ 80,645	(Schedule B)

Schedule A
Present Value of Tax Benefits

Investment Credit		$100,000
Depreciation Tax Shield		
(as below)		238,100
Total		$338,100

(1)	(2)	(3) ACRS	(4) Cost	(5) Tax	(6) Discount	(7)
Year	Cost	Percentage	Recovery	Deduction (4×0.48)	Factor	Present Value $(5) \times (6)$
1	$1,000,000	0.09	$ 90,000	$ 43,200	0.833333	$ 36,000
2	1,000,000	0.19	190,000	91,200	0.694444	63,333
3	1,000,000	0.16	160,000	76,800	0.578704	44,444
4	1,000,000	0.14	140,000	67,200	0.482253	32,414
5	1,000,000	0.12	120,000	57,600	0.401878	23,148
6	1,000,000	0.10	100,000	48,000	0.334898	16,075
7	1,000,000	0.08	80,000	38,400	0.279082	10,717
8	1,000,000	0.06	60,000	28,800	0.232568	6,698
9	1,000,000	0.04	40,000	19,200	0.193807	3,721
10	1,000,000	0.02	20,000	9,600	0.161506	1,550
			$1,000,000	$480,000		$238,100

Schedule B
Annual Lease Equivalent (R)

$338,100 = R \times$ Discount Factor for 10 years at 20%
$338,100 = R \times 4.192472$
$\qquad R = $80,645$

Since W. T. Poor Company expects to have zero tax obligations, it would have a zero tax shield and no income tax against which the investment tax credit could be applied. Thus, they can in effect transfer these benefits to a profitable firm in exchange for lower leasing costs. The value of the tax shields to the lessee totals $338,100, or $80,645 annualized. The question for negotiation is how to split these benefits with W. T. Poor by reducing the lease cost to close the deal. However, the annual lease payment cannot be reduced by more than $80,645, for this would mean that Lots-a-Lease would concede all the benefits of ownership. Because Lots-a-Lease uses its cost of capital (20%) to evaluate projects, the lease package would have to yield 20% to be considered favorably as a capital budgeting project.   □

In sum, the lessee should probe the quality of the estimates attached to the variables that constitute the advantages of ownership: tax factors, the method of depreciation, salvage values, the rationale of the discount factor, and so on. Adjusting the estimates of key variables can result in a lower lease payment. Similarly, the lessor might trade a lower lease payment for a longer-term lease and reduced uncertainty.

Once agreement is reached on the viability of the estimates, the present value of the significant variables to the lessor can be determined. This raises the question of whether any portion of the present value can be transferred in the form of a lower rental. The limits of the transfer process are reached when the lease has a lower net present value than outright sale.

LEVERAGED LEASES

Leveraged leases are generally found in capital-intensive industries such as airlines, railroads, metallurgy, and maritime shipping. Such industries have a heavy investment per employee but enjoy large tax write-offs in investment credits and depreciation. On the other hand, to take advantage of tax deductions, one must first earn a commensurate taxable income. Herein lies the main spring of leveraged leasing.

Assume a capital-intensive firm that lacks suitable taxable income and seeks to expand its facilities. The firm will arrange with a manufacturer for equipment of a suitable design. After agreement on the equipment specifications, the asset is formally purchased (Figure 24–1) by an investor group (lessor)—commonly, commercial banks or insurance companies and their corporate affiliates. The investor-owners receive all the tax benefits associated with ownership and the residual values on termination of the lease. The investor-owners are in tax brackets where these deductions serve to reduce their effective tax rates. In brief, the company (now the lessee) has tax deductions, but not the offsetting income; the investor-owners (now the lessor) have the taxable income but lack the deductions to reduce their effective tax rates.

These tangible benefits to the lessor are further concentrated by leveraging the lease—splitting it into debt and equity portions. The lessor leverages equity by borrowing from 60% to 90% of the equipment cost from a long-term lender (generally an insurance company), who agrees to be repaid out of the lease payments over the period of the lease. The lender may be assigned the lease payments and given a lien on the equipment. Where this occurs, the lessor's credit is no longer involved because recourse can be taken only against the lessee directly. The interest rate on the term debt, therefore, reflects the credit standing of the lessee, not the lessor. Thus, leveraging permits the lessor(s) to advance only a fraction of the capital required to purchase the asset, while retaining the full

FIGURE 24–1   Participants in a Leveraged Lease Transaction

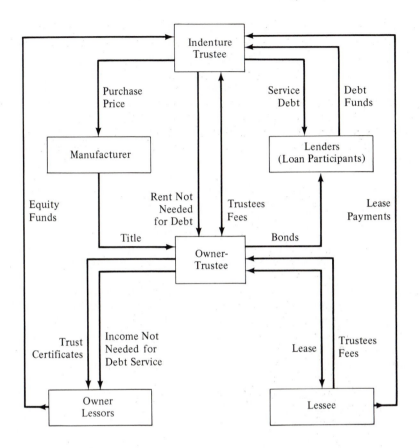

Definitions:

LESSEE (User)—The lessee selects the leased asset, makes the rental payments, and usually passes on the investment tax credit to the lessor.

LESSOR—There may be more than one lessor, depending on the size of the transaction. If there is more than one lessor, the lessors are sometimes referred to as equity holders, owner participants or owner trustees.

OWNER-TRUSTEE—Holds the title to the asset for the benefit of the lessors. He issues trust certificates to the lessors evidencing their beneficial interest as owners of the leased asset.

LENDERS—Lend the funds necessary to make up the full purchase price. (The Lessors must put up a minimum of 10% of the purchase price.) The loan is on a non-recourse basis to the lessor or owner trustee and is secured by a first lien on the equipment, by an assignment of the lease and an assignment of the lease rentals.

benefits of ownership. The investor group (lessor) looks for an investment in which its share of the lease payments plus the tax benefits yield a specified return on its fraction of the total investment.

Leveraged leasing allows a lessee-company to recapture some of its lost tax benefits through a lower effective cost of financing; that is, the lease payments will be significantly less than the normal debt service. Under the lease arrangement, the company (prospective lessee) passes on the tax benefits it cannot use to a lessor who can use them. The lessor, in this case, can use the tax deductions more effectively because its marginal tax rate is higher (has a higher tax shield) than the lessee company. In turn, the lessor reciprocates by conceding the company a lease payment rate below the interest rate on the company's long-term debt. The calculation assumes, however, that the lessee's effective tax rate will remain relatively low. If it should rise sharply, the company will miss the tax shelter it has conceded by foregoing ownership. The lease deal may turn sour when the deductions no longer have the desired impact on the effective tax rate. Just as the lessee's rising tax rate might reduce savings and make the lease uneconomical, the lessor's declining tax rate could eliminate its profit.

Leveraged leasing transactions, therefore, are oriented toward tax savings rather than convenience. For example, it was estimated in 1983 that a company could obtain the use of equipment under a tax-oriented lease for a rate 3 to 4 percentage points below its long-term borrowing rate. The lessee's cost in some instances was only 1% or 2%; occasionally, equipment was leased at a negative interest rate. Such magnanimous terms result from sharing the tax benefits. But uncertainties abound. An investment that may look attractive at one time may prove a poor choice with a change in tax rates, interest rates, or income level.

In evaluating the leveraged lease, we take the perspective of the lessor because the lessee's position remains as described in Chapter 23. There are several approaches to evaluating the leveraged lease. One of the most common —because of its compatibility with the criteria of accounting presentation—is the *multiple investment sinking fund method* (*MISF*). This can be illustrated in steps by a series of sequential problems.

□ EXAMPLE 4

Assume a lessor plans to acquire an asset costing $2,000,000 ($C$) and put it out to lease. The lessor plans to borrow 80% of the cost, he would incur $30,000 in legal fees (LE), and would have an investment tax credit of 10%. What is the lessor's investment (I)?

Solution:

Gross investment at risk (GI) (0.20 × $2,000,000)	$400,000
less	
Investment tax credit (0.10 × $2,000,000)	200,000
Net	$200,000
plus	
Legal expenses (LE)	30,000
Lessor's net investment at risk (I)	$230,000

Observe that the investment tax credit (ITC) is applied to the total cost of the asset (C), not to the investor's equity (I). But the lessor, while committing $430,000 of his or her own funds, receives the full $200,000 ITC. The cash flow of the lessor at this point is:

Cash Outflows:	
(GI)	$400,000
(LE)	30,000
Total	$430,000
Cash inflow (ITC)	200,000
Net cash outflow	$230,000

□

□ EXAMPLE 5

Assume the lessor plans a 10-year lease (N) and will depreciate the asset using ACRS, 5-year category. The lessor will amortize the nonrecourse loan (P) over the full term of the lease (N). The loan has a coupon rate of 12% (R).

(a) Determine the annual cost recovery.

(b) Determine the annual repayments on the nonrecourse loan by setting up an amortization schedule.

Solution: (a) Accelerated cost-recovery schedule:

(1) Period	*(2)* Cost	*(3)* ACRS Percentage	*(4)* Cost Recovery
1	$2,030,000	0.15	$ 304,500
2	2,030,000	0.22	446,600
3	2,030,000	0.21	426,300
4	2,030,000	0.21	426,300
5	2,030,000	0.21	426,300
		Total	$2,030,000

(b) The interest factor on 12% loan for 10 years is 5.650. Therefore, the annual repayment is $1,600,000 ÷ 5.650 = $283,186.

Loan Amortization Schedule

(1) Year	*(2)* Amortization	*(3)* Interest	*(4)* Principal *(2) − (3)*	*(5)* Balance *P − (4)*
0				$1,600,000
1	$283,186	$192,000	$ 91,186	1,508,814
2	283,186	181,058	102,128	1,406,686
3	283,186	168,802	114,384	1,292,302
4	283,186	155,076	128,110	1,164,192
5	283,186	139,703	143,483	1,020,709
6	283,186	122,485	160,701	860,008
7	283,186	103,201	179,985	680,023
8	283,186	81,603	201,583	478,440
9	283,186	57,413	225,773	252,667
10	283,186	30,320	252,866[a]	—

[a] Excess of $199 due to rounding.

□

□ EXAMPLE 6

Assume the lessor will charge an annual rental of $300,000 payable at the end of the year. The marginal tax rate (t_c) is 48%. Using the data from Example 5a and 5b, determine the lessor's taxable income and tax liability.

Solution:

(1) Year	(2) Rent	(3) Cost Recovery	(4) Interest	(5) Taxable Income (2) − [(3) + (4)]	(6) Tax Payment (5) × 0.48
1	$ 300,000	$ 304,500	$ 192,000	− $196,500	− $ 94,320
2	300,000	446,600	181,058	− 327,658	− 157,276
3	300,000	426,300	168,802	− 295,102	− 141,649
4	300,000	426,300	155,076	− 281,376	− 135,060
5	300,000	426,300	139,703	− 266,003	− 127,681
6	300,000	—	122,485	+ 177,515	+ 85,207
7	300,000	—	103,201	+ 196,799	+ 94,464
8	300,000	—	81,603	+ 218,397	+ 104,831
9	300,000	—	57,413	+ 242,587	+ 116,442
10	300,000	—	30,320	+ 269,680	+ 129,446
	$3,000,000	$2,030,000	$1,231,661	− $261,661	− $125,596

The lessor's interest concentrates on column (6). The negative values represent tax losses, which can be offset against taxable income from other sources. The lessor, *de facto* is "purchasing" a series of tax losses for an investment of $230,000. In this respect, under the Economic Recovery Act of 1981, the lessor must be a corporation. No longer may individuals per se act as lessors in a leveraged lease or sale and leaseback transaction.   □

□ EXAMPLE 7

Because the lessor is looking for tax deductions, the negative values are really positive inflows, i.e., tax reductions. The lessor's cash flow equals the tax payments saved plus the actual cash received (the excess of rentals over debt service). For year 1, the computation becomes:

	Rental	$300,000	
less	Debt service	283,186	
	Net	$ 16,814	(Changing sign from
plus	Tax savings	94,320	minus to plus)
	Total	$111,134	

Complete the conversion of the lessor's cash flows.

Solution:

(1) Period		(2) Cash Flows
0	Investment	− $400,000
0	Legal fees	− 30,000
1	ITC	+ 200,000
1		+ 111,134
2		+ 174,090
3		+ 158,463
4		+ 151,874
5		+ 144,495
6		− 68,393
7		− 77,650
8		− 88,017
9		− 99,628
10		− 112,632
	Total	+ $ 63,736

After conversion of signs, the lessor's cash flow is now a positive value.   □

☐ **EXAMPLE 8**

Assuming the cash flows from Example 7, a yield rate of 20% after tax during the years when the initial investment is being paid off, and a sinking fund earning rate of 4.5% after tax, complete the given schedule.

(1) Period	(2) Cash Flows	(3) Investment Balance	(4) Investment Repay (2) − (5)	(5) Investment Earnings (3) × 0.20	(6) Sinking Fund	(7) Sinking-Fund Earnings (6) × 0.045
0	− $430,000[a]	0	0	0	0	0
1	+ 311,134[a]	$430,000		$86,000		
2	+ 174,090					
3	+ 158,463					
4	+ 151,874					
5	+ 144,495					
6	− 68,393					
7	− 77,650					
8	− 88,017					
9	− 99,628					
10	− 112,632					
	+ $ 63,736					

[a] − $430,000 = I + LE = $400,000 + $30,000 (Period 0)
  + $311,134 = ITC + CF = $200,000 + $111,134 (Period 1)

Solution:

(1) Period	(2) Cash Flows	(3) Investment Balance	(4) Investment Repay (2) − (5)	(5) Investment Earnings (3) × 0.20	(6) Sinking Fund	(7) Sinking Fund Earnings (6) × 0.045
0	− $430,000	0	0	0	0	0
1	+ 311,134	$430,000	$225,134	$86,000	0	0
2	+ 174,090	204,866	133,117	40,973		
3	+ 158,463	71,749	71,749	14,350	$ 72,364	$ 3,256
4	+ 151,874	0	0	0	227,494	10,237
5	+ 144,495	0	0	0	382,226	17,200
6	− 68,393	0	0	0	331,033	14,896
7	− 77,650	0	0	0	268,279	12,073
8	− 88,017	0	0	0	192,334	8,655
9	− 99,628	0	0	0	101,361	4,561
10	− 112,632	0	0	0	≈ 0	
	+ $ 63,736					

To summarize:

1. The lessor has taxable income from other sources and needs tax deductions. Hence, tax losses of years 1 to 5 create cash inflows. If it were not for the savings of tax payments, the leveraged lease would have a negative net present value.

2. The yield under MISF is 20%, while the lessor has an investment outstanding through period 3. The yield rate is 20% after tax.

3. After the $430,000 investment is reduced to zero, the remaining cash flows accumulate as a sinking fund. The sinking fund earns interest at 4.5%.

4. When the cash flows turn negative, the sinking fund is drawn down to cover the taxes. The sinking fund is reduced to zero by the end of the lease term.

5. There is no change in the lessee's method of evaluation.   ☐

Two other methods of leverage lease evaluation fall into the traditional framework of net present value and the internal rate of return. We shall illustrate their application using the data from Example 8.

□ EXAMPLE 9

Take the cash flows from column 2, Example 8, and the lessor's equity investment, $430,000. Assuming the lessor has a cost of equity capital (K_e) equal to 20%, what is the NPV?

Solution:

(1) Period	(2) Cash Flow	(3) Discount Factor[a]	(4) Present Value (2) × (3)
1	+ $311,134	.833333	+ $259,278
2	+ 174,090	.694444	+ 120,896
3	+ 158,463	.578704	+ 91,703
4	+ 151,874	.482253	+ 73,242
5	+ 144,495	.401878	+ 58,069
6	− 68,393	.334898	− 22,905
7	− 77,650	.279082	− 21,670
8	− 88,017	.232568	− 20,470
9	− 99,628	.193807	− 19,309
10	− 112,632	.161506	− 18,191
		Total	+ $500,643

less	
Lessor's equity at risk (I)	430,000
Net present value	$ 70,643

[a] Discount Factors taken from Appendix C.

Observe that NPV would have been negative if cost of the asset (C) rather than the lessor's equity (I) had been used in the computation. This is typical of leveraged leasing. The lessor's risk investment is $430,000.

The present value of the tax savings under the lease exceeds the present value of the tax liabilities by $500,643. For these tax savings, the lessor has paid $430,000. □

□ EXAMPLE 10:

Using the data from Example 8, determine the internal rate of return.

Solution:

Internal Rate of Return on Equity Investment — 40%

(1) Period	(2) Cash Flow	(3) Discount Factor	(4) Present Value (2) × (3)
1	+ $311,134	0.714286	+ $222,239
2	+ 114,090	0.510204	+ 58,209
3	+ 158,463	0.364431	+ 57,749
4	+ 151,874	0.260308	+ 39,534
5	+ 144,495	0.185934	+ 26,867
6	− 68,393	0.132810	− 9,083
7	− 77,650	0.094865	− 7,366
8	− 88,017	0.067760	− 5,964
9	− 99,628	0.048400	− 4,822
10	− 112,632	0.034572	− 3,894
			+ $373,469

We use interpolation:

$$
0.20\begin{cases} 0.20 & 500,643 & +\$500,643 \\ ? & & +\ 430,000 \\ 0.40 & 373,469 & +\ 373,469 \end{cases} \quad \$70,643 \Big\}\$127,174
$$

Then,

$$
\frac{\$70,643}{\$127,174} \times 0.20 = 0.11
$$

and

$$
0.20 + 0.11 = 0.31 \text{ or } 31\% \text{ internal rate of return.} \qquad \square
$$

As we have observed, the magnitude of the internal rate of return is attributable to discounting the cash flows to equal the lessor equity investment, not the total cost of the asset. The departure from normal procedure is justified by the use of the nonrecourse loan to cover 80% of the asset cost. The lessor or lessors have only 20% of the asset cost at risk.

Finally, we note that the "purchase" of tax credits is perhaps more easily accomplished using the sale and leaseback arrangement under the provisions of the Economic Recovery Act of 1981. The ultimate effect of the Act on leverage leasing and leasing in general is too early to prognosticate.

LEASING AND THE COST OF CAPITAL

Recall that we have defined the cost of capital (K) as a weighted average of the incremental costs of each type of capital represented in the firm's capital structure; that is, a composite cost of the next dollar of debt, preferred stock, common stock, and retained earnings. In these chapters we note: (1) leasing is a *de facto* substitute for debt financing; (2) some financial-analysis models assume an equivalent loan equal to the purchase cost of the asset; (3) some financial models use the firm's incremental after-tax cost of debt to discount the cash flows of ownership and leasing in order to obtain the present-value cost of each alternative. The Financial Accounting Standards Board (FASB) has also recognized the essential nature of lease agreements as debt instruments:

> The *lessee* shall *record* a capital lease *as an asset* and *an obligation* equal to the present value at the beginning of the lease term of minimum lease payments during the lease term, *excluding* that portion of the payments representing executory costs such as insurance, maintenance, and taxes to be paid by the lessor, together with any profit thereon [emphasis added].[3]

Henceforth, capital leases will appear on the firm's balance sheet as an asset and liability in an amount equal to the present value of the adjusted lease payments. The capital lease is no longer a mere footnote to financial statements.

If the capital lease now gives rise to a recognizable asset and liability similar to the incurrence of debt, what is the cost of lease capital to be used in

---

[3]*Statement of Financial Accounting Standards No. 13, Accounting for Leases* (November 1976), p. 11.

calculating the firm's cost of capital? It cannot be the firm's incremental after-tax cost of debt capital, for this may be greater or less than the rate embedded in the lease. Neither can it be the firm's average cost of capital, for the latter is a weighted aggregate in which the cost of leased capital represents one component. Neither can the cost of leased capital represent that rate which equates the present value of the rental payments to equal the cost of the equipment; such a rate might incorporate other charges as well as an interest cost. In sum, the cost of leased capital *for a specific contract* need not be the same rate used in the preliminary financial analysis.

□ **EXAMPLE 11**   *Implicit Interest Cost*

Assume a lessee has the opportunity to enter upon a 5-year lease for a piece of equipment. The lessor will charge an annual rental of $8,000 and assume $1,000 in annual maintenance charges. What is the implicit interest rate in the proposed arrangement? The lessee's marginal tax rate is 40% and the purchase cost of the equipment is $25,000.

Solution: Assume the implicit rate will lie between 12% and 14%. Then:

	12%	14%
Before tax cash flows:		
Present value of lease payments		
$8,000 × 3.605 (12% for 5 years)	$28,840	
8,000 × 3.433 (14% for 5 years)		$27,464
less		
Present value of maintenance		
$1,000 × 3.605 (12% for 5 years)	3,605	
1,000 × 3.433 (14% for 5 years)		3,433
Present value of lease payments	$25,235	$24,031
less		
Purchase cost	25,000	25,000
Net present value	$ 235	−$ 969

Implicit interest before tax:

$$0.12 + \frac{\$235}{\$235 + \$969} \times 0.02 = 0.1239, \quad \text{or} \quad 12.39\%$$

Implicit interest rate after tax:

$$0.1239 \times (1 - 0.40) = 0.07434, \quad \text{or} \quad 7.434\%$$ □

The implicit interest as determined in Example 11 approximates the cost of leased capital. The closeness of the approximation depends upon the estimates of executory cost assumed by the lessor. By contrast, *the effective interest cost of the lease* (found by discounting the lessor's charges to equal the purchase cost of the asset) is:

$$\$25,000 = DF \times \$8,000$$
$$3.125 = DF$$

The discount factor of 3.125 equates to an effective interest cost greater than 18%. The 18%, on the other hand, covers executory costs included in the rental charges.

Thus, if the executory costs are assumed by the lessor, the cost of leased capital is the implicit interest rate as calculated in Example 11. If the executory costs are passed on to the lessee, the cost of leased capital is the *effective interest cost*, now the same as the implicit interest rate.

SUMMARY

This chapter concentrates on the position of the lessor. Two kinds of lessors are recognized: the lessor-dealer and the lessor-manufacturer. The differences in position arise from the vagaries of the income tax law. Leveraged leasing is an offspring of tax legislation. In fact, it is probably fair to say that, except where the lessor has economies of scale, leasing would not survive but for tax legislation. That is, except where the lessor has economies of scale, ownership is preferred over leasing. The intervention of tax legislation upsets the natural economic equilibrium.

QUESTIONS/PROBLEMS

1. A lessor may purchase equipment for $60,000. The equipment has a 3-year life (ACRS) and the lease will be for 3 years. The projected salvage value is $2,000. The lessor's after-tax marginal cost of capital is 10%, but the salvage will be discounted at 20%, owing to the higher rate of uncertainty connected to the estimate. Determine the annual lease payments, first assuming payments made at the start of each year and then at the end of each year. Assume a tax rate of 46%.

2. The Bunker brothers, who inherited their wealth from Big Daddy Bunker, have insufficient tax deductions to cover their taxable income. On the way to the ranch, the boys are pondering a leverage-lease proposition with the following terms: cost of asset, $1,000,000; nonrecourse debt, $800,000; equity, $200,000; legal fees, $15,000; investment tax credit, 10%; amortization of nonrecourse loan will cover 10 years with a nominal rate of 10%; rental, $130,000 payable at end of period; length of lease, 10 years; asset depreciated on an ACRS basis over 5 years. Evaluate the lease using each of the following, assuming a tax rate of 46%.

(a) A multiple-investment, sinking-fund method, assuming a yield rate of 20% and a sinking-fund earning rate of 5.5% after tax.

(b) Net present value.

(c) Internal rate of return.

3. Assume a lease proposal with the following terms: term lease (N), 8 years; asset life, 10 years; asset cost, $1,000,000; salvage value (S), $200,000 (estimated at end of lease); investment tax credit (ITC), $100,000 (received at end of first period); lessor's combined federal and state marginal tax rate (t_c), 50%; lessor's marginal cost of capital (K_{MC}), 15% (after tax); discount on salvage (K_S), 20% (after tax); operating expenses (O), $1,000 (paid at end of each period); cost recovery: ACRS.

What rental should be charged in each case?

(a) Rents paid at end of period, after tax and pretax.

(b) Rents paid at beginning of period, after tax and pretax.

4. NBM has the option of selling or leasing its new computer. The company's financial officer presents the following data: selling price of asset, $300,000; manufacturer's cost,

$150,000; marginal tax rate, 0.48; marginal cost of capital, 10%; investment tax credit payable at end of period 1, 0.10; depreciation on straight-line, no salvage anticipation, $18,750; lessor's cost of new debt, 5% after tax; length of lease and depreciable life of asset, 8 years. What is the pretax rental with the same NPV as outright sale?

5. The Grace Manufacturing Company can purchase new equipment for $50,000. Alternatively, the equipment can be leased for 10 years at $10,000. The lessor will pay $2,000 annual maintenance charges and assume insurance payments of $1,000. Grace has a marginal tax rate of 40%. What is the implicit interest rate, before and after tax, in the lease agreement?

Capital Budgeting for the Multinational Firm

The somewhat complicated evaluations of investment opportunities in national settings are rendered extremely complex in less familiar international environments. Capital budgeting theory does not change, but the application is bedeviled by varying institutional environments (differing governmental systems, tax laws, import and export regulations, etc.). In essence, capital budgeting in an international environment demands not only a grasp of theoretical concepts covered earlier in this text, but an intimate knowledge of local economic conditions and customs. Figure 25–1 gives an overall view of the unique variables attendant upon capital budgeting in an international setting.

In spite of the growing importance of the subject matter, the manifold number of variables and the uncertainty of their nature seems to deter model builders. This fact is unfortunate because the rapid growth in the number of multinational corporations and the difficulty of their decision settings necessitate sophisticated tools of analysis. Monte Carlo simulation, introduced in Chapter 22, is extended in Appendix 25A and has great potential for handling the complex multinational capital investment decisions. It can incorporate the interdependence of the large number of variables in the decision process and makes it possible to visualize the dynamics of business decisions in complex settings. Furthermore, the peculiarities of international risk can be efficiently introduced through simulation into the capital investment decision area.

CAPITAL BUDGETING PROCESS

The capital budgeting objective for the multinational corporation (MNC) is the same as for a domestic firm: to maximize the firm's value as expressed in terms of the market price of the common shares. Therefore, for any proposed

FIGURE 25–1   Multinational Capital Budgeting Environment

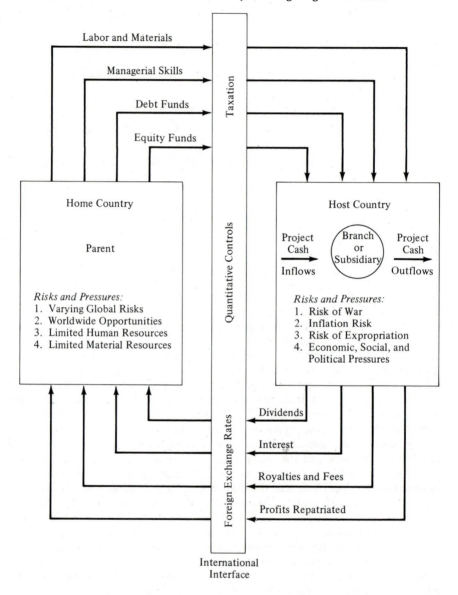

International
Interface

project to be attractive, firms insist that the discounted cash inflows exceed the discounted outflows where the discount rate reflects the risk associated with the project under evaluation.

The capital budgeting process for an MNC typically involves the following activities:

1. Identification of cash flows generated by the proposed project.
2. Identification of flows available for repatriation to the MNC.
3. Conversion of cash flows by means of exchange rates.
4. Adjustments to compensate for financial risks, including sensitivity analysis.
5. Selection of a minimum rate of return.
6. Calculation of investment profitability including sensitivity analysis.
7. Acceptance or rejection of the proposed investment.

Identification of Cash Flows Generated by the Project

The MNC first concentrates its analysis on the cash flows generated by the project. A budget statement is prepared which provides estimates for the project cash inflows and cash outflows over the designated evaluation period. Generally, an investment will be analyzed over a limited period of time (10 years is typical) rather than an attempt made to forecast flows indefinitely.

The initial *cash outflows* required by the project can be identified as the costs to acquire the land and fixed assets associated with the project. Attendant with all new investments are many other start-up costs that should be considered. Such costs include selling expenses, legal expenses, initial inventories, administrative and manufacturing staffing costs, and financing costs for debt and equity. For the most part these costs can be classified as the initial working capital and organizational costs.

Furthermore, the MNC must anticipate additional investments beyond its initial commitment. In reality, original investments are usually followed by a succession of further investments, some of which may be involuntary. If a project is started within a country which provides tariff protections for fledgling industries, it may be necessary to expand operations after tariffs are removed in order to compete with foreign markets. Moreover, some countries disallow total repatriation of cash flows, thereby making reinvestment mandatory. Finally, the new venture can be set up with a large debt structure, which will require the reinvestment of profits to provide greater "financial strength."

The cash flows represent typical operating revenues and expenses. First, the MNC develops a demand forecast from such factors as historical demands, alternative sources of products, general population growth, ease of entry into the industry by competitors, and the feasibility of serving nearby markets. From this forecast the sales projections over the project period are derived.

Second, the MNC forecasts its expected expenditures for operating the subsidiary and the fees or charges that it would expect to receive from the subsidiary. These forecasts can usually be obtained from the historical data of similar ventures. Such forecasting techniques as *percent of sales* or *simple linear regression* can be applied to the historical data to obtain reasonable estimates of the necessary expenditures.

Next, the MNC would review the tax structure of the host country. Analysis would include the income taxes, indirect taxes, and tax treaties enforced by local authorities. From these data, the estimated tax requirements can be projected.

The estimated sales, less the estimated expenses, will yield the after-tax profits from operations. These profits plus any depreciation write-offs will give the cash inflows from operations.

Identification of Cash Flows Available for Repatriation

The MNC would like to maximize the utility of the project cash throw-offs on a worldwide basis. The MNC may wish to reinvest the cash in other subsidiaries, pay dividends, pay debt obligations, or invest in new ventures. The profits from any project would have little value if the MNC could not use the cash throw-offs for these alternatives.

In essence, the MNC must determine which of the cash throw-offs it will be allowed to convert into other currencies for transfer elsewhere. The MNC must examine the existing laws pertaining to such subsidiary remittances as profits from operations, management and technical fees, royalties, loans, dividends. Moreover, a study of exchange controls in the past would be advisable to ascertain which remittances are more frequently restricted. Once the available cash flows for the MNC worldwide network have been identified, the budgeted statement for the parent may be prepared.

All anticipated remittances from the subsidiary will necessitate transactions in the foreign exchange markets. Thus, it is important that the cash flows be represented in the currencies of the two countries involved. This conversion will allow the MNC to visualize the effects of currency values and exchange rates.

Conversion of Cash Flows Using Exchange Rates

Two interrelated risks faced by the MNC are: (1) the risk associated with different rates of inflation in the host country of the subsidiary versus the home country of the parent company; and (2) the risk associated with unanticipated changes in foreign exchange rates over the life of the project under evaluation. As mentioned earlier, repatriated cash flows must be converted to the parent's currency using the foreign exchange market. However, it is also necessary to address the two risks just mentioned. Recent research by Dufey[1] and Shapiro[2] has indicated that the primary determinant of an MNC's exposure to these two risks is a function of whether the subsidiary is: (1) engaged in business whose nature is purely domestic, competing with imported goods, or by-and-large export-oriented; and/or (2) dependent for its inputs to the production process on nontraded domestic goods and services, traded inputs, or imported raw materi-

[1]Dufey, Gunter, "Corporate Finance and Exchange Rate Variations," *Financial Management* (Summer 1972), pp. 51–57.
[2]Shapiro, Alan C., "Exchange Rate Changes, Inflation and the Value of the Multinational Corporation," *Journal of Finance* (May 1975), pp. 485–502.

als. In addition to these factors, the MNC has the opportunity to hedge against inflation and foreign exchange risks.

The management of foreign-exchange risk is beyond our scope here; however the interested reader is referred to several recent, comprehensive works in this area.[3] Clearly, the impact of inflation and foreign-exchange risks impose new complexities on the capital budgeting decision process. However, the MNC should enter into a foreign direct-investment decision with its eyes open and with formal policies and strategies for coping with the additional risks. In addition, our recommended approach calls upon the use of sensitivity analysis in order to determine the variables that most critically impact the project under evaluation and the degree of variation necessary in order to jeopardize the project's viability.

Required Rates of Return and Adjustments for Risk

Before assigning a required rate of return to a particular project, it is necessary for an MNC to be certain that all risks peculiar to international activities have been defined and provided for in the total analysis. We have briefly discussed the international financial risks that might confront the MNC and have cited references for strategies to minimize losses. We also mentioned that analysis of foreign tax laws and repatriation policies would assist in the proper allocation of remittances for the purpose of making funds available to the worldwide network. However, all these strategies are operational in nature and do not assist in determining the profitability of a project when evaluating the decision to invest.

A highly recommended approach for risk adjustment suggests that an MNC perform a sensitivity analysis of the factors that would influence the profitability of a project. This implies an analysis of the risks, estimating their possible changes, and applying these changes to the elements of the prepared budget data. Not only will this method serve to incorporate the variable risks, it will educate responsible persons about the inherent risks and will facilitate anticipation of such risks during initial project evaluation.

Some of the possible sensitivity adjustments are as follows:

1. If inflation is expected in the near future, increased domestic prices could reduce domestic demands.

2. If devaluation is expected, increased foreign prices could increase domestic demands.

3. Expected inflation would increase the operating costs.

4. Expected inflation would increase asset replacement costs. If revaluation is allowed, increased depreciation write-offs would occur.

---

[3]See L. L. Jacque, "Management of Foreign Exchange Risk: A Review Article," *Journal of International Business Studies* (Spring/Summer 1981), pp. 81–101; David K. Eiteman and Arthur I. Stonehill, *Multinational Business Finance*, 2nd ed. (Reading, Mass: Addison-Wesley, Inc., 1979), Chapters 2, 3, and 4; Rita M. Rodriguez and E. Eugene Carter, *International Financial Management*, *2nd Edition* (Englewood Cliffs, N.J.: Prentice-Hall, Inc., 1979), Chapters 5–9; L. L. Jacque, *Management of Foreign Exchange Risk: Theory and Praxis* (Lexington, Mass: D. C. Heath, Inc., 1978).

5. The new subsidiary may cause undue contraction of sales for existing subsidiaries. An estimated value for these losses could be included in the cash outflows for the project.

6. The budget statement should be scheduled over the 10-year period, showing the expected annual flows. Realistically, the project will show a series of uneven cash flows with decreasing accuracy further ahead in the 10-year projection span.

7. Conversion of the budget elements using different exchange rates is important because the many transactions involving foreign exchange are quite often subject to different duties, tariffs, or other special exchange restrictions. One single rate may not represent the estimate range adequately.

8. Imposition of previously used exchange controls, not currently in effect (but most commonly used) could be injected in the statement.

As can be readily concluded, the objective of a sensitivity analysis is to anticipate as many contingencies as possible, thereby increasing the accuracy of the project's expected returns. Feeling reasonably confident that the budgeted statement has considered all risks, the MNC may now direct its attention to the project's required rate of return.

In the case of evaluating one separate investment opportunity, it is necessary to establish a minimum rate of return to be used as a cutoff point when deciding to accept or reject the investment. The most commonly accepted minimum rate used by firms has been their risk-adjusted cost of capital. For an MNC, this rate would represent its worldwide cost of acquiring additional funds adjusted to reflect project-specific risk. This rate is defined as the rate of return that must be realized to maintain the corporation's current stock price.

If an MNC perceives that greater risks are inherent with a particular investment, it may adjust for risk in a manner such as illustrated in Chapter 13. It could be perceived that the effects of inflation or exchange controls are also predictable, thus justifying an additional adjustment for risk.

Measuring the Profitability of the Investment

As intimated, the MNC is greatly concerned about its ability to recover its initial investment. This concern exists because the effects of inflation and exchange controls could ultimately restrict the repatriation of funds or greatly reduce the value of funds received. Consequently, discounted-cash-flow techniques for measuring profitability are highly recommended.

In essence, the attractiveness of any investment is based on the ability of its eventual cash inflows to exceed its required cash outflows. However, monies received in future years would be worth less in terms of purchasing power, owing to either inflation or devaluations. To measure the real value of future cash inflows, these inflows should be expressed in constant (current) values equivalent to the values of the outflows in the earlier years. If the inflows then exceed the outflows, the investment will contribute to maximizing the dollar value of the firm in present values.

It is the primary objective of discounted-cash-flow techniques to provide for the time value of money by expressing future flows in terms of present value. One final factor for imputing cash inflows has been introduced and that is to assign a terminal value to the project. It is expected that the assets of the subsidiary will have a salable value at the end of the designated period, either as an ongoing concern or through liquidation. In addition, this approach can be called upon to handle compensation received by the MNC in the event that expropriation has taken place.

Following our preference for the net-present-value (NPV) model, we recommend that MNC's evaluate the attractiveness of projects using Equation (1):

$$NPV = \sum_{t=0}^{T-1} \frac{\overline{R}_t}{(1+r')^t} + \frac{\overline{TINF}_T}{(1+r')^T} - I_o \tag{1}$$

where $\overline{R}_t$ = the parent company's expected (after-tax, after-exchange-rate adjustment) net cash flow in period t

$\overline{TINF}_T$ = the expected (after-tax, after-exchange-rate adjustment) terminal net cash inflow to the parent company when either expropriation takes place or the end of the planning period occurs

r' = the risk-adjusted discount rate appropriate for the project under evaluation

I_o = the initial (after-tax, after-exchange-rate adjustment) cash outflow required by the parent company to acquire the asset.

Equation (1) provides an evaluation mechanism to handle most projects under evaluation by the MNC. In addition, the various sensitivity adjustments recommended earlier can be easily implemented using Equation (1).

Where the firm is evaluating projects with a very high initial investment or with a high degree of uncertainty given the host-country environment, the methodology presented in Appendix 25A, "A Simulation-Based Multinational Capital Budgeting Approach," is justified. This later approach provides a more powerful methodology to handle risky conditions faced by the MNC.

Acceptance of Investment

Referring to the previous premises, for an investment to be acceptable, the NPV value must be positive when the cash flows are discounted at the risk-adjusted rate appropriate for the project under evaluation. Again this risk-adjusted rate is a function of the MNC's cost of capital, as well as the environmental risk that exists for a project of this type in the host country of the subsidiary.

Furthermore, the acceptance of a proposed investment does not necessarily imply that it will be implemented. Acceptance merely includes the investment with other accepted investment opportunities. The accepted investment must now appear more attractive than the others to be fully implemented. Finally, the investment's performance will continually be reviewed after implementation. If performance is poor, abandonment procedures may be considered.

COST OF CAPITAL

Risk differences cause the cost of funds from a particular source to be higher than the risk-free rate and account for the possibility of loss and prospect of gain. It is also apparent that the type of funding chosen affects fees, flotation costs, rates of interest paid, and indirect costs, such as minimum balance deposits required. However, it is important to note that for multinational corporations the risk or degree of variability for all the preceding factors differs with the host country involved. The differences relate to inflation rates, possible changes in regulations of MNC, balance of payments, variability in labor costs, and political changes. It is for this reason that subsidiary costs of capital should be examined for the effect on the company-wide cost of capital.

The cost of borrowing is expected to vary because of business risk, financial structure, variability of earnings, company size, money-market conditions, and other variables. The cost and availability of funds in the international capital markets adds another dimension.

Effective interest rates in different national money markets vary considerably, and because, in general, bond yields are lower in the United States, a cost differential on long-term borrowing exists. This is further widened by security flotation costs also being higher outside the United States. Interest rates in underdeveloped countries are usually much higher than in developed countries because of smaller local savings; capital flight, which reduces local fund supplies; continuous inflation; and higher business risk.

A study that compares the cost of equity capital of U.S. multinational firms and their domestic counterparts looks at the possibility of higher risk for business operations abroad and the implication that the cost of capital would automatically be higher because of the entry into foreign markets.[4] By using a version of the dividend valuation model over 28 quarters, a sample of 110 companies from the Fortune 500 was used to evaluate cost of equity capital. The multinational firms on the list were compared to their domestic counterparts on that list using the paired-difference test to detect statistically significant differences. Seven industries were covered, including the following: nonferrous metals, fabricated metals products, electrical machinery, other machinery, petroleum refining, chemical and allied products, food products, and companies without distinction by industry. Of the seven distinct industries, only the chemical and allied products industry showed noticeably higher costs of equity capital for multinational firms. Interestingly, the oil and nonferrous metals industries have both been prone to expropriation by foreign governments. Kohers states that by making distinct differences in the capitalization rates of companies in different industries and not necessarily by domestic or MNC status, investors appear to clearly differentiate investment risks and opportunities among industries. They do not tend to unfairly discriminate against foreign operations in their appraisal of common stock investment values. From these findings it was concluded that by becoming involved in foreign business activities a company does not automatically raise its cost of capital.

The cost of short-term and medium-term funds, as mentioned earlier, now becomes a matter of operating most profitably (and prudently) while in compliance with FASB-8 (to be discussed momentarily). Minimization of dollar investment exposure to currency devaluation leads to scheduled repatriation of dollars by dividend payments and maximum efficient utilization of local funding sources by constant comparison of short-term rates for various instruments such as

---

[4]Theodore Kohers, "The Effect of Multinational Operations on the Cost of Equity Capital: An Empirical Study," *Management International Review*, 1975.

overdrafts, notes, and so on. When borrowing becomes difficult as a result of the general lack of availability of funds and retention of dividends becomes necessary to augment working capital, forward hedging is an alternative to protect investments and its cost can be considered as a cost of funds. Ordinarily, forward cover against fall of currency, especially for a developing country, is expensive and considered prohibitive.

It is quite apparent from the preceding discussion in this section that risk may not be perceived as greater for a multinational firm than for a domestic company, but it definitely can take many more forms. It follows that a decision to commit capital internationally deserves careful analysis. Techniques to effectively determine the worth of a capital expenditure proposal have been the subjects of many books and papers. Brill surveyed the range of techniques in practice and presented an approach to treat subjective data that possesses certain desirable properties: [5]

1. It summarizes relevant investment decision information in a single figure.
2. It is useful for all types of proposals.
3. It permits appraisal in terms of a single set of standards.
4. It provides an easily computed index.
5. It is easily understood.
6. It is adjustable to allow for ranges of uncertainty.

A shortcoming of discounted-cash-flow calculations is that the discount rates are often adjusted with "not totally rational" values for risk. These values are arrived at by conventional approaches to risk analysis, which include sensitivity studies, adjustments to venture worth criteria, and the *three-level estimate* method. In sensitivity studies, the effects of unit changes in the many parameters governing the profitability of a contemplated venture are determined to establish which parameters are most significant. Management must subjectively evaluate the relevance of the variables, because the likelihood of their deviations is unknown. Adjustments to venture worth criteria to reflect levels of risk are based on the theory that the risk incurred is related to the rewards expected. Results can be inconsistent, and recognition of risk in computing cash flows is more effective. In the three-level estimate approach, optimistic, pessimistic and most likely cases are developed and intuitively assigned probabilities of occurrence. The analysis is treated as decision-under-risk to arrive at an expected value of investment worth for venture analysis. The subjectivity of the probability designations, in addition to the omission of the dimension of variability, leads to rejection of this approach in risk analysis for investments as well as project management.

The limitations of the techniques discussed above are better overcome by more advanced techniques that develop distributions of return through Monte Carlo simulation (see Appendix 25A). To overcome the requirement for knowledge of the distribution of each variable in the analysis, Brill proposes a method utilizing reasonable estimates of the parameter distributions, thereby validly incorporating the risk dimension in venture analysis. [6] The technique relies on the

[5] Martin Brill, *An Approach to Risk Analysis in the Evaluation of Capital Ventures* (Philadelphia: Drexel Institute of Technology, 1966).
[6] Ibid.

assumptions that venture analysis variables can be described by a beta distribution with ranges usually reliably obtained from experts representing a 95% confidence interval. Although still subjective, owing to the very nature of the task of prediction, the method is rational, useful, and meets the guidelines presented earlier. Major banks readily volunteer expertise and information on domestic and international banking and financial matters as part of their marketing approach to attract new customers. Such expertise, combined with a firm's knowledge of its own business, could be well applied in the simulation approach.

REPATRIATION VERSUS REINVESTMENT OF PROFITS

The decision process of whether to repatriate dividends or reinvest in the foreign subsidiary requires examination beyond the original commitment in terms of what is needed to protect or strengthen the original investment. This is, of course, based heavily on the reassessment of the subsidiary's market position for an extended period of time, nominally 10 years, and the related investment alternatives.[7] Considerations generally include ultimate remittability of the required investment expenditures. Rather than measure returns only in terms of the local currency, inflows available to the investor are a key consideration. Inflation and money valuation forecasts play an important part in the long-range reinvestment plan. As indicated by recent moves of Japanese and German manufacturers to obtain manufacturing sites in the United States, this country holds a favored position in the struggle against inflationary effects. For this reason, United States–based MNC's will also lean toward expansion and improvement of domestic plants while maintaining sales and service branches overseas.

The important judgment in formulating and screening alternatives is to learn whether proposed planning will remain feasible if host-country restrictions are expected to become more stringent.

Another factor that influences the remittance decision and, therefore, the reinvestment decision of many multinational companies is taxation. Tax objectives vary and can reflect varying emphasis among companies. Firms that are most tax-conscious will make every attempt to minimize the corporations' total tax burden and give this consideration higher priority than any others in the investment decision. This would come about by modeling the tax situation after the other project-related details and projections are evaluated. Alternatively the tax burden might be given equal weight with one or two other factors, such as the risk of leaving funds abroad or the subsidiary's requirements for funds. The latter point is considered in relation to the availability and cost of funds locally.

Some companies consider paying taxes to the United States on repatriated dividends a fact of doing business, and no effort is made to delay or avoid this obligation. However, they do try to avoid penalty taxes for paying too high or too low a dividend as might occur in Germany.[8] A few corporations, because of

---

[7]David B. Zenoff and Jack Zwick, *International Financial Management* (Englewood Cliffs, N.J.: Prentice-Hall, Inc., 1969), pp. 148, 149.
[8]Ibid., p. 415.

the minimal amounts involved, assign a low level of importance to any tax consideration relative to foreign dividends.

Foreign dividends exercised to suit the corporate plan regarding taxes, reinvestment, or dividends to stockholders are only one part of the total fund remittance framework. Other means include management fees, technical-service fees, royalties interest on parent loans, principal repayments on such loans, license fees, commissions on exports, and payments for merchandise obtained from the parent.[9] Basic decisions regarding fund remittances are centralized, with the goal of maximizing corporate worldwide placement of funds. Perception of the overall needs of the entire corporate network and availability of the necessary financial data can only occur at a central office. As indicated earlier, the corporate prerogative to control and dispense funds can be affected by the policy of a host country. This is increasingly evident on all forms of fund remittance, including pricing, as active surveillance of invoices by customs agents is conducted.

STATEMENTS 8 AND 52 OF THE FINANCIAL ACCOUNTING STANDARDS BOARD (FASB)

The foreign-investment decision setting is clouded by the existence of FASB rulings on foreign exchange translation of the financial statements of an MNF's subsidiaries. FASB-8, "Accounting for the Translation of Foreign Currency Transactions and Foreign Currency Financial Statements," was implemented January 1, 1976. The mandatory guidelines of FASB-8 (and its successor, FASB-52) had three major effects:

1. It required that foreign transactions be handled using both a current rate and a historical rate; the former is used for real assets carried at market value, cash, accounts receivable, and *all* liabilities; the latter is used for all real assets carried at original cost.

2. It required that all foreign exchange gains and losses be reflected in net income *during the period* in which the change in the exchange rate occurred.

3. The use of reserve accounts and the distinction between realized and unrealized foreign exchange gains and losses were eliminated.

In viewing the impact of FASB-8, it is important to identify three types of exposure faced by the MNC: (1) translation exposure; (2) transaction exposure; and (3) economic exposure. Translation exposure is the exposure of an MNC to foreign-exchange loss as the net assets of its foreign subsidiary are translated into the home-country currency. Transaction exposure is the exposure of an MNC to foreign-exchange loss due to a contractural obligation of its foreign subsidiary to deliver goods or services in the future. Economic exposure is the risk of loss to the MNC due to the long-term impact of foreign-exchange fluctuations on the valuation of the corporation. The FASB statements address only the first two of these exposures, while the third is also of significant importance to multinational firms.

---

[9]See Eiteman and Stonehill, *Multinational Business Finance*, p. 308.

FASB-8 was a highly controversial accounting standard because reported income showed great volatility due to the requirement that all translation gains and losses had to be shown in the current income statement. FASB-8 was replaced by FASB-52 "Foreign Currency Translation" in December 1981. FASB-52 imposes two major changes: (1) a mandatory use of an all-current rate method; and (2) a differing treatment for transaction and translation gains and losses. The first revision eliminates the use of historical exchange rates in translating financial statements. The second revision would charge only *transaction* gains and losses to current income; whereas, *translation* gains and losses would be handled in a manner akin to charging these to a stockholders' equity reserve account. Financial managers should be aware of the existence of such rulings by the FASB and they should incorporate the impact of such rulings into the capital project evaluation process.

SUMMARY

This chapter surveys the important area of capital budgeting for the multinational firm. The new dimensions and variables present in the international environment are outlined and discussed.

A seven-step approach is suggested to evaluate and select capital projects for the multinational firm.

The important area of the cost of capital for the multinational firm is discussed next. Following this, repatriation versus reinvestment of profits is addressed, since this trade-off is an important phase in the strategic planning area for the multinational firm. Finally, the impact of FASB-8 and FASB-52 was outlined.

The appendix that follows illustrates many of the techniques and concepts discussed in the chapter by showing a Monte Carlo simulation model for capital budgeting for the multinational firm.

APPENDIX 25A
SIMULATION-BASED MULTINATIONAL
CAPITAL BUDGETING APPROACH[10]

This appendix outlines a Monte Carlo simulation model for multinational capital budgeting. The model has been made as general as possible while not sacrificing ease of understanding and use. In order to provide adequate information and a flexible analysis, a two-stage simulation is recommended. First, each investment opportunity is evaluated in a uninational setting by the subsidiary proposing it. If it passes the first screening, it is then analyzed from the parent's point of view. This joint evaluation is of paramount importance. Indeed, a plant built in a foreign country can be a very profitable investment in itself, but

---

[10]The model presented in this appendix is based on André Fourcans and Thomas J. Hindelang, "Capital Budgeting for the Multinational Firm: A Simulation Approach," presented at The Financial Management Association Conference, October, 1975.

currency devaluations, tax differentials, and/or quantitive controls can make it significantly less attractive to the parent company. The proposed model handles both the case where the parent is considering a joint venture as well as a 100% participation.

The model provides an operational, theoretically sound, and mathematically powerful capital project ranking methodology wherein project uncertainty as well as environmental uncertainty (including all major international variables) are incorporated into the analysis. Based on this ranking of investment proposals (consisting of empirical risk-return characteristics for several relevant evaluation criteria), both the subsidiary and parent can select the set of projects that best meets its risk-return preferences, financing availabilities, and objectives for synergy considering interactions between current operations and new projects. The model's two-stage simulation approach utilizing all relevant international variables is consistent with prior research in the international capital budgeting area. The model focuses well on the behavioral theory of the MNC postulated by Stonehill and Nathanson,[11] wherein they suggest an independent financial evaluation of projects by both the parent and subsidiary; further, the model avoids the serious disadvantages the authors cite that prevail when a risk-adjusted discount rate is used to reflect political and foreign exchange uncertainties; last, the model provides helpful information in implementing the "uncertainty absorption" program suggested by the authors, as well as arriving at an operational approach for charging each period with the cost of such a program. The model capitalizes on the strengths of the most sophisticated approach recommended by Stobaugh[12] in analyzing foreign investment climates, namely, that of risk analysis, wherein the full range of international uncertainty and variable interactions are incorporated rather than just the "optimistic," "most likely," and "pessimistic" estimates. In addition, the recommended model is not burdened with the assumption of independence of variables as are some models.[13] Finally, the model addresses the important cultural, economic, and political aspects of the capital investment decision setting that Mauriel[14] points to as differentiating uninational from multinational operations.

Subsidiary Simulation

The subsidiary's evaluation of a given investment proposal utilizes mainly the direct project costs and revenues discussed immediately above. The analysis uses a uninational framework and considers the parent mainly as a source of funds to finance accepted projects. Furthermore, in order not to unduly complicate matters, it is assumed that the subsidiary only sells and buys inside the host country (this assumption could be relaxed, if desired).

---

[11] A. I. Stonehill and L. Nathanson, "Capital Budgeting and the Multinational Corporation," *California Management Review* (Summer 1968), pp. 39–54.

[12] R. B. Stobaugh, "How to Analyze Foreign Investment Climates," *Harvard Business Review* (September–October 1969), pp. 100–108.

[13] J. Chambers and S. Mullick, "Investment Decision Making in a Multinational Enterprise," *Management Accounting*, (August 1971), pp. 44–59.

[14] J. J. Mauriel, "Evaluation and Control of Overseas Operations," *Management Accounting* (May 1969), pp. 35–39.

TABLE 25A–1 Subsidiary Cash Flows

Inflows	*Outflows*
Revenue from sales	Initial outlay
Salvage value	Financing costs
	Operating costs
	Host country taxes

The technical details of this stage of the simulation are presented in three illustrations. Table 25A–1 lists the relevant cash inflows and outflows for the subsidiary.

Table 25A–2 defines the variables (both exogenous and endogenous) and formulates the identities of the simulation model. Figure 25A–1 on page 435 shows a flow chart of this part of the simulation.

As we can see from Table 25A–2, the main endogenous variables that determine an investment proposal's attractiveness are the total revenue, total costs, net income after taxes, and net cash inflow each year. From these measures the payback, NPV, and IRR are computed for each simulated observation of the proposal's useful life. Empirical distributions are derived for each of these three criteria based on all simulation runs. Of course, other criteria (e.g., discounted payback, equivalent annual savings, or growth in earnings per share) could be easily built into the model, depending on the needs of the individual firm.

Based on the empirical distributions of the criteria above, summary statistics (the expected value, standard deviation, measures of skewness, and so on) are computed and probability statements can be made about the likelihood that various ranges are achieved by each criterion measure. The subsidiary will then have the necessary data to rank the proposal relative to all others under consideration (which have been run through the simulation) on the basis of its risk preferences and its evaluation of the risk-return trade-offs of the various proposals. Given this ranking of proposals, a recommendation will be made to the parent company concerning the set of proposals that the subsidiary feels should be adopted depending on availability of capital.

Two details should be mentioned about the subsidiary simulation. First, the international variables dealing with inflation risks, expropriation risks, risk of war, and taxation have been built into the subsidiary simulation. The mechanics of handling inflation are discussed below and the treatment of host-country taxation is straightforward. The occurrence of expropriation or war was obtained through a Monte Carlo determination in each year of the proposal's useful life. When it is established that either of these two events has taken place, the associated percentage loss is generated from the appropriate input distribution. This result is used to derive the terminal cash inflow of the project as a proportion of current salvage value, the yearly cash inflow, and working capital accumulated to date because of the project.

Second, the risk-free rate relevant to the subsidiary company (which will usually be different from the risk-free rate for the parent) is used in the computation of the NPV and as the relevant hurdle rate for the final comparison in the IRR method. More will be said later about the risk-free rate.

TABLE 25A-2   Variables of the Subsidiary Simulation Model

Parameters:

SP_t	= selling price per unit in year t KS = subsidiary risk-free rate
DR_t	= depreciation rate for year t
MAX	= total number of simulation runs to be considered

Exogenous variables:

Stochastic variables with known probability distributions:

MG_t	= market growth rate for each year t
MS_t	= initial market size in number of units
SM_t	= share of the market for each year t
INV	= initial investment required by the proposal
N	= useful life of investment
FC_t	= total operating fixed costs in year t
VC_t	= variable operating costs per unit in year t
IC_t	= interest cost associated with the project in year t
OC_t	= other project related costs in year t
WC_t	= working-capital needs of the project in year t
TR_t	= tax rate for host country tax on project returns in year t
IR_t	= rate of inflation in year t
WAR_t	= probability that a war will break out in the host country during year t
$LWAR_t$	= % of loss suffered by the firm if a war occurs in year t
EX_t	= probability that expropriation will take place in host country in year t
LEX_t	= % of loss suffered by the firm if expropriation takes place in host country during year t

Endogenous variables:

$USAL_t$	= unit sales generated by the proposal in year t
REV_t	= total revenue generated by the proposal in year t
TC_t	= total costs associated with the project in year t
TAX_t	= host country tax on taxable income generated by project in year t
$NIAT_t$	= net income after host country tax generated by project in year t
NCI_t	= net cash inflow generated by project in year t
BV_t	= book value of the project at the end of year t
SV_t	= salvage value of the project at the end of year t
$TINF_n$	= terminal inflow if expropriation or war occurs during year n
$PAYB_m$	= payback period for the investment on the mth simulation run
NPV_m	= net present value for the investment on the mth simulation run
IRR_m	= discounted rate of return for the investment on the mth simulation run

Identities and operating equations:

BV_0	$= INV$	
DEP_t	$= (DR_t)(BV_{t-1})$	
BV_t	$= BV_{t-1} - DEP_t$	
MS_t	$= (MS_{t-1})(1 + MG_{t-1})$	$t = 2, 3, \ldots, N$
$USAL_t$	$= (MS_t)(SM_t)$	$t = 1, 2, \ldots, N$
REV_t	$= (SP_t)(USAL_t)$	$t = 1, 2, \ldots, N$
TVC_t	$= (VC_t)(USAL_t)$	$t = 1, 2, \ldots, N$
TC_t	$= TVC_t + FC_t + OC_t + DEP_t$	$t = 1, 2, \ldots, N$
TAX_t	$= (TR_t)(REV_t - TC_t)$	$t = 1, 2, \ldots, N$
$NIAT_t$	$= REV_t - TC_t - TAX_t$	$t = 1, 2, \ldots, N$
NCI_t	$= NIAT_t + DEP_t - WC_t$	$t = 1, 2, \ldots, N$
SV_n	$= (SV_{n-1} - DEP_n)(1 + IR_n)$	

TABLE 25A–2   (*continued*)

If expropriation (EX_n) occurs in year n, determine loss suffered (LEX_n), then:

$$TINF_n = (1 - LEX_n)(SV_n + NCI_n)$$

If war (WAR_n) occurs in year n, determine loss suffered ($LWAR_n$), then:

$$TINF_n = (1 - LWAR_n)(SV_n + NCI_n)$$

$PAYB_m$ = period i such that:

$$INV - \sum_{t=1}^{i} (NCI_t + IC_t) = 0$$

NPV_m is determined in the usual way:

$$NPV_m = \sum_{t=1}^{n} \frac{NCI_t}{(1 + KS)^t} - INV$$

IRR_m = discount rate r such that

$$\sum_{t=1}^{N} \frac{NCI_t}{(1 + r)^t} - INV = 0$$

Parent-Company Simulation

The parent company takes a more global view in its evaluation of potential projects. It utilizes the empirical data relative to the project per se (i.e., project net income after taxes and net cash inflows) developed by the subsidiary simulation but also incorporates the critical international variables associated with the transfer of funds. These additional risks and uncertainties are built into the framework so that the parent can adequately assess the situation before it commits funds to a given project in a specific country. Table 25A–3 on page 436 shows the cash flows from the parent's point of view.

Because the parent-company simulation model closely parallels that of the subsidiary company shown in Table 25A–2 and Figure 25A–1, they are not repeated. It should be mentioned that the identities and operating equations for the parent show that all cash flows which cross international boundaries are subject to foreign exchange adjustment, international taxation, and quantitative controls. In addition, the benefits to the parent company are dependent upon the direct savings in the operations, which are a result of the project as well as the dividends, profits repatriated, royalties, and interest received from the subsidiary, which are tied to the project. Both international and home country tax effects are taken into account in computing the net returns to the parent.

The same measures as before (i.e., internal rate of return, net present value, and payback) provide the criteria in the parent's evaluation of the worth of the project. Like each subsidiary, the parent can now rank all proposals on a worldwide basis using these empirical distributions and their associated statistics. The parent company's risk preferences and its evaluation of risk-return trade-offs of various proposals come into the analysis here. The parent company uses the relevant risk-free rate in the evaluation criteria.

FIGURE 25A–1   Flow Chart of Subsidiary Simulation

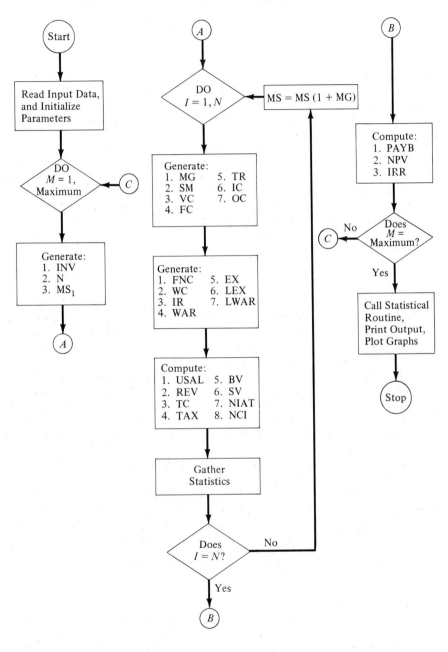

TABLE 25A-3   Parent-Company Cash Flows

Inflows	Outflows
Direct savings generated by the project	Equity funds provided
Profit repatriated	Loans provided
Dividends	Labor, material, and other costs
Royalties and fees	Transportation costs
Interest and loan repayments	Taxes paid on dividends, royalties, and profit repatriated

Mechanics of the Simulation

As noted above, the simulation is designed to be flexible and complete, yet not overly demanding on the user relative to necessary data inputs. However, it was also pointed out that the more precise the input specifications are, the more exact and helpful will be the results generated by the simulation. Thus, balancing these trade-offs, the decision-maker is asked to specify the exogenous variables as accurately as he can for as many years into the future as possible. It is realized, of course, that the farther into the future a user must estimate distributions, the greater is the degree of uncertainty. Offsetting this shortcoming are two countermeasures:

1. The discounting process weighs more distant years less significantly.
2. Sensitivity analysis is used to determine the impact of changes in the input variables on the decision criteria.

In order to make the variable estimation process as painless as possible, the user is given many alternatives to the method of specifying inputs:

1. The user can provide the parameters of any well-known distribution (e.g., binomial, uniform, normal, beta, and so on).
2. The user can input any discrete distribution that he or she feels is appropriate.
3. The user can specify that the distribution is a composite of various distributions.

Inflation is dealt with in two ways. First, it can be taken into consideration in the estimation of the exogenous variables by the user specifying a different distribution for each year of the anticipated useful life of the project. Second, the distribution can be shifted to the right, every year, by the expected percent inflation. This operation can be done for selling price, variable cost, and so on. If a single distribution is specified for all periods, the inflation factor is built into the simulation and taken into consideration in the yearly revision of the distributions for the exogenous variables.

One of the important strengths of the model is the way in which it handles interdependencies among related variables. Some interrelationships can be reflected exclusively by means of an informed and careful specification of the input distribution's exogenous variables, whereas the simulation model has built in self-checks in order to adequately handle other dependencies. Examples of the former strategy would be where the user would be reminded of the fact that expected high rates of inflation in any given year must be associated with larger expected changes in foreign exchange rates for that year; further, dividend rates and percent of profits repatriated should both reflect those risks associated with a given host country—inflation risk, war and expropriation risks, taxation policies, and quantitative controls. The technique, using built-in checks, is necessitated by the fact that only after the value of an exogenous variable is generated by the simulation will the appropriate domain for a related variable be determined. For example, there is a trade-off between fixed and variable costs associated with producing a product—it is reasonable to assume that a high level of fixed costs is generally associated with a lower variable cost per unit; thus, the model restricts the feasible values of the variable-cost distribution to the lower tail whenever the value of total fixed cost generated comes from the upper tail, and vice versa. Similar relationships are built in to reflect the trade-offs between market size and market growth rate and among selling price, demand relationships, and market share.

One final important point should be mentioned. Because of the two-stage analysis of investment proposals—first by the subsidiary and then by the parent—two different risk-free rates are used. The subsidiary uses its own rate in order to determine the proposal's relative ranking, and if the project should be recommended to the parent for acquisition. In a similar vein, the parent uses the risk-free rate of its home country to determine whether funds should be committed to the product. Such an approach gives a double, somewhat independent, more stringent screening of proposals. They must survive both cutoff points in order to be adopted by the multinational firm.

It must be strongly emphasized that both the parent and subsidiary simulations use the relevant risk-free rate (rather than the cost of capital or a risk-adjusted discount rate) in computing any project's net present value. Indeed, in both stages of the simulation, the discounting operation must only reflect discounting for futurity or the time value of money and not for the specific riskiness of the project under consideration. The risk element of each investment proposal is ascertained in the simulation runs themselves. As we have mentioned before in Chapter 22, and as Lewellen and Long point out, to discount cash flows on each simulation run "at a rate in excess of the default-free rate" (e.g., the risk-free rate) would impose improper double adjustment for uncertainty upon the project.[15] Thus, all that is required is to discount these empirical cash flows at the risk-free rate in order to arrive at an empirical NPV distribution which contains valuable information for both the expected return and riskiness of the project under consideration.

[15] W. G. Lewellen and M. S. Long, "Simulation vs. Single-Value Estimates in Capital Expenditure Analysis," *Decision Sciences*, 3, no. 4 (October 1972), 19–33.

Validation and Analysis of the Model's Output

The following discussion is aimed at providing insight to the users of the proposed simulation model in terms of interpreting the final results and utilizing them in the capital investment decision process. Several authors have pointed to such a gap in theory and practice: Bower and Lessard[16] found in their empirical work that simulation models were not used because of "the inability to translate results into simple measures executives could reconcile with their intuition and experience and use, with other measures, to make a judgment"; Lewellen and Long[17] point to this problem by asking: "What do you do with that impressive distribution of possible outcomes once you have simulated? How should the information be digested?" Mao and Helliwell found that their three sample firms had difficulty in conceptualizing and quantifying risk-return trade-offs.[18]

The simulation methodology not only permits managers to evaluate and compare the expected performance of different potential investments, but also presents an analytical approach to determine relationships among project variables and international factors.

The main output consists of the two empirical profiles of net present value (NPV) and internal rate of return (IRR) for both the parent company and for the subsidiary. Relevant statistical measures of central tendency variability and skewness are computed for each empirical distribution.

Figure 25A–2 gives an example of the main output. Curve I represents the IRR profile for the subsidiary, whereas curve II is for the parent. As can be quickly noted in this specific case, the IRR for the parent is everywhere lower than the subsidiary's IRR. However, this need not always be the case (it would depend on the influence of such factors as foreign exchange rates, tax differentials, and the relevant risk-free rates). The purpose of these two profiles is to make sure that the worthiness of the investment can be evaluated by all groups (parent's managers and possible partners in the country of the investment) with their possibly different aspirations. Therefore, an investment is considered attractive by a particular group only if the proposal meets the criteria of acceptability of that group.

How are these profiles used? As demonstrated by curve I of Figure 25A–2, there is a 98% probability that an IRR greater than or equal to 6% can be obtained, a 90% probability of the IRR exceeding 10%, a 50% probability of the IRR exceeding 15%, and a 10% probability of the IRR exceeding 22%. We know that the investment will be worthwhile (from the point of view of the subsidiary) if the IRR is at least equal to its risk-free rate. If we assume a subsidiary's risk-free rate of 10%, the chance of having an IRR $\geq$ 10% is 90 out of 100. The decision-makers will have to decide whether they are ready to take the risk implied: 90 chances out of 100 of having a "profitable" investment, but

[16] D. R. Lessard and R. S. Bower, "An Operational Approach to Risk Screening," *Journal of Finance* (May 1973), pp. 245–247.

[17] W. G. Lewellen and M. S. Long, "Reply to Comments by Bower and Lessard and Gentry," *Decision Sciences*, 4, no. 4 (October 1973), 575–576.

[18] J. C. T. Mao and J. F. Helliwell, "Investment Decision Under Uncertainty: Theory and Practice," *Journal of Finance*, 24, no. 2 (May 1969), 323–338.

FIGURE 25A–2

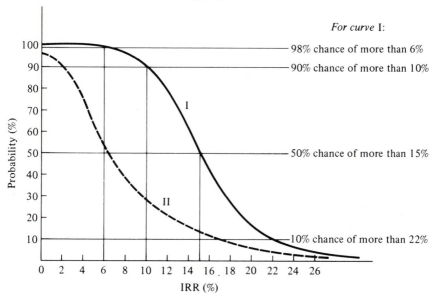

10 out of 100 of "losing money." The same analysis needs to be done with curve II from the point of view of the parent.

The statistics computed from the empirical distributions enable the subsidiary and the parent to evaluate risk-return trade-offs among various alternatives available. Furthermore, the analysis of the output data is rendered more sophisticated by the following elaborations. A statistical analysis subroutine using the multiple ranking criteria discussed by Kleijnen, Naylor, and Seaks analyzes and determines the order of the project desirability and whether statistically significant differences exist among the ranked projects.[19] The analysis is performed by each subsidiary and by the parent for all projects considered by the multinational firm. Such results are invaluable when the firms are faced with capital rationing and multiple, competing investment opportunities and risks.

Another significant benefit from the simulation approach is that sensitivity analysis can be performed. Decision-makers can change the distribution of each exogenous variable one at a time or several at a time and have a good understanding of the importance each variable has on the attractiveness of the investment. It allows an increased comprehension of the relationships among variables and their impact on the decision process. This information is extremely valuable, especially for the evaluation of the international variables, in particular for foreign exchange rates, which are difficult enough to forecast. If, for example, the final results are found to be affected very little by changes in

[19]J. P. C. Kleijnen, T. H. Naylor and T. G. Seaks, "The Use of Multiple Ranking Procedures to Analyze Simulations of Management Systems," *Management Sciences* (February 1972), pp. 245–257.

currency values, it is clear that the uncertainty of the investment is greatly reduced. On the contrary, high sensitivity to foreign exchange rates would warn the decision-maker to give special forecasting attention to this variable and to consider the addition of an annual cost for hedging against this risk (i.e., a cost for "uncertainty absorption" discussed above).

QUESTIONS/PROBLEMS

1. Discuss at least four major risks that multinational firms face in their capital budgeting activities.

2. Outline a general approach to capital budgeting for the multinational firm.

3. Discuss several "operating strategies" that multinational firms can use to reduce foreign exchange risks.

4. Discuss several strategies that can be implemented to reduce the impact of inflation on the multinational firm.

5. Mention several characteristics that could point to greater risk of expropriation for the multinational firm.

6. Based on the simulation model presented in Appendix 25A, do the following things:

   (a) Outline the suggested two-stage approach for capital investment evaluation by the multinational firm.

   (b) For both the parent company and the subsidiary, list the major cash inflows and outflows.

   (c) List the major "endogenous variables" that will be used to evaluate and rank capital projects.

   (d) Discuss why both the parent company and the subsidiary will utilize their respective risk-free rates in conjunction with the simulation.

   (e) Discuss how sensitivity analysis would be performed in conjunction with the simulation and why this is important.

26

BUSINESS COMBINATIONS

The acquisition of one corporation by another qualifies as a capital budgeting decision inasmuch as the project involves the alternative usage of investable funds. Corporate acquisitions, accordingly, stand or fall by the same criteria applied to all discretionary capital expenditures. Consistent with the assumptions of financial management, the presumed objective of a combination is to enhance the present worth of the joint enterprise and thereby improve the wealth position of the common stockholders measured by the market value of their shares.

The measure of a successful acquisition rests upon the market value of the stock. If the market value has increased, the increment in market value (post-combination) over the preacquisition values denotes the synergistic effects of the combination. The gain or loss to any one group of shareholders naturally depends upon the exchange ratios, as will be discussed in a following section. Because market values trade off risk and return, synergism results only if:

1. The combination increases earnings for the same level of risk.

2. The combination reduces risk while maintaining the same level of earnings.

3. Earnings and risk are both changed to improve the risk-return combination.

Equally proportionate increases in earnings and risk do not raise market values, although the financial statements may show higher earnings per share. The combination has merely moved up the security market line.

Synergism is not easy to obtain and is even more difficult to measure when achieved. The criterion assumes a linear relationship between market returns and risk (i.e., that the market is efficient). Time is also a factor. *Synergistic effects rarely appear in the fiscal period following the combination, and it may be many periods down the road before the full benefits of the combination are realized.* In the meantime, the acquiring firm may have entered upon other combinations and the national economy may have moved from one plateau to another. Under these circumstances, it becomes almost impossible to quantify precisely the synergistic effects of a single combination.

ACQUISITION STRATEGY

Many motivations, both personal and financial, inspire business combinations. Not all are consistent with the underlying assumption of financial management: to maximize the present worth of the firm or maximize the market value of the common shares. Nevertheless, whether a firm undertakes a single merger or pursues a policy of continued expansion by combination, it will enhance the probability of a successful venture by articulating an acquisition strategy. The components of an acquisition strategy relate to decisions on the following points:

1. Is internal or external expansion the preferable alternative?
2. What is the direction of expansion?
3. What is the legal form of expansion?
4. What are the appropriate accounting options to structure the combination?
5. What tax options will minimize the tax liabilities of the parties?
6. Is the combination liable to antitrust action?

The responses to these inquiries must be integrated into a comprehensive plan for intercorporate investments. They are discussed sequentially in the succeeding sections.

INTERNAL VERSUS EXTERNAL EXPANSION

A firm may expand either internally or externally. Thus far in our discussion of the capital investment process, we have limited our examination to the former, so it is valuable at this juncture to enumerate the primary advantages and disadvantages of internal expansion. This will provide a benchmark for comparison as we examine external expansion.

Internal expansion enjoys the following advantages:

1. The valuation process of expansion by combination is avoided.
2. There are fewer accounting and tax problems to resolve.
3. The problem of minority stockholders does not arise.
4. Subject to some qualification, the situation may diminish the likelihood of unfavorable antitrust action.
5. The firm has the opportunity to acquire new facilities designed and located specially to meet its operational requirements, and, as a corollary, management has the opportunity to entrench the firm as a low-cost producer.

The disadvantages inherent to internal expansion also warrant close consideration:

1. The availability of funds (retained earnings or issuance of new securities) limits the scope of the expansion programs.

2. The disbursal of funds to acquire new assets may drain liquidity.

3. The tempo of expansion depends upon the construction period or lead times of the assets concerned.

Alternatively, if the firm expands by combination, it will enjoy other advantages:

1. The funds available for expansion may be supplemented by the issuance of securities so that more expansion can be accomplished for the same dollar outlay and, as a corollary, to the extent the combination is financed by the exchange of securities, liquidity is conserved.

2. The firm secures additional facilities at once.

3. The acquisition may reduce the number of competitors or otherwise improve market control.

4. If the transaction meets IRS criteria, it may qualify as a tax-free exchange.

5. The combination may be the vehicle for recruiting new managerial talent.

Disadvantages associated with combination include the following:

1. The process of negotiation encompasses valuation problems, choice of accounting methodology and tax treatment, and the question of minority interests.

2. All things equal, the situation carries a higher probability of antitrust prosecution.

3. Depending upon the terms of exchange, the transaction may create a substantial tax liability for the selling corporation.

4. The acquiring firm may have to invest additional funds to integrate the facilities into its operational pattern.

5. The success of the combination depends upon the ability of management to mesh in a single operation two previously independent organizations. *The human equation in this regard presents a substantial challenge.*

Of the two approaches, internal expansion predominates, but expansion by combination is more common as the asset sizes increase.

DIRECTION OF EXPANSION

The achievement of synergistic effects depends upon the economic substance of the combination, that is, the earnings potential and risk posture of the joint enterprise. In terms of economic substance there are five basic classes of combinations, which are described below:

1. Vertical combination. The acquiring firm expands backward toward sources of supply or forward toward market outlets. The United States Steel Corporation, for example, sought a completely integrated system from the raw-material stage to the finished product. More recent illustrations of vertical combination include the acquisition of Conoco by DuPont (1981) and Pillsbury's acquisition of Burger King (1978). *Potentially, vertical combinations can stabilize the supply and/or demand schedules of the acquiring company, reduce inventories, facilitate production planning, and economize on working capital investment.*

2. Horizontal combination. This entails the amalgamation of competing firms at the same stage of the industrial process. Examples include the 1973 Coca Cola Bottling acquisition of Franzia Brothers Winery and McDonnell's acquisition of Douglas Aircraft Company (1967). *In addition to reducing the degree of competition, horizontal combinations offer the prospect of eliminating duplicate facilities and operations,* reducing the investment in working capital, a broadened product line, and better market control.

3. Product extension. This strategy unites companies which are functionally related in production and/or distribution but sell products that do not compete directly with one another. Examples include Sperry-Rand's acquisition of Univac (RCA) and American Express Co.'s acquisition of Shearson Loeb Rhoades (both in 1981).

4. Market extension. Mergers in this category add to the product market served by the acquiring firm; that is, the acquiring and acquired firms manufacture the same product but sell it in different geographic markets. Dairy, beer, cement, and oil producers are the most common source of market extension combinations.

5. Conglomerate combination. The conglomerate combines firms in different lines of endeavor. General Dynamics, for example, spans such diverse operations as aerospace manufacture, surface and subsurface marine vehicles, rubber and tire manufacture, and communications. *Among so diversified a collection of outputs, it seems difficult to envision operating economies, although risk pooling may reduce financing charges. On the other hand, the market value of the whole enterprise may increase through reducing the variance in total revenues by including firms that covary unequally with fluctuations in general business activity, by increasing capacity to leverage the capital structure, and by improving substandard earnings of the component units.*

It is easier to enumerate the theoretical advantages of different combinations than to achieve them in practice. Larger size does not invariably equate with greater efficiency. Problems of managerial effectiveness afflict all organizations, but they grow disproportionately with size. Paperwork proliferates and bureaucratic red tape discourages initiative. Moreover, the advantages of specialization can be lost with integration. Studies by the Federal Trade Commission and independent bodies suggest that the largest firms in an industry are not always the lowest-cost producers.

The particular direction of expansion varies with the circumstances of the day and the evolution of industry. Vertical and horizontal combinations dominated the scene in the nineteenth and the first half of the twentieth centuries. The 1950s saw the emergence of the conglomerate movement, which reached an apogee in the late sixties. By 1980, the statistics evidenced some deconglomeration as firms moved to simplify their corporate structures under the pressure of rising interest rates. Combinations also wax and wane with the business cycle—flourishing in prosperity and receding in recession. Tables 26–1 and 26–2 put an historical perspective on the types of combination in the post–World War II period.

TABLE 26–1 **Large Acquisitions in Manufacturing and Mining, by Year 1948–1978**

Year	Number of Acquisitions	Assets[a] ($ Millions)
1948	4	63.2
1949	6	89.0
1950	5	186.3
1951	9	201.5
1952	16	373.8
1953	23	779.1
1954	37	1,444.5
1955	67	2,165.7
1956	53	1,882.0
1957	17	1,202.3
1958	42	1,070.6
1959	49	1,431.1
1960	51	1,535.1
1961	46	2,003.3
1962	65	2,251.9
1963	54	2,535.8
1964	73	2,302.9
1965	64	3,253.7
1966	76	3,329.1
1967	138	8,258.5
1968	174	12,580.0
1969	138	11,043.2
1970	91	5,904.3
1971	59	2,459.9
1972	60	1,885.5
1973	64	3,148.8
1974	62	4,466.4
1975	59	4,950.5
1976	81	6,279.2
1977	100	9,004.2
1978[b]	110	10,705.5
Total	1,923	108,786.9

[a]Acquired firms with assets of $10 million or more.
[b]Figures for 1978 are preliminary.
NOTE: Not included in above tabulation are companies for which data are not publicly available. There were 523 such companies with assets of $13,802.9 million for period 1948–1978.
SOURCE: Bureau of Economics, Federal Trade Commission.

TABLE 26–2 Large Acquisitions in Manufacturing and Mining by Type of Acquisition, 1978; Compared with 1977, 1948–1977 and 1967–1977

Type of Acquisition	Number				Assets[a] (Millions)			
	1948–1977	1967–1977	1977	1978	1948–1977	1967–1977	1977	1978[b]
Horizontal	304	141	26	21	$15,236.6	$ 9,684.0	$ 1,183.9	$ 3,036.6
Vertical	183	73	4	13	8,474.7	4,031.9	752.8	1,619.3
Conglomerate	1,326	812	70	76	74,370.1	56,264.6	70,067.5	6,049.6
Product extension	791	448	38	37	33,707.7	22,709.9	2,863.1	2,999.0
Market extension	76	36	0	0	6,379.9	3,989.5	0.0	0.0
Other	459	328	32	39	34,282.5	29,565.2	4,204.4	3,050.6
Total	1,813	1,026	100	110	98,081.4	69,980.5	9,004.2	10,705.5

[a]Acquired firms with assets of $10 million or more.
[b]Figures for 1978 are preliminary.

NOTE: Not included in above tabulation are companies for which data were not publicly available. There were 489 such companies with assets of $12,738.0 million for period 1948–1977, 303 companies with assets of $8,442.2 million for period 1967–1977, 25 companies with assets of $962.9 million in 1977, and 34 companies with assets of $1,064.9 million in 1978.

SOURCE: Bureau of Economics, Federal Trade Commission.

LEGAL FORMS OF COMBINATION

Interrelated with the economic objective of expansion is the legal form of the combination. Economic objectives influence management structure (e.g., centralized versus decentralized management) and particular legal forms facilitate one or the other types of management structures. *Specifically, the form of combination impacts on the time required to effect the combination, the ease of financing, the degree of management control, the flexibility of the organization, the degree of permanence in the arrangement, and the tax liability of the enterprise.* The principal forms of combination —purchase of assets, mergers and consolidations, and formation of holding companies—are discussed below.

Purchase of Assets

As the term implies, the acquiring firm may purchase all or some of the seller's assets and assume all, some, or none of his liabilities. For example, the sale of the RCA computer division to Sperry-Univac falls into this category. The procedure has several advantages:

1. The sale may not require the approval of the selling corporation's stockholders. Unless the sale changes the character of the seller's business (the sale of goodwill or property forming an integral part of the business), the transaction would not require the consent of the stockholders.

2. In contrast to the merger approach described below, purchase of assets has an inherent flexibility. The acquiring corporation may purchase only those facilities pertinent to its operations and may or may not assume any liabilities. Consideration may take the form of cash, securities, or a combination thereof.

3. Tax shields may be created if the sale results in a capital loss to the seller.

4. The acquiring corporation does not inherit the personnel or management problems of the selling firm.

The disadvantages associated with the purchase of assets also warrant close attention:

1. If the sale requires the consent of the shareholders, the usual problems of minority rights arise. Creditors, however, cannot object in the absence of fraud, and their liens follow the property subject to the attachment.

2. If the selling firm realizes a large gain, substantial tax liabilities may be involved.

3. Some state laws mandate the approval of the seller's stockholders when the buyer purchases the assets by issuing stock in exchange for assets.

Merger and Consolidation

Technically speaking, in a merger, the acquiring firm assumes all the assets and liabilities of the seller and the latter is dissolved. Consolidation involves forming a new corporation which assumes the assets and liabilities of two or more selling corporations. The latter are then dissolved. The reader should bear in mind, however, that the term *merger* in *popular usage* describes all business combinations.

By way of illustration, in 1954, the Nash Corporation, renamed American Motors Corporation, acquired by *merger* the Hudson Motor Car Company. Hudson shareholders received two American Motors shares for each three Hudson shares. Nash stock exchanged share for share. In 1967, a new company, McDonnell Douglas Corporation, was formed to *consolidate* the McDonnell and Douglas corporations. Douglas shareholders received 1.75 shares of the new firm's common for each Douglas share. McDonnell shares were swapped on a one-to-one ratio.

Some advantages of the merger or consolidation include the following:

1. Taxes on intercorporate dividends may be eliminated.

2. Financial reporting is simplified by elimination of consolidated financial statements.

3. Centralization of authority is facilitated.

4. The tax expense of maintaining separate corporate entities is eliminated.

5. It may be possible to effect a merger or consolidation as a tax-free exchange.

Disadvantages must also be considered.

1. There may be some loss of goodwill. When a small company combines with a significantly larger firm, circumstances dictate the dissolution of the smaller organization. This may result in loss of some goodwill.

2. The arrangement is inflexible. The acquiring corporation must assume all the assets and liabilities of the seller, including those of only peripheral importance.

3. Stockholders of both corporations must assent to the combination. Dissenting stockholders may demand an appraisal of their holdings and payment in cash. Dissenters may also sue to test compliance with the legal formalities stipulated by state law.

4. Negotiators must wrestle with the question of valuation, choice of accounting method, and the tax status of the selling firm's shareholders.

5. The perennial managerial problem of blending two previously distinct organizations remains. The Penn Central combination is a prime example.

Holding Company

Generally speaking, any corporation that invests in the stock of another firm constitutes a holding company. Holding companies function in all fields of business but are common to public utilities and banking, where legal restrictions set geographic limits on the establishment of new facilities. Within the study of capital investment, we are concerned with two objectives of a holding company: investment and control. Control might signify majority ownership of the outstanding shares, but often, especially if the subsidiary is a large corporation with scattered stock ownership, the investor may secure *de facto* control with relatively few shares, perhaps only 20% of the outstanding stock.

There are two functional types of holding companies: pure holding companies and holding-operating companies. The former have no operating functions. The assets consist solely of holdings in subsidiary stocks, bonds, and loans, while the chief sources of income are the dividends, interest, and fees earned from providing services to the subsidiary units. The United States Steel Corporation and American Home Products were formed *initially* with the prime purpose of acquiring stocks in operating companies. The latter represents a mixed form. General Motors, initially organized as a pure holding company, was reorganized as an operating company by converting the subsidiary corporations into GM divisions. However, the company still retains subsidiary investments in General Motors Acceptance Corporation and various foreign affiliates.

Several factors recommend the holding company:

1. It is not necessary to secure the consent of stockholders of the subsidiary corporations, and the need to pay off dissenters does not arise.

2. The parent acquires a going concern intact without loss of goodwill; if cash is paid to purchase subsidiary stock, a sum far less than the net value of the subsidiary's assets need be invested to acquire control. The parent has only to gain sufficient outstanding shares to ensure control, and where the subsidiaries have large blocks of long-term debt outstanding, this can represent a small portion of the total assets brought under control. The pyramiding of debt leverages the parent's investment.

3. The parent need not assume the liabilities of the subsidiary corporations.

4. It may make possible a combination of enterprises which legislation would not permit under a single corporate roof. By the late 1960s, virtually all the nation's larger commercial banks converted their corporate structures to holding company form to enable them to undertake such diverse functions as data processing, insurance, mutual fund sales, investment advisory services, and leasing. As banks they could not participate in these activities.

5. The holding company organizational form facilitates decentralized operations over state and international boundaries.

Several factors that detract from the holding company organization must be considered:

1. The structure may prove unstable. If the subsidiary fails to pay dividends on its preferred or misses an interest payment, the parent's investment may be lost or its control jeopardized.

2. The income tax laws work to the disadvantage of the holding company. If the holding company owns less than 80% of the subsidiary's stock, it must pay a 15% tax on dividends received from the subsidiary. This creates three tiers of taxation: the operating companies on the original income earned, the parent holding company in receipt of dividends from the operating company, and the holding company's stockholders on the dividends they receive from the parent.

3. Maintaining separate corporate entities duplicates expenses: franchise taxes, annual meetings, officers' salaries, and so on.

4. Minority interests of the subsidiary corporations can prove troublesome. The minority is there to challenge intercorporate transfers, accounting methods, inventory control, or practices that appear to "exploit" the subsidiary corporations.

5. Because of historical abuses, the holding company device is regulated by the SEC under the Public Utility Holding Company Act of 1937 and the ICC under the Interstate Commerce Act.

To recapitulate, *an acquisition strategy should first define the economic substance of the combination, that is, whether the objective is to increase revenues, achieve operating economies, diversify, readjust the financial structure, or reduce the risk of ultimate failure.*[1] This will largely determine whether the combination is best accomplished by internal financing or by acquisition. It will also influence the management structure: the degree of centralization and the arrangement of line and staff functions.

Economic substance also influences the choice of accounting methodology; that is, the accounting system should record the nature of the economic event taking place. It should record the economic substance of the transaction on a basis that permits comparison of precombination and postcombination results and facilitate the prediction of future performance. At any rate, this represents the theory. In practice, the choice of accounting methodology—purchase or pooling—has become the source of much argumentation, and the suspicion persists that some recent combinations would not have taken place except for the accounting options available. Since the choice of accounting methodology can affect earnings per share, the accounting numbers figure prominently in an acquisition strategy.

THE ACCOUNTING DECISION

Copeland and Wojdak stated the essense of the accounting decision in business combinations:[2]

> The manipulative quality of the purchase-pooling decision rule derives from the fact that acquired assets may be valued differently under the two methods. If a merger is accounted for as a purchase, acquired assets are recorded at the fair value of the consideration given by the acquiring company; however, under the pooling method they are valued at their pre-acquisition book values.... *The method that minimizes asset values usually maximizes profits* [emphasis added].

Minimizing asset values on the books reduces future charges against income. Hence, if book values exceed market values, the decision rule dictates a purchase treatment. When this

---

[1]The reader will correctly observe that the statement oversimplifies the problem of motivation underlying merger activity. Mixed motives may predominate, the parties in interest having different objectives in fostering the combination. In some instances, the predominant objective may look to speculative gains from rising market prices or the issuance of new securities. The lurid details of "big killings" decorate business history books. Yet, if the combination survives, it must serve an economic purpose and indeed without some ostensible economic rationale, the stock market would probably not react positively to the announcement of the combination.

[2]Ronald M. Copeland and Joseph F. Wojdak, "Income Manipulation and the Purchase-Pooling Choice," *Journal of Accounting Research* (Autumn 1969), pp. 188–195.

condition is reversed, the pooling of interest is the appropriate treatment. But two assumptions underlie the rule: that management seeks to maximize future accounting incomes; and accounting numbers determine the market value of the common shares (i.e., the value of the combination).[3]

Empirical evidence supports the first assumption. Gagnon investigated a sample of 500 mergers from New York Stock Exchange listing applications for the period 1955–1958.[4] He found approximately 51% followed the proposed decision rule. Copeland-Wojdak showed a much higher incidence of maximizing behavior in the period 1966–1967.[5] They concluded:

> There has been a trend toward pooling since 1958... and the results strongly support the hypothesis that firms record mergers by the method that maximizes reported income.

A study by Anderson and Louderback covered the period 1967–1974.[6] They found about 86% of the surveyed firms followed the decision rule. Their findings seemingly lend support to an observation of Wyatt:[7]

> Accounting for a combination is commonly decided in advance of consummation of the transaction. That is, *the accounting treatment is one of the variables that must be firmed up before the final prize (in terms of exchange ratios) is determined* [emphasis added].

The accounting methodology is an important element in the overall acquisition strategy. It effects such factors as the earnings per share, asset values, and retained earnings of the combination. The major accounting options available in business combinations are purchase or pooling.

Purchase

Accounting Principles Board (APB) Opinion No. 16 defines a purchase as a "business combination of two or more corporations in which an important part of the ownership interests in the acquired corporation or corporations is eliminated." The notion is one of discontinuity in voting participation, financial structure, and accountability. The characteristics of a purchase transaction follow from the definition:

---

[3] Ibid.

[4] Jean-Marie Gagnon, "Purchase v. Pooling-of-Interests: The Search for a Predictor," *Empirical Research in Accounting: Selected Studies*, 1969. Supplement to *Journal of Accounting Research*, pp. 187–204.

[5] Ronald M. Copeland and Joseph F. Wojdak, "Income Manipulation and the Purchase-Pooling Choice," *Journal of Accounting Research* (Autumn 1969), pp. 188–195.

[6] John C. Anderson and Joseph G. Louderback III, "Income Manipulation and Purchase-Pooling: Some Additional Results," *Journal of Accounting Research* (Autumn 1975), pp. 338–343.

[7] Arthur R. Wyatt, "Discussion of Purchase v. Pooling-of-Interests: The Search for a Predictor," *Empirical Research in Accounting: Selected Studies*, 1967. Supplement to *Journal of Accounting Research*, pp. 187–204.

1. The acquiring corporation views the transaction as an investment; that is, if the value of the consideration (cash and/or securities) exceeds the *appraised* value of the assets acquired, the excess may be recorded as goodwill. APB Opinion No. 16 requires that the portion of the excess recorded as goodwill be amortized against earnings over some reasonable period. The charge against earnings, on the other hand, while lowering accounting net income, does not qualify as a tax deduction. Other things being equal, taxable income exceeds accounting income.

2. The surviving firm records the acquired assets at their cost (i.e., current value), not the book value to the selling corporation. A new basis of accountability is established, possibly resulting in higher depreciation charges against income with consequent effects on earnings after taxes.

3. Considerations may take the form of debt securities, stock, and/or cash. Securities issued by the acquiring corporation are deemed to have been issued at current market values. Debt securities and cash are frequently used to reduce the participation of the acquired firm's shareholders in the management of the surviving corporation. As a corollary, if the surviving corporation had acquired its own voting stock (Treasury stock) in contemplation of the combination, the transaction must be recorded as a purchase.

4. The seller corporation's liabilities become the obligations of the surviving firm. However, the seller's retained earnings are not added to those of the surviving firm. *Purchase accounting, in effect, capitalizes the retained earnings of the seller.* The basic notion is that one company cannot increase its retained earnings by buying another company.

As contrasted to pooling, purchasing suffers several disadvantages which can prove to be fatal impediments to a management seeking to demonstrate quickly the wisdom of the combination:

1. Given the presence of goodwill and/or a higher basis of accountability on depreciable assets, net income will be lower than if the transaction were consummated as a pooling.

2. There are negotiation problems. If the consideration includes cash, the seller may incur substantial taxable gains and demand a higher price to offset the tax bite. Or, the acquiring firm may wish to allocate the purchase price to assets that may be amortized to reduce taxable income while the seller may seek to allocate the purchase price against assets that reduce taxable gains. The objectives may be in juxtaposition.

3. The investor corporation requires earnings projections on the seller under a variety of purchase terms. This implies an understanding of the accounting methods adopted by the seller in calculating net income and an estimate of the current value of the seller's assets.

An important limitation of the purchase option should be mentioned at this point. *Under purchase, the acquiring corporation includes all of the seller's assets and liabilities in its consolidated statement, no matter when during the fiscal period the transaction was consummated. However, on the consolidated income statement, it picks up only the income of the seller applicable to the period between the transaction date and the end of the fiscal period.*

The choice between purchase or pooling depends upon the state of the economy, the earning capacity of the combining firms, their financial structures, and the objectives of the ownership interests. In general, focusing only on the accounting numbers, purchase is the choice if the book value of the acquired assets exceeds their fair market value and the effective yield on the financing used is less than the return on assets for the acquired company. This situation tends to be more prevalent in a period of declining business activity. Conversely, in a period of expansion, market values tend to exceed book values and pooling may seem the attractive option.

Pooling

APB Opinion No. 16 *describes pooling as a business combination in which the holders of substantially all the ownership interest in the constituent corporations become the owners of a single corporation that owns the assets and businesses of the constituent corporation. Continuity of voting participation and operation is the core of a pooling arrangement.* Some specific features of this accounting treatment include:

1. The acquisition is not viewed as an investment; rather, the two predecessor corporations combine into a single entity.

2. The original accounts (assets and liabilities) are carried over to the combined entity at book values. The transaction does not create a new basis of accountability or generate goodwill.

3. A pooling must be accomplished by an exchange of voting stock between previously independent companies. Bond and preferred stocks that alter the structure of ownership may not form part of the consideration. For the same reason, cash is ruled out along with Treasury stock acquired in contemplation of the merger.

4. Since assets and liabilities carry over at book values, the retained earnings of the seller corporation carry over to the combination.

5. On the same premises, the minority interest is left untouched by the pooling of the majority interests.

The *stated* capital of the pooled companies may be greater or less than the total capital of the individual units. If it is greater, the excess is deducted first from the total of any other contributed capital and then from the consolidated retained earnings. If it is less, the difference is reported on the consolidated balance sheet as excess over par.

Distinct advantages can accrue to management through executing a pooling of interests:

1. The transaction may qualify as a tax-free exchange if it also meets Internal Revenue criteria.

2. The transaction does not drain liquid assets or increase the debt/equity ratio of the combination.

3. All things equal, pooling results in a higher net income due to the absence of goodwill and no change in the basis of accountability.

4. Regardless of market values, the postcombination entity bears responsibility only for the dollar amounts that existed prior to the combination. Hence, if synergism results, pooling can create "instant growth" in earnings. As a general rule, pooling is desirable if the assets of the acquired company at book are undervalued in relation to actual or potential earning power.

5. Retention of retained earnings may permit the combination to write off any deficit on the books of the acquiring firm.

6. In contrast to the purchase transaction, the combination may pick up not only the assets and liabilities of the constituents but their *full income* irrespective of the transaction date—even after the close of the fiscal year or before the auditors arrive.

The advantages to pooling are easily demonstrated in a situation where all variables are constant except for the choice of accounting method. The real world, on the other hand, affords few instances for such simple laboratory comparisons. Instead, the relative advantage to pooling will depend upon the specific terms of the combination: the asset values, type and amounts of consideration, presence of goodwill, and so on. Earnings per share could be higher under purchase accounting depending upon the consideration mix and asset values. This complicates the researchers' problem of assessing whether security markets ignore accounting numbers in pricing the common shares of a business combination. The accounting effects may be clouded by the presence of other variables.

In summary, pooling sees nothing of significance in the event: Assets are the same as prior to the combination and the management structure remains mostly untouched. Hence, the accounting record should leave the relationships undisturbed and the market value of the shares issued to effect the combination is of no consequence for the accounting entries. Conversely, a significant change in voting rights or the sale of substantial portion of the business suggests a purchase transaction.

Accounting Methodology and Security Prices

Combination by purchase or pooling of interests can result in significant differences in earnings per share. Do security prices reflect these differences? Will the market price of the common shares be higher if the combination is effected as a pooling rather than a purchase? Does the accounting treatment convey important information to the user of financial statements? To this point, we have assumed that managements believe in the importance of accounting numbers in shaping security prices. They are not alone. It is also widely believed by business writers that stockholders of companies using pooling make abnormal gains from higher stock prices as a direct consequence of reporting relatively higher earnings.

For example, Copeland and Wojdak sampled 169 poolings[8] and estimated that earnings were overstated by 3% to 98.15%. Lintner agrees that companies which manipulate accounting numbers in mergers successfully mislead shareholders and raise the aggregate value of the combination even in a perfect

---

[8] Ronald M. Copeland and Joseph F. Wojdak, "Valuation of Unrecorded Goodwill in Merger-Minded Firms," *Financial Analysts Journal* (September-October 1969), pp. 57–62.

securities market.[9] Mosich gives a theoretical estimate of a 60% increase in stock price of a typical merging company choosing pooling instead of purchase accounting.[10]

On the significance of the accounting treatment for the user of financial statements, the FASB surveyed analysts using financial statements in making investment and credit decisions.[11] Most respondents expressed a greater need for appropriate disclosures about a combination rather than preference for a particular accounting method. With better disclosure, the analyst can adjust the statement amounts to reflect the economic and financial impact of the combination. Burton surveyed 210 financial analysts and found them evenly split as to whether purchase or pooling presented data more meaningfully.[12] Yet a survey of 64 financial analysts by Bullard showed a marked preference for purchase accounting.[13] In general, these and other surveys show no unanimity among users of financial statements regarding a preference for a particular accounting treatment, nor do they provide much information about why users of financial statements prefer a particular accounting treatment. Implicitly, however, the evidence points to a general conclusion; namely, analysts are alert to the effect on earnings of recording the combination as a purchase or pooling. It would seem they would allow for these effects in evaluating the combination.

Recent studies, looking at the informational content of alternative accounting methods and their effects on stock prices, seem to confirm the conclusion. These studies report that accounting manipulations not accompanied by real economic impacts (cash flows) have no statistically significant effects on stock prices. Apparently, the presence of alternative sources of information on corporate performance enables investors to look beyond the accounting numbers in assessing equity securities. Therefore, if the market is efficient, it will respond to the real economic consequences of the combination. Kaplan and Roll, Sunder, and Ball all report that differences in accounting methodology have no statistically significant effect on security prices, and accounting data are unimportant relative to the aggregate supply of information.

But the evidence leaves much room for reasonable doubt, and so the argument will continue unabated. It will take more substantial evidence than is currently available to convince businessmen that accounting strategy has neutral effects on the market value of the combination.

Tax Options

Accounting advantages may not harmonize with preferred tax treatments. An acquisition strategy to optimize tax benefits for the acquiring corporation

[9]J. Lintner, "Expectations, Mergers and Equilibrium in Purely Competitive Securities Markets," *American Economic Review* (1971), pp. 101–111.
[10]A. N. Mosich, "Impact of Merger Accounting on Post-Merger Financial Reports," *Management Accounting* (December 1965).
[11]Financial Accounting Standards Board, *Accounting for Business Combinations and Purchased Intangibles*, (August 19, 1976), pp. 36–40.
[12]John C. Burton, *Accounting for Business Combinations* (New York: Financial Executives Research Foundation, 1970).
[13]Ruth Harper Bullard, "The Effect of Accounting for Combinations on Investor Decisions," The University of Texas at Austin, August 1972.

may result in a lower earnings per share. For example, a cash transaction treated as a *taxable exchange* and a *purchase* may generate higher tax shields and increased cash flow but carry a lower earnings per share, owing to added depreciation charges and the amortization of goodwill. To further complicate the issue, the criteria for a tax-free exchange and pooling differ. Hence, it is sometimes possible to treat the acquisition as taxable to obtain depreciation tax shields and for accounting purposes as a pooling to secure higher earnings per share.

Tax strategies conflict and the tax objectives of the buyer and seller may not coincide. Tax objectives depend upon a comparison of the purchase price for the property acquired and the seller's tax basis on the stock or other assets sold. Where purchase price is less than the tax cost, the seller will likely opt for a taxable transaction. Conversely, if the purchase price exceeds the tax cost, the seller more often seeks a tax-free transaction. The buyer, on the other hand, would aim at tax-free exchange in the first instance and a taxable exchange in the second case. Then, too, the tax position of the shareholders may differ from the tax position of their corporation so that what is good for one may not under all circumstances meet the interests of the other. The issue arises depending on whether the corporation is disposing of assets or its stockholders are selling their shares in a takeover situation.

Buyer and seller may also disagree over the allocation of the purchase price in a taxable transaction. The buyer strives to allocate the purchase price to depreciable property in order to capture the tax shields. The seller, on the other hand, seeks to allocate the purchase price to assets that qualify for capital gains or to those assets where the tax basis approximates or exceeds their purchase cost. The seller will also resist the allocations to inventories, since gains on inventory investment are taxable as ordinary income.

Finally, a tax-free exchange does not imply forgiveness, only deferral. The seller does not pay a tax at the time he or she exchanges his or her stock for shares in the acquiring corporation. Instead, the tax basis of the original shares becomes the basis of the new shares, and the seller pays a tax calculated on this basis when he *subsequently* disposes of the new shares. In short, no tax is payable at the time of the stock swap. Further, if the seller wills the shares to his or her estate, they are valued to the estate on the basis of their current worth at time of death and the entire capital gain is thus avoided. The latter arrangement at best gives the seller a vicarious satisfaction—wherever he or she may be.

IDENTIFYING TAKE-OVER OPPORTUNITIES

The articulation of an acquisition strategy (covering economic substance, accounting methodology, tax objectives, as well as the pertinent options under the security and antitrust regulations) sets the stage for the process of identifying a potential merger partner. No matter what the particular techniques employed (and each practitioner has his own angle) selection requires a forecast of future earnings and assessment of risk. There are two fundamental approaches: present value analysis and capital asset pricing. These are discussed below.

Present-Value Analysis

When present-value analysis is used, the earnings of the acquired firm are projected and discounted at the investor's cost of capital to obtain a theoretical market price on the shares of the investee corporation. This is compared to the actual market price to determine the net present value of the investment.

Assume that Alpha, Inc., is considering the acquisition of 100% of Delta's voting shares. Alpha's cost of capital is 10%. Delta has maintained a constant payout ratio with the current dividend at $1 per share. Earnings are expected to grow at 9% annually. Delta's shares currently sell at $52. The *theoretical price* of Delta's shares, using the dividend valuation model from Chapter 8, is:

$$D_1 = D_0(1 + g) = \$1.00(1.09) \tag{1}$$
$$= \$1.09$$
$$P_0 = \frac{D_1}{K - g} = \frac{\$1.09}{0.10 - 0.09} = \$109$$

Because the theoretical price exceeds the market price (or cost of the investment) of $52, the NPV equals $57 per share. The situation, accordingly, warrants further investigation of Delta.

The NPV approach has several shortcomings. The analysis assumes that the acquired corporation will do as well after the combination as before (i.e., in the case of Delta, it will at least maintain the 9% growth rate). More important, if the acquired company is large relative to the size of the investor, the acquisition will likely change the risk-return characteristics of the surviving firm. This alters its cost of capital and upsets the calculation of NPV. Also, unless NPV is put on an expected value basis and the variance and covariances calculated, the method does not specifically assess the risk posture of the combination (i.e., the portfolio effects). Thus, the analysis at best provides only a point of departure for further investigation of a merger candidate.

Capital Asset Pricing

The NPV approach has the advantage of using concepts familiar to everyday financial practices. The CAPM (capital asset pricing model), however, enjoys theoretical superiority.[14] Following the procedures of Chapter 17, CAPM employs the security market line or the market price of risk as the hurdle rate in identifying a potential merger partner. A required return is calculated, $E(R_j^0) = R_F + [E(R_m) - R_F](B_j)$ and compared to an expected return, $E(R_j)$, calculated independently. If the expected return exceeds the required return, $E(R_j) > E(R_j^0)$, the acquiring firm has a potential merger partner. In this case $E(R_j)$ lies above the security market line.

In Table 26–3 we have assumed four possible states of the economy with related probabilities (P_S), and rates of return for the market index (R_m) and the potential merger partner (R_j). These rates of return depict the performance of

[14]Subject to the restrictive assumptions discussed in Chapter 18.

TABLE 26–3   Selecting a Merger Partner by CAPM

States of the Economy	P_S	R_m	R_j
Revival (S_1)	0.20	0.10	0.15
Prosperity (S_2)	0.50	0.15	0.20
Recession (S_3)	0.20	0.08	0.06
Depression (S_4)	0.10	0.06	0.03
	1.00		

Market Parameters

	P_S	R_m	$(P_S)(R_m)$	$R_m - E(R_m)$	$[R_m - E(R_m)]^2$	$[R_m - E(R_m)]^2 P_S$
S_1	0.20	0.10	0.020	-0.017	0.000289	0.0000578
S_2	0.50	0.15	0.075	$+0.033$	0.001089	0.0005445
S_3	0.20	0.08	0.016	-0.037	0.001369	0.0002738
S_4	0.10	0.06	0.006	-0.057	0.003249	0.0003249
			$E(R_m) = 0.117$		$\sigma_m^2 =$	0.0012010

Cov $R_j R_m$

	P_S	R_j	$(P_S)(R_j)$	$d_j =$ $R_j - E(R_j)$	$d_m =$ $R_m - E(R_m)$	$d_j d_m$	$d_j d_m P_S$
S_1	0.20	0.15	0.030	$+0.005$	-0.017	-0.000085	-0.0000170
S_2	0.50	0.20	0.100	$+0.055$	$+0.033$	$+0.001815$	$+0.0009075$
S_3	0.20	0.06	0.012	-0.085	-0.037	$+0.003145$	$+0.0006290$
S_4	0.10	0.03	0.003	-0.115	-0.057	$+0.006555$	$+0.0006555$
			$E(R_j) = 0.145$			$\text{Cov}(R_j, R_m) =$	0.0021750

Assume a 6% risk-free rate (R_F).
Then

$$B_j = \frac{\text{Cov}(R_j, R_m)}{\sigma_m^2} = \frac{0.0021745}{0.001201} = 1.81$$

Therefore,

$$E(R_j^0) = R_F + [E(R_m) - R_F]B_j \qquad (2)$$
$$= 0.06 + (0.117 - 0.06)1.81$$
$$= 0.163$$

the market index and the acquiring firm over the past business cycles (which are expected to hold for the future), or they may be projections of future performance allowing for deviations from past behavior. Either approach may be used. Note in Table 26–3 that the required rate of return $E(R_j^0) = 16.3\%$ exceeds the expected return $E(R_j) = 14.5\%$, so j would not qualify as a desirable merger partner.

The contribution of the acquired firm to the combination's variance-of-equity rate does not affect the accept or reject decision based upon the market price of risk, so diversification (the reduction of the variance) can be ignored. In the absence of synergy, $E(R_j^0) = E(R_j)$, each potential merger partner can be evaluated without reference to the firm's existing risk-return characteristics. CAPM simply assumes that the acquiring firm will always seek merger partners having estimated returns at least commensurate with their risk posture.

The Bargaining Area

After identifying the merger target, the implementation of an acquisition strategy requires identification of a bargaining area: maximum and minimum exchange ratios acceptable to the shareholders of the acquiring and acquired firms. For this purpose, the model developed by Larson and Gonedes offers a useful framework.[15] This model assumes the following:

1. The objective of the combination is to enhance the market value of the common shares.
2. The shareholders will not approve of the combination unless it promises to maintain or increase their wealth position measured by the market value of their holdings.
3. The price-earnings (P/E) ratio of the shares captures the risk-return characteristics of the merging firms. In other words, market price trades off risk and return.
4. The shares are publicly traded.
5. No synergism will eventuate in the first year of merger.
6. Bargaining is a condition of bilateral monopoly: one buyer of the shares and one seller.

The Larson-Gonedes Model requires the calculation of several components:

1. Precombination wealth position of the firms. This represents the market value of a common share 6 months to 1 year before the announcement of any merger. The objective is to establish the value of the equity shares uneffected by news of an impending combination:
(a) *Wealth of acquiring company* (W_A):

$$W_A = (P/E_A)(EPS_A) \qquad (3)$$

(b) *Wealth of acquired company* (W_B):

$$W_B = (P/E_B)(EPS_B)$$

2. Postcombination wealth position. This refers to the value of a common share (W_{AB}) after the combination or merger:

$$W_{AB} = (\Theta)(Y_A + Y_B) \times \frac{1}{S_A + (ER)S_B} \qquad (4)$$

where Θ = the expected P/E ratio after the combination
Y = total earnings of each entity for latest period prior to combination or first period earnings of the entity after the combination

[15]Kermit D. Larson and Nicholas J. Gonedes, "Business Combinations: An Exchange Ratio Determination Model," *The Accounting Review* (October 1969), pp. 720–728.

S_A = number of precombination shares of acquiring company
S_B = number of precombination shares of acquired company
ER = exchange ratio to affect the combination.

Note that for any given value of Θ, there is a corresponding exchange ratio.

3. *Wealth position of acquiring shareholders, postcombination.* The shareholders of the acquiring firm (A) will approve the combination if they *expect*:

$$W_{AB} \geq W_A \tag{5}$$

That is, the market value of their common shares will be equal to or greater than the precombination value. In other words, they anticipate the benefits of synergism.

4. *Wealth position of the acquired shareholders, postcombination.* The shareholders of the acquired firm (B) will approve the combination if they *expect*:

$$W_{AB} \geq \left(\frac{1}{ER} \right) W_B \tag{6}$$

where

$$ER = \frac{W_B}{W_A} \tag{7}$$

The same rationale for approval of the combination applies to the acquired shareholders.

5. Bargaining area.

(a) *Maximum exchange ratio.* The maximum exchange ratio acceptable to the shareholders of the acquiring company (ER_A) is that which leaves their wealth position unchanged ($W_{AB} = W_A$). A higher exchange ratio transfers wealth to the shareholders of the acquired company. It follows that the acquiring company will bargain for a lower exchange ratio.

$$ER_A = \frac{(\Theta)(Y_A + Y_B) - (P/E_A)(Y_A)}{(P/E_A)(Y_A)(1/S_A)(S_B)} \tag{8}$$

ER_A will increase at a constant rate as Θ increases (see Figure 26–1).

(b) *Minimum exchange ratio.* This designates the minimum number of shares of company A acceptable to the acquired shareholders (ER_B) that will leave their wealth position unchanged ($W_{AB} = (1/ER)W_B$). A lower exchange ratio would transfer wealth to the shareholders of the acquiring company. Hence, the acquired company will bargain for a higher exchange ratio.

$$ER_B = \frac{(P/E_B)(Y_B/S_B)(S_A)}{(\Theta)(Y_A + Y_B) - (P/E_B)(Y_B)} \tag{9}$$

The minimum exchange ratio varies inversely with theta (see Figure 26–1).

In Figure 26–1, the bargaining area is bounded by ER_A–E–ER_B. Here, the market value of the combination (V_{AB}) exceeds the precombination values of the separate entities (V_A and V_B), thereby creating synergism. To the left of the equilibrium, E, no merger would take place because both sets of shareholders

FIGURE 26-1   Business Combinations Bargaining Area

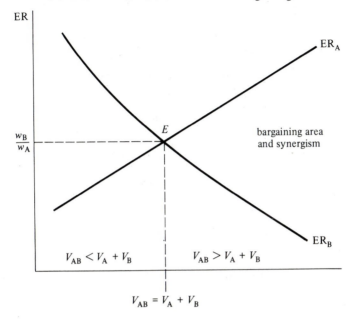

would be less well off. At E, their wealth positions remain unchanged; the exchange ratio equals the ratio of the market prices of the common shares for A and B; and Θ equals an average of the P/E ratios of A and B weighted by their total earnings, Y_A and Y_B.

□ **EXAMPLE 1**   *Larson-Gonedes Model*

Assume Air-Frames, Inc. is negotiating a merger with Windom Engines, Inc. The comparative data on the two corporations is as follows:

	Air-Frames, Inc. (A)	*Windom Engines, Inc. (B)*
Earnings per share	$2.87	$1.65
Dividends	$1.80 annually	$1.00
Growth rate	6%	7%
Book value per share	$26.50	$33
Market value per share	$43	$52
Shares outstanding	3 million	1 million
P/E	15	31.5
Total earnings (Y)	$8,610,000	$1,650,000
Total value of equity	$129,000,000	$52,000,000

Projected P/E of combination $(\Theta) = 25$

(a) Should the shareholders of both corporations approve the merger?

(b) What are the minimum and maximum exchange ratios for acquiring and acquired corporations?

(c) What is the total synergism projected? If the actual exchange ratio agreed upon is 1.2 A for 1 B, how is the synergism divided?

Solution:

(a) First, find the precombination wealth position [Equation (3)]:

$$\text{Air Frames, Inc.} \quad W_A = (15)(2.87) = \$43.05$$

$$\text{Windom Engines, Inc.} \quad W_B = (31.5)(1.65) = \$51.98$$

Then, find the postcombination wealth position [Equation (4)]:

$$W_{AB} = (25)(\$8,610,000 + \$1,650,000) \times \frac{1}{3,000,000 + (1.2)1,000,000}$$

$$= \$256,500,000 \times \frac{1}{4,200,000}$$

$$= \$61.07$$

The wealth position of Air-Frame shareholders [Equation (5)] is:

$$\$61.07 > \$43$$

Air-Frame shareholders should vote for merger.

The wealth position of Windom Engines shareholders [Equation (6)] is:

$$\$61.07 > \frac{1}{1.2} \times \$52$$

$$\$61.07 > \$43.33$$

Windom shareholders should vote for the merger.

(b) The maximum exchange ratio [Equation (8)] is:

$$ER_A = \frac{(25)(\$8,610,000 + \$1,650,000) - (15)(\$8,610,000)}{(15)(8,610,000)(1/3,000,000)(1,000,000)}$$

$$= \frac{\$256,500,000 - \$129,150,000}{\$129,150,000 \times 1,000,000/3,000,000}$$

$$= \frac{\$127,350,000}{43,050,000}$$

$$= 2.96 \text{ shares}$$

The minimum exchange ratio [Equation (9)] is:

$$ER_B = \frac{(31.5)(\$1,650,000/1,000,000)(3,000,000)}{(25)(\$8,610,000 + \$1,650,000) - (31.5)(\$1,650,000)}$$

$$= \frac{\$155,925,000}{\$256,500,000 - \$51,975,000}$$

$$= \frac{\$155,925,000}{\$204,525,000}$$

$$= 0.76 \text{ shares}$$

(c) To find synergism, assuming an actual exchange rate of 1.2 A = 1 B, use the following:

Postcombination value of common shares [Equation (4)]:
$61.07 × 4,200,000 = $256,494,000
Precombination value of common shares:
    Air-Frame, Inc. $43 × 3,000,000 = $129,000,000
    Windom Engines, Inc. $52 × 1,000,000 =   52,000,000 181,000,000
Total synergism $75,494,000

less

Amount to Air-Frame holders:
    $61.07 − $43 × 3,000,000 = 54,210,000
Amount to Windom holders $21,284,000

If the actual exchange ratio equals the ratio of market prices for the acquired and acquiring companies ($ER = MV_B/MV_A$), then the synergism will be divided proportionately; that is, the parties retain their same relative wealth positions as before the merger. If the actual exchange ratio exceeds the ratio of market values, then the shareholders of the acquired company do proportionately better; they have gained relatively. If the actual exchange ratio is less than the ratio of market values, the shareholders of the acquiring company gain relatively. These conclusions follow from the bargaining strategies derived from Equations (8) and (9).   □

Within the bargaining area, the final exchange ratio may depend upon a balance of factors representing the strengths and weaknesses of the firms in light of the merger objectives. These include the following:

1. Liquidity. In the McDonnell-Douglas merger, for example, Douglas had important contracts but had working-capital problems. McDonnell had the liquidity to rectify the deficiency, and this became an important element in effecting the combination. It is worth recalling that the primary cause of business failures in the 1970s among larger firms has been inadequate working capital.

2. Strategic assets. One firm may possess facilities, patents, and other special assets that enhance its bargaining power.

3. Management capabilities. If one firm possesses a particularly strong management team, it may figure prominently in assessing the future prospects of the combination.

4. Tax-loss carryovers. In a tax-free exchange, tax losses carry over to the acquiring corporation, but the principal purpose of the acquisition cannot look to the tax benefits. Assuming a legitimate business objective, tax-loss carryovers are attractive where the acquiring firm has income against which deductions may be applied. In a taxable exchange, the loss remains with the selling firm and may be applied against the gain from the sale of assets.

5. Reproduction cost. In a period of sustained inflation, it may be more economical to acquire assets through combination than by new construction. The factor may motivate mergers where the acquisition of fixed assets determines the objectives of expansion.

6. Investment value. Where the merger involves combination with a newly organized firm and/or the promotion of a new process, the amount of cash actually paid into the newcomer (investment value) may influence the exchange rate.

7. Market value. Probably the most common determinant of the final exchange ratio is the relative market value of the combined firms' shares. It is also the most logical element. If there exists an active market in the shares and if the market is efficient, the market will discount all that is known about the future prospects of the firms and reflect it in the market value of the shares.

8. Book values. Where conservative accounting practices have been followed, book values offer the advantage of convenience and speed in negotiation.

The reader may add other factors, such as earnings per share, dividend payout ratios, and so on. Suffice it to say, as the negotiations swing toward higher or lower exchange ratios, wealth is transferred from one group of shareholders to the other.

SUMMARY

A comprehensive merger theory has been slow in evolving. This should not be surprising because business combinations spring from different motivations and cover a time frame concomitant with the evolution of capitalism. Moreover, the available studies consider different time periods, employ dissimilar sample selection criteria, use disparate techniques in measuring the "effects" of business combinations, and apply varying statistical techniques in assessing results. The chameleon policies of government, which may channel business combinations in less than economically optimal directions, compound these problems. For example, Weston points out that the 1950 amendments to Section 7 of the Clayton Act enabled regulatory authorities virtually to abort horizontal and vertical mergers in which one of the parties has 10% or more of the defined market area. This change in the institutional structure contributed to the rising tide of conglomerate mergers.[16]

All the same, survey of the modern literature (1960–80) underscores the following characteristics of acquired firms:

They have a cost of capital higher than other firms in their industry. Merger lowers the cost of capital, thus facilitating investment in the acquired firms operations.

They are situated in an industry with favorable growth and profit opportunities. The acquiring firm has more funds than capital projects to absorb them. Investment opportunities are relatively more favorable in the acquired firm's industry than the acquiring firm's industry.

They have organizational and/or managerial capital of value in the upcoming combination.

[16] J. Fred Weston, "Developments in Finance Theory," *Financial Management*, (Summer, 1981), pp. 5–22.

They have lower P/E ratios and lower financial leverage than acquiring firms.

Their shareholders experience significant positive wealth effects from the market reaction to news of the combination or the tender offer.

QUESTIONS/PROBLEMS

1. Briefly discuss the elements of the acquisition decision.
2. What are the shortcomings of a present-value analysis in the acquisition decision?
3. Discuss how CAPM would be used in the acquisition decision and when it would point to an attractive merger.
4. Return to Air-Frames, Inc. Air-Frames has another merger opportunity with General Aviation. The latter has the following financial profile:

Earnings per share	$4.20
Annual dividend	$3.50
Growth rate	1%
Book value per share	$55
Market value per share	$41
Share Outstanding	2,000,000
P/E ratio	9.76
Total earnings	$8,400,000
Total value	$82,000,000
Projected P/E (Θ)	13
Proposed actual exchange ratio	0.95 A = 1 B

Determine each of the following.
(a) Precombination wealth position.
(b) Postcombination wealth position.
(c) Maximum and minimum exchange ratios.
(d) The amount and division of total synergism.
(e) Air-Frames has decided to evaluate General Aviation using the CAPM approach:

State of the Economy	P_S	R_m	General Aviation (R_j)
Revival (S_1)	0.20	0.20	0.15
Prosperity (S_2)	0.50	0.30	0.20
Recession (S_3)	0.20	0.16	0.09
Depression (S_4)	0.10	0.12	0.05

The risk-free rate is 10%. Is General Aviation worth consideration as a takeover prospect?

[17]Ibid.

Strategic Planning: The Financial Component

Strategic planning pertains to the establishment of goals and the progress of the firm in moving toward the defined targets. In periods of expanding economic activity, typical goals include increased market penetration through modification of product lines; additions to plant and equipment; added research and development spending; updating management training and personnel administration; the achievement of an optimal financial structure to minimize the cost of capital; and so forth. Many of these topics, the reader will observe, form the subject matter of capital budgeting—and not by coincidence. *Important components of the strategic plan are given concrete expression by the capital budget and the supporting decisions made in formulating a capital budget.*

Strategic planning does not relate solely to the balmy days of prosperity. Mistakes are made in the planning process that become sorely obvious during economic retrenchment. The strategic plan in a recession environment may stress retreat from indefensible positions and reductions in cost of operations to restore profit margins. The decision to abandon a project or subsidiary relies upon the same techniques of capital budgeting as those required by the initial evaluation of investment opportunities. In addition, decisions such as lease or own, lease or sell, refunding of corporate debt, buying up the firm's stock on the open market also relate to strategic planning but utilize capital budgeting evaluation techniques in execution.

Viable strategic planning demands a balanced relationship among the defined goals. If imbalances appear in the implementation, then some goals are necessarily compromised. This chapter centers on the problem of balancing growth (or shrinkage) in assets with other established financial policies enunciated in the strategic plan.

SUSTAINABLE GROWTH (STABLE PRICES)

In a strategic-planning context, the question of an appropriate growth rate over a defined long-term period takes the form: What rate of growth is sustainable with regard to established financial policies? Specifically, given the firm's target dividend-payout ratio and capital structure (long-term debt to equity), what percentage increase in sales can be maintained without necessitating a change in financial policy?[1] If sales grow at a higher rate, the firm can exercise a combination of options: increase debt, reduce dividend payout, improve operating performance to increase profit margins, or issue equity securities. Except for improved operating efficiency, each option alters established financial policies.[2]

For purposes of initial discussion, let us assume the following:

1. The book depreciation is adequate to recapture the value of existing assets.

2. The profit margin (P) on new sales (ΔS) corresponds to that of existing sales (S).

3. The firm has an established financial structure goal (L) without the sale of new common stock.

4. The firm has an established dividend payout rate (D); thus, the target retention ratio is $1 - D$.

5. New fixed assets at book values (F) represent a stated proportion of the change in physical volume of output (real sales).

6. New current assets (C) are a stated proportion of sales in nominal dollars.

7. The initial level of sales at the beginning of the period is represented by S and the change in sales during the period by ΔS.

8. The ratio of *total* assets to net sales is denoted by T; the ratio is constant for new and existing sales.

9. The firm will rely on retained earnings for equity financing—no new common stock is to be issued.

Assuming a stable price level for the moment as well as all of the symbols defined above, the sustainable growth rate (g^*) becomes:

$$g^* = \frac{\Delta S}{S} = \frac{P(1 - D)(1 + L)}{T - P(1 - D)(1 + L)} \tag{1}$$

---

[1] The reader will recall the distinction between *capital structure* (long-term debt to equity) and *financial structure* (total debt to equity).

[2] The discussion is based upon the following articles: Robert C. Higgins, "How Much Growth Can a Firm Afford?" *Financial Management* (Fall 1977) and "Sustainable Growth Under Inflation" *Financial Management* (Autumn 1981); and Dana J. Johnson, "The Behavior of Financial Structure and Sustainable Growth in an Inflationary Environment," *Financial Management* (Autumn 1981).

□ **EXAMPLE 1**   *Micro-Industries, Inc.*

Micro-Industries, Inc.
Balance Sheet
December 31, 198X

Assets	$	%	Liabilities and Equities	$	%
Cash	$10,000	(0.12)	Accounts payable	$ 5,000	(0.06)
Inventory	15,000	(0.18)	Bonds payable	30,000	(0.35)
Equipment	80,000	(0.94)	Capital stock (7,500 shares)	30,000	(0.35)
less: accumulated					
depreciation	20,000	(−0.24)	Retained earnings	20,000	(0.24)
	$85,000	(1.00)		$85,000	(1.00)

Micro-Industries, Inc.
Income Statement
December 31, 198X

Sales	$30,000	(10,000 units at $3.00)
less: cost of sales	8,000	
Gross Profit	$22,000	
less: selling and administrative expenses	11,000	
Net-operating income (EBIT)	$11,000	
less: interest (10%) on debt	3,500	
Earnings before taxes (EBT)	$ 7,500	

Profit Margin $(P) = 0.25$
Earnings per share (EPS) = $7,500/7,500 = $1.00 before taxes
Dividend payout ratio (D) = 33%, or $1.00 × 0.33 = 33¢ per share
Retention Ratio = $1 - D = 1 - 0.33 = 0.67$, or 67%
Total assets/sales ratio (T) = $85,000/$30,000 = 2.833
Financial structure objective $(L) = D/E$ = $35,000/$50,000 = 0.70
Price Trend (J) = +10% (revival); − 0.10% (recession)
Current assets/current sales (C) = $25,000/$30,000 = 0.833
Fixed assets/sales (F) = $80,000/$30,000 = 2.67

What is the sustainable rate of growth for Micro-Industries?

Solution:

$$g^* = \frac{0.25(1 - 0.33)(1 + 0.70)}{2.83 - 0.25(1 - 0.33)(1 + 0.70)} \tag{2}$$

$$= \frac{0.28475}{2.83 - 0.28475}$$

$$= 0.111875, \quad \text{or} \quad \approx 11.2\% \qquad\qquad □$$

Since assets must equal liabilities plus equity, growth-induced assets must be financed by new debt and/or an increase in retained earnings. Unless the actual growth rate (g) equals the sustainable growth rate (g^*), the profit margin, dividend payout ratio, debt/equity ratio, or total assets/sales ratio must change or the firm will be compelled to issue new equities.

Thus, the optimal growth is not simply the product of accepting all investments with a positive NPV or an IRR greater than or equal to K. Management may have to reflect explicitly upon the implications of higher growth rates and the revision of financial policies through lower dividend payout, increased leveraging, or sale of equities. These decisions have both financial and managerial control implications.

SUSTAINABLE GROWTH (RISING PRICE TREND)

Allowing for the effect of a rising price trend revises Equation (1) as follows:

$$g_R^* = \frac{(1+J)P(1-D)(1+L) - JC}{(1+J)C + F - (1+J)P(1-D)(1+L)} \tag{3}$$

Equation (3) is illustrated in the following example.

□ **EXAMPLE 2** *Micro-Industries Extended*

Take the same data on Micro-Industries, but now take a 10% rate of price increase into account. What is the real sustainable growth rate (g_R^*)?

Solution:

$$g_R^* = \frac{(1+0.10)0.25(1-0.33)(1+0.70) - (0.10)(0.833)}{(1+0.10)0.833 + 2.67 - (1+0.10)0.25(1-0.33)(1+0.70)} \tag{4}$$

$$= \frac{0.313225 - 0.0833}{3.5863 - 0.313225}$$

$$= \frac{0.229925}{3.273075}$$

$$= 0.0702473 \quad \text{or} \quad \approx 7\%$$ □

Overall, *given the assumptions of the model,* an upward trend in prices acts to reduce real sustainable growth unless offset by operating efficiencies. In the extreme case, inflation-induced increases in retained earnings and borrowing are more than offset by required increases in working capital investment. Higgins[3] estimates, for example, that real sustainable growth declines by 2.2% for every 5% increase in the rate of inflation. He further notes:

> To the extent that depreciation is insufficient to maintain the value of assets...sustainable growth is reduced.... If newly acquired assets are more profitable than existing assets in the sense of producing sales with a higher profit margin, offering a more rapid depreciation rate or generating more sales per dollar of assets...sustainable growth will rise.

Similarly sustainable growth (g^*) can rise if the firm intensifies asset utilization

---

[3] Higgins, *op. cit.*

by reducing the assets required to support a given level of sales. Otherwise, the firm can restore its sustainable rate of growth ($g*$) in an inflationary environment subject to the stipulated assumptions only by altering accepted financial policies (reducing dividend payout, increasing leverage, sale of new equity shares). All things considered, therefore, inflation has inimical effects on the sustainable rate of growth ($g*$). A sustainable growth rate different from $g*$ is inconsistent with established financial targets.

Johnson qualified the original Higgins model and the presumption of a constant *financial* structure. The former hinged the discussion on the rate of sustainable growth using a constant *capital* structure [long-term debt to equity ratio (L_L)]. Based upon Higgins assumptions, Johnson shows that total uses of funds are composed of the change in total nominal current assets, $[(S + \Delta S)(1 + J) - S]C$, plus new nominal fixed assets, $(\Delta S)F$. Sources of funds equal the increase in nominal debt plus retained earnings, $(S + \Delta S)(1 + J)P(1 - D)(1 + L)$. The real sustainable rate of growth (g_R) as restated by Johnson[4] using the Higgins assumptions becomes:

$$g_R = \frac{(1 + J)Y - JC}{F - (1 + g)Y + C(1 + J)} \tag{5}$$

where

$$Y = P(1 - D)(1 + L)$$

□ **EXAMPLE 3**

Using the data on Micro-Industries, determine the sustainable rate of growth by applying Equation (5).

Solution:

$$Y = 0.25(1 - 0.33)(1 + 0.70)$$
$$= 0.28475$$

Then,

$$g_R = \frac{(1 + 0.10).28475 - (0.10)(0.833)}{2.67 - (1 + 0.10)0.28475 + 0.833(1 + 0.10)} \tag{6}$$

$$= \frac{0.229925}{2.67 - 0.313225 + 0.9163}$$

$$= \frac{0.229925}{3.273075}$$

$$= 0.0702473, \quad \text{or} \quad \approx 7\%$$

This agrees with Higgins results from Equation (4) based upon a constant financial structure. However, Johnson by focusing on capital structure (long-term debt to equity) allows working capital to float with nominal sales.   □

The revised real sustainable rate of growth thus takes the form:

$$g_R = \frac{\Delta S}{S} = \frac{Y(1 + J) - WJ}{F - (1 + J)Y + W(1 + J)} \tag{7}$$

where $Y = P(1 - D)(1 + L_L)$
    W = the ratio of nominal net working capital to nominal sales

[4] Johnson, *op. cit.*

□ **EXAMPLE 4**

Assume the same data used in the preceding problems except that long-term debt to equity ratio (L_L) equals .60; and the ratio of net working capital to nominal sales (W) equals 0.67. What is the real sustainable growth based upon a constant *capital* structure?

Solution:

$$Y = 0.25(1 - 0.33)(1 + 0.60)$$

$$= 0.268$$

Then,

$$g_R = \frac{0.268(1 + 0.10) - (0.67)(0.10)}{2.67 - (1 + 0.10)0.268 + 0.67(1 + 0.10)} \tag{8}$$

$$= \frac{0.2948 - 0.067}{2.67 - 0.2948 + 0.737}$$

$$= \frac{0.2278}{3.1122}$$

$$= 0.0731958, \quad \text{or} \quad 7.3\%$$ □

Comparison of Equations (5) and (7) indicates that the incremental price-induced financing for current assets is partially offset by the price-adjusted rise in current liabilities. Thus, with a constant capital structure the real sustainable rate of growth is higher than that attainable were the firm to adhere to an established financial structure. In both cases (a target financial structure or a target capital structure), the sustainable rate is lower than that attainable under conditions of price stability. The reason for the latter phenomenon lies in the assumption that management uses historical-cost financial statements in describing the optimal financial or capital structures and in setting up target ratios. It follows that in the face of persistent inflation, management can maintain a stable capital structure over time only by using a constant dollar debt/equity ratio or one based upon market values.

Bear in mind our conclusions apply to any generalized upward trend in prices. Inflation (see Chapter 9) is a special, albeit extreme, case of an upward movement in prices.

SUSTAINABLE GROWTH (DOWNWARD TREND IN PRICES)

This section addresses the questions raised as the price level turns downward from the equilibrium, depicted in Equations (3) and (4). A priori, one would expect a slowdown in the rate of real sustainable growth. Applying Equation (3) for a *fixed financial structure*, we have:

$$g_R^* = \frac{(1 - 0.10)0.25(1 - 0.33)(1 + 0.70) - (-0.10)(0.833)}{(1 - 0.10)0.833 + 2.67 - (1 - 0.10)0.25(1 - 0.33)(1 + 0.70)} \tag{10}$$

$$= \frac{0.256275 - (-0.0833)}{3.4197 - 0.256275}$$

$$= \frac{0.339575}{3.163425}$$

$$= 0.1073441, \quad \text{or} \quad \approx 10.7\%$$

For a constant capital structure, applying Equation (7), we have:

$$g_R = \frac{0.268(1 - 0.10) - (0.67)(0.10)}{2.67 - (1 - 0.10)0.268 + 0.67(1 - 0.10)} \tag{11}$$

$$= \frac{0.2412 - 0.067}{2.67 - 0.2412 + 0.603}$$

$$= \frac{0.1742}{3.0318}$$

$$= 0.0574576, \quad \text{or} \quad \approx 5.7\%$$

Based upon the Johnson formulation [Equation (7)], the real sustainable growth rate drops to zero with a 28% decline in the price level and shows a negative rate at 30%. Improved productivity can wholly or partially offset declining growth rates by enhancing profit margins. Otherwise, the situation dictates a defensive strategy of building liquidity, reducing leverage or increasing dividend payouts in the presence of capital in excess of investment opportunities.

ESTABLISHING FINANCIAL POLICY IN RELATION TO A TARGET GROWTH RATE

Obviously, the preceding equations can be employed to solve for any unknown value, as illustrated in the following example.

□ EXAMPLE 5

Suppose that Micro-Industries, assuming a stable price level, establishes a target growth rate of 11.2% for the period covered by its strategic plan. What D/E is compatible with the stated objective?

Solution: Using the original Higgins model expressed in Equation (1), we have:

$$g^* = \frac{P(1 - D)(1 + L)}{T - P(1 - D)(1 + L)} \tag{12}$$

$$11.2 = \frac{0.25(1 - 0.33)(1 + L)}{2.83 - 0.25(1 - 0.33)(1 + L)}$$

$$11.2 = \frac{0.1675(1 + L)}{2.83 - 0.1675(1 + L)}$$

Let $(1 + L) = X$. Then,

$$11.2 = \frac{0.1675(X)}{2.83 - .1675(X)}$$

Let $Y = 0.1675(X)$:

$$0.112(2.83 - Y) = Y$$

$$0.112 \times 2.83 = Y + 0.112Y$$

$$0.112 \times 2.83 = 1.112Y$$

$$Y = \frac{0.112 \times 2.83}{1.112}$$

$$= 0.285$$

Then,

$$X = \frac{Y}{0.1675}$$

$$X = \frac{0.285}{0.1675}$$

$$X = 1.7$$

Since $X = (1 + L)$, $L = X - 1 = 1.7 - 1 = 0.70$. The D/E ratio consistent with the targeted growth rate is 0.70. □

In like manner, Micro-Industries might test the compatibility of other variables, such as the dividend payout policy, total assets to sales, profit margin on sales and so forth. The testing procedure can also incorporate projected price trends by using Equation (3). If we assume that the targeted growth rate is primarily dependent on capital budget items, then the manipulation of Equation (1) relates the significance of the capital budget for other key planning variables.

The Johnson models can, of course, be similarly utilized, as now demonstrated.

□ **EXAMPLE 6**

Posing the same question for Micro-Industries as raised in Example 5, determine g_R using Equation (7).

Solution:

$$g_R = \frac{Y(1+J) - WJ}{F - (1+J)Y + W(1+J)}$$

where $Y = P(1 - D)(1 + L_L)$

If we insert the disaggretated value of Y into the primary equation, g_R becomes:

$$g_R = \frac{[P(1 - D)(1 + L_L)](1+J) - WJ}{F - (1+J)[P(1 - D)(1 + L_L)] + W(1+J)} \tag{13}$$

$$0.073 = \frac{[0.25(1 - 0.33)(1 + L_L)](1 + 0.10) - (0.67)(0.10)}{2.67 - (1 + 0.10)[0.25(1 - 0.33)(1 + L_L)] + 0.67(1 + 0.10)}$$

$$0.073 = \frac{[0.1675(1 + L_L)](1.1) - 0.067}{2.67 - (1.1)[0.1675(1 + L_L)] + 0.737}$$

Let $X = (1 + L_L)$. Then,

$$0.073 = \frac{[0.1675(X)](1.1) - 0.067}{2.67 - (1.1)[0.1675(X)] + 0.737}$$

If $Z = 0.1675(X)$,

$$0.073 = \frac{Z(1.1) - 0.067}{2.67 - Z(1.1) + 0.737}$$

$$0.073(2.67 - 1.1Z + 0.737) = 1.1Z - 0.067$$

$$0.19491 - 0.0803Z + 0.053801 = 1.1Z - 0.067$$

$$0.19491 + 0.053801 + 0.067 = 1.1Z + 0.0803Z$$

$$0.315711 = 1.1803Z$$

$$0.2674836 = Z$$

Accordingly,

$$Z = 0.1675(X)0.2674836 = 0.1675(X)$$
$$X = 1.596917 \approx 1.6$$
$$X = (1 + L_L) = 1.6 = (1 + L_L)L_L = 0.60.$$

A long-term debt/equity ratio of 0.60 is compatible with a growth rate of 7.3%.   □

VALUATION

Of course, in developing the financial component of the strategic plan, management attempts to make decisions that maximize the market value of the firm. The market price on long-term debt and common stock reflects the quality of decisions made on the capital budget, the debt/equity ratio, the target growth rate, and the other variables displayed in the preceding formulas. To illustrate, let us again use Higgins model and the Micro-Industries data.

□ **EXAMPLE 7**

Micro-Industries has a financial structure composed of 37.5% long-term debt and 62.5% equity at book values. This structure is sustainable at a target growth rate of 11.2%. If Micro bonds sell at 80 and the P/E ratio is 8, what is the market value of the firm? Micro has a combined marginal tax rate (federal and state) of 50% and 3,750 common shares outstanding.

Solution I: This approach assumes that business risk and financial risk influence value (see Chapter 8). The method allows for the inclusion of income tax effects (see Table 8–1). Increased leveraging, therefore, will (up to a point) lower the average cost of capital and raise the value of the firm.

Net operating income (EBIT)	$11,000
Interest (10%)	3,500
Earnings before taxes (EBT)	$ 7,500
Taxes (0.50)	3,750
Earnings after taxes (EAT)	$ 3,750
Market value of common stock:	
EPS (after-tax) × P/E ratio	
× no. of shares = $1.00 × 8 × 3,750 =	$30,000
Market value of debt:	
30 bonds × $800	24,000
Market value of firm	$54,000

Cost of capital at market weights:

	After-Tax Cost	Weight	Total
Debt $= \dfrac{\$3,500}{24,000}(1 - 0.50)$	0.0729	0.375	0.0273
Equity $= \dfrac{7,500}{30,000}(1 + 0.50)$	0.125	0.625	0.0781
Weighted average cost of capital (K)			0.1054

Solution II: This alternative method of valuation assumes that the cost of capital (K) is influenced only by business risk with the financial risk discounted against the market worth of the common stock.

EBIT $(1 - 0.50) = \$11,000 \times 0.50$	$ 5,500
Cost of capital $(K) = 0.1054$	
Market value of the firm:	
$\dfrac{\$5,500}{0.1054} =$	$52,182
Market value of debt	24,000
Market value of common	$28,182
Cost of equity (K_e)	
$\dfrac{\$3,750}{\$28,182} = 0.133$	

In both solutions, the short-term debt ($5,000) was omitted. This was done on the assumption that the short-term debt carried no interest charge and offered no discount for prompt payment. Inclusion of the short-term debt would increase both solutions by $5,000. □

SUMMARY

This chapter attempts to underscore the interrelatedness of the financial elements that enter the articulation of the firm's strategic planning. The capital budget in greater or lesser degree affects the target growth rate. The latter, in turn, relates to specific levels of debt and equity financing, earnings retention, profit margins, productivity, and price trends. The sum of these factors influences the market value of the firm. The essence of strategic planning in the financial area is to balance these elements to achieve an optimal growth rate and related financial structure which will maximize the market value of the firm.

Financial theory dictates that the firm strive toward an optimal financial structure: that combination of debt and equity which minimizes the weighted average marginal cost of capital. This figure reflects the average risk posture of the firm and the reinvestment rate on retained cash flows. It is a rate which in conjunction with a given level of operating income maximizes the market value of the firm.

The optimal marginal cost of capital is not, as we have seen, a static calculation. It corresponds to the dynamic business and financial risks of the enterprise and to broad trends moving through the economic environment. In particular, with relation to the formulation of a strategic plan, a target growth rate implies a compatible set of established financial policies. Growth rates above and below the target rate eventually impel alterations in the financial or capital structure. Only by keeping the two in balance can a sustainable growth be realized.

In this respect, we should not equate growth with rising prices and retardation with falling prices. The firm's profit margin reflects trends in prices, production costs, and quantities. Cost-price movements are rarely synchronized.

Fixed costs by definition lag behind price level adjustments. A firm selling in a competitive market but buying in a monopolistic-competitive market might find its profit margin under pressure, although the prices show an upward trend. Conversely, declining prices may not adversely impact profit margins if management can improve the firm's output per worker-hour.

The reader will recognize that the chapter does not refer to portfolio effects or the capital asset pricing model in a strategic planning context. Problems of required return and systematic risk and the effect of a capital project on debt capacity manifestly have an important role in the specifics of strategic planning. These topics are covered extensively in Chapters 16–18 and the reader should easily relate them to the present theme.

QUESTIONS/PROBLEMS

1. Assume a dividend payout ratio of 40% and the following financial statements for Aloc Industries.

Aloc Industries
December 31, 198X
Balance Sheet

Assets		*Liabilities and Equity*	
Cash	$ 22,000	Current liabilities	$ 6,000
Accounts receivable	40,000	Long-term debt	12,000
Inventory	10,000	Capital stock	50,000
Fixed assets	41,000	Retained earnings	45,000
	$113,000		$113,000

Aloc Industries
December 31, 198X
Income Statement

Sales	$122,000
less	
Cost of sales	65,000
Gross profit	$ 57,000
less	
Selling and administrative expenses	22,000
Net operating income	$ 35,000
less	
Interest on long-term debt	$ 1,500
Earnings before taxes	$ 33,500

(a) Assume a stable price level.
    (i) Determine the sustainable rate of growth under each.
        (a) Fixed financial structure.
        (b) Fixed capital structure.
    (ii)   How might Aloc improve upon the sustainable rate of growth?

(b) Assume a rising price level of 20%.
   (i) Determine the *real* sustainable rate of growth under each.
       (a) Fixed financial structure.
       (b) Fixed capital structure.
   (ii) How might Aloc improve upon the *real* sustainable rate of growth?
(c) Assume a decline in prices of 25%.
   (i) Determine the *real* sustainable rate of growth under each.
       (a) Fixed financial structure.
       (b) Fixed capital structure.
   (ii) How might Aloc improve upon the *real* sustainable rate of growth?
2. What are the deficiencies of computing financial ratios and establishing financial policies based upon book values? How might this be overcome in regard to the establishment of financial policies?
3. If Aloc Industries sets a target growth rate of 25%, how will this objective affect the financial structure and the capital structure?
4. If, all other things equal, Aloc Industries reduces its cost of sales from $65,000 to $45,000, how will the change affect the sustainable growth rate?
5. Based upon the discussion in this chapter, which factors should Aloc Industries bear in mind when adding new capital projects to the existing mix in formulating the firm's strategic plan?

APPENDIX

Detailed Bibliography

CHAPTERS 1, 2, 3

Anderson, Leslie P., Vergil V. Miller, and Donald L. Thompson, *The Finance Function* (Scranton, Pa.: International Textbook Company, 1971).

Ang, J. S., "A Graphical Presentation of an Integrated Capital Budgeting Model," *Engineering Economist* (Winter 1978).

Anthony, R. N., "The Trouble with Profit Maximization," *Harvard Business Review*, 38 (November–December 1960) 126–134.

Bkara, S. and R. Wilson, "On the Theory of the Firm in an Economy with Incomplete Markets," *Bell Journal of Economics*, 5 (1974) 171–180.

Branch, Ben, "Corporate Objectives and Market Performance," *Financial Management*, 2 (Summer 1973), 24–29.

————, "The Impact of Operating Decisions on ROI Dynamics," *Financial Management*, 7 (Winter 1978), 54–60.

————, "The Laws of the Marketplace and ROI Dynamics," *Financial Management*, 9 (Summer 1980), 58–65.

Bunke, C. C., "A Group Profile of the Fortune 500 Chief Executives," *Fortune*, 93 (May 1976), 172–177 ff.

Ciscel, David H., and Thomas M. Carroll, "The Determinants of Executive Salaries: An Econometric Survey," *Review of Economics and Statistics*, 62 (February 1980), 7–13.

Cooley, Phillip L., "Managerial Pay and Financial Performances of Small Business," *Journal of Business*, 7 (September 1979), 267–276.

Davis, Keith, "Social Responsibility Is Inevitable," *California Management Review*, 19 (Fall 1970), 14–20.

De Alessi, Louis, "Private Property and Dispersion of Ownership in Large Corporations," *Journal of Finance*, 28 (September 1973), 839–851.

Dean, J., *Capital Budgeting* (New York: Columbia University Press, 1951).

De Angelo, Harry, and Edward M. Rice, "Anti-Takeover Charter Amendments and

Stockholder Wealth," Working Paper, Graduate School of Business Administration, University of Washington, 1980.

Dewing, A. S., *Financial Policy of Corporations*, 5th ed. (New York: The Ronald Press Company, 1953).

Donaldson, Gordon, "Financial Management in an Affluent Society," *Financial Executive*, 35 (April 1967), 52–60.

Durand, David, "Comprehensiveness in Capital Budgeting," *Financial Management*, 10 (Winter 1981), 7–14.

Elliott, J. W., "Control, Size, Growth, and Financial Performance in the Firm," *Journal of Financial and Quantitative Analysis*, 7 (January 1972), 1309–1320.

Fama, E. F., "Agency Problems and the Theory of the Firm," *Journal of Political Economy* (April 1980), 288–307.

————, "The Effects of a Firm's Investment and Financing Decisions on the Welfare of Its Security Holders," *American Economic Review*, 68 (September 1978), 272–284.

————, *Foundations of Finance* (New York: Basic Books, 1976).

Findlay, M. Chapman, III, and G. A. Whitmore, "Beyond Shareholder Wealth Maximization," *Financial Management*, 3 (Winter 1974), 25–35.

————, and Edward E. Williams, "Capital Allocation and the Nature of Ownership Equities," *Financial Management*, 1 (Spring 1972), 72–96.

Frankle, Alan W., and John C. Anderson, "The Impact of the Disclosure of the Environmental Effects of Organizational Behavior on the Market: Comment," *Financial Management*, 7 (Summer 1978), 76–78.

Friend, Irwin, "Recent Developments in Finance," *Journal of Banking and Finance*, 1 (October 1977), 103–117.

Fruhan, William E., Jr., *Financial Strategy* (Homewood, Ill.: Irwin, 1979).

Galbraith, J. K., *The New Industrial State* (Boston: Houghton Mifflin Company, 1967).

Gerstner, Louis V., and Helen M. Anderson, "The Chief Financial Officer as Activist," *Harvard Business Review*, 54 (September–October 1976), 100–106.

Grabowski, Henry G., and Dennis C. Mueller, "Managerial and Stockholder Welfare Models of Firm Expenditures," *Review of Economics and Statistics*, 54 (February 1972), 9–24.

Greene, T. L., *Corporation Finance* (New York: G. P. Putnam's Sons, 1897).

Grossman, S. J., and J. E. Stiglitz, "On Value Maximization and Alternative Objectives of the Firm," *Journal of Finance*, 32 (May 1977), 389–415.

Hakansson, Nils H., "The Fantastic World of Finance: Progress and the Free Lunch," *Journal of Financial and Quantitative Analysis*, 14 (November 1979), 717–734.

Hibdon, J. E., *Price and Welfare Theory* (New York: McGraw-Hill Book Company, 1969).

Hill, Lawrence W., "The Growth of the Corporate Finance Function," *Financial Executive*, 44 (July 1976), 36–43.

Jennergren, I. Peter, "On the Design of Incentives in Business Firms—A Survey of Some Research," *Management Science* (February 1980).

Jensen, Michael C., and William H. Meckling, "Theory of the Firm: Managerial Behavior, Agency Costs and Ownership Structure," *Journal of Financial Economics*, 3 (October 1976), 305–360.

————, and ————, "Can the Corporation Survive?" *Financial Analysts Journal* (January–February 1978).

Lee, Sang M., and A. J. Lerro, "Capital Budgeting for Multiple Objectives," *Financial Management* (Spring 1974).

Levy, Haim, and Marshall Sarnat, "A Pedagogic Note on Alternative Formulations of the Goal of the Firm," *Journal of Business*, 50 (October 1977), 526–528.

Lewellen, W. G., "Management and Ownership in the Large Firm," *Journal of Finance*, 26 (May 1969), 299–322.

Masson, Robert Tempest, "Executive Motivations, Earnings, and Consequent Equity Performance," *Journal of Political Economy*, 79 (November–December 1971), 1278–1292.

Mao, J. C. T., *Quantitative Analysis of Financial Decisions* (New York: Macmillan Publishing Co., 1969).

Moag, J. S., W. T. Carleton, and E. M. Lerner, "Defining the Finance Function: A Model-Systems Approach," *Journal of Finance*, 22 (December 1967), 543–556.

Moore, J. R., "The Financial Executive in the 1970s," *Financial Executive*, 35 (January 1967), 28–29, 32–34, 36.

Petty, J. W., D. F. Scott, Jr., and M. M. Bird, "The Capital Expenditure Decision-Making Process of Large Corporations," *The Engineering Economist* (Spring 1975).

Pinches, George E., "Myopia, Capital Budgeting and Decision Making," *Financial Management*, 11 (Autumn 1982), 6–19.

Pogue, G. A., and K. Lall, "Corporate Finance: An Overview," *Sloan Management Review* (Spring 1974), 19–38.

Sauvain, H., "Comment," *Journal of Finance*, 12, 4 (December 1967), 541.

Simkowitz, Michael A., and Charles P. Jones, "A Note on the Simultaneous Nature of Finance Methodology," *Journal of Finance*, 27 (March 1972), 103–108.

Solomon, Ezra, "What Should We Teach in a Course in Business Finance?" *Journal of Finance*, 21 (May 1966), 411–415.

Weston, J. Fred, "New Themes in Finance," *Journal of Finance*, 24 (March, 1974), 237–243.

―――――, *The Scope and Methodology of Finance* (Englewood Cliffs, N.J.: Prentice-Hall, Inc., 1966).

―――――, "Developments in Finance Theory," *Financial Management*, 10 (Summer 1981), 5–22.

Yarrow, G. K., "On the Predictions of Managerial Theories of the Firm," *Journal of Industrial Economics* (June 1976).

CHAPTERS 4, 5, 6, 7

Aggarwal, Raj, "Corporate Use of Sophisticated Capital Budgeting Techniques: A Strategic Perspective and a Critique of Survey Results," *Interfaces*, 10 (April 1980), 31–34.

Ang, J. S., and J. H. Chua, "Composite Measures for the Evaluation of Investment Performance," *Journal of Financial and Quantitative Analysis* (June 1979).

Bacon, Peter W., "The Evaluation of Mutually Exclusive Investments," *Financial Management*, 6 (Summer 1977), 55–58.

Bauman, W. Scott, "Investment Returns and Present Values," *Financial Analysts Journal*, 25 (November–December 1969), 107–118.

Beedles, William L., "A Note on Evaluating Non-Simple Investments," *Journal of Financial and Quantitative Analysis*, 13 (March 1978), 173–176.

Beenhakker, Henri L., "Sensitivity Analysis of the Present Value of a Project," *Engineering Economist*, 20 (Winter 1975), 123–149.

Beranek, William, "Some New Capital Budgeting Theorems," *Journal of Financial and Quantitative Analysis*, 13 (December 1978), 809–829.

Bernhard, Richard H., "'Modified' Rates of Return for Investment Project Evaluation—A Comparison and Critique," *Engineering Economist*, 24 (Spring 1979) 161–167.

―――――, "Some New Capital Budgeting Theorems: Comment," *Journal of Financial and*

Quantitative Analysis, 13 (December 1978), 825–829.

Bierman, Harold, Jr., "A Reconciliation of Present Value Capital Budgeting and Accounting," *Financial Management*, 6 (Summer 1977), 52–54.

Blume, Marshall E., "On the Assessment of Risk," *Journal of Finance*, 26 (March 1971), 1–10.

Bower, Richard S., and Dorothy H. Bower, "Risk and the Valuation of Common Stock," *Journal of Political Economy*, 77 (May–June 1969), 349–362.

Branch, Ben, "The Impact of Operating Decisions on ROI Dynamics," *Financial Management*, 7 (Winter 1978), 54–60.

Brick, John R., and Howard E. Thompson, "The Economic Life of an Investment and the Appropriate Discount Rate," *Journal of Financial and Quantitative Analysis*, 13 (December 1978), 831–846.

Brigham, Eugene F., and James L. Pappas, "Duration of Growth, Changes in Growth Rates, and Corporate Share Prices," *Financial Analysts Journal*, 22 (May–June 1966), 157–162.

————, "Hurdle Rate for Screening Capital Expenditure Proposals," *Financial Management*, 4 (Autumn 1975), 17–26.

————, and Richard H. Pettway, "Capital Budgeting by Utilities," *Financial Management*, 2 (Autumn 1973), 11–22.

Carter, E. Eugene, "Designing the Capital Budgeting Process," *TIMS Studies in the Management Sciences*, 5 (1977), 25–42.

Dean, Joel, *Capital Budgeting* (New York: Columbia University Press, 1951).

————, "Measuring the Productivity of Capital," *Harvard Business Review* (January–February 1954).

Dearden, John, "The Case Against ROI Control," *Harvard Business Review*, 47 (May–June 1969), 124–135.

de Faro, Clovis, "On the Internal Rate of Return Criterion," *Engineering Economist*, 19 (April–May 1974), 165–194.

————, "A Sufficient Condition for a Unique Nonnegative Internal Rate of Return: A Comment," *Journal of Financial and Quantitative Analysis*, 8 (September 1973), 683–684.

de la Mare, R. F., "An Investigation into the Discounting Formulae Used in Capital Budgeting Models," *Journal of Business Finance & Accounting* (Summer 1975).

Doenges, R. Conrad, "The 'Reinvestment Problem' in a Practical Perspective," *Financial Management*, 1 (Spring 1972), 85–91.

Donaldson, Gordon, "Strategic Hurdle Rates for Capital Investments," *Harvard Business Review*, 50 (March–April 1972), 50–58.

Dorfman, Robert, "The Meaning of the Internal Rate of Return," *Journal of Finance*, 36 (December 1981), 1010–1023.

Dudley, Carlton L., Jr., "A Note on Reinvestment Assumptions in Choosing Between Net Present Value and Internal Rate of Return," *Journal of Finance*, 27 (September 1972), 907–915.

Dyckman, Thomas R., and James C. Kinard, "The Discounted Cash Flow Investment Decision Model with Accounting Income Constraints," *Decision Sciences*, 4 (July 1973), 301–313.

Emery, Gary W., "Some Guidelines for Evaluating Capital Investment Alternatives with Unequal Lives," *Financial Management*, 11 (Spring 1982), 14–18.

Fama, Eugene F., "Components of Investment Performance," *Journal of Finance*, 27 (June 1972), 551–557.

————, "Multiperiod Consumption—Investment Decisions," *American Economic Review*, 60 (March 1970), 163–174.

————, and Merton H. Miller, *The Theory of Finance* (New York: Holt, Rinehart and Winston, Inc., 1972).

Fogler, H. Russell, "Ranking Techniques and Capital Rationing," *Accounting Review*, 47 (January 1972), 134–143.

Franklin, Peter J., "The Normal Cost Theory of Price and the Internal Rate of Return Method of Investment Appraisal: An Integration," *Journal of Business Finance and Accounting* (Spring 1977).

Gitman, Lawrence J., and John R. Forrester, Jr., "A Survey of Capital Budgeting Techniques Used by Major U.S. Firms," *Financial Management*, 6 (Fall 1977), 66–71.

Gonedes, Nicholas J., "Information-Production and Capital Market Equilibrium," *Journal of Finance*, 30 (June 1975), 841–864.

Gordon, Myron, *The Investment, Financing, and Valuation of the Corporation* (Homewood, Ill.: Richard D. Irwin, Inc., 1962).

Grinyer, J. R., "Relevant Criterion Rates in Capital Budgeting," *Journal of Business Finance and Accounting*, 1 (Autumn 1974), 357–374.

Grossman, Elliott S., *A Guide to the Determinants of Capital Investment*, Conference Board Report No. 721 (New York: Conference Board, 1977).

Haley, Charles W., and Lawrence D. Schall, *The Theory of Financial Decisions* (New York: McGraw-Hill Book Company, 1973), Chap. 5.

Hastie, Larry K., "One Businessman's View of Capital Budgeting," *Financial Management*, 3 (Winter 1974), 36–44.

Haynes, W. Warren and Martin B. Solomon, Jr., "A Misplaced Emphasis in Capital Budgeting," *Quarterly Review of Economics and Business* (February 1962).

Herbst, Anthony, "The Unique, Real Internal Rate of Return: Caveat Emptor!" *Journal of Financial and Quantitative Analysis*, 13 (June 1978), 363–370.

Hirshleifer, J., *Investment, Interest and Capital* (Englewood Cliffs, N.J.: Prentice-Hall, Inc., 1970).

————, "On the Theory of Optimal Investment Decision," *Journal of Political Economy*, 66 (August 1958).

Hoskins, Colin G., and Glen A. Mumey, "Payback: A Maligned Method of Asset Ranking," *Engineering Economist*, 25 (Fall 1979), 53–65.

Jarrett, Jeffrey E., "A Note on Investment Criteria and the Estimation Problem in Financial Accounting," *Journal of Business Finance & Accounting* (Summer 1980).

Jean, William H., "Terminal Value or Present Value in Capital Budgeting Programs," *Journal of Financial and Quantitative Analysis*, 6 (January 1971), 649–652.

————, "On Multiple Rates of Return," *Journal of Finance*, 23 (March 1968), 187–192.

Jeynes, Paul H., "The Significance of Reinvestment Rate," *Engineering Economist*, 9 (Fall 1965), 1–9.

Keane, Simon M., "The Internal Rate of Return and the Reinvestment Fallacy," *Journal of Accounting and Business Studies*, 15 (June 1979), 48–55.

Kim, Suk H., and Edward J. Farragher, "Current Capital Budgeting Practices," *Management Accounting*, 28 (June 1981), 26–30.

King, Paul, "Is the Emphasis of Capital Budgeting Theory Misplaced?" *Journal of Business Finance & Accounting* (Winter 1975).

Klammer, Thomas, "Empirical Evidence of the Adoption of Sophisticated Capital Budgeting Techniques," *Journal of Business*, 45 (July 1972), 387–397.

Lerner, Eugene M., and Willard T. Carleton, *A Theory of Financial Analysis* (New York: Harcourt Brace Jovanovich, 1966).

————, and A. Rappaport, "Limit DCF in Capital Budgeting," *Harvard Business Review*, 46 (September–October 1968), 133–138.

Lewellen, Wilbur G., Howard P. Lanser, and John J. McConnell, "Payback Substitutes for Discounted Cash Flow," *Financial Management*, 2 (Summer 1973), 17–23.

Lindsay, R. J., and A. W. Sametz, *Financial Management: An Analytical Approach* (Homewood, Ill.: Richard D. Irwin, Inc., 1967).

Lorie, J. H., and L. J. Savage, "Three Problems in Rationing Capital," *Journal of Business*, 28 (October 1955).

Machol, Robert E., and Eugene M. Lerner, "Risk, Ruin, and Investment Analysis," *Journal of Financial and Quantitative Analysis*, 4 (December 1969), 473–492.

Malkiel, Burton G., "Equity Yields, Growth, and the Structure of Share Prices," *American Economic Review*, 53 (December 1963), 467–494.

_____, and John G. Cragg, "Expectations and the Structure of Share Prices," *American Economic Review*, 40 (September 1970), 601–617.

Mao, James C. T., "The Internal Rate of Return as a Ranking Criterion," *Engineering Economist*, 11 (Winter 1966), 1–13.

_____, "A New Graphic Analysis of Fisher's Rate of Return," *Cost and Management*, 44 (November–December 1970), 24–27.

_____, *Quantitative Analysis of Financial Decisions* (New York: Macmillan Publishing Co., Inc., 1969), Chaps. 6, 7.

_____, "Survey of Capital Budgeting: Theory and Practice," *Journal of Finance*, 25 (May 1970), 349–360.

_____, "The Valuation of Growth Stocks: The Investment Opportunities Approach," *Journal of Finance*, 21 (March 1966), 95–102.

Meyer, Richard L., "A Note on Capital Budgeting Techniques and the Reinvestment Rate," *Journal of Finance*, 34 (December 1979), 1251–1254.

Murdick, Robert G., and Donald D. Deming, *The Management of Capital Expenditures* (New York: McGraw-Hill Book Company, 1968).

Norstrom, Carl J., "A Sufficient Condition for a Unique Nonnegative Internal Rate of Return," *Journal of Financial and Quantitative Analysis*, 7 (June 1972), 1835–1839.

Oblak, David· J., and Roy J. Helm, Jr., "Survey and Analysis of Capital Budgeting Methods Used by Multinationals," *Financial Management*, 9 (Winter 1980), 37–41.

Petry, Glenn H., "Effective Use of Capital Budgeting Tools," *Business Horizons*, 19 (October 1975), 57–65.

Petty, J. William, and Oswald D. Bowlin, "The Financial Manager and Quantitative Decision Models," *Financial Management*, 4 (Winter 1976), 32–41.

_____, David F. Scott, Jr., and Monroe M. Bird, "The Capital Expenditure Decision-Making Process of Large Corporations," *Engineering Economist*, 20 (Spring 1975), 159–172.

Pogue, Gerald A., and Kishore Lall, "Corporate Finance: An Overview," *Sloan Management Review*, 15 (Spring 1974), 19–38.

Porterfield, J. T., *Investment Decisions and Capital Costs* (Englewood Cliffs, N.J.: Prentice-Hall, Inc., 1965).

Pratt, John W., and John S. Hammond, III, "Evaluating and Comparing Projects: Simple Detection of False Alarms," *Journal of Finance*, 34 (December 1979), 1231–1242.

Rappaport, Alfred, "A Capital Budgeting Approach to Divisional Planning and Control," *Financial Executive*, 36 (October 1968), 47–63.

Renshaw, E., "A Note on the Arithmetic of Capital Budgeting Decisions," *Journal of Business*, 30 (July 1957).

Robichek, Alexander A., "Risk and the Value of Securities," *Journal of Financial and Quantitative Analysis*, 4 (December 1969), 513–538.

_____, and Stewart C. Myers, *Optimal Financing Decisions* (Englewood Cliffs, N.J.: Prentice-Hall, Inc., 1965), Chaps. 4–6.

_____, Donald G. Ogilvie, and John D. C. Roach, "Capital Budgeting: A Pragmatic Approach," *Financial Executive*, 37 (April 1969), 26–38.

_____, and James C. Van Horne, "Abandonment Value and Capital Budgeting," *Journal of Finance*, 22 (December 1967), 577–590.

Rosenblatt, Meir J., "A Survey and Analysis of Capital Budgeting Decision Process in Multi-Division Firms," *Engineering Economist*, 25 (Summer 1980), 259–273.

Schwab, Bernhard, and Peter Lusztig, "A Comparative Analysis of the Net Present Value and the Benefit-Cost Ratios as Measures of the Economic Desirability of Investments," *Journal of Finance*, 24 (June 1969), 507–516.

Searby, Frederick W. "Return to Return on Investment," *Harvard Business Review*, 53 (March–April 1975), 113–119.

Shank, John K., and A. Michael Burnell, "Smooth Your Earnings Growth Rate," *Harvard Business Review*, 54 (January–February 1974), 136–141.

Solomon, Ezra, "The Arithmetic of Capital-Budgeting Decisions," *Journal of Business*, 29 (April 1956), 124–129.

Stephen, Frank, "On Deriving the Internal Rate of Return from the Accountant's Rate of Return," *Journal of Business Finance and Accounting*, 3 (Summer 1976), 147–150.

Taggart, Robert A., Jr. "Capital Budgeting and the Financing Decision: An Exposition," *Financial Management*, 6 (Summer 1977), 59–64.

Teichroew, Daniel, Alexander A. Robichek, and Michael Montalbano, "An Analysis of Criteria for Investment and Financing Decisions under Certainty," *Management Science*, 12 (November 1965), 151–179.

Trippi, Robert R., "Conventional and Unconventional Methods for Evaluating Investments," *Financial Management*, 3 (Autumn 1974), 31–35.

Waters, Robert C., and Richard L. Bullock, "Inflation and Replacement Decisions," *Engineering Economist*, 21 (Summer 1976), 249–257.

Weaver, James B., "Organizing and Maintaining a Capital Expenditure Program," *Engineering Economist*, 20 (Fall 1974), 1–36.

Weingartner, H. M., "The Excess Present Value Index—A Theoretical Basis and Critique," *Journal of Accounting Research*, 1 (Autumn 1963), 213–224.

Welter, P., "Put Policy First in DCF Analysis," *Harvard Business Review*, 48 (January–February 1970), 141–148.

Whisler, William D., "Sensitivity Analysis of Rates of Return," *Journal of Finance*, 31 (March 1976), 63–70.

Wiar, Robert C., "Economic Implications of Multiple Rates of Return in the Leveraged Lease Context," *Journal of Finance*, 28 (December 1973), 1275–1286.

CHAPTER 8

Agmon, T., A. P. Ofer, and A. Tamir, "Variable Rate Debt Instruments and Corporate Debt Policy," *Journal of Finance* (December 1980).

Aivazian, V. A., and J. L. Callen, "Investment, Market Structure, and the Cost of Capital," *Journal of Finance* (March 1979).

Alberts, W. W., and S. H. Archer, "Some Evidence on the Effect of Company Size on the Cost of Equity Capital," *Journal of Financial and Quantitative Analysis* (March 1973).

Ang, J. S., "Weighted Average vs. True Cost of Capital," *Financial Management* (Spring 1974).

Archer, Stephen H., and LeRoy G. Faerber, "Firm Size and the Cost of Equity Capital," *Journal of Finance* (March 1966).

Arditti, Fred D., "The Weighted Average Cost of Capital: Some Questions on Its Definition, Interpretation and Use," *Journal of Finance* (September 1973).

————, H. Levy, and M. Sarnat, "Taxes, Capital Structure, and the Cost of Capital: Some Extensions," *Quarterly Review of Economics and Business* (Summer 1977).

_____, and J. M. Pinkerton, "The Valuation and Cost of Capital of the Levered Firm with Growth Opportunities," *Journal of Finance* (March 1978).

_____, "Risk and the Required Return on Equity," *Journal of Finance*, 22 (March 1967), 19–36.

_____, and Stephen A. Tysseland, "Three Ways to Present the Marginal Cost of Capital," *Financial Management* (Summer 1973), 63–67.

Auerbach, Alan, "Wealth Maximization and the Cost of Capital," *Quarterly Journal of Economics* (August 1979).

Barges, Alexander, *The Effect of Capital Structure on the Cost of Capital* (Englewood Cliffs, N.J.: Prentice-Hall, Inc., 1963).

Barnea, Amir, Robert A. Haugen, and Lemma W. Senbet, "Market Imperfections, Agency Problems, and Capital Structure: A Review," *Financial Management*, 10 (Summer 1981), 7–22.

_____, _____, and _____, "A Rationale for Debt Maturity Structure and Call Provisions in the Agency Theoretic Framework," *Journal of Finance* (December 1980).

Baron, David P., and Holmström Bengt, "The Investment Banking Contract for New Issues Under Asymmetric Information: Delegation and the Incentive Problem," *Journal of Finance* (December 1980).

_____, "Default Risk and the Modigliani-Miller Theorem: A Synthesis," *American Economic Review*, 66 (March 1976), 204–212.

_____, "Default Risk, Homemade Leverage, and the Modigliani-Miller Theorem," *American Economic Review*, 64 (March 1974), 176–182.

Baumol, William, and Burton G. Malkiel, "The Firm's Optimal Debt-Equity Combination and the Cost of Capital," *Quarterly Journal of Economics*, 81 (November 1967), 547–578.

Baxter, Nevins D., "Leverage, Risk of Ruin, and the Cost of Capital," *Journal of Finance*, 22 (September 1967), 395–404.

Bear, Robert M., and Anthony J. Curley, "Unseasoned Equity Financing," *Journal of Financial and Quantitative Analysis* (June 1978).

Beaver, W., P. Kettler, and M. Scholes, "The Association Between Market Determined and Accounting Determined Risk Measures," *The Accounting Review* (October 1970), 654–682.

Ben-Horim, Moshe, "Comment on 'The Weighted Average Cost of Capital as a Cutoff Rate,'" *Financial Management* (Summer 1979).

Ben-Shahar, Haim, "The Capital Structure and the Cost of Capital: A Suggested Exposition," *Journal of Finance*, 23 (September 1968), 639–653.

_____, and Abraham Ascher, "Capital Budgeting and Stock Valuation: Comment," *American Economic Review*, 57 (March 1967), 209–214.

Beranek, William, *The Effects of Leverage on the Market Value of Common Stocks* (Madison, Wis.: Bureau of Business Research and Service, University of Wisconsin, 1964).

_____, "The Cost of Capital, Capital Budgeting, and the Maximization of Shareholder Wealth," *Journal of Financial and Quantitative Analysis* (March 1975).

_____, "The Weighted Average Cost of Capital and Shareholder Wealth Maximization," *Journal of Financial and Quantitative Analysis* (March 1977).

Black, Fischer, and John C. Cox, "Valuing Corporate Securities: Some Effects on Bond Indenture Provisions," *Journal of Finance*, 31 (May 1976), 351–368.

_____, and Myron Scholes, "The Pricing of Options and Corporate Liabilities," *Journal of Political Economy*, 81 (May–June 1973), 637–654.

Block, Stanley, and Marjorie Block, "The Financial Characteristics and Price Movement

Patterns of Companies Approaching the Unseasoned Securities Market in the Late 1970s," *Financial Management* (Winter 1980).

Bodenhorn, Diran, "On the Problem of Capital Budgeting," *Journal of Finance*, 14 (December 1959), 473–492.

Bodie, Z., and B. M. Friedman, "Interest Rate Uncertainty and the Value of Bond Call Protection," *Journal of Political Economy* (February 1978).

Boness, A. James, "A Pedagogic Note on the Cost of Capital," *Journal of Finance*, 19 (March 1964), 99–106.

Boquist, J. A., G. A. Racetta, and G. G. Schlarbaum, "Duration and Risk Assessment for Bonds and Common Stocks," *Journal of Finance* (December 1975).

Boudreaux, Kenneth J., and Hugh W. Long, "The Weighted Average Cost of Capital as a Cutoff Rate: A Further Analysis," *Financial Management* (Summer 1979).

Bower, Richard S., and Dorothy H. Bower, "Risk and the Valuation of Common Stock," *Journal of Political Economy*, 77 (May–June 1969), 349–362.

Brennan, Michael J., "A New Look at the Weighted Average Cost of Capital," *Journal of Business Finance* (Spring 1973).

————, "Taxes, Market Valuation and Corporate Financial Policy," *National Tax Journal*, 23 (December 1970), 417–427.

————, and E. S. Schwartz, "Corporate Income Taxes, Valuation and the Problem of Optimal Capital Structure," *Journal of Business*, 51 (January 1978), 103–115.

Brewer, D. E., and J. Michaelson, "The Cost of Capital, Corporation Finance, and the Theory of Investment: Comment," *American Economic Review*, 55 (June 1965), 516–524.

Brigham, Eugene F., and Myron J. Gordon, "Leverage, Dividend Policy, and the Cost of Capital," *Journal of Finance*, 23 (March 1968), 85–104.

————, and Keith V. Smith, "The Cost of Capital to the Small Firm," *The Engineering Economist* (Fall 1967).

Budd, A. F., and R. H. Litzenberger, "Changes in the Supply of Money, the Firm's Market Value and Cost of Capital," *Journal of Finance* (March 1973).

Campbell, Tim S., "Optimal Investment Financing Decisions and the Value of Confidentiality," *Journal of Financial and Quantitative Analysis*, 14 (December 1979), 913–924.

Chambers, Donald R., Robert S. Harris, and John J. Pringle, "Treatment of Financing Mix in Analyzing Investment Opportunities," *Financial Management*, 11 (Summer 1982), 24–41.

Chen, Andrew H., and E. Han Kim, "Theories of Corporate Debt Policy: A Synthesis," *Journal of Finance*, 34 (May 1979), 371–384.

Craine, R. N., and J. L. Pierce, "Interest Rate Risk," *Journal of Financial and Quantitative Analysis* (November 1978).

Crockett, Jean, and Irwin Friend, "Capital Budgeting and Stock Valuation: Comment," *American Economic Review*, 57 (March 1967), 214–220.

De Angelo, Harry, and Ronald W. Masulis, "Optimal Capital Structure under Corporate and Personal Taxation," *Journal of Financial Economics*, 8 (March 1980), 3–29.

Dobrovolsky, S. P., "Economics of Corporation Internal and External Financing," *Journal of Finance* (March 1958).

Durand, David, "Costs of Debt and Equity Funds for Business: Trends and Problems of Measurement," reprinted in Ezra Solomon, ed., *The Management of Corporate Capital* (New York: The Free Press, 1959), pp. 91–116.

Ederington, L. H., "Uncertainty, Competition, and Costs in Corporate Bond Underwriting," *Journal of Financial Economics* (March 1975).

Edmister, R. O., "Commission Cost Structure Shifts and Scale Economies," *Journal of Finance* (May 1978).

Elliott, Walter J., "The Cost of Capital and U.S. Capital Investment: A Test of

Alternative Concepts," *The Journal of Finance* (September 1980).

Elton, Edwin J., and Martin J. Gruber, "The Effect of Share Repurchases on the Value of the Firm," *Journal of Finance* (March 1968).

Ezzamel, Mahmoud A., "Estimating the Cost of Capital for a Division of a Firm, and the Allocation Problem in Accounting: A Comment," *Journal of Business Finance & Accounting* (Spring 1980).

Ezzell, J. R., and R. B. Porter, "Flotation Costs and the Weighted Average Cost of Capital," *Journal of Financial and Quantitative Analysis* (September 1976).

_____, and _____, "Correct Specification of the Cost of Capital and Net Present Value," *Financial Management* (Summer 1979).

Fabozzi, F. J., and R. A. Hershkoff, "The Effect of the Decision to List on a Stock's Systematic Risk," *Review of Business and Economic Research* (Spring 1979).

Fama, Eugene F., "The Effects of a Firm's Investment and Financing Decisions on the Welfare of Its Security Holders," *American Economic Review*, 68 (June 1978), 272–284.

_____, and Merton H. Miller, *The Theory of Finance* (New York: Holt, 1972), Chap. 4.

Findlay, M. Chapman, III, "The Weighted Average Cost of Capital and Finite Flows," *Journal of Business Finance & Accounting* (1977).

Flath, David, and Charles R. Knoeber, "Taxes, Failure Costs, and Optimal Industry Capital Structure: An Empirical Test," *Journal of Finance*, 35 (March 1980), 99–117.

Fox, A. F., The Cost of Retained Earnings—A Comment," *Journal of Business Finance & Accounting* (4/4 1977).

Gahlon, James M., and James A. Gentry, "On the Relationship Between Systematic Risk and the Degree of Operating Financial Leverage," *Financial Management*, 11 (Summer 1982), 15–23.

Galai, Dan, and Ronald W. Masulis, "The Option Pricing Model and the Risk Factor of Stock," *Journal of Financial Economics*, 3 (January–March 1976), 53–81.

Gentry, James A., and Stephen A. Pyhrr, "Stimulating an EPS Growth Model," *Financial Management* (Summer 1973).

Gitman, Lawrence, and Vincent A. Mercurio, "Cost of Capital Techniques Used by Major U.S. Firms: Survey and Analysis of Fortune's 1000," *Financial Management*, 11 (Winter 1982), 21–29.

Glenn, David W.,"Super Premium Security Prices and Optimal Corporate Financing Decisions," *Journal of Finance*, 31 (May 1976).

Gordon, Myron J., and Clarence C. Y. Kwan, "Debt Maturity, Default Risk, and Capital Structure," *Journal of Banking and Finance*, 3 (December 1979) 313–329.

_____, and Paul J. Halper, "Cost of Capital for a Division of a Firm," *Journal of Finance* (September 1974).

_____, and L. I. Gould, "The Cost of Equity Capital: A Reconsideration," *Journal of Finance* (June 1978).

_____, and Eli Shapiro, "Capital Equipment Analysis: The Required Rate of Profit," *Management Science* (October 1956).

Gordon, Roger H., and Burton G. Malkiel, "Taxation and Corporation Finance," Working Paper, National Bureau of Economic Research, 1980.

Grier, P. and S. Katz, "The Differential Effects of Bond Rating Changes among Industrial and Public Utility Bonds by Maturity," *Journal of Business* (April 1976).

Gup, Benton E., and Samuel W. Norwood III, "Divisional Cost of Capital: A Practical Approach," *Financial Management*, 11 (Spring 1982), 20–24.

Hakansson, Nils H., "On the Dividend Capitalization Model under Uncertainty," *Journal of Financial and Quantitative Analysis* (March 1969).

Haley, Charles W., "Taxes, The Cost of Capital, and the Firm's Investment Decisions," *Journal of Finance* (September 1971).

_____, and L. D. Schall, "Problems with the Concept of the Cost of Capital," *Journal of Financial and Quantitative Analysis* (December 1978).

Hamada, Robert S., "The Effect of the Firm's Capital Structure on the Systematic Risk of Common Stocks," *Journal of Finance*, 27 (May 1972), 435–452.

_____, "Portfolio Analysis, Market Equilibrium, and Corporation Finance," *Journal of Finance*, 24 (March 1969), 13–31.

Harris, Robert S., "The Refunding of Discounted Debt: An Adjusted Present Value Analysis," *Financial Management* (Winter 1980).

Haugen, Robert A., and Lemma W. Senbet, "The Irrelevance of Bankruptcy Costs to the Theory of Optimal Capital Structure," *Journal of Finance*, 33 (June 1978), 383–394.

Heins, A. James, and Case M. Sprenkle, "A Comment on the Modigliani-Miller Cost of Capital Thesis," *American Economic Review*, 59 (September 1969), 590–592.

Hellwig, Martin F., "Bankruptcy, Limited Liability, and the Modigliani-Miller Theorem," *American Economic Review*, 71 (March 1981), 155–170.

Henderson, Glenn V., Jr., "Shareholder Taxation and the Required Rate of Return on Internally Generated Funds," *Financial Management* (Summer 1976).

_____, "In Defense of the Weighted Average Cost of Capital," *Financial Management* (Autumn 1979), 57–61.

Ibbotson, R. G., "Price Performance of Common Stock New Issues," *Journal of Financial Economics* (September 1975).

Jarrett, Jeffrey E., "Estimating the Cost of Capital for a Division of a Firm, and the Allocation Problem in Accounting," *Journal of Business Finance and Accounting* (Spring 1978).

Jensen, Michael C., and William E. Meckling, "Theory of the Firm: Managerial Behavior, Agency Costs and Ownership Structure," *Journal of Financial Economics*, 3 (October 1976), 305–360.

Johnson, K. B., T. G. Morton, and M. C. Findlay, III, "An Empirical Analysis of the Flotation Cost of Corporate Securities, 1971–1972," *Journal of Finance* (September 1975).

Keane, Simon M., "The Cost of Capital as a Financial Decision Tool," *Journal of Business Finance & Accounting* (Autumn 1978).

Keenan, Michael, and Rita M. Maldonado, "The Redundancy of Earnings Leverage in a Cost of Capital Decision Framework," *Journal of Business Finance and Accounting* (Summer 1976).

Kim, E. Han, "A Mean-Variance Theory of Optimal Structure and Corporate Debt Capacity," *Journal of Finance*, 33 (March 1978), 45–64.

_____, John J. McConnell, and Irwin Silberman, "Capital Structure Rearrangements and Me-First Rules in an Efficient Capital Market," *Journal of Finance*, 32 (June 1977), 789–810.

_____, Wilbur G. Lewellen, and John J. McConnell, "Financial Leverage Clienteles," *Journal of Financial Economics*, 7 (March 1979), 83–109.

Kim, Moon H., "Weighted Average vs. True Cost of Capital," *Financial Management* (Spring 1974).

Kolodny, R., P. Seely, and M. E. Polakoff, "The Effect of Compensating Balance Requirements on the Profitability of Borrowers and Lenders," *Journal of Financial and Quantitative Analysis* (December 1977).

Kraus, Alan, and Robert H. Litzenberger, "A State-Preference Model of Optimal Financial Leverage," *Journal of Finance*, 28 (September 1973), 911–922.

Kummer, D. R., and J. R. Hoffmeister, "Valuation Consequences of Cash Tender Offers," *Journal of Finance* (May 1978).

Lakonishok, Joseph, and Aharon R. Ofer, "The Value of General Price Level Adjusted Data to Bond Rating," *Journal of Business Finance & Accounting* (Spring 1980).

Lee, Sang M., and A. J. Lerro, "An Appraisal of Price Earnings, Dividends and Retained Earnings," *The Southern Journal of Business* (February 1978).

Lee, Wayne Y., and Henry H. Barker, "Bankruptcy Costs and the Firm's Optimal Debt Capacity," *Southern Economic Journal*, 43 (April 1977), 1453–1465.

Lerner, Eugene M., and Willard T. Carleton, "Financing Decisions of the Firm," *Journal of Finance*, 21 (May 1966), 202–214.

_____, and _____, "The Integration of Capital Budgeting and Stock Valuation," *American Economic Review*, 54 (September 1964), 327–346.

_____, and _____, *A Theory of Financial Analysis* (New York: Harcourt Brace Jovanovich, 1966).

Lewellen, Wilbur G., *The Cost of Capital* (Belmont, Calif.: Wadsworth Publishing Co., Inc., 1969), Chaps. 3, 4.

_____, "A Conceptual Reappraisal of Cost of Capital," *Financial Management* (Winter 1974).

Linke, Charles M., "Weighted Average vs. True Cost of Capital," *Financial Management* (Spring 1974).

Lintner, John, "Dividends, Earnings, Leverage, Stock Prices and the Supply of Capital to Corporations," *Review of Economics and Statistics*, 44 (August 1962), 243–269.

Litzenberger, Robert H., and James C. Van Horne, "Elimination of the Double Taxation of Dividends and Corporate Financial Policy," *Journal of Finance*, 33 (June 1978), 737–749.

_____, and Rao, C. U., "Portfolio Theory and Industry Cost-of-Capital Estimates," *Journal of Financial and Quantitative Analysis* (March 1972).

Livingston, M., "Taxation and Bond Market Equilibrium in a World of Uncertain Future Interest Rates," *Journal of Financial and Quantitative Analysis* (March 1979).

_____, "The Pricing of Premium Bonds," *Journal of Financial and Quantitative Analysis* (September 1979).

Long, Michael S. and George A. Rasette, "Stochastic Demand, Output and the Cost of Capital," *Journal of Finance* (May 1974).

Malkiel, Burton G., *The Debt-Equity Combination of the Firm and the Cost of Capital: An Introductory Analysis* (Morristown, N.J.: General Learning Press, 1971).

_____, and John G. Cragg, "Expectations and the Structure of Share Prices," *American Economic Review*, 60 (September 1970), 601–617.

Mandelker, G. and A. Raviv, "Investment Banking: An Economic Analysis of Optimal Underwriting Contracts," *Journal of Finance* (June 1977).

Masulis, Ronald W., "The Effects of Capital Structure Change on Security Prices: A Study of Exchange Offers," *Journal of Financial Economics*, forthcoming.

McConnell, John J., and Gary G. Schlarbaum, "Evidence on the Impact of Exchange Offers on Security Prices: The Case of Income Bonds," *Journal of Business*, 54 (January 1981), 65–85.

McDonald, John G., and Alfred E. Osborne, Jr., "Forecasting the Market Return on Common Stocks," *Journal of Business Finance & Accounting* (Summer 1974).

_____, "Market Measures of Capital Cost," *Journal of Business Finance* (Autumn 1970).

Merton, Robert C., "On the Pricing of Corporate Debt: The Risk Structure of Interest Rates," *Journal of Finance* (May 1974).

Miles, James A., and John R. Ezzell, "The Weighted Average Cost of Capital, Perfect Capital Markets, and Project Life: A Clarification," *Journal of Financial and Quantitative Analysis* (September 1980).

Miller, Merton H., "Debt and Taxes," *Journal of Finance*, 32 (May 1977), 266–268.

_____, and Myron S. Scholes, "Dividends and Taxes," *Journal of Financial Economics*, 6 (December 1978), 333–364.

_____, and Franco Modigliani, "Cost of Capital to Electric Utility Industry," *American Economic Review*, 56 (June 1966), 333–391.

Milne, F., "Choice over Asset Economics: Default Risk and Corporate Leverage," *Journal of Financial Economics*, 2 (June 1975), 165–185.

Modigliani, Franco, and M. H. Miller, "The Cost of Capital, Corporation Finance and the Theory of Investment," *American Economic Review*, 48 (June 1958), 261–297.

_____, and _____, "The Cost of Capital, Corporation Finance and the Theory of Investment: Reply," *American Economic Review*, 49 (September 1958), 655–669; "Taxes and the Cost of Capital: A Correction," ibid., 53 (June 1963), 433–443; "Reply," ibid., 55 (June 1965), 524–527; "Reply to Heins and Sprenkle," ibid., 59 (September 1969), 592–595.

Mumey, Glen A., *Theory of Financial Structure* (New York: Holt, Rinehart and Winston, Inc., 1969).

Myers, Stewart C., "Determinants of Corporate Borrowing," *Journal of Financial Economics*, 5 (November 1977), 147–175.

Nantell, Timothy J., and Robert C. Carlson, "The Cost of Capital as a Weighted Average," *Journal of Finance* (December 1975).

Ofer, A. R., and R. A. Taggart, Jr., "Bond Refunding: A Clarifying Analysis," *Journal of Finance* (March 1977).

Petry, Glenn H., "An Unidentified Corporate Risk—Using the Wrong Cost of Funds," *MSU Business Topics* (Autumn 1975).

Pinches, G. E., and J. C. Singleton, "The Adjustment of Stock Prices to Bond Rating Changes," *Journal of Finance* (*March* 1978).

Porterfield, James T. S., *Investment Decisions and Capital Costs* (Englewood Cliffs, N.J.: Prentice-Hall, Inc., 1965).

Reilly, F. K., and M. D. Joehnk, "The Association between Market-Determined Risk and Measures for Bonds and Bond Ratings," *Journal of Finance* (December 1976).

Reilly, Raymond R., and William E. Wecker, "On the Cost of Capital as a Weighted Average Cost of Capital," *Journal of Financial and Quantitative Analysis* (January 1973).

Rendleman, Richard J., "The Effects of Default Risk on the Firm's Investment and Financing Decisions," *Financial Management*, 7 (Spring 1978), 45–53.

Resek, Robert W., "Multidimensional Risk and the Modigliani-Miller Hypothesis," *Journal of Finance*, 25 (March 1970), 47–52.

Robichek, Alexander A., and Steward C. Myers, *Optimal Financing Decisions* (Englewood Cliffs, N.J.: Prentice-Hall, Inc., 1965).

Ross, Stephen A., "The Determination of Financial Structure: The Incentive-Signalling Approach," *Bell Journal of Economics*, 8 (Spring 1977), 23–40.

Rubinstein, Mark E., "A Mean-Variance Synthesis of Corporate Financial Theory," *Journal of Finance*, 28 (March 1973), 167–182.

Schall, Lawrence D., "Firm Financial Structure and Investment," *Journal of Financial and Quantitative Analysis*, 6 (June 1971), 925–942.

_____, "Valuation and Firm Investment and Financing Policies with Personal Tax Biases," *Journal of Business Research*, forthcoming.

Schneller, Meir I., "Taxes and the Optimal Capital Structure of the Firm," *Journal of Finance*, 35 (March 1980), 119–127.

Schwartz, Eli, "Theory of the Capital Structure of the Firm," *Journal of Finance*, 14 (March 1959).

_____, and J. Richard Aronson, "Some Surrogate Evidence in Support of the Concept of Optimal Capital Structure," *Journal of Finance*, 22 (March 1967), 10–18.

Scott, James H., Jr., "Bankruptcy, Secured Debt, and Optimal Capital Structure," *Journal of Finance*, 32 (March 1977), 1–20.

_____, "A Theory of Optimal Capital Structure," *Bell Journal of Economics*, 7 (Spring 1976), 33–54.

Seitz, Neil, "Shareholder Goals, Firm Goals, and Firm Financing Decisions," *Financial Management*, 11 (Autumn, 1982), 20–26.

Shapiro, Alan C., "In Defense of the Traditional Weighted Average Cost of Capital as a Cutoff Rate," *Financial Management* (Summer 1979).

Shiller, R. J., and F. Modigliani, "Coupon and Tax Effects on New and Seasoned Bond Yields and the Measurement of the Cost of Debt Capital," *Journal of Financial Economics* (June 1979).

Smith, C. W., Jr., "Alternative Methods for Raising Capital: Rights versus Underwritten Offerings," *Journal of Financial Economics* (December 1977).

————, "Option Pricing: A Review," *Journal of Financial Economics*, 3 (January–March 1976), 3–51.

————, and Jerold B. Warner, "On Financial Contracting: An Analysis of Bond Covenants," *Journal of Financial Economics*, 7 (June 1979), 117–161.

Soldofsky, Robert M., and Roger, L. Miller, "Risk-Premium Curves for Different Classes of Long-Term Securities, 1950–66," *Journal of Finance* (June 1969).

Solomon, Ezra, "Measuring a Company's Cost of Capital," *Journal of Business*, 28 (October 1955), 240–252.

————, *The Theory of Financial Management* (New York: Columbia University Press, 1963).

Stiglitz, Joseph E., "A Re-examination of the Modigliani–Miller Theorem," *American Economic Review*, 59 (December 1969), 784–793.

————, "On the Irrelevance of Corporate Financial Policy," *American Economic Review*, 64 (December 1974), 851–866.

Stoll, H. R., "The Pricing of Security Dealer Services: An Empirical Study of NASDAQ Stocks," *Journal of Finance* (September 1978).

Taggart, Robert A. Jr., "Taxes and Corporate Capital Structure in an Incomplete Market," *Journal of Finance*, 35 (June 1980), 645–660.

Tallman, Gary D., David F. Rush, and Ronald W. Melicher, "Competitive Versus Negotiated Underwriting Costs for Regulated Industries," *Financial Management* (Summer 1974).

Tepper, Irwin, "Revealed Preference Methods and the Pure Theory of the Cost of Capital," *Journal of Finance* (March 1973).

Tinsley, P. A., "Capital Structure, Precautionary Balances, and Valuation of the Firm: the Problem of Financial Risk," *Journal of Financial and Quantitative Analysis*, 5 (March 1970), 33–62.

Van Horne, James C., "Optimal Initiation of Bankruptcy Proceedings by Debt Holders," *Journal of Finance*, 31 (June 1976), 897–910.

Vickers, Douglas, "Profitability and Reinvestment Rates: A Note on the Gordon Paradox," *Journal of Business* (July 1966).

————, "The Cost of Capital and the Structure of the Firm," *Journal of Finance*, 25 (March 1970), 35–46.

Weinstein, M. I., "The Effect of a Rating Change Announcement on Bond Price," *Journal of Financial Economics* (December 1977).

Weston, J. Fred, "Investment Decisions Using the Capital Asset Pricing Model," *Financial Management* (Spring 1973), 25–33.

————, "A Test of Cost of Capital Propositions," *Southern Economic Journal*, 30 (October 1963), 105–112.

————, and W. Y. Lee, "Cost of Capital for a Division of a Firm: Comment," *Journal of Finance* (December 1977).

White, M. J., "Public Policy toward Bankruptcy: Me-first and Other Priority Rules," *Bell Journal of Economics*, 11 (Autumn 1980), 550–564.

White R. W., and P. A. Lusztig, "The Price Effects of Rights Offerings," *Journal of Financial and Quantitative Analysis* (March 1980).

Whitington, G., "The Profitability of Retained Earnings," *Review of Economics and Statistics* (May 1972).

Wippern, Ronald F., "Financial Structure and the Value of the Firm," *Journal of Finance*, 21 (December 1966), 615–634.

Wrightsman, Duayne, and James O. Harrigon, "Retention, Risk of Success, and the Price of Stock," *Journal of Finance* (December 1975).

Yawitz, J. B., "Risk Premia on Municipal Bonds," *Journal of Financial and Quantitative Analysis* (September 1978).

Zanker, F. W. A., "The Cost of Capital for Debt-Financed Investments," *Journal of Business Finance and Accounting*, 4, 3 (1977).

Zwick, B., "Yields on Privately Placed Corporate Bonds," *Journal of Finance* (March 1980).

CHAPTERS 9, 10, 11

Agrawall, S. P., "Accounting for the Impact of Inflation on a Business Enterprise," *Accounting Review* (October 1977).

Arditti, F. D., "Discounting the Components of an Income Stream: Reply," *Journal of Finance* (March 1977).

Baran, A., J. Lakonishok, and A. R. Ofer, "The Information Content of General Price Level Adjusted Earnings: Some Empirical Evidence," *Accounting Review* (January 1980).

Becker, S. W., J. Ronen, and G. H. Sorter, "Opportunity Costs—An Experimental Approach," *Journal of Accounting Research* (Autumn 1974).

Beja, Avraham, and Yair Aharoni, "Some Aspects of Conventional Accounting Profits in an Inflationary Environment," *Journal of Accounting Research* (Autumn 1977).

Beranek, W., *Analysis for Financial Decisions* (Homewood, Ill.: Richard D. Irwin, Inc., 1963), Chap. 11.

Bierman, H., Jr., and R. E. Dukes, "Limitations of Replacement Cost," *Quarterly Review of Economics and Business* (Spring 1979).

Brennan, M. J., "An Approach to the Valuation of Uncertain Income Streams," *Journal of Finance* (June 1973).

Brooks, L. D., and D. Buckmaster, "Price-Change Accounting Models and Disaggregated Monetary Gains and Losses," *Quarterly Review of Economics and Business* (Spring 1979).

Call, W. L., "General versus Specific Price-Level Adjustment: A Graphic Analysis," *Accounting Review* (January 1977).

Cargill, Thomas F., and Robert Meyer, "The Term Structure of Inflationary Expectations and Market Efficiency," *Journal of Finance*, 35 (March 1980), 57–70.

Carlson, John A., "Expected Inflation and Interest Rates," *Economic Inquiry*, 17 (October 1979), 597–608.

Chant, P. D., "On the Predictability of Corporate Earnings per Share Behavior," *Journal of Finance* (March 1980).

Coen, Robert M., "Investment Behavior, The Measurement of Depreciation and Tax Policy," *The American Economic Review* (March 1975).

Cross, Stephen, M., "A Note on Inflation, Taxation and Investment Returns," *Journal of Finance* (March 1980).

Darby, Michael R., "The Financial Effects of Monetary Policy on Interest Rates," *Economic Inquiry*, 13 (June 1975), 226–276.

Davidson, Sidney, and David F. Drake, "The 'Best' Tax Depreciation Method—1964," *Journal of Business*, 37 (July 1964), 258–260.

————, and ————, "Capital Budgeting and the 'Best' Tax Depreciation Method," *Journal of Business*, 34 (October 1961), 442–452.

Dopuch, N., and S. Sunder, "FASB's Statements on Objectives and Elements of Financial Accounting: A Review," *Accounting Review* (January 1980).

Dowsett, R. C., "Investment Advantages from Tax Credits and Accumulated Depreciation," *Financial Executive* (June 1966), 52 ff.

Drury, D. H., "Effects of Accounting Practice Divergence: Canada and the United States," *Jounral of International Business Studies* (Fall 1979).

Edwards, James W., *Effects of Federal Income Taxes on Capital Budgeting* (New York: National Association of Accountants, 1969).

Fabozzi, F. J., and L. M. Shiffrin, "Replacement Cost Accounting: Application to the Pharmaceutical Industry," *Quarterly Review of Economics and Business* (Spring 1979).

Fama, Eugene F., "Short-Term Interest Rates as Predictors of Inflation," *American Economic Review*, 65 (June 1975), 269–282.

————, and G. William Schwert, "Asset Returns and Inflation," *Journal of Financial Economics*, 5 (November 1977), 115–146.

Feldstein, Martin, Jerry Green, and Eytan Sheshinski, "Inflation and Taxes in a Growing Economy with Debt and Equity Finance," *Journal of Political Economy*, 86 (April 1978), S53–S70.

————, and Lawrence Summers, "Inflation, Tax Rules and the Long-Term Interest Rate," *Brookings Papers on Economic Activity*, 1 (1978), 61–109.

Findlay, M. C., III, and E. E. Williams, *An Integrated Analysis for Managerial Finance* (Englewood Cliffs, N.J.: Prentice-Hall, Inc., 1970), Chaps. 2, 7.

Fisher, Irving, *Appreciation and Interest* (New York: Macmillan, 1896).

Friedman, Benjamin M., "Price Inflation, Portfolio Choice and Nominal Interest Rates," *American Economic Review*, 70 (March, 1980), 32–48.

————, "Who Puts the Inflation Premium into Nominal Interest Rates," *Journal of Finance*, 33 (June 1978), 833–845.

Gee, K. P., and K. V. Peasnell, "A Comment on Replacement Cost as the Upper Limit of Value to the Owner," *Accounting and Business Research* (Autumn 1977).

Gheyara, Kelly, and James Boatsman, "Market Reaction to the 1976 Replacement Cost Disclosure," *Journal of Accounting and Economics* (August 1980).

Hackamack, Lawrence C., *Making Equipment-Replacement Decisions* (New York: American Management Association, 1969).

Hamada, Robert S., "Financial Theory and Taxation in an Inflationary World: Some Public Policy Issues," *Journal of Finance*, 34 (May 1979), 347–370.

Hendershott, Patric H., "Inflation, Resource Utilization, and Debt and Equity Returns," Working paper, National Bureau of Economic Research (June 1981).

————, and James C. Van Horne, "Expected Inflation Implied by Capital Market Rates," *Journal of Finance*, 28 (May 1973), 301–314.

Higgins, Robert C., "Sustainable Growth Under Inflation," *Financial Management*, 10 (Autumn 1981), 36–40.

Hong, Hai, "Inflation and the Market Value of the Firm: Theory and Tests," *Journal of Finance*, 32 (September 1977), 1031–1048.

Ibbotson, Roger G., and Rex A. Sinquefield, *Stocks, Bonds, Bills, and Inflation*. Charlottesville, Va.: Financial Analysts Research Foundation, 1979.

Ijiri, Yuji, "An Introduction to Corporate Accounting Standards: A Review," *Accounting Review* (October 1980).

————, "The Price-Level Restatement and its Dual Interpretation," *Accounting Review* (April 1976).

Kaplan, R. S., "Purchasing Power Gains on Debt: The Effect of Expected and Unexpected Inflation," *Accounting Review* (April 1977).

Kim, M. K., "Inflationary Effects in the Capital Investment Process: An Empirical Examination," *Journal of Finance* (September 1979).

Kistler, L. H., and C. P. Carter, "Replacement Cost Measures: Their Impact on Income, Dividends, and Investment Return," *Quarterly Review of Economics and Business* (Spring 1979).

Leech, S. A., D. J. Pratt, and W. G. W. Magill, "Company Assets Revaluations and Inflation in Australia, 1950 to 1975," *Journal of Business Finance & Accounting* (Winter 1978).

Lembke, V. C., and H. R. Toole, "Differences in Depreciation Methods and the Analysis of Supplemental Current-Cost and Replacement Cost Data," *Journal of Accounting Auditing and Finance* (Winter 1981).

Livnat, J., J. Ronen, and M. Swirski, "Disaggregation of Deviations in Cost Analysis," *OMEGA, The International Journal of Management Science*, Vol. 9, No. 1., 1981.

Mao, J. C. T., *Quantitative Analysis of Financial Decisions* (New York: Macmillan Co., 1969), 183 ff.

Marks, Kenneth R., and Warren A. Law, "Hedging Against Inflation with Floating-rate Notes," *Harvard Business Review*, 58 (March–April 1980), 106–112.

Modigliani, Franco, and Richard A. Cohn, "Inflation, Rational Valuation and the Market," *Financial Analysis Journal*, 35 (March–April 1979), 24–44.

Mundell, Robert, "Inflation and Real Interest," *Journal of Political Economy*, 71 (June 1963), 280–283.

Murray, Alan P., *Depreciation* (Cambridge, Mass.: International Tax Program, Harvard Law School, 1971).

Myers, J. H., "Depreciation Manipulation for Fun and Profit," *Financial Analysts Journal* (September 1969), 47–56.

Nelson, C. R., "Inflation and Capital Budgeting," *Journal of Finance* (June 1976), 923–931.

Osteryoung, J. S., D. E. McCarty, and K. Fortin, "A Note on the Optimal Tax Lives for Assets Qualifying for the Investment Tax Credit," *Accounting Review* (April 1980).

Perrin, J., "Inflation Accounting: Survey of Academic Opinion," *Journal of Business Financing & Accounting* (Spring 1976).

Piper, A. G., "Reporting the Effects of Inflation in Company Accounts in the United Kingdom," *Quarterly Review of Economics and Business* (Spring 1979).

Poengsen, Otto H., and Hubert Straub, "Inflation and the Corporate Investment Decision," *Management International Review*, Vol. 16, No. 4, 1976.

Popoff, Boris, "Replacement Cost as the Upper Limit of Value to the Owner," *Accounting and Business Research* (Autumn 1977).

Raby, William L., *The Income Tax and Business Decisions* (Englewood Cliffs, N.J.: Prentice-Hall, Inc., 1972).

Rappaport, Alfred, and Robert A. Taggart, Jr., "Evaluation of Capital Expenditure Proposals Under Inflation," *Financial Management*, 11 (Spring 1982), 5–13.

Ro, Byung, T., "The Adjustment of Security Returns to the Disclosure of Replacement Cost Accounting Information," *Journal of Accounting and Economics* (August 1980).

Samuelson, R. A., "Should Replacement-Cost Changes be Included in Income?" *Accounting Review* (April 1980).

Scheiner, J. H., and W. J. Morese, "The Impact of SEC Replacement Cost Reporting Requirements: An Analysis," *Quarterly Review of Economics and Business* (Spring 1979).

Schoenfeld, H. M. W., "Inflation Accounting—Development of Theory and Practice in Continental Europe," *Quarterly Review of Economics and Business* (Spring 1979).

Schwert, G. William, "The Adjustment of Stock Prices to Information About Inflation," *Journal of Finance*, 36 (March 1981), 15–30.

Shashua, L., and Y. Goldschmidt, "A Tool for Inflation Adjustment of Financial Statements," *Journal of Business Finance and Accounting* (Spring 1976).

Singh, S. P., "Inflation and the Profitability of Firms in Canada," *Journal of Business Finance & Accounting* (Winter 1975).

Stark, M. E., "A Survey of LIFO Inventory Application Techniques," *Accounting Review* (January 1978).

Sunder, S., "A Note on Estimating the Economic Impact of the LIFO Method of Inventory Valuation," *Accounting Review* (April 1976).

Tanzi, Vito, "Inflation Expectations, Economic Activity, Taxes, and Interest Rates," *American Economic Reveiw*, 70 (March 1980), 12–21.

Tatom, John A., and James E. Turley, "Inflation and Taxes: Disincentives for Capital Formation," *Review of the Federal Reserve Bank of St. Louis*, 60 (January 1978), 2–8.

Turnbull, S. M., "Discounting the Components of an Income Stream: Comment," *Journal of Finance* (March 1977).

Tysseland, M. S. and D. K. Gandhi, "Depreciation, Inflation and Capital Formation in Public Utilities: One Possible Approach towards a Solution," *Quarterly Reveiw of Economics and Business* (Spring 1979).

Van Horne, James C., *Financial Market Rates and Flows* (Englewood Cliffs, N.J.: Prentice-Hall, 1978), Chap. 5.

_____, and William F. Glassmire, Jr., "The Impact of Unanticipated Changes in Inflation on the Value of Common Stocks," *Journal of Finance*, 27 (December 1972), 1081–1092.

_____, "A Note on Biases in Capital Budgeting Introduced by Inflation," *Journal of Financial and Quantitative Analysis* (January 1971).

Vasarhelyi, M. A., and E. F. Pearson, "Studies in Inflation Accounting: A Taxonomization Approach," *Quarterly Review of Economics and Business* (Spring 1979).

Watts, Ross, L., and Jerold L. Zimmerman, "On the Irrelevance of Replacement Cost Disclosures for Security Prices," *Journal of Accounting and Economics* (August 1980).

Wilkens, E. N., "Forecasting Cash Flow: Some Problems and Applications," *Management Accounting* (October 1967), 26–30.

Winsen, J., and D. Ng, "Investor Behavior and Changes in Accounting Methods," *Journal of Financial and Quantitative Analysis* (December 1976).

Winston, Joseph K., "Capital Market Behaviour and Accounting Policy Decisions," *Accounting and Business Research* (Spring 1977).

Zimmer, R. K., and R. Gray, "Using Accelerated Depreciation in Capital Expenditure Analysis," *Management Service* (January 1969), 43–48.

CHAPTERS 12, 13, 14, 15

Adler, F. Michael, "On Risk-Adjusted Capitalization Rates and Valuation by Individuals," *Journal of Finance* (September 1970).

Aharony, Joseph, and Martin Loeb, "Mean-Variance vs. Stochastic Dominance: Some Empirical Findings on Efficient Sets," *Journal of Banking and Finance* (June 1977).

Alexander, G. J., "A Re-evaluation of Alternative Portfolio Selection Models Applied to Common Stocks," *Journal of Financial and Quantitative Analysis* (March 1978).

Ali, M. M., "Stochastic Dominance and Portfolio Analysis," *Journal of Financial Economics* (June 1975).

Amihud, Yakov, "A Note on Risk Aversion and Indifference Curves," *Journal of Financial and Quantitative Analysis* (September 1977).

_____, "General Risk Aversion and an Attitude towards Risk," *The Journal of Finance* (June 1980).

Ang, James S., and Wilbur G. Lewellen, "Risk Adjustment in Capital Investment Project Evaluations," *Financial Management*, 11 (Summer 1982), 5–14.

Arditti, Fred D., "Risk and the Required Return on Equity," *Journal of Finance* (March 1967).

Arrow, Kenneth J., *Essays in Risk Bearing* (Amsterdam: North Holland Press, 1970).

————, "Alternative Approaches to the Theory of Choice in Risk Taking Situations," *Econometrica* (October 1951).

Arzac, Enrique R., "Structural Planning Under Controllable Business Risk," *Journal of Finance* (December 1975).

Azzi, Corry, "Conglomerate Mergers, Default Risk and Homemade Mutual Funds," *American Economic Review*, 68 (March 1978), 161–172.

Baesel, Jerome B., "On the Assessment of Risk: Some Further Considerations," *Journal of Finance*, 29 (December 1974), 1491–1494.

Baker, H. K., M. B. Hargrove, and J. A. Haslem, "An Empirical Analysis of the Risk-Return Preferences of Individual Investors," *Journal of Financial and Quantitative Analysis* (September 1977).

Baron, David P., "On the Utility Theoretic Foundation of Mean-Variance Analysis," *Journal of Finance*, 32 (December 1977), 1683–1698.

————, "Investment Policy, Optimality, and the Mean-Variance Model: Review Article," *Journal of Finance* (March 1979).

Barry, C. B., and R. L., Winkler, "Nonstationarity and Portfolio Choice," *Journal of Financial and Quantitative Analysis* (June 1976).

Bar-Yosef, S., and R. Mesznik, "On Some Definitional Problems with the Method of Certainty Equivalents," *Journal of Finance* (December 1977).

Baum, S., R. C. Carlson, and J. V. Jucker, "Some Problems in Applying the Continuous Portfolio Selection Model to the Discrete Capital Budgeting Problem," *Journal of Financial and Quantitative Analysis* (June 1978).

Bawa, V. S., "Safety-First, Stochastic Dominance, and Optimal Portfolio Choice, *Journal of Financial and Quantitative Analysis* (June 1978).

————, "Optimal Rules for Ordering Uncertain Prospects," *Journal of Financial Economics* (March 1975).

————, E. J. Elton, and M. J. Gruber, "Simple Rules for Optimal Portfolio Selection in Stable Paretian Markets," *Journal of Finance* (September 1979).

————, "Admissible Portfolios for All Individuals," *Journal of Finance* (September 1976).

Beaver, William, Paul Kettler, and Myron Scholes, "The Association between Market Determined and Accounting Determined Risk Measures," *Accounting Review*, 45 (October 1970), 654–682.

————, and James Manegold, "The Association between Market Determined and Accounting Determined Measures of Systematic Risk: Some Further Evidence," *Journal of Financial and Quantitative Analysis*, 10 (June 1975).

————, and ————, "The Association between Market Determined and Accounting Determined Measures of Systematic Risk: Some Further Evidence," *Journal of Financial and Quantitative Analysis*, 12 (December 1977), 859–878.

Ben-Horim, M., and H. Levy, *Statistics: Decisions and Applications in Business and Economics* (New York: Random House, 1981).

Ben-Shahar, Haim, and Frank M. Werner, "Multiperiod Capital Budgeting under Uncertainty: A Suggested Application," *Journal of Financial and Quantitative Analysis*, 12 (December 1977), 859–878.

Beranek, William, "Some New Capital Budgeting Theorems," *Journal of Financial and Quantitative Analysis*, 13 (December 1978), 809–824.

Berg, Claus C., "Individual Decisions Concerning the Allocation of Resources for Projects with Uncertain Consequences," *Management Science Theory* (September 1974).

Bernoulli, D., "Exposition of a New Theory on the Measurement of Risk," *Econometrica* (January 1954).

Bey, Roger P., and J. Clayton Singleton, "Autocorrelated Cash Flows and the Selection of a Portfolio of Capital Assets," *Decision Sciences*, 8 (October 1978), 640–657.

Bierman, Harold Jr. and Jerome E. Hass, "Capital Budgeting Under Uncertainty: A Reformulation," *Journal of Finance* (March 1973).

————, and Warren H. Hausman, "The Resolution of Investment Uncertainty Through Time," *Management Science*, 18 (August 1972), 654–662.

Bildersie, John S., "The Association between a Market-Determined Measure of Risk and Alternative Measures of Risk," *Accounting Review*, 50 (January 1975), 81–98.

Blatt, John M., "Investment Evaluation Under Uncertainty," *Financial Management* (Summer 1979).

Blume, Marshall E., "Portfolio Theory. A Step Towards its Practical Application," *Journal of Business* (April 1970).

————, "Betas and Their Regression Tendencies," *Journal of Finance*, 30 (June 1975), 785–796.

————, "On the Assessment of Risk," *Journal of Finance*, 26 (March 1971), 1–10.

Bogue, M., and R. Roll, "Capital Budgeting of Risky Projects with Imperfect Markets for Physical Capital," *Journal of Finance* (May 1974), 601–613.

Bonini, Charles P., "Capital Investment Under Uncertainty with Abandonment Options," *Journal of Financial and Quantitative Analysis* (March 1977), 39–54.

————, "Comment on Formulating Correlated Cash Flow Streams," *Engineering Economist*, 20 (Spring 1975), 209–214.

————, "Evaluation of Project Risk in Capital Investments with Abandonment Options," *Research Paper 224*, Stanford Graduate School of Business, 1974.

Borch, K., *The Economics of Uncertainty* (Princeton, N.J.: Princeton University Press, 1968).

Boudreaux, Kenneth J., "Divestiture and Share Price," *Journal of Financial and Quantitative Analysis*, 10 (November 1975), 619–626.

Bower, Richard S., and Donald R. Lessard, "An Operational Approach to Risk-Screening," *Journal of Finance*, 28 (May 1973), 321–337.

Brealey, R. A., *An Introduction to Risk and Return from Common Stocks* (Cambridge: The M.I.T. Press, 1969).

————, and S. D. Hodges, "Playing with Portfolios," *Journal of Finance* (March 1975).

Brennan, M. J., "The Optimal Number of Securities in a Risky Asset Portfolio Where There Are Fixed Costs of Transacting: Theory and Some Empirical Results," *Journal of Financial and Quantitative Analysis* (September 1975).

————, "An Approach to the Valuation of Uncertain Income Streams," *Journal of Finance*, 28 (June 1973), 661–674.

Brenner, Meanachem and Seymour Smidt, "A Simple Model for Non-Stationarity of Systematic Risk," *Journal of Finance*, 32 (September 1977), 1801–1892.

————, "Asset Characteristics and Systematic Risk," *Financial Management*, 7 (Winter 1978), 33–39.

Brito, N. O., "Portfolio Selection in an Economy with Marketability and Short Sales Restrictions," *Journal of Finance* (May 1978).

Brumelle, Shelby L., and Bernhard Schwab, "Capital Budgeting with Uncertain Future Opportunities: A Markovian Approach," *Journal of Financial and Quantitative Analysis* (January 1973).

Bussey, Lynn E., and G. T. Stevens, Jr., "Formulating Correlated Cash Flow Streams," *Engineering Economist*, 18 (Fall 1972), 1–30.

Buzby, Stephen L., "Extending the Applicability of Probabilistic Management Planning and Control Models," *Accounting Review*, 49 (January 1974), 42–49.

Byrne, R., A. Charnes, A. Cooper, and K. Kortanek, "Some New Approaches to Risk," *Accounting Review*, 63 (January 1968), 18–37.

Carter, E. Eugene, *Portfolio Aspects of Corporate Capital Budgeting* (Lexington, Mass.: D.C. Heath & Company, 1974).

Castagna; A. D., and Z. P. Matolesy, "The Relationship between Accounting Variables and Systematic Risk and the Prediction of Systematic Risk," *Australian Journal of Management* (October 1978).

Celec, S. E., and R. H. Pettway, "Some Observations on Risk-Adjusted Discount Rates: A Comment," *Journal of Finance* (September 1979).

Chen, A. H., and A. J. Boness, "Effects of Uncertain Inflation on the Investment and Financing Decisions of a Firm," *Journal of Finance*, 30 (May 1975), 469–484.

————, "Portfolio Selection with Stochastic Cash Demand," *Journal of Financial and Quantitative Analysis* (June 1977).

————, Frank C. Jen, and Stanley Zionts, "The Joint Determination of Portfolio and Transaction Demands for Money," *Journal of Finance* (March 1974).

Chen, Houng-yhi, "Valuation Under Uncertainty," *Journal of Financial and Quantitative Analysis*, 2 (September 1967), 313–326.

Childs, Wendell M., "Management of Capital Expenditures," *Management Accounting* (January 1970), 37–40.

Cohen, Kalman J., and Edwin J. Elton, "Inter-Temporal Portfolio Analysis Based upon Simulation of Joint Returns," *Management Science*, 14 (September 1967), 5–18.

Constantinides, G. M., "Market Risk Adjustment in Project Valuation," *Journal of Finance* (May 1978).

Cooley, Philip L., Rodney L. Roenfeldt, and Naval K. Modani, "Interdependence of Market Risk Measures," *Journal of Business*, 50 (July 1977), 356–363.

Cord, Joel, "A Method for Allocating Funds to Investment Projects When Returns are Subject to Uncertainty," *Management Science* (January 1964).

Copeland, T. E., "A Probability Model of Asset Trading," *Journal of Financial and Quantitative Analysis* (November 1977).

Cox, J. C., J. E. Ingersoll, Jr., and S. A. Ross, "Duration and the Measurement of Basic Risk," *Journal of Business* (January 1979).

Cramer, R. H., and J. A. Seifert, "Measuring the Impact of Maturity on Expected Return and Risk," *Journal of Bank Research* (Autumn 1976).

Crum, Roy L., Dan J. Laughhunn, and John W. Payne, "Risk-Seeking Behavior and Its Implications for Financial Models," *Financial Management*, 10 (Winter, 1981), 20–27.

Cozzolino, John M., "A New Method for Risk Analysis," *Sloan Management Review*, 20 (Spring 1979), 53–65.

————, "Controlling Risk in Capital Budgeting: A Practical Use of Utility Theory for Measurement and Control of Petroleum Exploration Risk," *The Engineering Economist* (Spring 1980).

Dhingra, Harbans L., "Effects of Estimation Risk on Efficient Portfolios: A Monte Carlo Simulation Study," *Journal of Finance and Accounting* (Summer 1980).

Dickinson, J. P., "The Reliability of Estimation Procedures in Portfolio Analysis," *Journal of Financial and Quantitative Analysis* (June 1974).

Dimson, Elroy, "Risk Measurement when Shares are Subject to Infrequent Trading," *Journal of Financial Economics* (1979).

Dothan, Uri, and Joseph Williams, "Term-Risk Structures and the Valuation of Projects," *Journal of Financial and Quantitative Analysis*, 15 (November 1980), 875–906.

Dyl, Edward A., and Hugh W. Long, "Comments," *Journal of Finance* (March 1969), 88–95.

Edelman, Franz, and Joel S. Greenberg, "Venture Analysis: The Assessment of Uncertainty and Risk," *Financial Executive*, 37 (August 1969), 56–62.

Ekern, Steinar, "On the Inadequacy of a Probabilistic Internal Rate of Return," *Journal of Business Finance and Accounting*, 6, 2, 1979.

Elton, Edwin, and Martin J. Gruber, "Estimating the Dependence Structure of Share Prices—Implications for Portfolio Selection," *Journal of Finance*, 28 (December 1973), 1203–1232.

_____, _____, and M. W. Padberg, "Simple Criteria for Optimal Portfolio Selection," *Journal of Finance* (December 1976).

_____, _____, and _____, "Simple Criteria for Optimal Portfolio Selection: Tracing out the Efficient Frontier," *Journal of Finance* (March 1978).

_____, and _____, "Earnings Estimates and the Accuracy of Expectational Data," *Management Science*, 18 (April 1972), 409–424.

_____, and _____, "On the Optimality of Some Multi-period Portfolio Selection Criteria," *The Journal of Business* (April 1974).

_____, and _____, *Finance as a Dynamic Process* (Englewood Cliffs, N.J.: Prentice-Hall, Inc., 1975), Chap. 5.

Evans, Jack, and Stephen H. Archer, "Diversification and the Reduction of Dispersion: An Empirical Analysis," *Journal of Finance*, 23 (December 1968), 761–767.

Falk, Haim and James A. Heintz, "The Predictability of Relative Risk Over Time," *Journal of Business Finance and Accounting* (Spring 1977).

_____, and _____, "Assessing Industry Risk by Ratio Analysis," *Accounting Review* (October 1975).

Fairley, William B., and Henry D. Jacoby, "Investment Analysis Using the Probability Distribution of the Internal Rate of Return," *Management Science*, 21 (August 1975), 1428–1437.

Fama, Eugene F., "Risk-Adjusted Discount Rates and Capital Budgeting under Uncertainty," *Journal of Financial Economics*, 5 (1977), 3–24.

_____, "Components of Investment Performance," *Journal of Finance*, 27 (June 1972), 551–567.

_____, "Efficient Capital Markets: A Review of Theory and Empirical Work," *Journal of Finance*, 25 (May 1970), 333–417.

_____, "Efficient Capital Markets: Restatement of the Theory," *Journal of Finance*, forthcoming.

_____, "Multiperiod Consumption–Investment Decisions," *American Economic Review*, 60 (March 1970), 163–174.

_____, "Risk, Return, and Equilibrium," *Journal of Political Economy*, 79 (January–February 1971), 30–55.

_____, "Risk, Return, and Equilibrium: Some Clarifying Comments," *Journal of Finance*, 23 (March 1968), 29–40.

_____, and James D. MacBeth, "Risk, Return, and Equilibrium: Empirical Tests," *Journal of Political Economy*, 81 (May–June 1973), 607–636.

_____, and Merton H. Miller, *The Theory of Finance* (New York: Holt, Rinehart and Winston, Inc., 1972).

Fielitz, Bruce D., "Indirect versus Direct Diversification," *Financial Management* (Winter 1974).

Findlay, M. Chapman III, Arthur E. Gooding, and Wallace Q. Weaver, Jr., "On the Relevant Risk for Determining Capital Expenditure Hurdle Rates," *Financial Management*, 5 (Winter 1976), 9–16.

Fishburn, P. C., "Mean-Risk Analysis with Risk Associated with Below-Target Returns," *American Economic Review* (March 1977).

Fisher, L., and J. Lorie, "Some Studies of Variability of Returns on Investment in Common Stock," *Journal of Business* (April 1970), 99–134.

_____, "Determinants of Risk Premiums on Corporate Bonds," *Journal of Political Economy*, 67 (June 1959), 217–237.

Firth, Michael, "The Relationship between Stock Market Returns and Rates of Inflation," *Journal of Finance*, 31 (June 1979), 743–749.

Foster, G., *Financial Statement Analysis* (Englewood Cliffs, N.J.: Prentice-Hall, Inc., 1978).

Francis, Jack Clark, "Intertemporal Differences in Systematic Stock Price Movements," *Journal of Financial and Quantitative Analysis*, 10 (June 1975), 205–220.

Frankfurter, G. M. and T. J. Frecker, "Efficient Portfolios and Superfluous Diversification," *Journal of Financial and Quantitative Analysis* (December 1979).

_____, and Herbert E. Phillips, "Portfolio Selection: An Analytic Approach for Selecting Securities from a Large Universe," *Journal of Financial and Quantitative Analysis* (June 1980).

Fremgen, James M., "Capital Budgeting Practices: A Survey," *Management Accounting* (May 1973), 19–25.

Friedman, M., and L. J. Savage, "Utility Analysis of Choices Involving Risk," *Journal of Political Economy* (August 1948), 279–304.

_____, and _____, "The Expected Utility Hypothesis and the Measurability of Utility," *Journal of Political Economy* (December 1952).

Friend, I., and M. Blume, "Measurement of Portfolio Performances Under Uncertainty," *The American Economic Review* (September 1970), 561–575.

_____, and _____, "The Demand for Risky Assets," *American Economic Review* (December 1975).

Fuller, Russel J., and Kim Lang-Hoon, "Inter-Temporal Correlation of Cash Flows and the Risk of Multi-Period Investment Projects," *Journal of Financial and Quantitative Analysis* (December 1980).

Gallinger, George W., and Glenn V. Henderson, Jr., "The SML and the Cost of Capital," Research Paper, Arizona State University, 1981.

Gehr, Adam K., Jr., "Risk-Adjusted Capital Budgeting Using Arbitrage," *Financial Management*, 10 (Winter 1981), 14–19.

_____, "Risk and Return," *Journal of Finance*, 34 (September 1979), 1027–1030.

Gitman, L. J., "Capturing Risk Exposure in the Evaluation of Capital Budgeting Projects," *The Engineering Economist* (Summer 1977).

Goldsmith, D., "Transactions Costs and the Theory of Portfolio Selection," *Journal of Finance* (September 1976).

Gonedes, Nicholas J., "A Note on Accounting-Based and Market-Based Estimates of Systematic Risk," *Journal of Financial and Quantitative Analysis*, 10 (June 1975), 355–365.

Gonzalez, N., R. Litzenberger, and J. Rolfo, "On Mean Variance Models of Capital Structure and the Absurdity of Their Predictions," *Journal of Financial and Quantitative Analysis* (June 1977).

Graves, P. E., "Relative Risk Aversion: Increasing or Decreasing?" *Journal of Financial and Quantitative Analysis* (June 1979).

Grayson, F. Jackson Jr., *Decisions Under Uncertainty: Drilling Decisions by Oil and Gas Operators* (Boston: Division of Research, Harvard Business School, 1960).

Gregory D. D., "Multiplicative Risk Premiums," *Journal of Financial and Quantitative Analysis* (December 1978).

Gressis, N., G. C. Philippatos, and J. Hayya, "Multiperiod Portfolio Analysis and the Inefficiency of the Market Portfolio," *Journal of Finance* (September 1976).

Hadar, J., and W. R. Russell, "Rules for Ordering Uncertain Prospects," *American Economic Review* (March 1969).

Hakansson, Nils H., "Friedman-Savage Utility Functions Consistent with Risk Aversion," *Quarterly Journal of Economics* (August 1970).

_____, "Capital Growth and the Mean-Variance Approach to Portfolio Selection," *Journal of Financial and Quantitative Analysis*, 6 (January 1971), 517–558.

Haley, Charles W., and Lawrence D. Schall, *The Theory of Financial Decisions* (New York: McGraw-Hill Book Company, 1973), Chaps. 5–7.

Hall, Thomas W., "Post Completion Audit Procedure," *Management Accounting* (September 1975), 33–37.

Hamada, Robert S., "Investment Decision with a General Equilibrium Mean-Variance Approach," *Quarterly Journal of Economics*, 85 (November 1971), 667–683.

_____, "Portfolio Analysis, Market Equilibrium and Corporation Finance," *Journal of Finance*, 24 (March 1969), 13–32.

Hanoch, G., and H. Levy, "The Efficiency Analysis of Choices Involving Risk," *Review of Economic Studies* (July 1969).

Harvey, R. K., and A. V. Cabot, "A Decision Theory Approach to Capital Budgeting Under Risk," *Engineering Economist*, 20 (Fall 1974), 37–49.

Hastie, K. Larry, "One Businessman's View of Capital Budgeting," *Financial Management* (Winter 1974), 36–44.

Haugen, Robert A., and A. James Heins, "Risk and the Rate of Return on Financial Assets," *Journal of Financial and Quantitative Analysis*, 10 (December 1975), 775–784.

Hayes, Robert H., "Incorporating Risk Aversion into Risk Analysis," *Engineering Economist*, 20 (Winter 1975), 99–121.

Hertz, David B., "Investment Policies That Pay Off," *Harvard Business Review*, 46 (January–February 1968), 96–108.

_____, "Risk Analysis in Capital Investment," *Harvard Business Review*, 42 (January–February 1964), 95–106.

Hespos, Richard F., and Paul A. Strassmann, "Stochastic Decision Trees for the Analysis of Investment Decisions," *Management Science*, 11 (August 1965), 244–259.

Hicks, Carl F., Jr., and L. Lee Schmidt, Jr., "Post-Auditing the Capital Budgeting Decision," *Management Accounting* (August 1971), 24–32.

Hillier, Frederick S., "The Derivation of Probabilistic Information for the Evaluation of Risky Investments," *Management Science*, 9 (April 1963), 443–457.

_____, "A Basic Model for Capital Budgeting of Risky Interrelated Projects," *Engineering Economist*, 20 (Fall 1974), 37–49.

Hirshleifer, J., "Efficient Allocation of Capital in an Uncertain World," *American Economic Review*, 54 (May 1964), 77–85.

_____, "Investment Decisions Under Uncertainty: Applications of the Slate-Preference Approach," *Quarterly Journal of Economics*, 80 (May 1966), 252–277.

_____, *Investment, Interest and Capital* (Englewood Cliffs, N.J.: Prentice-Hall, Inc., 1970).

Hogan, William W., and James M. Warren, "Toward the Development of an Equilibrium Capital-Market Model Based on Semivariance," *Journal of Financial and Quantitative Analysis* (January 1974).

Hoskins, C. G., "Capital Budgeting Decision Rules for Risky Projects Derived from a Capital Market Model Based on Semivariance," *The Engineering Economist* (Summer 1978).

Hsia, Chi-Cheng, and Russell J. Fuller, "Capital Budgeting for Multiperiod Investments with Correlated Cash Flows: A Simplified Approach," Research Paper; Washington State University, 1981.

Hsiao, F. S. T., and W. J. Smith, "An Analytic Approach to Sensitivity Analysis of the Internal Rate of Return Model," *Journal of Finance* (May 1978).

Huang, C. C., I. Vertinsky, and W. T. Ziemba, "On Multiperiod Stochastic Dominance," *Journal of Financial and Quantitative Analaysis* (March 1978).

Huefner, Ronald L., "Sensitivity Analysis and Risk Evaluation," *Decision Sciences* (July 1972).

Jacob, N. , "The Measurement of Systematic Risk for Securities and Portfolios: Some Empirical Results," *Journal of Financial and Quantitative Analysis*, 6 (March 1971), 815–834.

_____, "A Limited Diversification Portfolio Selection Model for the Small Investor," *Journal of Finance* (June 1974).

Jaffe, Jeffrey P., and Larry J. Merville, "Stock Price Dependencies and the Valuation of Risky Assets with Discontinuous Temporal Returns," *Journal of Finance* (December 1974).

James, J. A., "Portfolio Selection with an Imperfectly Competitive Asset Market," *Journal of Financial and Quantitative Analysis* (December 1976).

Jarrett, Jeffrey E., "An Abandonment Decision Model," *Engineering Economist* (Fall 1973), 35–46.

Jean, W. H., "The Geometric Mean and Stochastic Dominance," *Journal of Finance* (March 1980).

Jensen, Michael C., "Capital Markets: Theory and Practice," *Bell Journal of Economics and Management Science*, 3 (Autumn 1972), 357–398.

————, *Studies in the Theory of Capital Markets* (New York: Praeger Publishers, Inc., 1972).

Johnson, K. H., and R. C. Burgess, "The Effects of Sample Sizes on the Accuracy of EV and SSD Efficiency Criteria," *Journal of Financial and Quantitative Analysis* (December 1975).

————, and D. S. Shannon, "A Note on Diversification and the Reduction of Dispersion," *Journal of Financial Economics*, 1 (December 1974), 365–372.

Joy, O. Maurice, and Jerry O. Bradley, "A Note on Sensitivity Analysis of Rates of Return," *Journal of Finance*, 28 (December 1973), 1255–1261.

————, "Abandonment Values and Abandonment Decisions: A Clarification," *Journal of Finance* (September 1976), 1225–1228.

Kean, Simon E., "The Investment Discount Rate—In Defence of the Market Rate of Interest," *Accounting and Business Research* (Summer 1976), 228–236.

Kearns, R. B., and R. C. Burgess, "An Effective Algorithm for Estimating Stochastic Dominance Efficient Sets," *Journal of Financial and Quantitative Analysis* (September 1979).

Keeley, Robert, and Randolph Westerfield, "A Problem in Probability Distribution Techniques for Capital Budgeting," *Journal of Finance*, 27 (June 1972), 703–709.

Kemp, Patrick S., "Post-Completion Audits of Capital Investment Projects," *Management Accounting* (August 1966), 49–54.

Kihlstrom, R. E., and J. J. Laffont, "A General Equilibrium Entrepreneurial Theory of Firm Formation Based on Risk Aversion," *Journal of Political Economy* (August 1979).

Klein, R. W., and V. S. Bawa, "The Effect of Estimation Risk on Optimal Portfolio Choice," *Journal of Financial Economics* (June 1976).

Klemkosky, R. C., and T. S. Maness, "The Predictability of Real Portfolio Risk Levels," *Journal of Finance* (May 1978).

————, and John D. Martin, "The Effect of Market Risk on Portfolio Diversification," *Journal of Finance* (March 1975).

————, and ————, "The Adjustment of Beta Forecasts," *Journal of Finance*, 30 (September 1975), 1123–1128.

Kryzanowski, Lawrence, Peter Lusztig, and Bernhard Schwab, "Monte Carlo Simulation and Capital Expenditure Decisions—A Case Study," *Engineering Economist*, 18 (Fall 1972), 31–48.

Kudla, Ronald J., "Some Pitfalls in Using Certainty-Equivalents: A Note," *Journal of Business Finance and Accounting* (Summer 1980).

Latane, H. A., and Donald L. Tuttle, "Decision Theory and Financial Management," *Journal of Finance* (May 1966).

Lessard, Donald P., and Richard S. Bower, "An Operational Approach to Risk Screening," *Journal of Finance*, 28 (May 1973), 321–338.

Levy, H., and M. Sarnat, "The Portfolio Analysis of Multiperiod Capital Investment Under Conditions of Risk," *Engineering Economist* (Fall 1970).

————, and ————, "The World Oil Crisis: A Portfolio Interpretation," *Economic Inquiry* (September 1975).

_____, and Y. Kroll, "Ordering Uncertain Options with Borrowing and Lending," *Journal of Finance* (May 1978).

_____, and Jacob Paroush, "Multi-Period Stochastic Dominance," *Management Science Application* (December 1974).

_____, and Marshall Sarnat, *Capital Investment and Financial Decisions*, 2nd ed. (Englewood Cliffs, N.J.: Prentice-Hall, 1982).

_____, "The Portfolio Analysis of Multiperiod Capital Investment under Conditions of Risk," *Engineering Economist*, 16 (Fall 1970), 1–19.

Levy, Robert A., "On the Short Term Stationarity of Beta Coefficients," *Financial Analysts Journal*, 27 (November–December 1971), 55–62.

Lewellen, W. G., "Some Observations on Risk Adjusted Discount Rates," *Journal of Finance* (September 1977).

_____, and Michael S. Long, "Simulation versus Single-Value Estimates in Capital Expenditure Analysis," *Decision Sciences*, 3 (1973), 19–33.

Lintner, John, "The Aggregation of Investors' Judgments and Preferences in Purely Competitive Security Markets," *Journal of Financial and Quantitative Analysis*, 4 (December 1969), 347–400.

_____, "The Evaluation of Risk Assets and the Selection of Risky Investments in Stock Portfolios and Capital Budgets," *Review of Economics and Statistics*, 47 (February 1965), 13–37.

_____, "Security Prices, Risk and Maximal Gains from Diversification," *Journal of Finance*, 20 (December 1965), 587–616.

Litzenberger, R. H., and A. P. Budd, "Secular Trends in Risk Premiums," *Journal of Finance*, 27 (September 1972), 857–864.

Lockett, A. Geoffrey, and Anthony E. Gear, "Multistage Capital Budgeting under Uncertainty," *Journal of Financial and Quantitative Analysis*, 10 (March 1975), 21–36.

Logue, D. E., and L. J. Merville, "Financial Policy and Market Expectations," *Financial Management* (Summer 1972), 37–44.

Lucken, J. A., and D. P. Stuhr, "Decision Trees and Risky Projects," *The Engineering Economist* (Winter 1978).

Magee, John F., "Decision Trees for Decision Making," *Harvard Business Review* (July–August 1964).

_____, "How to Use Decision Trees in Capital Investment," *Harvard Business Review* 42 (September–October 1964), 79–96.

Mao, James C. T., and John F. Helliwell, "Investment Decisions under Uncertainty: Theory and Practice," *Journal of Finance* (May 1969).

_____, "Survey of Capital Budgeting: Theory and Practice," *Journal of Finance* (May 1970), 349–360.

Markowitz, Harry M., "Portfolio Selection," *Journal of Finance* (March 1952).

_____, *Portfolio Selection* (New York: Wiley 1959).

Martin, A. D., "Mathematical Programming of Portfolio Selections," *Management Science* (January 1955), 152–166.

Martin, J. D., and A. J. Keown, "Interest Rate Sensitivity and Portfolio Risk," *Journal of Financial and Quantitative Analysis* (June 1977).

McEnally, R. W., and D. E. Upton, "A Re-examination of the Ex Post Risk-Return Tradeoff on Common Stocks," *Journal of Financial and Quantitative Analysis* (June 1979).

Meyer, J., "Further Applications of Stochastic Dominance to Mutual Fund Performance," *Journal of Financial and Quantitative Analysis* (June 1977).

_____, "Mean-Variance Efficient Sets and Expected Utility," *Journal of Finance* (December 1979).

Miller, Edward M., "Uncertainty Induced Bias in Capital Budgeting," *Financial Management* (Autumn 1978).

Modigliani, Franco, and Gerald A. Pogue, "An Introduction to Risk and Return," *Financial Analysts Journal* Part I (March/April 1974), Part II (May/June 1974).

Montgomery, John L., "Appraising Capital Expenditures," *Management Accounting* (September 1965), 3–10.

Murphy, Joseph E., Jr., and M. F. M. Osborne, "Games of Chance and the Probability of Corporate Profit or Loss," *Financial Management*, 8 (Summer 1979), 82–87.

Myers, Stewart C., "The Application of Finance Theory to Public Utility Rate Cases," *Bell Journal of Economics and Management Science*, 3 (Spring 1972), 58–97.

————, "Procedures for Capital Budgeting Under Uncertainty," *Industrial Management Review*, 9 (Spring 1968), 1–15.

————, "A Time-State Preference Model of Security Valuation," *Journal of Financial and Quantitative Analysis*, 3 (March 1968), 1–34.

Newhauser, John J., and Jerry A. Viscione, "How Managers Feel About Advanced Capital Budgeting Methods," *Management Review* (September 1973), 16–22.

Nielsen, N. C., "The Investment Decision of the Firm Under Uncertainty and the Allocative Efficiency of Capital Markets," *Journal of Finance*, 31 (May 1976), 587–601.

Obel, Borge, and James van der Weide, "On the Decentralized Capital Budgeting Problem under Uncertainty," *Management Science* (September 1979).

Pappas, James L., "The Role of Abandonment Value in Capital Asset Management," *Engineering Economist*, 22 (Fall 1976), 53–61.

Parkinson, M. "The Extreme Value Method for Estimating the Variance of the Rate of Return," *Journal of Business* (January 1980).

Perrakis, S., and J. Zerbinis, "Identifying the SSD Portion of the EV Frontier: A Note," *Journal of Financial and Quantitative Analysis* (March 1978).

————, "Certainty Equivalents and Timing Uncertainty," *Journal of Financial and Quantitative Analysis* (March 1975).

Peterson, D. E., and R. B. Haydon, *A Quantitative Framework for Financial Management* (Homewood, Ill.: Richard D. Irwin, Inc., 1969), pp. 404–434.

Petry, Glenn H., "Effective Use of Capital Budgeting Tools," *Business Horizons* (October 1975), 57–65.

Pettit, H. Richardson, and Randolph Westerfield, "A Model of Capital Asset Risk," *Journal of Financial and Quantitative Analysis*, 7 (March 1972), 1649–1668.

Petty, J. William, David F. Scott, Jr., and Monroe M. Bird, "The Capital Expenditure Decision-Making Process of Large Corporations," *Engineering Economist* (Spring 1975), 159–172.

————, and Oswald D. Bowlin, "The Financial Manager and Quantitative Decision Models," *Financial Management* (Winter 1976).

Phelps, E. S., "The Accumulation of Risky Capital: A Sequential Utility Analysis," *Econometrica*, 30 (1962), 729–743.

Philippatos, George C., and Nicolas Gressis, "Conditions of Equivalence Among E-V, SSD, and E-H Portfolio Selection Criteria—The Case for Uniform Normal and Lognormal Distributions," *Management Science Application* (February 1957).

Pogue, Gerald A., "An Extension of the Markowitz Portfolio Selection Model to Include Variable Transactions Costs, Short Sales, Leverage Policies and Taxes," *Journal of Finance*, 25 (December 1970), 1005–1027.

————, and Kishore Lall, "Corporate Finance: An Overview," *Sloan Management Review*, 15 (Spring 1974), 19–38.

Porter, R. B., R. P. Bey, and D. C. Lewis, "The Development of a Mean-Semivariance Approach to Capital Budgeting," *Journal of Financial and Quantitative Analysis* (November 1975).

————, and ————, "An Evaluation of the Empirical Significance of Optimal Seeking Algorithms in Portfolio Selection," *Journal of Finance* (December 1974).

Pratt, J. W. and J. S. Hammond, III, "Evaluating and Comparing Projects: Simple Detection of False Alarms," *Journal of Finance* (December 1979).

_____, "Risk Aversion in the Small and in the Large," *Econometrica* (January–April 1964).

Quirin, G. David, and John C. Wiginton, *Analyzing Capital Expenditures* (Homewood, Ill: Irwin, 1981).

Quirk, J. P., and R. Saposnik, "Admissibility and Measurable Utility Functions," *Review of Economic Studies* (February 1962).

Raiffa, H., *Decision Analysis* (Reading Mass: Addison-Wesley, 1968).

Rendleman, Richard J., Jr., "The Effects of Default Risk on the Firm's Investment and Financing Decisions," *Financial Management*, 7 (Spring 1978), 45–53.

Renwick, F. B., *Introduction to Investments and Finance* (New York: Macmillan Publishing Co., Inc., 1971).

Robichek, Alexander A., and Stewart C. Myers, "Conceptual Problems in the Use of Risk-Adjusted Discount Rates," *Journal of Finance*, 21 (December 1966), 727–730.

_____, *Optimal Financing Decisions* (Englewood Cliffs, N.J.: Prentice-Hall, Inc., 1965), Chap. 5.

_____, and James C. Van Horne, "Abandonment Value and Capital Budgeting," *Journal of Finance* (December 1967), 577–589.

_____, and James C. Van Horne, "Reply," *Journal of Finance* (March 1969), 96–97.

_____, and Richard A. John, "The Economic Determinants of Systematic Risk," *Journal of Finance*, 29 (May 1974), 439–447.

_____, "Interpreting the Results of Risk Analysis," *Journal of Finance*, 30 (December 1975), 1384–1386.

Robison, L. J., and P. J. Barry, "Risk Efficiency Using Stochastic Dominance and Expected Gain-Confidence Limits," *Journal of Finance* (September 1978).

Roll, Richard, and Marcus C. Bogue, "Capital Budgeting of Risky Projects with Imperfect Markets for Physical Capital," *Journal of Finance*, 29 (May 1974), 606–612.

Ross, S. A., "Return, Risk, and Arbitrage," in *Risk and Return in Finance*, I. Friend and J. L. Bicksler, eds., Vol. I, Section 9 (Cambridge: Ballinger Publishing Company, 1977).

_____, "A Simple Approach to the Valuation of Risky Streams," *Journal of Business* (July 1978).

Roy, A. D., "Safety First and the Holding of Assets," *Econometrica* (July 1952).

Salazar, Rudolfo C., and Subrata K. Sen, "A Simulation Model of Capital Budgeting under Uncertainty," *Management Science*, 15 (December 1968), 161–179.

Saniga, E., N. Gressis, and J. Hayya, "The Effects of Sample Size and Correlation on the Accuracy of the EV Efficiency Criterion," *Journal of Financial and Quantitative Analysis* (September 1979).

Saunders, Anthony, Charles Ward, and Richard Woodward, "Stochastic Dominance and the Performance of UK Unit Trusts," *Journal of Financial and Quantitative Analysis* (June 1980).

Schall, Lawrence D., and Gary L. Sundem, "Capital Budgeting Methods and Risk: A Further Analysis," *Financial Management*, 9 (Spring 1980), 7–11.

_____, "Asset Valuation, Firm Investment, and Firm Diversification," *Journal of Business*, 45 (January 1972), 11–28.

_____, "Firm Financial Structure and Investment," *Journal of Financial and Quantitative Analysis*, 6 (June 1971), 925–942.

Schlaifer, R., *Probability and Statistics for Business Decisions* (New York: McGraw-Hill Book Company, 1969).

_____, "A Simplified Model for Portfolio Analysis," *Management Science*, 10 (January 1963), 277–293.

Schlarbaum, Gary G., and George A. Racette, "Measuring Risk: Some Theoretical and Empirical Issues," *Journal of Business Research* (July 1974).

Schnell, James S., and Roy S. Nicolosi, "Capital Expenditure Feedback: Project Reappraisal," *Engineering Economist*, 19 (July–August 1974), 253–261.

Schneller, M. I., "Mean-Variance Portfolio Composition When Investors' Revision Horizon is Very Long," *Journal of Finance* (December 1975).

Schwab, Bernhard, "Conceptual Problems in the Use of Risk-Adjusted Discount Rates with Disaggregated Cash Flows," *Journal of Business Finance and Accounting* (Winter 1978).

_____, and P. Lusztig, "A Note on Abandonment Value and Capital Budgeting," *Journal of Financial and Quantitative Analysis* (September 1970), 377–379.

Schwartz, R. A., and D. K. Whitcomb, "The Time-Variance Relationship: Evidence on Autocorrelation in Common Stock Returns," *Journal of Finance* (March 1977).

Schwendiman, Carl J., and George E. Pinches, "An Analysis of Alternative Measures of Investment Risk," *Journal of Finance* (March 1975).

Scott, Robert C., and Philip A. Horvath, "On the Direction of Preference for Moments of Higher Order than the Variance," *Journal of Finance* (September 1980).

Senbet, L. W. and H. E. Thompson, "The Equivalence of Alternative Mean-Variance Capital Budgeting Models," *Journal of Finance* (May 1978).

Sharpe, William F., "A Simplified Model for Portfolio Analysis," *Management Science* (January 1963).

_____, "Efficient Capital Markets with Risk," *Research Paper* 71 (Stanford Graduate School of Business, 1972).

_____, *Portfolio Analysis and Capital Markets* (New York: McGraw-Hill Book Company, 1970).

_____, and Guy M. Cooper, "Risk-Return Classes of New York Stock Exchange Common Stocks," *Financial Analysts Journal*, 28 (March–April 1972), 46–54.

_____, *Investments*, 2nd Edition (Englewood Cliffs, N.J.: Prentice-Hall, Inc., 1982).

Shillinglaw, Gordon, "Profit Analysis for Abandonment Decisions," in Ezra Solomon, ed., *The Management of Corporate Capital* (New York: The Free Press, 1959), pp. 269–281.

Silvers, J. B., "Liquidity, Risk and Duration Patterns in Corporate Financing," *Financial Management*, 5 (Autumn 1976), 54–64.

Simkowitz, M. A., and W. L. Beedles, "Diversification in a Three-Moment World," *Journal of Financial and Quantitative Analysis* (December 1978).

Spahr, Ronald W., and Stanley A. Martin, "Project Pricing in Limited Diversification Portfolios," *Engineering Economist*, 26 (Spring 1981), 207–222.

Spies, Richard R., "The Dynamics of Corporate Capital Budgeting," *Journal of Finance* (June 1974), 829–845.

Stapleton, Richard C., "Portfolio Analysis, Stock Valuation and Capital Budgeting Rules for Risky Projects," *Journal of Finance*, 26 (March 1971), 95–118.

Sundem, Gary L., "Evaluating Simplified Capital Budgeting Models Using a Time-State Preference Metric," *Accounting Review*, 49 (April 1974), 306–320.

Tehranian, H., "Empirical Studies in Portfolio Performance Using Higher Degrees of Stochastic Dominance," *Journal of Finance* (March 1980).

Thompson, Donald J., II, "Sources of Systematic Risk in Common Stocks," *Journal of Business*, 49 (April 1976), 173–188.

Tobin, James, "Liquidity Preference as Behavior Towards Risk," *Review of Economic Studies*, 25 (February 1958), 65–86.

Turnbull, Stuart M., "Market Value and Systematic Risk," *Journal of Finance*, 32 (September 1977), 1125–1142.

Tuttle, Donald L., and Robert H. Litzenberger, "Leverage, Diversification and Capital Market Effects on a Risk-Adjusted Capital Budgeting Framework," *Journal of Finance*, 23 (June 1968), 427–443.

Vandell, Robert F., and Paul J. Stonich, "Capital Budgeting: Theory or Results?" *Financial Executive* (August 1973), 46–56.

Van Horne, James C., "The Analysis of Uncertainty Resolution in Capital Budgeting for New Products," *Management Science*, 15 (April 1969), 376–386.

________, "Capital-Budgeting Decisions Involving Combinations of Risky Investments," *Management Science*, 13 (October 1966), 84–92.

________, *The Function and Analysis of Capital Market Rates* (Englewood Cliffs, N.J.: Prentice-Hall, Inc., 1970).

________, "Capital Budgeting under Conditions of Uncertainty as to Project Life," *Engineering Economist*, 17 (Spring 1972), 189–199.

________, "The Variation of Project Life as a Means for Adjusting for Risk," *Engineering Economist*, 21 (Spring 1976), 151–158.

________, "Optimal Initiation of Bankruptcy Proceedings by Debt Holders," *Journal of Finance*, 31 (June 1976), 897–910.

Vernon, Thomas H., "Capital Budgeting and the Evaluation Process," *Management Accounting* (October 1972), 19–24.

Von Neumann, J. and O. Morgenstern, *Theory of Games and Economic Behavior*, (Princeton, N.J.: Princeton University Press, 1953).

Vickson, R. G., "Stochastic Dominance for Decreasing Absolute Risk Aversion," *Journal of Financial and Quantitative Analysis* (December 1975).

________, and M. Altmann, "On the Relative Effectiveness of Stochastic Dominance Rules: Extension to Decreasingly Risk-Averse Utility Functions," *Journal of Financial and Quantitative Analysis* (March 1977).

Wachowicz, John M., Jr., and Ronald E. Shrieves, "An Argument for 'Generalized' Mean-Coefficient or Variation Analysis," *Financial Management* (Winter 1980).

Wallingford B. A., "A Survey and Comparison of Portfolio Selection Models," *Journal of Financial and Quantitative Analysis* (June 1967).

Weaver, James B., "Organizing and Maintaining a Capital Expenditure Program," *Engineering Economist* (Fall 1974), 1–35.

Weinwurm, Ernest H., "Utilization of Sophisticated Capital Budgeting Techniques in Industry," *Engineering Economist* (Summer 1974), 271–272.

Whisler, William D., "Sensitivity Analysis of Rates of Return," *Journal of Finance*, 31 (March 1976), 63–70.

Whitmore, G. A., "The Theory of Skewness Preference," *Journal of Business Administration* (Spring 1975).

Williams, J. T., "A Note on Indifference Curves in the Mean-Variance Model," *Journal of Financial and Quantitative Analysis* (March 1977).

Winkler, Robert L., and Christopher B. Barry, "A Bayesian Model for Portfolio Selection and Revision," *Journal of Finance* (March 1975).

Ziemba, W. T., C. Parkan, and R. Brooks-Hill, "Calculation of Investment Portfolios with Risk Free Borrowing and Lending," *Management Science Application* (October 1974).

Zinn, C. D., W. G. Lesso, and B. Motazed, "A Probabilistic Approach to Risk Analysis in Capital Investment Projects," *The Engineering Economist* (Summer 1977).

CHAPTERS 16, 17, 18

Alexander, Gordon J., and Norman L. Chervany, "On the Estimation and Stability of Beta," *Journal of Financial and Quantitative Analysis* (March 1980).

Andrews, Victor L., "Sterile Promises in Corporate Capital Theory," *Financial Management*, 8 (Winter 1979), 7–11.

Baesel, Jerome B., "On the Assessment of Risk: Some Further Considerations," *Journal of Finance*, 29 (December 1974), 1491–1494.

Barry, C. B., "Effects of Uncertain and Non-Stationary Parameters upon Capital Market Equilibrium Conditions," *Journal of Financial and Quantitative Analysis* (September 1978).

Beja, Avraham, and Barry Goldman, "On the Dynamic Behavior of Prices in Disequilibrium," *The Journal of Finance* (May 1980).

Ben-Horim, Moshe, and Haim Levy, "Total Risk, Diversifiable Risk: A Pedagogic Note," *Journal of Financial and Quantitative Analysis* (June 1980).

Bierman, Harold, Jr., and Warren H. Hausman, "The Resolution of Investment Uncertainty Through Time," *Management Science*, 18 (August 1972), 654–662.

Black, F., M. C. Jensen, and M. Scholes, "The Capital Asset Pricing Model: Some Empirical Tests," in M. C. Jensen, ed., *Studies in the Theory of Capital Markets* (New York: Praeger Publishers, Inc., 1972).

————, "Capital Market Equilibrium with Restricted Borrowing," *Journal of Business* (1972).

Blume, M. E., "Betas and Their Regression Tendencies: Some Further Evidence," *Journal of Finance* (March 1979).

————, and Irwin Friend, "A New Look at the Capital-Asset Pricing Model," *Journal of Finance*, 28 (March 1973), 19–34.

————, "On the Assessment of Risk," *Journal of Finance*, 26 (March 1971), 1–10.

————, and Z. Bodie, "Common Stocks as a Hedge Against Inflation," *Journal of Finance*, 31 (May 1976), 459–470.

Bolton, S. E., and J. H. Crockett, "The Influence of Liquidity Services on Beta," *Review of Business and Economic Research* (Spring 1978).

————, S. J. Kretlow, and J. H. Oakes, "The Capital Asset Pricing Model under Certainty," *Review of Business and Economic Research* (Fall 1978).

Bower, Richard S., and Donald Lessard, "An Operational Approach to Risk-Screening," *Journal of Finance*, 28 (May 1973), 321–337.

Boyer, Marcel, Sverre Storoy, and Thore Sten, "Equilibrium in Linear Capital Market Networks," *Journal of Finance* (December 1975).

Breeden, D. T., "An Intertemporal Asset Pricing Model with Stochastic Consumption and Investment Opportunities," *Journal of Financial Economics* (June 1979).

Brennan, Michael J., "Taxes, Market Valuation and Corporate Finance Policy," *National Tax Journal*, 23 (1970).

Brenner, Menachem and Seymour Smidt, "Asset Characteristics and Systematic Risk," *Financial Management* (Winter 1978).

Brito, N. O., "Marketability Restrictions and the Valuation of Capital Assets under Uncertainty," *Journal of Finance* (September 1977).

Brown, S. L., "Autocorrelation, Market Imperfections, and the CAPM," *Journal of Financial and Quantitative Analysis* (December 1979).

Casabona, Patrick A. and Ashok Vora, "The Bias of Conventional Risk Premiums in Empirical Tests of the Capital Asset Pricing Model, *Financial Management*, 11 (Summer 1982), 90–95.

Chen, A. H., E. H. Kim, and S. J. Kon, "Cash Demand, Liquidation Costs and Capital Market Equilibrium under Uncertainty," *Journal of Financial Economics* (September 1975).

Cheng, Pao L., and Robert R. Grauer, "An Alternative Test of the Capital Asset Pricing Model," *The American Economic Review* (September 1980).

Cohn, Richard A. and D. Lessard, "The Effect of Inflation on Stock Prices: International Evidence," *Journal of Finance*, 36 (May 1981), 277–289.

Conine, Thomas E., Jr., "Debt Capacity and the Capital Budgeting Decision: A Comment," *Financial Management*, 9 (Spring 1980), 20–22.

Cornell, B., and J. K. Dietrich, "Mean-Absolute-Deviation Versus Least-Squares Regression Estimation of Beta Coefficients," *Journal of Financial and Quantitative Analysis* (March 1978).

Crockett, Jean and Irwin Friend, "Capital Budgeting and Stock Valuation Comment," *American Economic Review* (March 1967).

Eddy, A. R., "Interest Rate Risk and Systematic Risk: An Interpretation," *Journal of Finance* (May 1978).

Elgers, P. T., J. R. Haltiner, and W. H. Hawthorne, "Beta Regression Tendencies: Statistical and Real Causes," *Journal of Finance* (March 1979).

Epstein, Larry G., and Stuart M. Turnbull, "Capital Asset Prices and the Temporal Resolution of Uncertainty," *The Journal of Finance* (June 1980).

Evans, Jack, and Stephen H. Archer, "Diversification and the Reduction of Dispersion: An Empirical Analysis," *Journal of Finance*, 23 (December 1968), 761–767.

Everett, James E., and Bernhard Schwab, "On the Proper Adjustment for Risk Through Discount Rates in a Mean-Variance Framework," *Financial Management* (Summer 1979).

Fabozzi, F. J., and J. C. Francis, "Beta as a Random Coefficient," *Journal of Financial and Quantitative Analysis* (March 1978).

Fabry, Jaak, and Willy van Grembergen, "Further Evidence on the Stationarity of Betas and Errors in their Estimates," *Journal of Banking and Finance* (October 1978).

Fama, Eugene F., "Components of Investment Performance," *Journal of Finance*, 27 (June 1972), 551–567.

————, "Efficient Capital Markets: A Review of Theory and Empirical Work," *Journal of Finance*, 25 (May 1970), 333–417.

————, "Efficient Capital Markets: Restatement of the Theory," *Journal of Finance*, forthcoming.

————, "Multiperiod Consumption–Investment Decision," *American Economic Review*, 60 (March 1970), 163–174.

————, "Risk, Return, and Equilibrium," *Journal of Political Economy*, 79 (January–February 1971), 30–55.

————, "Risk, Return, and Equilibrium: Some Clarifying Comments," *Journal of Finance*, 23 (March 1968), 29–40.

————, and James D. MacBeth, "Risk, Return, and Equilibrium: Empirical Tests," *Journal of Political Economy*, 81 (May–June 1973), 607–636.

————, and Merton H. Miller, *The Theory of Finance* (New York: Holt, Rinehart and Winston, Inc., 1972).

————, Lawrence Fisher, Michael Jensen, and Richard Roll, "The Adjustment of Stock Prices to New Information," *International Economic Review* (February 1969).

Foster, G., "Asset Pricing Models: Further Tests," *Journal of Financial and Quantitative Analysis* (March 1978).

Francis, Jack Clark, "Intertemporal Differences in Systematic Stock Price Movements," *Journal of Financial and Quantitative Analysis*, 10 (June 1975), 205–220.

Frankfurter, G. M., "The Effect of 'Market Indexes' on the Ex-Post Performance of the Sharpe Portfolio Selection Model," *Journal of Finance* (June 1976).

Friend, Irwin, and Randolph Westerfield, "Co-Skewedness and Capital Asset Pricing," *The Journal of Finance* (September 1980).

————, and ————, "Risk and Capital Asset Prices," *Journal of Banking and Finance*, forthcoming.

Friend, L., R. Westerfield, and M. Granito, "New Evidence on the Capital Asset Pricing Model," *Journal of Finance* (June 1978).

Gahlon, James M., and D. Roger Stover, "Debt Capacity and the Capital Budgeting Decision: A Caveat," *Financial Management*, 8 (Winter 1979), 55–59.

Gentry, James and John Pike, "An Empirical Study of the Risk-Return Hypothesis Using Common Stock Portfolios of Life Insurance Companies," *Journal of Financial and Quantitative Analysis* (June 1970).

Goldberg, M. A., and A. Vora, "Bivariate Spectral Analysis of the Capital Asset Pricing Model," *Journal of Financial and Quantitative Analysis* (September 1978).

Grauer, R. R., "Generalized Two Parameter Asset Pricing Models: Some Empirical Evidence," *Journal of Financial Economics* (March 1978).

Hakansson, Nils H., "Capital Growth and the Mean-Variance Approach to Portfolio Selection," *Journal of Financial and Quantitative Analysis*, 6 (January 1971), 517–558.

Haley, Charles W., and Lawrence D. Schall, *The Theory of Financial Decision* (New York: McGraw-Hill Book Company, 1973), Chaps. 5–7.

Hamada, Robert S., "Investment Decision with a General Equilibrium Mean-Variance Approach," *Quarterly Journal of Economics*, 85 (November 1971), 667–683.

_____, "Multiperiod Capital Asset Prices in an Efficient and Perfect Market: A Valuation or Present Value Model Under Two Parameter Uncertainty," unpublished ms., University of Chicago, 1972.

_____, "Portfolio Analysis, Market Equilibrium and Corporation Finance," *Journal of Finance*, 24 (March 1969), 13–32.

_____, "Discussion," *Journal of Finance*, 32 (May 1977), 333–336. Comments on Myers and Turnball article.

Harris, Richard G., "A General Equilibrium Analysis of the Capital Asset Pricing Model," *Journal of Financial and Quantitative Analysis* (March 1980).

Hayes, Robert H., "Incorporation Risk Aversion into Risk Analysis," *Engineering Economist*, 20 (Winter 1975), 99–121.

Hess, A. C., "The Riskless Rate of Interest and Market Price of Risk," *Quarterly Journal of Economics* (August 1975).

Hill, Ned C., and Bernell K. Stone, "Accounting Betas, Systematic Operating Risk, and Financial Leverage: A Risk-Composition Approach to the Determinants of Systematic Risk," *Journal of Financial and Quantitative Analysis* (September 1980).

Hillier, Frederick S., "A Basic Model for Capital Budgeting of Risky Interrelated Projects," *Engineering Economist*, 17 (October–November 1971), 1–30.

_____, "The Derivation of Probabilistic Information for the Evaluation of Risky Investments," *Management Science*, 9 (April 1963), 443–457.

Hirshleifer, Jack, "Investment Decisions Under Uncertainty: Applications of the State-Preference Approach," *Quarterly Journal of Economics*, 80 (May 1966), 252–277.

_____, *Investment, Interest and Capital* (Englewood Cliffs, N.J.: Prentice-Hall, Inc., 1970).

Jahankhani, A., "E-V and E-S Capital Asset Pricing Models: Some Empirical Tests," *Journal of Financial and Quantitative Analysis* (September 1976).

Jarrow, Robert, "Heterogeneous Expectations, Restrictions on Short Sales, and Equilibrium Asset Prices," *Journal of Finance* (December 1980).

Jensen, Michael C. (Editor), *Studies in the Theory of Capital Markets* (New York: Praeger Publishers, 1972).

_____, "Capital Markets: Theory and Practice," *Bell Journal of Economics and Management Science*, 3 (Autumn 1972), 357–398.

_____, "Risk, the Pricing of Capital Assets, and the Evaluation of Investment Portfolios," *Journal of Business*, 42 (April 1969), 167–247.

Johnson, K. H., and D. S. Shannon, "A Note on Diversification and the Reduction of Dispersion," *Journal of Financial Economics*, 1 (December 1974), 365–372.

Jones-Lee, M. W., and D. S. Poskitt, "An Existence Proof for Equilibrium in a Capital Asset Market," *Journal of Business Finance & Accounting* (Autumn 1975).

Klemosky, R. C., and J. D. Martin, "The Adjustment of the Beta Forecasts," *Journal of Finance* (September 1975).

Kon, S. L., and F. C. Jen, "Estimation of Time-Varying Systematic Risk and Performance for Mutual Fund Portfolios: An Application of Switching Regression," *Journal of Finance* (May 1978).

Kraus, Alan, and Robert H. Litzenberger, "Market Equilibrium in a Multiperiod State Preference Model with Logarithmic Utility," *Journal of Finance* (December 1975).

Kymn, K. O., and W. P. Page, "A Microeconomic and Geometric Interpretation of Beta in Models of Discrete Adaptive Expectations," *Review of Business and Economic Research* (Spring 1978).

Lakonishok, Josef, "Stock Market Returns Expectations: Some General Properties," *The Journal of Finance* (September 1980).

Landskroner, Y., "Intertemporal Determination of the Market Price of Risk," *Journal of Finance*, (December 1977).

Lee, C. F., and F. C. Jen, "Effects of Measurement Errors on Systematic Risk and Performance Measure of a Portfolio," *Journal of Finance and Quantitative Analysis* (June 1978).

_____, "On the Relationship between the Systematic Risk and the Investment Horizon," *Journal of Financial and Quantitative Analysis* (December 1976).

_____, "Performance Measure, Systematic Risk, and Errors-in-Variables Estimation Method," *Journal of Economics and Business* (Winter 1977).

Leland, H., "Production Theory and the Stock Market," *Bell Journal of Economics*, 5 (1974) 125–144.

Levitz, G. D., *A Study of the Usefulness of Beta Analysis in the Management of Common Stock Portfolios* (New York: Brown Brothers, Harriman & Co., 1972).

Levy, Haim, and Marshall Sarnat, "The Portfolio Analysis of Multiperiod Capital Investment Under Conditions of Risk," *Engineering Economist*, 16 (Fall 1970), 1–19.

_____, "The CAPM and Beta in an Imperfect Market," *Journal of Portfolio Management* (Winter 1980).

Levy, Robert A., "On the Short Term Stationarity of Beta Coefficients," *Financial Analysts Journal*, 27 (November–December 1971), 55–62.

Lewellen, Wilbur G., Ronald C. Lease, and Gary G. Schlarbaum, "Portfolio Design and Portfolio Performance: the Individual Investor," *Journal of Economics and Business* (Spring/Summer 1980).

Lin, Winston T., and Frank C. Jen, "Consumption, Investment, Market Price of Risk, and the Risk-Free Rate," *Journal of Financial and Quantitative Analysis*, (December 1980).

Lintner, John, "The Valuation of Risk Assets and the Selection of Risky Investments in Stock Portfolios and Capital Budgets," *Review of Economics and Statistics* (February 1965), 13–37.

_____, "The Aggregation of Investors' Judgements and Preferences in Purely Competitive Security Markets," *Journal of Financial and Quantitative Analysis*, 4 (December 1969), 347–400.

_____, "Security Prices, Risk and Maximal Gains from Diversification," *Journal of Finance*, 20 (December 1965), 587–616.

Litzenberger, Robert H., and Alan P. Budd, "Corporate Investment Criteria and the Valuation of Risk Assets," *Journal of Financial and Quantitative Analysis* (December 1970).

_____, and O. M. Joy, "Target Rates of Return and Corporate Asset and Liability Structure under Uncertainty," *Journal of Financial and Quantitative Analysis* (March 1971).

Logue, D. E., and L. J. Merville, "Financial Policy and Market Expectations," *Financial Management* (Summer 1972), 37–44.

Markowitz, H., "Portfolio Selection," *The Journal of Finance* (March 1952), 77–91.

Merton, Robert C., "Capital Budgeting in the Capital Asset Pricing Model," unpublished note, 1973.

————, "An Intertemporal Capital Asset Pricing Model," *Econometrica*, 45, 5 (September 1973), 867–887.

————, "Theory of Finance from the Perspective of Continuous Time," *Journal of Financial and Quantitative Analysis*, 10 (November 1975), 659–674.

Milne, Frank, and Clifford Smith, Jr., "Capital Asset Pricing with Proportional Transaction Costs," *Journal of Financial and Quantitative Analysis* (June 1980).

Modigliani, Franco, and Gerald A. Pogue, "An Introduction to Risk and Return," *Financial Analysts Journal*, 30 (March–April 1974), 68–80, and (May–June 1974), 69–86.

————, and R. Cohn, "Inflation, Rational Valuation and the Market," *Financial Analysts Journal*, 35 (March–April 1979), 24–44.

Mossin, Jan, "Equilibrium in a Capital Asset Market," *Econometrica*, 34, 4 (October 1966), 768–783.

————, *Theory of Financial Markets* (Englewood Cliffs, N.J.: Prentice-Hall, Inc., 1973), Chaps. 7–8.

Myers, Stewart C., and Stuart M. Turnbull, "Capital Budgeting and the Capital Asset Pricing Model: Good News and Bad News," *Journal of Finance*, 32 (May 1977), 321–332.

Nielson, N. C., "The Investment Decision of the Firm under Uncertainty and the Allocative Efficiency of Capital Markets," *Journal of Finance* (May 1976).

Officer, R. R., "Seasonality in Australian Capital Markets: Market Efficiency and Empirical Issues," *Journal of Financial Economics* (*March* 1975).

Owen, Joel, and Ramon Rabinovitch, "The Cost of Information and Equilibrium in the Capital Asset Market," *Journal of Financial and Quantitative Analysis* (September 1980).

Perrakis, Stylianos, "Capital Budgeting and Timing Uncertainty Within the Capital Asset Pricing Model," *Financial Management* (Autumn 1979).

Pettit, R. Richardson, and Randolph Westerfield, "Using the Capital Asset Pricing Model and the Market Model to Predict Security Returns," *Journal of Financial and Quantitative Analysis*, 9 (September 1974), 579–606.

Pogue, Gerald A., "An Extension of the Markowitz Portfolio Selection Model to Include Variable Transaction Costs, Short Sales, Leverage Policies and Taxes," *Journal of Finance*, 25 (December 1970), 1005–1027.

————, and Kishore Lall, "Corporate Finance: An Overview," *Sloan Management Review*, 15 (Spring 1974), 19–38.

Rabinovitch, R., and J. Owen, "Nonhomogeneous Expectations and Information in the Capital Asset Market," *Journal of Finance*, (May 1979).

Reinganum, Marc R., "The Arbitrage Pricing Theory: Some Empirical Results," *Journal of Finance*, 36 (May 1981), 313–321.

Rendleman, Richard J. Jr., "Ranking Errors in CAPM Capital Budgeting Applications," *Financial Management* (Winter 1978).

Rhee, S. Ghon, and Franklin L. McCarthy, "Corporate Debt Capacity and Capital Budgeting Analysis," *Financial Management*, 11 (Summer 1982), 42–50.

Robichek, Alexander A., and Stewart C. Myers, "Conceptual Problems in the Use of Risk-Adjusted Discount Rates," *Journal of Finance*, 21 (December 1966), 727–730.

————, *Optimal Financing Decisions* (Englewood Cliffs, N.J.: Prentice-Hall, Inc., 1965).

————, and Richard A. Cohn, "The Economic Determinants of Systematic Risk," *Journal of Finance* (May 1974).

Roenfeldt, R. L., G. L. Griepentrof, and C. C. Pflaum, "Further Evidence on the Stationarity of Beta Coefficients," *Journal of Financial and Quantitative Analysis* (March 1978).

Roll, Richard, "Ambiguity When Performance is Measured by the Securities Market Line," *Journal of Finance*, 33 (September 1978), 1051–1069.

_____, "A Critique of the Asset Pricing Theory's Tests: Part I: On Past and Potential Testability of the Theory," *Journal of Financial Economics* (March 1977).

_____, and S. Ross, "An Empirical Investigation of the Arbitrage Pricing Theory," *Journal of Finance* (December 1980).

_____, and Marcus C. Bogue, "Capital Budgeting of Risky Projects with Imperfect Markets for Physical Capital," *Journal of Finance*, 29 (May 1974), 606–612.

Ross, S. A., "The Capital Asset Pricing Model (CAPM), Short-Sale Restrictions and Related Issues," *Journal of Finance* (March 1977).

_____, "The Current Status of the Capital Asset Pricing Model (CAPM)," *Journal of Finance* (June 1978).

Rubinstein, Mark E., "A Comparative Statics Analysis of Risk Premiums," *Journal of Business*, 46 (October 1973).

_____, "A Mean-Variance Synthesis of Corporate Financial Theory," *Journal of Finance*, 28 (March 1973), 167–182.

Schall, Lawrence D., "Asset Valuation, Firm Investment, and Firm Diversification, *Journal of Business*, 45 (January 1972), 11–28.

_____, "Firm Financial Structure and Investment," *Journal of Financial and Quantitative Analysis*, 6 (June 1971), 925–942.

Schlaifer, R., *Probability and Statistics for Business Decisions* (New York: McGraw-Hill Book Company, 1969).

_____, "A Simplified Model for Portfolio Analysis," *Management Science*, 10 (January 1963), 277–293.

Scholes, M., and J. Williams, "Estimating Betas from Nonsynchronous Data," *Journal of Financial Economics* (December 1977).

Scott, E., and S. Brown, "Biased Estimators and Unstable Betas," *Journal of Finance* (March 1980).

Sharpe, William F., "Capital Asset Prices: A Theory of Market Equilibrium Under Conditions of Risk," *Journal of Finance*, 19 (September 1964), 425–442.

_____, "Efficient Capital Markets with Risk," *Research Paper* 71, Stanford Graduate School of Business, 1972.

_____, *Portfolio Analysis and Capital Markets* (New York: McGraw-Hill Book Company, 1970).

_____, and Guy M. Cooper, "Risk–Return Classes of New York Stock Exchange Common Stocks," *Financial Analysts Journal*, 28 (March–April 1972), 46–54.

Smith, K. V., "The Effect of Intervaling on Estimating Parameters of the Capital Asset Pricing Model," *Journal of Financial and Quantitative Analysis* (June 1978).

Stapleton, Richard C., "Portfolio Analysis, Stock Valuation and Capital Budgeting Decision Rules for Risky Projects," *Journal of Finance* (March 1971).

_____, and M. G. Subrahmanyam, "Market Imperfections, Capital Market Equilibrium and Corporation Finance," *Journal of Finance* (May 1977).

_____, and _____, "Marketability of Assets and the Price of Risk," *Journal of Financial and Quantitative Analysis* (March 1979).

_____, "Portfolio Analysis, Stock Valuation and Capital Budgeting Rules for Risky Projects," *Journal of Finance*, 26 (March 1971), 95–118.

Sundem, Gary L., "Evaluating Simplified Capital Budgeting Models Using a Time-State Preference Metric," *Accounting Review*, 49 (April 1974), 306–320.

Theobald, Michael, "An Analysis of the Market Model and Beta Factors Using U.K. Equity Share Data," *Journal of Business Finance and Accounting* (Spring 1980).

Tobin, James, "Liquidity Preference as Behavior Towards Risk," *Review of Economic Studies*, 25 (February 1958), 65–86.

Trauring, M., "A Capital Asset Pricing Model with Investors' Taxes and Three Categories of Investment Income," *Journal of Financial and Quantitative Analysis* (September 1979).

Treynor, J. L., "Toward a Theory of Market Value of Risky Assets," unpublished manuscript.

Turnbull, S. M., "Value and Systematic Risk," *Journal of Finance* (September 1977).

Tuttle, Donald L., and Robert H. Litzenberger, "Leverage, Diversification and Capital Market Effects on a Risk-Adjusted Capital Budgeting Framework," *Journal of Finance*, 23 (June 1968), 427–443.

Umstead, D. A., and G. L. Bergstrom, "Dynamic Estimation of Portfolio Betas," *Journal of Financial and Quantitative Analysis* (September 1979).

Van Horne, James C., "The Analysis of Uncertainty Resolution in Capital Budgeting for New Projects," *Management Science*, 15 (April 1969), 376–386.

————, "Capital-Budgeting Decisions Involving Combinations of Risky Investments," *Management Science*, 13 (October 1966), 84–92.

————, *The Function and Analysis of Capital Market Rates* (Englewood Cliffs, N.J.: Prentice-Hall, Inc., 1970).

von Neumann, J., and O. Morgenstern, *Theory of Games and Economic Behavior*, 2nd ed. (Princeton, N.J.: Princeton University Press, 1947).

Wells, C., "The Beta Revolution: Learning to Live With Risk," *Institutional Investor* (September 1971), 21–64.

Weston, J. Fred, "Developments in Finance Theory," *Financial Management*, 10 (Summer 1981), 5–22.

————, "Investment Decisions Using the Capital Asset Pricing Model," *Financial Management* (Spring 1973).

Williams, J. T., "Capital Asset Prices with Heterogeneous Beliefs," *Journal of Financial Economics* (November 1977).

CHAPTER 19

Beale, E. M. L., *Mathematical Programming in Practice* (Pitman, 1968).

Charnes, A., and W. W. Cooper, *Management Models and Industrial Applications of Linear Programming*, Vols. I and II (New York: John Wiley & Sons, Inc., 1961).

Dantzig, G. B., *Linear Programming Extensions* (Princeton, N.J.: Princeton University Press, 1963).

Dorfman, R., P. A. Samuelson, and R. M. Solow, *Linear Programming and Economic Analysis* (New York: McGraw-Hill Book Company, 1958).

Gale, D., *The Theory of Linear Economic Models* (New York: McGraw-Hill Book Company, 1960).

Gass, S. I., *Linear Programming: Methods and Applications*, 3rd ed. (New York: McGraw-Hill Book Company, 1969).

Karlin, S., *Mathematical Methods and Theory in Games, Programming and Economics*, Vol. I (Reading, Mass.: Addison-Wesley Publishing Co., Inc., 1959).

Koopmans, T. C., ed., *Activity Analysis of Production and Allocation, Proceeding of a Conference* (New York: John Wiley & Sons, Inc., 1951).

Kuhn, H. W., and A. W. Tucker, eds., *Linear Inequalities and Related Systems* (Princeton, N.J.: Princeton University Press, 1956).

Lasdon, L., *Optimization Theory for Large Systems* (New York: Macmillan Publishing Co., Inc., 1970).

Orchard–Hays, W., *Advanced Linear-Programming Computing Techniques* (New York: McGraw-Hill Book Company, 1968).

Zionts, S., *Linear and Integer Programming* (Englewood Cliffs, N.J.: Prentice-Hall, Inc., 1974).

CHAPTERS 20, 21, 22

Linear and Integer Programming

Baumol, W. J., and R. E. Quandt, "Investment and Discount Rates Under Capital Rationing—A Programming Approach," *Economic Journal*, 75 (June 1965), 317–329.

Beale, E. M. L., *Mathematical Programming in Practice* (Pitman, 1968).

Bey, R. P., and R. B. Porter, "An Evaluation of Capital Budgeting Portfolio Models Using Simulated Data," *Engineering Economics* (Fall 1977).

Bhaskar, Krish, "Linear Programming and Capital Budgeting: The Financing Problem," *Journal of Business Finance and Accounting* (Summer 1978).

Bradley, Stephen, and Sherwood C. Frey, Jr. "Equivalent Mathematical Programming Models of Pure Capital Rationing," *Journal of Financial and Quantitative Analysis*, 13 (June 1978), 345–361.

Burton, R. M., and W. W. Damon, "On the Existence of a Cost of Capital Under Pure Capital Rationing," *Journal of Finance* (September 1974).

Carleton, W. T., "Linear Programming and Capital Budgeting Models: A New Interpretation," *Journal of Finance* (December 1969), 825–833.

Charnes, A., and W. W. Cooper, *Management Models and Industrial Applications of Linear Programming*, Vols. I and II (New York: John Wiley & Sons, Inc., 1961).

———, ———, and M. H. Miller, "Application of Linear Programming to Financial Budgeting and the Costing of Funds," *Journal of Business*, 32 (January 1959), 20–46.

Cheng, Pal L., and John P. Shelton, "A Contribution to the Theory of Capital Budgeting —The Multi-Investment Case," *Journal of Finance* (December 1963).

Dantzig, G. B., *Linear Programming and Extensions* (Princeton, N.J.:Princeton University Press, 1963).

Dorfman, R., P. A. Samuelson, and R. M. Solow, *Linear Programming and Economic Analysis* (New York: McGraw-Hill Book Company, 1958).

Ederington, L. H., and W. R. Henry, "On Costs of Capital in Programming Approaches to Capital Budgeting," *Journal of Financial and Quantitative Analysis* (December 1979).

Elton, Edwin J., "Capital Rationing and External Discount Rates," *Journal of Finance* (June 1970), 573–584.

———, and Martin J. Gruber, *Finance as a Dynamic Process* (Englewood Cliffs, N.J.: Prentice-Hall, Inc., 1975), Chaps. 7, 8.

Fama, Eugene E., and Merton H. Miller, *The Theory of Finance* (New York: Holt, Rinehart and Winston, Inc., 1972), Chap. 3.

Fogler, H. Russell, "Ranking Techniques and Capital Rationing," *Accounting Review*, 47 (January 1972), 134–143.

Freeland, J. R., and M. J. Rosenblatt, "An Analysis of Linear Programming Formulations for the Capital Rationing Problem," *Engineering Economist* (Fall 1978).

Gale, D., *The Theory of Linear Economic Models* (New York: McGraw-Hill Book Company, 1960).

Gass, S. I., *Linear Programming: Methods and Applications*, 3rd ed. (New York: McGraw-Hill Book Company, 1969).

Goldberger, Juval and Jacob Paroush, "Capital Budgeting of Interdependent Projects," *Management Science* (July 1977).

Haley, Charles W., "Taxes, the Cost of Capital and the Firm's Investment Decisions," *Journal of Finance*, 26 (September 1971), 901–918.

———, and Lawrence D. Schall, "A Note on Investment Policy with Imperfect Capital Markets," *Journal of Finance*, 27 (March 1972), 93–96.

Hughes, John S., and Wilbur G. Lewellen, "Programming Solutions to Capital Rationing Problems," *Journal of Business Finance & Accounting*, (Winter 1974).

Karlin S., *Mathematical Methods and Theory in Games, Programming and Economics*, 1 (Reading, Mass.: Addison-Wesley Publishing Co., Inc., 1977).

Keown, Arthur J., and John D. Martin, "An Integer Goal Programming Model for Capital Budgeting in Hospitals," *Financial Management*, 5 (Autumn 1976), 28–35.

Koopmans, T. C., ed., *Activity Analysis of Production and Allocation, Proceeding of a Conference* (New York: John Wiley & Sons, Inc., 1951).

Krainer, Robert E., "A Neglected Issue in Capital Rationing—The Asset Demand for Money," *Journal of Finance* (December 1966).

Kuhn, H. W., and A. W. Tucker, eds., *Linear Inequalities and Related Systems* (Princeton, N.J.: Princeton University Press, 1956).

Lerner, Eugene M., and Alfred Rappaport, "Limit DCF in Capital Budgeting," *Harvard Business Review*, 46 (July–August 1968), 133–139.

Lorie, J. H., and L. J. Savage, "Three Problems in Rationing Capital," *Journal of Business*, 28, 4 (October 1955), 229–239.

Lusztig, P., and B. Schwab, "A Note on the Application of Linear Programming to Capital Budgeting," *Journal of Financial and Quantitative Analysis*, 3 (December 1968), 427–431.

Manne, A. S., "Optimal Dividend and Investment Policies for a Self-Financing Business Enterprise," *Management Science*, 15, 3 (November 1968), 119–129.

Mao, J. C. T., *Quantitative Analysis of Financial Decisions* (New York: Macmillan Publishing Co., Inc., 1969), 266–280.

Martin, A. D., "Mathematical Programming of Portfolio Selections," *Management Science*, (January 1955), 152–166.

McClain, J. O., "Linear Programming Is a Shrinking Watermellon and Optimality Is a Black Hole," *Interfaces*, 10 (June 1980), 106–107.

Merville, L. J., and L. A. Tavis, "A Generalized Model for Capital Investment," *Journal of Finance*, 28, 1 (March 1973), 109–118.

Moag, J. S., and E. M. Lerner, "Capital Budgeting Decisions Under Imperfect Market Conditions," *Journal of Finance*, 25 (June 1970), 613–621.

Myers, Stewart C., "Interactions of Corporate Financing and Investment Decisions—Implications for Capital Budgeting," *Journal of Finance*, 29 (March 1974), 1–26.

————, "A Note on Linear Programming and Capital Budgeting," *Journal of Finance*, 27 (March 1972), 89–92.

————, and Gerald A. Pogue, "A Programming Approach to Corporate Financial Management," *Journal of Finance* (May 1974).

Ophir, T., "Optimum Capital Budgeting Lessons of a Linear Programming Formulation," Research No. 6, The Hebrew University, Israel.

Orchard-Hays, W., *Advanced Linear-Programming Computing Techniques* (New York: McGraw-Hill Book Company, 1968).

Peterson, D. E., and R. B. Haydon, *A Quantitative Framework for Financial Management* (Homewood, Ill.: Richard D. Irwin, Inc., 1969), 404–434.

————, and D. J. Laughhunn, "Capital Expenditure Programming and Some Alternative Approaches to Risk," *Management Science*, 17 (January 1971), 320–336.

Petty, J. William, David F. Scott, Jr., and Monroe M. Bird, "The Capital Expenditure Decision-Making Process of Large Corporations," *Engineering Economist*, 20 (Spring 1975), 159–172.

Rychel, Dwight F., "Capital Budgeting with Mixed Integer Linear Programming: An Application," *Financial Management*, 6 (Winter 1977), 11–19.

Sealey, C. W. Jr., "Utility Maximization and Programming Models for Capital Budgeting," *Journal of Business Finance and Accounting* (Autumn 1978).

Spies, Richard R., "The Dynamics of Corporate Capital Budgeting," *Journal of Finance* (June 1974).

Teichroew, Daniel, Alexander A. Robichek, and Michael Montalbano, "An Analysis of Criteria for Investment and Financing Decisions Under Certainty," *Management Science*, 12 (November 1965), 151–179.

————, ————, and ————, "Mathematical Analysis of Rates of Return Under Certainty," *Management Science*, 11 (January 1965), 395–403.

Weingartner, H. Martin, "Capital Budgeting of Interrelated Projects: Survey and Synthesis," *Management Science*, 12 (March 1966), 485–516.

————, "Capital Rationing: n Authors in Search of a Plot," *Journal of Finance*, 32 (December 1977), 1403–1431.

————, "The Excess Present Value Index—A Theoretical Basis and Critique," *Journal of Accounting Research*, 1 (Autumn 1963), 213–224.

————, "The Generalized Rate of Return," *Journal of Financial and Quantitative Analysis*, 1 (September 1966), 1–29.

————, *Mathematical Programming and the Analysis of Capital Budgeting Problems* (Englewood Cliffs, N.J.: Prentice-Hall, Inc., 1963).

Whitmore, G. A., and L. R. Amey, "Capital Budgeting Under Rationing: Comments on the Lusztig and Schwab Procedure," *Journal of Financial and Quantitative Analysis*, 8 (January 1973), 127–135.

Zionts, S. *Linear and Integer Programming* (Englewood Cliffs, N.J.: Prentice-Hall, Inc., 1974).

Goal Programming

Ashton, D. J., and D. R. Atkins, "Multicriteria Programming for Financial Planning," *Journal of Operational Research Society*, 30 (March 1979) 259–270.

Fandel, G., and T. Cal (eds.), *Multiple Criteria Decision Making Theory and Application*, (New York: Springer-Verlag, 1980).

Fourcans, A., and Thomas J. Hindelang, "The Incorporation of Multiple Goals in the Selection of Capital Investments," paper presented at Financial Management Association Meeting, October 1973.

Hawkins, Clark A., and Richard A. Adams, "A Goal Programming Model for Capital Budgeting," *Financial Management*, 3 (Spring 1974), 52–57.

Hemming, T., *Multiobjective Decision Making under Certainty*, (Stockholm: Economic Research Institute, Stockholm School of Economics, 1978).

Ignizio, James P., "An Approach to the Capital Budgeting Problem with Multiple Objectives," *Engineering Economist*, 21 (Summer 1976), 259–272.

————, *Goal Programming and Extensions* (Lexington, Mass.: Lexington Books, 1977).

Ijiri, Y., *Management Goals and Accounting for Control* (Amsterdam: North-Holland Publishing Co., 1965).

Keown, Arthur J., and John D. Martin, "Capital Budgeting in the Public Sector: A Zero-One Goal Programming Approach," *Financial Management*, 7 (Summer 1978), 21–27.

Lee, Sang M., *Goal Programming for Decision Analysis* (Philadelphia: Auerbach Publishing Co., 1972).

————, and A. J. Lerro, "Capital Budgeting for Multiple Objectives," *Financial Management* (Spring 1974), 58–66.

Merville, L. J., and L. A. Tavis, "Financial Planning in a Decentralized Firm Under Conditions of Competitive Capital Markets," *Financial Management*, 6 (Fall 1977) 17–23.

Sealey, C. W., Jr., "Financial Planning With Multiple Objective," *Financial Management*, 7 (Winter 1978), 17–23.

Wacht, Richard F., and David T. Whitford, "A Goal Programming Model for Capital Investment Analysis in Nonprofit Hospitals," *Financial Management*, 5 (Summer 1976), 37–47.

Monte Carlo Simulation and Decision Trees

Carter, E. E., *Portfolio Aspects of Corporate Capital Budgeting* (Lexington, Mass.: Lexington Books, 1974).

Chambers, J. C., and S. K. Mullick, "Investment Decision Making in a Multinational Enterprise," *Management Accounting* (August 1971).

Cohen, K. J., and E. J. Elton, "Intertemporal Portfolio Analysis Based on Simulation of Joint Returns," *Management Science*, 14 (September 1967), 5–18.

Fourcans, A., and T. J. Hindelang, "A Simulation Approach to Capital Budgeting for the Multinational Firm," paper presented to the 1976 Financial Management Association Conference, Montreal, Canada, October 1976.

Hertz, David B., "Investment Policies That Pay Off," *Harvard Business Review*, 46 (January–February 1968), 96–108.

————, "Risk Analysis in Capital Investment," *Harvard Business Review*, 42 (January–February 1964), 95–106.

Hespos, Richard F., and Paul A. Strassmann, "Stochastic Decision Trees for the Analysis of Investment Decisions," *Management Science*, 11 (August 1965), 244–259.

Lewellen, Wilbur G., and Michael S. Long, "Simulation Versus Single-Value Estimates in Capital Expenditure Analysis," *Decision Sciences*, 3 (1973), 19–33.

Kryzanowski, Lawrence, Peter Lusztig, and Bernhard Schwab, "Monte Carlo Simulation and Capital Expenditure Decisions—A Case Study," *Engineering Economist*, 18 (Fall 1972), 31–48.

Magee, J. F., "How to Use Decision Trees in Capital Investment," *Harvard Business Review*, 42 (September–October 1964), 79–96.

Naylor, T. H., J. L. Balintfy, D. S. Burdick, and K. Chu, *Computer Simulation Techniques* (New York: John Wiley & Sons, Inc., 1966).

————, and A. J. Mastai, "Investment in an Automated Warehouse: A Monte Carlo Simulation and Post-Optimality Analysis," *Proceedings of the 1971 Conference on Systems, Networks and Computers*, Mexico City, January 1971.

Philippatos, G. C., *Financial Management: Theory and Techniques* (San Francisco: Holden-Day, Inc., 1973), Chap. 21.

Robichek, Alexander A., "Interpreting the Results of Risk Analysis," *Journal of Finance*, 30 (December 1975), 1384–1386.

Salazar, R. C., and S. K. Sen, "A Simulation Model of Capital Budgeting Under Uncertainty," *Management Science*, 15 (December 1968), 161–179.

Shannon, R. E., *System Simulation: The Art and Science* (Englewood Cliffs, N.J.: Prentice-Hall, Inc., 1975).

Sundem, Gary L., "Evaluating Capital Budgeting Models in Simulated Environments," *Journal of Finance*, 30 (September 1975), 977–992.

Thuesen, G. J., "Nuclear vs. Fossil Power Plants: Evolution of Economic Evaluation Techniques," *The Engineering Economist*, 21 (Fall 1975), 21–38.

Stochastic Programming

Bernhard, Richard H., "Mathematical Programming Models for Capital Budgeting—A Survey, Generalization, and Critique," *Journal of Financial and Quantitative Analysis*, 4 (June 1969), 111–158.

Byrne, R., A. Charnes, W. W. Cooper, and K. Kortenek, "A Chance-Constrained Programming Approach to Capital Budgeting," *Journal of Financial and Quantitative Analysis*, 2 (December 1967), 339–364.

_____, A. Charnes, W. W. Cooper, and K. Kortenek, "A Discrete Probability Chance Constrained Capital Budgeting Model–I and II," *Opsearch*, 6 (December 1969) 171–198, 226–261.

Charnes, A., and W. W. Cooper, "Deterministic Equivalents for Optimizing and Satisficing Under Chance Constraints," *Operations Research*, 11 (January 1963), 18–39.

Farrer, D. F., *The Investment Decision Under Uncertainty* (Englewood Cliffs, N.J.: Prentice-Hall, Inc. 1962).

Hillier, Frederick S., "A Basic Model for Capital Budgeting of Risky Interrelated Projects," *Engineering Economist*, 20 (Fall 1974), 37–49.

_____, "Chance-Constrained Programming with 0–1 or Bounded Continuous Decision Variables," *Management Science*, 14 (September 1967), 34–57.

_____, "The Derivation of Probabilistic Information for the Evaluation of Risky Investments," *Management Science*, 9 (April 1963), 443–457.

_____, *The Evaluation of Risky Interrelated Investments* (Amsterdam: North-Holland Publishing Co. 1969).

Lockett, A. Geoffrey, and Anthony E. Gear, "Multistage Capital Budgeting Under Uncertainty," *Journal of Financial and Quantitative Analysis*, 10 (March 1975), 21–36.

Myers, S. C., "Procedures for Capital Budgeting Under Uncertainty," *Industrial Management Review*, 9 (Spring 1968), 1–15.

Naslund, B., "A Model for Capital Budgeting Under Risk," *Journal of Business*, 39 (April 1966), 257–271.

_____, and A. Whinston, "A Model of Multi-Period Investment Under Uncertainty," *Management Science*, 9 (January 1962), 184–200.

Thompson, H. E., "Mathematical Programming, the Capital Asset Pricing Model and Capital Budgeting of Interrelated Projects," *The Journal of Finance*, 31, 1 (March 1976), 125–131.

Wilson, Robert B., "Investment Analysis Under Uncertainty," *Management Science*, 15 (August 1969), 650–664.

CHAPTERS 23, 24

Allen, C. L., J. D. Martin, and P. F. Anderson, "Debt Capacity and the Lease-Purchase Problem: A Sensitivity Analysis," *Engineering Economist* (Winter 1978).

American Institute of Certified Public Accountants, Accounting Principles Board, *Opinion 5*, "Reporting of Leases in Financial Statements of Lessee" (September 1964), and *Opinion 31*, "Disclosure of Lease Commitments by Lessees" (June 1973).

American Management Association, *Taking Stock of Leasing: A Practical Appraisal* (New York, 1965).

Anderson, Paul E., *Financial Aspects of Industrial Leasing Decisions: Implications for Marketing* (East Lansing: Division of Research, Graduate School of Business Administration, Michigan State University, 1977).

_____, and John D. Martin, "Lease vs. Purchase Decisions: A Survey of Current Practice," *Financial Management*, 6 (Spring 1977), 41–47.

Anthony, R. N., and S. Schwartz, *Office Equipment, Buy or Rent?* (Boston: Management Analysis Center, Inc., 1957).

Archer, W. R. V., "Lease or Buy Decisions," *Accountant*, 162, 4964 (February 5, 1970), 193–196.

Ashton, D. J., "The Reasons for Leasing—A Mathematical Programming Framework," *Journal of Business Finance & Accounting* (Summer 1978).

Athanaspoulos, Peter J., and Peter W. Bacon, "The Evaluation of Leveraged Leases," *Financial Management*, 9 (Spring 1980), 76–80.

Axelson, Kenneth S., "Needed: A Generally Accepted Method for Measuring Lease Commitments," *Financial Executive*, 39 (July 1971), 40–52.

Basi, Bart A., "Tax Aspects of Leasing: Lessee's Viewpoint," *Tax Executive*, 27, 4 (July 1975), 365–378.

Batkin, A., "Leasing vs. Buying; A Guide for the Perplexed," *Financial Executive*, 41 (June 1973), 63–68.

Beechy, T. H., "The Cost of Leasing: Comment and Correction," *Accounting Review*, 45 (October 1970), 769–773.

————, "Quasi-Debt Analysis of Financial Leases," *Accounting Review*, 44 (April 1969), 375–381.

Benjamin, James J., and Robert H. Strawser, "Developments in Lease Accounting," *CPA Journal*, 46, 11 (November 1976), 33–36.

Bierman, Harold, Jr., "Accounting for Capitalized Leases: Tax Considerations," *Accounting Review*, 48, 2 (April 1973), 421–424.

Bloomfield, E. C., and M. A. Ronald, "The Lease Evaluation Solution," *Accounting and Business Research* (Autumn 1979).

Bower, Richard S., "Issues in Lease Financing," *Financial Management* (Winter 1973).

————, and Dorothy H. Bower, "Risk and the Valuation of Common Stock," *Journal of Political Economy* (May–June 1969).

————, Frank G. Herringer, and J. Peter Williamson, "Lease Evaluation," *Accounting Review*, 41 (April 1966), 257–265.

Bowles, G. N., "Some Thoughts on the Lease Evaluation Solution," *Accounting and Business Research* (Spring 1977).

Bowman, R. G., "The Debt Equivalence of Leases: An Empirical Investigation," *Accounting Review* (April 1980).

Brealey, R. A., and C. M. Young, "Debt, Taxes and Leasing—A Note," *Journal of Finance* (December 1980).

Capettini, Robert, and Howard Toole, "Designing Leveraged Leases: A Mixed Integer Linear Programming Approach," *Financial Management*, 10 (Autumn 1981), 15–23.

Chamberlain, Douglas C., "Capitalization of Lease Obligations," *Management Accounting*, 57 (December 1975), 37–42.

Chasteen, Lanny G., "Implicit Factors in the Evaluation of Lease vs. Buy Alternatives," *Accounting Review*, 48 (October 1973), 764–767.

Cooper, Kerry, and Robert H. Strawser, "Evaluation of Capital Investment Projects Involving Asset Leases," *Financial Management*, 4 (Spring 1975), 44–49.

————, and ————, "Evaluation of Capital Investment Projects Involving Asset Leases," *Financial Management*, 4 (Spring 1975), 44–49.

Copeland, Thomas E., and J. Fred Weston, "A Note on the Evaluation of Cancellable Operating Leases," *Financial Management*, 11 (Summer 1982), 60–67.

Crawford, Peggy J., Charles P. Harper, and John J. McConnell, "Further Evidence on the Terms of Financial Leases," *Financial Management*, 10 (Autumn 1981), 7–14.

Davidson, Sidney, and Roman L. Weil, "Lease Capitalization and Inflation Accounting," *Financial Analysts Journal*, 34 (November–December 1975), 22–29.

Defliese, Philip L., "Accounting for Leases: A Broader Perspective," *Financial Executive*, 42 (July 1974), 14–23.

Doenges, R. Conrad, "The Cost of Leasing," *Engineering Economist*, 17 (Fall 1971), 31–44.

Dyl, Edward A., and Stanley A. Martin, Jr., "Setting Terms for Leveraged Leases," *Financial Management*, 6 (Winter 1977), 20–27.

Elliott, Grover S., "Leasing of Capital Equipment," *Management Accounting*, 57 (December 1975), 39–42.

Fawthrop, R. A., and Brian Terry, "The Evaluation of an Integrated Investment in Lease-Financing," *Journal of Business Finance and Accounting*, 3 (Autumn 1976), 79–112.

_____, "Debt Management and the Use of Leasing Finance in UK Corporate Financing Strategies," *Journal of Business Finance and Accounting*, 2 (Autumn 1975), 295–314.

Ferrara, William L., "The Case for Symmetry in Lease Reporting," *Management Accounting*, 59 (April 1978), 17–24.

_____, "Lease vs. Purchase: A Quasi-Financing Approach," *Management Accounting*, 56 (January 1974), 21–26.

_____, "Should Investment and Financing Decisions Be Separated?" *Accounting Review*, 41 (January 1966), 106–114.

_____, and Joseph F. Wojdak, "Valuation of Long-Term Leases," *Financial Analysts Journal*, 25 (November–December 1969), 29–32.

_____, "Capital Budgeting and Financing or Leasing Decision," *Management Accounting*, 49 (July 1968), 55–63.

Financial Accounting Standards Board, *Financial Accounting Standard—No. 13 Accounting For Leases*. Original Pronouncements as of July 1, 1978 (Stamford, Conn.: Financial Accounting Standards Board, 1978).

Findlay, M. Chapman, III, "A Sensitivity Analysis of IRR Leasing Models," *Engineering Economics*, 20 (Summer 1975), 231–241.

_____, "Financial Lease Evaluation: Survey and Synthesis," Paper presented at Eastern Finance Association Meetings, Stores, Connecticut, (April 12, 1973).

Finnerty, Joseph E., Rick N. Fitzsimmons, and Thomas W. Oliver, "Lease Capitalization and Systematic Risk," *Accounting Review* (October 1980).

Ford, Allen, and Jack E. Gaumnitz, "The Lease or Sell Decision," *Financial Management*, 7 (Winter 1978), 69–74.

Franks, J. R., and S. D. Hodges, "Valuation of Financial Lease Contracts: A Note," *Journal of Finance*, 33 (May 1978), 617–639.

Gant, D. R., "A Critical Look at Lease Financing," *Controller*, 29 (June 1961), 274–277, 311–312.

_____, "Illusion in Lease Financing," *Harvard Business Review*, 37 (March–April 1959), 121–142.

Gaumnitz, Jack E., and Allen Ford, "The Lease or Sell Decision," *Financial Management*, 7 (Winter 1978), 69–74.

Gordon, Myron J., "A General Solution to the Buy or Lease Decision: A Pedagogical Note," *Journal of Finance*, 29 (March 1974), 245–250.

Griesinger, F. K., "Pros and Cons of Leasing Equipment," *Harvard Business Review*, 33 (March–April 1955), 75–89.

Grimlund, Richard A., and Robert Capettini, "A Note on the Evaluation of Leveraged Leases and Other Investments," *Financial Management*, 11 (Summer 1982), 68–72.

Gritta, Richard D., "The Impact of the Capitalization of Leases on Financial Analysis," *Financial Analysts Journal*, 30 (March–April 1974), 1–6.

Hamel, H. G., *Leasing in Industry* (New York: National Industrial Conference Board, 1968).

Hawkins, D. F., and M. M. Wehle, *Accounting for Leases* (New York: Financial Executives Research Foundation, 1973).

Henderson, G. V., Jr., "A Decision Format for Lease or Buy Analysis," *Review of Business & Economic Research* (Fall 1976).

Hindelang, Thomas J., and Robert E. Pritchard, *Making the Lease Buy Decision*, 2nd Edition, (New York: AMACOM, 1984).

Honic, Lawrence E., and Stephen C. Colley, "An After-Tax Equivalent Payment Approach to Conventional Lease Analysis," *Financial Management*, 4 (Winter 1975), 28–35.

Idol, Charles R., "A Note on Specifying Debt Displacement and Tax Shield Borrowing Opportunities in Financial Lease Valuation Models," *Financial Management*, 9 (Summer 1980), 24–29.

Jackson, J. F., Jr., *An Evaluation of Finance Leasing* (Austin, Tex.: Bureau of Business Research, University of Texas, 1967).

Jenkins, David O., "Purchase or Cancelable Lease," *Financial Executive*, 38 (April 1970), 26–31.

Johnson, Keith B., and Thomas B. Hazuka, "The NPV-IRR Debate in Lease Analysis," *Mississippi Valley Journal*.

Johnson, R. W., and W. G. Lewellen, "Analysis of the Lease or Buy Decision," *Journal of Finance*, 27 (September 1972), 815–823.

Kalata, John, J. Dennis, G. Campbell, and Ian K. Shumaker, "Lease Financing Reporting," *Financial Executive*, 45 (March 1977), 34–40.

Keller, Thomas F., and Russell J. Peterson, "Optimal Financial Structure, Cost of Capital, and the Lease or Buy Decision," *Journal of Business Finance and Accounting*, 1 (Autumn 1974), 405–414.

Kim, E. Han, Wilbur G. Lewellen, and John J. McConnell, "Sale-and-Leaseback Agreements and Enterprise Valuation," *Journal of Financial and Quantitative Analysis*, 13 (December 1978), 871–883.

Knutson, P. H., "Leased Equipment and Divisional Return on Capital," *N.A.A. Bulletin*, (November 1962), 15–20.

Law, W. A., and M. C. Crum, *Equipment Leasing and Commercial Banks* (Chicago: Association of Reserve City Bankers, 1963).

Lee, Wayne T., John D. Martin, and Andrew J. Senchack, "The Case for Using Options to Evaluate Salvage Values in Financial Leases," *Financial Management*, 11 (Autumn 1982), 33–44.

Levy, Haim, and Marshall Sarnat, "Leasing, Borrowing, and Financial Risk," *Financial Management*, 8 (Winter 1979), 47–54.

Levy, L. E., "Off Balance Sheet Financing," *Management Accounting*, 51 (May 1969), 12–14.

Lewellen, Wilbur G., and Douglas R. Emery, "On the Matter of Parity Among Financial Obligations," *Journal of Finance*, 36 (March 1981), 97–111.

_____, Michael S. Long, and John J. McConnell, "Asset Leasing in Competitive Capital Markets," *Journal of Finance*, 31 (June 1976), 787–798.

Long, Michael S., "Leasing and the Cost of Capital," *Journal of Financial and Quantitative Analysis*, 12 (November 1977), 579–586.

MacEachron, W. D., "Leasing: A Discounted Cash-Flow Approach," *Controller*, 29 (May 1961), 213–219.

Martin, John D., Paul E. Anderson, and Arthur J. Keown, "Lease Capitalization and Stock Price Stability: Implication for Accounting," *Journal of Accounting, Auditing and Finance*, 2 (Winter 1979), 151–164.

McGugan, Vince J., and Richard E. Caves, "Integration and Competition in the Equipment Leasing Industry," *Journal of Business*, 47 (July 1974), 382–396.

McLean, J. H., "Economic and Accounting Aspects of Lease Financing," *Financial Executive*, 31 (December 1963), 18–23.

Metz, D. H., *Leasing Standards and Procedures* (Kaukauna, Wis.: Thomas Publications, 1968).

Middleton, K. A., "Lease Evaluation: Back to Square One," *Accounting and Business Research* (Spring 1977).

Miller, Merton H., and Charles W. Upton, "Leasing, Buying, and the Cost of Capital Services," *Journal of Finance*, 31 (June 1976), 787–798.

Mitchell, G. B., "After-Tax Cost of Leasing," *Accounting Review*, 45 (April 1970), 308–314.

Morgan, Eleanor, Julian Lowe, and Cyril Tomkins, "The UK Financial Leasing Industry—A Structural Analysis," *The Journal of Industrial Economics* (June 1980).

Moyer, Charles R., "Lease Evaluation and the Investment Tax Credit: A Framework for Analysis," *Financial Management*, 4 (Summer 1975), 39–44.

Myers, Stewart C., David A. Dill, and Alberto J. Bautista, "Valuation of Financial Lease Contracts," *Journal of Finance*, 31 (June 1976), 799–819.

Nantell, Timothy J., "Equivalence of Lease versus Buy Analyses," *Financial Management*, 2 (Autumn 1973), 61–65.

Ofer, Ahorn R., "The Evaluation of the Lease versus Purchase Alternatives," *Financial Management*, 5 (Summer 1976), 67–72.

Olsen, Robert A., "Lease vs. Purchase or Lease vs. Borrow: Comment," *Financial Management*, 7 (Summer 1978), 82–83.

Parker, G. G. C., "The Lease: Use Without Ownership," *Columbia Journal of World Business*, 5 (September–October 1970), 77–82.

Peat, Marwick, Mitchell & Co., *1981 Economic Recovery Act Tax Act Leases* (New York: Peat, Marwick, Mitchell & Co., 1981).

Peller, Philip R., John E. Stewart, and Bejamin S. Neuhausen, "The 1981 Tax Act: Accounting for Leases," *Financial Executive* (January 1982), 16–26.

Perg, Wayne E., "Leveraged Leasing: The Problem of Changing Leverage," *Financial Management*, 7 (Autumn 1978), 47–51.

Reilly, F., "A Direct Cost Lease Evaluation Method," *Bank Administration* (July 1972), 22–26.

Roberts, Gordon S., and Arthur C. Gudikunst, "Equipment Financial Leasing Practices and Costs: Comment," *Financial Management*, 7 (Summer 1978), 79–81.

Roenfeldt, Rodney L., and James B. Henry, "Lease vs. Debt Purchase of Automobiles," *Management Accounting*, 58, 4 (October 1976), 49–54.

————, and J. S. Osteryoung, "Analysis of Financial Leases," *Financial Management* (Spring 1973), 74–87.

Sartoris, William L., and Ronda S. Paul, "Lease Evaluation—Another Capital Budgeting Decision," *Financial Management*, 2, 2 (Summer 1973), 46–52.

Sax, F. S., "Lease or Purchase Decision—Present Value Method," *Management Accounting*, 47 (October 1965), 55–61.

Schahner, Leopold, "The New Accounting for Leases," *Financial Executive*, 46 (February 1978), 40–47.

Schall, Lawrence D., "The Lease-or-Buy and Asset Acquisition Decisions," *Journal of Finance*, 29 (September 1974), 1203–1214.

Smith, Bruce D., "Accelerated Debt Repayment in Leveraged Leases," *Financial Management*, 11 (Summer 1982), 73–80.

Sorensen, Ivar W., and Ramon E. Johnson, "Equipment Financial Leasing Practices and Costs: An Empirical Study," *Financial Management*, 6 (Spring 1977), 33–40.

Thulin, W. B., "Own or Lease: Underlying Financial Theory," *Financial Executive*, 32 (April 1964), 23–24, 28–31.

————, *Leasing of Industrial Equipment* (New York: McGraw-Hill Book Company, 1963).

Uttal, Bro, "The Lease Is Up on Itel's Lavish Living," *Fortune* (October 8, 1979), 106–119.

Vancil, Richard F., "Lease or Borrow: Steps in Negotiation," *Harvard Business Review*, 39 (November–December 1961), 238–259.

————, "Lease or Borrow: New Method of Analysis," *Harvard Business Review*, 39 (September–October 1961), 122–136.

————, "Lease or Borrow: Steps in Negotiation," *Harvard Business Review*, 39 (November–December 1961), 138–159.

————, and Robert N. Anthony, "The Financial Community Looks at Leasing," *Harvard Business Review*, 37 (November–December 1959), 113–130.

Vanderwicken, P., "The Powerful Logic of the Leasing Boom," *Fortune* (November 1973).

Van Horne, James C., "The Cost of Leasing with Capital Market Imperfections," *Engineering Economist*, 23 (Fall 1977), 1–12.

Westbrook, David N., "Accounting for Long-Term Leases," *Cost and Management*, 48 (May–June 1974), 54–58.

Weston, J. F., and R. Craig, "Understanding Lease Financing," *California Management Review*, 2 (Winter 1960), 67–75.

Wiar, Robert C., "Economic Implications of Multiple Rates of Return in the Leverage Lease Context," *Journal of Finance*, 28 (December 1973), 1275–1286.

Wilson, C. J., "The Operating Lease and the Risk of Obsolescence," *Management Accounting*, 55 (December 1973), 41–44.

Wyman, Harold E., "Financial Lease Evaluation under Conditions of Uncertainty," *Accounting Review*, 48 (July 1973), 489–493.

CHAPTER 25

Ankrom, Robert K., "Top-Level Approach to the Foreign Exchange Problem," *Harvard Business Review* (July–August 1974).

Brill, Martin, *An Approach to Risk Analysis in the Evaluation of Capital Ventures* (Philadelphia: Drexel Institute of Technology, 1966).

Carter, E. Eugene, and Rita M. Rodriguez, *International Financial Management* 2nd Edition (Englewood Cliffs, N.J.: Prentice-Hall, Inc., 1979).

Chambers, J., S. Mullock, and D. Smith, "The Use of Simulation Models at Corning Glass Works," in A. Schrieber, ed., *Corporate Simulation Models*.

Dunlop, J., F. Harbison, C. Kerr, and C. Meyers, *Industrialism and Industrial Man* (Cambridge, Mass.: Harvard University Press, 1960).

Einzig, P., *Foreign Exchange Crises* (New York: Macmillan Publishing Co., Inc., 1970).

Eiteman, David K., and Stonehill, Arthur I., *Multinational Business Finance* 3rd Edition (Reading, Mass.: Addison-Wesley Publishing Co., Inc., 1982).

Feierbend, I., "Conflict, Crisis, and Collision: A Study of International Stability," *Psychology Today* (May 1968).

Friedman, W. G., and G. Kalmanoff, *Joint International Business Ventures* (New York: Columbia University Press, 1961).

Harbison, F., and C. Meyers, *Education, Manpower, and Economic Growth* (New York: McGraw-Hill Book Company, 1966).

"Hedging Against the Franc's Fall," *Business Week* (January 31, 1977), 70–72.

Hertz, D. B., "Investment Policies That Pay Off," *Harvard Business Review* (January 1968), 96–108.

————, "Risk Analysis in Capital Investment," *Harvard Business Review* (January 1964), 95–106.

Hillier, F. S., *The Evaluation of Risky Interrelated Investments* (New York: American Elsevier Publishing Co., 1969).

Kohers, Theodore, "The Effect of Multinational Operation on the Cost of Equity Capital: An Empirical Study," *Management International Review* (1975).

Lessard, D. R., and R. S. Bower, "An Operational Approach to Risk Screening," *Journal of Finance* (May 1973), 245–257.

_____, *International Financial Management* (Boston: Warren, Gorham, and Lamont, 1979).

Lewellen, W. G., and M. S. Long, "Reply to Comments by Bower & Lessard and Gentry," *Decision Sciences*, 4, 4 (October 1973), 575–576.

_____, and M. S. Long, "Simulation vs. Single-Value Estimates in Capital Expenditure Analysis," *Decision Sciences*, 3, 4 (October 1972), 19–33.

Lietaer, Bernard, "Managing Risks in Foreign Exchange," *Harvard Business Review* (March 1970), 127–138.

Mao, J. C. T., and J. F. Helliwell, "Investment Decision Under Uncertainty: Theory and Practice," *Journal of Finance*, 24, 2 (May 1969), 323–338.

Mauriel, J. J. "Evaluation and Control of Overseas Operations," *Management Accounting* (May 1969), 35–39.

Naylor, T. H., *Computer Simulation Experiments with Models of Economic Systems* (New York: John Wiley & Sons, Inc., 1971).

Robbins, Sidney M., and Robert B. Stobaugh, *Money in the Multinational Enterprise* (New York: Basic Books, Inc., 1973).

Rutenberg, David P., "Maneuvering Liquid Assets in a Multinational Company," *Management Science* (June 1970).

Shannon, R. E., *System Simulation: The Art & Science* (Englewood Cliffs, N.J.: Prentice-Hall, Inc., 1975).

Shapiro, Alan C., "Capital Budgeting for the Multinational Corporation," *Financial Management* (Spring, 1978), pp. 7–16.

_____, *Multinational Financial Management* (Boston: Allyn and Bacon, Inc., 1981).

Singer, H. W., *International Development: Growths and Change* (New York: McGraw-Hill Book Company, 1964).

Smith, Dennis E., "Requirements for an 'Optimizer' for Computer Simulations," *Naval Research Logistics Quarterly*, 20, 1 (March 1973), 161–179.

Stobaugh, R. B. "How to Analyze Foreign Investment Climates," *Harvard Business Review* (September–October 1969), 100–108.

_____, *Multinational Financial Management* (Boston: Allyn & Bacon, Inc., 1982).

Stonehill, Arthur D., and Leonard Nathanson, "Capital Budgeting and the Multinational Corporation," *California Management Review* (Summer 1968).

Truitt, J. F., "Expropriation of Private Foreign Investment: A Framework to Consider the Post World War II Experience of British and American Investors," unpublished D.B.A. dissertation, Indiana University, 1971.

Zenoff, David B., and Jack Zwick, *International Financial Management* (Englewood Cliffs, N.J.: Prentice-Hall, Inc., 1969).

CHAPTERS 26, 27

Adams, Walter, *The Structure of American Industry* (New York: Macmillan Publishing Co., Inc., 1982), 218–248, 432–434.

Alberts, William W., and Segall, Joel E., *The Corporate Merger* (Chicago: University of Chicago Press, 1966).

AICPA, Inc., *Accounting for Business Combinations* (Chicago: Commerce Clearing House, 1973), pp. 901–942, 5321–5361.

_____, *Accounting Principles Board Opinions 16–17* (August 1970).

_____, *Accounting Research Bulletin No. 48—Business Combinations* (January 1957).

Ansoff, H. Igor, *Acquisition Behavior of U.S. Manufacturing Firms, 1946–65* (Nashville, Tenn.: Vanderbilt University Press, 1971).

Backman, Jules, "An Economist Looks at Accounting for Business Combinations," *Financial Analysts Journal* (July–August 1970), 39–48.

Bagley, Edward R., *Beyond the Conglomerates: The Impact of the Supercorporations on the Future Life and Business* (New York: AMACOM, 1975).

Bailey, Elizabeth, and Ann F. Friedlaender, "Market Structure and Multiproduct Industries," *Journal of Economic Literature* (September 1982), 1024–1048.

Bock, Betty, *Antitrust Issues in Conglomerate Acquisitions: Tracking a Moving Target* (New York: National Industrial Conference Board, 1969).

————, *Mergers and Markets* (New York: National Industrial Conference Board, 1969).

————, *Statistical Games and The "200 Largest" Industrials: 1954 and 1968* (New York: National Industrial Conference Board, 1970).

Bradley, James W., and Donald H. Korn, *Acquisition and Corporate Development* (Massachusetts: Lexington Books, 1981), 64.

Briloff, Abraham J., "Dirty Pooling—How to Succeed in Business Without Really Trying," *Barron's* (July 15, 1968).

————, "Grime Shelter," *Barron's* (October 25, 1971).

————, "Much Abused Goodwill," *Barron's* (April 18, 1969).

————, *Unaccountable Accounting* (New York: Harper & Row, Inc., 1972).

————, "You Deserve a Break...," *Barron's* (July 8, 1974).

Brozen, Yale, *Mergers in Perspective* (Washington D.C.: American Enterprise Institute for Public Policy Research, 1982).

Buzzell, Robert D., "Is Vertical Integration Profitable?," *Harvard Business Review* (January–February, 1983).

Catlett, George R., and Norman O. Olson, *Accounting for Goodwill* (New York: AICPA, 1968).

Chaikin, Sol C., "Deindustrializing America," *Foreign Affairs* (Spring 1982).

Committee of Experts on Restrictive Business Practices, *Mergers and Competitive Policy: A Report* (Paris: Organization for Economic Co-operation and Development, 1974).

Conglomerate Mergers and Acquisitions (New York: St. John's Law Review Association, 1970).

Conn, Robert L., "Performance of Conglomerate Firms: Comments," *The Journal of Finance* (June 1973), 754–758.

Curley, Anthony J., "Conglomerate Earnings Per Share: Real and Transitory Growth," *The Accounting Review* (July 1971), 519–528.

Daughen, Joseph R., and Peter Binzen, *The Wreck of the Penn Central*, (New York: Little, Brown and Co., 1971).

Dirks, Raymond L., and Leonard Gross, *The Great Wall Street Scandal*, (New York: McGraw-Hill Book Company, 1974).

Editors of Fortune, *The Conglomerate Commotion* (New York: Viking Press, Inc., 1970).

Foster, William C., "Does Pooling Present Fairly?" *CPA Journal* (December 1974), 36–41.

————, "The Illogic of Pooling," *Financial Executive* (December 1974), 16–21.

————, "Setting Standards for Treasury Shares," *Financial Executive* (February 1974), 48–52.

"Gimmick for All Seasons," *Forbes* (October 1, 1975), 60–62.

Gray, E., *Chrome Colossus (GM and Its Times)* (New York: McGraw-Hill Book Company, 1980).

Gunther, Samuel P., "Lingering Pooling Problems," *The CPA Journal* (June 1973), 459–463.

Harvey, John L., and Albert Newgarden, *Management Guide to Mergers & Acquisitions* (New York: John Wiley & Sons, Inc., 1969).

Hawkins, David E., *Corporate Financial Reporting* (Homewood, Ill.: Richard D. Irwin, Inc., 1971).

Higgins, Robert C., "Sustainable Growth Under Inflation," *Financial Management*, 10 (Autumn 1981), 36–40.

_____, "How Much Growth Can a Firm Afford?" *Financial Management*, 6 (Fall 1977).

Holbrook, Steward H., *The Age of Moguls* (New York: Doubleday, 1954).

Husband, William H., and James C. Dockeray, *Modern Corporation Finance*, (Homewood, Illinois: Richard D. Irwin, Inc., 1966), 598–599, 600–602.

Hutchinson, G. Scott, *The Business of Acquisitions and Mergers* (New York: Presidents Publishing House, 1968).

Johnson, Dana J., "The Behavior of Financial Structure and Sustainable Growth in an Inflationary Environment," *Financial Management*, 10 (Autumn 1981), 30–35.

Keenan, Michael, and Lawrence J. White, *Mergers and Acquisitions* (Lexington, Mass.: D. C. Heath and Co., 1982).

Kemp, Bernard A., *Understanding Merger Activity* (New York: New York University, 1969).

Knortz, Herbert C., "The Realities of Business Combinations," *Financial Analysts Journal* (July–August 1970), 28–32.

Laporte, Lowell, *Merger Policy in the Smaller Firm* (New York: National Industrial Conference Board, 1969).

Lewellen, Wilbur G., "A Pure Financial Rationale for the Conglomerate Merger," *The Journal of Finance* (May 1971), 532–533.

Libby, Robert, "The Early Impact of APB Opinions No. 16 & 17, An Empirical Study," *CPA Journal* (October 1972), 839–842.

Linowes, David F., *Managing Growth Through Acquisitions* (New York: AMA, 1968).

Little, Arthur D., Inc., *Mergers and Acquisitions* (Cambridge, Mass.: 1963).

Lynch, Harry H., *Financial Performance of Conglomerates* (Boston: Harvard University Press, Division of Research, 1971).

Marrow, Alfred J., David G. Powers, and Stanley E. Seashore, *Management By Participation* (New York: Harper & Row, Inc., 1967).

Markam, J. W., *Conglomerate Enterprise and Public Policy* (Boston: Harvard University, Graduate School of Business Administration, 1973).

Mase, Myles La Grange, *Management Problems of Corporate Acquisitions* (Cambridge, Mass.: Harvard University Press, 1962).

_____, and George C. Montgomery, *Management Problems of Corporate Acquisitions* (Massachusetts: Division of Research, 1971).

Mason, R. Hal and Maurice B. Gondzwaard, "Performance of Conglomerate Firms: A Portfolio Approach," *The Journal of Finance*, 31 (March 1976), 39–48.

Mautz, R. K., *Financial Reporting By Diversified Companies* (New York: Financial Executives Research Foundation, 1968).

McCarthy, George D., *Acquisitions and Mergers* (New York: The Ronald Press Company, 1963).

McCord, Jim, and Robert J. Oziel, *Conglomerates & Cogenerics* (New York: Practicing Law Institute, 1970).

Meyers, Gustavus, *History of Great American Fortunes* (New York: Random, House, 1936).

Miller, Malcolm C., "Goodwill—An Aggregation Issue," *The Accounting Review* (April 1973), 286–291.

Mueller, Dennis C., "The Effects of Conglomerate Mergers: A Survey of Empirical Evidence," *Journal of Banking and Finance*, I: 339 (1977).

Mueller, Willard F., "Conglomerates: A Nonindustry," in Walter Adams, *The Structure of American Industry* (New York: Macmillan Publishing Co., Inc., 1982).

Narver, John C., *Conglomerate Mergers and Market Competition* (Berkeley, Calif.: University of California Press, 1967).

Nelson, Ralph Lowell, *Merger Movements in American Industry* (Princeton, N.J.: Princeton University Press, 1959), 1895–1956.

Nicholson, John W., "Treasury Stock and Pooling of Interest," *CPA Journal* (October 1973), 913–915.

PBA Accounting Principles (New York: AICPA, 1973).

Pivar, Samuel, "Implementation of APB Opinions Nos. 16 & 17," *CPA Journal* (October 1973), 58–65.

Reich, Robert B., "Making Industrial Policy," *Foreign Affairs* (Spring 1982).

Reid, Samuel Richardson, *Mergers, Managers, and the Economy* (New York: McGraw-Hill Book Company, 1968).

Renshaw, Edward F., "The Theory of Financial Leverage and Conglomerate Mergers," *California Management Review* (Fall, 1968).

Report of the Federal Trade Commission on the Merger Movement, 1968.

Salter, Malcolm S. and Wolf A. Weinhold, *Diversification Through Acquisition*, New York: The Free Press (1979).

Samuels, John Malcolm, *Readings on Mergers & Takeovers* (New York: St. Martin's Press, 1972).

Sapienza, Samuel R., "Pooling Theory & Practice in Business Combinations," *Accounting Review* (April, 1962), 263–278.

Sauerhaft, Stan, *The Merger Game* (New York: T. Y. Crowell, Inc., 1971).

Seidman, J. S., "Pooling Must Go," *Barron's* (July 1 1968).

Short, Robert A., *Business Mergers* (Englewood Cliffs, N.J.: Prentice-Hall, Inc., 1967).

Steiner, Peter Otto, *Mergers: Motives Effects Policies* (Ann Arbor, Mich.: University of Michigan Press, 1976).

Strage, Mark, *Acquisition and Merger Negotiations* (New York: Presidents Publishing House, 1971).

Tearney, Michael G., "Accounting for Goodwill: A Realistic Approach," *Journal of Accountancy* (July 1973), 41–45.

Townsend, Harry, *Scale, Innovation, Merger and Monopoly* (Oxford: Pergamon Press, 1968).

Wakefield, B. Richard, "The Accounting Principles Board on the Wrong Track," *Financial Analysts Journal* (July–August 1973), 33–36.

Welcome to Our Conglomerate—You're Fired! (New York: Delacorte Press, 1971).

Weston, J. Fred and S. K. Monsinghka, "Tests of the Efficiency Performance of Conglomerate Firms," *The Journal of Finance* (September 1971), 919–936.

Winslow, John F., *Conglomerates Unlimited* (Bloomington, Ind.: Indiana University Press, 1973).

Wyatt, Arthur R., *A Critical Study of Accounting For Business Combinations* (New York: AICPA, 1963).

————, "Inequities in Accounting for Business Combinations," *Financial Executive* (December 1972), 28–35.

————, and Donald E. Kieso, *Business Combinations: Planning and Action* (Scranton, Pa.: International Textbook Company, 1969).

APPENDIX B

Compound Interest and Annuity Tables[a]

1.00 %
ANNUAL

		Amount Of 1	Amount Of 1 Per Period	Sinking Fund Payment	Present Worth Of 1	Present Worth Of 1 Per Period	Periodic Payment To Amortize 1	Constant Annual Percent	Total Interest	Annual Add-on Rate	
		What a single $1 deposit grows to in the future. The deposit is made at the beginning of the first period.	What a series of $1 deposits grow to in the future. A deposit is made at the end of each period.	The amount to be deposited at the end of each period that grows to $1 in the future.	What $1 to be paid in the future is worth today. Value today of a single payment tomorrow.	What $1 to be paid at the end of each period is worth today. Value today of a series of payments tomorrow.	The mortgage payment to amortize a loan of $1. An annuity certain, payable at the end of each period, worth $1 today.	The annual payment, including interest and principal, to amortize completely a loan of $100.	The total interest paid over the term on a loan of $1. The loan is amortized by regular periodic payments.	The average annual interest rate on a loan that is completely amortized by regular periodic payments.	
		$S=(1+i)^n$	$S_{\overline{n}}=\dfrac{(1+i)^n-1}{i}$	$\dfrac{1}{S_{\overline{n}}}=\dfrac{i}{(1+i)^n-1}$	$V^n=\dfrac{1}{(1+i)^n}$	$A_{\overline{n}}=\dfrac{1-V^n}{i}$	$\dfrac{1}{A_{\overline{n}}}=\dfrac{i}{1-V^n}$				
YR											**YR**
1	1	1.010000	1.000000	1.00000000	0.990099	0.990099	1.01000000	101.00	0.010000	1.00	1
2	2	1.020100	2.010000	0.49751244	0.980296	1.970395	0.50751244	50.76	0.015025	0.75	2
3	3	1.030301	3.030100	0.33002211	0.970590	2.940985	0.34002211	34.01	0.020066	0.67	3
4	4	1.040604	4.060401	0.24628109	0.960980	3.901966	0.25628109	25.63	0.025124	0.63	4
5	5	1.051010	5.101005	0.19603980	0.951466	4.853431	0.20603980	20.61	0.030199	0.60	5
6	6	1.061520	6.152015	0.16254837	0.942045	5.795476	0.17254837	17.26	0.035290	0.59	6
7	7	1.072135	7.213535	0.13862828	0.932718	6.728195	0.14862828	14.87	0.040398	0.58	7
8	8	1.082857	8.285671	0.12069029	0.923483	7.651678	0.13069029	13.07	0.045522	0.57	8
9	9	1.093685	9.368527	0.10674036	0.914340	8.566018	0.11674036	11.68	0.050663	0.56	9
10	10	1.104622	10.462213	0.09558208	0.905287	9.471305	0.10558208	10.56	0.055821	0.56	10
11	11	1.115668	11.566835	0.08645408	0.896324	10.367628	0.09645408	9.65	0.060995	0.55	11
12	12	1.126825	12.682503	0.07884879	0.887449	11.255077	0.08884879	8.89	0.066185	0.55	12
13	13	1.138093	13.809328	0.07241482	0.878663	12.133740	0.08241482	8.25	0.071393	0.55	13
14	14	1.149474	14.947421	0.06690117	0.869963	13.003703	0.07690117	7.70	0.076616	0.55	14
15	15	1.160969	16.096896	0.06212378	0.861349	13.865053	0.07212378	7.22	0.081857	0.55	15
16	16	1.172579	17.257864	0.05794460	0.852821	14.717874	0.06794460	6.80	0.087114	0.54	16
17	17	1.184304	18.430443	0.05425806	0.844377	15.562251	0.06425806	6.43	0.092387	0.54	17
18	18	1.196147	19.614748	0.05098205	0.836017	16.398269	0.06098205	6.10	0.097677	0.54	18
19	19	1.208109	20.810895	0.04805175	0.827740	17.226008	0.05805175	5.81	0.102983	0.54	19
20	20	1.220190	22.019004	0.04541531	0.819544	18.045553	0.05541531	5.55	0.108306	0.54	20
21	21	1.232392	23.239194	0.04303075	0.811430	18.856983	0.05303075	5.31	0.113646	0.54	21
22	22	1.244716	24.471586	0.04086372	0.803396	19.660379	0.05086372	5.09	0.119002	0.54	22
23	23	1.257163	25.716302	0.03888584	0.795442	20.455821	0.04888584	4.89	0.124374	0.54	23
24	24	1.269735	26.973465	0.03707347	0.787566	21.243387	0.04707347	4.71	0.129763	0.54	24
25	25	1.282432	28.243200	0.03540675	0.779768	22.023156	0.04540675	4.55	0.135169	0.54	25
26	26	1.295256	29.525631	0.03386888	0.772048	22.795204	0.04386888	4.39	0.140591	0.54	26
27	27	1.308209	30.820888	0.03244553	0.764404	23.559608	0.04244553	4.25	0.146029	0.54	27
28	28	1.321291	32.129097	0.03112444	0.756836	24.316443	0.04112444	4.12	0.151484	0.54	28
29	29	1.334504	33.450388	0.02989502	0.749342	25.065785	0.03989502	3.99	0.156956	0.54	29
30	30	1.347849	34.784892	0.02874811	0.741923	25.807708	0.03874811	3.88	0.162443	0.54	30
31	31	1.361322	36.132740	0.02767573	0.734577	26.542285	0.03767573	3.77	0.167948	0.54	31
32	32	1.374941	37.494068	0.02667089	0.727304	27.269589	0.03667089	3.67	0.173468	0.54	32
33	33	1.388690	38.869009	0.02572744	0.720103	27.989693	0.03572744	3.58	0.179005	0.54	33
34	34	1.402577	40.257699	0.02483997	0.712973	28.702666	0.03483997	3.49	0.184559	0.54	34
35	35	1.416603	41.660276	0.02400368	0.705914	29.408580	0.03400368	3.41	0.190129	0.54	35
36	36	1.430769	43.076878	0.02321431	0.698925	30.107505	0.03321431	3.33	0.195715	0.54	36
37	37	1.445076	44.507647	0.02246805	0.692005	30.799510	0.03246805	3.25	0.201318	0.54	37
38	38	1.459527	45.952724	0.02176150	0.685153	31.484663	0.03176150	3.18	0.206937	0.54	38
39	39	1.474123	47.412251	0.02109160	0.678370	32.163033	0.03109160	3.11	0.212572	0.55	39
40	40	1.488864	48.886373	0.02045560	0.671653	32.834686	0.03045560	3.05	0.218224	0.55	40
41	41	1.503752	50.375237	0.01985102	0.665003	33.499689	0.02985102	2.99	0.223892	0.55	41
42	42	1.518790	51.878989	0.01927563	0.658419	34.158108	0.02927563	2.93	0.229576	0.55	42
43	43	1.533978	53.397779	0.01872737	0.651900	34.810008	0.02872737	2.88	0.235277	0.55	43
44	44	1.549318	54.931757	0.01820441	0.645445	35.455454	0.02820441	2.83	0.240994	0.55	44
45	45	1.564811	56.481075	0.01770505	0.639055	36.094508	0.02770505	2.78	0.246727	0.55	45
46	46	1.580459	58.045885	0.01722775	0.632728	36.727236	0.02722775	2.73	0.252476	0.55	46
47	47	1.596263	59.626344	0.01677111	0.626463	37.353699	0.02677111	2.68	0.258242	0.55	47
48	48	1.612226	61.222608	0.01633384	0.620260	37.973959	0.02633384	2.64	0.264024	0.55	48
49	49	1.628348	62.834834	0.01591474	0.614119	38.588079	0.02591474	2.60	0.269822	0.55	49
50	50	1.644632	64.463182	0.01551273	0.608039	39.196118	0.02551273	2.56	0.275637	0.55	50

[a] SOURCE: *Thorndike Encyclopedia of Banking and Financial Tables*, Warren, Gorham and Lamont, Inc., New York, pp. 6–352 through 6–373. Used with permission.

COMPOUND INTEREST AND ANNUITY TABLE

2.00 %
ANNUAL

		Amount Of 1	Amount Of 1 Per Period	Sinking Fund Payment	Present Worth Of 1	Present Worth Of 1 Per Period	Periodic Payment To Amortize 1	Constant Annual Percent	Total Interest	Annual Add-on Rate	
		What a single $1 deposit grows to in the future. The deposit is made at the beginning of the first period.	What a series of $1 deposits grow to in the future. A deposit is made at the end of each period.	The amount to be deposited at the end of each period that grows to $1 in the future.	What $1 to be paid in the future is worth today. Value today of a single payment tomorrow.	What $1 to be paid at the end of each period is worth today. Value today of a series of payments tomorrow.	The mortgage payment to amortize a loan of $1. An annuity certain, payable at the end of each period, worth $1 today.	The annual payment, including interest and principal, to amortize completely a loan of $100.	The total interest paid over the term on a loan of $1. The loan is amortized by regular periodic payments.	The average annual interest rate on a loan that is completely amortized by regular periodic payments.	
		$S=(1+i)^n$	$S_{\overline{n}}=\dfrac{(1+i)^n-1}{i}$	$\dfrac{1}{S_{\overline{n}}}=\dfrac{i}{(1+i)^n-1}$	$V^n=\dfrac{1}{(1+i)^n}$	$A_{\overline{n}}=\dfrac{1-V^n}{i}$	$\dfrac{1}{A_{\overline{n}}}=\dfrac{i}{1-V^n}$				
YR											**YR**
1	1	1.020000	1.000000	1.00000000	0.980392	0.980392	1.02000000	102.00	0.020000	2.00	1
2	2	1.040400	2.020000	0.49504950	0.961169	1.941561	0.51504950	51.51	0.030099	1.50	2
3	3	1.061208	3.060400	0.32675467	0.942322	2.883883	0.34675467	34.68	0.040264	1.34	3
4	4	1.082432	4.121608	0.24262375	0.923845	3.807729	0.26262375	26.27	0.050495	1.26	4
5	5	1.104081	5.204040	0.19215839	0.905731	4.713460	0.21215839	21.22	0.060792	1.22	5
6	6	1.126162	6.308121	0.15852581	0.887971	5.601431	0.17852581	17.86	0.071155	1.19	6
7	7	1.148686	7.434283	0.13451196	0.870560	6.471991	0.15451196	15.46	0.081584	1.17	7
8	8	1.171659	8.582969	0.11650980	0.853490	7.325481	0.13650980	13.66	0.092078	1.15	8
9	9	1.195093	9.754628	0.10251544	0.836755	8.162237	0.12251544	12.26	0.102639	1.14	9
10	10	1.218994	10.949721	0.09132653	0.820348	8.982585	0.11132653	11.14	0.113265	1.13	10
11	11	1.243374	12.168715	0.08217794	0.804263	9.786848	0.10217794	10.22	0.123957	1.13	11
12	12	1.268242	13.412090	0.07455960	0.788443	10.575341	0.09455960	9.46	0.134715	1.12	12
13	13	1.293607	14.680332	0.06811835	0.773033	11.348374	0.08811835	8.82	0.145539	1.12	13
14	14	1.319479	15.973938	0.06260197	0.757875	12.106249	0.08260197	8.27	0.156428	1.12	14
15	15	1.345868	17.293417	0.05782547	0.743015	12.849264	0.07782547	7.79	0.167382	1.12	15
16	16	1.372786	18.639285	0.05365013	0.728446	13.577709	0.07365013	7.37	0.178402	1.12	16
17	17	1.400241	20.012071	0.04996984	0.714163	14.291872	0.06996984	7.00	0.189487	1.11	17
18	18	1.428246	21.412312	0.04670210	0.700159	14.992031	0.06670210	6.68	0.200638	1.11	18
19	19	1.456811	22.840559	0.04378177	0.686431	15.678462	0.06378177	6.38	0.211854	1.12	19
20	20	1.485947	24.297370	0.04115672	0.672971	16.351433	0.06115672	6.12	0.223134	1.12	20
21	21	1.515666	25.783317	0.03878477	0.659776	17.011209	0.05878477	5.88	0.234480	1.12	21
22	22	1.545980	27.298984	0.03663140	0.646839	17.658048	0.05663140	5.67	0.245891	1.12	22
23	23	1.576899	28.844963	0.03466810	0.634156	18.292204	0.05466810	5.47	0.257366	1.12	23
24	24	1.608437	30.421862	0.03287110	0.621721	18.913926	0.05287110	5.29	0.268906	1.12	24
25	25	1.640606	32.030300	0.03122044	0.609531	19.523456	0.05122044	5.13	0.280511	1.12	25
26	26	1.673418	33.670906	0.02969923	0.597579	20.121036	0.04969923	4.97	0.292180	1.12	26
27	27	1.706886	35.344324	0.02829309	0.585862	20.706898	0.04829309	4.83	0.303913	1.13	27
28	28	1.741024	37.051210	0.02698967	0.574375	21.281272	0.04698967	4.70	0.315711	1.13	28
29	29	1.775845	38.792235	0.02577836	0.563112	21.844385	0.04577836	4.58	0.327572	1.13	29
30	30	1.811362	40.568079	0.02464992	0.552071	22.396456	0.04464992	4.47	0.339498	1.13	30
31	31	1.847589	42.379441	0.02359635	0.541246	22.937702	0.04359635	4.36	0.351487	1.13	31
32	32	1.884541	44.227030	0.02261061	0.530633	23.468335	0.04261061	4.27	0.363539	1.14	32
33	33	1.922231	46.111570	0.02168653	0.520229	23.988564	0.04168653	4.17	0.375656	1.14	33
34	34	1.960676	48.033802	0.02081867	0.510028	24.498592	0.04081867	4.09	0.387835	1.14	34
35	35	1.999890	49.994478	0.02000221	0.500028	24.998619	0.04000221	4.01	0.400077	1.14	35
36	36	2.039887	51.994367	0.01923285	0.490223	25.488842	0.03923285	3.93	0.412383	1.15	36
37	37	2.080685	54.034255	0.01850678	0.480611	25.969453	0.03850678	3.86	0.424751	1.15	37
38	38	2.122299	56.114940	0.01782057	0.471187	26.440641	0.03782057	3.79	0.437182	1.15	38
39	39	2.164745	58.237238	0.01717114	0.461948	26.902589	0.03717114	3.72	0.449675	1.15	39
40	40	2.208040	60.401983	0.01655575	0.452890	27.355479	0.03655575	3.66	0.462230	1.16	40
41	41	2.252200	62.610023	0.01597188	0.444010	27.799489	0.03597188	3.60	0.474847	1.16	41
42	42	2.297244	64.862223	0.01541729	0.435304	28.234794	0.03541729	3.55	0.487526	1.16	42
43	43	2.343189	67.159468	0.01488993	0.426769	28.661562	0.03488993	3.49	0.500267	1.16	43
44	44	2.390053	69.502657	0.01438794	0.418401	29.079963	0.03438794	3.44	0.513069	1.17	44
45	45	2.437854	71.892710	0.01390962	0.410197	29.490160	0.03390962	3.40	0.525933	1.17	45
46	46	2.486611	74.330564	0.01345342	0.402154	29.892314	0.03345342	3.35	0.538857	1.17	46
47	47	2.536344	76.817176	0.01301792	0.394268	30.286582	0.03301792	3.31	0.551842	1.17	47
48	48	2.587070	79.353519	0.01260184	0.386538	30.673120	0.03260184	3.27	0.564888	1.18	48
49	49	2.638812	81.940590	0.01220396	0.378958	31.052078	0.03220396	3.23	0.577994	1.18	49
50	50	2.691588	84.579401	0.01182321	0.371528	31.423606	0.03182321	3.19	0.591160	1.18	50

COMPOUND INTEREST AND ANNUITY TABLE

3.00 %
ANNUAL

		Amount Of 1	Amount Of 1 Per Period	Sinking Fund Payment	Present Worth Of 1	Present Worth Of 1 Per Period	Periodic Payment To Amortize 1	Constant Annual Percent	Total Interest	Annual Add-on Rate		
		What a single $1 deposit grows to in the future. The deposit is made at the beginning of the first period.	What a series of $1 deposits grow to in the future. A deposit is made at the end of each period.	The amount to be deposited at the end of each period that grows to $1 in the future.	What $1 to be paid in the future is worth today. Value today of a single payment tomorrow.	What $1 to be paid at the end of each period is worth today. Value today of a series of payments tomorrow.	The mortgage payment to amortize a loan of $1. An annuity certain, payable at the end of each period, worth $1 today.	The annual payment, including interest and principal, to amortize completely a loan of $100.	The total interest paid over the term on a loan of $1. The loan is amortized by regular periodic payments.	The average annual interest rate on a loan that is completely amortized by regular periodic payments.		
		$S=(1+i)^n$	$S_{\overline{n}}=\dfrac{(1+i)^n-1}{i}$	$\dfrac{1}{S_{\overline{n}}}=\dfrac{i}{(1+i)^n-1}$	$V^n=\dfrac{1}{(1+i)^n}$	$A_{\overline{n}}=\dfrac{1-V^n}{i}$	$\dfrac{1}{A_{\overline{n}}}=\dfrac{i}{1-V^n}$					
YR												**YR**
1	1	1.030000	1.000000	1.00000000	0.970874	0.970874	1.03000000	103.00	0.030000	3.00	1
2	2	1.060900	2.030000	0.49261084	0.942596	1.913470	0.52261084	52.27	0.045222	2.26	2
3	3	1.092727	3.090900	0.32353036	0.915142	2.828611	0.35353036	35.36	0.060591	2.02	3
4	4	1.125509	4.183627	0.23902705	0.888487	3.717098	0.26902705	26.91	0.076108	1.90	4
5	5	1.159274	5.309136	0.18835457	0.862609	4.579707	0.21835457	21.84	0.091773	1.84	5
6	6	1.194052	6.468410	0.15459750	0.837484	5.417191	0.18459750	18.46	0.107585	1.79	6
7	7	1.229874	7.662462	0.13050635	0.813092	6.230283	0.16050635	16.06	0.123544	1.76	7
8	8	1.266770	8.892336	0.11245639	0.789409	7.019692	0.14245639	14.25	0.139651	1.75	8
9	9	1.304773	10.159106	0.09843386	0.766417	7.786109	0.12843386	12.85	0.155905	1.73	9
10	10	1.343916	11.463879	0.08723051	0.744094	8.530203	0.11723051	11.73	0.172305	1.72	10
11	11	1.384234	12.807796	0.07807745	0.722421	9.252624	0.10807745	10.81	0.188852	1.72	11
12	12	1.425761	14.192030	0.07046209	0.701380	9.954004	0.10046209	10.05	0.205545	1.71	12
13	13	1.468534	15.617790	0.06402954	0.680951	10.634955	0.09402954	9.41	0.222384	1.71	13
14	14	1.512590	17.086324	0.05852634	0.661118	11.296073	0.08852634	8.86	0.239369	1.71	14
15	15	1.557967	18.598914	0.05376658	0.641862	11.937935	0.08376658	8.38	0.256499	1.71	15
16	16	1.604706	20.156881	0.04961085	0.623167	12.561102	0.07961085	7.97	0.273774	1.71	16
17	17	1.652848	21.761588	0.04595253	0.605016	13.166118	0.07595253	7.60	0.291193	1.71	17
18	18	1.702433	23.414435	0.04270870	0.587395	13.753513	0.07270870	7.28	0.308757	1.72	18
19	19	1.753506	25.116868	0.03981388	0.570286	14.323799	0.06981388	6.99	0.326464	1.72	19
20	20	1.806111	26.870374	0.03721571	0.553676	14.877475	0.06721571	6.73	0.344314	1.72	20
21	21	1.860295	28.676486	0.03487178	0.537549	15.415024	0.06487178	6.49	0.362307	1.73	21
22	22	1.916103	30.536780	0.03274739	0.521893	15.936917	0.06274739	6.28	0.380443	1.73	22
23	23	1.973587	32.452884	0.03081390	0.506692	16.443608	0.06081390	6.09	0.398720	1.73	23
24	24	2.032794	34.426470	0.02904742	0.491934	16.935542	0.05904742	5.91	0.417138	1.74	24
25	25	2.093778	36.459264	0.02742787	0.477606	17.413148	0.05742787	5.75	0.435697	1.74	25
26	26	2.156591	38.553042	0.02593829	0.463695	17.876842	0.05593829	5.60	0.454396	1.75	26
27	27	2.221289	40.709634	0.02456421	0.450189	18.327031	0.05456421	5.46	0.473234	1.75	27
28	28	2.287928	42.930923	0.02329323	0.437077	18.764108	0.05329323	5.33	0.492211	1.76	28
29	29	2.356566	45.218850	0.02211467	0.424346	19.188455	0.05211467	5.22	0.511325	1.76	29
30	30	2.427262	47.575416	0.02101926	0.411987	19.600441	0.05101926	5.11	0.530578	1.77	30
31	31	2.500080	50.002678	0.01999893	0.399987	20.000428	0.04999893	5.00	0.549967	1.77	31
32	32	2.575083	52.502759	0.01904662	0.388337	20.388766	0.04904662	4.91	0.569492	1.78	32
33	33	2.652335	55.077841	0.01815612	0.377026	20.765792	0.04815612	4.82	0.589152	1.79	33
34	34	2.731905	57.730177	0.01732196	0.366045	21.131837	0.04732196	4.74	0.608947	1.79	34
35	35	2.813862	60.462082	0.01653929	0.355383	21.487220	0.04653929	4.66	0.628875	1.80	35
36	36	2.898278	63.275944	0.01580379	0.345032	21.832252	0.04580379	4.59	0.648937	1.80	36
37	37	2.985227	66.174223	0.01511162	0.334983	22.167235	0.04511162	4.52	0.669130	1.81	37
38	38	3.074783	69.159449	0.01445934	0.325226	22.492462	0.04445934	4.45	0.689455	1.81	38
39	39	3.167027	72.234233	0.01384385	0.315754	22.808215	0.04384385	4.39	0.709910	1.82	39
40	40	3.262038	75.401260	0.01326238	0.306557	23.114772	0.04326238	4.33	0.730495	1.83	40
41	41	3.359899	78.663298	0.01271241	0.297628	23.412400	0.04271241	4.28	0.751209	1.83	41
42	42	3.460696	82.023196	0.01219167	0.288959	23.701359	0.04219167	4.22	0.772050	1.84	42
43	43	3.564517	85.483892	0.01169811	0.280543	23.981902	0.04169811	4.17	0.793019	1.84	43
44	44	3.671452	89.048409	0.01122985	0.272372	24.254274	0.04122985	4.13	0.814113	1.85	44
45	45	3.781596	92.719861	0.01078518	0.264439	24.518713	0.04078518	4.08	0.835333	1.86	45
46	46	3.895044	96.501457	0.01036254	0.256737	24.775449	0.04036254	4.04	0.856677	1.86	46
47	47	4.011895	100.396501	0.00996051	0.249259	25.024708	0.03996051	4.00	0.878144	1.87	47
48	48	4.132252	104.408396	0.00957777	0.241999	25.266707	0.03957777	3.96	0.899733	1.87	48
49	49	4.256219	108.540648	0.00921314	0.234950	25.501657	0.03921314	3.93	0.921444	1.88	49
50	50	4.383906	112.796867	0.00886549	0.228107	25.729764	0.03886549	3.89	0.943275	1.89	50

COMPOUND INTEREST AND ANNUITY TABLE

4.00 %
ANNUAL

		Amount Of 1	Amount Of 1 Per Period	Sinking Fund Payment	Present Worth Of 1	Present Worth Of 1 Per Period	Periodic Payment To Amortize 1	Constant Annual Percent	Total Interest	Annual Add-on Rate		
		What a single $1 deposit grows to in the future. The deposit is made at the beginning of the first period.	What a series of $1 deposits grow to in the future. A deposit is made at the end of each period.	The amount to be deposited at the end of each period that grows to $1 in the future.	What $1 to be paid in the future is worth today. Value today of a single payment tomorrow.	What $1 to be paid at the end of each period is worth today. Value today of a series of payments tomorrow.	The mortgage payment to amortize a loan of $1. An annuity certain, payable at the end of each period, worth $1 today.	The annual payment, including interest and principal, to amortize completely a loan of $100.	The total interest paid over the term on a loan of $1. The loan is amortized by regular periodic payments.	The average annual interest rate on a loan that is completely amortized by regular periodic payments.		
		$S=(1+i)^n$	$S_{\overline{n}}=\dfrac{(1+i)^n-1}{i}$	$\dfrac{1}{S_{\overline{n}}}=\dfrac{i}{(1+i)^n-1}$	$V^n=\dfrac{1}{(1+i)^n}$	$A_{\overline{n}}=\dfrac{1-V^n}{i}$	$\dfrac{1}{A_{\overline{n}}}=\dfrac{i}{1-V^n}$					
YR												YR
1	1	1.040000	1.000000	1.00000000	0.961538	0.961538	1.04000000	104.00	0.040000	4.00	1
2	2	1.081600	2.040000	0.49019608	0.924556	1.886095	0.53019608	53.02	0.060392	3.02	2
3	3	1.124864	3.121600	0.32034854	0.888996	2.775091	0.36034854	36.04	0.081046	2.70	3
4	4	1.169859	4.246464	0.23549005	0.854804	3.629895	0.27549005	27.55	0.101960	2.55	4
5	5	1.216653	5.416323	0.18462711	0.821927	4.451822	0.22462711	22.47	0.123136	2.46	5
6	6	1.265319	6.632975	0.15076190	0.790315	5.242137	0.19076190	19.08	0.144571	2.41	6
7	7	1.315932	7.898294	0.12660961	0.759918	6.002055	0.16660961	16.67	0.166267	2.38	7
8	8	1.368569	9.214226	0.10852783	0.730690	6.732745	0.14852783	14.86	0.188223	2.35	8
9	9	1.423312	10.582795	0.09449299	0.702587	7.435332	0.13449299	13.45	0.210437	2.34	9
10	10	1.480244	12.006107	0.08329094	0.675564	8.110896	0.12329094	12.33	0.232909	2.33	10
11	11	1.539454	13.486351	0.07414904	0.649581	8.760477	0.11414904	11.42	0.255639	2.32	11
12	12	1.601032	15.025805	0.06655217	0.624597	9.385074	0.10655217	10.66	0.278626	2.32	12
13	13	1.665074	16.626838	0.06014373	0.600574	9.985648	0.10014373	10.02	0.301868	2.32	13
14	14	1.731676	18.291911	0.05466897	0.577475	10.563123	0.09466897	9.47	0.325366	2.32	14
15	15	1.800944	20.023588	0.04994110	0.555265	11.118387	0.08994110	9.00	0.349117	2.33	15
16	16	1.872981	21.824531	0.04582000	0.533908	11.652296	0.08582000	8.59	0.373120	2.33	16
17	17	1.947900	23.697512	0.04219852	0.513373	12.165669	0.08219852	8.22	0.397375	2.34	17
18	18	2.025817	25.645413	0.03899333	0.493628	12.659297	0.07899333	7.90	0.421880	2.34	18
19	19	2.106849	27.671229	0.03613862	0.474642	13.133939	0.07613862	7.62	0.446634	2.35	19
20	20	2.191123	29.778079	0.03358175	0.456387	13.590326	0.07358175	7.36	0.471635	2.36	20
21	21	2.278768	31.969202	0.03128011	0.438834	14.029160	0.07128011	7.13	0.496882	2.37	21
22	22	2.369919	34.247970	0.02919881	0.421955	14.451115	0.06919881	6.92	0.522374	2.37	22
23	23	2.464716	36.617889	0.02730906	0.405726	14.856842	0.06730906	6.74	0.548108	2.38	23
24	24	2.563304	39.082604	0.02558683	0.390121	15.246963	0.06558683	6.56	0.574084	2.39	24
25	25	2.665836	41.645908	0.02401196	0.375117	15.622080	0.06401196	6.41	0.600299	2.40	25
26	26	2.772470	44.311745	0.02256738	0.360689	15.982769	0.06256738	6.26	0.626752	2.41	26
27	27	2.883369	47.084214	0.02123854	0.346817	16.329586	0.06123854	6.13	0.653441	2.42	27
28	28	2.998703	49.967583	0.02001298	0.333477	16.663063	0.06001298	6.01	0.680363	2.43	28
29	29	3.118651	52.966286	0.01887993	0.320651	16.983715	0.05887993	5.89	0.707518	2.44	29
30	30	3.243398	56.084938	0.01783010	0.308319	17.292033	0.05783010	5.79	0.734903	2.45	30
31	31	3.373133	59.328335	0.01685535	0.296460	17.588494	0.05685535	5.69	0.762516	2.46	31
32	32	3.508059	62.701469	0.01594859	0.285058	17.873551	0.05594859	5.60	0.790355	2.47	32
33	33	3.648381	66.209527	0.01510357	0.274094	18.147646	0.05510357	5.52	0.818418	2.48	33
34	34	3.794316	69.857909	0.01431477	0.263552	18.411198	0.05431477	5.44	0.846702	2.49	34
35	35	3.946089	73.652225	0.01357732	0.253415	18.664613	0.05357732	5.36	0.875206	2.50	35
36	36	4.103933	77.598314	0.01288688	0.243669	18.908282	0.05288688	5.29	0.903928	2.51	36
37	37	4.268090	81.702246	0.01223957	0.234297	19.142579	0.05223957	5.23	0.932864	2.52	37
38	38	4.438813	85.970336	0.01163192	0.225285	19.367864	0.05163192	5.17	0.962013	2.53	38
39	39	4.616366	90.409150	0.01106083	0.216621	19.584485	0.05106083	5.11	0.991372	2.54	39
40	40	4.801021	95.025516	0.01052349	0.208289	19.792774	0.05052349	5.06	1.020940	2.55	40
41	41	4.993061	99.826536	0.01001738	0.200278	19.993052	0.05001738	5.01	1.050712	2.56	41
42	42	5.192784	104.819598	0.00954020	0.192575	20.185627	0.04954020	4.96	1.080688	2.57	42
43	43	5.400495	110.012382	0.00908989	0.185168	20.370795	0.04908989	4.91	1.110865	2.58	43
44	44	5.616515	115.412877	0.00866454	0.178046	20.548841	0.04866454	4.87	1.141240	2.59	44
45	45	5.841176	121.029392	0.00826246	0.171198	20.720040	0.04826246	4.83	1.171811	2.60	45
46	46	6.074823	126.870568	0.00788205	0.164614	20.884654	0.04788205	4.79	1.202574	2.61	46
47	47	6.317816	132.945390	0.00752189	0.158283	21.042936	0.04752189	4.76	1.233529	2.62	47
48	48	6.570528	139.263206	0.00718065	0.152195	21.195131	0.04718065	4.72	1.264671	2.63	48
49	49	6.833349	145.833734	0.00685712	0.146341	21.341472	0.04685712	4.69	1.295999	2.64	49
50	50	7.106683	152.667084	0.00655020	0.140713	21.482185	0.04655020	4.66	1.327510	2.66	50

COMPOUND INTEREST AND ANNUITY TABLE   5.00 % ANNUAL

		Amount Of 1	Amount Of 1 Per Period	Sinking Fund Payment	Present Worth Of 1	Present Worth Of 1 Per Period	Periodic Payment To Amortize 1	Constant Annual Percent	Total Interest	Annual Add-on Rate
		What a single $1 deposit grows to in the future. The deposit is made at the beginning of the first period.	What a series of $1 deposits grow to in the future. A deposit is made at the end of each period.	The amount to be deposited at the end of each period that grows to $1 in the future.	What $1 to be paid in the future is worth today. Value today of a single payment tomorrow.	What $1 to be paid at the end of each period is worth today. Value today of a series of payments tomorrow.	The mortgage payment to amortize a loan of $1. An annuity certain, payable at the end of each period, worth $1 today.	The annual payment, including interest and principal, to amortize completely a loan of $100.	The total interest paid over the term on a loan of $1. The loan is completely amortized by regular periodic payments.	The average annual interest rate on a loan that is completely amortized by regular periodic payments.
		$S=(1+i)^n$	$S_{\overline{n}}=\dfrac{(1+i)^n-1}{i}$	$\dfrac{1}{S_{\overline{n}}}=\dfrac{i}{(1+i)^n-1}$	$V^n=\dfrac{1}{(1+i)^n}$	$A_{\overline{n}}=\dfrac{1-V^n}{i}$	$\dfrac{1}{A_{\overline{n}}}=\dfrac{i}{1-V^n}$			
YR											**YR**
1	1	1.050000	1.000000	1.00000000	0.952381	0.952381	1.05000000	105.00	0.050000	5.00	1
2	2	1.102500	2.050000	0.48780488	0.907029	1.859410	0.53780488	53.79	0.075610	3.78	2
3	3	1.157625	3.152500	0.31720856	0.863838	2.723248	0.36720856	36.73	0.101626	3.39	3
4	4	1.215506	4.310125	0.23201183	0.822702	3.545951	0.28201183	28.21	0.128047	3.20	4
5	5	1.276282	5.525631	0.18097480	0.783526	4.329477	0.23097480	23.10	0.154874	3.10	5
6	6	1.340096	6.801913	0.14701747	0.746215	5.075692	0.19701747	19.71	0.182105	3.04	6
7	7	1.407100	8.142008	0.12281982	0.710681	5.786373	0.17281982	17.29	0.209739	3.00	7
8	8	1.477455	9.549109	0.10472181	0.676839	6.463213	0.15472181	15.48	0.237775	2.97	8
9	9	1.551328	11.026564	0.09069008	0.644609	7.107822	0.14069008	14.07	0.266211	2.96	9
10	10	1.628895	12.577893	0.07950457	0.613913	7.721735	0.12950457	12.96	0.295046	2.95	10
11	11	1.710339	14.206787	0.07038889	0.584679	8.306414	0.12038889	12.04	0.324278	2.95	11
12	12	1.795856	15.917127	0.06282541	0.556837	8.863252	0.11282541	11.29	0.353905	2.95	12
13	13	1.885649	17.712983	0.05645577	0.530321	9.393573	0.10645577	10.65	0.383925	2.95	13
14	14	1.979932	19.598632	0.05102397	0.505068	9.898641	0.10102397	10.11	0.414336	2.96	14
15	15	2.078928	21.578564	0.04634229	0.481017	10.379658	0.09634229	9.64	0.445134	2.97	15
16	16	2.182875	23.657492	0.04226991	0.458112	10.837770	0.09226991	9.23	0.476319	2.98	16
17	17	2.292018	25.840366	0.03869914	0.436297	11.274066	0.08869914	8.87	0.507885	2.99	17
18	18	2.406619	28.132385	0.03554622	0.415521	11.689587	0.08554622	8.56	0.539832	3.00	18
19	19	2.526950	30.539004	0.03274501	0.395734	12.085321	0.08274501	8.28	0.572155	3.01	19
20	20	2.653298	33.065954	0.03024259	0.376889	12.462210	0.08024259	8.03	0.604852	3.02	20
21	21	2.785963	35.719252	0.02799611	0.358942	12.821153	0.07799611	7.80	0.637918	3.04	21
22	22	2.925261	38.505214	0.02597051	0.341850	13.163003	0.07597051	7.60	0.671351	3.05	22
23	23	3.071524	41.430475	0.02413682	0.325571	13.488475	0.07413682	7.42	0.705147	3.07	23
24	24	3.225100	44.501999	0.02247090	0.310068	13.798642	0.07247090	7.25	0.739302	3.08	24
25	25	3.386355	47.727099	0.02095246	0.295303	14.093945	0.07095246	7.10	0.773811	3.10	25
26	26	3.555673	51.113454	0.01956432	0.281241	14.375185	0.06956432	6.96	0.808672	3.11	26
27	27	3.733456	54.669126	0.01829186	0.267848	14.643034	0.06829186	6.83	0.843880	3.13	27
28	28	3.920129	58.402583	0.01712253	0.255094	14.898127	0.06712253	6.72	0.879431	3.14	28
29	29	4.116136	62.322712	0.01604551	0.242946	15.141074	0.06604551	6.61	0.915320	3.16	29
30	30	4.321942	66.438848	0.01505144	0.231377	15.372451	0.06505144	6.51	0.951543	3.17	30
31	31	4.538039	70.760790	0.01413212	0.220359	15.592811	0.06413212	6.42	0.988096	3.19	31
32	32	4.764941	75.298829	0.01328042	0.209866	15.802677	0.06328042	6.33	1.024973	3.20	32
33	33	5.003188	80.063771	0.01249004	0.199873	16.002549	0.06249004	6.25	1.062171	3.22	33
34	34	5.253348	85.066959	0.01175545	0.190355	16.192904	0.06175545	6.18	1.099685	3.23	34
35	35	5.516015	90.320307	0.01107171	0.181290	16.374194	0.06107171	6.11	1.137510	3.25	35
36	36	5.791816	95.836323	0.01043446	0.172657	16.546852	0.06043446	6.05	1.175640	3.27	36
37	37	6.081407	101.628139	0.00983979	0.164436	16.711287	0.05983979	5.99	1.214072	3.28	37
38	38	6.385477	107.709546	0.00928423	0.156605	16.867893	0.05928423	5.93	1.252801	3.30	38
39	39	6.704751	114.095023	0.00876462	0.149148	17.017041	0.05876462	5.88	1.291820	3.31	39
40	40	7.039989	120.799774	0.00827816	0.142046	17.159086	0.05827816	5.83	1.331126	3.33	40
41	41	7.391988	127.839763	0.00782229	0.135282	17.294368	0.05782229	5.79	1.370714	3.34	41
42	42	7.761588	135.231751	0.00739471	0.128840	17.423208	0.05739471	5.74	1.410578	3.36	42
43	43	8.149667	142.993339	0.00699333	0.122704	17.545912	0.05699333	5.70	1.450713	3.37	43
44	44	8.557150	151.143006	0.00661625	0.116861	17.662773	0.05661625	5.67	1.491115	3.39	44
45	45	8.985008	159.700156	0.00626173	0.111297	17.774070	0.05626173	5.63	1.531778	3.40	45
46	46	9.434258	168.685164	0.00592820	0.105997	17.880066	0.05592820	5.60	1.572697	3.42	46
47	47	9.905971	178.119422	0.00561421	0.100949	17.981016	0.05561421	5.57	1.613868	3.43	47
48	48	10.401270	188.025393	0.00531843	0.096142	18.077158	0.05531843	5.54	1.655285	3.45	48
49	49	10.921333	198.426663	0.00503965	0.091564	18.168722	0.05503965	5.51	1.696943	3.46	49
50	50	11.467400	209.347996	0.00477674	0.087204	18.255925	0.05477674	5.48	1.738837	3.48	50

COMPOUND INTEREST AND ANNUITY TABLE

6.00 %
ANNUAL

		Amount Of 1	Amount Of 1 Per Period	Sinking Fund Payment	Present Worth Of 1	Present Worth Of 1 Per Period	Periodic Payment To Amortize 1	Constant Annual Percent	Total Interest	Annual Add-on Rate		
		What a single $1 deposit grows to in the future. The deposit is made at the beginning of the first period.	What a series of $1 deposits grow to in the future. A deposit is made at the end of each period.	The amount to be deposited at the end of each period that grows to $1 in the future.	What $1 to be paid in the future is worth today. Value today of a single payment tomorrow.	What $1 to be paid at the end of each period is worth today. Value today of a series of payments tomorrow.	The mortgage payment to amortize a loan of $1. An annuity certain, payable at the end of each period, worth $1 today.	The annual payment, including interest and principal, to amortize completely a loan of $100.	The total interest paid over the term on a loan of $1. The loan is amortized by regular periodic payments.	The average annual interest rate on a loan that is completely amortized by regular periodic payments.		
		$S=(1+i)^n$	$S_{\overline{n}}=\dfrac{(1+i)^n-1}{i}$	$\dfrac{1}{S_{\overline{n}}}=\dfrac{i}{(1+i)^n-1}$	$V^n=\dfrac{1}{(1+i)^n}$	$A_{\overline{n}}=\dfrac{1-V^n}{i}$	$\dfrac{1}{A_{\overline{n}}}=\dfrac{i}{1-V^n}$					
YR											**YR**
1	1	1.060000	1.000000	1.00000000	0.943396	0.943396	1.06000000	106.00	0.060000	6.00	1
2	2	1.123600	2.060000	0.48543689	0.889996	1.833393	0.54543689	54.55	0.090874	4.54	2
3	3	1.191016	3.183600	0.31410981	0.839619	2.673012	0.37410981	37.42	0.122329	4.08	3
4	4	1.262477	4.374616	0.22859149	0.792094	3.465106	0.28859149	28.86	0.154366	3.86	4
5	5	1.338226	5.637093	0.17739640	0.747258	4.212364	0.23739640	23.74	0.186982	3.74	5
6	6	1.418519	6.975319	0.14336263	0.704961	4.917324	0.20336263	20.34	0.220176	3.67	6
7	7	1.503630	8.393838	0.11913502	0.665057	5.582381	0.17913502	17.92	0.253945	3.63	7
8	8	1.593848	9.897464	0.10103594	0.627412	6.209794	0.16103594	16.11	0.288288	3.60	8
9	9	1.689479	11.491316	0.08702224	0.591898	6.801692	0.14702224	14.71	0.323200	3.59	9
10	10	1.790848	13.180795	0.07586796	0.558395	7.360087	0.13586796	13.59	0.358680	3.59	10
11	11	1.898299	14.971643	0.06679294	0.526788	7.886875	0.12679294	12.68	0.394722	3.59	11
12	12	2.012196	16.869941	0.05927703	0.496969	8.383844	0.11927703	11.93	0.431324	3.59	12
13	13	2.132928	18.882138	0.05296011	0.468839	8.852683	0.11296011	11.30	0.468481	3.60	13
14	14	2.260904	21.015066	0.04758491	0.442301	9.294984	0.10758491	10.76	0.506189	3.62	14
15	15	2.396558	23.275970	0.04296276	0.417265	9.712249	0.10296276	10.30	0.544441	3.63	15
16	16	2.540352	25.672528	0.03895214	0.393646	10.105895	0.09895214	9.90	0.583204	3.65	16
17	17	2.692773	28.212880	0.03544480	0.371364	10.477260	0.09544480	9.55	0.622562	3.66	17
18	18	2.854339	30.905653	0.03235654	0.350344	10.827603	0.09235654	9.24	0.662418	3.68	18
19	19	3.025600	33.759992	0.02962086	0.330513	11.158116	0.08962086	8.97	0.702796	3.70	19
20	20	3.207135	36.785591	0.02718456	0.311805	11.469921	0.08718456	8.72	0.743691	3.72	20
21	21	3.399564	39.992727	0.02500455	0.294155	11.764077	0.08500455	8.51	0.785095	3.74	21
22	22	3.603537	43.392290	0.02304557	0.277505	12.041582	0.08304557	8.31	0.827003	3.76	22
23	23	3.819750	46.995828	0.02127848	0.261797	12.303379	0.08127848	8.13	0.869405	3.78	23
24	24	4.048935	50.815577	0.01967900	0.246979	12.550358	0.07967900	7.97	0.912296	3.80	24
25	25	4.291871	54.864512	0.01822672	0.232999	12.783356	0.07822672	7.83	0.955668	3.82	25
26	26	4.549383	59.156383	0.01690435	0.219810	13.003166	0.07690435	7.70	0.999513	3.84	26
27	27	4.822346	63.705766	0.01569717	0.207368	13.210534	0.07569717	7.57	1.043823	3.87	27
28	28	5.111687	68.528112	0.01459255	0.195630	13.406164	0.07459255	7.46	1.088591	3.89	28
29	29	5.418388	73.639798	0.01357961	0.184557	13.590721	0.07357961	7.36	1.133809	3.91	29
30	30	5.743491	79.058186	0.01264891	0.174110	13.764831	0.07264891	7.27	1.179467	3.93	30
31	31	6.088101	84.801677	0.01179222	0.164255	13.929086	0.07179222	7.18	1.225559	3.95	31
32	32	6.453387	90.889778	0.01100234	0.154957	14.084043	0.07100234	7.11	1.272075	3.98	32
33	33	6.840590	97.343165	0.01027293	0.146186	14.230230	0.07027293	7.03	1.319007	4.00	33
34	34	7.251025	104.183755	0.00959843	0.137912	14.368141	0.06959843	6.96	1.366346	4.02	34
35	35	7.686087	111.434780	0.00897386	0.130105	14.498246	0.06897386	6.90	1.414085	4.04	35
36	36	8.147252	119.120867	0.00839483	0.122741	14.620987	0.06839483	6.84	1.462214	4.06	36
37	37	8.636087	127.268119	0.00785743	0.115793	14.736780	0.06785743	6.79	1.510725	4.08	37
38	38	9.154252	135.904206	0.00735812	0.109239	14.846019	0.06735812	6.74	1.559669	4.10	38
39	39	9.703507	145.058458	0.00689377	0.103056	14.949075	0.06689377	6.69	1.608857	4.13	39
40	40	10.285718	154.761966	0.00646154	0.097222	15.046297	0.06646154	6.65	1.658461	4.15	40
41	41	10.902861	165.047684	0.00605886	0.091719	15.138016	0.06605886	6.61	1.708413	4.17	41
42	42	11.557033	175.950545	0.00568342	0.086527	15.224543	0.06568342	6.57	1.758703	4.19	42
43	43	12.250455	187.507577	0.00533312	0.081630	15.306173	0.06533312	6.54	1.809324	4.21	43
44	44	12.985482	199.758032	0.00500606	0.077009	15.383182	0.06500606	6.51	1.860266	4.23	44
45	45	13.764611	212.743514	0.00470050	0.072650	15.455832	0.06470050	6.48	1.911522	4.25	45
46	46	14.590487	226.508125	0.00441485	0.068538	15.524370	0.06441485	6.45	1.963083	4.27	46
47	47	15.465917	241.098612	0.00414768	0.064658	15.589028	0.06414768	6.42	2.014941	4.29	47
48	48	16.393872	256.564529	0.00389765	0.060998	15.650027	0.06389765	6.39	2.067087	4.31	48
49	49	17.377504	272.958401	0.00366356	0.057546	15.707572	0.06366356	6.37	2.119515	4.33	49
50	50	18.420154	290.335905	0.00344429	0.054288	15.761861	0.06344429	6.35	2.172214	4.34	50

COMPOUND INTEREST AND ANNUITY TABLE

7.00 %
ANNUAL

		Amount Of 1	Amount Of 1 Per Period	Sinking Fund Payment	Present Worth Of 1	Present Worth Of 1 Per Period	Periodic Payment To Amortize 1	Constant Annual Percent	Total Interest	Annual Add-on Rate		
		What a single $1 deposit grows to in the future. The deposit is made at the beginning of the first period.	What a series of $1 deposits grow to in the future. A deposit is made at the end of each period.	The amount to be deposited at the end of each period that grows to $1 in the future.	What $1 to be paid in the future is worth today. Value today of a single payment tomorrow.	What $1 to be paid at the end of each period is worth today. Value today of a series of payments tomorrow.	The mortgage payment to amortize a loan of $1. An annuity certain, payable at the end of each period, worth $1 today.	The annual payment, including interest and principal, to amortize completely a loan of $100.	The total interest paid over the term of $1. The loan is amortized by regular periodic payments.	The average annual interest rate on a loan that is completely amortized by regular periodic payments.		
		$S=(1+i)^n$	$S_{\overline{n}}=\dfrac{(1+i)^n-1}{i}$	$\dfrac{1}{S_{\overline{n}}}=\dfrac{i}{(1+i)^n-1}$	$V^n=\dfrac{1}{(1+i)^n}$	$A_{\overline{n}}=\dfrac{1-V^n}{i}$	$\dfrac{1}{A_{\overline{n}}}=\dfrac{i}{1-V^n}$					
YR												**YR**
1	1	1.070000	1.000000	1.00000000	0.934579	0.934579	1.07000000	107.00	0.070000	7.00	1
2	2	1.144900	2.070000	0.48309179	0.873439	1.808018	0.55309179	55.31	0.106184	5.31	2
3	3	1.225043	3.214900	0.31105167	0.816298	2.624316	0.38105167	38.11	0.143155	4.77	3
4	4	1.310796	4.439943	0.22522812	0.762895	3.387211	0.29522812	29.53	0.180912	4.52	4
5	5	1.402552	5.750739	0.17389069	0.712986	4.100197	0.24389069	24.39	0.219453	4.39	5
6	6	1.500730	7.153291	0.13979580	0.666342	4.766540	0.20979580	20.98	0.258775	4.31	6
7	7	1.605781	8.654021	0.11555322	0.622750	5.389289	0.18555322	18.56	0.298873	4.27	7
8	8	1.718186	10.259803	0.09746776	0.582009	5.971299	0.16746776	16.75	0.339742	4.25	8
9	9	1.838459	11.977989	0.08348647	0.543934	6.515232	0.15348647	15.35	0.381378	4.24	9
10	10	1.967151	13.816448	0.07237750	0.508349	7.023582	0.14237750	14.24	0.423775	4.24	10
11	11	2.104852	15.783599	0.06335690	0.475093	7.498674	0.13335690	13.34	0.466926	4.24	11
12	12	2.252192	17.888451	0.05590199	0.444012	7.942686	0.12590199	12.60	0.510824	4.26	12
13	13	2.409845	20.140643	0.04965085	0.414964	8.357651	0.11965085	11.97	0.555461	4.27	13
14	14	2.578534	22.550488	0.04434494	0.387817	8.745468	0.11434494	11.44	0.600829	4.29	14
15	15	2.759032	25.129022	0.03979462	0.362446	9.107914	0.10979462	10.98	0.646919	4.31	15
16	16	2.952164	27.888054	0.03585765	0.338735	9.446649	0.10585765	10.59	0.693722	4.34	16
17	17	3.158815	30.840217	0.03242519	0.316574	9.763223	0.10242519	10.25	0.741228	4.36	17
18	18	3.379932	33.999033	0.02941260	0.295864	10.059087	0.09941260	9.95	0.789427	4.39	18
19	19	3.616528	37.378965	0.02675301	0.276508	10.335595	0.09675301	9.68	0.838307	4.41	19
20	20	3.869684	40.995492	0.02439293	0.258419	10.594014	0.09439293	9.44	0.887859	4.44	20
21	21	4.140562	44.865177	0.02228900	0.241513	10.835527	0.09228900	9.23	0.938069	4.47	21
22	22	4.430402	49.005739	0.02040577	0.225713	11.061240	0.09040577	9.05	0.988927	4.50	22
23	23	4.740530	53.436141	0.01871393	0.210947	11.272187	0.08871393	8.88	1.040420	4.52	23
24	24	5.072367	58.176671	0.01718960	0.197147	11.469334	0.08718960	8.72	1.092536	4.55	24
25	25	5.427433	63.249038	0.01581052	0.184249	11.653583	0.08581052	8.59	1.145263	4.58	25
26	26	5.807353	68.676470	0.01456103	0.172195	11.825779	0.08456103	8.46	1.198587	4.61	26
27	27	6.213868	74.483823	0.01342573	0.160930	11.986709	0.08342573	8.35	1.252495	4.64	27
28	28	6.648838	80.697691	0.01239193	0.150402	12.137111	0.08239193	8.24	1.306974	4.67	28
29	29	7.114257	87.346529	0.01144865	0.140563	12.277674	0.08144865	8.15	1.362011	4.70	29
30	30	7.612255	94.460786	0.01058640	0.131367	12.409041	0.08058640	8.06	1.417592	4.73	30
31	31	8.145113	102.073041	0.00979691	0.122773	12.531814	0.07979691	7.98	1.473704	4.75	31
32	32	8.715271	110.218154	0.00907292	0.114741	12.646555	0.07907292	7.91	1.530333	4.78	32
33	33	9.325340	118.933425	0.00840807	0.107235	12.753790	0.07840807	7.85	1.587466	4.81	33
34	34	9.978114	128.258765	0.00779674	0.100219	12.854009	0.07779674	7.78	1.645089	4.84	34
35	35	10.676581	138.236878	0.00723396	0.093663	12.947672	0.07723396	7.73	1.703189	4.87	35
36	36	11.423942	148.913460	0.00671531	0.087535	13.035208	0.07671531	7.68	1.761751	4.89	36
37	37	12.223618	160.337402	0.00623685	0.081809	13.117017	0.07623685	7.63	1.820763	4.92	37
38	38	13.079271	172.561020	0.00579505	0.076457	13.193473	0.07579505	7.58	1.880212	4.95	38
39	39	13.994820	185.640292	0.00538676	0.071455	13.264928	0.07538676	7.54	1.940084	4.97	39
40	40	14.974458	199.635112	0.00500914	0.066780	13.331709	0.07500914	7.51	2.000366	5.00	40
41	41	16.022670	214.609570	0.00465962	0.062412	13.394120	0.07465962	7.47	2.061045	5.03	41
42	42	17.144257	230.632240	0.00433591	0.058329	13.452449	0.07433591	7.44	2.122108	5.05	42
43	43	18.344355	247.776496	0.00403590	0.054513	13.506962	0.07403590	7.41	2.183543	5.08	43
44	44	19.628460	266.120851	0.00375769	0.050946	13.557908	0.07375769	7.38	2.245338	5.10	44
45	45	21.002452	285.749311	0.00349957	0.047613	13.605522	0.07349957	7.35	2.307481	5.13	45
46	46	22.472623	306.751763	0.00325996	0.044499	13.650020	0.07325996	7.33	2.369958	5.15	46
47	47	24.045707	329.224386	0.00303744	0.041587	13.691608	0.07303744	7.31	2.432760	5.18	47
48	48	25.728907	353.270093	0.00283070	0.038867	13.730474	0.07283070	7.29	2.495873	5.20	48
49	49	27.529930	378.999000	0.00263853	0.036324	13.766799	0.07263853	7.27	2.559288	5.22	49
50	50	29.457025	406.528929	0.00245985	0.033948	13.800746	0.07245985	7.25	2.622992	5.25	50

COMPOUND INTEREST AND ANNUITY TABLE

8.00 %
ANNUAL

	Amount Of 1	Amount Of 1 Per Period	Sinking Fund Payment	Present Worth Of 1	Present Worth Of 1 Per Period	Periodic Payment To Amortize 1	Constant Annual Percent	Total Interest	Annual Add-on Rate	
	What a single $1 deposit grows to in the future. The deposit is made at the beginning of the first period.	What a series of $1 deposits grow to in the future. A deposit is made at the end of each period.	The amount to be deposited at the end of each period that grows to $1 in the future.	What $1 to be paid in the future is worth today. Value today of a single payment tomorrow.	What $1 to be paid at the end of each period is worth today. Value today of a series of payments tomorrow.	The mortgage payment to amortize a loan of $1. An annuity certain, payable at the end of each period, worth $1 today.	The annual payment, including interest and principal, to amortize completely a loan of $100.	The total interest paid over the term on a loan of $1. The loan is amortized by regular periodic payments.	The average annual interest rate on a loan that is completely amortized by regular periodic payments.	
	$S=(1+i)^n$	$S_n=\dfrac{(1+i)^n-1}{i}$	$\dfrac{1}{S_n}=\dfrac{i}{(1+i)^n-1}$	$V^n=\dfrac{1}{(1+i)^n}$	$A_n=\dfrac{1-V^n}{i}$	$\dfrac{1}{A_n}=\dfrac{i}{1-V^n}$				
YR										YR
1	1.080000	1.000000	1.00000000	0.925926	0.925926	1.08000000	108.00	0.080000	8.00	1
2	1.166400	2.080000	0.48076923	0.857339	1.783265	0.56076923	56.08	0.121538	6.08	2
3	1.259712	3.246400	0.30803351	0.793832	2.577097	0.38803351	38.81	0.164101	5.47	3
4	1.360489	4.506112	0.22192080	0.735030	3.312127	0.30192080	30.20	0.207683	5.19	4
5	1.469328	5.866601	0.17045645	0.680583	3.992710	0.25045645	25.05	0.252292	5.05	5
6	1.586874	7.335929	0.13631539	0.630170	4.622880	0.21631539	21.64	0.297892	4.96	6
7	1.713824	8.922803	0.11207240	0.583490	5.206370	0.19207240	19.21	0.344507	4.92	7
8	1.850930	10.636628	0.09401476	0.540269	5.746639	0.17401476	17.41	0.392118	4.90	8
9	1.999005	12.487558	0.08007971	0.500249	6.246888	0.16007971	16.01	0.440717	4.90	9
10	2.158925	14.486562	0.06902949	0.463193	6.710081	0.14902949	14.91	0.490295	4.90	10
11	2.331639	16.645487	0.06007634	0.428883	7.138964	0.14007634	14.01	0.540840	4.92	11
12	2.518170	18.977126	0.05269502	0.397114	7.536078	0.13269502	13.27	0.592340	4.94	12
13	2.719624	21.495297	0.04652181	0.367698	7.903776	0.12652181	12.66	0.644783	4.96	13
14	2.937194	24.214920	0.04129685	0.340461	8.244237	0.12129685	12.13	0.698156	4.99	14
15	3.172169	27.152114	0.03682954	0.315242	8.559479	0.11682954	11.69	0.752443	5.02	15
16	3.425943	30.324283	0.03297687	0.291890	8.851369	0.11297687	11.30	0.807630	5.05	16
17	3.700018	33.750226	0.02962943	0.270269	9.121638	0.10962943	10.97	0.863700	5.08	17
18	3.996019	37.450244	0.02670210	0.250249	9.371887	0.10670210	10.68	0.920638	5.11	18
19	4.315701	41.446263	0.02412763	0.231712	9.603599	0.10412763	10.42	0.978425	5.15	19
20	4.660957	45.761964	0.02185221	0.214548	9.818147	0.10185221	10.19	1.037044	5.19	20
21	5.033834	50.422921	0.01983225	0.198656	10.016803	0.09983225	9.99	1.096477	5.22	21
22	5.436540	55.456755	0.01803207	0.183941	10.200744	0.09803207	9.81	1.156706	5.26	22
23	5.871464	60.893296	0.01642217	0.170315	10.371059	0.09642217	9.65	1.217710	5.29	23
24	6.341181	66.764759	0.01497796	0.157699	10.528758	0.09497796	9.50	1.279471	5.33	24
25	6.848475	73.105940	0.01367878	0.146010	10.674776	0.09367878	9.37	1.341969	5.37	25
26	7.396353	79.954415	0.01250713	0.135202	10.809978	0.09250713	9.26	1.405185	5.40	26
27	7.988061	87.350768	0.01144810	0.125187	10.935165	0.09144810	9.15	1.469099	5.44	27
28	8.627106	95.338830	0.01048891	0.115914	11.051078	0.09048891	9.05	1.533689	5.48	28
29	9.317275	103.965936	0.00961854	0.107328	11.158406	0.08961854	8.97	1.598938	5.51	29
30	10.062657	113.283211	0.00882743	0.099377	11.257783	0.08882743	8.89	1.664823	5.55	30
31	10.867669	123.345868	0.00810728	0.092016	11.349799	0.08810728	8.82	1.731326	5.58	31
32	11.737083	134.213537	0.00745081	0.085200	11.434999	0.08745081	8.75	1.798426	5.62	32
33	12.676050	145.950620	0.00685163	0.078889	11.513888	0.08685163	8.69	1.866104	5.65	33
34	13.690134	158.626670	0.00630411	0.073045	11.586934	0.08630411	8.64	1.934340	5.69	34
35	14.785344	172.316804	0.00580326	0.067635	11.654568	0.08580326	8.59	2.003114	5.72	35
36	15.968172	187.102148	0.00534467	0.062625	11.717193	0.08534467	8.54	2.072408	5.76	36
37	17.245626	203.070320	0.00492440	0.057986	11.775179	0.08492440	8.50	2.142203	5.79	37
38	18.625276	220.315945	0.00453894	0.053690	11.828869	0.08453894	8.46	2.212480	5.82	38
39	20.115298	238.941221	0.00418513	0.049713	11.878582	0.08418513	8.42	2.283220	5.85	39
40	21.724521	259.056519	0.00386016	0.046031	11.924613	0.08386016	8.39	2.354406	5.89	40
41	23.462483	280.781040	0.00356149	0.042621	11.967235	0.08356149	8.36	2.426021	5.92	41
42	25.339482	304.243523	0.00328684	0.039464	12.006699	0.08328684	8.33	2.498047	5.95	42
43	27.366640	329.583005	0.00303414	0.036541	12.043240	0.08303414	8.31	2.570468	5.98	43
44	29.555972	356.949646	0.00280152	0.033834	12.077074	0.08280152	8.29	2.643267	6.01	44
45	31.920449	386.505617	0.00258728	0.031328	12.108402	0.08258728	8.26	2.716428	6.04	45
46	34.474085	418.426067	0.00238991	0.029007	12.137409	0.08238991	8.24	2.789936	6.07	46
47	37.232012	452.900152	0.00220799	0.026859	12.164267	0.08220799	8.23	2.863776	6.09	47
48	40.210573	490.132164	0.00204027	0.024869	12.189136	0.08204027	8.21	2.937933	6.12	48
49	43.427419	530.342737	0.00188557	0.023027	12.212163	0.08188557	8.19	3.012393	6.15	49
50	46.901613	573.770156	0.00174286	0.021321	12.233485	0.08174286	8.18	3.087143	6.17	50

COMPOUND INTEREST AND ANNUITY TABLE

9.00 %
ANNUAL

		Amount Of 1	Amount Of 1 Per Period	Sinking Fund Payment	Present Worth Of 1	Present Worth Of 1 Per Period	Periodic Payment To Amortize 1	Constant Annual Percent	Total Interest	Annual Add-on Rate		
		What a single $1 deposit grows to in the future. The deposit is made at the beginning of the first period.	What a series of $1 deposits grow to in the future. A deposit is made at the end of each period.	The amount to be deposited at the end of each period that grows to $1 in the future.	What $1 to be paid in the future is worth today. Value today of a single payment tomorrow.	What $1 to be paid at the end of each period is worth today. Value today of a series of payments tomorrow.	The mortgage payment to amortize a loan of $1. An annuity certain, payable at the end of each period, worth $1 today.	The annual payment, including interest and principal, to amortize completely a loan of $100.	The total interest paid over the term of $1. The loan is amortized by regular periodic payments.	The average annual interest rate on a loan that is completely amortized by regular periodic payments.		
		$S=(1+i)^n$	$S_{\overline{n}}=\frac{(1+i)^n-1}{i}$	$\frac{1}{S_{\overline{n}}}=\frac{i}{(1+i)^n-1}$	$V^n=\frac{1}{(1+i)^n}$	$A_{\overline{n}}=\frac{1-V^n}{i}$	$\frac{1}{A_{\overline{n}}}=\frac{i}{1-V^n}$					
YR												YR
1	1	1.090000	1.000000	1.00000000	0.917431	0.917431	1.09000000	109.00	0.090000	9.00	1
2	2	1.188100	2.090000	0.47846890	0.841680	1.759111	0.56846890	56.85	0.136938	6.85	2
3	3	1.295029	3.278100	0.30505476	0.772183	2.531295	0.39505476	39.51	0.185164	6.17	3
4	4	1.411582	4.573129	0.21866866	0.708425	3.239720	0.30866866	30.87	0.234675	5.87	4
5	5	1.538624	5.984711	0.16709246	0.649931	3.889651	0.25709246	25.71	0.285462	5.71	5
6	6	1.677100	7.523335	0.13291978	0.596267	4.485919	0.22291978	22.30	0.337519	5.63	6
7	7	1.828039	9.200435	0.10869052	0.547034	5.032953	0.19869052	19.87	0.390834	5.58	7
8	8	1.992563	11.028474	0.09067438	0.501866	5.534819	0.18067438	18.07	0.445395	5.57	8
9	9	2.171893	13.021036	0.07679880	0.460428	5.995247	0.16679880	16.68	0.501189	5.57	9
10	10	2.367364	15.192930	0.06582009	0.422411	6.417658	0.15582009	15.59	0.558201	5.58	10
11	11	2.580426	17.560293	0.05694666	0.387533	6.805191	0.14694666	14.70	0.616413	5.60	11
12	12	2.812665	20.140720	0.04965606	0.355535	7.160725	0.13965606	13.97	0.675808	5.63	12
13	13	3.065805	22.953385	0.04356656	0.326179	7.486904	0.13356656	13.36	0.736365	5.66	13
14	14	3.341727	26.019189	0.03843417	0.299246	7.786150	0.12843417	12.85	0.798064	5.70	14
15	15	3.642482	29.360916	0.03405888	0.274538	8.060688	0.12405888	12.41	0.860883	5.74	15
16	16	3.970306	33.003399	0.03029991	0.251870	8.312558	0.12029991	12.03	0.924799	5.78	16
17	17	4.327633	36.973705	0.02704625	0.231073	8.543631	0.11704625	11.71	0.989786	5.82	17
18	18	4.717120	41.301338	0.02421229	0.211994	8.755625	0.11421229	11.43	1.055821	5.87	18
19	19	5.141661	46.018458	0.02173041	0.194490	8.950115	0.11173041	11.18	1.122878	5.91	19
20	20	5.604411	51.160120	0.01954648	0.178431	9.128546	0.10954648	10.96	1.190930	5.95	20
21	21	6.108808	56.764530	0.01761663	0.163698	9.292244	0.10761663	10.77	1.259949	6.00	21
22	22	6.658600	62.873338	0.01590499	0.150182	9.442425	0.10590499	10.60	1.329910	6.05	22
23	23	7.257874	69.531939	0.01438188	0.137781	9.580207	0.10438188	10.44	1.400783	6.09	23
24	24	7.911083	76.789813	0.01302256	0.126405	9.706612	0.10302256	10.31	1.472541	6.14	24
25	25	8.623081	84.700896	0.01180625	0.115968	9.822580	0.10180625	10.19	1.545156	6.18	25
26	26	9.399158	93.323977	0.01071536	0.106393	9.928972	0.10071536	10.08	1.618599	6.23	26
27	27	10.245082	102.723135	0.00973491	0.097608	10.026580	0.09973491	9.98	1.692842	6.27	27
28	28	11.167140	112.968217	0.00885205	0.089548	10.116128	0.09885205	9.89	1.767857	6.31	28
29	29	12.172182	124.135356	0.00805502	0.082155	10.198283	0.09805502	9.81	1.843616	6.36	29
30	30	13.267678	136.307539	0.00733635	0.075371	10.273654	0.09733635	9.74	1.920091	6.40	30
31	31	14.461770	149.575217	0.00668560	0.069148	10.342802	0.09668560	9.67	1.997254	6.44	31
32	32	15.763329	164.036987	0.00609619	0.063438	10.406240	0.09609619	9.61	2.075078	6.48	32
33	33	17.182028	179.800315	0.00556173	0.058200	10.464441	0.09556173	9.56	2.153537	6.53	33
34	34	18.728411	196.982344	0.00507660	0.053395	10.517835	0.09507660	9.51	2.232604	6.57	34
35	35	20.413968	215.710755	0.00463584	0.048986	10.566821	0.09463584	9.47	2.312254	6.61	35
36	36	22.251225	236.124723	0.00423505	0.044941	10.611763	0.09423505	9.43	2.392462	6.65	36
37	37	24.253835	258.375948	0.00387033	0.041231	10.652993	0.09387033	9.39	2.473202	6.68	37
38	38	26.436680	282.629783	0.00353820	0.037826	10.690820	0.09353820	9.36	2.554452	6.72	38
39	39	28.815982	309.066463	0.00323555	0.034703	10.725523	0.09323555	9.33	2.636186	6.76	39
40	40	31.409420	337.882445	0.00295961	0.031838	10.757360	0.09295961	9.30	2.718384	6.80	40
41	41	34.236268	369.291865	0.00270789	0.029209	10.786569	0.09270789	9.28	2.801023	6.83	41
42	42	37.317532	403.528133	0.00247814	0.026797	10.813366	0.09247814	9.25	2.884082	6.87	42
43	43	40.676110	440.845665	0.00226837	0.024584	10.837950	0.09226837	9.23	2.967540	6.90	43
44	44	44.336960	481.521775	0.00207675	0.022555	10.860505	0.09207675	9.21	3.051377	6.93	44
45	45	48.327286	525.858734	0.00190165	0.020692	10.881197	0.09190165	9.20	3.135574	6.97	45
46	46	52.676742	574.186021	0.00174160	0.018984	10.900181	0.09174160	9.18	3.220113	7.00	46
47	47	57.417649	626.862762	0.00159525	0.017416	10.917597	0.09159525	9.16	3.304977	7.03	47
48	48	62.585237	684.280411	0.00146139	0.015978	10.933575	0.09146139	9.15	3.390147	7.06	48
49	49	68.217908	746.865648	0.00133893	0.014659	10.948234	0.09133893	9.14	3.475608	7.09	49
50	50	74.357520	815.083556	0.00122687	0.013449	10.961683	0.09122687	9.13	3.561343	7.12	50

COMPOUND INTEREST AND ANNUITY TABLE

**10.00 %
ANNUAL**

		Amount Of 1	Amount Of 1 Per Period	Sinking Fund Payment	Present Worth Of 1	Present Worth Of 1 Per Period	Periodic Payment To Amortize 1	Constant Annual Percent	Total Interest	Annual Add-on Rate		
		What a single $1 deposit grows to in the future. The deposit is made at the beginning of the first period.	What a series of $1 deposits grow to in the future. A deposit is made at the end of each period.	The amount to be deposited at the end of each period that grows to $1 in the future.	What $1 to be paid in the future is worth today. Value today of a single payment tomorrow.	What $1 to be paid at the end of each period is worth today. Value today of a series of payments tomorrow.	The mortgage payment to amortize a loan of $1. An annuity certain, payable at the end of each period, worth $1 today.	The annual payment, including interest and principal, to amortize completely a loan of $100.	The total interest paid over the term on a loan of $1. The loan is amortized by regular periodic payments.	The average annual interest rate on a loan that is completely amortized by regular periodic payments.		
		$S=(1+i)^n$	$S_{\overline{n}}=\frac{(1+i)^n-1}{i}$	$\frac{1}{S_{\overline{n}}}=\frac{i}{(1+i)^n-1}$	$V^n=\frac{1}{(1+i)^n}$	$A_{\overline{n}}=\frac{1-V^n}{i}$	$\frac{1}{A_{\overline{n}}}=\frac{i}{1-V^n}$					
YR												YR
1	1	1.100000	1.000000	1.00000000	0.909091	0.909091	1.10000000	110.00	0.100000	10.00	1
2	2	1.210000	2.100000	0.47619048	0.826446	1.735537	0.57619048	57.62	0.152381	7.62	2
3	3	1.331000	3.310000	0.30211480	0.751315	2.486852	0.40211480	40.22	0.206344	6.88	3
4	4	1.464100	4.641000	0.21547080	0.683013	3.169865	0.31547080	31.55	0.261883	6.55	4
5	5	1.610510	6.105100	0.16379748	0.620921	3.790787	0.26379748	26.38	0.318987	6.38	5
6	6	1.771561	7.715610	0.12960738	0.564474	4.355261	0.22960738	22.97	0.377644	6.29	6
7	7	1.948717	9.487171	0.10540550	0.513158	4.868419	0.20540550	20.55	0.437838	6.25	7
8	8	2.143589	11.435888	0.08744402	0.466507	5.334926	0.18744402	18.75	0.499552	6.24	8
9	9	2.357948	13.579477	0.07364054	0.424098	5.759024	0.17364054	17.37	0.562765	6.25	9
10	10	2.593742	15.937425	0.06274539	0.385543	6.144567	0.16274539	16.28	0.627454	6.27	10
11	11	2.853117	18.531167	0.05396314	0.350494	6.495061	0.15396314	15.40	0.693595	6.31	11
12	12	3.138428	21.384284	0.04676332	0.318631	6.813692	0.14676332	14.68	0.761160	6.34	12
13	13	3.452271	24.522712	0.04077852	0.289664	7.103356	0.14077852	14.08	0.830121	6.39	13
14	14	3.797498	27.974983	0.03574622	0.263331	7.366687	0.13574622	13.58	0.900447	6.43	14
15	15	4.177248	31.772482	0.03147378	0.239392	7.606080	0.13147378	13.15	0.972107	6.48	15
16	16	4.594973	35.949730	0.02781662	0.217629	7.823709	0.12781662	12.79	1.045066	6.53	16
17	17	5.054470	40.544703	0.02466413	0.197845	8.021553	0.12466413	12.47	1.119290	6.58	17
18	18	5.559917	45.599173	0.02193022	0.179859	8.201412	0.12193022	12.20	1.194744	6.64	18
19	19	6.115909	51.159090	0.01954687	0.163508	8.364920	0.11954687	11.96	1.271390	6.69	19
20	20	6.727500	57.274999	0.01745962	0.148644	8.513564	0.11745962	11.75	1.349192	6.75	20
21	21	7.400250	64.002499	0.01562439	0.135131	8.648694	0.11562439	11.57	1.428112	6.80	21
22	22	8.140275	71.402749	0.01400506	0.122846	8.771540	0.11400506	11.41	1.508111	6.86	22
23	23	8.954302	79.543024	0.01257181	0.111678	8.883218	0.11257181	11.26	1.589152	6.91	23
24	24	9.849733	88.497327	0.01129978	0.101526	8.984744	0.11129978	11.13	1.671195	6.96	24
25	25	10.834706	98.347059	0.01016807	0.092296	9.077040	0.11016807	11.02	1.754202	7.02	25
26	26	11.918177	109.181765	0.00915904	0.083905	9.160945	0.10915904	10.92	1.838135	7.07	26
27	27	13.109994	121.099942	0.00825764	0.076278	9.237223	0.10825764	10.83	1.922956	7.12	27
28	28	14.420994	134.209936	0.00745101	0.069343	9.306567	0.10745101	10.75	2.008628	7.17	28
29	29	15.863093	148.630930	0.00672807	0.063039	9.369606	0.10672807	10.68	2.095114	7.22	29
30	30	17.449402	164.494023	0.00607925	0.057309	9.426914	0.10607925	10.61	2.182377	7.27	30
31	31	19.194342	181.943425	0.00549621	0.052099	9.479013	0.10549621	10.55	2.270383	7.32	31
32	32	21.113777	201.137767	0.00497172	0.047362	9.526376	0.10497172	10.50	2.359095	7.37	32
33	33	23.225154	222.251544	0.00449941	0.043057	9.569432	0.10449941	10.45	2.448480	7.42	33
34	34	25.547670	245.476699	0.00407371	0.039143	9.608575	0.10407371	10.41	2.538506	7.47	34
35	35	28.102437	271.024368	0.00368971	0.035584	9.644159	0.10368971	10.37	2.629140	7.51	35
36	36	30.912681	299.126805	0.00334306	0.032349	9.676508	0.10334306	10.34	2.720350	7.56	36
37	37	34.003949	330.039486	0.00302994	0.029408	9.705917	0.10302994	10.31	2.812108	7.60	37
38	38	37.404343	364.043434	0.00274692	0.026735	9.732651	0.10274692	10.28	2.904383	7.64	38
39	39	41.144778	401.447778	0.00249098	0.024304	9.756956	0.10249098	10.25	2.997148	7.68	39
40	40	45.259256	442.592556	0.00225941	0.022095	9.779051	0.10225941	10.23	3.090377	7.73	40
41	41	49.785181	487.851811	0.00204980	0.020086	9.799137	0.10204980	10.21	3.184042	7.77	41
42	42	54.763699	537.636992	0.00185999	0.018260	9.817397	0.10185999	10.19	3.278120	7.81	42
43	43	60.240069	592.400692	0.00168805	0.016600	9.833998	0.10168805	10.17	3.372586	7.84	43
44	44	66.264076	652.640761	0.00153224	0.015091	9.849089	0.10153224	10.16	3.467418	7.88	44
45	45	72.890484	718.904837	0.00139100	0.013719	9.862808	0.10139100	10.14	3.562595	7.92	45
46	46	80.179532	791.795321	0.00126295	0.012472	9.875280	0.10126295	10.13	3.658096	7.95	46
47	47	88.197485	871.974853	0.00114682	0.011338	9.886618	0.10114682	10.12	3.753901	7.99	47
48	48	97.017234	960.172338	0.00104148	0.010307	9.896926	0.10104148	10.11	3.849991	8.02	48
49	49	106.718957	1057.189572	0.00094590	0.009370	9.906296	0.10094590	10.10	3.946349	8.05	49
50	50	117.390853	1163.908529	0.00085917	0.008519	9.914814	0.10085917	10.09	4.042959	8.09	50

COMPOUND INTEREST AND ANNUITY TABLE

11.00 %
ANNUAL

		Amount Of 1	Amount Of 1 Per Period	Sinking Fund Payment	Present Worth Of 1	Present Worth Of 1 Per Period	Periodic Payment To Amortize 1	Constant Annual Percent	Total Interest	Annual Add-on Rate		
		What a single $1 deposit grows to in the future. The deposit is made at the beginning of the first period.	What a series of $1 deposits grow to in the future. A deposit is made at the end of each period.	The amount to be deposited at the end of each period that grows to $1 in the future.	What $1 to be paid in the future is worth today. Value today of a single payment tomorrow.	What $1 to be paid at the end of each period is worth today. Value today of a series of payments tomorrow.	The mortgage payment to amortize a loan of $1. An annuity to amortize, certain, payable at the end of each period, worth $1 today.	The annual payment, including interest and principal, to amortize completely a loan of $100.	The total interest paid over the term on a loan of $1. The loan is completely amortized by regular periodic payments.	The average annual interest rate on a loan that is completely amortized by regular periodic payments.		
		$S=(1+i)^n$	$S_{\overline{n}}=\dfrac{(1+i)^n-1}{i}$	$\dfrac{1}{S_{\overline{n}}}=\dfrac{i}{(1+i)^n-1}$	$V_n=\dfrac{1}{(1+i)^n}$	$A_{\overline{n}}=\dfrac{1-V_n}{i}$	$\dfrac{1}{A_{\overline{n}}}=\dfrac{i}{1-V_n}$					
YR												**YR**
1	1	1.110000	1.000000	1.00000000	0.900901	0.900901	1.11000000	111.00	0.110000	11.00	1
2	2	1.232100	2.110000	0.47393365	0.811622	1.712523	0.58393365	58.40	0.167867	8.39	2
3	3	1.367631	3.342100	0.29921307	0.731191	2.443715	0.40921307	40.93	0.227639	7.59	3
4	4	1.518070	4.709731	0.21232635	0.658731	3.102446	0.32232635	32.24	0.289305	7.23	4
5	5	1.685058	6.227801	0.16057031	0.593451	3.695897	0.27057031	27.06	0.352852	7.06	5
6	6	1.870415	7.912860	0.12637656	0.534641	4.230538	0.23637656	23.64	0.418259	6.97	6
7	7	2.076160	9.783274	0.10221527	0.481658	4.712196	0.21221527	21.23	0.485507	6.94	7
8	8	2.304538	11.859434	0.08432105	0.433926	5.146123	0.19432105	19.44	0.554568	6.93	8
9	9	2.558037	14.163972	0.07060166	0.390925	5.537048	0.18060166	18.07	0.625415	6.95	9
10	10	2.839421	16.722009	0.05980143	0.352184	5.889232	0.16980143	16.99	0.698014	6.98	10
11	11	3.151757	19.561430	0.05112101	0.317283	6.206515	0.16112101	16.12	0.772331	7.02	11
12	12	3.498451	22.713187	0.04402729	0.285841	6.492356	0.15402729	15.41	0.848327	7.07	12
13	13	3.883280	26.211638	0.03815099	0.257514	6.749870	0.14815099	14.82	0.925963	7.12	13
14	14	4.310441	30.094918	0.03322820	0.231995	6.981865	0.14322820	14.33	1.005195	7.18	14
15	15	4.784589	34.405359	0.02906524	0.209004	7.190870	0.13906524	13.91	1.085979	7.24	15
16	16	5.310894	39.189948	0.02551675	0.188292	7.379162	0.13551675	13.56	1.168268	7.30	16
17	17	5.895093	44.500843	0.02247148	0.169633	7.548794	0.13247148	13.25	1.252015	7.36	17
18	18	6.543553	50.395936	0.01984287	0.152822	7.701617	0.12984287	12.99	1.337172	7.43	18
19	19	7.263344	56.939488	0.01756250	0.137678	7.839294	0.12756250	12.76	1.423688	7.49	19
20	20	8.062312	64.202832	0.01557564	0.124034	7.963328	0.12557564	12.56	1.511513	7.56	20
21	21	8.949166	72.265144	0.01383793	0.111742	8.075070	0.12383793	12.39	1.600597	7.62	21
22	22	9.933574	81.214309	0.01231310	0.100669	8.175739	0.12231310	12.24	1.690888	7.69	22
23	23	11.026267	91.147884	0.01097118	0.090693	8.266432	0.12097118	12.10	1.782337	7.75	23
24	24	12.239157	102.174151	0.00978721	0.081705	8.348137	0.11978721	11.98	1.874893	7.81	24
25	25	13.585464	114.413307	0.00874024	0.073608	8.421745	0.11874024	11.88	1.968506	7.87	25
26	26	15.079865	127.998771	0.00781258	0.066314	8.488058	0.11781258	11.79	2.063127	7.94	26
27	27	16.738650	143.078636	0.00698916	0.059742	8.547800	0.11698916	11.70	2.158707	8.00	27
28	28	18.579901	159.817286	0.00625715	0.053822	8.601622	0.11625715	11.63	2.255200	8.05	28
29	29	20.623691	178.397187	0.00560547	0.048488	8.650110	0.11560547	11.57	2.352559	8.11	29
30	30	22.892297	199.020878	0.00502460	0.043683	8.693793	0.11502460	11.51	2.450738	8.17	30
31	31	25.410449	221.913174	0.00450627	0.039354	8.733146	0.11450627	11.46	2.549694	8.22	31
32	32	28.205599	247.323624	0.00404329	0.035454	8.768600	0.11404329	11.41	2.649385	8.28	32
33	33	31.308214	275.529222	0.00362938	0.031940	8.800541	0.11362938	11.37	2.749770	8.33	33
34	34	34.752118	306.837437	0.00325905	0.028775	8.829316	0.11325905	11.33	2.850808	8.38	34
35	35	38.574851	341.589555	0.00292749	0.025924	8.855240	0.11292749	11.30	2.952662	8.44	35
36	36	42.818085	380.164406	0.00263044	0.023355	8.878594	0.11263044	11.27	3.054696	8.49	36
37	37	47.528074	422.982490	0.00236416	0.021040	8.899635	0.11236416	11.24	3.157474	8.53	37
38	38	52.756162	470.510564	0.00212535	0.018955	8.918590	0.11212535	11.22	3.260763	8.58	38
39	39	58.559340	523.266726	0.00191107	0.017077	8.935666	0.11191107	11.20	3.364532	8.63	39
40	40	65.000867	581.826066	0.00171873	0.015384	8.951051	0.11171873	11.18	3.468749	8.67	40
41	41	72.150963	646.826934	0.00154601	0.013860	8.964911	0.11154601	11.16	3.573386	8.72	41
42	42	80.087569	718.977896	0.00139086	0.012486	8.977397	0.11139086	11.14	3.678416	8.76	42
43	43	88.897201	799.065465	0.00125146	0.011249	8.988646	0.11125146	11.13	3.783813	8.80	43
44	44	98.675893	887.962666	0.00112617	0.010134	8.998780	0.11112617	11.12	3.889552	8.84	44
45	45	109.530242	986.638559	0.00101354	0.009130	9.007910	0.11101354	11.11	3.995609	8.88	45
46	46	121.578568	1096.168801	0.00091227	0.008225	9.016135	0.11091227	11.10	4.101964	8.92	46
47	47	134.952211	1217.747369	0.00082119	0.007410	9.023545	0.11082119	11.09	4.208596	8.35	47
48	48	149.796954	1352.699580	0.00073926	0.006676	9.030221	0.11073926	11.08	4.315485	8.99	48
49	49	166.274619	1502.496533	0.00066556	0.006014	9.036235	0.11066556	11.07	4.422612	9.03	49
50	50	184.564827	1668.771152	0.00059924	0.005418	9.041653	0.11059924	11.06	4.529962	9.06	50

COMPOUND INTEREST AND ANNUITY TABLE

12.00 %
ANNUAL

	Amount Of 1	Amount Of 1 Per Period	Sinking Fund Payment	Present Worth Of 1	Present Worth Of 1 Per Period	Periodic Payment To Amortize 1	Constant Annual Percent	Total Interest	Annual Add-on Rate	
	What a single $1 deposit grows to in the future. The deposit is made at the beginning of the first period.	What a series of $1 deposits grow to in the future. A deposit is made at the end of each period.	The amount to be deposited at the end of each period that grows to $1 in the future.	What $1 to be paid in the future is worth today. Value today of a single payment tomorrow.	What $1 to be paid at the end of each period is worth today. Value today of a series of payments tomorrow.	The mortgage payment to amortize a loan of $1. An annuity certain, payable at the end of each period, worth $1 today.	The annual payment, including interest and principal, to amortize completely a loan of $100.	The total interest paid over the term on a loan of $1. The loan is amortized by regular periodic payments.	The average annual interest rate on a loan that is completely amortized by regular periodic payments.	
	$S = (1+i)^n$	$S_{\overline{n}} = \dfrac{(1+i)^n - 1}{i}$	$\dfrac{1}{S_{\overline{n}}} = \dfrac{i}{(1+i)^n - 1}$	$V^n = \dfrac{1}{(1+i)^n}$	$A_{\overline{n}} = \dfrac{1 - V^n}{i}$	$\dfrac{1}{A_{\overline{n}}} = \dfrac{i}{1 - V^n}$				
YR										YR
1	1.120000	1.000000	1.00000000	0.892857	0.892857	1.12000000	112.00	0.120000	12.00	1
2	1.254400	2.120000	0.47169811	0.797194	1.690051	0.59169811	59.17	0.183396	9.17	2
3	1.404928	3.374400	0.29634898	0.711780	2.401831	0.41634898	41.64	0.249047	8.30	3
4	1.573519	4.779328	0.20923444	0.635518	3.037349	0.32923444	32.93	0.316938	7.92	4
5	1.762342	6.352847	0.15740973	0.567427	3.604776	0.27740973	27.75	0.387049	7.74	5
6	1.973823	8.115189	0.12322572	0.506631	4.111407	0.24322572	24.33	0.459354	7.66	6
7	2.210681	10.089012	0.09911774	0.452349	4.563757	0.21911774	21.92	0.533824	7.63	7
8	2.475963	12.299693	0.08130284	0.403883	4.967640	0.20130284	20.14	0.610423	7.63	8
9	2.773079	14.775656	0.06767889	0.360610	5.328250	0.18767889	18.77	0.689110	7.66	9
10	3.105848	17.548735	0.05698416	0.321973	5.650223	0.17698416	17.70	0.769842	7.70	10
11	3.478550	20.654583	0.04841540	0.287476	5.937699	0.16841540	16.85	0.852569	7.75	11
12	3.895976	24.133133	0.04143681	0.256675	6.194374	0.16143681	16.15	0.937242	7.81	12
13	4.363493	28.029109	0.03567720	0.229174	6.423548	0.15567720	15.57	1.023804	7.88	13
14	4.887112	32.392602	0.03087125	0.204620	6.628168	0.15087125	15.09	1.112197	7.94	14
15	5.473566	37.279715	0.02682424	0.182696	6.810864	0.14682424	14.69	1.202364	8.02	15
16	6.130394	42.753280	0.02339002	0.163122	6.973986	0.14339002	14.34	1.294240	8.09	16
17	6.866041	48.883674	0.02045673	0.145644	7.119630	0.14045673	14.05	1.387764	8.16	17
18	7.689966	55.749715	0.01793731	0.130040	7.249670	0.13793731	13.80	1.482872	8.24	18
19	8.612762	63.439681	0.01576300	0.116107	7.365777	0.13576300	13.58	1.579497	8.31	19
20	9.646293	72.052442	0.01387878	0.103667	7.469444	0.13387878	13.39	1.677576	8.39	20
21	10.803848	81.698736	0.01224009	0.092560	7.562003	0.13224009	13.23	1.777042	8.46	21
22	12.100310	92.502584	0.01081051	0.082643	7.644646	0.13081051	13.09	1.877831	8.54	22
23	13.552347	104.602894	0.00955996	0.073788	7.718434	0.12955996	12.96	1.979879	8.61	23
24	15.178629	118.155241	0.00846344	0.065882	7.784316	0.12846344	12.85	2.083123	8.68	24
25	17.000064	133.333870	0.00749997	0.058823	7.843139	0.12749997	12.75	2.187499	8.75	25
26	19.040072	150.333934	0.00665186	0.052521	7.895660	0.12665186	12.67	2.292948	8.82	26
27	21.324881	169.374007	0.00590409	0.046894	7.942554	0.12590409	12.60	2.399411	8.89	27
28	23.883866	190.698887	0.00524387	0.041869	7.984423	0.12524387	12.53	2.506828	8.95	28
29	26.749930	214.582754	0.00466021	0.037383	8.021806	0.12466021	12.47	2.615146	9.02	29
30	29.959922	241.332684	0.00414366	0.033378	8.055184	0.12414366	12.42	2.724310	9.08	30
31	33.555113	271.292606	0.00368606	0.029802	8.084986	0.12368606	12.37	2.834268	9.14	31
32	37.581726	304.847719	0.00328033	0.026609	8.111594	0.12328033	12.33	2.944970	9.20	32
33	42.091533	342.429446	0.00292031	0.023758	8.135352	0.12292031	12.30	3.056370	9.26	33
34	47.142517	384.520979	0.00260064	0.021212	8.156564	0.12260064	12.27	3.168422	9.32	34
35	52.799620	431.663496	0.00231662	0.018940	8.175504	0.12231662	12.24	3.281082	9.37	35
36	59.135574	484.463116	0.00206414	0.016910	8.192414	0.12206414	12.21	3.394309	9.43	36
37	66.231843	543.598690	0.00183959	0.015098	8.207513	0.12183959	12.19	3.508065	9.48	37
38	74.179664	609.830533	0.00163980	0.013481	8.220993	0.12163980	12.17	3.622312	9.53	38
39	83.081224	684.010197	0.00146197	0.012036	8.233030	0.12146197	12.15	3.737017	9.58	39
40	93.050970	767.091420	0.00130363	0.010747	8.243777	0.12130363	12.14	3.852145	9.63	40
41	104.217087	860.142391	0.00116260	0.009595	8.253372	0.12116260	12.12	3.967667	9.68	41
42	116.723137	964.359478	0.00103696	0.008567	8.261939	0.12103696	12.11	4.083552	9.72	42
43	130.729914	1081.082615	0.00092500	0.007649	8.269589	0.12092500	12.10	4.199775	9.77	43
44	146.417503	1211.812529	0.00082521	0.006830	8.276418	0.12082521	12.09	4.316309	9.81	44
45	163.987604	1358.230032	0.00073625	0.006098	8.282516	0.12073625	12.08	4.433131	9.85	45
46	183.666116	1522.217636	0.00065694	0.005445	8.287961	0.12065694	12.07	4.550219	9.89	46
47	205.706050	1705.883752	0.00058621	0.004861	8.292822	0.12058621	12.06	4.667552	9.93	47
48	230.390776	1911.589803	0.00052321	0.004340	8.297163	0.12052321	12.06	4.785110	9.97	48
49	258.037669	2141.980579	0.00046686	0.003875	8.301038	0.12046686	12.05	4.902876	10.01	49
50	289.002190	2400.018249	0.00041666	0.003460	8.304498	0.12041666	12.05	5.020833	10.04	50

COMPOUND INTEREST AND ANNUITY TABLE

13.00 %
ANNUAL

	Amount Of 1	Amount Of 1 Per Period	Sinking Fund Payment	Present Worth Of 1	Present Worth Of 1 Per Period	Periodic Payment To Amortize 1	Constant Annual Percent	Total Interest	Annual Add-on Rate	
	What a single $1 deposit grows to in the future. The deposit is made at the beginning of the first period.	What a series of $1 deposits grow to in the future. A deposit is made at the end of each period.	The amount to be deposited at the end of each period that grows to $1 in the future.	What $1 to be paid in the future is worth today. Value today of a single payment tomorrow.	What $1 to be paid at the end of each period is worth today. Value today of a series of payments tomorrow.	The mortgage payment to amortize a loan of $1. An annuity certain, payable at the end of each period, worth $1 today.	The annual payment, including interest and principal, to amortize completely a loan of $100.	The total interest paid over the term on a loan of $1. The loan is amortized by regular periodic payments.	The average annual interest rate on a loan that is completely amortized by regular periodic payments.	
	$S=(1+i)^n$	$S_{\overline{n}}=\dfrac{(1+i)^n-1}{i}$	$\dfrac{1}{S_{\overline{n}}}=\dfrac{i}{(1+i)^n-1}$	$V^n=\dfrac{1}{(1+i)^n}$	$A_{\overline{n}}=\dfrac{1-V^n}{i}$	$\dfrac{1}{A_{\overline{n}}}=\dfrac{i}{1-V^n}$				
YR										**YR**
1	1.130000	1.000000	1.00000000	0.884956	0.884956	1.13000000	113.00	0.130000	13.00	1
2	1.276900	2.130000	0.46948357	0.783147	1.668102	0.59948357	59.95	0.198967	9.95	2
3	1.442897	3.406900	0.29352197	0.693050	2.361153	0.42352197	42.36	0.270566	9.02	3
4	1.630474	4.849797	0.20619420	0.613319	2.974471	0.33619420	33.62	0.344777	8.62	4
5	1.842435	6.480271	0.15431454	0.542760	3.517231	0.28431454	28.44	0.421573	8.43	5
6	2.081952	8.322706	0.12015323	0.480319	3.997550	0.25015323	25.02	0.500919	8.35	6
7	2.352605	10.404658	0.09611080	0.425061	4.422610	0.22611080	22.62	0.582776	8.33	7
8	2.658444	12.757263	0.07838672	0.376160	4.798770	0.20838672	20.84	0.667094	8.34	8
9	3.004042	15.415707	0.06486890	0.332885	5.131655	0.19486890	19.49	0.753820	8.38	9
10	3.394567	18.419749	0.05428956	0.294588	5.426243	0.18428956	18.43	0.842896	8.43	10
11	3.835861	21.814317	0.04584145	0.260698	5.686941	0.17584145	17.59	0.934256	8.49	11
12	4.334523	25.650178	0.03898608	0.230706	5.917647	0.16898608	16.90	1.027833	8.57	12
13	4.898011	29.984701	0.03335034	0.204165	6.121812	0.16335034	16.34	1.123554	8.64	13
14	5.534753	34.882712	0.02866750	0.180677	6.302488	0.15866750	15.87	1.221345	8.72	14
15	6.254270	40.417464	0.02474178	0.159891	6.462379	0.15474178	15.48	1.321127	8.81	15
16	7.067326	46.671735	0.02142624	0.141496	6.603875	0.15142624	15.15	1.422820	8.89	16
17	7.986078	53.739060	0.01860844	0.125218	6.729093	0.14860844	14.87	1.526343	8.98	17
18	9.024268	61.725138	0.01620085	0.110812	6.839905	0.14620085	14.63	1.631615	9.06	18
19	10.197423	70.749406	0.01413439	0.098064	6.937969	0.14413439	14.42	1.738553	9.15	19
20	11.523088	80.946829	0.01235379	0.086782	7.024752	0.14235379	14.24	1.847076	9.24	20
21	13.021089	92.469917	0.01081433	0.076798	7.101550	0.14081433	14.09	1.957101	9.32	21
22	14.713831	105.491006	0.00947948	0.067963	7.169513	0.13947948	13.95	2.068549	9.40	22
23	16.626629	120.204837	0.00831913	0.060144	7.229658	0.13831913	13.84	2.181340	9.48	23
24	18.788091	136.831465	0.00730826	0.053225	7.282883	0.13730826	13.74	2.295398	9.56	24
25	21.230542	155.619556	0.00642523	0.047102	7.329985	0.13642523	13.65	2.410648	9.64	25
26	23.990513	176.850098	0.00565451	0.041683	7.371668	0.13565451	13.57	2.527017	9.72	26
27	27.109279	200.840611	0.00497907	0.036888	7.408556	0.13497907	13.50	2.644435	9.79	27
28	30.633486	227.949890	0.00438693	0.032644	7.441200	0.13438693	13.44	2.762834	9.87	28
29	34.615839	258.583376	0.00386722	0.028889	7.470088	0.13386722	13.39	2.882150	9.94	29
30	39.115898	293.199215	0.00341065	0.025565	7.495653	0.13341065	13.35	3.002320	10.01	30
31	44.200965	332.315113	0.00300919	0.022624	7.518277	0.13300919	13.31	3.123285	10.08	31
32	49.947090	376.516078	0.00265593	0.020021	7.538299	0.13265593	13.27	3.244990	10.14	32
33	56.440212	426.463168	0.00234487	0.017718	7.556016	0.13234487	13.24	3.367381	10.20	33
34	63.777439	482.903380	0.00207081	0.015680	7.571696	0.13207081	13.21	3.490407	10.27	34
35	72.068506	546.680819	0.00182922	0.013876	7.585572	0.13182922	13.19	3.614023	10.33	35
36	81.437412	618.749325	0.00161616	0.012279	7.597851	0.13161616	13.17	3.738182	10.38	36
37	92.024276	700.186738	0.00142819	0.010867	7.608718	0.13142819	13.15	3.862843	10.44	37
38	103.987432	792.211014	0.00126229	0.009617	7.618334	0.13126229	13.13	3.987967	10.49	38
39	117.505798	896.198445	0.00111582	0.008510	7.626844	0.13111582	13.12	4.113517	10.55	39
40	132.781552	1013.704243	0.00098648	0.007531	7.634376	0.13098648	13.10	4.239459	10.60	40
41	150.043153	1146.485795	0.00087223	0.006665	7.641040	0.13087223	13.09	4.365761	10.65	41
42	169.548763	1296.528948	0.00077129	0.005898	7.646938	0.13077129	13.08	4.492394	10.70	42
43	191.590103	1466.077712	0.00068209	0.005219	7.652158	0.13068209	13.07	4.619330	10.74	43
44	216.496816	1657.667814	0.00060326	0.004619	7.656777	0.13060326	13.07	4.746543	10.79	44
45	244.641402	1874.164630	0.00053357	0.004088	7.660864	0.13053357	13.06	4.874011	10.83	45
46	276.444784	2118.806032	0.00047196	0.003617	7.664482	0.13047196	13.05	5.001710	10.87	46
47	312.382606	2395.250816	0.00041749	0.003201	7.667683	0.13041749	13.05	5.129622	10.91	47
48	352.992345	2707.633422	0.00036933	0.002833	7.670516	0.13036933	13.04	5.257728	10.95	48
49	398.881350	3060.625767	0.00032673	0.002507	7.673023	0.13032673	13.04	5.386010	10.99	49
50	450.735925	3459.507117	0.00028906	0.002219	7.675242	0.13028906	13.03	5.514453	11.03	50

COMPOUND INTEREST AND ANNUITY TABLE

**14.00 %
ANNUAL**

		Amount Of 1	Amount Of 1 Per Period	Sinking Fund Payment	Present Worth Of 1	Present Worth Of 1 Per Period	Periodic Payment To Amortize 1	Constant Annual Percent	Total Interest	Annual Add-on Rate	
		What a single $1 deposit grows to in the future. The deposit is made at the beginning of the first period.	What a series of $1 deposits grow to in the future. A deposit is made at the end of each period.	The amount to be deposited at the end of each period that grows to $1 in the future.	What $1 to be paid in the future is worth today. Value today of a single payment tomorrow.	What $1 to be paid at the end of each period is worth today. Value today of a series of payments tomorrow.	The mortgage payment to amortize a loan of $1. An annuity certain, payable at the end of each period, worth $1 today.	The annual payment, including interest and principal, to amortize completely a loan of $100.	The total interest paid over the term on a loan of $1. The loan is amortized by regular periodic payments.	The average annual interest rate on a loan that is completely amortized by regular periodic payments.	
		$S=(1+i)^n$	$S_{\overline{n}}=\dfrac{(1+i)^n-1}{i}$	$\dfrac{1}{S_{\overline{n}}}=\dfrac{i}{(1+i)^n-1}$	$V^n=\dfrac{1}{(1+i)^n}$	$A_{\overline{n}}=\dfrac{1-V^n}{i}$	$\dfrac{1}{A_{\overline{n}}}=\dfrac{i}{1-V^n}$				
YR											**YR**
1	1	1.140000	1.000000	1.00000000	0.877193	0.877193	1.14000000	114.00	0.140000	14.00	1
2	2	1.299600	2.140000	0.46728972	0.769468	1.646661	0.60728972	60.73	0.214579	10.73	2
3	3	1.481544	3.439600	0.29073148	0.674972	2.321632	0.43073148	43.08	0.292194	9.74	3
4	4	1.688960	4.921144	0.20320478	0.592080	2.913712	0.34320478	34.33	0.372819	9.32	4
5	5	1.925415	6.610104	0.15128355	0.519369	3.433081	0.29128355	29.13	0.456418	9.13	5
6	6	2.194973	8.535519	0.11715750	0.455587	3.888668	0.25715750	25.72	0.542945	9.05	6
7	7	2.502269	10.730491	0.09319238	0.399637	4.288305	0.23319238	23.32	0.632347	9.03	7
8	8	2.852586	13.232760	0.07557002	0.350559	4.638864	0.21557002	21.56	0.724560	9.06	8
9	9	3.251949	16.085347	0.06216838	0.307508	4.946372	0.20216838	20.22	0.819515	9.11	9
10	10	3.707221	19.337295	0.05171354	0.269744	5.216116	0.19171354	19.18	0.917135	9.17	10
11	11	4.226232	23.044516	0.04339427	0.236617	5.452733	0.18339427	18.34	1.017337	9.25	11
12	12	4.817905	27.270749	0.03666933	0.207559	5.660292	0.17666933	17.67	1.120032	9.33	12
13	13	5.492411	32.088654	0.03116366	0.182069	5.842362	0.17116366	17.12	1.225128	9.42	13
14	14	6.261349	37.581065	0.02660914	0.159710	6.002072	0.16660914	16.67	1.332528	9.52	14
15	15	7.137938	43.842414	0.02280896	0.140096	6.142168	0.16280896	16.29	1.442134	9.61	15
16	16	8.137249	50.980352	0.01961540	0.122892	6.265060	0.15961540	15.97	1.553846	9.71	16
17	17	9.276464	59.117601	0.01691544	0.107800	6.372859	0.15691544	15.70	1.667562	9.81	17
18	18	10.575169	68.394066	0.01462115	0.094561	6.467420	0.15462115	15.47	1.783181	9.91	18
19	19	12.055693	78.969235	0.01266316	0.082948	6.550369	0.15266316	15.27	1.900600	10.00	19
20	20	13.743490	91.024928	0.01098600	0.072762	6.623131	0.15098600	15.10	2.019720	10.10	20
21	21	15.667578	104.768418	0.00954486	0.063826	6.686957	0.14954486	14.96	2.140442	10.19	21
22	22	17.861039	120.435996	0.00830317	0.055988	6.742944	0.14830317	14.84	2.262670	10.28	22
23	23	20.361585	138.297035	0.00723081	0.049112	6.792056	0.14723081	14.73	2.386309	10.38	23
24	24	23.212207	158.658620	0.00630284	0.043081	6.835137	0.14630284	14.64	2.511268	10.46	24
25	25	26.461916	181.870827	0.00549841	0.037790	6.872927	0.14549841	14.55	2.637460	10.55	25
26	26	30.166584	208.332743	0.00480001	0.033149	6.906077	0.14480001	14.49	2.764800	10.63	26
27	27	34.389906	238.499327	0.00419288	0.029078	6.935155	0.14419288	14.42	2.893208	10.72	27
28	28	39.204493	272.889233	0.00366449	0.025507	6.960662	0.14366449	14.37	3.022606	10.80	28
29	29	44.693122	312.093725	0.00320417	0.022375	6.983037	0.14320417	14.33	3.152921	10.87	29
30	30	50.950159	356.786847	0.00280279	0.019627	7.002664	0.14280279	14.29	3.284084	10.95	30
31	31	58.083181	407.737006	0.00245256	0.017217	7.019881	0.14245256	14.25	3.416029	11.02	31
32	32	66.214826	465.820186	0.00214675	0.015102	7.034983	0.14214675	14.22	3.548696	11.09	32
33	33	75.484902	532.035012	0.00187958	0.013248	7.048231	0.14187958	14.19	3.682026	11.16	33
34	34	86.052788	607.519914	0.00164604	0.011621	7.059852	0.14164604	14.17	3.815965	11.22	34
35	35	98.100178	693.572702	0.00144181	0.010194	7.070045	0.14144181	14.15	3.950463	11.29	35
36	36	111.834203	791.672881	0.00126315	0.008942	7.078987	0.14126315	14.13	4.085473	11.35	36
37	37	127.490992	903.507084	0.00110680	0.007844	7.086831	0.14110680	14.12	4.220952	11.41	37
38	38	145.339731	1030.998076	0.00096993	0.006880	7.093711	0.14096993	14.10	4.356857	11.47	38
39	39	165.687293	1176.337806	0.00085010	0.006035	7.099747	0.14085010	14.09	4.493154	11.52	39
40	40	188.883514	1342.025099	0.00074514	0.005294	7.105041	0.14074514	14.08	4.629806	11.57	40
41	41	215.327206	1530.908613	0.00065321	0.004644	7.109685	0.14065321	14.07	4.766781	11.63	41
42	42	245.473015	1746.235819	0.00057266	0.004074	7.113759	0.14057266	14.06	4.904052	11.68	42
43	43	279.839237	1991.708833	0.00050208	0.003573	7.117332	0.14050208	14.06	5.041590	11.72	43
44	44	319.016730	2271.548070	0.00044023	0.003135	7.120467	0.14044023	14.05	5.179370	11.77	44
45	45	363.679072	2590.564800	0.00038602	0.002750	7.123217	0.14038602	14.04	5.317371	11.82	45
46	46	414.594142	2954.243872	0.00033850	0.002412	7.125629	0.14033850	14.04	5.455571	11.86	46
47	47	472.637322	3368.838014	0.00029684	0.002116	7.127744	0.14029684	14.03	5.593951	11.90	47
48	48	538.806547	3841.475336	0.00026032	0.001856	7.129600	0.14026032	14.03	5.732495	11.94	48
49	49	614.239464	4380.281883	0.00022830	0.001628	7.131228	0.14022830	14.03	5.871186	11.98	49
50	50	700.232988	4994.521346	0.00020022	0.001428	7.132656	0.14020022	14.03	6.010011	12.02	50

COMPOUND INTEREST AND ANNUITY TABLE

**15.00 %
ANNUAL**

		Amount Of 1	Amount Of 1 Per Period	Sinking Fund Payment	Present Worth Of 1	Present Worth Of 1 Per Period	Periodic Payment To Amortize 1	Constant Annual Percent	Total Interest	Annual Add-on Rate		
		What a single $1 deposit grows to in the future. The deposit is made at the beginning of the first period.	What a series of $1 deposits grow to in the future. A deposit is made at the end of each period.	The amount to be deposited at the end of each period that grows to $1 in the future.	What $1 to be paid in the future is worth today. Value today of a single payment tomorrow.	What $1 to be paid at the end of each period is worth today. Value today of a series of payments tomorrow.	The mortgage payment to amortize a loan of $1. An annuity certain, payable at the end of each period, worth $1 today.	The annual payment, including interest and principal, to amortize completely a loan of $100.	The total interest paid over the term on a loan of $1. The loan is amortized by regular periodic payments.	The average annual interest rate on a loan that is completely amortized by regular periodic payments.		
		$S=(1+i)^n$	$S_{\overline{n}}=\dfrac{(1+i)^n-1}{i}$	$\dfrac{1}{S_{\overline{n}}}=\dfrac{i}{(1+i)^n-1}$	$V^n=\dfrac{1}{(1+i)^n}$	$A_{\overline{n}}=\dfrac{1-V^n}{i}$	$\dfrac{1}{A_{\overline{n}}}=\dfrac{i}{1-V^n}$					
YR												YR
1	1	1.150000	1.000000	1.00000000	0.869565	0.869565	1.15000000	115.00	0.150000	15.00	1
2	2	1.322500	2.150000	0.46511628	0.756144	1.625709	0.61511628	61.52	0.230233	11.51	2
3	3	1.520875	3.472500	0.28797696	0.657516	2.283225	0.43797696	43.80	0.313931	10.46	3
4	4	1.749006	4.993375	0.20026535	0.571753	2.854978	0.35026535	35.03	0.401061	10.03	4
5	5	2.011357	6.742381	0.14831555	0.497177	3.352155	0.29831555	29.84	0.491578	9.83	5
6	6	2.313061	8.753738	0.11423691	0.432328	3.784483	0.26423691	26.43	0.585421	9.76	6
7	7	2.660020	11.066799	0.09036036	0.375937	4.160420	0.24036036	24.04	0.682523	9.75	7
8	8	3.059023	13.726819	0.07285009	0.326902	4.487322	0.22285009	22.29	0.782801	9.79	8
9	9	3.517842	16.785842	0.05957402	0.284262	4.771584	0.20957402	20.96	0.886166	9.85	9
10	10	4.045558	20.303718	0.04925206	0.247185	5.018769	0.19925206	19.93	0.992521	9.93	10
11	11	4.652391	24.349276	0.04106898	0.214943	5.233712	0.19106898	19.11	1.101759	10.02	11
12	12	5.350250	29.001667	0.03448078	0.186907	5.420619	0.18448078	18.45	1.213769	10.11	12
13	13	6.152788	34.351917	0.02911046	0.162528	5.583147	0.17911046	17.92	1.328436	10.22	13
14	14	7.075706	40.504705	0.02468844	0.141329	5.724476	0.17468844	17.47	1.445639	10.33	14
15	15	8.137062	47.580411	0.02101705	0.122894	5.847370	0.17101705	17.11	1.565256	10.44	15
16	16	9.357621	55.717472	0.01794769	0.106865	5.954235	0.16794769	16.80	1.687163	10.54	16
17	17	10.761264	65.075093	0.01536686	0.092924	6.047161	0.16536686	16.54	1.811237	10.65	17
18	18	12.375454	75.836357	0.01318629	0.080805	6.127966	0.16318629	16.32	1.937353	10.76	18
19	19	14.231772	88.211811	0.01133635	0.070265	6.198231	0.16133635	16.14	2.065391	10.87	19
20	20	16.366537	102.443583	0.00976147	0.061100	6.259331	0.15976147	15.98	2.195229	10.98	20
21	21	18.821518	118.810120	0.00841679	0.053131	6.312462	0.15841679	15.85	2.326753	11.08	21
22	22	21.644746	137.631638	0.00726577	0.046201	6.358663	0.15726577	15.73	2.459847	11.18	22
23	23	24.891458	159.276384	0.00627839	0.040174	6.398837	0.15627839	15.63	2.594403	11.28	23
24	24	28.625176	184.167841	0.00542983	0.034934	6.433771	0.15542983	15.55	2.730316	11.38	24
25	25	32.918953	212.793017	0.00469940	0.030378	6.464149	0.15469940	15.47	2.867485	11.47	25
26	26	37.856796	245.711970	0.00406981	0.026415	6.490564	0.15406981	15.41	3.005815	11.56	26
27	27	43.535315	283.568766	0.00352648	0.022970	6.513534	0.15352648	15.36	3.145215	11.65	27
28	28	50.065612	327.104080	0.00305713	0.019974	6.533508	0.15305713	15.31	3.285600	11.73	28
29	29	57.575444	377.169693	0.00265133	0.017369	6.550877	0.15265133	15.27	3.426888	11.82	29
30	30	66.211772	434.745146	0.00230020	0.015103	6.565980	0.15230020	15.24	3.569006	11.90	30
31	31	76.143538	500.956918	0.00199618	0.013133	6.579113	0.15199618	15.20	3.711882	11.97	31
32	32	87.565068	577.100456	0.00173280	0.011420	6.590533	0.15173280	15.18	3.855450	12.05	32
33	33	100.699829	664.665524	0.00150452	0.009931	6.600463	0.15150452	15.16	3.999649	12.12	33
34	34	115.804803	765.365353	0.00130657	0.008635	6.609099	0.15130657	15.14	4.144423	12.19	34
35	35	133.175523	881.170156	0.00113485	0.007509	6.616607	0.15113485	15.12	4.289720	12.26	35
36	36	153.151852	1014.345680	0.00098586	0.006529	6.623137	0.15098586	15.10	4.435491	12.32	36
37	37	176.124630	1167.497532	0.00085653	0.005678	6.628815	0.15085653	15.09	4.581692	12.38	37
38	38	202.543324	1343.622161	0.00074426	0.004937	6.633752	0.15074426	15.08	4.728282	12.44	38
39	39	232.924823	1546.165485	0.00064676	0.004293	6.638045	0.15064676	15.07	4.875224	12.50	39
40	40	267.863546	1779.090308	0.00056209	0.003733	6.641778	0.15056209	15.06	5.022483	12.56	40
41	41	308.043078	2046.953854	0.00048853	0.003246	6.645025	0.15048853	15.05	5.170030	12.61	41
42	42	354.249540	2354.996933	0.00042463	0.002823	6.647848	0.15042463	15.05	5.317834	12.66	42
43	43	407.386971	2709.246473	0.00036911	0.002455	6.650302	0.15036911	15.04	5.465872	12.71	43
44	44	468.495017	3116.633443	0.00032086	0.002134	6.652437	0.15032086	15.04	5.614118	12.76	44
45	45	538.769269	3585.128460	0.00027893	0.001856	6.654293	0.15027893	15.03	5.762552	12.81	45
46	46	619.584659	4123.897729	0.00024249	0.001614	6.655907	0.15024249	15.03	5.911154	12.86	46
47	47	712.522358	4743.482388	0.00021082	0.001403	6.657310	0.15021082	15.03	6.059908	12.89	47
48	48	819.400712	5456.004746	0.00018328	0.001220	6.658531	0.15018328	15.02	6.208798	12.93	48
49	49	942.310819	6275.405458	0.00015935	0.001061	6.659592	0.15015935	15.02	6.357808	12.98	49
50	50	1083.657442	7217.716277	0.00013855	0.000923	6.660515	0.15013855	15.02	6.506927	13.01	50

COMPOUND INTEREST AND ANNUITY TABLE

16.00 %
ANNUAL

		Amount Of 1	Amount Of 1 Per Period	Sinking Fund Payment	Present Worth Of 1	Present Worth Of 1 Per Period	Periodic Payment To Amortize 1	Constant Annual Percent	Total Interest	Annual Add-on Rate	
		What a single $1 deposit grows to in the future. The deposit is made at the beginning of the first period.	What a series of $1 deposits grow to in the future. A deposit is made at the end of each period.	The amount to be deposited at the end of each period that grows to $1 in the future.	What $1 to be paid in the future is worth today. Value today of a single payment tomorrow.	What $1 to be paid at the end of each period is worth today. Value today of a series of payments tomorrow.	The mortgage payment to amortize a loan of $1. An annuity certain, payable at the end of each period, worth $1 today.	The annual payment, including interest and principal, to amortize completely a loan of $100.	The total interest paid over the term on a loan of $1. The loan is amortized by regular periodic payments.	The average annual interest rate on a loan that is completely amortized by regular periodic payments.	
		$S=(1+i)^n$	$S_{\overline{n}}=\dfrac{(1+i)^n-1}{i}$	$\dfrac{1}{S_{\overline{n}}}=\dfrac{i}{(1+i)^n-1}$	$V^n=\dfrac{1}{(1+i)^n}$	$A_{\overline{n}}=\dfrac{1-V^n}{i}$	$\dfrac{1}{A_{\overline{n}}}=\dfrac{i}{1-V^n}$				
YR											**YR**
1	1	1.160000	1.000000	1.00000000	0.862069	0.862069	1.16000000	116.00	0.160000	16.00	1
2	2	1.345600	2.160000	0.46296296	0.743163	1.605232	0.62296296	62.30	0.245926	12.30	2
3	3	1.560896	3.505600	0.28525787	0.640658	2.245890	0.44525787	44.53	0.335774	11.19	3
4	4	1.810639	5.066496	0.19737507	0.552291	2.798181	0.35737507	35.74	0.429500	10.74	4
5	5	2.100342	6.877135	0.14540938	0.476113	3.274294	0.30540938	30.55	0.527047	10.54	5
6	6	2.436396	8.977477	0.11138987	0.410442	3.684736	0.27138987	27.14	0.628339	10.47	6
7	7	2.826220	11.413873	0.08761268	0.353830	4.038565	0.24761268	24.77	0.733289	10.48	7
8	8	3.278415	14.240093	0.07022426	0.305025	4.343591	0.23022426	23.03	0.841794	10.52	8
9	9	3.802961	17.518508	0.05708249	0.262953	4.606544	0.21708249	21.71	0.953742	10.60	9
10	10	4.411435	21.321469	0.04690108	0.226684	4.833227	0.20690108	20.70	1.069011	10.69	10
11	11	5.117265	25.732904	0.03886075	0.195417	5.028644	0.19886075	19.89	1.187468	10.80	11
12	12	5.936027	30.850169	0.03241473	0.168463	5.197107	0.19241473	19.25	1.308977	10.91	12
13	13	6.885791	36.786196	0.02718411	0.145227	5.342334	0.18718411	18.72	1.433393	11.03	13
14	14	7.987518	43.671987	0.02289797	0.125195	5.467529	0.18289797	18.29	1.560572	11.15	14
15	15	9.265521	51.659505	0.01935752	0.107927	5.575456	0.17935752	17.94	1.690363	11.27	15

17.00 %
ANNUAL

YR											**YR**
1	1	1.170000	1.000000	1.00000000	0.854701	0.854701	1.17000000	117.00	0.170000	17.00	1
2	2	1.368900	2.170000	0.46082949	0.730514	1.585214	0.63082949	63.09	0.261659	13.08	2
3	3	1.601613	3.538900	0.28257368	0.624371	2.209585	0.45257368	45.26	0.357721	11.92	3
4	4	1.873887	5.140513	0.19453311	0.533650	2.743235	0.36453311	36.46	0.458132	11.45	4
5	5	2.192448	7.014400	0.14256386	0.456111	3.199346	0.31256386	31.26	0.562819	11.26	5
6	6	2.565164	9.206848	0.10861480	0.389839	3.589185	0.27861480	27.87	0.671689	11.19	6
7	7	3.001242	11.772012	0.08494724	0.333195	3.922380	0.25494724	25.50	0.784631	11.21	7
8	8	3.511453	14.773255	0.06768989	0.284782	4.207163	0.23768989	23.77	0.901519	11.27	8
9	9	4.108400	18.284708	0.05469051	0.243404	4.450566	0.22469051	22.47	1.022215	11.36	9
10	10	4.806828	22.393108	0.04465660	0.208037	4.658604	0.21465660	21.47	1.146566	11.47	10
11	11	5.623989	27.199937	0.03676479	0.177810	4.836413	0.20676479	20.68	1.274413	11.59	11
12	12	6.580067	32.823926	0.03046558	0.151974	4.988387	0.20046558	20.05	1.405587	11.71	12
13	13	7.698679	39.403993	0.02537814	0.129892	5.118280	0.19537814	19.54	1.539916	11.85	13
14	14	9.007454	47.102672	0.02123022	0.111019	5.229299	0.19123022	19.13	1.677223	11.98	14
15	15	10.538721	56.110126	0.01782209	0.094888	5.324187	0.18782209	18.79	1.817331	12.12	15

COMPOUND INTEREST AND ANNUITY TABLE

**18.00 %
ANNUAL**

		Amount Of 1	Amount Of 1 Per Period	Sinking Fund Payment	Present Worth Of 1	Present Worth Of 1 Per Period	Periodic Annual Payment To Amortize 1	Constant Annual Percent	Total Interest	Annual Add-on Rate		
		What a single $1 deposit grows to in the future. The deposit is made at the beginning of the first period.	What a series of $1 deposits grow to in the future. A deposit is made at the end of each period.	The amount to be deposited at the end of each period that grows to $1 in the future.	What $1 to be paid in the future is worth today. Value today of a single payment tomorrow.	What $1 to be paid at the end of each period is worth today. Value today of a series of payments tomorrow.	The mortgage payment to amortize a loan of $1. An annuity certain, payable at the end of each period, worth $1 today.	The annual payment, including interest and principal, to amortize completely a loan of $100.	The total interest paid over the term on a loan of $1. The loan is amortized by regular periodic payments.	The average annual interest rate on a loan that is completely amortized by regular periodic payments.		
		$S=(1+i)^n$	$S_{\overline{n}}=\dfrac{(1+i)^n-1}{i}$	$\dfrac{1}{S_{\overline{n}}}=\dfrac{i}{(1+i)^n-1}$	$V^n=\dfrac{1}{(1+i)^n}$	$A_{\overline{n}}=\dfrac{1-V^n}{i}$	$\dfrac{1}{A_{\overline{n}}}=\dfrac{i}{1-V^n}$					
YR												**YR**
1	1	1.180000	1.000000	1.00000000	0.847458	0.847458	1.18000000	118.00	0.180000	18.00	1
2	2	1.392400	2.180000	0.45871560	0.718184	1.565642	0.63871560	63.88	0.277431	13.87	2
3	3	1.643032	3.572400	0.27992386	0.608631	2.174273	0.45992386	46.00	0.379772	12.66	3
4	4	1.938778	5.215432	0.19173867	0.515789	2.690062	0.37173867	37.18	0.486955	12.17	4
5	5	2.287758	7.154210	0.13977784	0.437109	3.127171	0.31977784	31.98	0.598889	11.98	5
6	6	2.699554	9.441968	0.10591013	0.370432	3.497603	0.28591013	28.60	0.715461	11.92	6
7	7	3.185474	12.141522	0.08236200	0.313925	3.811528	0.26236200	26.24	0.836534	11.95	7
8	8	3.758859	15.326996	0.06524436	0.266038	4.077566	0.24524436	24.53	0.961955	12.02	8
9	9	4.435454	19.085855	0.05239482	0.225456	4.303022	0.23239482	23.24	1.091553	12.13	9
10	10	5.233836	23.521309	0.04251464	0.191064	4.494086	0.22251464	22.26	1.225146	12.25	10
11	11	6.175926	28.755144	0.03477639	0.161919	4.656005	0.21477639	21.48	1.362540	12.39	11
12	12	7.287593	34.931070	0.02862781	0.137220	4.793225	0.20862781	20.87	1.503534	12.53	12
13	13	8.599359	42.218663	0.02368621	0.116288	4.909513	0.20368621	20.37	1.647921	12.68	13
14	14	10.147244	50.818022	0.01967806	0.098549	5.008062	0.19967806	19.97	1.795493	12.82	14
15	15	11.973748	60.965266	0.01640278	0.083516	5.091578	0.19640278	19.65	1.946042	12.97	15

**19.00 %
ANNUAL**

YR											**YR**
1	1	1.190000	1.000000	1.00000000	0.840336	0.840336	1.19000000	119.00	0.190000	19.00	1
2	2	1.416100	2.190000	0.45662100	0.706165	1.546501	0.64662100	64.67	0.293242	14.66	2
3	3	1.685159	3.606100	0.27730789	0.593416	2.139917	0.46730789	46.74	0.401924	13.40	3
4	4	2.005339	5.291259	0.18899094	0.498669	2.638586	0.37899094	37.90	0.515964	12.90	4
5	5	2.386354	7.296598	0.13705017	0.419049	3.057635	0.32705017	32.71	0.635251	12.71	5
6	6	2.839761	9.682952	0.10327429	0.352142	3.409777	0.29327429	29.33	0.759646	12.66	6
7	7	3.379315	12.522713	0.07985490	0.295918	3.705695	0.26985490	26.99	0.888984	12.70	7
8	8	4.021385	15.902028	0.06288506	0.248671	3.954366	0.25288506	25.29	1.023080	12.79	8
9	9	4.785449	19.923413	0.05019220	0.208967	4.163332	0.24019220	24.02	1.161730	12.91	9
10	10	5.694684	24.708862	0.04047131	0.175602	4.338935	0.23047131	23.05	1.304713	13.05	10
11	11	6.776674	30.403546	0.03289090	0.147565	4.486500	0.22289090	22.29	1.451800	13.20	11
12	12	8.064242	37.180220	0.02689602	0.124004	4.610504	0.21689602	21.69	1.602752	13.36	12
13	13	9.596448	45.244461	0.02210215	0.104205	4.714709	0.21210215	21.22	1.757328	13.52	13
14	14	11.419773	54.840909	0.01823456	0.087567	4.802277	0.20823456	20.83	1.915284	13.68	14
15	15	13.589530	66.260682	0.01509191	0.073586	4.875863	0.20509191	20.51	2.076379	13.84	15

COMPOUND INTEREST AND ANNUITY TABLE

		Amount Of 1	Amount Of 1 Per Period	Sinking Fund Payment	Present Worth Of 1	Present Worth Of 1 Per Period	Periodic Payment To Amortize 1	Constant Annual Percent	Total Interest	Annual Add-on Rate		
		What a single $1 deposit grows to in the future. The deposit is made at the beginning of the first period.	What a series of $1 deposits grow to in the future. A deposit is made at the end of each period.	The amount to be deposited at the end of each period that grows to $1 in the future.	What $1 to be paid in the future is worth today. Value today of a single payment tomorrow.	What $1 to be paid in the future at the end of each period is worth today. Value today of a series of payments tomorrow.	The mortgage payment to amortize a loan of $1. An annuity certain, payable at the end of each period, worth $1 today.	The annual payment, including interest and principal, to amortize completely a loan of $100.	The total interest paid over the term on a loan of $1. The loan is amortized by regular periodic payments.	The average annual interest rate on a loan that is completely amortized by regular periodic payments.		
		$S=(1+i)^n$	$S_{\overline{n}}=\dfrac{(1+i)^n-1}{i}$	$\dfrac{1}{S_{\overline{n}}}=\dfrac{i}{(1+i)^n-1}$	$V^n=\dfrac{1}{(1+i)^n}$	$A_{\overline{n}}=\dfrac{1-V^n}{i}$	$\dfrac{1}{A_{\overline{n}}}=\dfrac{i}{1-V^n}$					
YR												YR
1	1	1.200000	1.000000	1.00000000	0.833333	0.833333	1.20000000	120.00	0.200000	20.00	1
2	2	1.440000	2.200000	0.45454545	0.694444	1.527778	0.65454545	65.46	0.309091	15.45	2
3	3	1.728000	3.640000	0.27472527	0.578704	2.106481	0.47472527	47.48	0.424176	14.14	3
4	4	2.073600	5.368000	0.18628912	0.482253	2.588735	0.38628912	38.63	0.545156	13.63	4
5	5	2.488320	7.441600	0.13437970	0.401878	2.990612	0.33437970	33.44	0.671899	13.44	5
6	6	2.985984	9.929920	0.10070575	0.334898	3.325510	0.30070575	30.08	0.804234	13.40	6
7	7	3.583181	12.915904	0.07742393	0.279082	3.604592	0.27742393	27.75	0.941967	13.46	7
8	8	4.299817	16.499085	0.06060942	0.232568	3.837160	0.26060942	26.07	1.084875	13.56	8
9	9	5.159780	20.798902	0.04807946	0.193807	4.030967	0.24807946	24.81	1.232715	13.70	9
10	10	6.191736	25.958682	0.03852276	0.161506	4.192472	0.23852276	23.86	1.385228	13.85	10
11	11	7.430084	32.150419	0.03110379	0.134588	4.327060	0.23110379	23.12	1.542142	14.02	11
12	12	8.916100	39.580502	0.02526496	0.112157	4.439217	0.22526496	22.53	1.703180	14.19	12
13	13	10.699321	48.496603	0.02062000	0.093464	4.532681	0.22062000	22.07	1.868060	14.37	13
14	14	12.839185	59.195923	0.01689306	0.077887	4.610567	0.21689306	21.69	2.036503	14.55	14
15	15	15.407022	72.035108	0.01388212	0.064905	4.675473	0.21388212	21.39	2.208232	14.72	15

YR											YR
1	1	1.250000	1.000000	1.00000000	0.800000	0.800000	1.25000000	125.00	0.250000	25.00	1
2	2	1.562500	2.250000	0.44444444	0.640000	1.440000	0.69444444	69.45	0.388889	19.44	2
3	3	1.953125	3.812500	0.26229508	0.512000	1.952000	0.51229508	51.23	0.536885	17.90	3
4	4	2.441406	5.765625	0.17344173	0.409600	2.361600	0.42344173	42.35	0.693767	17.34	4
5	5	3.051758	8.207031	0.12184674	0.327680	2.689280	0.37184674	37.19	0.859234	17.18	5
6	6	3.814697	11.258789	0.08881950	0.262144	2.951424	0.33881950	33.89	1.032917	17.22	6
7	7	4.768372	15.073486	0.06634165	0.209715	3.161139	0.31634165	31.64	1.214392	17.35	7
8	8	5.960464	19.841858	0.05039851	0.167772	3.328911	0.30039851	30.04	1.403188	17.54	8
9	9	7.450581	25.802322	0.03875620	0.134218	3.463129	0.28875620	28.88	1.598806	17.76	9
10	10	9.313226	33.252903	0.03007256	0.107374	3.570503	0.28007256	28.01	1.800726	18.01	10
11	11	11.641532	42.556129	0.02349286	0.085899	3.656403	0.27349286	27.35	2.008421	18.26	11
12	12	14.551915	54.207661	0.01844758	0.068719	3.725122	0.26844758	26.85	2.221371	18.51	12
13	13	18.189894	68.759576	0.01454343	0.054976	3.780098	0.26454343	26.46	2.439065	18.76	13
14	14	22.737368	86.949470	0.01150093	0.043980	3.824078	0.26150093	26.16	2.661013	19.01	14
15	15	28.421709	109.686838	0.00911686	0.035184	3.859263	0.25911686	25.92	2.886753	19.25	15

YR											YR
1	1	1.300000	1.000000	1.00000000	0.769231	0.769231	1.30000000	130.00	0.300000	30.00	1
2	2	1.690000	2.300000	0.43478261	0.591716	1.360947	0.73478261	73.48	0.469565	23.48	2
3	3	2.197000	3.990000	0.25062657	0.455166	1.816113	0.55062657	55.07	0.651880	21.73	3
4	4	2.856100	6.187000	0.16162922	0.350128	2.166241	0.46162922	46.17	0.846517	21.16	4
5	5	3.712930	9.043100	0.11058155	0.269329	2.435570	0.41058155	41.06	1.052908	21.06	5
6	6	4.826809	12.756030	0.07839430	0.207176	2.642746	0.37839430	37.84	1.270366	21.17	6
7	7	6.274852	17.582839	0.05687364	0.159366	2.802112	0.35687364	35.69	1.498115	21.40	7
8	8	8.157307	23.857691	0.04191521	0.122589	2.924702	0.34191521	34.20	1.735322	21.69	8
9	9	10.604499	32.014998	0.03123536	0.094300	3.019001	0.33123536	33.13	1.981118	22.01	9
10	10	13.785849	42.619497	0.02346344	0.072538	3.091539	0.32346344	32.35	2.234634	22.35	10
11	11	17.921604	56.405346	0.01772882	0.055799	3.147338	0.31772882	31.78	2.495017	22.68	11
12	12	23.298085	74.326950	0.01345407	0.042922	3.190260	0.31345407	31.35	2.761449	23.01	12
13	13	30.287511	97.625036	0.01024327	0.033017	3.223277	0.31024327	31.03	3.033163	23.33	13
14	14	39.373764	127.912546	0.00781784	0.025398	3.248675	0.30781784	30.79	3.309450	23.64	14
15	15	51.185893	167.286310	0.00597778	0.019537	3.268211	0.30597778	30.60	3.589667	23.93	15

COMPOUND INTEREST AND ANNUITY TABLE

35.00 %
ANNUAL

		Amount Of 1	Amount Of 1 Per Period	Sinking Fund Payment	Present Worth Of 1	Present Worth Of 1 Per Period	Periodic Payment To Amortize 1	Constant Annual Percent	Total Interest	Annual Add-on Rate		
		What a single $1 deposit grows to in the future. The deposit is made at the beginning of the first period.	What a series of $1 deposits grow to in the future. A deposit is made at the end of each period.	The amount to be deposited at the end of each period that grows to $1 in the future.	What $1 to be paid in the future is worth today. Value today of a single payment tomorrow.	What $1 to be paid at the end of each period is worth today. Value today of a series of payments tomorrow.	The mortgage payment to amortize a loan of $1. An annuity certain, payable at the end of each period, worth $1 today.	The annual payment, including interest and principal, to amortize completely a loan of $100.	The total interest paid over the term on a loan of $1. The loan is amortized by regular periodic payments.	The average annual interest rate on a loan that is completely amortized by regular periodic payments.		
		$S=(1+i)^n$	$S_{\overline{n}\mid}=\dfrac{(1+i)^n-1}{i}$	$\dfrac{1}{S_{\overline{n}\mid}}=\dfrac{i}{(1+i)^n-1}$	$V^n=\dfrac{1}{(1+i)^n}$	$A_{\overline{n}\mid}=\dfrac{1-V^n}{i}$	$\dfrac{1}{A_{\overline{n}\mid}}=\dfrac{i}{1-V^n}$					
YR												**YR**
1	1	1.350000	1.000000	1.00000000	0.740741	0.740741	1.35000000	135.00	0.350000	35.00		1
2	2	1.822500	2.350000	0.42553191	0.548697	1.289438	0.77553191	77.56	0.551064	27.55		2
3	3	2.460375	4.172500	0.23966447	0.406442	1.695880	0.58966447	58.97	0.768993	25.63		3
4	4	3.321506	6.632875	0.15076419	0.301068	1.996948	0.50076419	50.08	1.003057	25.08		4
5	5	4.484033	9.954381	0.10045828	0.223014	2.219961	0.45045828	45.05	1.252291	25.05		5
6	6	6.053445	14.438415	0.06925968	0.165195	2.385157	0.41925968	41.93	1.515558	25.26		6
7	7	8.172151	20.491860	0.04879987	0.122367	2.507523	0.39879987	39.88	1.791599	25.59		7
8	8	11.032404	28.664011	0.03488695	0.090642	2.598165	0.38488695	38.49	2.079096	25.99		8
9	9	14.893745	39.696415	0.02519119	0.067142	2.665308	0.37519119	37.52	2.376721	26.41		9
10	10	20.106556	54.590160	0.01831832	0.049735	2.715043	0.36831832	36.84	2.683183	26.83		10
11	11	27.143850	74.696715	0.01338747	0.036841	2.751884	0.36338747	36.34	2.997262	27.25		11
12	12	36.644198	101.840566	0.00981927	0.027289	2.779173	0.35981927	35.99	3.317831	27.65		12
13	13	49.469667	138.484764	0.00722101	0.020214	2.799387	0.35722101	35.73	3.643873	28.03		13
14	14	66.784051	187.954431	0.00532044	0.014974	2.814361	0.35532044	35.54	3.974486	28.39		14
15	15	90.158469	254.738482	0.00392559	0.011092	2.825453	0.35392559	35.40	4.308884	28.73		15

40.00 %
ANNUAL

YR												**YR**
1	1	1.400000	1.000000	1.00000000	0.714286	0.714286	1.40000000	140.00	0.400000	40.00		1
2	2	1.960000	2.400000	0.41666667	0.510204	1.224490	0.81666667	81.67	0.633333	31.67		2
3	3	2.744000	4.360000	0.22935780	0.364431	1.588921	0.62935780	62.94	0.888073	29.60		3
4	4	3.841600	7.104000	0.14076577	0.260308	1.849229	0.54076577	54.08	1.163063	29.08		4
5	5	5.378240	10.945600	0.09136091	0.185934	2.035164	0.49136091	49.14	1.456805	29.14		5
6	6	7.529536	16.323840	0.06126010	0.132810	2.167974	0.46126010	46.13	1.767561	29.46		6
7	7	10.541350	23.853376	0.04192279	0.094865	2.262839	0.44192279	44.20	2.093460	29.91		7
8	8	14.757891	34.394726	0.02907422	0.067760	2.330599	0.42907422	42.91	2.432594	30.41		8
9	9	20.661047	49.152617	0.02034480	0.048400	2.378999	0.42034480	42.04	2.783103	30.92		9
10	10	28.925465	69.813664	0.01432384	0.034572	2.413571	0.41432384	41.44	3.143238	31.43		10
11	11	40.495652	98.739129	0.01012770	0.024694	2.438265	0.41012770	41.02	3.511405	31.92		11
12	12	56.693912	139.234781	0.00718211	0.017639	2.455904	0.40718211	40.72	3.886185	32.38		12
13	13	79.371477	195.928693	0.00510390	0.012599	2.468503	0.40510390	40.52	4.266351	32.82		13
14	14	111.120068	275.300171	0.00363240	0.008999	2.477502	0.40363240	40.37	4.650854	33.22		14
15	15	155.568096	386.420239	0.00258786	0.006428	2.483930	0.40258786	40.26	5.038818	33.59		15

TAble of tHE NORMAl DisTRibuTiON

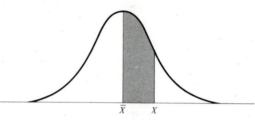

The table of areas of the normal curve between $\bar{X}$ and X for Z values is computed as follows:

$$Z = \frac{X - \bar{X}}{\sigma}$$

z	.00	.01	.02	.03	.04	.05	.06	.07	.08	.09
0.0	.0000	.0041	.0080	.0120	.0160	.0199	.0239	.0279	.0319	.0359
0.1	.0398	.0438	.0478	.0517	.0557	.0596	.0636	.0675	.0714	.0753
0.2	.0793	.0832	.0871	.0910	.0948	.0987	.1026	.1064	.1103	.1141
0.3	.1179	.1217	.1255	.1293	.1331	.1368	.1406	.1443	.1480	.1517
0.4	.1554	.1591	.1628	.1664	.1700	.1736	.1772	.1808	.1844	.1879
0.5	.1915	.1950	.1985	.2019	.2054	.2088	.2123	.2157	.2190	.2224
0.6	.2257	.2291	.2324	.2357	.2389	.2422	.2454	.2486	.2517	.2549
0.7	.2580	.2611	.2642	.2673	.2704	.2734	.2764	.2794	.2823	.2852
0.8	.2881	.2910	.2939	.2967	.2995	.3023	.3051	.3078	.3106	.3133
0.9	.3159	.3186	.3212	.3238	.3264	.3289	.3315	.3340	.3365	.3389
1.0	.3413	.3438	.3461	.3485	.3508	.3531	.3554	.3577	.3599	.3621
1.1	.3643	.3665	.3686	.3708	.3729	.3749	.3770	.3790	.3810	.3830
1.2	.3849	.3869	.3888	.3907	.3925	.3944	.3962	.3980	.3997	.4015
1.3	.4032	.4049	.4066	.4082	.4099	.4115	.4131	.4147	.4162	.4177
1.4	.4192	.4207	.4222	.4236	.4251	.4265	.4279	.4292	.4306	.4319
1.5	.4332	.4345	.4357	.4370	.4382	.4394	.4406	.4418	.4429	.4441
1.6	.4452	.4463	.4474	.4484	.4495	.4505	.4515	.4525	.4535	.4545
1.7	.4554	.4564	.4573	.4582	.4591	.4599	.4608	.4616	.4625	.4633
1.8	.4641	.4649	.4656	.4664	.4671	.4678	.4686	.4693	.4699	.4706
1.9	.4713	.4719	.4726	.4732	.4738	.4744	.4750	.4756	.4761	.4767
2.0	.4772	.4778	.4783	.4788	.4793	.4798	.4803	.4808	.4812	.4817
2.1	.4821	.4826	.4830	.4834	.4838	.4842	.4846	.4850	.4854	.4857
2.2	.4861	.4864	.4868	.4871	.4875	.4878	.4881	.4884	.4887	.4890
2.3	.4893	.4896	.4898	.4901	.4904	.4906	.4909	.4911	.4913	.4916
2.4	.4918	.4920	.4922	.4925	.4927	.4929	.4931	.4932	.4934	.4936
2.5	.4938	.4940	.4941	.4943	.4945	.4946	.4948	.4949	.4951	.4952
2.6	.4953	.4955	.4956	.4957	.4959	.4960	.4961	.4962	.4963	.4964
2.7	.4965	.4966	.4967	.4968	.4969	.4970	.4971	.4972	.4973	.4974
2.8	.4974	.4975	.4976	.4977	.4977	.4978	.4979	.4979	.4980	.4981
2.9	.4981	.4982	.4982	.4983	.4984	.4984	.4985	.4985	.4986	.4986
3.0	.4987	.4987	.4987	.4988	.4988	.4989	.4989	.4989	.4990	.4990

APPENDIX D

Answers to Selected Problems

Chapter 2

3. $ 690.29
4. $4952.70
6. $206,723
8. $8340.70

Chapter 3

1. $20,456.03
3. $14,205.15
5. $42,818.29
7. $717.34
9. $400,000
10. $636,547.87, $74,367.57
11. $8291.14
13. (a) $1598.89
    (b) $190,330.15
    (c) $52,616.01
    (d) $1937.82

Chapter 4

1. 4.54 years
3. Project A: 3 years, B = 4 years, C = $3\frac{3}{4}$ years
5. Discounted payback period is 12 years.
7. Select Project B
8. $3,605

Chapter 5

1. $NPV_A = \$1,009.16$, $NPV_B = \$2,326.29$, $PI_A = 1.05$, $PI_B = 1.08$
2. $NPV = -\$6,142$, $IRR = 6.28\%$
5. $IRR = 18.125\%$
7. $NPV = \$5,055$, $PI = .922$
9. $EAC_{New} = \$4,703,487$, $EAC_{Rebuild} = \$5,447,401$

Chapter 6

12.

K	NPV_I	NPV_{II}
20%	18,494.44	13,611.11
30%	15,809.47	11,301.78
40%	13,573.47	9,387.76
45%	12,590.73	8,549.35
49%	11,860.01	7,927.12

15. Present value of $\$5860 = \$5051.72$; $NPV_I = 19,726.52$;
   $NPV_{II} = 14,673.01$; $NPV_I - NPV_{II} = 5053.51$ (error due to rounding)
17. I and Loan combined becomes 8,000.

Chapter 7

7. (a) $NPV_A = \$6,699$, $NPV_B = \$7,135$
   (b) $IRR_A \cong 21.8\%$, $IRR_B \cong 18.25\%$
   (e) $NPV_A^* > NPV_B^*$
9. $NPV_{GR}^* > NPV_{RZ}^*$
11. $NPV_H^* > NPV_S^*$
13. $NPV_A^* > NPV_B^*$
15. $NPV_A^* > NPV_B^*$
17. $NPV_P^* > NPV_O^*$
19. $NPV_{Bo}^* > NPV_{Be}^*$

Chapter 8

1. After-tax 4.186%
3. $K_i = 0.0485$, $_nK_p = 0.0513$, $_nK_e = 0.1096$, $K_{mc} = 8.02\%$

Chapter 11

1. (a) $18,000;
   (b) old truck: $6,320, new truck: $9,400;
   (c) difference in years 1 to 10 is $3040.
3. (a) same;
   (b) old truck: $6,640, new truck: $9,200;
   (c) difference in years 1–5, $2,560 and years 6–10, $4,520.

5. (a) $22,000;
   (b) old truck$_{1-5}$: $6,640, new truck$_{1-5}$: $9,200, old truck$_{6-10}$: $6,160, and new truck$_{6-10}$: $9,200;
   (c) difference$_{1-5}$ = $2,560, difference$_5$ = $10,000, and difference$_{6-10}$ = $3,040.
7. $2,881,100
10. year 1: $55,160; year 2: $1,406,400

Chapter 12

5. (a) $\bar{R}_A$ = $4,000, $\bar{R}_B$ = $4,000;   (b) MAD$_A$ = $400, MAD$_B$ = $800;
   (c) σ_A^2 = $300,000, σ_B^2 = $1,200,000;   (d) σ_A = $548, σ_B = $1,095;
   (e) SV$_A$ = $150,000, SV$_B$ = $600,000;   (f) D_A = .137, D_B = .274
7. (a) $\bar{A}_w$ = $3,500, $\bar{A}_x$ = $4,390, $\bar{A}_y$ = $4,900, $\bar{A}_z$ = $4,750;
   (b) Only a .03 increase in the probability of a "good" economy will shift the preferred alternative from Y to Z.
8. $\bar{A}$ = $1,153.58, σ_A = $264.69

Chapter 13

1. $\overline{CE}$ = $6,352
3. $\overline{RAR}_A$ = $265, $\overline{RAR}_B$ = $-$6.275
5. $\overline{RAR}$ = $-$5,127, $\overline{CE}$ = $263
7. (a) $\overline{CE}_A$ = 8.6, $\overline{CE}_B$ = 8.48;
   (b) Independent: σ_A = 7.54 and σ_B = 7.98, Perfectly correlated: σ_A = 12.28, σ_B = 12.81
   (c) Independent: Pr$_A$ = .8729 and Pr$_B$ = .8554; Perfectly correlated: Pr$_A$ = .7580 and Pr$_B$ = .7454

Chapter 14

1. σ_A = $16,426.46, σ_B = $66,394.65, Cov$_{AB}$ = $89,735,217.46
2. σ_{12}^2 = 0.19, σ_{13}^2 = 2.82, σ_{14}^2 = 0.94, σ_{23}^2 = 1.324, σ_{24}^2 = 3.4406, σ_{34}^2 = 0.94
3. $\bar{R}_x$ = $200, $\bar{R}_y$ = $175, σ_x^2 = 2,000, σ_y^2 = 6,875, σ_p^2 = 2,218.75
6. .814 invested equally in A & B and .186 invested in the risk-free security
7. Portfolio 2 is optimal: L = 0.1413

Chapter 15

4. (a) NPV = $403;   (b) end of year 3
5. (e) σ = $4,173; skewness = 1.005; V = 3.07; $\overline{NPV}$ = $1,358

Chapter 16

1. α = 0.047, β = 0.5
3. (a) 0.0001;   (b) 0.00017;   (c) 0.000025;   (d) 0.0001933
5. $\pm$ 2.37%
6. (a) E(R$_p$) = 0.10088;   (b) 0.884;   (c) 0.0111
7. 2 and 3 are overpriced
9. (a) β_1 = .24, β_2 = 1.62, β_3 = .56;   (b) 1 and 2 overpriced

Chapter 17

1. (a) $E(R_1)=0.115$, $\beta_1=3.154$, $E(R_2)=0.037$, $\beta_2=1.426$, $E(R_3)=0.07$, $\beta_3=0.4776$;
   (b) $\text{Cov}(R_{P_1}, R_m)=.012745$, $\text{Cov}(R_{P_2}, R_m)=.005761$, $\text{Cov}(R_{P_3}, R_m)=.00193$
   (c) $\beta_1=3.154$, $\beta_2=1.426$, $\beta_3=.4776$
   (d) $R_1^0=.019$, $R_2^0=.0415$, $R_3^0=.054$

Chapter 18

5. (a) $E(\bar{R}_{1t})=1.2933$, $E(\bar{R}_{2t})=.2595$, $E(\bar{R}_{3t})=.2724$
   (b) $\beta_1=21.3101$, $\beta_2=6.1560$, $\beta_3=4.8429$
   (c) $E(R_1)=2.5572$, $E(R_2)=.8587$, $E(R_3)=.70116$
   (d) Reject all three projects.

Chapter 19

1. 133.3 units of product X; 500 units of product Y; $3,649.99 profit
3.

Value	S_1	S_2	S_3	S_4	S_5
Δ^+	∞	25	∞	∞	100
Δ^-	116.667	200	650	16.667	50

5. $P_2=\$2.00$, $P_5=\$2.50$, $P_1=P_3=P_4=0$
7. (a) $X_1=250$ acres, $X_2=625$ acres, $X_3=0$
   (b) Profit = $32,500
   (c) $S_3=125$
   (d) $.125 for each additional dollar of capital; $2.50 for each additional man-day of labor; nothing for additional acreage
   (f) This is the amount by which the objective function decreases if the farmer is forced to plant 1 acre of soybeans.
   (g) $28.75 = (70)(1.25) + (8)(2.50) + (1)(0)$
9.

Value	S_1	S_2	S_3
Δ^+	$3.33	$2.86	$8.75
Δ^-	$2.00	$4.00	∞

11. $X_1=500$; $X_2=450$; $S_3=50$; profit = $33,000

Chapter 20

4. Completely accept projects 5, 6, 8, and 10; partially accept projects 4 and 9. NPV = $300.88
6. Completely accept projects 1, 2, 3, 4, 5, 6, 8, 11, and 12; partially accept projects 7 and 10; cash inflow = $2237.71

5. (a) Completely accept projects 1, 2, 3, 4, 5, 6, 8, and 11; partially accept projects 9, 10, and 12; all budgeted funds are exhausted.

Project	Shadow Price
11	$144.64
6	85.67
2	39.11
3	29.64
5	21.90
4	18.72
1	5.74
8	0.14

Chapter 21

1. Constraints are:
$$X_1 + X_3 + X_5 \leq 1$$
$$X_6 \leq X_3$$
$$X_2 + X_4 + X_7 + X_{10} \geq 2$$
$$2X_7 \leq X_8 + X_9$$
$$X_5 + X_9 + X_{59} \leq 1$$
$$X_1 + X_2 + X_3 + X_4 + X_5 + X_6 + X_7 + X_8 + X_9 + X_{10} \geq 5$$

2. The Integer LP formulation for the TUB Company is:

$$\text{Max NPV} = 60X_1 + 80X_2 + 55X_3 + 50X_4 + 25X_5 + 100X_6$$
$$+ 90X_7 + 40X_8 + 75X_9 + 75X_{10} + 156X_{11}$$

Subject to:

Budget Year 1: $250X_1 + 300X_2 + 275X_3 + 225X_4 + 150X_5$
$$+ 400X_6 + 200X_7 + 350X_8 + 250X_9 + 175X_{10}$$
$$+ 446.25X_{11} \leq 2000$$

Budget Year 2: $200X_1 + 250X_2 + 250X_3 + 225X_4 + 250X_5$
$$+ 150X_6 + 150X_7 + 50X_8 + 100X_9 + 175X_{10}$$
$$+ 403.75X_{11} \leq 1500$$

Budget Year 3: $100X_1 + 150X_2 + 175X_3 + 50X_4 + 150X_5$
$$+ 0X_6 + 100X_7 + 25X_8 + 150X_9 + 175X_{10}$$
$$+ 170X_{11} \leq 1000$$

Project Interrelationships:

(1) $X_6 + X_7 \leq 1$
(2) $X_2 + X_6 \leq 1$
(3) $X_7 \leq X_8$
(4) $X_9 + X_{10} = 1$
(5) $X_2 + X_4 + X_{11} \leq 1$

Project Acceptance:

$$X_j = \{0, 1\} \qquad j = 1, 2, \ldots, 10, 11$$

Note: Decision variable X_{11} is the acceptance of the complementary Project X_2 and X_4.

Author Index[1]

Adams, R. A., 346
Anderson, J. C., 451
Andrews, V. L., 275
Archer, S. H., 254

Balintfy, J. L., 363
Baumol, W. J., 325, 337
Bell M. D., 381
Benstead, J. C., 133, 147
Bird, M. M., 58
Blume, M. E., 278
Bodie, Z., 280
Bonini, C. P., 240
Bower, R. S., 281, 438
Brill, M., 427
Bullard, R. H., 455
Burdick, D. S., 363
Burton, J. C., 455
Burne, R., 377, 378

Carter, E. E., 373, 423
Chambers, J. C., 372, 431
Charnes, A., 309, 339, 377, 378
Christy, G. A., 241
Chu, K., 363
Clarke, A. C. M., 240
Cohen, K. J., 256, 372
Cohn, R. A., 280
Conine, T. E., Jr., 272
Cooper, W. W., 309, 339, 377, 378
Copeland, R. M., 450–51, 454

Dantzig, G. B., 294
Davey, J., 8
Doenges, R. C., 78
Dufey, G., 422
Dyer, J. S., 339

Eiteman, D. K., 423, 429
Elton, E. J., 372
Evans, J., 254

Fama, E. F., 66
Farrar, D. F., 380
Feinberg, A., 339
Fisher, Irving, 6, 66, 338
Forrester, J. R., Jr., 58, 59
Fourcans, A., 338, 372, 430

Gagnon, J. M., 451
Gahlon, J. M., 272
Geoffrion, A. M., 337, 339
Gitman, L. J., 58, 59
Gomory, R. E., 337, 338
Gonedes, N. J., 459
Groff, G. K., 360–61, 363

Hamada, R. S., 267
Hawkins, C. A., 346
Helliwell, J. F., 438
Hertz, D. B., 364–67, 372
Hespos, R. D., 167
Higgins, R. C., 467, 469–70, 472, 474
Hillier, F. S., 240, 378
Hindelang, T. J., 338, 372, 430
Hirshleifer, J., 66, 325
Horngren, C. T., 138

Ignizio, J. P., 339, 341, 348
Ijiri, Y., 339

Jacque, L. L., 423
Jean, W. H., 66
Johnson, D. J., 467, 470, 472, 473
Johnson, K. H., 254
Johnson, R. W., 391

Kaplan, R. S., 455
Keane, S. M., 73
Kim, S. H., 241
Kleijnen, J. P. C., 439
Kohners, T., 426
Kortenek, K., 377, 378
Kryzanowski, L., 372

Lanser, H. P., 33
Larson, K. D., 459
Lawler, E. E., 381
Lee, S. M., 339, 341
Lerner, E. M., 338
Lessard, D. R., 280, 281, 438
Levitz, G. D., 278–79
Levy, R. A., 278
Lewellen, W. G., 33, 370, 391, 437, 438
Lintner, J., 454–55
Logue, D. E., 278
Long, M. S., 370, 437, 438
Lorie, J. H., 308, 309, 346
Louderback, J. G., III, 451
Lusztig, P., 372

MacDonald, J. G., 57
Magee, J. F., 167
Mao, J. C. T., 66, 381, 438
Markowitz, H., 198, 253, 277, 380
Martin, J. D., 268, 272
Mastai, A. J., 372
Mauriel, J. J., 431
McConnell, J., 33
Merritt, A. J., 49
Merville, L. J., 278
Miller, M. H., 66, 268, 272, 309
Modigliani, F., 268, 272, 280
Mosich, A. N., 455
Muff, J. F., 360, 361, 363
Mullick, S. K., 372, 431
Myers, S. C., 267

Naslund, B., 377–79
Nathanson, L., 431
Nauss, R., 337, 338
Naylor, T. H., 363, 439

Petry, G. H., 57, 58, 59
Pettway, R. H., 336–37
Pflomm, N. E., 36, 221, 222
Philippatos, G. C., 372
Pogue, J. A., 256

[1]This index includes authors who have been referred to directly in the text. The page(s) noted correspond to chapter footnotes or source lines. A complete bibliography by chapters is included as Appendix A.

555

SUbjEct INdEx [1]

Abandonment, project, 3–4, 6, 8, 29, 118, 425, 466
  decision trees for, 229, 232–37
  discounted cash flow and, 53–55
  under risk conditions, 221, 229, 232–42
Accelerated cost recovery system (ACRS), 134–38
  in lease analysis: lessee, 385, 387–89, 393, 398
    lessor, 404, 405, 407, 411, 417
Accounting, business-combination decision, 450–56
  methodology of, 6, 443, 450, 454–55
Accounting net income, assumptions of, 4, 350–58
Accounting Principles Board, Opinion No. 16, 451–53
Acquisition, corporate, 441
  strategy of, 2, 7, 8, 442–44, 456, 463
Acquisition, new asset, 147–52, 447–48
Algorithms, 287, 288, 310, 311, 346, 348, 374, 378, 381
Analysis derived from capital budgeting, 2–5
Analyst's role in forecasting, 124
Annual (capital) charge (see Equivalent annual charge)
Annuities:
  compound sum of, 14–15
  future value and, 10, 14–15, 18, 19, 21
  present value of, 18–22
Annuity tables, 14, 529–47
Arbitrage pricing theory (APT) research, 204
Asset depreciation range, 134–36n

Assets:
  acquisition/disposal of, 4, 140, 147–56
  balancing growth with, 466–70
  depreciable value of, 134–36, 138–45
  replacement chains of, 93–98
  risk-free: portfolio effects, 211, 213
  useful life of, 134, 137, 138, 143–45
Assumptions, capital budgeting:
  about capital acquisitions programs, 3–5, 275–77
  about capital asset pricing, 275–77
  about budgeting, 29–31
  about investment decisions, 308
  about lease or purchase projects, 387–92
  of linear programming, 289–91, 305
  of math programming models, 288–91, 305
  See also Reinvestment assumptions
At-risk rule, 144
Audit, post-completion, 220–31
Audit forms, standard post-completion, 223–31

Beta value:
  in CAPM single index, 245–49, 252, 259, 267–69, 273
  of firm, 267–69, 272, 273
  of portfolio, 253–55
  in project evaluation, 264–67
  stability of, 278–79
Bonds, 13, 16, 384, 426
  cost of debt and, 116–17, 119–20
  holding companies for, 449

Book values, 140, 141, 145, 352, 450, 453, 467, 474
Business combination, 1
  classes of, 443–47
  legal forms of, 447–50
  synergistic effects of, 441, 443, 459, 460, 462, 463
  vertical or horizontal, 444, 446
Business risk, 31, 160, 161
  cost of capital and, 110–13

Capital abandonment idea, 2, 6, 8
Capital acquisitions program, 3–5, 8
Capital asset, 1, 3
  defined, 139n
  depreciating of, 134–39, 144–45
  growth of, 466–75
Capital asset pricing model (CAPM), 172, 198, 244–85, 457–59, 476
  assumptions about, 275–78
  cost of capital with, 245, 267–73
  vs. covariance technique, 255–60
  efficiency critique of, 275–85
  firm valuation process and, 263, 267–73
  merger partner selected by, 257–59
  in project evaluation, 263–67, 272, 273
  security market performance with, 280–81
  single-index model for, 245–52
Capital budgeting, 3, 5
  during inflation period, 5–6
  managerial overview of, 6–8
  simulation applied to, 364–73
    under risk conditions, 373–81

Market value:
and strategic planning, 471, 474–76
of tax shelter, 268–69, 272
Martin-Scott (formulation) model, 268, 272
Mathematical programming (MP) models, 85, 286–305, 360–81
McDonnell-Douglas merger, 463
Mean absolute deviation (MAD) in risk/return, 162–64
Merger, 447–48, 456–64
accounting asset values and, 450–51
Modigliani-Miller tax model, 268, 272
Monte Carlo simulation:
for multinational capital investment, 419, 427, 430–40
for multiperiod analysis, 240, 360–64
Mortgage project's IRR, 63–64
MPSX packaged LP program, 294, 312
Multinational corporation (MNC), 372, 419–40
Multiperiod analysis:
in CAPM, 281–84
under conditions of certainty, 308–26, 330–58
under conditions of risk, 360–81
Multiple investment sinking fund method (MISF), 410–14
Mutually exclusive projects:
DCF ranking evaluation, mostly NPV, 64–76
evaluation of, 84–100
IP constraints for, 331–32

Net present value (NPV)
model, 27, 28, 40–100 passim, 124–31 passim, 237–39, 281, 309–60 passim, 367–723, 80, 384–95, 400–416, 425–38, 457
basic model of, elaborated, 82–84
certainty equivalent value analogous to, 177, 179, 181–83, 185
comparisons to, 58–62, 64–76
for complex projects, 44–45, 124
for corporation takeover, 457
cost of capital and, 106, 108
described, 28, 40–41, 177
determination of, 41–42
deviation over useful life of project, 177–85 passim
increased by abandonment, 237–39, 242
for lease-purchase: lessee perspective, 384, 388–95

lessor perspective, 400, 403–6, 413–14, 416
maximization of, 309–11, 314, 315, 317, 319, 326, 331–60 passim
comprehensive model of, 349–50, 352–53, 355, 357–58
goal programming for, 309, 338, 342–50, 352, 353, 355, 357–59
integer programming for, 331–32, 334–36, 338
shareholder wealth by, 57–62, 64–76, 309–60 passim
for multinational firm project profit, 425, 432–34, 437, 438
mutually exclusive project evaluation by, 82–100
profile construction of, 42–44, 65–68
in quadratic programming, 380
in sensitivity analysis, 124, 126, 129–31
simulation for, 367–72
superiority among techniques of, 57–76, 281
See also following abbreviated entries of NPV
Net present value, risk-adjusted, 177–85, 207
ΔNPV (negative), 41, 45, 47, 284, 391–95, 413
NPV* (positive), 41, 42, 45, 46, 48, 49, 105, 131, 207, 469
in mutually exclusive projects, 83–85, 89–95, 97–100
NPV equations, 40–42, 54, 66–68, 82–83, 310, 331, 350, 380, 425, 434
for lease payment, 405–6
for mutually exclusive projects, 89, 91, 92, 95, 97, 99
for owners vs. leasing, 393–95
NPV profile, 42–44
in mutually exclusive projects, 65–68, 85, 87, 88, 100
Nonlinear programming (NLP), 289, 290
under uncertainty (NLPUU), 298, 373, 378, 380

Operating loss, 138, 141–42, 145
Ownership vs. leasing, 383–97

Payback method, 27, 31–36, 58, 377, 432, 434
including cost of funds, 33–35
frequent uses of, 34, 35, 176
Perpetuities, 18, 22–23

PERT/critical-path-monitoring systems, 8, 219
Plants and equipment:
acquisition of, 147–51, 155–56, 466
CAPM for, 244 n
investment level for, 135
projects for, 1, 7, 29, 34, 241
sale of, 152–53
Plants for lease, 384, 386
Pooling business, 451–55
Portfolio, identification of, 278–84
Portfolio, minimum-risk project, 107, 204–9, 211–12
Portfolio effect, 193, 198–213, 244, 260
of minimum risk, 204–9, 211–12
Portfolio parameters under CAPM, 252–60, 272
Portfolio standard deviation of investment combinations, 198–214, 253–55, 257
Portfolio theory, 211–13
Preferred stock:
capital costs and, 112, 114–15, 119, 415
in pooling, 453–54
See also Portfolio effects; Securities; Shareholding; Stock; Wealth maximization
Prentice-Hall tax service, 140
Prerequisite projects, 333
(see also Mutually exclusive projects)
Present value (PV), 3, 18–21, 100
of annuity, 18, 21–22
discounting cash flow to, 28, 40–43, 45–47, 50, 53, 54
for identifying merger partner, 456–57
in key variables determination, 126, 130–31
set by lessor-dealer, 400–408, 414–16
of perpetuity, 23
procedures discounting cash-flows to, 27–28
See also Equivalent annual charge; Internal rate of return; Net present value; Profitability index
Present value of investment tax credit value, 400–403, 405, 415
Price-earnings ratio (P/E), 459–61, 465
Price trends, 126, 129
sustainable growth and, 469–72, 475, 476
Primal theory, LP maximization, 302–4
Probability distribution, return, 160–62, 164, 165, 241
Production extension, 444, 446
Productive models of present value cash flow, 19